NO MAN'S LAND

by

JOHN TOLAND

Also by John Toland
Published by Ballantine Books:

ADOLF HITLER

NO MAN'S LAND

1918, The Last Year of the Great War

John Toland

BALLANTINE BOOKS • NEW YORK

Maps by Rafael Palacios

Grateful acknowledgment is made for permission to quote portions from the following:

The Ebb and the Flow of Battle, by P. J. Campbell. Reprinted by permission of the publisher, Hamish Hamilton, Ltd., London.

In the Cannon's Mouth, by P. J. Campbell. Reprinted by permission of the publisher, Hamish Hamilton, Ltd., London.

Excerpt from *Fighting the Flying Circus*, by Edward V. Rickenbacker. Copyright 1919 by David Edward Rickenbacker. Reprinted by permission of Doubleday & Company, Inc.

Through a Lens Darkly, by Franz Seldte. Reprinted by permission of the publisher, Hutchinson Publishing Group Limited, London.

With the German Guns, by Herbert Sulzbach. Reprinted by permission of the publisher, Frederick Warne, Ltd., London.

Fatalist at War, by R. Binding. Reprinted by permission of the publisher, George Allen and Unwin, London.

Diary of a Dying Empire, by Hans Peter Hanssen. Reprinted by permission of the publisher, Indiana University Press.

The Kaiser and His Court, edited by Walter Gorlitz. Reprinted by permission of the publisher, Harcourt Brace Jovanovich.

An English Wife in Berlin, by Princess Evelyn Blucher. Reprinted by permission of the publisher, Constable, London.

Memoirs of a British Agent, by R. H. Lockhart. Copyright R. H. Bruce Lockhart 1932. Macmillan London, Ltd. Reprinted by permission.

A Frenchman in Khaki, by Paul Maze. Wm. Heinemann, Ltd., London. Reprinted by permission.

Journey into Revolution, by Albert Rhys Williams. Copyright © 1969 by Abert Rhys Williams. Reprinted by permission of Times Books, a division of Quadrangle/The New York Times Co., Inc.

From *Our Times Over Here, Vol. V,* by Mark Sullivan. Copyright 1933 by Charles Scribner's Sons; renewal copyright © 1961 by Mark Sullivan, Jr. Reprinted by permission of the publisher.

Library of Congress Catalog Card Number: 78-22761

ISBN 0-345-33577-5

This edition published by arrangement with Doubleday & Co., Inc.

Printed in Canada

First Ballantine Books Edition: February 1982
Seventh Printing: February 1990

To all those who were there

Contents

vii

Part 5 WAR AND PEACE

List of Maps

Cast of Principal Characters

American

President Woodrow Wilson
Colonel Edward M. House, his chief adviser
Secretary of State Robert Lansing
Secretary of War Newton Baker
General John J. Pershing, commander A.E.F. in France
General Tasker Bliss, U.S. representative on Supreme War Council
Colonel George Marshall, operations officer of First Army
Brigadier General Douglas MacArthur, commander 84th Infantry Brigade
Lieutenant Colonel George S. Patton, 304th Tank Brigade
Gunnery Sergeant Paradise, Marines
Private First Class James W. Rose, 1st Division
Floyd Gibbons, Chicago *Tribune*

British

George V, King of England
David Lloyd George, Prime Minister
Arthur J. Balfour, Foreign Secretary
Lord Reading, Ambassador to Washington
Lord Derby, Minister of War, later Ambassador to France
Lord Milner, his successor as Minister of War
Winston Churchill, Minister of Munitions
Andrew Bonar Law, War Cabinet
Maurice Hankey, Secretary of War Cabinet
Sir George Riddell, publisher, intimate friend of Lloyd George
Herbert Asquith, former Prime Minister, leader of Minority
Colonel Charles A'Court Repington, military correspondent of the London *Morning Post*
General Sir William Robertson, Chief of Imperial General Staff
General Sir Henry Wilson, his successor
Major General Sir Frederick Maurice, Director of Military Operations

At the Front

Field Marshall Sir Douglas Haig, Commander-in-Chief British forces

General Sir Herbert Lawrence, his chief of staff

General Sir Julian Byng, commander Third Army

General Sir Hubert Gough, commander Fifth Army

General Sir Henry Rawlinson, his successor (army renamed Fourth Army)

Sergeant Paul Maze, special assistant to Gough and later Rawlinson

Lieutenant Colonel Graham Seton Hutchison, 33rd Division

Chaplain E. V. Tanner, 2nd Battalion, Worcestershire Regiment

Captain Arthur Behrend, heavy artillery officer

Captain R. S. Cockburn, 20th Division Reinforcement Battalion

Herbert Asquith, artillery officer

Lieutenant Patrick Campbell, artillery officer

W. A. Tucker, XI Corps Cyclist Battalion

Private H. Howard Cooper, King's Own Lancasters

French

Premier Georges Clemenceau

President Raymond Poincaré

General (later Marshal) Ferdinand Foch, Chief of General Staff

General Maxime Weygand, his chief of staff

Colonel E. Herbillon, liaison officer between Paris and High Command

General Henri Pétain, Commander-in-Chief French armies

General Charles Mangin, commander French Tenth Army

General Henri Mordacq, head of military cabinet

German

Wilhelm II, Emperor of Germany

Crown Prince Wilhelm

Chancellor Count Georg von Hertling

Max, Prince of Baden, his successor

Foreign Minister Richard von Kühlmann

Rear Admiral Paul von Hintze, his successor

F. W. B. von Berg, chief of Kaiser's civil cabinet

Colonel Hans von Haeften, head military department,
Foreign Ministry
Admiral Georg von Müller, chief of Kaiser's Naval
cabinet
Friedrich Ebert, leader of German Social Democrats
Matthias Erzberger, centrist leader in Reichstag
Hans Hanssen, deputy in Reichstag
Evelyn Blücher, English wife of Prince Blücher

At the Front
Field Marshtal Paul von Hindenburg
Quartermaster General Erich Ludendorff
Quartermaster General Wilhelm Groener, his successor
Colonel Mertz von Quirnheim, Supreme Command
Headquarters
Baron Manfred von Richthofen, the Red Baron
Colonel Georg von Bruchmüller, artillery expert
Lieutenant Herbert Sulzbach, artillery officer
Lieutenant Rudolf Binding, artillery officer
Lieutenant Ernst Jünger, infantry officer
Franz Seldte, head of motion picture unit

Russia
V. I. Lenin
Leon Trotsky, Commissar for Foreign Affairs and later
Commissar for War
Georgi Chicherin, his successor as Commissar for
Foreign Affairs

Foreigners in Russia
David R. Francis, American Ambassador
Maddin Summers, American Consul-General in Moscow
DeWitt Poole, his successor
Norman Armour, secretary of American Embassy in
Vologda
General William S. Graves, commander of A.E.F. to
Siberia
Raymond Robins, chief of American Red Cross Mission
to Russia
Albert Rhys Williams
R. H. Bruce Lockhart, British secret agent
Joseph Noulens, French Ambassador
Captain Jacques Sadoul, members of French Military
Mission
Count Wilhelm Mirbach, German Ambassador

WESTERN FRONT
1918

ENGLAND
Dover

NORTH
SEA

Ostend   Brugge   Zeebrugge   Ghent

Calais   Dunkirk   FLANDERS   Passchendaele   CANAL

ENGLISH CHANNEL

Boulogne   Eperlecques   Ypres   Kemmel   Wytschaete   BELGIUM
Hazebrouck   Bailleul   Armentières   LYS
LYS   Lille   Tournai
La Bassé
Béthune
Lens   Drocourt   SCARPE
Montreuil   St. Pol   Douai
Arras   Quéant   Cambrai   SENSÉE
Doullens   Bapaume
Abbeville   SOMME   Albert
Dieppe   SCARPE   Péronne
Amiens   Villers-   St. Quentin
Dury   Bretonneux
Moreuil   Nesle   SOMME
AVRE   Montdidier   F   R   A   N   CE
Rouen   Ressons-sur-Matz   Laon
Beauvais   Compiègne   AISNE
Clermont   Soissons
OISE   Villers-   Fère-en-Tardenois
Cotterêts   Dormans
Chantilly   Belleau   Château-Thierry
PARIS   Meaux   MARNE
SEINE   Versailles

■■■ Front Line Mar. 21, 1918
─── Farthest German Advances in 1918
─── Armistice Line Nov. 11, 1918

xiv

EUROPE, NOV. 11. 1918

Murmansk
Archangel

NORWAY
SWEDEN
FINLAND

Ekaterinburg

ATLANTIC
OCEAN

RUSSIA

Petrograd

IRELAND
ENGLAND
HOLLAND
London
BELGIUM

Moscow

DEN.

Riga

Berlin
Spa
GERMANY
POLAND

Brest-
Litovsk

Paris
LUX.
SWITZ.

Kiev UKRAINE

FRANCE
Vienna
AUSTRIA-
HUNGARY

Bordeaux

PORT.
SPAIN

ITALY
SERBIA

RUMANIA
BULGARIA

BLACK SEA

PERSIA

Rome

Constantinople

GREECE

TURKEY

MESOPOTAMIA

Damascus
PALESTINE
Jerusalem

ARABIA

ALGERIA

MEDITERRANEAN SEA

0   MILES   500

TRIPOLITANIA

EGYPT

Brussels

U M

Mons

Maubeuge

Avesnes

OISE

TO SPA
50 MILES

GERMANY

LUXEMBOURG

Sedan

C   E

Craonne

AISNE

L
O
R
R
A
I
N
E

Binarville

Montfaucon

Reims
VESLE

Varennes

Verdun

Metz

CHAMPAGNE

AIRE

MEUSE

MOSELLE

Épernay
MARNE

Châlons

AISNE

St. Mihiel

Pont-à-
Mousson

0   MILES   30
0   KM   30

Bar-le-Duc

pagaeias

XV

Prologue

On New Year's Day, 1918, Europe was close to bankruptcy after almost three and a half years of a war which had killed and maimed millions of soldiers, ravaged the land and brought hunger and misery to countless civilians. Each side had gone into battle with faith in the justice of its cause and the invincibility of its armed might. Both the Allies and the Central Powers had expected a quick and easy triumph, with battle itself envisaged as some kind of grand adventure.

But year after year passed in bloody deadlock with gains and losses in bitter trench warfare measured by yards. Men of many nations were still dying to no avail on many fronts in Belgium, France, Italy, the Balkans, Mesopotamia and Palestine.

The only hope of Allied victory now appeared to be America, which had entered the war with enthusiasm the previous April. "The United States is destined to be the deciding factor in the world war," Admiral Sir David Beatty, commander of Great Britain's Grand Fleet, cabled the New York *Times* on that first of January. But little more than 100,000 half-trained American soldiers were in France. A vast army would soon be on the way—"at least 5,000,000" if General Pershing got his way. This meant a combat force greater by one quarter than the entire Allied armies on the Western Front, where the war would eventually be won or lost.

America was indeed the hope of the Allies, but not a few leading Britons wondered that day if her troops would arrive in time to stave off defeat. Lord Milner, a member of the War Cabinet, saw "little prospect of military success for us." Sir George Riddell, an intimate friend of Lloyd George, was even gloomier. At lunch with Winston Churchill he said, "If the war continues for another twelve months, in attempting to annihilate Germany we may annihilate ourselves." Churchill, still trying to live down his support of the disastrous Gallipoli campaign, had not lost his nerve or optimism. "We must fight on to a finish. You never know when the Germans will crash."

There was reason for pessimism. The year 1917 had been one of near disaster, not so much because of German might as of the Allies' own failings and bad luck. First had come the failure of the great French spring offensive conceived by General Robert Georges Nivelle, an affable, vain man with an explosive temper and little experience in high command. Convinced he could win the war with one massive blow, he was tricked by the Germans,

1

who secretly withdrew their front line troops, then pulverized the advancing French armor and men with artillery. The horrendous death toll ignited mutinies throughout the French Army. It took executions, tempered by concessions from the new army commander, General Henri Pétain, to quell the troops, but much of the French élan that had held the Germans at bay earlier in the war was lost.

Allied misfortune was compounded that June when the British launched their own attack in Flanders to end the war. It opened on the morning of the seventh. Nineteen huge mines, containing almost a million pounds of explosives, detonated simultaneously on the front near Ypres. At his study in London, Lloyd George heard the distant rumble and felt the shock. Then came a tremendous barrage from 2,330 guns and howitzers. From the British lines 80,000 men rushed and soon reached their first objectives. But this early success was an illusion and three and a half months later the long campaign finally ended. Cost: 244,897 casualties. Gain: Less than six miles. The British troops groused and made up more caustic poems and songs, but they did not mutiny.

Those at home had also suffered during 1917 from severe German bombing raids as well as shortages in food and clothing caused by the enemy's U-boat depredations. Food queues and profiteering had become a national institution at the expense of nerves, but there were no riots. The British temper was frayed but not unraveled and the people could still joke. But behind the humor lay deep dissatisfaction. The workers were discontented with their lot; the middle classes felt that they, as usual, were carrying the heaviest burden; and almost everyone was growing weary of the eternal squabbling in high places.

France on that New Year's Day was still trying to recover from the Nivelle fiasco. Although the mutiny had been crushed, the French leaders feared another if their troops were pressed too hard. The watchword was defense; the goal the lowest possible casualties. This state of mind was not only limited but dangerous, since it was accompanied by a wave of defeatism and pacifism throughout the nation. Intellectuals joined with the bourgeoisie in an attempt to propagandize for peace. Romain Rolland and Henri Barbusse were among those authors who shared the fear of leading financiers that Britain would establish an industrial hegemony after the war. Traitors were also secretly working for peace with Germany. An extraordinary adventurer named Bolo organized a vast network of treason. Among those on his payroll was Senator Charles Humbert, and the arrest of these two in September had helped bring down the government of Premier Painlevé.

He was replaced in mid-November by Georges Clemenceau, onetime Socialist mayor of Montmartre, Dreyfusard, premier of the republican cabinet of 1906–9, and a staunch anti-German who had advocated strong defense measures before the war. He was a freethinker and free soul, unorthodox in private as well as public

2

life. As a country schoolteacher in Virginia, he had watched Grant's men march into Richmond in 1865. Once married to an American, he was as attracted to women as Lloyd George, whose affair with his secretary was a known secret. Both men were fighters, and without such aggressive leadership the war would probably be lost. For months Clemenceau had led the campaign against the pacifists, and although many detested him, including President Poincaré, he was supported by both right- and left-wing patriots. Everyone knew that his nickname, the Tiger, was apt. He took over with confidence, and his ministerial declaration electrified the nation with its ruthless brevity. Treason, he said, would be dealt with summarily. "No more pacifist campaigns, no more German machinations. Neither treason, nor half-treason: war, nothing but war." He met with the Council of Ministers but once a week and became, in effect, a one-man government.

Discipline and spirit were restored despite rationing of gas, electricity, and coal. Cinemas and theaters were shut down four days a week to conserve fuel, and the only museum in Paris open was the Invalides, featuring a patriotic exhibition of war trophies. Cafes and restaurants closed early and the dark streets of the City of Light were almost deserted by 10 P.M. Yet these annoyances, as well as the scarcity of vegetables, cheese, sugar, and meat, were accepted by the people. At last they had a leader they could trust.

Their allies in Italy, while not enduring such suffering, were still in a state of depression from the defeat of their army seven weeks earlier at Caporetto, a town near the Austro-Hungarian border. In one battle alone 275,000 Italians had surrendered to the Austrians. They did manage to re-form their lines and the civilians were now being rallied by the poet D'Annunzio and an unknown editor in Milan named Mussolini.

The catastrophes of the Allies in 1917 were shared by the Germans. While world attention centered on the terrible losses endured by the British in Flanders, it went generally unnoticed that Germany had been dealt equally high casualties. Despite the glorious victory at Caporetto, her main ally, Austria-Hungary, was disintegrating. The Habsburg Empire was decaying, and young Emperor Karl, who had succeeded Emperor Franz Josef in 1916, was secretly attempting to negotiate a peace through several Bourbon princes.

Germany had entered the war with a political unity which began to disintegrate after the "hunger" winter of 1916–17. With hardship, popular unrest grew and the workers demanded political rights. While the parties of the center and left combined in an attempt to bring these about peacefully, their demands were refused by the real rulers, the Kaiser and the military. The situation became critical after the March Revolution in Russia, which helped inspire 300,000 German workers to stage strikes in Berlin and Leipzig. More alarming was the spread of mutiny in parts of the fleet.

3

By the New Year the British naval blockade had brought acute food and clothing shortages. Almost everything was *ersatz*. Bread was now made from sawdust and potato peels and powdered with chalk instead of flour. People were forced to eat dogs and cats ("roof rabbits"). There was almost no milk and little meat, and, except for the well-to-do, the nation was becoming accustomed to living in overcoats.

Even so, the military leaders were confident of victory, for Russia was practically out of the war. A few weeks previously the Bolsheviks had overthrown the Socialist Provisional Government of Kerensky, then promptly appealed to the Germans for peace negotiations. Although the first round of talks at Brest-Litovsk had ended on New Year's Eve after a German demand for annexation of the Baltic States and Poland, Quartermaster General Erich Ludendorff, the driving force of the German Supreme Command, was confident that the Bolsheviks would sign the peace treaty when negotiations resumed in a few days.

He was so sure that the bulk of the eighty divisions on the Eastern Front could soon be transferred to the west that he was planning a massive attack on that front designed to bring quick final victory. For the first time in the war, Germany would have the advantage of numbers. It was an intoxicating concept to military leaders who had already come close to victory against heavy odds in manpower, artillery and aircraft. They had at last attained the object of three years' strivings and longings, wrote Field Marshal Paul von Hindenburg, Chief of the General Staff. "No longer threatened in the rear, we could turn to the great decision in the West and must now address ourselves to this passage of arms."

Smelling a decisive victory if their plans could be implemented without interference, the Supreme Command decided that the moment had come to press for complete dominance. Ludendorff went into action immediately. During the Crown Council meeting on January 2, 1918, at Bellevue Castle, he insisted on even harsher peace terms once the Brest-Litovsk negotiations with Russia resumed. He made no attempt to mask his fury when the Kaiser objected to his demand for outright annexations of Polish territory. As the assemblage listened in shock, Ludendorff declared that the frontier as drawn by the Kaiser could not be considered final—not before Ludendorff himself studied the case. The distressed monarch looked to Hindenburg for help, but he agreed with his forceful subordinate. Ludendorff then insisted that the Brest-Litovsk treaty be accelerated as much as possible "with a view to a blow to be struck in the West."

Two days later he forced the issue by threatening to resign. There was an immediate flood of telegrams to Wilhelm II urging him not to dismiss the Fatherland's military genius. More important, Hindenburg agreed to give Ludendorff his full support, and the climax came on January 7, when the field marshal personally presented a petition to the Kaiser, replete with underlined phrases. It read like an ultimatum and contained a querulous list of complaints that made it sound as if Hindenburg were a school principal admonishing an unruly student. "The events of January 2 have made the most painful impression on General Ludendorff and myself, and have shown us that Your Majesty disregards our opinion in a matter of vital importance for the existence of the German Fatherland. . . . In order to secure the political and economic situation in the world which we need, *we must defeat the Western Powers.*" To accomplish this, he declared, the Kaiser would have to decide between the views of the diplomats and those of the Supreme Command. Unable to stand up to this direct challenge to his authority, Wilhelm capitulated without a protest. With Ludendorff now probably the most influential man in Germany, the Supreme Command expedited preparations for the great spring offensive that would solve all their problems. And Germany was bound on a course of final victory—or final defeat.

Part 1

OPERATION MICHAEL

Chapter One

THUNDER IN THE WEST

1.

ON the brisk sunny morning of March 18, 1918, the Western Front appeared to be as quiet as it had been since the beginning of the year. But Field Marshal Douglas Haig, commander of the British troops, was convinced this was only the calm before a massive German offensive. He and the recently dismissed Chief of the Imperial General Staff, Sir William Robertson, had been warning since January that it was imminent; they pleaded for additional men, but Prime Minister Lloyd George and his War Cabinet had no intention of pouring more troops into a front that had already squandered the cream of Britain's manhood.

Instead Lloyd George pressed for an extensive "sideshow" offensive in Palestine while merely holding on in the west. He was determined to keep the bulk of Britain's reserves at home, partly from fear of an Irish rebellion but primarily to check Haig's wasteful offensives. He had never liked the Western Front with its frightful losses, and depriving Haig of troops would force him to stay on the defensive—and so save many lives. As a result a bitter struggle had been waged between the Prime Minister and his generals, ending with the firing of Robertson. The wounds suffered in this contest were bandaged but not healed. The bitterness remained. Another such confrontation could bring disaster to the empire. Lloyd George also dearly wished to get rid of Haig but dared not go that far yet, since the field marshal's wife had been Maid of Honor to Queen Alexandra and he himself was highly esteemed by King George.

Haig's concern on March 18 was not for his own precarious position. That morning British ground observers reported abnormal road traffic up forward. Many German staff cars were sighted, and officers were seen studying General Sir Hubert Gough's Fifth Army front.

General Pétain, the French field commander, shared Haig's fears but felt sure the blow would fall on his troops, not on the

British. Eight days previously the Germans had abruptly placed into service a completely new code, a sign to both Pétain and Haig that the big push was coming. The French code expert Captain Georges Painvin, with the help of a New York lawyer, Hugo Berthold, broke the code and by now the Allied cryptanalysts were reading enemy front-line messages better than German code clerks themselves. But these experts still could only guess when and where the attack would come.

It seemed obvious to Haig that he would be the target. The French had not yet recovered from their own disastrous spring offensive of 1917, and it would be just like the brilliant Ludendorff, Haig reasoned, to strike at the strongest enemy point, not the weakest.

Haig was most concerned about Arras, the keystone of his entire defense system. If the Germans broke through here, they could split his front in two and race for the coast in two directions. The Ypres area on the north flank also worried him, for this too was a gateway to the channel ports of Dunkirk, Calais, and Boulogne. These places were essential not only for supply but for escape back to England in the event of total collapse. The field marshal had sixty-two infantry and cavalry divisions to hold a front of 126 miles. Gough's Fifth Army had the longest frontage of any of Haig's four other armies, forty-two miles, yet had the least number of men to defend it. But his persistent requests for more troops were rejected. There were simply not enough men to go around. And Haig felt he could not take troops from the more sensitive Arras sector. Moreover, Gough's right wing adjoined the French and he would get assistance from them in an emergency; Haig and Pétain, out of apprehension of their own superiors, had privately arranged that if one of them were attacked the other would send immediate aid.

The long spell of dry weather along the British front ended on March 19. Light rain fell periodically throughout the day. The sky was dull with overcast skies making morning air reconnaissance impossible. Haig had visitors from England for lunch, including the energetic Minister of Munitions, Winston Churchill. He revealed that, with the approval of the War Cabinet, he was proceeding with the manufacture of four thousand tanks.

After dinner Haig's chief of staff, General Sir Herbert Lawrence, brought in reports based on interrogations of prisoners, indicating that the enemy probably intended to attack tomorrow or the next day, the twenty-first. Haig felt prepared. Batteries had received their allotment of ammunition for the battle, 1,200 rounds including 300 gas shells. Large air forces had also been concentrated along the front, but they were being kept under cover until the battle began.

Gough also felt prepared but still was deeply concerned about his skimpy forces. He was writing his wife: "I expect a bombardment will begin tomorrow night, last six or eight hours, and then will come the German infantry on Thursday, 21st . . . Every one

7

is calm and very confident. All is ready." At forty-seven, Gough was by far the youngest of Haig's army commanders. A short man with a long, lean face, he was noted for his terrier tenacity and courage. He had a rare relationship with his men, who felt he was one commander who understood the hellish life of the trenches.

Major W. E. Grey, of the 2nd London Regiment, found that evening "strangely still and peaceful; few of war's usual discordant noises disturbed the last quiet hours of the departing day. The whole country side was instinct with the sweetness and vigour of approaching spring; woodland scents filled the keen, crisp air; a gentle breeze played among the yet leafless branches of the trees; and away from the line, only the Very lights, waxing and waning noiselessly above the tree-tops, served to dispel the illusion, bred of the enshrouding darkness, that peace had returned to this beautiful land. Yet over all there was a presage of impending disaster."

Earlier that afternoon Herbert Asquith, an artillery officer—son of the former prime minister and present opposition leader—also found an odd quiet at his observation post: ". . . the only sign of bloodshed was a dead hare which an infantryman had shot with his rifle and was carrying in from the edge of No Man's Land. In the German lines and behind them there was no single human being in view." But he guessed there probably was an overwhelming force of artillery lying hidden in the placid landscape beyond. Asquith called up the gunners and advised them to have their gas gloves ready and to apply "undimming mixture" to the goggles of their respirators.

At his headquarters in Montreuil, Haig wrote his wife: "The enemy is rather threatening for the moment. I therefore think it will be better for me to delay coming over to see you for a week." He was very disappointed at having to put off seeing his wife and their son, born four days earlier, "but under the circumstances it is right that I should do so. Everyone is in good spirits and only anxious that the enemy should attack. And if he did attack on Saturday, and I was in England, it might lead to 'talk!' " He hoped that she would, as she had so often done in this war, "show that example of patience and determination to do one's duty, which has made me so proud of you." He had received, he concluded, a mass of letters of congratulations—"many from poor people quite unknown to me. How happy it makes one to feel that so many kindly thoughts and prayers are being lavished *on us three* at this time."

Mist now shrouded the Fifth Army and its neighbor to the north, the Third Army, deadening sounds while adding an eerie sense of apprehension. At about 9 P.M. British raiders of the 61st Division brought thirteen prisoners back from No Man's Land. Several of these talked freely to interrogators. A preliminary German bombardment would start at 4:40 A.M. and the infantry would come over the top about 9:30 A.M. Visibly nervous, they asked to be sent to the rear as soon as possible. This information was sent to artillery units and, as planned and rehearsed, numerous batteries were hastily moved to different firing positions.

Asquith was one who got the news. He also got orders to destroy all secret documents. He and his captain made a fire of cherry wood in the corner of their dugout, piling on the mass of papers that had come up from headquarters.

Every man not on duty lay down for a night's sleep, "but all of us," recalled Gough, "felt perfectly certain that we would be wakened before morning by the roar of battle."

German troops were plodding in seemingly endless columns to the front with transport trains and trucks among them. "No rest the whole night long," recalled pilot Rudolf Stark, "and always this roaring and surging, like the approaches of a thunderstorm." In the villages of Picardy, German soldiers ignored strict orders and the air rang with their triumphant songs as they marched forward.

Lieutenant Rudolf Binding, an aide-de-camp on the staff of a new division, was explaining in a letter why he hadn't written for almost two weeks.* "To-morrow there will be nothing to keep secret, for then hell breaks loose . . . Of course, I know that I cannot entirely escape the day which is so relentlessly approaching. It is a tremendous thing for every one of us. Aeschylus says that a drama ought to excite Hope and Fear, but here is one already showing behind the curtain and awakening both of these sensations before it even rises. It will be a drama like a Greek Tragedy, with a fate hanging over it, shaped and created by man alone, and ready to descend on the head of him who is responsible. . . .

"We are all going as light as possible. All unnecessary baggage has been ruthlessly prohibited; we all left it willingly behind, buoyed up by a final hope. The organization is really great, but it was, of course, impossible to keep the secret. In Brussels every child knows that the offensive is to begin on March 21st."

2.

Late in February the War Cabinet in London had doubted there would be an offensive in the west despite two disquieting reports: one from the Royal Flying Corps that everything pointed to an impending major attack near St. Quentin; and another, from Clemenceau, that captured German documents indicated that March 10 was a likely date for the enemy offensive, since Crown Prince Wilhelm was heard to remark that he would be in Calais on March 20 and in Paris on April 15. These reports were followed a few days later by another from Major General Sir Frederick Maurice, Director of Military Operations. He told the Cabinet in person that the Germans would be ready by mid-March and that the attack would probably come on the British front. "They still believe in an attack on Italy," Maurice noted sarcastically in his diary, "because nothing much is heard about it."

* Binding became an important member of German postwar authors who idealized the virtues shown at the front and, to an extent, prepared the psychological atmosphere that helped bring Adolf Hitler to power.

Haig had no doubts. On March 2, a cold, frosty day, he had told his commanders that they must be ready "as soon as possible to meet a big hostile offensive of prolonged duration." He was pleased with recent tours of his three armies and was "only afraid that the enemy would find our front so very strong that he will hesitate to commit his Army to the attack with the almost certainty of losing very heavily."

The next day Haig learned that the enemy now had 182 divisions in the west. *"Troop movements and prisoners' statements,"* he underlined in his diary, *"all indicate that an offensive on a big scale will take place during the present month."*

In London, General Maurice agreed with Haig that an attack would probably take place soon on the Cambrai front. On March 4 he told the new Chief of the Imperial General Staff, General Henry Wilson, that he thought it was a certainty. But Wilson replied that he was afraid it wouldn't come and didn't think the Cambrai/St. Quentin front likely because of the devastated area and the Somme River. Maurice wrote that evening: "I go by evidence of preparation—point of junction of French and ourselves always a favourite with the Germans and the road to Paris." The next morning his constant warnings had some effect on the War Cabinet. Even though Lloyd George remained dubious, its members, Maurice wryly noted, "are at last beginning to think attack on us likely."

The awakening in London was reflected in the War Office and that day Lord Derby, the War Minister, wrote to Haig:

> It looks now as if an attack might come within a very short time on your front, and on that part of the front of which Gough is in command. You know my feelings with regard to that particular officer [three months earlier he had warned Haig that many in London blamed Gough for the failure at Ypres in 1917]. While personally I have no knowledge of his fighting capacity, still, it has been borne in upon me from all sides, civil and military, that he does not have the confidence of the troops he commands, and that is a very serious feeling to exist with regard to a Commander at such a critical time as the present. I believe the Prime Minister has also spoken to you on the subject . . . if by any chance you yourself have any doubts on the subject, I hope by this indefinite order . . . to give you a loophole which would make your task easier if you desired to make a change . . .

Haig did not accept the offer, nor was there substance in the charge that the Fifth Army commander lacked the confidence of his troops. The gossip about Gough had probably been generated by Liberal politicians who still hated him for threatening to resign in 1914 rather than fight against the Northern Ireland volunteers. Gough ignored the attempts to oust him and devoted himself to the task of strengthening his lines.

At the German Supreme Command, staff officers were studying his positions. The Fifth Army *was* the primary target, and a key point would be its III Corps, the extreme right wing of the British line along the River Oise. This, figured the Germans, would be extremely sensitive, since it was a junction with the French. Any junction was weak, and particularly one with troops of a different nationality.

Two days after Derby's letter was dispatched, Haig visited the Fifth Army, but it had nothing to do with the War Minister's warning. This was merely a tour of army sectors. His first point of call was III Corps, and what he found disturbed him. It had a very wide front to defend with three divisions, even though much of the front featured river and marsh obstacles. "On the whole I don't like the position," he wrote, and ordered a division from another army to move south to reinforce Gough.

Haig also was concerned by XVIII Corps, well organized as it was. Although every detail had been thought out, "they were taking it too much for granted that enemy would do what they had planned that he should do."

Despite his apprehension, Haig had no thought of wishing to remove Gough, particularly just before an important battle. Moreover he understood Gough's problem, which was his own—a lack of manpower. "The French handed over to him a wide front with no defences, and Gough has not enough labour for the work."

As late as March 14, Lloyd George still refused to take the offensive seriously, and on that day Haig crossed the Channel to sound yet another warning. The Prime Minister's response was to do his best to get Haig to say that the Germans would not attack. Haig refused. Then the Prime Minister charged that Haig had given his opinion that the Germans would only attack against small portions of the British front. "I never said that!" was the bristling retort.

"Would you attack if you were a German general," asked the Prime Minister.

"The German Army and its leaders seem drunk with their success in Russia and the Middle East, so it is impossible to foretell what they may not attempt. In any case, we must be prepared to meet"—and he accented the next words—"*a very strong attack on a 50-mile front, and for this, drafts are urgently required.*"

By this time Ludendorff's offensive had a code name, Michael, and orders had been issued in the Kaiser's name to launch the first infantry attack at 9:40 A.M., March 21. Preparations for the assault were progressing methodically. On March 15 a young artillery lieutenant of the Eighteenth Army wrote in his diary: "One can only be amazed again and again at the careful work done by headquarters and at the preparations being made down to the last detail—that is after all the source of our greatness . . . all kinds of new equipment are in evidence, things that were lacking in 1914." That day ammunition dumps were completed and on March 16 the sixty-two divisions of the assault force marched westward toward final positions singing to the accompaniment of bands, *"Muss i denn, muss i denn."*

On March 18, Baron Manfred von Richthofen's squadron turned back a large force of British fighter planes that had infiltrated the front. In a wild melee he shot down his sixthy-sixth enemy plane while his men were accounting for eight others. That evening Ludendorff and Hindenburg left Spa to be nearer the front. They set up an augmented Operations Branch at Avesnes. The recent bright weather had turned into violent rainstorms, and Hindenburg noted that tension among his staff had increased. He hoped the clouds and rain would shroud their final preparations. "But had we really any grounds for hoping that the enemy had not got wind of what we were about?" Although enemy artillery fire had died down, enemy fliers kept coming over. "But all this supplied no definite date on which to answer the question: 'Can our surprise succeed?'"

Ludendorff's orders were loose. Unlike the preparations, there were no detailed objectives or times. "There must be no rigid adherence to plans made beforehand." The strongest form of attack was to be envelopment. In general the Germans would smash through the Fifth and Third Armies before wheeling northwest to envelop Arras—which Haig regarded as "the backbone and centre" of the British defensive system.

Gray columns of troops were marching through the rain on the night of the nineteenth, and as they neared the front were led forward by guides, wrapped in capes. The last trench mortars and batteries were brought up under cover of night. After midnight clouds cleared and stars appeared. But before dawn of March 20 a dense ground mist filled the valleys and crept to the crest of the ridges, obscuring the entire Fifth Army front. Although lighter mist to the north also masked the Third Army lines, once the sun rose the fog along the entire front began to disperse. But soon the skies began to cloud and on the German side rain pelted down. An unfavorable wind also sprang up. This concerned Ludendorff, for artillery bombardment relied on gas for its effect. Fog also would impede the movements of Ludendorff's troops. He feared it would prevent, as he put it, "our superior training and leadership from reaping its full reward."

At 11 A.M. his meteorologist, Lieutenant Dr. Schmaus, submitted his report. It was not "strikingly favorable but it did indicate that the attack was possible." At noon Hindenburg and Ludendorff decided to take a chance; the army groups were told to proceed on schedule. "Now it could no longer be stopped," wrote Ludendorff. "Everything must run its course. G.H.Q., higher commanders and troops had all done their duty. The rest was in the hands of fate."

Ludendorff's superstitious confidence in his own fate was revealed at lunch. "Do you know what it says for tomorrow in the *Brüdergemeinde* [book of the Moravian Brothers]? It is the day of the Chosen People. Now can we not look upon the offensive that begins tomorrow with confidence?"

During the day a captive German balloon escaped its moorings, drifted over the French lines, and was shot down. Papers in the basket revealed detailed plans of a massive attack on March 26 near Reims. General Pétain took the German ruse seriously, but Gough was still positive the blow was coming directly at him in a few hours, and that afternoon sent a curt message to his commanders: "Prepare for attack."

An important member of his staff was touring the front lines on a motorbike. Described by Churchill as "unique and undefinable," Paul Maze's duties puzzled visiting officers. He was a Frenchman who had attended an English public school and was determined to serve with the British. Son of a well-to-do merchant, he had been taught to paint by Pissarro, Dufy, and other noted artists who were fed well by Madame Maze. Gough, a friend, agreed to put Maze on his staff if he would get a commission in the French Army. Maze, a tall handsome man in his late twenties, returned a few weeks later in a resplendent uniform (designed by himself) and a huge sword. He also had a title that was resounding to English ears: *maréchal des logis*. In French it meant he was a sergeant major.

Maze was instructed to roam Fifth Army on his own initiative, making sketches of trenches, emplacements, and strategic terrain features. He was also to visit corps, division, battalion, and company headquarters gathering news and impressions. He was to be, in short, Gough's eyes and ears. He had already been saved at the last moment from being shot as a spy and had been decorated several times for bravery.

That evening he reported to Gough at his forward headquarters in Nesle. After remarking that he "expected the storm to break over the Fifth Army that night," the general was interrupted by the telephone. It was Haig's chief of staff. When Gough insisted that he should move his two reserve divisions, General Lawrence, ten years older but junior in rank and at his post only two months, began giving Gough "a little lecture on the conduct of military operations in accordance with the teachings of the great Masters." What particularly irritated Gough was that his junior "purred on the telephone like a damned pussycat." Finally Gough could take no more condescension and explained, "I shall fight the blighters in my battle zone as long as we can hold them there. Good night, good night." He turned to Maze and told him to report early in the morning.

Maze changed his dirty clothes and had dinner in Nesle. Later as he walked through the streets "the place seemed plunged in perfect peace. Not a sound came from the lines."

Lieutenant Binding was writing home that the German preparations were "quite inconceivable in detail, and can only be described as the last word. The troops are packed in position so tight that those in front have been there for the last ten days. For weeks past ammunition has been hauled and hauled, night after night, to be piled in mountains round the guns. All that is to be poured out on the enemy in four hours from now." Each attacking division had been provided with first-class remounts from the Quartermaster General's reserve. "God knows how Ludendorff has got them together. I am still 200 short for the Division, but they are to be given me when we advance, or during the battle. Naturally the railways have been working day and night at this business; waiting for thousands of trains with men, horses, guns, wagons, ammunition, tools, rations, bridging material, and a hundred other things was a trying business for everybody."

At midnight the Kaiser's special train left Spa bound for Ludendorff's advance headquarters. It was scheduled to arrive just before the first storm troops attacked. At the front a white mist was slowly rising from the wet earth and spreading slowly across the trenches, the shattered woods and the wrecked villages. Behind this curtain lay sixty-two German divisions. Nineteen were preparing to smash into Third Army's six divisions plus only two in reserve. Forty-three were to hit Gough's thirteen, also with two in reserve. The British would be outnumbered by more than three to one. Padres went along the whole Fifth Army front giving absolution and communion to Catholics.

Shortly after midnight Gough's divisions issued the code word, "Bustle!" "It meant "Man battle stations," and thousands of Britons in billets and bivouac silently crept forward into position.

Chapter Two

THE GREAT ATTACK
MARCH 21–24

1.

NEAR the north flank of Gough's Fifth Army, Lieutenant Patrick Campbell had barely fallen asleep when he heard someone calling his name. It was the signaler sergeant who had raised the gas curtain of the shelter and was shining a flashlight at the young artillery officer. "Captain's orders, sir," he said. "He wants you to go up to the top of the hill." Campbell was to take a good look and send back information.

It was 4 A.M., March 21, and Campbell thought, Blast the captain and his nervousness. He was leisurely taking off his pajamas when the sergeant returned. "Sir, he wants you to go quickly." Campbell asked was there any noise about? "No, sir," he answered quietly. "Only mist."

14

Campbell put on his soft hat. No need to wear a steel helmet in a war like this. But as he set out with two signalers he heard for the first time the sound of gunfire. It was normal for early morning but heavier than usual, so he went back for a helmet and also pulled his gas mask around to alert position in front. He had brought a feeling of inferiority with him to France, but was discovering he could do about as well as the other subalterns, even if he did occasionally stutter.

As he walked up the hill in the extremely thick fog, holding a telephone line as a guide, he expected the noise to die down, but it seemed to intensify. It made him uneasy. Shellfire was always frightening. In August 1917, in front of Ypres he had been caught in a heavy bombardment. He could still hear the screeching of shells, the screams of pain, the terrifying explosions, the vicious fragments of iron rushing down and biting deeply into the earth. He had been paralyzed. He had no power over his limbs; his face was burning, his throat was parched. There was lime juice in his water bottle but he couldn't move his arm to get it. Such fear was debasing, abject. The bombardment had turned him into "another person, one out of whom all courage had been poured away." His fear haunted him and he thought if he had something to do he might forget it. Afterward he had read Trollope's *Framley Parsonage*. "It was delightful. Nothing happens in the book. And one day, I thought, we may return to a life in which nothing ever happens."

On that morning of March 21, the old fear returned once he came to a break in the telephone wire. Unable to find the line ahead in the fog, he felt alone and lost. The fury of the guns increased. Gas shells! They made a different sound as they burst. He smelled the sickly mustard gas mixed with the clammy odor of fog, and scrambled into his gas mask. Something *was* happening up front and he didn't know what it was.

It was 4:40 A.M. and the most massive bombardment in history had begun. Along a front of more than fifty miles, some 6,000 guns, more than 2,500 of which were heavy or superheavy, simultaneously began pounding the Third and Fifth Armies. The bombardment was a carefully orchestrated program devised by Germany's leading artillery expert, Lieutenant Colonel Georg Bruchmüller, nicknamed "Durchbruchmüller" (Breakthrough Müller). The hellish din was such that when 2,500 British guns answered the additional noise was hardly noticeable.

To a German artilleryman like Lieutenant Herbert Sulzbach it sounded "as if the world were coming to an end." His guns were saturating the enemy artillery with gas shells and every so often the gas and smoke were so bad he had to take a break. The gunners, their shirts already drenched with sweat, kept ramming shells automatically into the breeches. They were in such good spirits and put up such a rapid rate of fire that orders were no longer necessary.

At a forward observation post, Walter Bensen had his telescope blown over by concussion from a British shell. He was unharmed but the sentry nearby had crumpled into a little heap, rifle still held by a lifeless hand. Bensen set up the telescope but the view was shrouded in fog. Then something unexpected happened—the wind shifted and gas drifted back. Bensen snapped on his mask.

Bruchmüller's plan was to first concentrate on enemy artillery positions. Just north of the junction between the Third and Fifth Armies, the first shells wakened the adjutant of a British heavy artillery unit. Captain Arthur Behrend felt everything vibrating—the ground, his dugout, his bed. He lit a candle and grabbed a telephone only to find no messages were coming through. The door opened and the colonel—in spectacles, pajamas, and gum boots—burst in. "Any report from the O.P.?"

As Behrend replied a great crash half lifted him out of bed and blew out the candle. He was shaken. The war had seemed far away. Since Christmas not a shell had fallen within a thousand yards of their headquarters. Life on the Bapaume front had been "delightful—a succession of invigorating canters across the overgrown downs to the batteries, joyrides to Amiens through the snowy wastes of the Somme, early-morning partridge shoots over the fields around our headquarters."

Now a big shell had fallen in the roadway ten yards from his dugout. After the colonel hurried off, other shells exploded nearby thick and fast. It was impossible to keep his candle lit. The door of the dugout blew off its hinges. "The fascinating smell of high explosive and ravaged earth drugged and bewlidered me." Behrend never could remember how long he stayed in bed. Probably five minutes. He was trembling with excitement. Or was it fear? He was powerless to move. "There was nothing to do, and one might just as well be killed decently in bed instead of half naked while struggling into one's shirt." Yet in minutes, to his own surprise, he became accustomed to the inferno and he longed for action. He hastily dressed. If he were captured it would be better to be prepared. So he put on his new tunic, the one with the chevrons on it.

Fifth Army batteries were being similarly pounded. Near the north flank Lieutenant E. C. Allfree felt a bit excited and wondered what they were in for. He put on his Sam Browne belt, though as a rule artillery officers had little need for revolvers. As he was about to go outside, his major entered to tell him that he was not needed and it was beastly thick with gas outside. No need exposing oneself unnecessarily. Allfree hated to feel he was skulking down in a dugout, but the major told him he'd probably be more useful if he stayed where he was as present. Allfree adjusted his box respirator and went through the double curtains. He got a whiff of gas and it didn't sound at all nice outside. A wounded man was brought in and soon the major reappeared and said Allfree could now relieve Godfrey.

Allfree found the sunken road outside covered with thick mist. "Shells were falling everywhere. It was a perfect hell—no words

16

can describe how utterly beastly it was, so I am not afraid of exaggerating." The eyepieces of his gas mask immediately fogged and he had to feel his way up the road to the guns. The layers had stripped off their respirators to see better, retaining the nose clip and mouthpiece, but even so they could not see the lamps on the aiming pickets in the mist. Allfree sent out a man with a flashlight to hold over the picket, but this did little good. He went to the "maproom" and took the magnetic reading of their target. Then, armed with a prismatic compass, he laid the guns as accurately as he could.

A few miles to his rear in the ruins of Nurlu, Winston Churchill thought the first explosions were from British twelve-inch guns. "And then, exactly as a pianist runs his hands across the keyboard from treble to bass, there arose in less than one moment the most tremendous cannonade I shall ever hear." To the north and south, the intense roar and reverberation rolled toward him and through the chinks on the papered window the flame of the bombardment lit his little cabin like flickering firelight. Outside he met General Tudor. "This is *it*," he said. "I have ordered all our batteries to open. You will hear them in a minute." But the German shells made such a din that he could not distinguish the roar of friendly artillery.

In the center of Gough's lines, Herbert Asquith found the bombardment "more like a convulsion of nature than the work of man." As he went from gun to gun, checking the angles of fire, he sucked at the tube of his gas mask. In the pitch dark, the only lights were the flashes from his own guns or the flaming cores of exploding shells. "The noise was so great and varied, so many different chords of sound being mingled in this vast tornado, that an order could barely be heard even when it was shouted through a megaphone at a range of a few yards."

At the southern flank of the Fifth Army, Private Frank Gray of the Royal Berkshire regiment had endured many fierce bombardments before but nothing like this one. "It was a great, even awe-inspiring noise, one roll, one roar, which never diminished and never increased, and which, indeed, imagination refused to conceive could be increased. It was a noise unimaginably vast, in which there were no disintegrating items, in whose whole overpowering effect there were no fractions of noise. It came and overwhelmed me in an unpausing, irresistible, and endless wave of sound. Then came messages in rapid succession: 'Stand by!' 'Stand to!' and finally, 'Man battle positions!'" In the wan, fog-shrouded light the men paraded in battle order quietly, as if on review at home, then moved calmly toward the front "under this sky afire, and over this quaking earth, to take up their appointed positions."

The noise wakened Gray's army commander at 5:10 A.M. Back in Nesle the noise was dull but so sustained and steady that it at once gave Gough "the impression of some crushing, smashing power." He jumped out of bed and telephoned the General Staff to find out where the bombardment was falling. The answer was startling: all four of his own corps were being heavily hit. Third Army reported bombardment on about ten miles of the southern part of their front. "This at once opened my eyes to the magnitude of the attack on Fifth Army." It dispelled any hope that he could thin out some unthreatened part of his line to concentrate more troops against the main thrust. His problem had become simplified but "far more terrible and menacing." His entire spare line was involved and he had few reserves to throw into weakened areas.

After issuing a few orders, and warning all concerned, he peered out the window into a dense fog. The Germans wouldn't attack for several hours, so there was nothing more to be done. He went back to bed for a short sleep.

About an hour later the German guns shifted concentration from enemy batteries to the front lines. "Machine-gun posts were blown sky-high—along with human limbs," recalled one gunner at the north flank of Fifth Army. "Men were coughing and vomiting from the effects of gas, and men were blinded. The whole earth around us turned into an inferno—akin to the 'Three Divisions' described in Dante's description of hell."

This intense firing let up near 7 A.M., and officers let the men go down into tunnels for breakfast, but before they finished their meal shelling reopened and shortly afterward came the shout that Germans were in the front-line trenches. They had crawled through the mist unseen. But such attacks were sporadic and the British infantrymen prepared for the main assault, which was bound to come any moment.

By 8:30 A.M. Gough was shaved, dressed, and back at the telephone. There were no reports of any German advance but, convinced of the magnitude of the attack, he ordered his two reserve divisions to start forward. Then he called Haig's headquarters and asked authority to do so. General Davidson, head of operations, gave him permission. This pleased Gough, but his request for more reserves brought a chilling response. Four divisions were being sent to Third Army and only one to the Fifth. "You cannot expect it for seventy-two hours," said Davidson. The question came into Gough's mind: "Could we last as long?"

Impatient at the sparse reports coming in, Gough was tempted to jump into his car and visit his brigades and divisions. But that involved a trip of 140 miles and would take him out of direct contact with his own headquarters. He decided to stay where he was for the time being.

One of his best sources of information, Sergeant Maze, the French artist, was pacing up and down in front of headquarters, eager to see the general. He was told to wait for further news and had a second breakfast. It was 9:30 by the time he finished, and he was so impatient he set off by motorcycle on his own initiative to see what was going on at their junction with the Third Army. Maze headed for General Congreve's headquarters, VII Corps.

18

"Through the thick fog," he recalled, "the noise of roaring cannon was like thunder."

The Kaiser's train had just arrived at the little station near Avesnes and as he was driven toward Hindenburg's headquarters he could hear the distant, indefinite roll of thunder. He was impatient. The main infantry assault would start in a few minutes and he wanted to be present.

At 9:35 A.M. some 3,500 mortars opened rapid fire on the British front lines. Three German armies—the Seventeenth, Second, and Eighteenth—were lined up from north to south. More than a million men awaited the word to attack. They would be preceded by specially trained storm troops and be supported by thirty-nine divisions. Two of the armies, Marwitz's Second and Hutier's Eighteenth, were preparing to assault Gough. Below's Seventeenth would hit the Third Army.

Lieutenant Ernst Jünger, a young company commander of a Hanover regiment, stood in front of his dugout, watch in hand.* He was to lead a unit of storm troops and had just learned his battalion commander was dead. Heavy shells were falling in a narrow circle around his company. Earlier during the first minutes of their own bombardment the men had run along the trench shouting deliriously at each other. They were exulting over German power and burning with impatience for the attack. Now they were so shaken by enemy shells that it took coarse jokes to cheer and distract them. Jünger led his men over the top so they could take up their position in No Man's Land and be ready to charge at the enemy front at exactly 9:40. There were shouts of vengeance for their fallen battalion commander as they moved forward. Their spirit was returning and, upon finding attack battalions on both sides eagerly waiting for the signal to move, they too became intoxicated with the fever to fight. As far as Jünger could see there were masses of men. With such might they would surely break through! The decisive battle was about to begin. The stake was the possession of the world. He felt the significance of that hour, yet was amazed at the general air of intense excitment. Officers were standing upright nervously bantering with each other. Occasionally a short mortar round scattered earth over them but no one even ducked. "The roar of the battle had become so terrific that we were scarcely in our right senses." They were all mad, beyond reckoning, and had "gone over the edge of the world into superhuman perspectives." Death meant nothing, their lives were dedicated to the Fatherland.

Jünger's orderly handed him a full canteen and he took a long drink of liquor. It tasted like water. He tried to light the traditional cigar but the match was blown out three times. At last came

---

* Like Binding, Jünger belonged to those postwar German authors who kept alive the mystique of war. The most influential and eloquent of the group, Jünger—never pro-Hitler—contributed materially to the Führer's success.

9:40! The fire lifted and the waves of gray men swept forward impelled by rage, alcohol and the thirst for blood. Jünger was ahead of the others, gripping a revolver in his right hand, a bamboo riding crop in his left. He was boiling with a fury that later amazed him. "The overpowering desire to kill winged my feet. Rage squeezed bitter tears from my eyes."

He leaped over the front line, which was scarcely recognizable. Then surprisingly came a chatter of machine-gun fire from the second line. Jünger and the men with him leaped into a shell hole. In mid-flight there came a frightful crack. Shrapnel screeched but by a miracle no one was hit. Jünger scrambled out of the hole and trotted down a sunken road, its smashed dugouts yawning on the banks. He was alone—and then he saw, ten feet away, his first enemy, a crouched man, apparently wounded. Jünger ground his teeth and jammed the muzzle of his revolver to the soldier's temple. Crying out in terror, the Tommy pulled out a photograph, thrusting it toward Jünger. He conquered his rage. How could you shoot a man in front of his loved ones?

A few miles to the south, another German lieutenant, Heinrich Lamm, led his platoon into the first fogbound enemy trench with a triumphant "Hurrah!" The area was gassed so they donned masks. He stepped on something soft. A dead Englishman. He went into the next trench, also thick with fog, and shouted. A few Tommies appeared with hands in air. Lamm sent them to the rear and continued to roll up the trench. He took off his stifling mask. He coughed and sneezed but there was no gas. He leaped into the next trench followed by thirty men. He didn't recognize them but they wanted a leader. He shouted, "Prisoners out!" and, after a moment, an enemy officer and some twenty men filed out. A wounded German led them to the rear. He came upon another English officer, who shouted encouragement to his men but was finally forced to surrender. He spoke a little German, so Lamm told him to take his five men to the rear. They shook hands. Noticing he carried a nice leather jacket, Lamm said, "You don't need it any more. The war is over for you." The Englishman graciously handed it over—as a present.

When the sun broke through and the mist cleared, Lamm led a group toward Hargicourt. Suddenly he saw his own company and joined them. As they advanced up the road his good friend Speckhard was hit by a grenade. His arm was blown off and Lamm watched the life gush out of him. First Lamm wept, then shouted, "Speckhard, I'll avenge you!" With fixed bayonet he led his platoon into a trench, but his rage began to dissipate once he saw the piles of dead Tommies. He came upon one who, like Speckhard, had lost an arm. It lay like a package across his knees. Beyond was another man—alive but with both legs gone. He looked up with such a sad expression that Lamm wanted to cry. The miserable sight took away all his fighting spirit for the day. "Water, drink!" the Tommy whispered. Lamm gave him his own canteen, filled with tea and rum. The wounded man gulped down every drop, then the bottle fell from his fingers and he died. There goes the soul of a hero, thought Lamm, and he said aloud, "It's good your family doesn't know how you had to die."

By now Lieutenant Jünger had joined his company on the road. He was boiling hot and ripped off his coat. "Lieutenant Jünger now casts off his cloak!" he theatrically announced several times, and his men laughed as though it were a great joke. They came to the end of the embankment. Jünger saw fire coming out of a dugout window. He shot through the cloth. A man ripped off the cloth and tossed in a grenade. Explosion, smoke, silence.

After cleaning out the dugouts they stormed up the bank, and for the first time in his three years of war Jünger saw large groups of men engaged in hand-to-hand fighting. He leaped into the first trench and, as he stumbled around the first traverse, collided with an English officer with open tunic and tie hanging loose. Jünger seized him by the throat and flung him against the sandbanks. An elderly German major shouted, "Shoot the hound dead," but Jünger headed for the lower trench. It "seethed" with the enemy. He was firing with such ferocity that he kept pressing the trigger even after the last shot. His men were tossing grenades among the British. He saw a dish-shaped helmet spinning in the air. After a minute the battle was over. The enemy were scrambling out of their trenches "by battalions." They fled to the rear, stumbling over each other and leaving behind piles of bodies. A German noncom gaped at the sight with mouth open. Still mastered by bloodlust, Jünger snatched away the noncom's rifle and brought down a khaki figure more than 150 yards away. "He snapped together like the blade of a knife and lay still."

2.

To the south the left flank of Fifth Army was also being overrun. Just when Lieutenant Campbell thought things were quieting down, he saw several figures running toward his battery out of the fog. Germans? What an absurd idea! But why were they running?

"Jerry's through!" panted one of them, out of breath and obviously bewildered and terrified.

"What's happened?"

"Jerry's through," repeated the soldier. "He's in Epéhy; we've got no officers left." The fog had already swallowed the other men and in a moment he too disappeared.

Campbell reported the incident and was told to keep a sharp lookout for enemy. By the time he got back to his position the fog had dissipated and the hills and valleys lay bathed in bright sunshine. He looked and looked but there was nothing to see. No Germans. No British. Only sunlight on bare hillsides. "Was there a battle being fought? I could see nothing of it. Everything looked the same as on any other day."

A few miles away, at Allfree's battery, they could see Germans swarming up the rise from Epéhy. They were circling to the right. While Allfree was directing fire on them, he was handed a message from brigade: "Pull out at once, and retire to rear position; I am sending horse teams from heavy battery." Allfree gave the order to cease fire, pull out and limber up. Moments after each gun was attached to its limber (the detachable forepart of the carriage, consisting of two wheels), two eight-horse heavy gun teams came thundering up. As the roar of battle grew closer, their first big gun was hastily hitched behind one of the teams. Allfree ordered it to move off but was told the drivers refused to leave without an officer and had brought a horse for him.

"Oh, damn, I suppose they can't," said Allfree. "Find Mr. Godfrey." He soon appeared. "Here you are, Godfrey, my boy. Here's a chance for you to clear out of this Hell. Get on that horse and take these guns back to the rear position. Number 1 is ready to move off now, and Number 2 can follow you in a minute."

"Do you mean it?"

"Of course I mean it. They have to go out at once. Are you ready to leave?"

"Rather!" Godfrey leaped into the saddle and was off in a canter. Behind him the heavy gun lumbered and bumped over the rough field. The second big gun never got away. Its wheels caught in a bank and one of the horses slipped into a shell hole. The drivers lashed the other horses in a supreme effort to get free just as the horse in the hole plunged to get out. The traces snapped in two places, and before a new harness could be sent back the entire battery had to leave to avoid capture.

To the right in the center of the Fifth Army lines a deadly battle was going on for Manchester Hill, which looked like the hump of a camel facing St. Quentin. It stood in the way of the German advance, and Lieutenant Colonel Wilfred Elstob, commander of the 16th Manchester, knew it. He was not a professional soldier but a schoolmaster who had joined as a private. He was called "Big Ben" by his men, who knew that his exhortations were not mere rhetoric. "There is only one degree of resistance," he told them, "and that is to the last round and to the last man." The two forward companies had been quickly surrounded and headquarters overrun. Rallying cooks, bakers, and clerks, Elstob led the counterattack with revolver, grenades, and finally bayonet. He almost single-handedly repelled the second attack and seemed indestructible. He was wounded but ignored it. He was also thrown into the air by a shell explosion but emerged from the smoke dusting himself off. By the time the fog disappeared a mass of dead and wounded Manchester men surrounded the little hill. But it was still in British hands and, as Elstob cheerfully kept reporting, it would stay that way.

At other points along Gough's line, Germans were streaming west. Nikolaus Schulenberg of Wilhelmsburg was enjoying the spoils of war. His outfit looted an abandoned mess hall where bacon was sizzling on the stove and "half a cow was on the table." He and his comrades filled their haversacks with "so-called German hamburgers" and cigarettes. They all lit up and set out for the next objective. They advanced so far and so quickly that they almost ran into their own barrage. Groups of prisoners passed them. They were pale and some were still shaking with fear. The bombardment, they said, had been sheer hell. Other prisoners walked back "cheekily with a fag in their mouths." But even these cocky ones "were speechless at our massed infantry assault."

Sergeant Maze managed to motorcycle safely to Fifth Army's northernmost corps headquarters, but almost every office was empty. General Congreve and most of his staff had gone off to the divisions. "A dog, its tail between its legs, was slinking round the huts, stopping to turn and snarl at the artillery roaring five miles away." Maze decided to go up further front and somehow managed to get through the block barrage at the entrance of Heudecourt. "Artillery limbers rushed past, the drivers with a look of fear and haste in their eyes. Nobody could tell me what had really happened so far." He became paralyzed by terror and anxiety as shells flew overhead to crash into houses. Last night he had gone down the same road, but now every familiar landmark was gone. Suddenly there came a terrific clatter of firing from the left of the 9th Division front. He left his bike to follow signalers who were uncoiling a wire from headquarters to their batteries. As he stumbled forward shapeless figures ran through the fog past him. Shells fell nearby and the place reeked of gas. He was the only one not wearing a mask and he nervously slipped on his own. He came to a gun and had to shout to the officer in command. They expected the Germans to break through at any moment.

Maze moved forward and from the sound of rifle fire deduced that the enemy had penetrated into the forward battle zone. On the left the violence of the firing rose unevenly from different areas, indicating imminent further penetration. A jagged piece of shrapnel thumped into his shell hole and startled him to his feet. He scrambled out and started down the road before the Germans broke through. Shells were falling on all sides. Through the smoke and fog Maze saw an officer hurrying to the rear and trotted along beside him to find out that Gauche Wood had just fallen to the Boche. Everywhere Maze went he got meager information, so he decided to head back to Congreve's headquarters. As he was searching for his motorcycle, the fog suddenly split and let through the blue sky.

Haig reported to London that there was heavy bombardment between the Scarpe and the Oise rivers. General Maurice rang back to ask if infantry had attacked and was told it had. He promptly informed General Wilson that the big battle had started. The Chief of Staff was dubious; it would come further north.

When the War Cabinet met at 11:30 A.M., Wilson told about the bombardment, adding that it might be nothing more than a big raid. The information received so far, he concluded, gave no

23

cause for anxiety. "He hasn't got our manpower position into his head," Maurice noted in his diary, "and in spite of his Versailles war game wants the Boche to put in a heavy attack on us. So would I if we had the men but we haven't."

The noted war commentator for the London *Morning Post*, Colonel Repington, was far more concerned than Wilson. A bitter foe of Lloyd George's policies, he commented in his diary: "Only the valour of the British soldier can atone for the follies of the War Cabinet." The Secretary to the Cabinet, Maurice Hankey, was equally concerned and wrote in his diary: "It is one of the most decisive moments of the world's history, but I think our fellows will hold them up." He also mentioned he had lunch with Lloyd George, but there is no record of what matters they discussed.

The Germans also had superiority in the air. For the first time they outnumbered the Allies, 730 aircraft to 579. During the morning almost all the German attacks were low level because of the fog and the need to support the infantry. But soon after midday the fog thinned and the British began floating observation balloons. Effectively protected by fighter planes, the balloonists sent back valuable information on the confused movements along the front while directing effective artillery fire on German reserve units. British observation planes were also ranging over the German lines; they returned with information that masses of Germans were moving forward and all roads feeding into the front lines were "packed with troops."

These reports convinced Gough that he could not fight it out successfully in the battle zone but must carry out a delaying action. Otherwise his army would be completely annihilated. But how could he maintain an intact if battered line against such overwhelming odds until Haig and Pétain sent up sufficient reserves to hold the ground? Haig could send him only one division in three days and another a day later. The French hoped to have one division ready in two days and two more in three days.

Just as Gough was setting out for lunch, General Humbert, commander of the French Third Army, in reserve just to the south, arrived. It was a most opportune moment for good news, and Gough said he was certainly glad to see him with his army. "But," said Humbert regretfully, "I have only the flag on my car." This was something of an exaggeration. He also had his aide and a skeleton staff. The troops taken from him several weeks earlier, he explained, had not yet been returned.

After lunch Gough ordered the 3rd Cavalry Division to move down at once to support III Corps of General Butler, then telephoned his four corps commanders that he was going to visit them all. He started the tour about 3 P.M., first drving to Butler, who held the right flank. This was his first battle as commander. "I found him perhaps a little anxious," wrote Gough, "but this, of course, was very natural in view of the situation." The loss of ground and guns weighed heavily on Butler, but Gough told him

24

not to worry. The corps had fought against terrible odds, "and now the only thing that mattered was to take the right steps to meet the menacing storm." Gough eased Butler's mind considerably with the news that the 3rd Cavalry Division was already on its way to reinforce him. Butler's job was to draw back his entire corps behind the Crozat Canal.

Gough's next stop was at XVIII Corps, and here he got a much different reception. He found General Maxse and his staff "cheerful, active and confident." Their nine battalions in the forward zone had fought stoutly, sacrificing themselves to delay the enemy. These troops had been practically annihilated, but the battle zone still held. Gough told Maxse to hold out as long as he could on the morrow and then withdraw his right flank to keep touch with Butler's corps at the Crozat Canal.

He was also to keep contact with his neighbor on the left. On the way to this corps, XIX, Gough's aide remarked that Maxse's corps seemed confident they could hold against all odds. "My dear boy," said Gough, "quite apart from their casualties in the battle zone, they have lost the better part of nine battalions forward. . . . How long do you think he can go on taking casualties like that?" Gough found that XIX Corps had lost less ground than III Corps while facing the heaviest odds. The lines were thin, with only two divisions, and any reserves were far behind it. But Gough had faith in the sixty-year-old commander, General Herbert Watts, a spare, quiet, modest man. He was also possessed of sound judgment and courage.

His final call was to Congreve's VII Corps. Gough arrived long after Sergeant Maze had left, only to find that the right flank had been pushed back considerably. But Congreve, acting with decision and energy, had built up a new front with a reserve brigade. "Well done, Walter," said Gough. "Hang on as long as you can. Every hour we hold the Germans up improves our prospects." He was trusting Pétain to honor his commitment to return troops to the Fifth Army at once in case of such an attack, not aware that Pétain, while keeping the letter of the agreement, was moving with deliberation. He had his own lines to think of and still believed the documents found in the balloon calling for an attack on Champagne were genuine. Even though Pétain had reserves amounting to fifty divisions, he was not releasing a single man or gun until pressed. The Germans had predicted he would do so. "It need not be anticipated," one officer informed Ludendorff more than two months earlier, "that the French will run themselves off their legs and hurry at once to help their Entente comrades. They will wait first and see if their own front is not to be attacked also, and decide to support their ally only when the situation has been quite cleared up." Such shrewd thinking had led to the fake orders in the balloon.

At the center of the Fifth Army lines the reports of "Big Ben" Elstob from Manchester Hill ended that afternoon with one to the acting brigade commander, H. S. Poyntz, announcing that very few men were left, he had been wounded again, and the end was nearly come. "Goodbye," he said to Poyntz, and hung up. The enemy had brought up field guns to a range of about sixty yards. This murderous barrage, combined with steady machine-gun fire, abruptly ended at 4:30 P.M. It was all over. But the schoolmaster from Manchester standing on the fire step, rifle in hand, shouted, "Never!" when asked to surrender. He was shot through the head.

Lieutenant Jünger was still alive. After leading the capture of the sunken road, he had pushed forward. In a hollow he saw with delight his friend Lieutenant Breyer, strolling nonchalantly throught heavy machine-gun fire, walking stick in hand and a long green huntsman's pipe in his mouth. Draped over his shoulder was his rifle as if he were out shooting hares.

By late afternoon Jünger was near Vraucourt. It was time to rest and he decided to relax in a dugout. A young Tommy lay in front of it. After surrendering he had made a break for it and Jünger had to shoot him through the head. It was a strange feeling, he thought, to look into the eyes of a man you've killed. Inside the dugout he found white bread, jam, and a stone jar full of ginger beer. He read some English newspapers "that abounded in the most tasteless invective against the 'Huns.' "

At Hindenburg's headquarters there was satisfaction over the unprecedented success of the day, but the stubborn resistance of the British Third Army was disconcerting. There were higher casualties then expected, and Hindenburg was merely satisfied with the first day. But the Kaiser was exultant. He could only see the enormous gains in the south. He returned to his train determined to give Hindenburg the Iron Cross with Golden Rays, last awarded to Field Marshal Blücher in 1814. The average front-line soldier shared the Kaiser's elation, for most of them saw only the day's victories. "Perhaps I am born to fulfill my life's work, my aim in life with this battle," wrote Reinhard Muth to his family. He would die in action the next day.

There was little cheer that night at Lieutenant Campbell's battery near the north flank of Gough's army. Only a man named Griffith was in the mood for talking. And he was shut up peremptorily when he looked up from his diary and said brightly, "I see that it's the first day of spring and in some ways it has been a real springlike day, hasn't it?"

Further south, there was a general exodus toward the Crozat Canal. Other columns were falling back on Nesle, Gough's headquarters. He was telephoning Haig's chief of staff to tell of the number of divisions thrown at him by the Germans and the masses still in the rear. The push, Gough added, would surely continue the next day and probably continue with unabated fury for many days. How could his tired and attenuated line keep fighting without support? "That was the question, and it was a grave one,"

Gough wrote later. "Lawrence did not seem to grasp the seriousness of the situation; he thought that 'the Germans would not come on again the next day'; 'after the severe losses they had suffered,' he thought they 'would be busy clearing the battlefield,' 'collecting their wounded, reorganising and resting their tired troops.' I disagreed emphatically, but I failed to make much impression."

Not at all fatigued, Gough walked down to his operations center to get the latest information from the front. He queried his liaison officers on what they had learned in their travels behind the battle zone. He also talked to Paul Maze, who had come back exhausted from his long tour, and then sent him off with a message to the French Army headquarters in the south. Maze was so weary that he was only half conscious of the road sliding under him. He delivered the message, then lay down for an hour's sleep before returning to Nesle.

At Montreuil, Haig was sending out a message of congratulations to the Third and Fifth Armies for communication to all ranks. Considering the great strength of the attack he felt that the day's results were "highly creditable to the British troops." War correspondent Philip Gibbs was far more concerned. In his war dispatch of the day he told of a possible German enveloping movement that could capture many British men and guns. "It is a menace which cannot be taken lightly, and at the present moment our troops are fighting not only for their lives, but also for the fate of England and all our race."

3.

At 2:30 in the morning of the second day of the offensive, March 22, Private Frank Gray got orders granting him leave in England. To him it was almost a reprieve from death—"permission to leave this awful battle!" His commanding officer released him at once but didn't know how Gray could get away; he was on his own. His sergeant told him that a train left Flavy-le-Martel, a village near the southern boundary of the Fifth Army, at 7:15 every morning. If it wasn't running he could follow the tracks.

He set out in the darkness with his heavy infantry pack and three days' rations, soon coming onto the main road. He found it swirling with traffic, all going west. There were guns of all sorts and sizes, some drawn by horses, others by "caterpillars." There were lorries, empty and full, limbers, ammunition, infantrymen. Most eloquent to him were the ambulances, sometimes alone, sometimes in convoys. He pushed on against this endless flow and, when shells began to fall nearby, decided to head cross-country. It was easy to find his way from the flashes of guns and bursting of shells, but as he continued he became nervously conscious that nobody else seemed to be going his way and he began tumbling into the shell holes that pocked the area. Finally he reached the little railway station and followed a group of old civilians into a boxcar. They looked at him so curiously he feared they would take him for a deserter. Luckily an interpreter examined his papers, vouched for him, and explained it was the last train that would leave Flavy-le-Martel. The refugees offered him food and drink. Shells exploded nearby and one old woman said, *"Pas bon, monsieur,"* and he solemnly replied, *"Pas bon, madame."* The train jerked into motion and he left the battlefiield.

Gray didn't know that most of the troops and guns in his section were already being moved west from the Crozat Canal to dubious safety. It was difficult to tell it was dawn because of the dense yellowish mist. It was worse than yesterday. It was cold and raw.

In some places the thick curtain of mist would rise about three feet, then suddenly fall. During one of these lifts a company of the 5th Duke of Cornwall's Light Infantry got its first glimpse of a horde of Boche. It was such an awesome sight that the commanding officer tried to shout, "Fifteen rounds rapid!" but could only croak. He tried again and this time made himself heard. "It seemed minutes before the men started shooting," recalled Lieutenant R. G. Ross, "but to get things going one officer plugged away with his revolver, and actually fired all his rounds before our men realized what was happening. It was a glorious ten minutes we had. We were positive nothing could break our lines: the men were cool and collected, bombs were thrown and [rifle] grenades fired. The casualties were terrible to the Germans, because they were in close formation. Then down came the mist again and our view was obstructed. We waited patiently, gripping rifles and revolvers as we had never gripped them before. At last the mist cleared and we found to our surprise some of the most daring of the enemy on our wire just about twenty yards in front of us."

Ross was sure that the Germans would have to fall back, but machine-gun fire started to come from the left. Friendly troops on the left had given way and fled to the rear. On small and large scale the same situation recurred throughout the day.

Further north, at the junction of the Fifth and Third Armies, the acting commander of Campbell's battery was depressed. "O, my God!" said Captain Bingley. "I can't stand another day like yesterday!" As the fog lifted, news began to come in. The enemy had penetrated their battle line at several points. "O, my God!" said Bingley. Then word came that a division on their right had lost the whole battle line. Another "O, my God!" Then the enemy was in Roisel. "O, my God!" said Bingley. "It will be another Sedan."

Campbell studied a map. Roisel was five miles due south. That meant the Boche were halfway to Péronne already and their own battery was in danger of having retreat cut off. "We ought to be doing something," said one officer. "Why aren't we firing?" One reason was that they didn't know the positions of their own men or of the enemy and all telephone wires to the front were cut. Someone suggested that they at least fire on their old abandoned lines, but Captain Bingley said they must conserve ammunition. Then came a report that Chapel Hill, their own main line of defense, had been captured, but still Bingley did nothing. "We must wait for the Colonel's orders. He will tell us what to do." The worst mistake, he said, was to act on one's own initiative, for afterward one always found that the worst possible thing had been done. Bingley could not sit still and kept walking out to the line of guns despite the bombardment, which did not frighten him. It was, thought Campbell, "responsibility he feared, or losing his guns, or being taken prisoner."

To the south the intact bridges over the Crozat Canal were jammed with retreating traffic. Lieutenant Colonel J. G. Birch had brought his battalion of the King's Royal Rifle Corps up from reserve to stem the tide. He found some dismounted cavalry units holding the canal line, but there were only a few men and no trenches. His own men quickly dug in under cover of the thick mist. As it suddenly lifted Birch was shocked to see enemy field guns just across the canal; German infantry began sniping at the defenders. All at once rifle fire came from their own side of the canal. Germans had crossed to seize a high ridge. Two hand grenades crashed against Birch's helmet. Duds! A third exploded only ten feet to his left. Something was wrong with his left ear and steel splinters had cut through his riding breeches and were sticking in his thigh. He leaped into a shell hole. Looking up, he saw a circle of rifles pointing down at him. Indignantly he called out in German, "We don't treat prisoners like that!" Surprised, the Germans lowered their weapons. One said, "Stop, he speaks German." They searched Birch, taking his money, wristwatch, and binoculars, but missing his valuable silver cigarette case, which he had slipped down his breeches. When they began eying his London-made riding boots, Birch edged along the road and asked a German doctor to send him down the line, as he was slightly wounded. "Nobody can go down the line," was the answer, "unless he helps carry a wounded German trooper." Birch agreed and set out for St. Quentin at one end of a heavy, clumsy stretcher with no straps to take the weight off the shoulders.

Crown Prince Wilhelm was being shown the ruins of St. Quentin. It was an unforgettable sight. Recently a flourishing town, it was now a dead heap of stones from English artillery. Long columns of his infantrymen were marching past, eager to get into the battle up ahead. "All round me cheerful faces, cheers and shouts at my car, which had great difficulty in threading its way forward, an irresistible onward march, the beating pulse of a victorious army which knows no law but 'Forward, on the heel of the enemy!'" The Kaiser's eldest son made his way through a heap of ruins to the headquarters of the 231st Division. "I found a group of officers feverishly at work, writing as fast as they could, the telephone to their ears and on their faces an expression of tired but composed satisfaction under the customary mask of quiet responsibility." He shook hands with men and officers before proceeding to the battlefield. "In sorrowful contemplation we gazed on the dead, and with grateful emotion on the wounded, to whom we were fortunately in a position to render some little service of love." On all sides were captured trenches, guns, and vast quantities of war material. Ahead the fire and flame of battle were advancing slowly but steadily. "And over all the horror of the scene and its alternating impressions was the shining spring sun which after long months of doubt filled me with fresh confidence and longing hopes for the future."

In Germany, the news of the great offensive was being devoured at breakfast. "With the old élan and spirit of 1914," reported the *Vossische Zeitung*, "our battalions stormed over the ground and broke the enemy's resistance all along the line. It is unanimously declared that the defenders fought bravely, but the British leadership was not equal to the colossal blow."

Having just learned that Butler's III Corps had been unable to man satisfactorily the Crozat Canal line during the night, Gough asked the French Sixth Army on the right for infantry assistance. General Duchêne felt that he could not lend his reserves but recommended to higher headquarters that a reserve division of Pétain's be sent immediately to Butler's aid. Pétain agreed but insisted that this division, the 125th, remain under French command.

It was welcome news to Gough, for it meant that he might be able, once the French arrived, to pull back III Corps into reserve. He went to breakfast. A little earlier he had given Paul Maze new instructions, explaining that he wanted the Fifth Army "to retire gradually, fighting a rear-guard action all the time and holding on the strategically valuable ground as long as possible." The vital thing, he said, was to make sure that units kept in touch with each other and did not withdraw without warning units alongside. He asked the sergeant, who, because of their personal relationship and Maze's initiative, had become a quasi liaison officer, to help him do this and to start with III Corps. Maze was fatigued as he headed southwest on his motorcycle. It was still misty as he passed the corps gun positions. There was plenty of artillery left. He saw cavalry regiments digging positions behind the Crozat Canal. The front seemed comparatively quiet, but as he neared his destination a heavy enemy barrage opened, spreading northward along the canal. The mist cleared and ahead he saw Tergnier wreathed in smoke.

Minutes after he passed, the vanguard of four German divisions began crossing the canal and piercing the III Corps lines.

Not long after Maze left Nesle, General Gough received a telephone call from Congreve revealing that the latter had misunderstood last evening's instructions concerning withdrawal. Gough had deliberately given verbal orders. Writing down his concept of gradual, fighting withdrawal might have set off a general retreat that could get out of hand. But Congreve had misunderstood his real intent, so might the three other corps commanders. Gough pondered the matter some time and finally at 10:45 dispatched a formal order:

> To all corps, Fifth Army. In the event of serious hostile attack corps will fight rearguard actions back to forward line of Rear Zone, and if necessary to rear line of Rear Zone. Most important that corps should keep close touch with each other and corps belonging to Armies on flanks.

This task completed, Gough set out for a tour of the north. In his absence an operations officer took it upon himself to telephone all corps the heartening but misleading news that the French were sending reinforcements and that it was possible III Corps could be put into reserve. In his conversation with Maxse's XVIII Corps, the operations officer mentioned that Gough was presently planning to hold the line along the Somme and the canal.

This information did not reach Maxse himself until noon. Combined with the order to pull back, he took it to mean that he should withdraw all the way to the Somme. He, in turn, ordered his three forward divisions to disengage and set up new lines on the river. It was a difficult decision that would undoubtedly bring censure, but Maxse, a commander of experience and ability, felt that the precarious position of his corps demanded it. His entire left flank had been exposed since early morning by the withdrawal of his neighbor on the right, III Corps.

But Maxse's decision endangered General Watts, his neighbor on the left. Watts had already ordered the retirement of his two forward divisions but had no idea that Maxse was going all the way back to the Somme and, to his dismay, found his right flank hanging in air. His own withdrawal was orderly and he was careful to keep connected with Congreve on his left. Since Gough was away from his own headquarters, he didn't learn of Maxse's withdrawal until it was under way. He did his best to stop it but it was too late. All he could do now was try to stabilize the line.

At his headquarters, Haig was writing reassuringly to his wife: "You will see we had a great battle yesterday and have done very well. Reports this morning state that our men are in great heart, and had very good targets yesterday. It was a case of 'kill, kill, all day long.' So the enemy must have lost severely." (Lady Haig noted on the letter: "Douglas writes optimistically because remember I am in bed. He really looked terribly anxious when he was at home.")

At his headquarters, Pétain did not know of the latest development and was sending a reassuring report to Paris. There was "no need to be very anxious," for he had made his arrangements: ". . . all that is necessary is for the British to hold on the Somme—and that river seems easy to hold . . . It will be a battle which we will take up in the best of condition."

The right flank of the Third Army was also in peril at the salient near its junction with the Fifth. More trouble was discovered further north once the mist completely disappeared in early afternoon of March 22. The Germans had penetrated to Vraucourt village. A special air reconnaissance brought back such an alarming report that three companies of tanks with infantry in support were ordered to counterattack.

Lieutenant Jünger was leading an assault on Vraucourt. The enemy were Scotsmen and they fought fiercely. The ground was soon heaped with bodies. "It was a nerve-scourging spot. We dashed over the still warm muscular bodies, displaying powerful knees below their kilts, or crept on over them." Abruptly the Jünger storm troops were brought to a halt by bombs and rifle grenades. "Tommy's counterattacking!" went the cry. Jünger, gathering a handful of men, organized a nucleus of resistance behind a broad traverse. Missiles were exchanged at a few yards' distance. "A man of the 76th, close to me, shot off cartridge after cartridge, looking perfectly wild and without thought of cover, till he collapsed in streams of blood." A bullet had smashed into his head and he was now doubled up in a corner of the trench, head leaning against his side. Blood poured out as if it came from a bucket. Snorting death rattles came at intervals, then stopped. Jünger seized the dead man's rifle and began firing.

At Lieutenant Campbell's battery not a shot had yet been fired. It was past midafternoon by the time he was finally ordered to climb to the top of the hill "and for Christ's sake try to find out what's happening." It was a relief to be doing something definite at last. Campbell kept climbing a thousand yards from the battery until the telephone wire ran out. Here he got a good view and could see up to the crest of Chapel Hill. He lay on the ground and put his field glasses up to his eyes. Germans! Thousands of them pouring down the side of Chapel Hill! "It was the chance of a lifetime. Never before had I seen Germans to shoot at."

He yelled, "BATTERY ACTION!" to the signaler behind him, then pulled out a map and hastily worked out the range and angle of fire. The Germans were spurting down the hill in waves and short rushes. Excitement made Campbell slow. He was interrupted by his signaler relaying a message from Bingley: "Captain says we can't fire. Guns are all packed up, ready to move."

Campbell rushed to the telephone. "THE BOCHE WILL BE HERE IN TEN MINUTES!" he screamed. He wanted to add "unless we can stop him" but had to stop for breath. In the pause he heard the calm voice of the signaler on the other end repeating the message to Bingley. "Mr. Campbell says the Boche will be here in ten minutes, sir." It sounded as if the Germans had been invited to tea and would be a few minutes late.

"What's this? What's this?" It was Bingley himself. "What do you mean, ten minutes? You must be mistaken. We've had no orders. The Colonel would have told me."

Campbell tried to control himself. He realized it had been stupid to say ten minutes since the Boche were three thousand yards away. Then it occurred to him that British infantrymen were in between and the Germans coming down the hill were about to attack them. "There are waves of Germans coming down the hill," he said as calmly as possible. "We must fire on them." The dialogue that followed could have come out of a black comedy.

"They must be our own men," said Bingley.

"They're Germans. I can see the shape of their helmets and the colour of their uniforms."

"The guns are all packed up," protested Bingley. "I'm expecting the Colonel's order to move back any minute."

"We must fire," insisted Campbell, in his slight stutter. "No one else is firing at them."

"That shows they are our own people."

"They're Germans. No one else is firing because there's no one left."

"Are you sure they're Germans?"

"Absolutely certain."

"Well," he reluctantly said like a father to a pleading son, "you can have two guns. But you must be careful with the ammunition."

Campbell seethed. For weeks they had been firing hundreds of rounds every night without knowing where they fell. Now in broad daylight they had the whole German army to shoot at and he was supposed to hoard ammunition. He gave orders to the signaler and waited to see where the ranging shells detonated. The first two fell so far to the right that Campbell almost missed them. He corrected the line. The next pair burst harmlessly high in the sky. He corrected the fuse. By the time shells were bursting at the right height the first waves of enemy were out of sight.

Shells were now exploding around Campbell, but he was too excited to care in his eager search for more Germans. He saw a large group running down the hill and shouted, "FIRE!" over his shoulder. This was better. Some of the Germans were ducking their head. "FIVE ROUNDS RAPID," he shouted, but no shells passed overhead.

"Captain says we must go in now," said the signaler as if they were being hustled home to dinner. "Order's come and we're to go back. He's told guns to stop firing."

Campbell seized the phone and asked for Bingley. Gone. He asked for any officer. All gone. "What are we to do, sir?" asked the signaler. "We've got to go back," said Campbell, and walked down the hill without saying another word. He was bitterly disappointed with himself. One of the other officers would surely have ordered the guns to go on firing, whatever Bingley said.

Some fifteen air miles to the south the situation was even more desperate at the battery of former Prime Minister Asquith's son. Both flanks were now threatened but they continued to fire. They had been doing so for almost thirty-six hours with scarcely any rest. The recoil mechanism of two guns now had to be run by hand. The men's eyes were inflamed by gas, their faces lined with fatigue. But upon receiving an order to fall back to the town of Ham, they were amazed. That was a ten-mile march by road, and such an order was beyond their experience; ". . . it dawned on us at last that the reinforcements we had imagined were creatures of our own fancy."

The march back was somber. Great shells from long-range German guns roared overhead to fall on villages far behind the battlefield. Wounded hobbled along the road since there were no ambulances, nor could they be loaded on the limbers since the guns had to be ready to go into action again at any moment. During one halt Asquith at last became conscious that he had eaten almost nothing since the battle started. He remembered there was a piece of chocolate in his pocket and found it nestling against a small edition of *Pickwick Papers*. As he ravenously ate the worn chocolate the mere thought of Pickwick added "a startling emphasis to the scene that surrounded us."

They found shells falling in Ham, some of them aimed at the Somme canal bridges. The people had vanished in such haste that the shutters of many shops were unclosed. At the butcher's meat was still hanging on hooks; dresses and hats adorned the windows of the draper. A civilian ran out and handed one of Asquith's comrades a large box of eggs; he didn't want the Boche to get them.

British were also retreating on the southern flank of the Third Army. Germans had broken through in several places to converge on Bapaume. Late in the afternoon British batteries were ordered to move behind the town in case of a breakthrough. As the guns moved back along the Cambrai-Bapaume highway, their officers wondered why the Germans were not pounding the vital road with long-range guns. It would have created chaos.

This road also seemed wide open to an infantry attack, and the 2nd Tank Battalion was ordered to block the way. The order came as a surprise to young subalterns of one company who had been sunning themselves and listening to the twittering of birds. Action was the last thing they imagined. They knew there was a war somewhere out there, but it didn't even remotely seem to concern them. Lieutenant R. Watson Kerr had just been unexpectedly called back to his unit from a gunnery course. As he got his tank under way, he shouted to the reconnaissance officer, "Where's the front line?" There was none. "Well, where's the Boche then?"

"Do you see there?" The other was pointing over the sunny fields ahead. Kerr could see no signs of war. "Well, just walk right on and you'll soon find the Boche."

Kerr experienced a slight thrill, but after rumbling several miles cross-country with several other tanks he got a bigger one. Empty shell casings, "pip-squeaks," began to drop all around. Friendly guns must be firing nearby. To his right he saw a battery of field guns firing in the open. To his amazement, the artillerymen began shouting, "The tanks! The tanks!" Their officer flourished his cap enthusiastically.

Kerr and his colleague sheepishly waved back. Those artillerymen must have been pretty desperate to cheer like that. The tanks crept forward, their commanders searching for supporting infantry. They had not been told they were on their own. Kerr saw a knoll ahead and brought his tank gently up the slope wondering, Where are those Germans? "Then suddenly I saw them. Battalions of them against the distant skyline, a swarming mass marching towards us in the open country. My driver and I could not believe our eyes at first." He could have sworn they were marching to music. He was sure he saw horses, ornamental harnesses sparkling, banners and an orderly glitter. "Here was the Drang nach Paris in full marching order in brilliant sunlight and with nobody apparently to stop it but ourselves. And what a target!"

Kerr could hear the gunner on his left blazing away and, exalted, he got his own Hotchkiss ready. He opened fire. Strip after strip rattled through the gun and he could see the imposing mass of attackers melt against the horizon. It was fantastic, incredible, and was over in a moment. "Had I actually seen what I had seen? Or was I dreaming?" Only the bare hill remained. He was startled when a small, fat German soldier darted up from under the nose of his tank and ran wildly ahead. He looked comical with his equipment dangling and jangling all round him. Kerr laughed, drew his pistol, opened the steel flap in front and fired. The little fat German sprawled to the ground unharmed. It was funny until Kerr saw a network of trenches swarming with enemy machine-gunners. The Germans were even more startled and many began scrambling to the woods behind. Kerr charged them, the tank bumping and swaying perilously on the uneven ground. Inside, the noise, heat, and fumes increased. Then came a fierce rattling of shells followed instantly by splashes of hot metal against his tank. Kerr knew he had to get out of this deathtrap. He shouted to the driver and the big tank slowly began to mount the trench, its tracks biting into the loose soil, its tail dipping dangerously low. The earth in front crunched away and the vehicle climbed further. All at once the engine stopped and there was silence.

Kerr turned and stared at the driver. It was the end. Then he shouted, "Come on, get her going again!" His voice sounded hideously loud in the cavernous silence. They swung around the starting handle. Miracle! The engine spluttered into life again. They plowed out of the dangerous ground and headed down the valley for home. Out of the fumes on the grass a khaki figure waved pleadingly. Kerr recognized a member of a friend's crew. Kerr waved back and made for him. The man sprang up and ran across the open. After a few steps he was shot down. He struggled to his feet and Kerr saw that his face was yellow. Gas! He shouted to open the door. Two of the crew pulled in the wounded man. He slumped heavily and Kerr wondered if he would get back alive. Their "bus" was now roaring full speed down the valley. Another tank suddenly emerged ahead and made for them. A German? No, it was one of their own company heading for the hell he had just left. "Good luck!" thought Kerr, and waved to its officer.

The gallant counterattack did save Bapaume, but of the twenty-five tanks that went out only nine returned and 70 per cent of the personnel were either killed or captured.

A few miles to the south Donald Boyd's battery was firing a slow barrage at the oncoming enemy. He was sent on his bicycle to help place the wagon line nearby in case of retreat. A flight of shells abruptly fell in the midst of the column, throwing their metal along the ground. Boyd signaled the teams to retire over the hill. They reversed and trotted off in perfect order, but the next salvo caught them. Three teams vanished in the smoke, finally struggled into sight pitching and falling. Boyd knew that he had to shoot the wounded horses at once. As shells continued to fall, he crawled from one to another, dispatching them. His hand grew so unsteady he had to rest the Webley on his left forearm to level the barrel over the brainpan. One horse stared and started to rise. Blood gushed onto Boyd's coat. "The last horse kicked and relaxed with a groan and as I watched him, feeling as though my inner creature had been emptied out, I saw the kind, confiding light in his eyes die, as if a dirty cloud had flowed into them." He walked back to the battery in a deep orange sunset that seemed sinister. He told his major about the shelling.

"This is going to be a fight to a finish," said the officer. "To the end."

Some miles further south Lieutenant Pat Campbell's battery was on its way back to Nurlu. Almost everything was left behind including two thousand rounds of the ammunition which Captain Bingley had ordered him to conserve. Campbell remembered he had left his rug and, without a word to anyone, galloped back to the old position. Two men were there. Germans? No, English officers. One sat in Bingley's green canvas chair. "Time you got out," shouted Campbell. "The Boche will be here in a few minutes." He saw they were padres.

"Most of our men who are left have been taken prisoner," said the man in the chair. "Our place is with them." He handed Campbell his name and address. "Write to my wife."

Campbell shook hands with them both, grabbed his rug, a writing case containing his 1917 diary, a letter from a girl, and the book he was reading. He galloped off hoping to get back before anyone realized he had gone. On the way he almost rode into three Scottish machine-gunners. One was wounded and the others were wheeling him along on a bicycle. They were stuck on a rise, and before Campbell, who was Scotch-Irish himself, grasped fully what he was doing he said, "We can put him on my horse." Campbell led the horse with the two others following. He was so involved in bemoaning the delay that he didn't notice the other two Scotsmen had somehow gotten in front and were riding away on the bicycle. "I shouted. But they did not hear me, or may not have wanted to, and the sound of my own voice made me realize how alone I was. Alone with a wounded soldier in the middle of a battle!" The battlefield was silent, deserted. The shadows were beginning to lengthen. It was beautiful. The abandoned guns on the side of the road looked out of place, incongruous with the peaceful scene. Nothing marred the quiet dignity of the downs except those deserted guns—and a wounded man on a horse. Well, he had got himself into a proper mess. His charge was in pain and, to support him on the horse, Campbell put the rug around his shoulder and told him to carry the writing case. The sun was a great red ball at the edge of the horizon by the time Campbell came to a field ambulance. The doctor in charge at first refused to take the wounded man. "I can't leave him for the Boche," argued Campbell, "and I can't go on leading him all over France. I've got to find my battery."

He won the argument and thankfully galloped off in search of his battery. The enemy was shelling a crossroad in Nurlu. The retreating column would wait for a shell to burst, and then a half-dozen wagons would dash madly across to safety. One too many went as Campbell approached. Dead men and horses sprawled across the road. One man was struggling to get up. Another pulled him out of the way of other thundering wagons. It was a padre who asked, "Are you a doctor?" Campbell shook his head. "Then go away. In God's name, go quickly."

Campbell turned as he was riding away. There was the screech of an incoming shell. The padre didn't move. Fortunately the shell burst harmlessly into a house. At last Campbell found his battery. As he sat down to eat there came an order to retreat still further. He stuffed biscuits into his pocket and mounted his horse. All his strength was gone. Excitement and the sense of responsibility had kept him going that day, but as darkness fell he knew he was finished. "And as my strength had gone, so had my courage, and instead of wanting to be up in the front of the battle I was eager to go back, to get as far away as possible from the enemy, to go more quickly, not to be held up on the road, the road was packed with other transport, we were stuck, we should never get away." For the first time he realized the magnitude of their defeat and it overcame him. "This was the most catastrophic defeat that Britain had ever suffered, and it seemed to me that I was partly responsible for the disaster. I could have stopped the enemy at Chapel Hill. I ought to have done so." If he had kept his head he could have fired that two thousand rounds of ammunition left behind. "That was my job—to kill Germans, not to go galloping about with a rug or taking a wounded Scottish machine-gunner on my horse." *

* Some weeks later Campbell was awarded the Military Cross "for directing the fire of his battery from a most forward position, inflicting heavy casualties on the advancing enemy, exposing himself to great danger and supplying much valuable information throughout." He was distressed to read it and at first felt unhappy whenever he caught sight of the purple and white

37

To left and right the blackness of night was bright with explosions. Petrol stores and ammunition dumps were being destroyed to keep them from the enemy. Huts blazed on all sides. A corporal riding beside Campbell said nervously, "Some of the lads is saying, sir, that we're luring Jerry on. What do you think, sir?"

From his white, anxious face, it was obvious that Campbell, as an officer, should give reassurance. But he could not help. He was as unhappy as the corporal, and more despondent. "I don't know," he said. "I don't know what to think." About all he really wanted out of life was to be an author—a live one.

To the south, a few miles east of Gough's headquarters at Nesle, which was about to be abandoned, Captain R. S. Cockburn of the 20th Division Reinforcement Battalion was startled by the shouts of a strange officer. "Fall in your men at once! They're coming here already! Their cavalry are on the road outside the village!"

Cockburn didn't believe him until the other explained he was the staff officer of a division and had just come from headquarters. "It's quite true what I tell you. There's not a minute to spare!" Cockburn took a closer look and recognized him; they had gone to school together. Cockburn ran back to his own hut, sent off the transport, then roused his men. The road outside was already in disorder and he decided to picket the village: first, to stop any enemy breaking through; second, to collect stragglers. He sent off an officer on horseback to report to Brigade what was happening here at Matigny, and asked for orders.

For the first time he began to feel the pathos of retreat. "I cannot tell you how depressing it was to stand on the road and watch the endless stream of men, horses, motor cars, motor lorries, ambulances, mules, artillery and other limbers, and guns, moving past us with scarcely an interval between them. Wretched, mud-stained soldiers limped along, often without equipment or rifles. There were wounded men, too, with labels dangling from their coats, trying to avoid being crushed by the traffic, or sitting down by the roadside from sheer fatigue, their heads in their hands."

Gough was far north visiting the commander of the Third Army, General Julian Byng. Gough was worried about the gap opening between the two armies, and Byng agreed to order his right-flank corps to make a limited withdrawal. This done, Gough headed south for his new headquarters at Villers-Bretonneux, since Nesle was already in danger of falling. He drove through the darkness along the Somme, occasionally stopping to chat with small groups of men. They looked cheerful but he saw they were fatigued. Some were sleeping at rest stops.

At 8 P.M. Gough telephoned Haig: "Parties of all arms of the enemy are through our Reserve Line." Haig approved his decision

---

ribbon on his tunic. But his colleagues seemed to think it was all right for him to have a medal and he soon became proud of it. "By the time the War came to an end I no longer even felt regret at my failure to kill Germans on Chapel Hill."

to fall back and defend the line of the Somme and to hold the Péronne bridgehead. Then the field marshal telephoned Pétain for his support. The Frenchman agreed to do his utmost. His earlier confidence shaken, he now doubted if the British would "really be able to hold on to the Somme." He ordered General Humbert, commander of the French Third Army, to assume command the following noon of all French and British troops at the south end of the battlefield. Humbert's mission was "to insure the holding of the line of the Crozat Canal and of the Somme."

In London, Chief of Staff Henry Wilson finally concluded this was indeed the great offensive. "I don't understand," he wrote in his diary, "why we are giving ground so quickly nor how the Boches get through our Battle Zone apparently so easily."

Already Lloyd George was having second thoughts about his new Chief of the Imperial General Staff. Admittedly Wilson had "the nimblest intelligence amongst the soldiers of high degree." He was witty, sharp-tongued, and could expound a military problem with lucidity. But he was "whimsical almost to the point of buffoonery," responding to a grave problem facetiously and with droll frivolity. He would even jest over matters of life and death. "This habit," thought Lloyd George, "detracted from the weight and authority which his position and capacity ought to have given to his counsel." Still, he was a brilliant staff officer and there was no one better fitted for the post available—and where could one find any more delightful companion to ease the boredom of long conferences?

His appearance was as arresting as his characteristics. He was extremely tall. His willowy figure seemed to climb up and up indefinitely to be topped by a face of fascinating ruggedness. Of this he was inordinately proud and boasted that he had once received a postcard addressed to the ugliest man in London. At conferences he would indulge in clowning. To illustrate trench warfare, he once reversed his cap so only the red band showed like that of a German soldier, then bent his towering frame, face level with a table, using his cane to take potshots at the conferees. Such antics were irresistible to some people and tickled the Prime Minister himself. His secretary and mistress, Frances Stevenson, found Wilson possessed of great charm. "A typical Irishman," she wrote, "he was the best company in the world . . . We enjoyed his gay and amusing—often deliberately challenging—conversation, his easy manner, and even his contempt for the 'frocks,' as he called the politicians. He was in every way the complete opposite of Robertson, whom he succeeded."

Wilson's Irish ebullience had made him a favorite of the French. Despite his poor command of their language, he understood the emotional, rhetorical manner of the Latins and in debate knew how to gain their vote with a joke. He did things no other British leader would dare attempt. Once he strode into Clemenceau's room at a time when the press was criticizing the Frenchman's age, grabbed the Tiger, and whirled him in a wild dance around the room until his black skullcap flew off. "Just," he told the delighted Clemenceau, "to show them how young we really are."

But Haig distrusted him almost as much as he did his own great enemy, Lloyd George. "They are both humbugs," he wrote his wife, "and it is difficult to decide exactly what is at the bottom of the mind of each of them. Wilson, I fancy, has plans more deeply laid than the other. But we'll see—meantime, both profess great friendship for me." He didn't add that Wilson's bizarre sense of humor, especially in discussion of grave subjects, was highly distasteful.

As for Wilson, he was equally critical of Haig, and, after a recent meeting, noted in his diary: "I have never seen him so stupid and un-accommodating. He is a remarkably stupid narrow prejudiced insular person." Under the strain of the present military crisis, this clash of personalities was even more pronounced and the still unsettled feud between London and the field generals threatened to break out anew in dead earnest.

4.

Saturday, March 23, was another day of retreat. It dawned bitter cold, and fog once more covered most of the battlefield. North of the strategic town of Bapaume, Captain Arthur Behrend was wakened by his colonel, who thrust a message from Corps into his hand and turned on the light. Behrend read with dismay that the Germans had broken through at Mory. "We have no troops left to put in the line."

"Wake up the others and tell them to dress," said the colonel. "Tell an officer of each battery to stand by the phone." Behrend passed on the bad news, then stood by the doorway watching and listening. To the northeast big guns were pounding and the sky flickered incessantly. All at once a great flash obliterated the darkness. It came from one of their own sixty-pounder batteries at the end of the village. This shell and others ripped overhead with hollow blasting roars. A flock of startled birds exploded from the church and kept wheeling overhead.

After breakfast Behrend was vainly trying to estimate how much ammunition was left, when he heard the sounds of bagpipes and drums. He ran outside. 'It was magnificent and too moving for words. No music, not even the trumpets of the French cavalry . . . has stirred me as deeply as the sobbing, skirling pipes of the 51st [Highland] Division playing their survivors back to the battle, and I shivered with pride as I stood there watching these grim Highlanders swing by—every man in step, every man bronzed and resolute. Could these be the weary, dirty men who came limping past us yesterday in ragged twos and threes, asking pitifully how much further to Achiet-le-Grand? Who could behold such a spectacle and say that the pomp and circumstance of War is no more?"

There was music down south in the Fifth Army too. Just west

of Ham, the Cornwalls, digging in after their long withdrawal of yesterday, were ordered by a desperate brigadier to drop picks and shovels and attack the village of Verlaines. "Off we go in good artillery formation," recalled one officer. "The mist has cleared and it is quite hot—a good day for tennis." Suddenly he heard martial music. It was a band of the 7th Cornwalls, trying to cheer up the men. After two miles they came on the village. They extended, fixed bayonets, and trudged on hot, exhausted, and hungry. Several men fainted. The rest jogged forward and most of the Germans in the village bolted. "As we pass through . . . I see a half a loaf of stale bread and a bottle of lukewarm wine on the ground which I pick up as I rush on." Nearing the crest of a ridge, they advanced in short rushes. "When we halt I pass the bread along the men and eat some myself as it seems one's only chance of ever getting food inside you."

Captain C. N. Tyacke urged on the next rush and they were on the crest. "We are now getting it in the neck from machine gun and rifle fire especially from snipers in the houses, Tyacke is shot through the heart." They had overrun their objective. "The men are knocked out as they lie and the stretcher bearers, who were splendid, all killed. We get our Lewis guns on to about twelve Boches who run from the houses and scupper them. I get a rifle and kill one to my intense satisfaction." There were other valiant British counterattacks but for the most part it turned into a desperate retreat to safety.

Many miles to the rear, Mildred Aldrich, an American living in France, was sitting in her garden listening to the faraway roar of guns. Then at 7:20 A.M. she heard an explosion from the direction of Paris. As she was wondering what it meant, church bells all along the valley began sounding the alert.

In Paris something had exploded on the stone pavement in front of a house on the Quai de la Seine. What was it? Civilians thought it was an air bomb, but to soldiers it sounded like a 77 mm. high explosive shell. There was not much excitement, since no one was hurt and there was little damage. Twenty minutes later came another tremendous explosion a mile and a half away in front of the Gare de l'Est. Whatever it was landed near one of the busiest Métro stations and there was panic. Eight people were dead, thirteen others injured. Police headquarters informed President Poincaré, Premier Clemenceau, and the Artillery Office. Artillery and aviation officers, together with explosions experts, were rushed to the scene. In the next hour and twenty-four minutes, five more explosions hit Paris, the last in the suburb town of Châtillon. This one upset the experts' calculations but at least brought some appearance of action. The sirens began to shriek. It was alarming, since it was the first time the alert had sounded in daytime. Buses and taxis stopped to spill out passengers who joined the rush for shelter. The Métro stations were jammed. Some trains were canceled. The busy Saturday crowd was in flight but there

FIRST
LUDENDORFF OFFENSIVE
MAR. 21– APR. 5

MILES 15
KM 15
N

Lens

Vimy

SCARPE

Arras

GER.
SEVENTEENTH
ARMY
BELOW

BR.
THIRD ARMY
BYNG

Doullens

Quéant

Cambrai

Mory

Achiet-
le-Grand

Vraucourt

Achiet-le-Petit

Bapaume

ANCRE

Mesnil

Heudecourt

GER.
SECOND
ARMY
MARWITZ

Albert

Nurlu

Épehy

Maricourt

Hangicourt

Sailly-le-Sec

Bray

Péronne

Roisel

Amiens

SOMME

Villers-
Bretonneux

VII CORPS
CONGREVE

St. Quentin

GER. EIGHTEENTH ARMY HUTIER

BR.
FIFTH ARMY
GOUGH

Matigny

XIX CORPS
WATTS

SOMME

Moreuil

Nesle

Ham

CROZAT CANAL

Flavy-le-Martel

Roye

XVIII CORPS
MAXSE

CANAL DU NORD

AVRE

Montdidier

III CORPS
BUTLER

Tergnier

Noyon

OISE

—— Front Line Mar. 21
– – – Front Line Apr. 5
···· Army Boundaries

FR. SIXTH ARMY
DUCHÊNE

was no panic. By 9:30 A.M. the experts realized that the projectiles might be coming from the German lines—and the nearest ones were sixty-seven miles away. Guns of such size would have to be positioned up to ten miles further back and that would make the range up to seventy-seven miles. Incredible.

The shells were coming from a great gun located in woods near Laon, some seventy-five miles from Paris. It was a monstrous thing, as long as a ten-story building. Its carriage was twenty-five feet high. The first shell climbed to a height of twenty-five miles and took exactly 176 seconds to reach Paris. Fifteen shots were fired that morning and officers and Krupp technicians were not at all surprised or dejected to discover that the sizzling hot gun already showed signs of wear and would probably last only for another forty-five shots. It was not the only gun of its kind. There were six others and two of these were located in the same woods. The celebration was heightened by the announcement that the Kaiser would arrive about 1 P.M. to witness the next firings.

That morning Wilhelm couldn't stay away from the front lines and, following in his son's footsteps of the previous day, was visiting the area near St. Quentin with Hindenburg. Their car, so recalled Colonel Birch, who had been captured the day before, stopped at the head of a column of prisoners. The Kaiser got out of the car and talked to the British in a rather gruff voice. "Well, gentlemen, you have fought very bravely but . . ." and he lapsed into German, "God is with us." He asked where a British regiment was but no one answered. The Kaiser put his foot on the running board and Birch noticed he was wearing rather crude riding breeches with leather gaiters bound with straps. Certainly not very regal garb.

The automobile drove off, destination Laon and the big guns, but within the hour another procession of cars approached. It too stopped and Crown Prince Wilhelm stepped out of one of the vehicles. Birch was amused that "Little Willie's" outfit was much smarter than his father's and had a "London made" look about it. His English was also better. "Hurrah," he said, "the war will soon be over. We are today already bombarding Paris, and in 15 days we shall be in London. Hurrah, the war is nearly over." The prisoners did not reply and when he drew out a large gold case to offer cigarettes, no one accepted.

German newspapers were celebrating the victory in the west. "Away with all petty whining over an agreement and reconciliation with the fetish of peace," said the *Deutsche Zeitung.* "Away with the miserable whimpering of those people who even now would prevent the righteous German hatred of England and sound German vengeance. The cry of victory and retaliation rages throughout Germany with renewed passion."

Germania was equally belligerent and confident. "There can be no lasting peace and long period of quiet in the world until the presumptuous notion that the Anglo-Saxons are the chosen people is victorious or defeated. We are determined to force with the sword the peace which our adversaries did not see fit to confide to our honest word."

At 9:30 A.M. Ludendorff had issued new orders: Seventeenth Army would "attack with full force" up toward Arras, the keystone of Haig's defense system. The Second Army would advance near the junction of the British Third and Fifth Armies; and the Eighteenth would advance a few miles north of Nesle with strong forces coming by way of Ham.

The streets of Nesle were jammed with vehicles heading toward Gough's new headquarters in Villers-Bretonneux. The inhabitants rushed about anxiously, not knowing whether they were to go or stay. Some called to each other from doorsteps to windows; others were trying in vain to persuade lorry drivers to cart them and some furniture to the rear. Sergeant Maze was still gathering material for Gough. He first pumped General Uniacke, the Fifth Army artillery commander, who admitted he had lost many guns but was getting replacements from General Headquarters. As Maze left town long lines of XVIII Corps lorries were driving into the town. General Maxse was taking over Gough's former headquarters. Cycling past one of the hospitals, Maze saw nurses in their long coats, holding little bags, waiting by the side of the road for lorries. They reminded him of passengers standing by the lifeboats of a sinking ship after a collision in the fog.

The Kaiser was so eager to see the big guns that he arrived at the site ahead of time. He examined the installation with great interest and was suitably impressed when Number 1 Paris Gun resumed firing at 12:57. He left after a few rounds to inspect the two other guns.

The first round fell at exactly 1 P.M. in the Tuileries Gardens, injuring no one. Fifteen minutes later the second barely missed the statue in the center of the Place de la République. Two people were killed, nine wounded. By 2:45 P.M. the twenty-fifth and final projectile of the day landed in or near Paris. Sixteen civilians in all were killed, and while the damage could not compare to the terrifying aerial bombing on the night of January 30, today's raid struck a new terror into Parisians. Bombardment by artillery was a terrifying experience that even shook hardened soldiers.

Taking advantage of the improved weather, the Royal Flying Corps was out in strength harassing the advancing gray waves and their supply columns. Sopwith Camels shot down hundreds of horses pulling German artillery. But the British retreat continued, and from north to south they were fighting rearguard action as they destroyed equipment and burned papers.

The Germans had broken through on both sides of the junction between the Third and Fifth Armies and were threatening Bapaume and Péronne. British infantry holding a line on the road between those two towns saw Germans appear over the horizon.

44

After a few shots they got orders to retire quickly. "And now followed the saddest and most terrible part of the retreat," wrote Private R. D. Fisher of the London Regiment. "It was terrible not because of danger, for the enemy was following us with a half-mile's distance, but because of the utterly exhausted condition of the men, after half-a-week without sleep, moving, moving, digging, digging, and having very little to eat or drink. As we went along other men appeared from all sides to join us, so that in half-an-hour we had grown from a small party into an immense line numbering thousands of retreating men, tramping dejectedly along, across the open country. We could see neither the front nor rear of the column, nor did we have any idea where it was going." Units became jumbled and the men were so fatigued and dispirited that order was impossible. They dragged along, each at his own pace, throwing away equipment. In places five or six moved abreast while others were drifting back alone. But all went in the same, unknown direction. "Often as we passed the water-filled shell-holes, men would dash out to fill a mess-tin or water-bottle, ignoring the few officers who reprimanded them, for the water was probably poisonous or foul. At times, too, men fell out and sat on the ground, too exhausted, or without the spirit to continue."

They tramped on until someone exclaimed, "German cavalry! They are surrounding us!" There was panic flight. A few officers and noncoms near Fisher shouted to make a stand, and thirty men, bayonets fixed, lined a shallow trench. But there were no Germans coming and, after five minutes, Fisher and the others clambered out of the trench and followed the retreating mob.

General Congreve allowed time for the civilians and rear installations to evacuate Péronne before the order was given to abandon it. At the casualty clearing stations quick and terrible decisions were being made to determine which men were going to die and had to be left behind. The streets were jammed with retreating troops and the roads out of towns were congested, since the adjoining fields were too torn up for traffic. "Some infantry were able to make their way across the fields," reported VII Corps, "but the masses on the roads were such that had the enemy's aircraft been active, enormous damage could have been done." Pilot Rudolf Stark did manage to get through to Péronne and flew over the town at a hundred meters. He saw the enemy artillery in retreat. Many khaki figures lay scattered on the ground. Then his engine began sputtering and he had to turn back.

British reinforcements heading east toward the crumbling front were appalled by the headlong retreat to the Somme. "Dumps of kits and valises lay on the side of the road, disorganized transport and guns were moving to the rear, all intermingled with pathetic groups of refugees," recalled Lieutenant Richard Gale, a machine-gunner of the 42nd Division. "Canteens had been abandoned and their stores of spirit rifled. This was a retreat with all the horrors of panic. There was, as far as we knew, nothing behind us and the

Channel ports, save this wretched rabble that seemed to have lost all cohesion and will to fight."

The sad plight of the civilians distressed H. E. L. Mellersh, a company commander. "Old women in black dresses there were; bent old men trundling wheelbarrows; girls in their Sunday best—to wear it the best way to save it; farm carts loaded with the miscellany of hens, pigs, furniture, children, mattresses, bolsters; moody cows being whacked and led by little boys. There were ambulances coming down the road too and British Army lorries with the bright painted Divisional signs on them. At the back of one of these sat a row of Army nurses. They waved; and we cheered. I think it was a shock to all of us, to realize that nurses were so near to the fighting and were also having to retreat. But for a moment we felt heroic—were we not going forward to protect them?"

Early that afternoon a calm and cheerful Haig visited Gough at Villers-Bretonneux. Gough hoped that his superior had come with a new strategy and expected orders, but Haig had apparently come only to listen. Finally Gough said that his troops would fight as long as they could but that casualties were far exceeding the reinforcements. "Well, Hubert," said Haig, "one can't fight without men." He didn't mention it but was surprised to find that Gough's troops were already behind the Somme, and as Haig drove back to his own advance headquarters at Dury to see Pétain, he was thinking, "I cannot make out why the Fifth Army has gone so far back without making some kind of a stand." At 4 P.M. he saw Pétain, who said that he was putting two armies under General Fayolle on the southern flank to operate in the Somme Valley. The important thing, he stressed, was to keep the French and British in touch with one another. He reiterated that he was anxious to do all he could to support the British and keep in touch with them, then revealed his doubt that the latter could be done. If contact *was* lost, he said, almost as a prediction, the enemy would drive a wedge between the two forces, "then probably the British will be rounded up and driven into the sea."

His gloom chilled Haig, who was convinced that such a catastrope "must be prevented even at the cost of drawing back the north flank on the sea coast." The two men were talking at cross-purposes, for each was obsessed by his own nation's strategic interest: Britain's to bolster its north flank, to maintain a clear line to the Channel ports, and, if need be, escape home; France's to save Paris, the heart of France, at all costs.

Ludendorff had foreseen that these conflicting national concerns would affect over-all strategy in a divided command, and was telling General H. H. von Kuhl and Colonel von der Schulenberg, "The object now is to separate the French and British by a rapid advance on either side of the Somme. The Seventeenth Army will conduct the attack against the British north of the Somme to drive them into the sea. They will keep attacking at new places in order to bring the entire British front to ruin . . . South of the

46

Somme, operations will be conducted offensively against the French by a wheel to the line Amiens–Montdidier–Noyon, followed by an advance south-westward. In so doing, the Second Army must press forward on both sides of the Somme towards Amiens keeping in close touch with the Eighteenth Army."

Success of this plan was based on the premise that the armies of Gough and Byng were already defeated. If Ludendorff were correct, it would mean sudden victory for Germany. The next forty-eight hours would bring the answer.

Earlier that day Sir George Riddell drove out to Walton Heath to find his good friend Lloyd George waiting for him. "I must go back to London at once," the Prime Minister said. "The news is very bad. I fear it means disaster. Come with me!" On the way back to the city he told Riddell that the Germans had broken through and the Third and Fifth Armies had been defeated. He complained that Haig had made no preparation for the attack even though Henry Wilson had foreseen and warned of it. It would have been amusing if Haig, Repington, and Maurice could have listened to this revision of fact from the back seat.

The Prime Minister decided to postpone the daily Cabinet meeting and to take matters in hand at the War Office itself. In extremity, he was always at his best and he again rose to the crisis. "I invited the Staff to meet me there in order to see what could be done to throw all available reinforcements into France with the greatest attainable celerity." A pledge had been given in Parliament that those under nineteen years of age should not be sent overseas unless there was a national emergency. That emergency had arisen, he said. He also saw to it that the 170,000 troops in England would be moved across the Channel as fast as ships could take them. The usual rate was 8,000 a day, but he raised this to 20,000 by hastily scraping together the necessary shipping.

Later that afternoon he called a Cabinet meeting at the War Office to consider the situation and approve the measures taken earlier. They discussed French tardiness in helping Haig, and it was suggested that either the Prime Minister or Lord Milner leave at once for Paris to put political pressure on their ally. But General Wilson wisely observed that it was undesirable for ministers to interfere between Haig and Pétain until these two had had a chance to adjust matters between themselves. The two men, he said, were scheduled to meet that day to discuss the problem.

General Maurice was asked to supply the latest figures of comparison between enemy and Allied forces and reported that the German rifle strength had increased to 1,402,800, while the Allied strength had decreased to 1,418,000. "War Cabinet in a panic," commented Maurice in his diary, "and talking of arrangements for falling back on Channel ports and evacuating our troops to England." War commentator Repington wrote in his: "The Cabinet much rattled . . . All the blindness and folly of the War Cabinet for a year past are now bearing their bitter fruits." Wilson finished his with predictable flippancy: *"Le bon dieu est boche."*

That evening Ludendorff was jubilant. "The superiority of German leaders and troops made itself felt to the full," he wrote in the daily report. "On the battlefield between the Scarpe and Oise, within a period of three days from the 21st to the 23rd instant, the English Army suffered the greatest defeat in British history. The successes achieved in the great victory are such as have not been nearly approached by the Entente since the beginning of the battle of positions in the western theater." He did not know that Erich, his youngest son, had just died in a plane crash. On the last evening before he left to fight in the great offensive, the youth had told his mother not to be sad. "Remember that I love my profession with my whole heart and although I have gone through a great deal I wouldn't have missed a moment of this last year." Then he confided that his highest ambition was to be a general like his father, and he was always very hurt when he heard people whispering, "Naturally, he is Ludendorff's son." He wanted above all to be recognized and respected for his own sake. Frau Ludendorff was alone when she learned by telephone of her son's death.* "I felt the full force of the blow. I do not know what happened. I only know that I collapsed and from that day onwards for years I was always sick and sorry."

It had been a day of triumph for the Kaiser. After his visit to the mammoth Paris Gun he returned to his private train. "The battle is won," he shouted to the guard on the platform. "The English have been utterly defeated!" At dinner with his staff the communiqué was read telling of the great victory under the personal leadership of His Majesty the Emperor. He drank a champagne toast to the army and its great leaders, quickly followed by one from his chief adjutant, Colonel General Hans von Plessen: "To our War Lord and leader!"

Premier Clemenceau and General Pétain were dining at Supreme Command Headquarters when confirmation of the German success arrived. The somber information did not faze Clemenceau, who remained calm and full of confidence as Pétain explained that it was essential to stop the Germans or at least delay them. The problem was that there were no divisions available. Pétain continued eating, then suddenly exclaimed to General Duval, the Director of Aviation, "Take the telephone!" Duval, astonished, lay down his fork and rose. Then his face brightened when he realized this meant that Pétain was going to throw all available air forces into the battle on the southern flank. The German divisions wait-

---

* Weeks later the Mayor of Nesle, still in German hands, reported that two unknown German airmen had been found nearby. Ludendorff went to the area immediately and identified his son. The body was returned to Supreme Headquarters at Avesnes, and later brought to Berlin, where young Ludendorff was interred next to his brother.

ing for dawn to begin their attack would be mercilessly bombed that night.

Lloyd George was having dinner as guest of the American Ambassador, Walter Hines Page. The dinner was in honor of the U. S. Secretary of War, Newton Baker, and present were two other Americans, General Biddle and Admiral William Sims, as well as Lords Balfour and Derby. Little was said about the battle raging across the Channel. Lloyd George and Balfour relaxed by reviewing their political careers and especially their old-time political battles. In those days they had delighted in putting each other "in a hole," but now they were colleagues. "The whole talk was lively and bantering, and accompanied with much laughter," recalled Page, but he noticed that occasionally Lloyd George would send out a secretary who would return and whisper something in his ear. "This battle means one thing," he said, at last referring to what was on everyone's mind, the inevitability of giving Foch over-all command of Allied forces. "That is a generalissimo."

"Why couldn't you have taken this step long ago?" asked Admiral Sims.

"If the Cabinet two weeks ago had suggested placing the British Army under a foreign general," he promptly replied, "it would have fallen. Every cabinet in Europe would also have fallen, had it suggested such a thing."

After he left Page's, Lloyd George summoned Lord Milner, a member of his War Cabinet. One of them would have to go to France at once to see why the arrangements for mutual help had failed. There seemed to be endless maneuvering between Pétain and Haig without any results. "It was therefore decided," wrote Lloyd George, "that nothing would put an end to this calamitous manoeuvering but the direct intervention of the meddling politicians." The two agreed that there was only one effective thing to do: put General Foch in charge of both armies. They also agreed that the Prime Minister had to stay in London and that it would be foolhardy to send Lord Derby, the War Minister. He was too much a weakling for such a critical mission. He was regarded as "the flabby jelly" by Maurice Hankey, the Secretary of the War Cabinet, and by Haig as "a very weak-minded fellow, I am afraid, and like the feather pillow, bears the mark of the last person who sat on him!" Lloyd George instructed Milner to leave early the next morning, authorizing him to do his utmost to restore Allied relations "by conferring upon Foch the necessary authority to organise a reserve and to control its disposition."

Haig's letter to his wife that day was realistic. "Situation is serious," he wrote, "but keep cheerful, as you always have done. The enemy has brought his *whole* strength against us."

5.

Sunday, March 24, was a day of crisis. At 2 A.M. a French corporal, Georges Gaudy, wakened with a start as the column of trucks carrying his regiment up to the front lines came to an abrupt stop.

There was a clatter as a long line of artillerymen on horseback moved past in the opposite direction. It was obvious from the pace that the horses were tired and were pulling empty limbers and wagons. Someone said the English were retreating and they had no guns.

"Where do you come from?" Gaudy called to a Briton. "D'you think they'll break the front?"

Another British voice shouted, "It's all over! They're going to Paris!"

At Gough's headquarters, Colonel Edward Beddington was called from his bed and told that Brigadier Seely, commander of the Canadian Cavalry Brigade, insisted on seeing him. "Bring him in," said Beddington reluctantly, and slipped on his dressing gown.

"Hallo, Beddington," said Seely, "I think you and your army commander would like to know what they are saying in London about this battle." Beddington lost his temper and "cursed him up hill and down dale" for waking him for such drivel.

At dawn it was bitter cold and once more a thick mist overhung the Somme Valley. Cold rime settled on the men's uniforms and numbed hands. In Paris it was clear but chilly, and those bound for Mass walked briskly. At 6:50 A.M. there came a dull boom. A shell smashed into a house on the Rue de Meaux, killing one and wounding fourteen. This time there was no wait, and sirens began screeching as buses and Métro trains were brought to a halt. This shell had come from the Number 1 Paris Gun. Nine minutes later Number 3 launched a shell that exploded almost in front of Notre Dame de la Croix, where a crowd was hurrying to Palm Sunday services. Two were killed, eighty wounded. The terror continued at short intervals.

There was also terror in Amiens even though the advancing Germans were far from that city. The inhabitants were convinced that this was the ultimate goal of the Boche. Once it fell, the way to the coast was open. Observation balloons had already blossomed behind the city. Yesterday these great bags were in front, where now could be heard the ominous drumfire of big guns. Wounded infantrymen were shuffling back.

"What's it like out there, chum?" asked a man from a British reserve division, the 35th, which was about to head east. The man took a proffered cigarette and stowed it in the breast pocket of his bloodstained tunic. "You're a bit late for the fun over t'other side of the hill," he said with a decided Tyne-side accent. His audience was attentive. "Jerry is coming over yon hills in thousands, and it's bluddy murder is that, but you Jocks will get some good hunting with the bayonet I'll be bound. So long." He shuffled off wearily, painfully. Someone remarked that it was Palm Sunday, and someone else wondered who could have imagined they would be spending it in this hellish inferno. Then the call to fall in came and they started marching to the northeast, their destination the chaotic area between two beleaguered British armies.

*   *   *

Out there the mist began to rise about 7:30 and the sun broke through brilliantly. Lieutenant Pat Campbell felt washed out, frightened. Orders had just come to send an officer out front with an artillery piece and a hundred rounds. He was to engage the enemy over open sights and hold up his advance. It was Campbell's turn and this was a suicide job. It was asking to be killed.

"Shall I go?" he said, wanting to pretend that he had volunteered.

His superior did not answer, for he was trying to figure which man would be the least loss to the battery. "No, I'll send Griffith." Campbell's relief must have been obvious. It was unfair, Griffith was given all the rotten jobs, but Campbell could not have offered again, and could not help admiring Griffith as he rode away with his gun. He seemed utterly unconcerned and only worried about the breakfast he had missed.

"They'll give him his breakfast in heaven," remarked Lieutenant Hughes, who had risen from the rank of sergeant, as they all watched the little suicide group clatter down the hill. Engaging the enemy over open sights meant that they could see you as easily as you could see them. Once Griffith appeared over the skyline he and his party would be slaughtered.

British infantrymen were already falling back from the front, and the battery got word to continue the withdrawal. Hughes came back, shouting that he had orders to retrieve Griffith. "But he knows he's got to come back on his own," argued Campbell. Hughes would surely be captured or killed for nothing.

"Got to obey orders," said Hughes crossly, adding that it was some crazy idea of Brigade's. By luck they all returned safely. Griffith had taken his gun behind a hill and opened fire without having any idea whether he was hurting the enemy. After a dozen rounds, the breech jammed, and while a sergeant tried to repair it Griffith sat on the ground and began to eat his breakfast. "Can you beat it!" Hughes told the others. "Sitting on his arse, eating his grub, and old Jerry on both sides of him."

There was even greater confusion to the south. Near Nesle, Captain Cockburn saw Germans advancing over a hill straight ahead. In response to this emergency, two companies of the divisional reinforcement battalion were dispatched to a line on the ridge in front of Nesle just behind Cockburn's own ridge. His company was already digging in across the enemy's line of advance. Bullets were smacking past him in greater numbers, near enough to make his ears ring. Then he saw khaki troops on the right retiring. "They were coming back like a disorderly crowd, and it made us angry to see them strolling along as though nothing mattered in the world."

At this critical moment a Scottish brigade started toward the enemy. It was "a fine sight" to see them advance steadily in many lines, in formation. "The men might have been exercising on the parade ground at Aldershot, they were so calm." The captain's

51

men, inspired, jumped out of their holes and joined the attack, cheering and shouting. Gray figures began running back over the open fields and the British chasing after, cheering.

But the Germans were too strong and even the Scotsmen finally had to turn back. There was already a mad withdrawal behind Cockburn. He laughed to see the brigadier and his staff frantically escaping on horseback. "They had little control over the situation in any event, and it did not matter much where they went."

Cockburn gathered his men and as many stragglers as possible and they all dug in. Hundreds of Germans were emerging over the skyline in several extended columns. Here and there a man dropped, but they came on resolutely. Suddenly the troops on Cockburn's left began pulling back hastily and in disorder. Some ran full speed. "It was disgusting to watch, and as this withdrawal meant that we were left in the air, so to speak, you may imagine our alarm and anger." He consulted with the temporary battalion commander and they agreed to stay in their trenches.

In a nearby village, Lieutenant H. E. L. Mellersh's orderly burst in shouting, "Sir! Sir! The Germans are coming over!" Mellersh, a schoolboy not so long ago, rushed out of his command post to the left position, a waist-high trench. A swish of machine-gun bullets whipped overhead. Men from the front came running toward him. They were British and he was horrified. Mellersh jumped out to meet their officer, who shouted, "Boche over the river!" Had he seen them? asked Mellersh. No, but everyone on his left was retiring. "But dash it all!" protested Mellersh, and managed to persuade the other man to stop retiring just as a runner arrived with orders from his superior, Captain Jacks, to withdraw. Mellersh started to do so but this seemed so ridiculous that he hastened to Jacks and told him the men were retiring only because everyone else was doing so. Could he take his own troops back? Jacks agreed and the men glumly followed Mellersh back to the waist-high trench. "Was I being noble, was I being foolhardy? I don't think it was really either. My sense of fitness, of logicality, was outraged." Just then, as he scanned the scene out front with field glasses, a shell landed almost on top of him. "With no warning I heard the explosion, like a thousand doors slamming. For the moment I think I was senseless. Then my brain began to work. I was dead! No, I wasn't. I began to yell. It seemed to me, rightly or wrongly, that no noise came out of my mouth at all. Then I came at least partly to my senses. My field glasses had been blown out of my hands, and my tin hat off my head. As I looked at my hands, which were black, they began to ooze blood; my face and one knee felt in the same condition." His orderly was beside him urging him to get moving. "Limping, dazed and cowed, a very different person from a couple of minutes ago, I followed him."

As the morning wore on it became alarmingly evident that the German advance was increasing, particularly in the south. French divisions had arrived with artillery, but the fluid conditions of battle made cooperation with the British difficult. The Somme line was crumbling and Gough wondered "how much longer would the officers and men be able to stand the tremendous strain?" The British Third Army was also imperiled. Bapaume was being assaulted from several sides and would have to be evacuated within hours. Disaster threatened the British, and if it had not been for the Royal Flying Corps the masses of men and equipment fleeing west would have been at the mercy of the German Air Force. At every point along the front, British fighter pilots drove off marauders. Before the mass air battle finished, the RFC claimed forty-two enemy aircraft and only eleven of their own planes were missing. Even Richthofen's circus was no match for the inspired British airmen that day. In more than a hundred sorties, seven of the German pilots were killed, and the sole victory was scored by Richthofen. The hero of the day was Captain J. L. Trollope, setting a record by shooting down six Germans. He would have had seven if his machine gun had not jammed.

By 10 A.M. the reports were so alarming that Pétain told Colonel E. Herbillon, his liaison officer to Paris, to leave at once and give Clemenceau the following message: "The situation is becoming even more serious, for the Germans have crossed the Somme and a possible break with the British army must be envisaged." Pétain promised to do what he could to avoid this and was hastily bringing in divisions, "but the persistence of the British retreat, and Douglas Haig's obstinacy in continually leaning to the north" made Pétain fear that he would be unable to hold the link. He assured Clemenceau that he would "cover Paris at all costs" and urgently requested the Premier to press the British to come toward the French "without which they will be separated, and, in that case, Douglas Haig will find himself in a situation where he will be unable to hold out." It was imperative, Pétain concluded, that he and Clemenceau meet that evening to settle the matter.

Just as Herbillon was setting off for Paris, Pétain summoned him back. The situation had worsened in the past half hour and he might have to make grave decisions. Rarely had anyone found Pétain in such a state, and later in the morning Minister of Munitions Loucheur also noticed it. "I have often seen him during the war, in the most difficult hours, always in control of himself, with a calmness which was impressive and at the same time reassuring." But on that day, he was indeed "worked up."

Pétain's alarm was transmitted to Clemenceau, who tried to pass it on to Poincaré, but the President thought their fears unjustified. The break between the French and English had not yet happened; the Allies were merely hard pressed. He did his utmost to calm the Tiger, who could already see their mines occupied, their army turned, and Paris itself threatened. "I fear greatly the contact that will take place between Clemenceau and Pétain this evening," Poincaré wrote in his diary. "Oh for the magnificent sang-froid of Joffre! Clemenceau, the romantic, the neurotic: France defending itself as far as the Pyrenees. Pétain, the critical mind. May not all this lead us to disaster?"

Minister Loucheur was so uneasy that he sought solace from Foch. "It is serious, very serious," the French Chief of Staff replied calmly, "but it is in no sense desperate. You understand, I refuse to speak of a possible retreat. There can be no question of a retreat." Both Haig and Pétain were resisting magnificently. "The situation can be likened to a double door: each of the Generals is behind his half of the door without knowing who should push first in order to close the door. I quite understand their hesitation: the one who pushes first risks having his right or left wing turned."

Foch could see that two distinct battles were being fought: one by Haig for the ports, and one by Pétain for Paris. This would surely result in a separation of the two armies—and certain defeat. The Allied Governments must intervene quickly or all was lost. Taking it on his own responsibility, he now asked for a meeting with Clemenceau to settle the matter. He did so with some reluctance, for a feud, as bitter as that between Haig and Lloyd George, existed between him and Clemenceau, whom he regarded as an unbridled rake.* On his part the Tiger, a freethinker, never could stand Catholic generals, and Foch in particular. At a recent important meeting in London the two had argued until Clemenceau lost his temper. Gesticulating, he shouted, much to the embarrassment of the British, "Silence!" like a schoolmaster. "Clemenceau then thoroughly sat on Foch!" recalled Haig.

Still smarting from this chastisement, Foch now composed a note to Clemenceau calling attention to the danger of carrying on coalition warfare in the present crisis with no generalissimo to direct a unified battle. Otherwise, he concluded, the Allies would risk "going into a battle entailing the gravest consequences, inadequately prepared, inadequately equipped, and inadequately directed."

The long-range shelling of Paris added to Clemenceau's apprehension. By 12:26 P.M. twenty-three shells had fallen in or near the city, then the bombardment stopped. Throughout the long morning there were no signs of panic, for Parisians could adjust to anything, it seemed. Already they had nicknamed the gun Big Bertha after a member of the Krupp munitions family.

While the German officers of the Paris Guns were at lunch, their chief was called to the phone. It was Supreme Command with congratulations: the people of Paris were completely demoralized. As the gun crews were drinking a toast an explosion rattled the windows. It had to be a heavy shell from a French railway gun. How had the enemy learned of their location? Five minutes later another shell crashed in the clearing. The commander decided to cease the bombardment. Perhaps the French were merely lucky.

* General Wilson was informed by Major General Sir C. Sackville-West, familiarly known as "Tit Willow," that Pétain was plotting the downfall of Foch. Wilson was convinced that Clemenceau was in the conspiracy. "They are all beginning to whisper that Foch is 'guggu,' that his judgment is gone, that he is ill, etc. The usual thing."

54

Just after 3 P.M. another heavy shell burst near Number 1 gun. Six men were seriously injured.

In Paris, Foch was handing Clemenceau his note. The Premier read it and said in alarm, "*You* are not going to desert me, you!"

"I am not going to desert you," said Foch. "But nothing is ready."

"The Commanders-in-Chief are in agreement," said Clemenceau. "I have lunched with Haig and I am going to dine with Pétain."

"Battles are not directed over the luncheon table," said Foch. The other reiterated that he was in agreement with Haig and Pétain. "What more can I do?"

"Each one of us must shoulder his own responsibilities and without delay; that is why I have handed you this note."

6.

By midafternoon the reserve 35th Division, which had left Amiens in the morning, had crossed the Somme and marched into the Third Army area to Maricourt. To the surprise of Private P. E. Williamson, a signaler, he met withdrawing units of the famous 51st Highland Division. Battle-stained with many walking wounded, they had retained their good humor. They had helped themselves to abandoned YMCA stores, carrying away shirts, socks, pants, bottles of wine, tins of beer, cases of whiskey and cigarettes. Some of the Scots, including officers, had drunk too much and were giving voice to their favorite ditties as they ambled or staggered by. "From their unwashed weary faces and bedraggled kilts it was obvious to our curious gaze that continuous fighting and lack of sleep had taken its toll hence no one could begrudge them this demonstration of elation now that tension was relaxed."

Someone asked a tall, lean Highlander who was toting a pile of cigarette tins as well as a Lewis gun, "Where's the auction, Mac?" A fancy shawl under his helmet added a comic touch. "Yon storemen telt us to help our sels before they fired the canteen and we couldna leave this loot to the bastut Germans, mon. Youse laddies mun gang there at the gildy."

From the top of the ridge the newcomers saw an amazing sight. "As far as the eye could travel the whole countryside below us was dotted with burning villages, marquees, stores, and field hospitals creating dense columns of smoke, for as the various units had retreated under sheer weight of numbers of the grey mass it was impossible to stem, every effort had been made to destroy or render useless anything of value to them." The heavy gun duels had stopped, but the din of machine guns and rifles was terrific. Then a tremendous explosion shook the earth, for a large ammunition dump half a mile ahead, along the Arras–Bapaume road, had gone up and a huge mushroom of smoke mounted into the sky.

A few miles south Lieutenant Gilbert Laithwaite, of the Lancashire Fusiliers, was watching British shells bursting in the Bapaume—Péronne road. Suddenly a column in single file appeared on the eastern skyline, beyond the road. The column grew and grew until there was a long line of silhouettes stretched out for several miles. "It's the Boche, get ready!" shouted an officer. "Prepare to distribute fire at 2,000 yards." In the afternoon sun the figures began to look strangely familiar in shape and color. Looking through a telescope, Laithwaite clearly saw their packs and the cross straps of their equipment. He handed the telescope to another man. "I believe they are Boche dressed in our stuff," he said, then realized they were British. The line kept moving until a shell burst in their midst, then it abruptly turned left. The men were coming down the ridge toward their own lines. Shells began to fall among them, "at first a few then thickly; it was an incredible sight, and a dreadful position—to see one's own comrades killed before one's eyes in this slow deliberate manner, by guns which one could not see and without being able to lend a hand to help them." As the shells kept bursting, there came the raucous chatter of a machine gun. "It was an imposing sight. Our men advanced nearly a mile before they reached the Péronne road, and I never saw a man run: it was an extraordinary sensation to see shells bursting among men who leave those who fall and carry on—the impression given by the trudging lines with their heads forward was that they must be dog-weary and utterly exhausted, but they never ran, and they stuck that heavy shelling and enfilade machine-gun-fire." Before leaving their position the order had gone out that any man who ran or fell out would be shot. Not a single man had disobeyed.

It was another busy day for Paul Maze. General Gough had sent him south to see how the right flank of Maxse's XVIII Corps was faring. He cycled through Villeselve and cut through a wood where the wagons of a French division had halted. To his dismay he saw infantrymen of the French 9th Division falling back. Then he realized they were conforming with the retirement of one of their divisions on the right. The whole right wing was retreating, and that would seriously affect the British divisions fighting north of them. He began searching for French headquarters, and when he finally did locate a staff they were entirely preoccupied with the problem of getting their troops safely through the wooded country. Maze knew he could not stem the tide of withdrawal but hoped to delay it by explaining the dangerous consequences to the British on their left.

"But they must also withdraw," said a French colonel.

Maze had to get this information to General Maxse at his new headquarters in Roye. He found him talking to General Robillot, commander of the French II Cavalry Corps, who had promised Gough to launch a counterattack next morning south of Nesle. Robillot's troops were about to take position behind Maxse's corps. "No two men could have presented a bigger contrast than these two Generals: General Maxse, very quiet, sitting grimly at his table, and the rather exuberant French General dressed in the palest blue with two rows of medals tinkling on his broad chest." Once Robillot's troops arrived, it meant that Maxse would come under his command. This arrangement was already causing complications, for the French had not yet realized the exhausted state of the British troops after four days' hard fighting; and their plans therefore were often out of tune with the reality of the situation. Maze was instructed to see that the arriving French troops reached their proper position.

After Maze left, Gough himself arrived at Roye and, following a briefing by Maxse, telephoned Robillot. They coordinated plans for a joint British-French attack on the Germans northeast of Nesle and hoped that this would drive the enemy back over the Somme to restore the river line in this sector. The attack was set for 8 A.M. and a barrage table was agreed upon.

The situation at Nesle was deteriorating. At dusk Cockburn saw British troops running out of the village of Mesnil-St. Nicaise as if hotly pursued. German lights went up from the village. That meant the village was taken and the Boche were attacking in force. There was no use in staying, so Cockburn pulled back his men to a position close to the railway, northeast of Nesle.

He started back to Brigade to tell what had happened. "Well, are you not glad to have finished the fighting?" he asked a prisoner he was escorting to the rear.

"Oh, the war is so bad wherever you are, that it is all the same whether you are fighting or not," replied the German, and he would say no more.

Ahead Cockburn could make out the gaunt, scarred houses and tall chimneys of Nesle. Soon they were walking down the dark cobbled deserted streets. He handed over his prisoner and reported to the brigade commander. "The Germans are now at Mesnil-St. Nicaise," he said as they both examined a map by flashlight. He pointed to where his men had fallen back. "It was easy to see that the General knew little of the situation, while another Brigadier who was with him appeared to be as ignorant." They had no idea what was really going on out front.

It was dark by the time the Kaiser returned to his train. He had spent the day near the front and was, so Admiral Georg von Müller, chief of the Naval cabinet, wrote in his diary, "impressed by the horrors of the battlefield and the scarred countryside. He said that the members of Parliament should be brought here to see what war was actually like. This remark was followed by the usual abuse levelled at the Reichstag, that monkey house . . ."

7.

March 24 had been another hectic day for Chief of Staff Henry Wilson. First General French, who had once commanded all the British armies on the Western Front, urged him for about the twentieth time to get rid of his successor, Haig; then he saw Lord Milner off at Charing Cross for France. At 5 P.M. he got a telephone call that Péronne had fallen and the British were retreating to the Ancre River. He phoned Lloyd George at Walton Heath to come back to town, and moments later got a call himself from Foch "asking me what I thought of the situation, and we are of one mind that someone must catch hold, or we shall be beaten. I said I would come over and see him."

At 7 P.M. Wilson met Lloyd George, Bonar Law (a member of the War Cabinet), and Jan Smuts (South African Minister of Defence) at 10 Downing Street, informing them that he was going to France. They all agreed that the situation was grave and that the plans of Haig and Pétain for mutual assistance were entirely inadequate. Dinner followed with the Churchills, Lloyd George, and Hankey. Wilson pressed the Prime Minister hard to conscript not only the country but Ireland and was pleased when Winston backed him up. Churchill also agreed, once Wilson finished, by telling Lloyd George in his sprightly manner, "You will come out of this bang top or bang bottom."

"A moving day," the Chief of Staff wrote in his diary. "We are very near a crash. Lloyd George has on the whole been buoyant. Bonar Law most depressing. Smuts talked much academic nonsense. Winston a real gun in a crisis, and reminded me of August, 1914."

Lloyd George may have seemed in good spirits to Wilson, but by the time he returned to Walton he was wan and depressed. "Things look very bad," he told Riddell. "I fear it means disaster. They have broken through, and the question is what there is behind to stop them. The absence of the reserves is the most serious factor." The French were bringing up reserves but they might be too late. "I may go to France on Tuesday. Meanwhile I must send all the men I can. Unless President Wilson hurries up, he may be too late. He has wasted too much time; he has been nine months in the war and has done very little which is of real service at the front." He went on to say that one of the disasters of the war was not appointing Henry Wilson earlier to high command. "They have wrongly regarded him as a farceur, just because he will joke on all occasions. But what does that matter?"

Clemenceau was once more dining with Pétain, at his headquarters in Compiègne, who reported the news in his usual somber manner. Not only had the Germans crossed the Somme but Haig was still tending to bring back his troops to the north. This threatened to widen the breach between the French and British forces. Pétain urged Clemenceau to bring pressure on the English to keep in touch with the French Army and not force *him* to extend his own line indefinitely to meet them.

The previous day Clemenceau had been depressed, but the grim news of the new day seemed to have made him more resolved. He was displeased at Pétain's exaggerated pessimism and frowned at the charge that if defeat came "it would be the fault of the British." Clemenceau now agreed with Poincaré that a supreme effort should be made "to close the gap" between the French and

British and they should not quit Paris. Moreover he blamed Pétain "for not doing quickly enough what was necessary, under the pretext that he might be attacked at Champagne."

Although Clemenceau didn't voice disapproval, Pétain must have felt it, for he set off after dinner, in an unsettled, glum mood, to see Haig. They met at the field marshal's advance headquarters in Dury at 11 P.M. From the first Pétain struck Haig "as very much upset, almost unbalanced and most anxious." He handed the Briton a copy of an order to all French armies: first, the primary mission was to keep the French armies together as a solid whole; second, liaison with the British would be maintained if possible.

Perturbed, Haig asked him to concentrate as large a force as possible about Amiens astride the Somme. But Pétain morosely shook his head, for he could not possibly allow General Fayolle to concentrate his reserve army group on Amiens. Any moment he expected the Germans to launch a major attack in Champagne. In fact, he had already ordered Fayolle to fall back southwestward toward Beauvais if the Germans advanced any further toward Amiens. Why? To cover Paris. He explained that he had attended a Cabinet meeting that morning in Paris and had orders from his government to "cover Paris at all costs." *

Haig was alarmed. Pétain's order to Fayolle would separate the British from the French flank and so allow the Germans to penetrate between the two armies. "Do you mean to abandon my right flank," Haig bluntly asked. After a silence the sad-faced Pétain nodded. "It is the only thing possible, if the enemy compels the Allies to fall back still further."

Haig was stunned. Covering Paris meant that it was no longer the basic principle of French strategy to keep in touch with the British Army. Though he was a stubborn man with a weather eye for British national interest, it had never occurred to him to separate his line from the French. They could win only if they were welded together. As his car rushed him through the night to his main headquarters at Montreuil, he came to the conclusion that a generalissimo must be chosen to direct the war. That man should be Foch, whom he had once disparaged as "a méridional [southerner] and a great talker." But he knew that Foch's "strategical ideas were in conformity with the orders given me by Lord Kitchener when I became C. in C. and that he was a man of great courage and decision as shown during the fighting at Ypres in October and November, 1914."

Upon reaching his château, near Montreuil, Haig cabled both Milner and Wilson about the serious change in French strategy.

* After the war Haig asked Poincaré about this meeting and was met with blank incomprehension. "From what he said," Haig wrote in his diary, "the President was evidently quite unaware that at the most critical moment of the German offensive in March, 1918, Pétain had given orders to dispose his army so as to cover Paris from the German advance, instead of continuing to have as its main strategical objective the maintenance, at all costs, of close touch with the British Army . . ."

He asked them to come over at once in order to arrange that Foch "or some other determined General who would fight, should be given supreme control of the operations in France." He also wrote his wife that he was glad the Government was finally getting awake to the need for reinforcements. "So far they have expected me to fight battles without men."

In Compiègne there was a nervous hubbub throughout Pétain's headquarters. The general's own qualms had seeped down the chain of command. The word had been passed from office to office that the palace was to be evacuated by eight the next morning. Mountains of baggage and boxes were piled in every corner of the palace yard. In the courtyard a hundred trucks, packed together, were being hastily loaded. A crowd of officers stood about "like a band of emigrants" waiting for a chance of leaving as early as possible.

General Poidron, in charge of the move, rushed out in a rage. "What are you doing there, gentlemen?" he shouted. "Who said we were leaving? Go back to your offices, get the typewriters unpacked and get on with your work." This was the first comic relief on an otherwise gloomy day, and everybody laughed. As typewriters were being unloaded, another order came to reload them. The move to the rear was reaffirmed.

Chapter Three

"GOD GRANT THAT IT MAY NOT BE TOO LATE"
General Foch, March 26

"IF THEY DO NOT BREAK US NOW, THEY WILL BREAK US LATER"
Lord Milner, March 27

MARCH 25–APRIL 6

1.

LITTLE was happening on the other battlefronts, in Italy, the Balkans and the Middle East; and world attention was still focused on the retreat in France. It continued through the early morning hours of Monday, March 25. Lieutenant Campbell had been ordered to go and find out where the enemy was and to send back information. He set off at 4:30 A.M. in utter darkness, up a hill and toward Maricourt, a village on the road to Albert. Campbell was feeling depressed. The exhaustion and continuous anxiety of the four days of battle had undermined his confidence and strength. "I was afraid, I felt alone, none of the others in the hut had woken when I went out, I should have felt less discouraged if one of them had been awake and had wished me luck before I started. And as for the battle, it seemed as though we should go on retreating forever. I could see no end to it."

Hardly a gun was firing as he passed through a wood and came to a road. He could sense he had come to the edge of a cliff, and to the south the Somme was somewhere below. He was to wait here until daylight, and it was not too long in coming. The valley was hidden in fog but the sun began dissolving the mist. Two hundred feet below in an almost sheer drop lay the river. The spectacular sight took away his breath. He looked into the valley. The war seemed to have stopped. "The guns were silent, we were alone, there was neither friend nor foe in sight, only the grey ruin of a church by the river, lit by the morning sun, like an old ruined abbey in the middle of deserted land." Then to his dismay he saw Major John, the commander of one of the other batteries, coming up the hill. He was the most disliked and dreaded officer in the entire brigade. "Without fear himself he expected others to be equally unafraid; he despised you if you showed fear; and I had been feeling afraid ever since I woke up." Campbell knew that the major, who was always doing crazy things, would expect him to go on some crazy enterprise. On the night the battery blew up its guns, John had gone forward to find the enemy, leaving orders for his own battery to stand. Of course, it hadn't. What was the point of being taken prisoner? It had retreated, never expecting to see its commander again. But John had somehow escaped capture and had gone berserk when he found that everyone had decamped.

This fearsome man was coming up the hill and Campbell hoped he wouldn't recognize him and would pass by. But John knew everyone and said in his unpleasant voice, "What's happening here?" He ended the sentence as usual with a short, disagreeable laugh. Campbell said there was no sign of the enemy and began looking through his field glasses, hoping to give the impression he was doing a useful job.

"No, there's nothing for us to do here," the major said. "We'll go on to Maricourt and find out what's happening there."

It was as Campbell had feared. *We'll* go! Yes, go out looking for trouble! But an extraordinary thing happened. As he walked beside the resolute John, he no longer felt afraid, and found himself striding erectly, not bending down to be nearer the ground. John began talking to the young lieutenant as if he were an equal, as one soldier to another. He admitted he had thought everything was lost on the night the batteries were blown up. "No plan of retreat, no reserves, no generalship!" he exclaimed. It was so satisfying for Campbell to hear a major criticizing the staff and higher headquarters the way the subalterns did among themselves.

At Maricourt, which was on a high plateau, the two came to a trench where a half-dozen infantrymen were standing. They

61

shouted to get down; they were under enemy observation. "I think you're mistaken," John said casually, and deliberately jumped across the trench toward the German line. He stood erectly on top of a little mound. "You can see for yourselves that there are no Germans within a thousand yards of us." Campbell wondered what he would do next, and decided it was the right moment to eat one of the sandwiches his servant had made the night before. He offered one to John. "I don't see why I should deprive you of your breakfast," he said, and, when Campbell said he had more than enough, remarked that they looked very appetizing. That was the last word to describe the thick slices of bread, smeared with butter and containing a slab of bully beef, but it indicated that John was as indifferent to food as to danger.

To the wonder of the infantrymen, the two artillerymen sat on top of the trench, legs dangling inside, discussing other wars and other generals—Napoleon, Clive, Marlborough. When the major got up to go, Campbell wanted to go with him. He would have followed wherever he led, to whatever danger. But John told him to stay and supply headquarters with accurate information. Even after he left, Campbell's courage remained high. His confidence had returned and he began to believe that the war was not lost after all. He believed John's announcement that the Germans had missed their chance and would have great difficulty moving their guns across the devastated area. There would be further retreat for several days but then reserves would come up and stem the tide. Campbell no longer wanted to retreat. He rested his elbows on the parapet of the trench, exposing himself more than necessary to observe enemy positions. Suddenly the telephone wire just overhead snapped. One of the ends fell on his helmet with a tinny sound. He heard the snap of a rifle. A sniper had narrowly missed him. His confidence began to ebb as he moved to another part of the trench. "Now I was careful when I looked over the edge." Fear had returned, but it was the end of depression and panic.

It was a fine bright morning. At 6:50 A.M. a shell from a Paris Gun landed in the French capital without hurting anyone. Ten minutes later a second shell, the fifty-third, smashed onto the Rue Tandou, this time killing one and wounding another. The short interval indicated that there was more than one big gun. The two explosions created a scene of comedy in the midst of tragedy. Gendarmes running to the scenes of destruction began blowing whistles and beating drums. With their sense of the ridiculous, Parisians burst into laughter. The gendarmes continued their drum beating, since they had orders to do so, but did so sheepishly, miserably, as if they were performers in a very bad show. One pedestrian exclaimed, *"Ooh, là, là! regardez là, c'est Napoléon, le petit caporal."* The terrifying tension since Saturday was relieved.

The first projectile had come from Number 3 gun; the second from Number 1. But as firing continued rapidly, the third round, from the Number 3 gun, ended in a deafening roar as its breech was blown off. Seventeen of the crew were killed or wounded. Firing on Number 1 was discontinued to find out what happened to the other gun. Moreover Number 1 was undershooting its target. It was decided to evacuate the position and send the gun back to the Krupp works to be rebored. There would be no more firing for at least three days.

At the front, the French-British counterattack toward Nesle was held up, for the French could not move into position in time and requested a three-hour postponement until 11 A.M. The British agreed, but their ally never did get into place and probably had never taken the operation seriously, since the French division commander later remarked, "It was only a project."

It was unfortunate, as the Germans were also massing for their own attack in the same area. The British assault force saw figures advancing through the mist and mistook them for French. Consequently the Germans broke through and this gap between the corps of Maxse and Watts became wider with each hour. To add to Gough's woes, he had been placed in a frustrating position by an order issued that morning: all of his troops above the Somme had been placed under Third Army and all those to the south taken over by the French under General Fayolle. This cut off Gough from Haig's headquarters as regards military operations. At the same time he was getting no orders from General Fayolle, whom he had seen for only a few minutes. He had to carry on as best he could without any defined authority.

One battalion of French infantrymen did attack Nesle. Seeing them in the distance, Captain Cockburn was heartened. He pointed to where the Germans were, and watched in approval as the men in blue advanced. "How admirably calm these Frenchmen were!" They drove the Germans back, but a half hour later the French could be seen falling back from Nesle. "There was now considerable disorder in their ranks, and they streamed past us on the road to Roye as if all were lost! Our own men, meanwhile—heaven alone could tell to which units they belonged as the confusion was so great—on seeing the French retiring, started to retire also. They did not run—nobody ran—but walked back slowly with a forlorn air, like sheep."

The French commander, smartly dressed in bright blue uniform with greatcoat thrown open, approached as if he were walking in the Bois de Boulogne. When Cockburn asked what he intended doing, the Frenchman, eying him as if he might be a spy, said, "Who are you, sir?"

"I am only a British officer with these men here, and I want to know if it is possible to make a stand somewhere."

"*Ah, bon!*" he said, and explained that the Boche had worked around his left, forcing him to retire. "The enemy, as you can see, are still advancing on our left and I propose to retire as far as that" —he indicated a spot a few hundred yards down the road—"and to form up so as to face north."

"Very well, I will join you with what men I can, and support you."

But some of the French troops had no intention of obeying their commander and were already streaking to the rear. "Oh, that miserable morning!" recalled Cockburn. He and other British officers kept blowing their whistles to get the men to halt and dig. Several times they persuaded one group to stop, but as soon as they started to dig, another group would retire and it would set everyone on the retreat. The officers did what they could, but with machine-gun bullets spraying the area and without horses it was impossible to control so many troops. Even so a mixed French-British unit at last did dig in along a row of short trees by the roadside and a defense line was finally established.

General Henry Wilson had just arrived at Haig's headquarters in Montreuil. "Briefly," Haig said, "everything depends on whether the French can and will support us *at once* with 20 divisions of good quality, north of the Somme." Clemenceau, he added, must take a far-reaching decision immediately "so that the *whole* of the French Divisions may be so disposed as to be able to take turns in supporting the British front as we are *now confronting the weight* of the German Army single-handed."

Wilson was not at all impressed. "D.H. is cowed," he wrote in his diary. "He said that unless the 'whole French Army' came up we are beaten and it would be better to make peace on any terms we could. I pointed out that in his present flush of success the Boche would only consent to make peace if we laid down our arms which was out of the question, and he agreed. After much talk I told him that in my opinion we must get greater unity of action, and I suggested that Foch should co-ordinate the action of both C. in C.s. In the end Douglas Haig agreed. I could not help reminding him that it was he with Clemenceau's assistance, who killed my plan of a General Reserve, nor could I resist reminding him of what I had both told him and written to him on the 6th of March —that without a General Reserve he would be living on the charity of Pétain. An impossible situation, for here is the attack I foresaw and predicted in January in full blast, and really no arrangements to meet it." *

He seemed to have forgotten that it was Haig who had protested so often that a great offensive was coming in the spring and that he had belittled it. Moreover Haig's mind that day was clearer than his. Wilson no longer regarded Foch with unrestricted admiration and later that afternoon proposed to General Weygand, Foch's chief of staff, that Clemenceau take over as commander-in-chief of the Allied armies, whereas it was Haig who had initiated the idea of choosing Foch as generalissimo.

---

* Unfortunately a number of the published diaries of the leading men of this era, including those of General Wilson and Colonel House, do not include some of the most revealing passages. The unexpurgated diaries of Henry Wilson reveal not only a brilliant, biting wit but add dimension to some of the crucial arguments of the day. In the above quotation from the Wilson diaries, for example, the first three sentences were deleted from the version edited by Major General Sir C. E. Caldwell.

Just before 3 P.M. the French Premier met with Lord Milner at the Ministry of War in Paris. Clemenceau declared that it was necessary "at all costs to maintain the connection with the French and British Armies, and that both Haig and Pétain must at once throw in their reserves to stop the breach." After Pétain's depressing words to Haig the previous night, this was a significant development. The Tiger went on to say that "it would be necessary to bring pressure to bear upon Pétain to do more in that direction."

After this meeting the two men, accompanied by Foch and Loucheur, left for a conference in Compiègne with Pétain and Poincaré. At the Gard du Nord, Clemenceau was accosted by the Director of Railway Communications, who said, "If you do not save Amiens, everything is lost! It is the center of all our communications."

"Well, we are going to try to," was the reply.

The meeting was held at a château on the outskirts of Compiègne, since the city itself was under constant bombardment. Poincaré presided as Pétain described the greatly disorganized condition of Gough's Fifth Army and claimed that it had ceased to exist as an army. He himself had already sent fifteen divisions to help stem the tide, and six of these were already heavily engaged. That was all he could spare at the moment, since he was faced with the task of defending the road to Paris. He was also being threatened from the valley of the Oise and perhaps from the direction of Champagne.

Foch challenged this glum appraisal and said that the greatest danger point was the Amiens area, where the Germans had broken through the Franco-British front and caused a large gap between the two armies. This front had to be re-established and liaison restored between the two forces even if some risks were entailed elsewhere. Clemenceau and Poincaré appeared to agree and the former asked, "How can the British cooperate in this plan?"

Lord Milner could not answer. Unfortunately Haig and Wilson were too busy to be there, so Milner suggested that they all meet the next day. The others assented and, after the conference broke up, Milner privately told Clemenceau that he had misgivings "whether Pétain on his side was prepared to take sufficient risks in order to bring up all possible French reserves, on which, as it seemed to me, everything depended." The Premier shared his qualms.

Now they needed Haig's consent. This was promptly given and he proposed they all meet at Doullens, which lay some twenty miles north of Amiens, and about the same distance behind German-occupied Bapaume. The time was set for eleven the next morning.

Haig and Wilson had been conferring simultaneously at Abbeville with General Weygand. Haig handed the Frenchman a note setting forth his requests and intention. He asked that the French place at least twenty divisions behind Amiens "for the purpose of acting against the flank of the German attack on the British Army." Weygand took this to mean that Haig had decided to transfer the British resistance west of Amiens. "The British Army," said Haig, "will have to fight falling back slowly and covering the Channel ports."

2.

There was already a feeling of near panic on the road leading to the site of tomorrow's conference. Captain Behrend's heavy artillery unit parked in line along the highway near Forceville, and he was sent to a nearby château to report to brigade headquarters. The commander, General Marshall, and the brigade major were sitting in a large, beautifully furnished salon. After Behrend told them the news and started out, an orderly entered. "Come back!" shouted the general, and asked Behrend how long it would take to get to his own colonel. About four minutes, he answered. "Then get off as quickly as you can and tell him to continue to retreat *at once*. The Germans captured Albert half an hour ago. Make for Doullens. Either the Brigade Major or I will be at the Town Hall to give you fresh orders. Hurry up—Forceville is only six miles from Albert."

Behrend ran to his motorcycle. He tore so furiously down the road to Forceville that people rushed to get out of the way and turned to stare. His colonel was standing complacently in the middle of town, proudly surveying the neatly lined brigade. Drivers were wiping down their trucks; gunners were polishing their guns. Half of the brigade was already in billets; the rest enjoying themselves in *estaminets*. The street became a bedlam of shouts and whistles, and within twelve minutes the heavy artillery was on the retreat again "and with real dismay in our hearts." They didn't know that Albert was still in British hands. Even so, the enemy was less than five miles away.

German movie cameramen were not far behind in the shattered town of Bapaume. It was bare and desolate, not at all the pleasant garrison town where their chief, Franz Seldte, had drained many a mug of beer two years earlier.* It was a wilderness but what a wealth of subjects to photograph! "The masses of English prisoners, the lines of tents and corrugated iron huts, and the strangely laid out cemeteries, and then the crossing of the battered positions with their fallen German attackers and English defenders; it all made up a tremendous, overwhelming spectacle."

Seldte's car forced its way through the rubble. Could this really be Bapaume? German labor battalions and English prisoners were laboriously cleaning the streets. Where were the friendly houses and shops? Where was the Hôtel de Ville, where he had so eagerly listened to lectures on art? Near stumps of walls he finally recognized the pedestal of the monument that had stood in front of the

* He later became leader of the *Stahlhelm* (Steel Helmet), a paramilitary, nationalist group of veterans. Not all its members shared Hitler's goals, but Seldte became a member of the Führer's first cabinet.

Town Hall. Wrecked Bapaume was swarming with activity, and Seldte ran off eighty meters of film of the marketplace, forty of prisoners, and sixty of heavy railway guns and batteries. The sound of battle drew him and he told the driver to head northwest where a battle was raging for Achiet-le-Grand.

This was familiar ground. Seldte clenched his teeth and his heart pounded. Ahead was the village where his unit had begun the long, savage Battle of the Somme two years earlier, during which each side suffered more than half a million casualties; and the attackers, the Allies, only gained a thin strip of territory about thirty miles wide. He had to see it again now, help retake it. The sound of battle increased. English shells began falling on both sides of the road. They abandoned the car, removed their gear, and started across the fields toward the railway embankment running from Arras to Paris. He led his group forward by a sunken road. Ahead lay broad green fields and the ruined houses of Achiet-le-Petit, where a frenzied infantry battle was raging. They pressed on to a long green hedge behind which infantry reserves were preparing to advance. Seldte asked an officer what was the outfit? It was the 39th Infantry. Seldte felt a severe shock. His youngest brother belonged to that Alsatian division and was up ahead under heavy fire. He knew what it meant to lead an infantry company into action and accosted an artillery officer who was peering ahead through his glasses. Were the Alsatians up ahead? Did he know Lieutenant Heinrich Seldte? The officer surveyed Seldte. "I see you're an old Front soldier. You know what war is. Pull yourself together. Your brother fell in the attack this morning. I knew him very well and thought a lot of him."

Seldte clicked his heels and saluted stiffly. "Is it certain?" He was aware how pale his face must look.

"Yes, I'm sorry to say it is. I heard it myself from the battalion." He added sympathetically that it was the soldier's lot. "We've all got to face it, and you've been through it yourself, I see." Seldte glanced at his useless left arm and nodded. "Thank you very much but I was thinking of my mother."

Moments later another officer asked if he was the brother of Lieutenant Seldte and shook his hand warmly. "Your brother was severely wounded this morning." Seldte thought he had misunderstood. "Only badly wounded and not . . . ?" It was severe, confirmed the other, but Seldte felt like shouting with joy. His brother was still alive! "Then he'll pull through. He's a tough lad." He must find him.

But first he had to make the most of the fading afternoon light to film the battle of Achiet-le-Petit. The wan sky was already reddening. From a raised position he shot a panorama of the attack on the village. The English obliged by dropping a few heavy shells. "The fall of the shells and the pyramids of the explosions, tree high, would be very effective on the screen," he thought grimly. Then he shouted to his crew, "Lie down!" Falling splinters howled and shrieked uncomfortably near. A gray violet twilight set in. He had to get back to headquarters and supply text and description so that the courier could rush the films to Berlin. He took a last long look at the village which held so many memories, and started back to Bapaume.

At the south end of the battlefield, Sergeant Maze, Gough's one-man information bureau, was sleeping on a patch of withered grass in a small wood. He had been on the move all day, giving reassurance that the French were arriving in force and that the situation, though serious, was being taken in hand. He always spoke loudly so everyone could hear the good news. He had gone from place to place, gleaning information, trying to keep in touch with brigade staffs which were constantly on the move. He was wakened by the rattle of horse-drawn carts and the sandpaper-scraping tread of retiring troops. In the fading daylight he saw blue uniforms intermingled with the khaki. They were all threading their way through the edge of a wood toward a village. Armored cars were moving up just as enemy shrapnel burst overhead with vicious sharp cracks.

Maze wanted to see what was happening on the right, and walked through the wood, which resounded with the echo of guns. Spinning rockets rose into the writhing smoke, and sharp firing broke out nearby. He rushed back to his motorcycle and set out to locate the British 18th Division. He came upon a large group of German prisoners, then found General Sadleir-Jackson, whose brigade had made the counterattack. He looked smart and bright, his moustache curled up as usual. "We've given the blighters hell," he said, "and have stopped them for a while. I am going to hold on here as long as I can; I wish you would go and tell the French corps."

Maze set off for Noyon, where he found the French corps headquarters in an old building. General Pellé, a distinguished-looking and charming man, told Maze that he did not intend defending Noyon. His troops were falling back on the canal. Orderlies and officers had already packed their papers and were waiting anxiously for the word to leave as Pellé calmly took his time "until he had settled everything to his perfect satisfaction."

Tired and dazed, Maze started down the dark road toward Amiens. His legs felt numb and all he could see was a circle of silver spray made by the glare of his headlight into the pouring rain. Water sizzled on the hot engine. In his imagination he could see village after village falling like ninepins into the enemy's hands, but he was somewhat cheered when the rays of his light showed almost constant desolation. The advancing Boche would soon taste the discomforts their shells had wrought.

Nearby Captain Cockburn received an order to withdraw to an assembly position just east of Roye, where the entire division was to concentrate and reorganize. They were to leave at midnight and Cockburn had the embarrassing task of telling this to the French.

He felt ashamed to be leaving them to fight on their own. He found the dapper French captain and showed him the orders.

"And we are warned that we shall be attacked at dawn!" he announced in dismay. After apologizing, Cockburn was asked, "Are you going to take away your machine guns as well?" Yes, he replied, everything was to go. "Well," said the Frenchman, "I can't hinder you from carrying out your orders."

Henry Wilson arrived in Paris about 10 P.M. and after a talk with Lord Milner went to see Foch regardless of the late hour. He suggested that Clemenceau take over-all command of the Allied armies with Foch as technical adviser. This, he added, would ensure "a closer cooperation between the armies and a better utilization of all available reserves." Foch had already been warned of this scheme by Weygand and both felt it was impractical. It was not Clemenceau's business to conduct the armies. Who would govern in his place? His work was heavy enough already.

Far from simplifying matters, Foch pointed out that "it was likely to make them still more difficult." As for himself, Foch did not wish to command anything. He only wanted to have the same sort of position he had held during the Battle of Ypres, when General Joffre delegated him to get the British and French to work more closely together. Now, however, he wished "to be placed in that position with a more distinct and higher authorization, that of both the Allied Governments." Wilson was pliable enough to change his mind on the spot and agreed to suggest at tomorrow's meeting in Doullens that both sides commission Foch to "co-ordinate the military action" of the two commanders-in-chief, Pétain and Haig. Foch would be the generalissimo.

General John J. Pershing, the American commander, already regarded by his allies as a difficult and obstinate man, arrived in Compiègne prepared to offer Pétain use of American troops in the crisis. Although there were now about 325,000 Americans in France, Pershing felt that only four of his divisions were of assault quality: the 1st, 2nd, 26th, and 42nd. These and other units had already been sent to quiescent British or French areas for training but as yet had seen little real action.

Pershing found General Pétain and his chief of staff preparing to move back to safer headquarters at Chantilly. The American was surprised to find the usually confident and nonchalant attitude of Pétain "entirely gone and he wore a very worried expression." They hastily went over the maps of the latest positions which Pétain thought he could hold. But the French general said that he had few reserves and would like to see the American troops placed into the line to replace French units which were needed at the present battlefront.

Pershing agreed to this as long as the Americans would be united as a corps. Pétain argued that the American division and corps staffs didn't have enough experience to justify placing on them the responsibility of holding a front-line sector. Pershing a bit stiffly replied that he was "willing and anxious to do what was best to meet the present emergency" but wished it understood "that it shall be the policy to work towards the organization of an American Corps on the front under the command of their own corps commander."

Pétain agreed in principle but said it was impossible at present to fix any date for the organization of an American corps. In this crisis manpower was the essential. Pershing concurred—also in principle—assuring Pétain that he wished to help "in every possible way during the present crisis and that he could be counted on to do his utmost." American divisions stood ready to go into battle and "were to do so."

How reassuring, said Pétain, who knew what little training the Americans had, but he would not like to see American divisions in battle so soon. The best instructed Americans should be given some experience in open warfare first. It was not an altogether successful meeting, for Pershing was eager to engage his troops under American leadership and Pétain looked upon the Americans only as strong, healthy replacements. It was obvious that a contest of national pride and wills was brewing.

3.

Tuesday, March 26, dawned bright and cold. It was the day that could decide the fate of the war. "Bomb and shoot up everything that can be seen," ordered Major General Salmond, commander of the Royal Flying Corps in France. "Very low flying necessary. All risks to be taken. Urgent."

That morning Sergeant Maze finally located General Maxse. He was in a bad mood, for his XVIII Corps counterattack at Nesle had failed. The French, he said, had never appeared and the British right flank had been left exposed. By now it was apparent that the French were being driven back southward toward the Avre River, while Maxse's troops were withdrawing as arranged to the west. This meant that the two forces were separating and the gap was becoming wider each hour, leaving an unprotected hole for the enemy to come through. The French had taken all of Maxse's guns and his order to have them returned had been ignored. He instructed Maze to go immediately to the French Fourth Army and explain the matter personally to General Humbert. Maze raced the twenty-six miles to Humbert's headquarters near the Avre. It was shocking to find himself abruptly in a luxurious paneled room facing a "hypermilitary" commander. Humbert, distinguished and formal, stood in front of a table laden with maps. Officers were receiving orders and saluting smartly with click of spurs and clang of sword. The dignified atmosphere contrasted greatly with the anxious world of the Fifth Army he had just left.

At last it was his turn. Two sharp black eyes behind spectacles turned on him. Humbert curtly asked what he wanted. Feeling even shabbier then he was, Maze said that he had come from General Maxse to ask for the immediate release of British artillery.

XVIII Corps was fighting without a single gun. Humbert turned to an officer who knew nothing, then said, "I will go into the matter at once."

Maze asked for a written order to help him get the artillery released. "Very well," said Humbert. While Maze waited he tried to impress on the general the grave consequences of the French retirement to the south. Humbert didn't appreciate advice from a sergeant. "We are looking after that," he said curtly, and handed him the order.

Maze now began a search for the artillery, and when he located it his order was greeted with skepticism. How could artillery be released because of a piece of paper? Maze drew himself up. "I am the *maréchal des logis!*" he said with authority. "The guns come back!" The French officer, hearing only the *"maréchal"* of the lowly title "sergeant major," was flustered. The stylish cut of Maze's uniform, though battle-stained, was obviously that of a high-ranking officer and so was his imperious manner. The guns were released.

To the north Allied leaders were converging on the provincial town of Doullens. Columns of trucks transporting reserves to the front filled the roads with dust. These columns met traffic retreating from the front: heavy guns, ambulances, army transport of every size and sort, civilian carts loaded with possessions. The congestion on all sides of the town was appalling.

Captain Behrend's artillery brigade was having difficulty making its way into Doullens from the east. Besides all the military traffic, the road was crowded with refugees and a straggling company of the Chinese Labour Corps, China's contribution to the Allied cause. "They were behaving more like school children unexpectedly let out of school; they grinned at everyone and everything, and trickled in twos and threes into every estaminet they passed." Some of the Chinese carried huge bundles on their heads; others had no possessions. Some were helping refugees push wheelbarrows or pull handcarts; others chased happily after British trucks hoping in vain for a lift. On the outskirts of Doullens, two Chinese entered a lingerie shop. When they were promptly ejected "they stood on the pavement chattering and gesticulating like angry monkeys."

Behrend was impressed by the great activity around the Hôtel de Ville. There were so many magnificent cars outside that he figured very important people must be inside. He thought that he even saw Field Marshal Haig's car flying its miniature Union Jack. There were also big French cars. What was going on inside?

Haig was the first to arrive in Doullens. He looked exhausted and anxious, having had little sleep in forty-eight hours. The little clock at the top of the solid but rather ornate three-story building pointed to eleven. In a large, high-ceilinged room on the second floor he met with the commanders of his First, Second, and Third

71

Armies—Horne, Plumer, and Byng. Conspicuously absent was General Gough, who was now officially under General Fayolle.

Haig explained that his object was to gain time to enable the French to come and support them. "To this end we must hold our ground, especially on the right of our Third Army on the Somme, where *we must not give up any ground*. The covering of Amiens is of first importance to the success of our cause; on the other hand, I must not so extend our line through enemy pressing our centre making it bulge, and thus extending our front as to risk its breaking."

"In the south near the Somme," commented Byng, "the enemy is very tired and there is no real fighting taking place there. Friend and foe are, it seems, dead beat and seem to stagger up against each other." Haig nodded. It was true. In fact, the entire battle seemed to be slowing down.

The French delegation from Paris was next to appear. On the way Clemenceau had confided to General Henri Mordacq, chief of the Premier's Military Cabinet, that he was going to take advantage of the British debacle to force upon them the unity of command. He was in good humor, looking forward to the confrontation.

The Tiger arrived at the Doullens Hôtel de Ville moments after Haig had entered. Then Poincaré's car pulled up. They were told that Haig was holding a meeting inside and that General Wilson and Lord Milner had not arrived. The main conference would not begin for some time. Since it was rather cold, the French walked briskly about the square to keep warm. Mordacq was impressed by the imperturbability of the British troops which were retiring "sedately" through the town. Occasionally their conversation was interrupted by violent cannonading of German guns only a few miles away. "That is why under a calm exterior the pangs of anxiety gnawed at every heart," recalled Mordacq. "But time was going on, and still the English did not arrive."

The Mayor of Doullens approached Poincaré. "If Amiens is taken," he asked, "will you make peace?"

"It is not I who has the right to make war or peace; but if you want my advice, I tell you frankly that I am personally opposed to a peace made the day after a defeat; it would be disastrous."

Clemenceau came over. He appeared gay but drew the President aside to reveal dejectedly that Pétain was contemplating the retreat of the French Army to the south while the British Army retired toward the north. "Pétain is annoying because of his pessimism. Do you know what he told me? And I wouldn't repeat it to anyone but you. He said, 'The Germans will beat the British in open country; after they will beat us too.' Do you think a general should talk, or even think like that?"

Foch arrived, charged with energy and bursting with fighting spirit. He confirmed the story about Pétain, then said, "It is necessary to draw up a minute of proceedings of the coming conference."

"What good will that do?" said Clemenceau.

"To fix responsibilities," said Foch, and wandered off. He wanted to visit the little schoolhouse where he and his staff had established themselves in 1914. His thoughts went back to those critical days and the battles of the Yser and of Ypres. Comparing their number, armament, and supplies then with now, "I could not permit myself for a moment to admit that, powerfully reinforced as we were, we could allow ourselves to be beaten in 1918, when, with means so relatively meager, we had conquered in 1914."

On his walk back to the Town Hall he overheard a colleague say that it might be wise to evacuate Paris. "Paris!" interrupted Foch. "Paris has nothing to do with it! Paris is a long way off! It is where we now stand that the enemy will be stopped. We have only to say, 'He shall not pass!' and he shall not pass. I guarantee you that. Believe me, success is three-quarters achieved when we are convinced that we cannot fall back farther and the order is sent forth to resist where we stand at this very moment." These words acted like a tonic on that small group, but could it overcome the gloom that Pétain would surely bring to the meeting? He was walking in another part of the garden, tense of face and filled with anxiety.

Fifteen minutes before noon, Milner and Wilson finally appeared. Clemenceau hurried up to the former, startling him with the announcement that Haig had just declared he would be obliged to uncover Amiens and fall back on the Channel ports. "I feel sure there has been some misunderstanding about this," said Milner, and suggested that he have a short talk with the field marshal before the conference convened. Clemenceau readily agreed. The two Britons went upstairs to see Haig, who quickly cleared up Milner's concern. The French, he explained, had misunderstood his view about Amiens. All he had meant to say was that with his limited forces he would be outflanked and unable to cover Amiens unless the French came to his assistance. At any rate "he was fully determined to stand his ground as long as he could, and, with some assistance from the French on his right flank, he believed he ought to be able to do so." His entire object, he explained, was to have a fighting French general in supreme command who would hold Amiens. "I can deal with a man but not with a committee," he said, and was agreeable to Wilson's suggestion that Foch be that man. Milner was delighted to find that Haig "so far from resenting—as I had been led to believe he might do—the thought of Foch's interference, he rather welcomed the idea of working with the latter, about whom his tone was altogether friendly."

The stage was at last set for the conference. It was 12:20 P.M. Rarely has such an important conference taken place under such dramatic circumstances. Along with the recurrent sound of artillery came the rumble and rattle of British tanks maneuvering into position at the eastern edge of town in case of a German breakthrough. The conferees gathered around an oval table. Poincaré, the chairman, sat on one side with Haig on his left and Milner and Wilson on his right. Across the table, facing a great curtain that separated them from the large Council Chamber, were Pétain, Weygand, General Archibald Montgomery (chief of staff of the British Fourth Army), Clemenceau, and Foch. At either end of the table were Paul Loucheur (Minister of Munitions) and General Lawrence (Haigh's chief of staff) with his back to a high window and balcony facing the town square. The table was lit overhead by a large crystal chandelier.

The impetuous Clemenceau immediately brought up the question of Amiens. Haig wore a look of concern, realizing that the outcome of the war might depend on what happened in that room. He explained, as he had to Milner, that he had been misunderstood and meant to hold his ground north of the Somme. He had no intention of withdrawing his troops to the Channel ports. He was throwing in all the reserves he could spare from the north. In fact, doing so at some risk. A mention of his Fifth Army brought an emotional interruption from Pétain that it was "broken." This irritated Wilson, who made a sharp, sarcastic rejoinder.

Pétain now took the floor. Haig thought he had a "terrible look . . . the appearance of a Commander who was in a funk and has lost his nerve." He explained the situation, stressing all the difficulties he had encountered since March 21. It was a gloomy picture but he brightened momentarily to announce that since the meeting yesterday at Compiègne he had looked for all possible resources to cope with the situation and was happy to announce that he could perhaps throw twenty-four divisions into the battle. He added that these divisions, of course, were far from fresh. In such a situation "it was essential not to be deceived by illusions, but to look realities in the face, and accordingly it must be realized that a fairly considerable time was necessary to get these units ready to take part in operations."

To Milner he gave "a certain impression of coldness and caution, as of a man playing for safety." He did not seem happy or convinced, and, upon announcing that he was doing everything possible to send all available troops to Amiens, the restless Foch could not control himself. "We must fight in front of Amiens," he exclaimed, "we must fight where we are now. As we have not been able to stop the Germans on the Somme, we must not now retire a single inch!"

This was the fighting talk Haig had been waiting for. "If General Foch will consent to give me his advice," he said spiritedly, "I will gladly follow it." A nervous silence fell upon the meeting. Clemenceau and Milner exchanged looks across the table. Milner asked whether he could have a word alone with the Premier. They went into a corner. "We must make an end of this," said Clemenceau. "What do you propose?" An artful manipulator, he intended leaving it to the English to make the request that the French had been preaching for months. Milner said that Foch appeared to be the man who had the greatest grasp of the situation. Could he not be placed in a position of general control? Clemenceau agreed with a straight face, not revealing that it had been his own idea. He said he would first have to consult Pétain. While the two Frenchmen were conferring in one corner, Milner and Haig were in another. The field marshal was "not only quite willing but really pleased."

A few minutes later Clemenceau showed a note to Milner which had been approved, if somewhat reluctantly, by Pétain:

> General Foch is charged by the British and French Governments to co-ordinate the action of the Allied Armies on the Western Front. He will work to this end with the Generals-in-Chief who are asked to furnish him with all necessary information.

Haig had no objections and Milner signed the final draft. On his own responsibility he committed the War Cabinet to stand behind Foch, entrusting to him the fate of the British Empire. Poincaré adjourned the meeting with words that both sides applauded: "I believe, gentlemen, that we have worked well for victory." As the meeting broke up there was a unity that must have seemed impossible at noon. The conferees were men of conflicting views and temperaments. The French and British were out of step because of differing languages, tastes, manners, and national interests. Egos and wills clashed on all sides. The freethinker Clemenceau distrusted Foch because he was a Catholic. Foch, a family man, could not condone the sexual excursions of the tempestuous Clemenceau. Wilson thought Haig was a pompous, narrowminded Scotsman; and Haig decried Wilson's outlandish Irish antics. Yet today all personal and national clashes had evaporated in the crisis. No single man could take the credit for the success of the meeting, even though each of them secretly thought himself responsible. There was only one man at odds with the others—Pétain. At bottom he was not a fighter by temperament like Foch, Haig, Clemenceau, and the others.

As they were leaving the Hôtel de Ville, Wilson revealed that Gough was going to be removed. He would be replaced by Rawlinson. Haig agreed, ate a box lunch, and then headed for Beaurepaire, his château outside of Montreuil. Wilson had lunch at the Hôtel des Quatre Fils Aymon with Milner. Clemenceau and Foch also dined there and on the way the former was so delighted with the day's work that he patted the extremely tall Wilson on the head and called him *"un bon garçon."* As they sat down to eat, Clemenceau chided Foch. "Well, you have had your own way," he said.

"Yes! A nice mess! You give me a lost battle, and tell me to win it."

"Anyhow, you have got what you wanted!"

"You should not say that," protested Loucheur. "General Foch is accepting the command because he loves his country, certainly not for his own pleasure."

Despite the triumph, Clemenceau did not enjoy his meal. He

had a stomach-ache, ate almost nothing, and yawned almost incessantly.

During the lunch, Foch was already mentally drawing up the detailed arrangements for carrying out his line of action. He must keep the French and British forces together in order to save Amiens. Instead of a British battle to cover the Channel ports and a French battle to cover Paris, they must fight a joint battle to protect Amiens, the connecting link between the two armies. He must explain all this in person to those principally concerned, and as soon as he left the restaurant drove to Dury to see General Gough. Foch was visibly excited upon entering Gough's room. Once they were alone he began assailing the Fifth Army commander in French. The latter spoke the language fairly well but was not equipped to carry on a brisk argument. "All these facts placed me at a distinct disadvantage, and exposed me to considerable surprise. Foch was peremptory, rude, and excited in his manner."

First he asked, "Why are you at your headquarters and not with your troops in the fighting line?" Gough said he was waiting for orders from Foch. "You should not wait for me in that way without doing anything, or else your Corps Commanders will be on your heels, and everyone will stampede. Go forward; the whole line will stand fast, and so will your own men." Gough was stunned. This was unfair advice given to a man who had tirelessly traveled from one end of his command to the other the past five days. Foch began shooting more questions without ever waiting for an answer. "Why couldn't you fight as we fought in the first battle of Ypres in 1914? Why did your Army retire? What were your orders to the Army?"

Gough was more surprised than indignant that he wasn't given a chance to reply properly. The answers were simple. He was at his headquarters because he had been ordered to meet Foch there. His task, moreover, was not to lead a battalion or a company but to attend to what was going on along his extended front. Fifth Army was not holding the ground as it had done in 1914 because the odds the past days were more than doubled. In the First Battle of Ypres the Germans had not the massed superiority to maintain a continuous battle for more than a day.

He kept his temper and told Foch his orders had been to fight a rearguard action and gain time for the Allies to send up more reserves. Foch became even more excited. "There must be no more retreat," he shouted. "The line must be held now at all costs!" So saying, he stalked out of the room. Gough was now angry. Foch had not even inquired into the position of the divisions of the Fifth Army, nor their strength or condition. And what about the fresh French divisions on his right flank which were falling back faster than his own exhausted troops? He was insulted that a British general officer should be subjected to such rudeness. Stung, he telephoned Haig, who commiserated with him and then started out for a ride. As Haig was mounting his horse, Milner and Wilson drove up. "He certainly looked much less tired and in much better spirits than he had done earlier in the day," noted the former, and the latter thought he was "ten years younger to-night than he was yesterday afternoon." Haig remarked that he was greatly pleased with the new arrangement with Foch, but when Gough's relief was again brought up, Haig defended his subordinate stoutly. "Whatever the opinion at home might be and no matter what Foch might have said, I consider that he dealt with a difficult situation very well. He never lost his head, was always cheery, and fought hard."

Gough was still fighting hard and devoting himself to gathering bits and pieces of reserve forces to stem the German wave. He scraped up a force under Brigadier Carey—electrical and mechanical engineers, surveyors, grooms, sanitary service men, men back from leave, tunnelers and miners, signalers, sniping instructors, and five hundred American engineers. These two thousand men, armed with rifles, were thrust into the gap between the British and French, along with the last regular reinforcements, two composite battalions, and a Canadian motorized machine-gun battery. That evening he phoned Haig's chief of staff that the situation was a bit brighter: the energy of the attacks seemed to be weakening, and "the Germans were becoming worn out and very tired." Also the enemy, except those supported by machine guns, were falling back under counterattacks. "If GHQ could send me three fresh divisions, I could push the Germans in front of us back as far as the Somme." General Lawrence laughed. "It's good to hear you have plenty of fight left." But there were no reinforcements at the moment.

The Germans at the front were still advancing and felt that victory was near. Newspapers back home were boasting of the terrifying effect the Paris Guns were having on the citizens. The *Berliner Tageblatt* claimed that Clemenceau was under bitter attack and a quarter of the capital had already been badly damaged. "The rigorous censorship of Paris papers prevents the French people from knowing the truth, the fearful hours which the population of Paris spent in cellars . . ." Their Swiss correspondent added that the bombardments had disrupted the entire public life of the capital. "All rich people are leaving Paris. The railway stations are filled with those making their escape. Many theaters play in cellars."

Not a shell had fallen on the city that day, but it was true that the stations were crammed with struggling crowds trying to escape Big Bertha and a possible German breakthrough. Every conversation, recalled Michel Corday, "began with the question: 'Have you heard anything?'" There were rumors that the Germans had reached Albert, captured Roye, and that Pétain had left Compiègne. These rumors happened to be true, and public figures did their best to still the voices of panic. "We must shut our ears and hold our tongues," wrote Anatole France. "What worries me is that there are so many things which we must not know . . . Some young Americans who came to see me have brought reassuring messages: they declare that the war will not last another three years."

Foch was just reaching his home, worn by the events of the day. His wife was not at all pleased to learn of his new command; it saddled him with too heavy a burden. He said thoughtfully, "God grant that it may not be too late." A boyhood friend, Colonel Graeff, was similarly alarmed:

"Do you realize what it involves?"

"Yes," said Foch. "I fully realize it. I shall succeed."

Milner and Wilson had left Haig's château to cross the Channel by destroyer. Accompanied by Winston Churchill, they arrived at Victoria Station at 10:45 P.M. The three drove at once to 10 Downing Street to report to the Prime Minister. The past forty-eight hours had been tense ones for the War Cabinet. Christopher Addison, Minister of Reconstruction, had never seen Lloyd George "look so troubled and anxious since he has been Prime Minister." One was not inclined to do much work, observed Addison. "Everything was submerged in the news from the Front."

Wilson and Milner reported that they had agreed to make Foch "co-ordinating authority" over the whole Western Front, and that the French were at last putting in all their reserves. Milner remarked that their own army commanders were "cool as cucumbers and in great heart." Everything behind the front was orderly and even some of the remnants of Gough's shattered army were cheery and in good spirits. Wilson summed it up: "The chances are now slightly in favour of us."

The Kaiser returned to his train in ecstasy from another day at the front. His troops had scored brilliant victories, he announced, and ordered a toast in champagne. His spirits were so high, recalled Admiral von Müller in his diary, that he declared, "If an English delegation comes to sue for peace it must kneel before the German standard since it is a question here of a victory of the monarchy over democracy."

At nearby Avesnes, Ludendorff was pleased that a wide gap had opened between the British and French lines, but was unhappy with progress in the north, where it was becoming apparent that the offensive was flagging. In a violent fit of anger, he telephoned Crown Prince Rupprecht of Bavaria. He was dissatisfied, he said, with the chief of staff of the Seventeenth Army and threatened to fire him. He ordered a new plan of operations put into effect: they would concentrate the offensive in the south since he was convinced that Gough's army was completely shattered. "I expected completely to cut off the English from the French by having the Second and Eighteenth German Armies advance round the left wing of the French near Noyon." If he succeeded it could mean the end of the war.

4.

It was after midnight when General Congreve told Major General Sir John Monash, the commander of the Australian 3rd Division, that his own corps line from Albert to Bray had given way. "The enemy is now pushing westwards and if not stopped tomorrow will certainly secure all the heights overlooking Amiens. What you must try and do is to get your division deployed across his path." There was a good line of old trenches running toward Sailly-le-Sec. "Occupy them, if you can't get further east."

Monash, an engineer by profession, was a German Jew by descent, and his parents had emigrated to Australia to escape prosecution. He was a thorough, methodical man with an original approach to warfare. Smooth cooperation among all arms was his creed and he himself likened an operation plan to an orchestral composition. He worked until dawn getting his troops on the move, using thirty two-decker London buses to transport infantrymen to the threatened area. By midday the situation was well in hand, but it would take at least another four hours to get his men into place—and German patrols could already be seen coming over the skyline.

The good news brought back to London the previous night by Milner and Wilson was already dissipated by alarming reports from the front. Milner himself was deeply concerned and on that morning of March 27 expressed his feeling to Lloyd George in a letter:

> . . . If there is a great disaster, we are as a Government "down and out" whatever we do, and we may as well fall gloriously over a big effort to relieve the situation.
>
> If, on the other hand, "the plague is stayed," we are in for a long dragging fight. It must be a year before the Americans can make their weight felt. We and the French can at the best *hold* the Germans. We are not strong enough to do more, and we shall not do that, unless we can prevent our army dwindling away . . . It is simply deluding ourselves to think that the Germans, after such success as they have had, in Italy and in France . . . *will not continue to press us for all they are worth.* They are certain to keep on pushing, and if they do not break us now, they will break us later . . . .
>
> Unless we can hold out another year, and that depends on what we do now—when people are thoroughly frightened and prepared for anything, a bad peace is a certainty.
>
> I should prefer to let someone else make it . . .

It was in this atmosphere that the War Cabinet met late that morning. "The situation is very desperate," wrote Christopher Addison in his diary, "but, on the whole, it is a little better than it was on Monday, which is the best that can be said of it." At the meeting Lloyd George "decided to press the Americans to let us have 300,000 men at the earliest possible moment," and to permit their trained units to be put in the front lines at once as replacements. He hastily composed a message addressed to President Wilson and the American public that epitomized the Government's desperation: "We are at the crisis of the War . . . time is vital. It is impossible to exaggerate the importance of getting American reinforcements across the Atlantic in the shortest possible space of time."

President Wilson had been urged by his Assistant Secretary of the Navy a few days earlier to send American troops into the breach. Otherwise, warned Franklin Roosevelt, the Allies would be beaten. "Roosevelt," he replied, "I don't want to put our troops in to stop up that hole. What you predict may happen but my hunch is that it won't happen. It is my responsibility and not yours; and I'm going to play my hunch." President Wilson had already agreed to a British request sent the day before, asking that four American divisions be used at once to hold the line and relieve French units being sent north to help Haig, but the new plea could run contrary to American interest. Secretary of War Newton Baker was in Paris and he and Pershing would have to make recommendations before any action could be taken.

That morning Pershing had shown that he was as opposed to amalgamation of his troops into the Allied command structure as he had been before the Ludendorff offensive. When the Permanent Military Representatives of the Supreme War Council * urged him to accept temporary amalgamation until the German attack had been stemmed, he said he would allow use of some infantry and machine-gun units in the emergency, but that was all. After Pershing left the meeting, the American representative at Versailles, General Tasker Bliss, ordinarily a model of restraint, was enraged. "General Pershing expressed only his personal opinion," he said, "and . . . it is the Military Representatives who must make a decision." It seemed likely that the smoldering differences between Pershing and the Supreme War Council's Military Representatives would break out into open conflict.

The Kaiser was again up front. His entourage was shown forty English guns which had been "shelled to pieces" in a forest near Péronne. Admiral von Müller was appalled at the devastation. "Towns and villages razed, all the fruit trees smashed and miles of shell holes and barbed-wire entanglements."

In the homeland, Germans were celebrating the continuing advances. Berlin was gay with flags and bells rang out triumphantly. The English wife of Prince Blücher felt sick to read of the British

---

* The Supreme War Council, located in Versailles, was a political organization of the four major allies designed to coordinate over-all strategy. With both political and military members, it was a unique institution devised to cope with the unprecedented problems of coalition warfare. Its principal function was to prepare joint recommendations on grand strategy which were then referred to the various governments for decision.

debacle, of the terrible effect of new gases. She hated to hear newsmen shouting out the latest victories. It almost made one believe that the Germans had crossed the Channel. She watched a troop of prisoners in English and French uniforms herded past her window. "I felt a great wave of bitterness and hatred overflowing my heart, hatred for all those in this and other countries who were the cause of this hell-being-let-loose on the earth, and I turned away from the window with an indignant sob in my throat as I heard the sound of church bells imperatively summoning the nation to rejoice . . ."

Gough spent the day visiting his hard-pressed units, which were doing their best to obey Foch's order to hold ground at any cost. Upon returning to his own headquarters he found Haig's military secretary. Not having any idea why he was there, Gough invited him to tea. "He then asked to see me alone," recalled Gough, "and told me as nicely as he could that the Chief thought I and my Staff must be very tired, so he had decided to put in Rawlinson and the Staff of the Fourth Army to take command."

Surprised and hurt, Gough said, "All right," and only asked when Rawlinson would take over. The next day was the answer. But he had no time to brood. Late in the afternoon Beddington brought word of another crisis. Germans in force had crossed the Somme near Watts's XIX Corps right flank and were apparently driving southwest toward Carey Force. "Have the French anyone they can send us?" asked Gough, and learned that the French had instructed Fifth Army to use its own XVIII Corps.

"Then you'll have to divert the 61st Division," Gough told Beddington. "How quickly can they get here?" They had to come by foot and would take about ten hours. "That's no good, they're tired out already, poor devils. Get every wagon you can, all our busses, cars, everything. Put them aboard and motor them round."

Orders were sent out repeating General Foch's order to hold the line and promising that help from the 61st Division was on its way. Well after midnight, General Watts telephoned Gough. He realized what Foch had ordered and that help was on the way, but his corps would be broken up if they didn't withdraw before dawn.

"Very well," said Gough, "I will ask Foch—but in any case get all arrangements made to pull back." He told Beddington to get Foch on the phone. It was 3 A.M., March 28, when Foch was roused from his bed. Gough said he must pull back his XIX Corps at once. Foch knew that the French on Gough's right had already retreated six miles without permission. He didn't mention this but gave Gough grudging permission to fall back, yielding as little ground as possible.

It was dawn by the time forward units got the order to retire. It was drizzling and there was a thick mist. The men retreated stubbornly, inflicting casualties on the enemy. It was an orderly operation carried on with a new spirit of confidence.

In Paris that morning Pershing was meeting with Secretary of War Baker and General Bliss. Pershing argued that the request by the Military Representatives would put American units entirely in the hands of the Supreme War Council and would "without doubt destroy all possibility of forming an American army." He turned angrily to Bliss. How could he have signed such a ridiculous request?

Baker soothed Pershing. You are quite right, he said. We cannot lose control of our troops. What did Pershing suggest? He was willing to make some concessions to continue only as long as the situation demanded it.

They also discussed Foch's assignment as generalissimo. All three agreed that this step should not have been taken without an American present, but Pershing, somewhat surprisingly, had no objections. Joint command, he said, was long overdue and wholehearted American cooperation should be expressed at once. He set out by car for Foch's headquarters at Clermont-sur-Oise.

He left a Paris whose railroad stations were still congested with people fleeing to safety. It was a city of rumors, and British Ambassador Lord Bertie was the recipient of many, including one that Gough had been "ungummed" and sent home, and another that the French Ministers for Foreign Affairs, War, and Marine were fleeing to Tours.

Unaware that his commander was being relieved that day, Sergeant Maze continued to carry out Gough's instructions. He found General Malcolm, commander of the 66th Division, with two other division commanders. The front that these three units now held was so small and the troops so few that brigades amalgamated to form a battalion. Looking tired and gray, Malcolm asked Maze what reserves there were behind. Were any coming? Maze told him that the two-thousand-man Carey Force was the only reserve. "What a pity," said Malcolm. "Had we fresh troops we could walk back to where we were a few days ago." The sergeant promised to cable Malcolm's wife that he was all right, and left for Dury to see Gough. Late in the afternoon he met cars filled with French officers and from the pennons guessed they were generals. Assuming they were leading some reserves, he stopped to give them some information.

He was sharply questioned by one of the generals. Who was he? What unit did he belong to? Maze said he was attached to General Gough. "He is not in command any more," said the general. Suddenly realizing this was Foch, Maze saluted in consternation and sped on toward Dury. The streets were crowded with trucks marked with the Boar—the Fourth Army emblem. Other lorries with the Fox of the Fifth Army were being loaded. He found Gough in the small garden outside his office. Looking up, he said that he no longer commanded the Fifth Army. "But before I tell you what has happened, if you have any urgent news you must give it to General Rawlinson, who is now in command. I have arranged with him for you to continue doing the work for him that you have been doing for me. He is a fine soldier; you will like him."

Maze followed Gough into the office to meet Rawlinson and his chief of staff, General Archibald Montgomery. Then he and Gough returned to the garden. The latter told how abrupt and short Foch had been with him and the deprecatory remarks made about the Fifth Army troops. But Gough neither complained nor passed an opinion. His thoughts were still on the problems the Fifth Army was facing. "We must win the war," he said as they parted. "We must not let our personal feelings distract us for a moment from our purpose."

Pershing's trip that afternoon to see Foch was slowed by roads jammed with troop-filled trucks, artillery, and supply wagons. Upon arrival in Clermont-sur-Oise he found no one who knew Foch's whereabouts. Finally a guide was located who brought the party through a stand of tall poplars to a small farmhouse hidden among the trees.

Inside Foch, Pétain, Loucheur, and Clemenceau were leaning over maps, marking the infiltrations of the Germans as couriers bustled in and out. As soon as Pershing intimated that he had come to see Foch, the others discreetly went out to the lawn. After much thought, Pershing had concluded that this was no time for purely national considerations. Concessions must be made at such a perilous moment. Deeply moved, he said in French that the Americans were now ready and anxious to do their part in the crisis. Foch listened with excitement. Such generosity he would never forget. Unable to restrain himself, the impetuous Gascon seized Pershing's arm and bustled him outside to Clemenceau and the others gathered in the garden where a cherry tree was in full bloom. "Repeat what you told me!" exclaimed Foch. Again in a French more fluent than he imagined he could speak, Pershing emotionally said, "I have come to tell you that the American people would consider it a great honor for our troops to be engaged in the present battle. I ask for this in their name and my own. At this moment there are no questions but of fighting. Infantry, artillery, aviation, all that we have are yours; use them as you wish. More will come, in numbers equal to requirements. I have come especially to tell you that the American people will be proud to take part in the greatest battle of history."

The French—with the exception of Pétain, who grumbled that the use of American troops had already been discussed—were in raptures. "What a noble gesture! What an admirable impulse!" thought Foch, and with emotion announced that he wanted the U.S. 1st Division to immediately take up positions before Montdidier, the center of the German drive.

The spontaneity and generosity of Pershing's offer also warmed Clemenceau. On his way back to Paris in the rain as he passed the gutted buildings and ravaged fields behind Montdidier, his spirits rose. The Germans had shot their bolt! They would advance no further. For the first time that week, he slept soundly.

5.

There was rejoicing throughout France and England at release of the news the next day, March 29. "General Pershing yesterday took, in the name of his country, action which was grand in its simplicity, and of moving beauty," wrote *La Liberté.* "In a few words, without adornment, but in which vibrated an accent of chivalrous passion, General Pershing made to France the offer of an entire people." Lord Reading, the British Ambassador in Washington, conveyed his Government's thanks to Wilson for "the instant and comprehensive measures" which the President had taken in response to the request for American aid. "It seals the unity of the Allied forces in France," said the *Westminster Gazette,* "and so far from weakening the determination to provide all possible reinforcement from this country, it will, we are confident, give it fresh energy."

At ten that Good Friday morning King George V, who was visiting France, saw his friend Douglas Haig, who thought he "looked as if he has been suffering from anxiety and 'funk.' I told him that I thought the Allies were fortunate that the attack had fallen on the British and not on the French, because the latter could not have withstood it." They discussed forcing conscription upon Ireland. The King was opposed, but Haig strongly pressed his view not only to get more troops but "for the good of Ireland."

Haig hurried from there to Abbeville, a town about halfway to Amiens, to meet Foch, who was late as usual but full of apologies. "He tells me that he is doing all he can to expedite the arrival of French Divisions, and until they come we can only do our best to hold on to our present positions." Haig gathered from the conversation that the French would have enough troops in four days to start an offensive. Still he wondered, "But will they?"

The morning was damp and there was a high wind, but by afternoon the sun was out. In Paris there was still a mass exodus. Big Bertha had been silent for three days, but that afternoon those who had come to the fashionable church of St. Gervais to hear a sacred concert were shocked by a tremendous explosion overhead. A shell had fallen into the dome of the cathedral, smashing a vital supporting pillar. Tons of stone tumbled onto the trapped congregation. Rescue workers rushing to the scene found an avalanche of debris over the worshipers. Eighty-eight were killed, sixty-eight injured. General Francfort was dead, so were a members of the Swiss Legation, the daughter of the Belgian Consul General, several soldiers, and French, British, and American civilians.

Clemenceau, hastening to the church, stood unnecessarily long under a tottering arch. It was another case of his deliberate courting of danger during these anxious days. At the front he was so reckless that even his ardent admirer, General Mordacq, was ashamed of his chief's *coquetterie.* Some of those close to Clemen-

84

ceau guessed that he felt guilty to be alive while so many brave men perished. His abrupt changes from despair to boastful confidence concerned his friends, as did his bravado before reporters and his malicious jabs of wit at the expense of rivals and discomfited generals. But there was no denying the exhilarating effect his spirit had on the pessimistic. Earlier in the day he had marched through the corridors of the Chamber of Deputies, which was a marketplace for panic rumors, and managed to still fears with his swagger. Yes, he said, when asked if the front had cracked. "There were breaks, plenty of breaches. Then I summoned Foch and I said to him: 'A little pasting up here, some more there. After that, we will assemble reserves.'" It was bad taste but good psychology and the mounting fear was quelled.

Gough's replacement, General Rawlinson, sent Maze to learn what was happening at Moreuil. If the town fell, the road to Amiens, less than fifteen miles to the northwest, would be open. The sergeant found a battle raging on the heights just outside the town. As he approached the bridge over the Avre he could see French troops gesticulating as they ran pell-mell from the town. There was General Mesple, who commanded a French group, revolver in one hand, map in the other, trying to corral a crowd of intoxicated poilus who had obviously broken into wine cellars. "While the kind old General was clutching hold of two of them, the others were slipping past brandishing bottles and hurling invectives at him." He called to Maze, "Take out your revolver!" then fired a shot himself.

These men were startled into obedience, but the main problem was to bring up fresh troops to stem the attack on Moreuil. Maze could see German soldiers on the ridge beyond the town, and they were falling as they were cut down by the volleys of retiring French troops. But how long could the thin line hold?

The Germans were also having trouble with drunkards. Lieutenant Binding saw one unruly group bound east driving a herd of cows. Others carried hens under one arm, while swigging wine. Some had evidently sacked stores, for they carried writing paper, colored notebooks, and other loot. Several men were draped in curtains and others wore top hats. They could hardly walk as they staggered to the rear. Binding was shocked. In the distance he could see the cathedral of Amiens, their goal. If they took it, the war would be over—and men were getting drunk and looting!

Early the following morning, Saturday, March 30, the Canadian Cavalry Brigade was ordered to prepare to move out of their bivouac ten miles west of Moreuil. At dawn it was drizzling as they saddled up and stood by. Two hours later the commander of the British 2nd Cavalry Division arrived to inform the Canadian commander, Brigadier Jack Seely, that the enemy was pouring troops into the Moreuil Wood on the Amiens side of the ridge. "Go to the support of the infantry just beyond Gastel, this side of the

Moreuil Ridge. Don't get too heavily involved—you will be needed later."

Leaving the brigade two miles behind, Seely rode ahead with his brigade major, and his aide-de-camp, Captain Prince Antoine of Orléans. The prince and he were both dashing characters who gravitated where the fighting was the thickest. At a crossroad Seely met the French general who commanded the division on his right. He warned that the enemy was advancing in overwhelming force, and strong detachments were already in Moreuil only two miles to the right. His right flank was unprotected and he was withdrawing his troops.

Seely saw that the situation was desperate. If the enemy were not stopped, the main line from Amiens to Paris would be broken and the French and British forces compelled to fall back—the French toward Paris, the British toward the Channel ports. "I knew that moment to be the supreme event of my life. I believed that if nothing were done the retreat would continue, and the war would be lost." He looked back at the spire of Amiens Cathedral. In some strange way it had inspired him throughout the war. He began to think of sayings from his boyhood: "Death is better than dishonour," and "By Faith ye shall move mountains." He told the French general, "We must retake the Moreuil Ridge." His listener agreed it should be seized or all would be lost—but it was impossible. "I have ample troops, and will send the orders now," said Seely. "Will you send orders to stand fast in Moreuil?"

"But your poor little force cannot do it. The Germans have a whole division in the woods this side of the ridge."

"I have the whole of the British cavalry coming to support me, and following me, le 'grand push' Foch."

The Frenchman looked dubious but said he would send orders. Seely ordered his brigade major, Connolly, to capture the ridge. Then, like heroes out of Dumas, Seely (nicknamed Galloping Jack), the Prince of Orléans and an orderly, carrying a little red pennant, raced down the hill followed by the signal troop. They thundered across a bridge, through a wheat field, and onto a road leading to the front. A few bullets flew past as they rode through their own front-line troops who were lying down, firing. "We are going to retake the ridge," Seely shouted to a young captain. "Fire on both sides of us, as close as you can while the rest of us go up."

The captain rose to his knees. "Good luck to you, sir!"

The infantry opened fire as the little group galloped up the ridge. Five of the signal troop were shot off their horses but seven reached the wood and began firing. As his orderly planted the red pennant at the point of the wood, Seely turned to see his brigade charging full speed up toward him. Seely noted how curious it was that galloping horses seemed to magnify in power and number. His brigade looked like a mighty host as it swept over the open country. The general rode up to Lieutenant G. M. Flowerdew, commander of the leading squadron of Lord Strathcona's Horse, and told him that this was the most adventurous task of all but he was confident they would succeed. Flowerdew, a mild-looking young man, smiled gently as they started forward. "I know, sir. I know it is a splendid moment. I will try not to fail you."

Ahead of them two squadrons of the Dragoons had turned into the wood and were engaging the enemy despite heavy losses. "The air was alive with bullets," recalled Seely, "but nobody minded a bit. It was strange to see the horses roll over like rabbits, and the men, when unwounded, jump up and run forward, sometimes catching the stirrups of their still mounted comrades."

Gordon Muriel Flowerdew wheeled his troops into line. Frank Rees, an infantryman in the shallow trenches, could not believe his eyes when he beheld a jingling, jangling troop of cavalry canter up and turn into line behind him. For some reason, Jerry was holding his fire as the cavalry moved ahead a dozen paces. Suddenly the German battery that had been pounding the trenches the past forty-eight hours opened up with a crash. The next five minutes were hell. Out front, Rees could see stumbling, falling, screaming horses. Men sprawled on the ground, some running, some trying to turn to hold their horses. Then came the chilling chatter of machine guns. Bullets were tearing into the cavalry, Rees wasn't sure whether the charge developed, but he thought he saw horses in some controlled group galloping into the faint haze. It was Flowerdew's squadron. With a wild shout he had led a charge at a long, thin column of Germans marching into the woods. A hundred yards ahead of the others, Flowerdrew plunged into the enemy, wielding his saber. He wheeled about and charged back again.

Rees could see only confusion, horses galloping free as the troopers tried to catch them. He would never forget their courage as they ran through the deadly fire to retrieve their mounts. Would the infantrymen have done it? The only thing the P.B.I. (Poor Bloody Infantry) could do now was look on helplessly. Rees dared not fire his rifle. Even if Jerry had come over the top, they could not have fired. They were helpless with all those horses and men in front. A Cockney next to him shouted to one of the troopers, "Oo are you?"

"Strathcona's Horse!"

"Strathcona's Orse! You'll be bloody bully beef if yer don't get art the way!"

Flowerdew and his men slaughtered many Germans, but in minutes 70 percent of their own comrades were dead from rifle and machine-gun fire. The enemy broke and ran. Flowerdew was on the ground, with bullets in both thighs and two in his chest. "Carry on, boys!" he shouted, then uttered his last words, "We have won."

Seely found the survivors of the desperate charge in a small ditch bordering the wood. They were manning enemy machine guns. At their side lay German bodies, seventy killed by sword thrust alone and another two or three hundred by machine guns. Over eight hundred horses were lost by Seely's men in a few brief minutes; three hundred men died or were wounded. The Germans fought as courageously. Hundreds had stood their ground and were shot at point-blank range.

As Seely on horseback led dismounted troops through the wood, he came upon a handsome young Bavarian propped against a tree, blood pouring from a bayonet thrust in his throat. Seely shouted down in German, "Lie still, a stretcher-bearer will look after you." The young Bavarian seized a rifle, shouted, *"Nein, nein. Ich will ungefangen sterben!"* He fired, then collapsed as Seely galloped on unharmed.

The infantrymen who witnessed the charge thought it was all a wicked waste and imagined that someone in GHQ had had an attack of heroics at other men's expense. What difference if that German battery had not been silenced and the little strip of ground out front retaken? They did not realize that the Canadian troopers had gone on to retake Moreuil Ridge, and that Amiens had been saved—at least for the moment. Cavalry armed with sabers should have been wiped out by artillery firing point-blank and machine guns manned by dug-in crews—but for the gallant spirit of Seely, Flowerdew, and others.

Soon after General Rawlinson, Gough's replacement, got the news of Moreuil Ridge, he was visited by Clemenceau and Winston Churchill. The latter had been sent over by Lloyd George to find out whether the French were going to make a genuine effort to stop the German onrush. He instructed Churchill to see everybody. "Use my authority. See Foch. See Clemenceau."

As the three enjoyed an improvised lunch set out on a table—meat, bread, pickles, whiskey and soda—Rawlinson remarked that Haig would join them in a few minutes. Almost immediately the field marshal's long gray car pulled up at the door. He and Clemenceau retired to an adjoining room while Loucheur and Churchill remained with Rawlinson, who told them there had just been a success. "We have taken a wood. Jack Seely, with the Canadian Cavalry, has just stormed the Bois de Moreuil."

"Will you be able to make a front?"

"No one can tell. We have hardly anything between us and the enemy except utterly exhausted, disorganized troops. There is a chap called Carey with a few thousand officers and men raked up anyhow from school and depots, who is holding about six miles of front here." He pointed at a map. "All the Fifth Army infantry are dead to the world from want of sleep and rest. Nearly all the formations are mixed or dissolved. The men are just crawling slowly backwards; they are completely worn out. D.H. [Haig] is trying to get some reinforcements out of Clemenceau."

"Do you think you will be here tomorrow night?" asked Churchill. Rawlinson made a grimace which was not encouraging.

In the other room Clemenceau agreed to support the British energetically so they could hold the high ground the Canadian Cavalry had just retaken. He talked freely of his fear that Pétain and Foch would squabble. "Pétain is a very nervous man and sometimes may not carry out all he has promised."

As they were rejoining the others, Clemenceau said in English, "I have done what you wished. Never mind what has been arranged before. If your men are tired and we have fresh men at hand, our men shall come at once and help you. And now, I claim my reward." Rawlinson asked what that was. "I wish to pass the river and see the battle." Rawlinson protested but Clemenceau could not be stopped. He and Churchill went forward until they could hear the crack of rifles in the woods; shells began dropping on the road ahead. Churchill suggested they get out of their car and take a look. The Moreuil Wood lay not far ahead. They could see stragglers and groups of led horses, perhaps from Seely's brigade. Clemenceau, completely oblivious of shrapnel, climbed a promontory for a better look. Shells landed only a hundred yards away but he was as cool as he had been yesterday standing under the tottering arch of St. Gervais church. He was as irresponsible as a boy on holiday, ignoring the pleas of the French staff officers to withdraw.

At the road a shell burst among the horses. One, streaming with blood, staggered toward Clemenceau, who, despite his seventy-six years, agilely seized the bridle. As the Premier reluctantly returned to the car, he grinned at Churchill and said in an undertone, "*Quel moment délicieux!*"

It was night by the time they reached Paris. Churchill was exhausted, but Clemenceau, apparently immune to fatigue, was still jocular and lively. "This sort of an excursion is all right for a single day," said Churchill. "But you ought not to go under fire too often."

"*C'est mon grand plaisir.*"

The following day, Easter, the last day of March, was showery with bright intervals. There was little action on the front except south of the Somme. Haig attended the Church of Scotland services at 9:30 A.M.

Back in England there was a rush to buy newspapers. Had the Germans broken through? In London's Hyde Park groups were fearfully debating what was going on. Outside Charing Cross Station crowds gathered to cheer the Red Cross ambulances bringing wounded from the front. The rumble of battle could be clearly heard in coastal towns, and even on the high ground of Wimbledon M. MacDonagh felt "a curious atmospheric sensation—a kind of pulsation in regular beats . . . it was the guns, the terrible cannonade of the Great Battle in France which was shaking the earth literally."

Just before dinner, Lloyd George was roused to excitement by a message from his ambassador in Washington, Lord Reading, that President Wilson would send 120,000 men per month to France if Britain could provide the shipping. The Prime Minister boasted to Riddell and other guests that this was the biggest thing he had accomplished all week. "At last I have stirred Wilson into action. I sent a message for Reading to read at a dinner at which he was the guest.* That had the effect. These 480,000 will be invaluable. We must publish the joyful news."

"You must not be too joyful," cautioned the Prime Minister's secretary. "You have not yet got the men."

"The news will hearten the French," he insisted, and suggested that they call General Wilson. "He will be very pleased. He calls President Wilson his 'cousin.' " A moment later Lloyd George was on the telephone. "Well, General, I have some good news for you. Your 'cousin' has agreed to send 120,000 men per month for the next three months." The President was evidently "in a fright," he added, and wanted the British to make the first announcement of the offer. But Henry Wilson had his suspicions. "The whole thing sounds a little fishy," he wrote in his diary that night.

In the meantime Lloyd George was so keyed up he also was impelled to telephone the Cabinet Secretary, Hankey. After relaying the news, he said, somewhat cockily, "Now you can sleep tonight."

"This is a good Easter egg," Hankey jotted down in his diary, "and it seems that the prayers I mumbled at early Communion this morning are already in a fair way to be answered. Nevertheless I doubt not the future has many terrible things in store for us, and that we shall need stout hearts and firm faith for many a day to come."

On April 1 the news from the front was better, and Foch wrote Clemenceau that evening: ". . . the enemy's initiative seems now blocked and paralyzed." The respite continued for another twenty-four hours, a fitting prelude to another important Allied conference, this to be held at Beauvais, some forty-five miles north of Paris. Foch felt that the powers conferred upon him at Doullens were "insufficient to cover even the present defensive operations." They would be far more inadequate to carry out the strategic employment of Allied armies in the near future, since the Americans obviously would play an increasing role. The present role of coordinator was not sufficient, he felt, for the larger program, so a meeting was called for April 3.

Lloyd George agreed and decided to attend so he could override Haig if necessary. On the morning of the third at ten, the two met near Montreuil and drove in the same car toward Beauvais. To Haig, the Prime Minister looked "as if he had been thoroughly frightened, and he seemed still in a funk." They talked about the retreat of the Fifth Army, and Haig was convinced that his companion was looking for a scapegoat. He himself championed Gough. "He had few reserves," said Haig, "a very big front entirely without defensive works, recently taken over from the French, and

---

* He was referring to a reading of his plea for help to the Lotos Club in New York on March 27, and was wrong on two counts. The President was not there; moreover, Lloyd George's appeal, which was directed to the American people rather than to the administration, so outraged Wilson that he considered asking for Reading's recall. Only the urgent appeals of Colonel House, Wilson's chief adviser, and Sir William Wiseman, covert head of British Intelligence in the United States, prevented him from doing so.

the weight of the enemy's attack fell on him." Moreover, despite a most difficult situation, Gough had never really lost his head.

Lloyd George grumbled that a man who had neither held the Somme bridges nor destroyed them should not be employed again. "I can not condemn an officer unheard," said Haig stiffly, "and if you wish him suspended, you must send me an order to that effect." He was thinking, *What a cur the Prime Minister is!* and could not "resist a feeling of distrust of him and of his intentions."

As for the coming meeting, Lloyd George felt that Foch's powers should be increased. Haig saw no need for this; things were getting on quite well. Field Marshal and Prime Minister were at odds about almost everything. When Lloyd George proudly reported that he had concluded arrangements for shipping the new American troops to France, he was incensed that Haig didn't express more relief. He never expected gratitude from such a man, but it was annoying to find him "cool and sniffy about it." Haig didn't seem to think much of American help; they would be only a massive wave of untrained rabble.

Haig was also annoyed. What a fatiguing companion Lloyd George was in an automobile! "He talks and argues so! And he appears to me to be a thorough impostor." Halfway to their destination, both men were relieved to change partners. The Prime Minister got into another car with General Lawrence, while Haig was joined by Wilson, who lately had put himself out to be charming to Haig, who, in turn, was beginning to think he had underestimated Wilson. The Chief of Staff was playing a part, for he still had little regard for the austere Scotsman. "He seems to me to have lost grip of the situation. He took most languid interest in the new American scheme for which I gave L.G. full credit. He can't understand why Foch does not attack and is prepared to carry an attack two days after the French have started theirs. I said I supposed Foch was delaying because he had not enough guns up yet. D.H. is a very stupid man."

The British party reached Beauvais about 1 P.M., and while they ate lunch Clemenceau sat with them. To Hankey the Premier looked tired and rather worried as if he had been sleeping badly. But he joked a bit and seemed full of courage. Afterward Lloyd George confided to Hankey that he thought the Doullens arrangement was too vague and that Foch should be given greater and more direct authority.

General Pershing had arrived early, so he had plenty of time to stroll around the historic old town. He took his time enjoying the cathedral, a Gothic structure of the thirteenth century. He then sauntered to the Hôtel de Ville, where the conference would take place. But the British were again late, and he had to wait an hour.

The meeting was not called to order until 3 P.M. At Doullens there had been an atmosphere of tension and even fright, but here there was an air of growing confidence that the German push could be stopped. "We have come together to settle a very simple question regarding the functions of General Foch," began Clemenceau. "I think we are all in agreement as to the coordination of Allied action, but there is some difference in the understanding of General Foch's powers as conferred upon him at the Doullens conference of March 26th. General Foch will explain his difficulties."

Foch succinctly stated his case. The powers given to him at Doullens were conferred when the battle was at a crisis. Today the front lines were practically at a standstill. "There should be authority to prepare for action and direct it. So we are right back where we were before, and nothing can be done until an action starts again."

Haig sat as still as a statue, but Lloyd George spiritedly supported Foch. "We have had more than three years of this war, and we have not had unity of action during that time. During the last year we have had two kinds of strategy, one by Haig and another by Pétain, both different, and nothing has been gained."

Haig flushed. Last year, he retorted angrily, he was under the orders of General Nivelle. Lloyd George warned Haig not to interrupt. "I did not refer to that period," he said. Moreover Nivelle's strategy had achieved the most valuable results of 1917, since it had put the British in possession of Vimy Ridge. Haig struggled to control himself from refuting this distortion of history while his enemy got back to the issue, strongly supporting Foch's desire for authority to prepare for action. "I think the resolution made at Doullens should be modified so that we may have a better understanding," said Haig, and asked to hear what the Americans had to say.

General Bliss, the American representative at the Supreme War Council in Versailles, said that the Doullens resolution gave Foch no authority to act except in conference with Haig and Pétain. General Pershing, making notes in pencil, now read from them: "The principle of unity of command is undoubtedly the correct one for the Allies to follow. I do not believe that it is possible to have unity of action without a supreme commander." So far there had been no unity, and coordination between two or three armies was impossible without a generalissimo. "Each commander-in-chief is interested in his own army, and cannot get the other commander's point of view or grasp the problem as a whole." The success of the Allied cause depended on immediate action in this matter. "I am in favor of conferring the supreme command upon General Foch."

The volatile Lloyd George sprang from his chair to grasp Pershing's hand. "I agree fully with General Pershing. This is well put." He turned to Haig for his opinion. The field marshal must have felt the others were conspiring against him. "We have had practically complete unity of action," he protested. "I have always cooperated with the French, whom I regard as in control of the strategical questions of the war." Hadn't he always worked well with both Nivelle and Pétain? "I agree with General Pershing's general idea that there should be unity of command, but I think we have had it."

At last Pétain was given a chance to talk. It was obvious that he and Foch disliked each other. He repeated almost exactly what Haig had said and a few minutes later antagonized Pershing. This came when a draft of a resolution was submitted which omitted reference to an American army. "There is no such thing," said Pétain. American units were either in training or amalgamated with the British or French. Pershing was not eloquent and tended to start every sentence with "er, er, er." But he could not be cowed. He jutted out his jaw. "There may not be an American army in force functioning now but there soon will be, and I want this resolution to apply to it when it becomes a fact." He looked challengingly around the table. It was obvious this was a strong and determined individual, not to be trifled with. The necessary addition was made. The resolution charged Foch with the coordination of the action of the Allied armies on the Western Front and "to this end there is conferred on him all the powers necessary for its effective realization. To the same end, the British, French and American Governments confide in General Foch the strategic direction of military operations." Henceforth Haig and Pétain were responsible only for the tactical direction of their armies.

Those present scribbled their names at the bottom of the document. Pershing thought it was a momentous achievement, and Haig got some consolation when his urgent request for a French offensive to begin "as soon as possible" was promised by both Foch and Pétain. *But will they ever attack?* he thought. He doubted whether the French Army, as a whole, was now fit for an offensive.

As the conferees filed out of the room, Lloyd George gaily accosted Foch. "And now which must I bet on, Ludendorff or Foch?" he asked.

"You can first back me, and you will win. For Ludendorff has got to break through us, and this he can no longer do. As for us, our present business is to stop him, which we shall certainly accomplish. Later on, when our turn comes to break through him—that is another matter; it will be seen then what we can do." But he was not completely happy with the arrangement. Unless he had the power to issue orders to Haig and Pétain, there would always be the problem of interpretation. He had never heard of an office in the army as coordinator. "What am I? I am Monsieur Foch, very well known . . ." he said, smiling, "but still Monsieur Foch." Lloyd George sympathized and promised to do his best to get his War Cabinet to suggest that Foch be called *Général-en-Chef*. Would that satisfy Foch? "That is a different matter altogether," said the Frenchman. "If that were done there would be no more difficulties."

On the drive to the port of Boulogne the Churchill party picnicked on the roadside from the luncheon basket Clemenceau had brought to Beauvais. It was completely dark by the time they reached the Channel port. At the dock a Scottish regiment of eighteen- and nineteen-year-olds was just disembarking from a steamer. In the glimmer of the dimmed arc lights they looked pale and pathetically young to Hankey. In a few days they would be thrown against experienced Germans.

Soon the British party was boarding a "P" boat, a new craft invented to fight submarines. They were warned that a German submarine was in the neighborhood, but the crossing was uneventful. "On the whole a satisfactory day," wrote Wilson in his diary.

Early the next afternoon, April 4, Gough was summoned to see Haig and was told to return to England immediately. "The orders don't come from me, Hubert," added Haig. They originated with Lloyd George and his Cabinet, who blamed Gough greatly, especially for not holding the line at the Somme.

"Never mind now, sir," said Gough, determined to say nothing to add to Haig's burdens or to offer any protests. "I know the tremendous problems you have to deal with, sir, so I am not going to say anything."

"You will have every chance to defend yourself, Hubert. There is to be an enquiry."

There was nothing more for Gough to say except, "Thank you."

Haig extended his hand. "I'm sorry to lose you, Hubert. Goodbye."

Gough was met at Charing Cross by his wife, Nora. She sensed that something was wrong, and in the taxi on the way to Waterloo he revealed what had happened. She was too amazed to say anything at first, then became indignant and angry.

At a Cabinet meeting, Lord Derby was informing his colleagues that he was investigating the Fifth Army reverse. "The heads of the enquiry," he said, "have already been drawn up." Lloyd George also took the opportunity to attack Haig's chief of staff. Lawrence, he said, was a very ordinary person for such a position. At this point, General Smuts chimed in to say that Haig had already proved his "complete impotence" as commander-in-chief. "There was no doubt," Wilson recorded in his diary, "that the feeling of the Cabinet was, I think, unanimously against Haig and the whole GHQ."

On that fourth of April the Germans resumed their attacks in a final effort to take Amiens, but steady rain made the battlefield a giant mudhole. Rifles became clogged and it was so diffcult to move that little advance was made.

"The slippery ground is against us, for every step forward one slides back two, and the ground rises all the way," wrote Lieutenant Binding in his diary that night. His division was attacking north of Moreuil Ridge, and he was appalled by the awfulness of that wasteland. "There is nothing like it on earth, nor can be. A desert is always a desert; but a desert which tells you all the time that it used not to be a desert is appalling. That is the tale which is told by the dumb, black stumps of the shattered trees which still stick up where there used to be villages. They were completely flayed by the splinters of the bursting shells, and they stand there like corpses upright . . . There are miles upon miles of flat, empty, broken, and tumbled stone-quarry, utterly purposeless and useless, in the middle of which stand groups of these blackened stumps of dead trees, poisoned oases, killed for ever." That ghastly, devastated area should remain as a memorial. "No road, no well, no settlement out to be made there, and every ruler, leading statesman, or president of a republic ought to be brought to see it, instead of swearing an oath on the Constitution, henceforth and for ever. Then there would be no more wars."

6.

Although America had declared war almost a year earlier, it was, except to the few facing death on the battlefields of France, still almost like a show—unreal, romantic, and exciting. The millions of men already killed brutally on the Western Front alone were little more than statistics to the Americans. Europe, too, had entered the war in 1914 with equal exuberance and innocence. America had yet to feel the tragedy; the greatest concern of many of those in uniform was that they would arrive at the front too late for the Big Show.

The popular songs mirrored the spirit of the day. There was a cryptic, saucy tune, "Good-morning, Mr. Zip, Zip, Zip (With your hair cut just as short as mine!)" and the sentimental "Keep the home fires burning, while your hearts are yearning; Though your lads are far away, they dream of home." Another, "Long Boy," celebrated the country hick going off to battle the Kaiser: "Good-bye, Ma! Good-bye, Pa! Good-bye, Mule, with yer old hee-haw! I may not know what this war's about, But you bet, by gosh, I'll soon find out." Most popular by far were a paean to sweet melancholy, "There's a long, long trail a-winding Into the land of my dreams," and George M. Cohan's rousing, jaunty "Over There," which perfectly expressed the brash optimism of the soldiers who were beginning to called themselves doughboys: *

> Over there, over there,
> Send the word, send the word, over there,
> That the Yanks are coming, the Yanks are coming,
> The drums rum-tumming everywhere.
> So prepare, say a pray'r.

* "A 'doughboy,'" according to an explanation printed in 1887, "is a small round doughnut served to sailors. . . . Early in the Civil War the term was applied to the large globular brass buttons on the infantry uniform, from which it passed, by a natural transition, to the infantryman himself." This is a far more likely theory than another, that it came from the word "adobe," which was applied by Spaniards in the Southwest to army personnel.

Send the word, send the word to beware,
We'll be over, we're coming over,
And we won't be back till it's over over there.

This was a common feeling throughout the United States. With little thought of blood and death, the Yanks were coming and the Allies had nothing to worry about. The war was still a game and Broadway was making the most of it. On the evening of April 4, D. W. Griffith's new motion picture, *Hearts of the World*, had its premiere in New York City. It was a special performance exclusively for representatives of the American and Allied Governments, state and municipal officials, and distinguished public citizens. It was a story of the great war starring Lillian and Dorothy Gish, and much of it had been filmed near the front lines.

The first scenes had been shot in England, where everyone wanted to cooperate. Winston Churchill volunteered to write a script and Lady Paget offered her estate as a location. Here King George, Queen Mary, the Queen Mother, Alexandra, and scores of other notables served as extras. The company then moved to France, filming scenes in a destroyed village just behind the front. "We worked quickly, intensely, quietly—with no shouting from Mr. Griffith," recalled Lillian Gish, "only hurried, tense orders, followed at once with precision by the three of us." They moved to a dugout for a quick lunch and then went closer to the front. "We were in range of long-distance guns. Shells and shrapnel fell close enough to make us nervous."

The motion picture was awaited with expectation. On the night it opened, a number of other movies and plays about the war were playing on Broadway to enthusiastic audiences. Another movie, *Over the Top*, starring Sergeant Guy Empey, the author, had opened a few days earlier, as had a stage extravaganza, *An American Ace*, with a cast of 150. Also showing was a patriotic play, *Her Country*, and there was *The Kaiser, the Beast of Berlin*.

Throughout the showing of *Hearts of the World*, the audience spontaneously applauded scene after scene and at the end everyone rose, shouting for Griffith until he appeared. Emotionally wrought, he said he could not make a speech and only wanted those present to pray for and support the men fighting in the war which the flickering shadows on the screen . . . But his voice broke and he could not finish the sentence.

On the real battlefield, the German attacks on Amiens continued the next day, April 5, but again were repulsed. It was the end of the great offensive. Huge gobs of territory had been seized, and Ludendorff was convinced that it was a brilliant feat that would go down in history. "What the English and French had not succeeded in doing we had accomplished, and that in the fourth year of the war." His armies had driven to a depth of forty miles, occupying 1,200 square miles of territory, more than the Allies had gained since the beginning of the war. Almost 90,000 British prisoners were taken, as well as 975 guns; 164,000 casualties had been inflicted on the British and 70,000 on the French.

But victory had been costly. It extended the German front and lost thousands of its best storm troops while exhausting seventy divisions. More important, the great breakthrough had failed, and the Allied lines, strengthened by two conferences which brought a united command, were still intact.

Ludendorff put all this behind him and set his operations officers working on a second grand attack, one further to the north. This surely would succeed in tearing asunder the English and French and bring final victory.

German industrialists had little doubt that he would succeed, and were already dividing up France. Ernst von Borsig, partner in a leading machine-manufacturing firm, called for "the acquisition of the iron district of Briey and Longwy . . . a question of life and death for the German iron industry." The Christian labor unions shared the same views; and on April 6, the *Deutsche Metallarbeiter*, organ of the Christian metal and foundry workers' union, also demanded the Briey-Longwy basin. Many Germans on the home front could taste the fruits of victory, while most of those at the front only hoped for a decent peace.

Hans Schröder, an airman, wanted to see what war on the ground looked like and was wandering through the woods near Bapaume. The sight of the British who died from gas was ghastly. "They lay as they fell when the fatal gas surprised them. The butt ends of their rifles were pressed against their cheeks; their right hands still grasped hand-grenades. There were whole lines of sharpshooters in this position. Then we came to a machine-gun nest, with the gunner still taking aim while the second and third men worked the belt, and the officer lay there with his glasses at his eyes. The useless gas-masks covering their faces gave them the appearance of fantastic apes." A pestilential odor still rose from the tortured ground, and Schröder wished that little children of all nations could see all this to impress on them this principle: "War is Murder!"

Part 2

CRISIS

Chapter Four

RED DAWN IN THE EAST
JANUARY 4–MARCH 16

1.

DURING the critical days of the March retreat on the Western Front, Pershing was only the figurehead of American adamancy. He was merely following the directives of President Wilson, who went far beyond Pershing's simple insistence on a unified American army under American officers. The idealistic and intellectual Wilson had entered the war reluctantly, and his ultimate goals were far different from those of his allies. While they fought primarily for survival of their way of life and continuance of empire, Woodrow Wilson, formerly president of Princeton University, envisaged a brave new world of eternal peace and justice, united in a democratic league of nations. He had led his country into battle with a noble double-edged slogan: this shall be a war to end all wars, in order to make the world safe for democracy.

The inevitable clash between idealism and pragmatism was already coming to a head in Russia. Both England and France saw the new Bolshevik state as a deadly peril, while Wilson, who knew little about Russia and whose new concept of her new political philosophy was still vague, was prepared to accept the Soviet Government into his democratic community of nations. He was guided in this direction by his chief adviser, Colonel Edward House, who had earned this honorary title by his sagacious counsel to several governors of Texas. House's ambition was not for high political office; he wanted to be the gray eminence of Washington. The diminutive colonel reveled in living in the shadow of the towering Wilson. He had made himself indispensable to the President "by supplying reliable information, by insinuating advice without offense, by expressing dissent usually by silence, and by taking care not to oversell himself or his ideas."

From the first, House had opposed any Allied military intervention in Bolshevik Russia and therefore found himself in complete disagreement with the French and British. "God only knows

98

who is right," he wrote in the meticulous, detailed diary he kept, "but, at least I feel that I am on the safe side when I advise that literally nothing be done further than that an expression of sympathy be offered for Russia's efforts to weld herself into a virile democracy, and to proffer our financial, industrial, and moral support in every way possible."

Consequently, House had persuaded the President to deliver, early in 1918, a major speech on America's war aims that would not only rally the Allied peoples, if not their governments, to a liberal peace settlement, but also include "an answer to the demand of the Bolsheviks for an explanation of the objects of the war, such an answer as might persuade Russia to stand by the Allies in their defense of democratic and liberal principles." In other words, he hoped that a friendly posture toward the Soviets, who were about to renew peace negotiations at Brest-Litovsk, would encourage them to turn down Germany's arbitrary demands and stay in the war.

On January 4, 1918, House had come to Washington armed with extensive material and recommendations compiled by a distinguished group of private experts, including Professor Charles Seymour, of Yale, and Walter Lippmann. His task was to help Wilson prepare the speech.

The two men got down to serious work the next morning, a Saturday. They labored behind locked doors, for Wilson wanted little advice from such as Robert Lansing, whom he considered a dullard, preferring to be his own Secretary of State. "We actually got down to work at half-past ten," recalled House, "and finished remaking the map of the world, as we would have it, at half-past twelve o'clock." They approached it systematically, "first outlining general terms, such as open diplomacy, freedom of the seas, removing of economic barriers, establishment of equality of trade conditions, guarantees for the reduction of national armaments, adjustment of colonial claims, general association of nations for the conservation of peace. Then we began on Belgium, France, and other territorial adjustments."

House kept urging open diplomacy. "I said there was nothing he could do that would better please the American people and the democracies of the world, and that it was right and must be the diplomacy of the future. I asked him to lay deep stress upon it and to place it first." He also suggested the removal of trade barriers and something on freedom of the seas, finally framing this paragraph: "Absolute freedom of navigation upon the seas, outside territorial waters, alike in peace and in war."

Wilson himself typed out a final version of the speech, cautiously avoiding any invective or generalized charges. He was careful to point out that America had no wish to injure postwar Germany by arms or economic sanctions, nor had she any intention of meddling with Germany's constitutional institutions. The following afternoon he read the finished speech to House, who was deeply moved. He felt that it was the most important document that Wilson had ever penned. "You will either be on the crest of the wave after it's delivered," he commented, "or reposing peacefully in the depths." They were both most anxious about how America would receive this abrupt entrance into European affairs. They were also fearful of other points: Alsace and Lorraine, the freedom of the seas, and the leveling of commercial barriers.

Tuesday, January 8, was bright and cold, but Wilson played a few holes of golf with his wife before returning to the White House at 11:30 A.M. Only then did he instruct his secretary, Joseph Patrick Tumulty, to inform Vice-President Thomas Marshall and Speaker of the House Champ Clark that he would be at the Capitol in thirty minutes to address a joint session of Congress.

Having addressed that body only four days earlier, he caught everyone by surprise and there was a wild scramble to round up enough senators and congressmen to fill the House. The only ambassador in the diplomatic gallery was Sir Cecil Spring Rice, who was about to be replaced as British Ambassador by Lord Reading. There were few spectators in the visitors' gallery when Mrs. Wilson arrived at noon, attended by four relatives and Colonel House.

As Wilson was led to the speaker's stand, there was only scattered applause. Even those members of his own Cabinet who learned the news in time to be on hand had no idea that Wilson was about to deliver a historic speech embodying America's war aims. The President began quietly, undramatically, with a surprisingly sympathetic portrayal of Soviet diplomacy at the current peace talks with Germany in Brest-Litovsk. "The Russian representatives have insisted, very justly, very wisely, and in the true spirit of democracy, that the conferences they have been holding with the Teutonic and Turkish statesmen should be held with open, not closed doors, and all the world has been an audience, as was desired." The Allies, he went on, had been utterly candid about their war aims, unlike the Central Powers. There was no confusion of counsel among the Allies, no uncertainty of principle or vagueness of detail. "There is, moreover, a voice calling for these definitions of principle and of purpose which is, it seems to me, more thrilling and more compelling than any of the many moving voices with which the troubled air of the world is filled. It is the voice of the Russian people. They are prostrate and all but helpless, it would seem, before the grim power of Germany, which has hitherto known no relenting and no pity. Their power, apparently, is shattered. And yet their soul is not subservient. They will not yield either in principle or in action. Their conception of what is right, of what is humane and honorable for them to accept, has been stated with frankness, a largeness of view, a generosity of spirit, and a universal human sympathy which must challenge the admiration of every friend of mankind; and they have refused to compound their ideals or desert others that they themselves may be safe."

It was a pity that he had not consulted the unassuming but

shrewd Lansing, who was aware that the Bolshevik negotiators were hardly voicing the motives and sentiments of a Russian people completely ignorant of what was going on at Brest-Litovsk. Wilson's equation of Bolshevism and the Russian people was a distortion of history; Lenin and Trotsky themselves would have ridiculed the naïve description of themselves as humane and honorable, of having a generosity of spirit, and refusing to desert others that they themselves may be safe.

As yet Wilson's calm, measured tones had aroused little show of enthusiasm, but now he began to speak with force and feeling of the Russian people. "They call us to say what it is we desire, in what, if in anything, our purpose and our spirit differ from theirs; and I believe that the people of the United States would wish me to respond, with utter simplicity and frankness. Whether their present leaders believe it or not, it is our heartfelt desire and hope that some way may be opened whereby we may be privileged to assist the people of Russia to attain their utmost hope of liberty and ordered peace." At last there was applause. An atmosphere of growing excitement came over the big room as visitors continued to file into the galleries and more senators and representatives edged quietly into their seats.

The basic American war aim, he continued, was unselfish: that the world be made fit and safe to live in; that all nations be assured of justice and fair dealing. "The program of the world's peace, therefore, is our program; and that program, the only possible program, as we see it, is this . . ." His words struck home and there was rapt silence as he began listing the fourteen points * of

* The Fourteen Points:

I.—Open covenants of peace, openly arrived at, after which there shall be no private international understandings of any kind but diplomacy shall proceed always frankly and in the public view.

II.—Absolute freedom of navigation upon the seas, outside territorial waters, alike in peace and in war, except as the seas may be closed in whole or in part by international action for the enforcement of international covenants.

III.—The removal, so far as possible, of all economic barriers and the establishment of an equality of trade conditions among all the nations consenting to the peace and associating themselves for its maintenance.

IV.—Adequate guarantees given and taken that national armaments will be reduced to the lowest point consistent with domestic safety.

V.—Free, open-minded, and absolutely impartial adjustment of all colonial claims, based upon a strict observance of the principle that in determining all such questions of sovereignty the interests of the populations concerned must have equal weight with the equitable claims of the Government whose title is to be determined.

VI.—The evacuation of all Russian territory and such settlement of all questions affecting Russia as will secure the best and freest cooperation of the other nations of the world in obtaining for her an unhampered and unembarrassed opportunity for the independent determination of her own political development and national policy and assure her of a sincere welcome into the society of free nations under institutions of her own choosing; and, more than a welcome, assistance also of every kind that she may need and may herself desire. The treatment accorded Russia by her sister nations in the months to come will be the acid test of their good will, of their comprehension of her needs as distinguished from their own interests, and of their intelligent and unselfish sympathy.

his program: open diplomacy, freedom of the seas, reduction of armaments, impartial adjustment of colonial claims, evacuation of all Russian and Belgium territory. But when he reached the next point, the restoration of all French territory, including Alsace-Lorraine, which had been seized by Prussia in 1871, there was a spontaneous burst of cheering. "Senators and representatives," wrote John Dos Passos, "jumped on chairs and waved their arms as if they were at a football game."

The President smiled, waiting patiently for the hubbub to subside, and then went on till he reached the last and fourteenth point: a demand for a League of Nations. The Allies, he said, were willing to fight to the end for these "essential rectifications of wrong and assertions of right." Nor had they any jealousy of German greatness. "We do not wish to injure her or to block in any way her legitimate influence or power. We do not wish to fight her either with arms or with hostile arrangements of trade if she is willing to associate herself with us and other peace-loving nations of the world in covenants of justice and law and fair dealing." The people of the United States, he concluded, were "ready to devote their lives, their honor, and everything they possess" to this princi-

---

VII.—Belgium, the whole world will agree, must be evacuated and restored, without any attempt to limit the sovereignty which she enjoys in common with all other free nations. No other single act will serve as this will serve to restore confidence among the nations in the laws which they themselves have set and determined for the government of their relations with one another. Without this healing act the whole structure and validity of international law is forever impaired.

VIII.—All French territory should be freed and the invaded portions restored, and the wrong done to France by Prussia in 1871 in the matter of Alsace-Lorraine, which has unsettled the peace of the world for nearly fifty years, should be righted, in order that peace may once more be made secure in the interest of all.

IX.—A readjustment of the frontiers of Italy should be effected along clearly recognizable lines of nationality.

X.—The peoples of Austria-Hungary, whose place among the nations we wish to see safeguarded and assured, should be accorded the freest opportunity of autonomous development.

XI.—Rumania, Serbia, and Montenegro should be evacuated; occupied territories restored; Serbia accorded free and secure access to the sea; and the relations of the several Balkan States to one another determined by friendly counsel along historically established lines of allegiance and nationality; and international guarantees of the political and economic independence and territorial integrity of the several Balkan States should be entered into.

XII.—The Turkish portions of the present Ottoman Empire should be assured a secure sovereignty, but the other nationalities which are now under Turkish rule should be assured an undoubted security of life and an absolutely unmolested opportunity of autonomous development, and the Dardanelles should be permanently opened as a free passage to the ships and commerce of all nations under international guarantees.

XIII.—An independent Polish State should be erected which should include the territories inhabited by indisputably Polish populations, which should be assured a free and secure access to the sea, and whose political and economic independence and territorial integrity should be guaranteed by international covenant.

XIV.—A general association of nations must be formed under specific covenants for the purpose of affording mutual guarantees of political independence and territorial integrity to great and small states alike.

ple of justice to all peoples and nationalities. "The moral climax of this the culmination and final war for human liberty has come, and they are ready to put their own strength, their own integrity and devotion to the test."

Throughout America the first response was concurrence by all political parties. Theodore Roosevelt and Senator Borah, who rarely agreed on anything, approved, as did the Socialists. The Republican New York *Tribune*, usually a harsh critic of Wilson, labeled the Fourteen Points speech a second Emancipation Proclamation. "As Lincoln freed the slaves of the South half a century ago, Mr. Wilson now pledges his country to fight for the liberation of the Belgian and the Pole, the Serb and the Rumanian . . . The President's words are the words of a hundred million . . . Today, as never before, the whole nation marches with the President, certain alike of the leader and the cause."

The British, however, were not at all enthusiastic about Wilson's call for freedom of the seas, and the London *Times* doubted that "the reign of righteousness was within our reach." While the French were similarly skeptical, there was relief at the statement about Alsace-Lorraine. "President Wilson's words," said *La Liberté*, "will make his name popular to the remotest villages of France." As for the Italian leaders, they were unhappy at Wilson's demand for a mere "readjustment of the frontiers of Italy . . . along clearly recognizable lines of nationality." They wanted more territory than that.

The European Allies were not at all ready to accept the idealistic American program, nor did Germany respond to Wilson's invitation to join the community of "peace-loving nations." The regime, of course, was insulted by the President's call for the surrender of Alsace-Lorraine, and even the Socialist *Vorwärts* suspected Wilson of attempting "to deceive Russia about a general peace and lure her once more into the morass of blood of the world war."

2.

And what of Russian reaction? "It is a great step toward the peace of the world," Lenin told an American official in good English, but then not only criticized the colonial clause but said the message was incomplete. "This is all very well as far as it goes, but why not formal recognition [of the Bolshevik regime], and when?" Yet he saw to it that *Izvestia*, the government paper, printed the entire speech. "The conditions laid down by President Wilson," it commented, "represent a great victory in the great struggle for a democratic peace; and we may hope to find in the American people an actual ally in the struggle."

The party paper, *Pravda*, was a truer mirror of Lenin's personal suspicions of Wilson's motives. "Of course," editorialized that paper, "we are not for a moment in doubt about the real significance of the compliments of this representative of the American stock market . . . We know that Wilson is the representative of the American imperialistic dictatorship, chastising its own workers, and poor people with prisons, forced labor, and death sentences." And a few days later, Lenin himself reported to the party, "The war with England and America will go on for a long time; the aggressive imperialism of both groups has unmasked itself finally and completely."

Most American officials in Russia were opposed to Wilson's friendly gesture to Russia and looked upon the Bolsheviks as a menace to democracy. Opposing them was Raymond Robins, head of the American Red Cross Mission. He could have stepped out of a Horatio Alger novel. Born on Staten Island, he became a farmhand and miner in Tennessee, Colorado, Arizona, and Mexico, then prospected for gold in Alaska for three years and returned in 1900 a wealthy young man. In the Klondike he was so shocked by its lawless life that he was fired with the spirit of reform and became involved in social work in Chicago. He threw himself into the muck of Chicago politics with a young attorney, Harold Ickes. Together they ran as reform candidates and managed to elect a reform mayor and then keep him in office.

Robins directed part of his amazing energy to the labor movement, helping to organize and conduct strikes. Another part went into religion, and he spent a year lecturing throughout the country for the "Men and Religion Forward Movement in Behalf of the Christian Life of Men and Boys." He became an ardent supporter of Theodore Roosevelt and in 1916 was chairman of the Progressive National Convention.

It was only natural that such as impressionable idealist was inspired by the ardor of the Bolsheviks. They reminded him of the radicals he had met and worked with in the Midwest; and the northern landscape of Russia wakened youthful memories of his beloved Yukon, inspiring in him a renewal of his faith in human progress and glory of God. In the next few weeks Robins, who held the rank of a U. S. Army lieutenant colonel, donned boots and rough clothes like any good proletarian. He became a constant visitor at Soviet headquarters in the Smolny Institute, talking to Lenin and Trotsky far more often than any other foreigner in the forward, man-to-man style they both liked.

At the end of January, Robins received a welcome ally in his fight for Allied cooperation with the Soviets. His name was R. H. Bruce Lockhart and he came, surprisingly, as a special representative of Lloyd George. Lockhart was also a secret agent and his instructions were vague.* He was to establish unofficial relations

---

* The British could show imagination in their choice of unofficial representatives. In 1917 they sent novelist Somerset Maugham to Petrograd as their top secret agent. "I set off in high spirits with unlimited money at my disposal," wrote Maugham in his autobiography, "and four devoted Czechs to act as Liaison officers between me and Professor Masaryk . . . I went as a private agent, who could be disavowed if necessary, with instructions to get in touch with parties hostile to the Government and devise a scheme that would keep Russia in the war and prevent the Bolsheviks, supported by the Central Powers, from seizing power."

with the Soviets but he undertook the mission with the understanding that "our two main objects in the war are (1) the defeat of German militarism and (2) the suppression of Bolshevism." At the same time his own experience as acting British Consul General in Moscow during most of 1917 had convinced him that Bolshevism would last; that there was no hope of keeping Russia in the war; and that British policy "should now aim at achieving an anti-German peace in Russia."

Consequently, he soon became a confederate of Robins. They met at a dinner, approaching each other warily like two dogs meeting for the first time. "Are you free?" finally asked Robins. "You can not handle this Russian story from Downing Street or anywhere else. It is too much of an original outdoor situation that you have got to shift from day to day."

Lockhart was impressed by Robins, who, with his black hair and aquiline features, reminded him of an Indian chief. "I am absolutely free," said Robins. The next morning he brought Lockhart to Bolshevik headquarters at the Smolny Institute and on their way back the American talked openly about himself. "The life of the mission and my own life and supplies here are being dealt with on the basis that this thing is an international social revolutionary situation opposed to all governments, but more opposed right now, because it is nearer to them, to the German militarists than anything else, and that we can do business with them on tha basis." Robins warned his new acquaintance that there was gossip in Petrograd that he himself was really a representative of Wall Street. "Let us assume that I am here to capture Russia for Wall Street and American business men. Let us assume that you are a British wolf and I am an American wolf, and that when this war is over we are going to eat each other up for the Russian market; let us do so in perfectly frank, man fashion, but let us assume at the same time that we are fairly intelligent wolves, and that we know that if we do not hunt together in this hour the German wolf will eat us both up, and then let us go to work. Even," he added, "if we do sing a different song."

Lockhart himself was more of a sophisticate and not so ideologically bound. "But I believe your song," he said when next they met, "and I am going to work that way." From that moment, according to Robins, they were "in absolute agreement on every move."

The two combined forces with another free spirit, Captain Jacques Sadoul, of the French Military Mission, who had once served as aide to Albert Thomas, the French Socialist leader. A genuine radical himself, Sadoul regarded both Robins and Lockhart as representatives of capitalism and secretly did not trust them. The two bourgeois gentlemen worked with Sadoul but got along with each other better. In fact, they ate almost every breakfast together. Lockhart realized that the American had made a very good impression on the Bolsheviks and "of all foreigners Robins was the only man whom Lenin was willing to see and who ever succeeded in imposing his own personality on the unemotional Bolshevik leader."

When Trotsky, as a protest against Germany's harsh demands, dramatically walked out of the Brest-Litovsk negotiations on February 10, Lockhart and Robins redoubled their efforts to gain aid for the beleaguered Soviets. During a luncheon given in Robins' honor by Lockhart, the American was moody and silent. Only after the guests assembled in the smoking room later did he come to life. He spoke movingly of the need to support the Bolsheviks, analyzing the arguments against recognition, and demolishing the theory that the Soviets were working for a German victory. He ridiculed the current rumors that Trotsky was an enemy agent, praising him as a "four kind son of a bitch but the greatest Jew since Christ. If the German General Staff bought Trotsky, they bought a lemon." He indignantly attacked the Allies for "playing the German game in Russia," then abruptly, dramatically pulled a piece of paper from his pocket.

"I can see him now," recalled Lockhart. "Consciously or not, he had provided himself with an almost perfect setting. Before him a semi-circle of stolid Englishmen. Behind him the roaring log-fire, its tongues of flame reflected in weird shadows on the yellow-papered walls. Outside, through the window, the glorious view of the slender spire of Peter and Paul with the great fire-ball of the setting sun casting rays of blood on the snow-clad waters of the Neva. Once again he pushed his hair back with his hand and shook his head like a lion."

"Have any of you read this?" Robins asked. "I found it this morning in one of your newspapers." In an emotional low voice he began to read Major John McCrae's famous poem:

> We are the Dead. Short days ago
> We lived, felt dawn, saw sunset glow,
> Loved and were loved, and now we lie
>   In Flanders Fields.
> Take up our quarrel with the foe:
> To you from failing hands we throw
> The Torch; be yours to hold it high.
> If ye break faith with us who die
> We shall not sleep, though Poppies grow
>   In Flanders Fields.

There was "an almost deathly silence" as Robins turned to stare out the window. Finally, squaring his shoulders, he about-faced. "Boys!" he exclaimed. "I guess we're all here for one purpose—to see that the German General Staff don't win this war." He took three long strides, wrung his host's hand, said, "Goodbye, Lockhart," and in four more strides was out the door. There was not a laugh or a grin from any of the group. Every man had been deeply moved.

Lockhart met Trotsky a few days later for the first time and expressed Britain's willingness to reach a *modus vivendi* with the Bolsheviks but would not tolerate their agitation in England. What about English support of the anti-Bolsheviks in Russia? Trotsky angrily retorted. Lockhart acknowledged Trotsky's complaints had some justification and the Russian finally said he was ready to cooperate with the Allies, if not for love, for expediency. "Now is the opportunity for the Allied Governments," were his last words, leaving Lockhart convinced that he was ready to make a deal. Lockhart cabled London that he was sure that if Trotsky were handled tactfully he would be a valuable asset against Germany. "Policy I advocate is one of expediency," he advised. "Trotsky will co-operate with us so long as it suits him. Our attitude should be the same."

3.

There was consternation in Petrograd on February 23, when the Germans sent a demand that Russia give up all her Baltic, Polish, and Belorussian provinces. Lockhart cabled London that aid should be promptly offered to the Bolsheviks. They would probably not promote Allied interests, but, he felt, they would impede and delay German economic penetration. The British agent then went to the Smolny Institute for an interview with Trotsky. The Commissar of Foreign Affairs was in a bad temper and, with a scowl, asked Lockhart if any message had come in from London offering aid. The Englishman replied in the negative but gave assurance that support would not be withheld providing the Bolsheviks made a genuine effort to keep half of Russia from falling to the Germans.

"You have no message," grumbled Trotsky. "But I have. While you are trying to throw dust in my eyes, your countrymen and the French have been intriguing against us with the Ukrainians, who have already sold themselves to the Germans. Your country is working for Japanese intervention in Siberia . . . Your Lloyd George is like a man playing roulette and scattering chips on every number."

Even so Trotsky remained determined to continue the war, and that evening the majority of the Petrograd Soviet agreed with him. But Lenin insisted on signing the peace treaty despite jeers and catcalls. "In our day wars are not won by mere enthusiasm but by technical superiority," he told the assemblage. "Give me an army of 100,000 men which will not tremble before the enemy, and I will not sign this peace. Can you raise an army? Can you give me anything but prattle and the drawing up of pasteboard figures?"

His reason won, and early next morning a telegram was dispatched to Berlin accepting the German terms. It was 6 A.M. when the exhausted Lenin walked out of the hall, his ears ringing with epithets of "Traitor! Judas! German spy!"

Predictably the sixty-seven-year-old American Ambassador, David Francis, was disgusted with the Bolshevik submission. He cabled Washington: "In my judgment terms of peace make Russia a German province with good prospects of becoming ally. I renew my recommendation for immediate possession of Vladivostok, Murmansk, Archangel."

But Robins was exultant. "What an hour!" he wrote in his diary that night. "The tide is flood. The Revolution and Allied cause and Democracy and Russia and America all in the melting pot."

By the end of February all of the Allied embassies had fled Petrograd for safer quarters some 350 air miles east in Vologda. Lockhart stayed in the capital and the following day had his first interview with Lenin. The British agent had arrived "a little forlorn," since his position was vaguer than ever. It was the first time he had ever seen Lenin and he found no superman—only a short, rather plump man with a thick neck, round, red face, high intellectual forehead, and short, stubbly beard. He looked "more like a provincial grocer than a leader of men." But his steely eyes were arresting. Lockhart found him amazingly frank. Peace negotiations had not broken down, as rumored, he said. The terms, of course, were scandalous. What could one expect from a militarist regime? Yes, they would probably be accepted, the next day. And they would undoubtedly be ratified by an overwhelming majority of the Party.

He could not guess how long the peace would last, but they were transferring the Government from Petrograd to Moscow, and if necessary would withdraw to the Urals. However they fought would be their business. They would not be "a cat's-paw for the Allies." If the Entente understood this, there was an excellent opportunity for cooperation. He did not try to hide the fact that Anglo-American capitalism was about as hateful to the Bolsheviks as German militarism. But the latter was the more immediate danger. He hoped the Allies would cooperate on these terms, but he doubted it. He was even willing to accept military support if the Germans continued their aggression. "At the same time I am convinced that your Government will never see things in this light. It is a reactionary Government. It will co-operate with Russian reactionaries."

Lockhart remarked that he feared that the Germans, with peace in their pocket, would now throw the forces in the east against the Western Front. What if they crushed the Allies? The Germans would steal all of Russia's grain, then.

Lenin smiled. "Like all your countrymen you are thinking in concrete military terms. You ignore the psychological factors. This war will be settled in the rear and not in the trenches."

Thoughtfully Lockhart returned home to find a batch of telegrams from the Foreign Office complaining about the peace. How could Lockhart call the Bolsheviks anti-German when they were willing to give half of Russia away? While attempting to write an answer, the phone rang. It was Trotsky. He said that he had just received word that the Japanese were about to land troops in Siberia. What did Lockhart propose to do about it? How could he justify his mission after such hostility?

Next came a telegram from Robins, advising Lockhart to join him in Vologda. He managed to get Robins on the telephone and said that he was "going to see things through to the bitter end" in Petrograd, and asked him to pass on to Francis the disturbing news of the Japanese landing. If it took place, that would ruin any chance of Allied-Bolshevik cooperation. A final telegram came from his wife in London, cryptically informing him that his actions were not approved in London. If he were not careful, it would be the end of his career.

The next day, Saturday, he wired London: "There are still considerable possibilities of organizing resistance to Germany and I shall remain in the country as long as there is the slightest hope."

But on Sunday, March 3, the peace treaty was finally signed at Brest-Litovsk. It was a harsh militaristic peace which showed the world that the true ruler of Germany was not the Reichstag, nor the Chancellor, nor even the Kaiser. It was Ludendorff.

A summons from Trotsky brought Robins from Vologda to the capital posthaste on March 5. "Colonel Robins," he said, "do you still want to beat the peace?"

"Mr. Commissar, you know the answer to that question."

"The time has come to be definite. We have talked and talked about help from America. Can you produce it? Can you get a definite promise from your Government? If you can, we can even now beat the peace. I will oppose ratification at Moscow, and beat it."

"But Mr. Commissar, you have always opposed ratification. The question is, what about Lenin? He is on the other side, and, if you will pardon me, it is he, not you, who is running this show."

Trotsky bridled. "You are mistaken! Lenin realizes that the threat of the German advance is so great that if he can get economic co-operation and military support from the Allies he will refuse the Brest peace, retire, if necessary, from both Petrograd and Moscow to Ekaterinburg, re-establish the front in the Urals, and fight with Allied support against the Germans."

Would Lenin agree to *that?* asked Robins with some suprise.

"He will."

"In writing?"

Trotsky bared his teeth in a frightening grin. "Do you want us to give you our lives? The Germans are thirty miles from Petrograd. How soon will *your* people be within thirty miles?"

But Robins refused to pass on a verbal message to Washington. He wanted something specific. "It's got to be written. I'll bring my interpreter back here with me. You tell him what you mean—in Russian. He'll write it down in English. Then you and Lenin will read it in English and say you understand it and will promise me to go through with it. Otherwise, I can't handle it."

Trotsky yielded. "Be back at four," he said.

At that hour Robins was back at Trotsky's office with his interpreter. The Commissar waved a paper, his offer to America, then brought the two Americans to Lenin's room. The Bolshevik chief abruptly left a meeting and led the procession to the Hall of the Council of the People's Commissars. The four men seated themselves at a long table, and Robins' interpreter began translating the message into English. It began with a series of questions based on the premise that the Bolsheviks would break the peace treaty and Germany would resume its advance. Could the Soviets rely on the support of the Allies? What kind of support would be furnished, particularly by the United States? Would the Allies, and particularly America, prevent the Japanese from invading Siberia?

After his interpreter read this aloud, Robins said to Lenin, "Does the translation give your understanding of the document?" "Yes," said Lenin, and Robins asked another question. "If the United States Government answers this document affirmatively, will you oppose the ratification of the Peace of Brest-Litovsk at the All-Russian Congress of Soviets at Moscow?"

"Yes."

As Robins left he felt that he was the messenger of history, holding the fate of Russia and America in his hands. He brought the document to Harold Williams, a New Zealander, who used his job as correspondent for the New York *Times* to cover his role as a British secret agent. Anti-Bolshevik himself, Williams promised to cable a story for his paper that the treaty would not be ratified and that war with Germany would probably recommence.

4.

Robins cabled Trotsky's proposal to Washington, but long before it reached its destination the fate of the tottering Bolshevik regime had just taken a turn for the better. President Wilson had been persuaded by Colonel House to reconsider a recent decision to let Japan know that America was willing to condone their limited intervention in Siberia. The President wired Tokyo on that eventful March 5 that intervention would generate "hot resentment" in Russia and that the whole question might play into the hands of the enemies of Russia, and particularly of the Russian Revolution, "for which the Government of the United States entertains the greatest sympathy, in spite of all the unhappiness and misfortune which for the time being has sprung out of it."

The following Sunday, March 10, the President received a note from House urging him to send an encouraging message to the Congress of the Soviets, about to convene to ratify the Brest-Litovsk peace treaty. "Our proverbial friendship for Russia could be reaffirmed and you could declare our purpose to help in her efforts to weld herself into a democracy." Wilson took this advice and the following day dispatched a message promising the Congress of the Soviets that America would "avail itself of every opportunity to secure for Russia once more complete sovereignty and independence in her own affairs and full restoration to her great role in the life of Europe and the modern world. The whole heart of the people of the United States is with the people of Russia in the attempt to free themselves forever from autocratic government and become the masters of their own life."

That same Monday, March 11, the Bolshevik Government and party headquarters shifted to Moscow. It was a symbolic move, since Petrograd was historically oriented to Western culture. Moscow, where the czars before Peter the Great had resided in the Kremlin, was more rooted in Russian history and nationalism.

Raymond Robins was also in Moscow and on the next day personally handed to Lenin the Wilson telegram. Forty-eight hours later, just before the opening of the Congress, he had tea with Lenin and his sister. "What have you heard from your Government?" Lenin asked regarding the Trotsky questionnaire. "Nothing," replied the American.

"You will not hear," said Lenin. "Neither the American Government nor any of the allied Governments will cooperate, even against the Germans, with the workmen's and peasants' revolutional Government of Russia."

Robins smiled and said he thought differently, for he was convinced that Wilson's telegram of sympathy had been inspired by his own message transmitting Trotsky's offer.

At the first session of the Congress, held in the stately Hall of the Nobles, the telegram from Wilson was read by Chairman Yakov Sverdlov. After some perfunctory applause Sverdlov read a resolution adopted by the Central Executive Committee in answer to Wilson: "The Congress expresses its gratitude to the American people, above all the laboring and exploited classes of the United States, for the sympathy expressed to the Russian people by President Wilson through the Congress of Soviets in the days of severe trials."

It went on, in terms calculated to provoke the Allies, ". . . to express to all peoples perishing and suffering from the horrors of imperialistic war its warm sympathy and firm belief that the happy time is not far distant when the laboring masses of all countries will throw off the yoke of capitalism and will establish a socialistic state of society, which alone is capable of securing just and lasting peace as well as the culture and well-being of all laboring people."

"Comrades," said Sverdlov after considerable applause, "allow me to consider this applause a sufficient answer that you all join this resolution." It was a direct insult to Wilson and was obviously intended as such. "We slapped the President of the United States in the face," Gregory Zinoviev, a prominent Bolshevik, told a Petrograd audience a few days later.

All that day the Congress argued about ratification of the treaty. Again Lenin was denounced, but he warned that peace was necessary to buy time. The tempestuous debate continued with neither Lenin nor his war-minded opponents relenting. For two days it seemed as if Lenin was almost alone in his fight for peace, but as the evening of March 16 wore on, it became apparent that his arguments were gaining adherents. At 11:30 P.M. he beckoned to

Robins, who was sitting on a step of the platform. "What have you heard from your Government?" asked Lenin.

"Nothing."

"What has Lockhart heard?"

"Nothing."

"I am now going to the platform and the peace will be ratified."

Robins was downcast. If only favorable answers to Trotsky's questions had come from America, the Soviets would have defied the Germans. So Robins imagined, but it is difficult to believe that the most encouraging words from Wilson could have turned Lenin from peace.

He spoke persuasively from about an hour and twenty minutes. "It's no use approaching German generals with a copy of Karl Marx in one hand and of Friedrich Engels in the other. Those books are in German. But German generals cannot understand them." Again he spoke of the absolute necessity for a breathing space, then called for a vote.

From all over the great hall red cards were held up in favor of ratification. Other red cards shot up against. Robins disconsolately sat on the steps and heard the final result called out: Abstaining, 115. Against ratification, 261. For ratification, 784.

Peace had come to Russia—despite Robins and Lockhart.

The German Supreme Command was delighted. At last they were free to launch their great offensive in the West and bring the war to an end.

Chapter Five

"WITH OUR BACKS TO THE WALL . . ."
Haig

APRIL 6–22

1.

BY the beginning of April, there was still no significant action on other fronts, and the Allied leaders could concentrate their concern on the West, where another major German offensive was momentarily expected. This second blow, in fact, was almost ready to be launched and had been given the effeminate code name Georgette. Designed as a "second act" to Michael, it was aimed at the northern half of Haig's lines in the Flanders plains: a stretch of some twenty-five miles between La Bassée Canal and Ypres. The country north of the canal was flat, drained by many streams and ditches and dotted by orchards and prosperous villages. The main thrust would be at Armentières, already made famous by song, which lay two miles behind the British lines. Once this city was taken the German spearhead would drive straight ahead some fifteen miles to the vital rail center of Hazebrouck. When this fell, Haig, his back to the Channel, would have little alternative except escape to England.

Although this attack could not be compared in scope to Michael, it threatened an area much more vital to the British. Here they could not afford to lose the ground they had in March. "The prospects which opened for us if we made good progress in such an operation were very alluring," wrote Hindenburg, "but the exertion of the attack was faced with most serious obstacles. In the first place, it was clear that we were dealing with the strongest English group at this point." Then there was the forbidding terrain on either side of Armentières: to the south the low-lying meadows of the Lys River, and to the north Mount Kemmel and other wooded hills. In the spring the Lys area was often a marsh for weeks on end, but that year the weather had been so dry that experts predicted the assault could begin in early April. Every day was critical because of the growing strength of the American forces. There were already more than 325,000 officers and men in France.

For some time Haig had feared an attack between Arras and La Bassée Canal. It concerned him also that the sector just above the canal was held by two Portuguese divisions. He was well aware that Portugal was no longer a reliable ally. Many of the soldiers sympathized with the revolution then going on in Portugal. Moreover, while officers were allowed home leave, the men were not and they had just spent a miserably cold and wet winter. Things were so bad that one division had already been removed by Haig—and this forced the remaining Portuguese troops to defend an extremely wide front. Evidence on April 6 indicated the possibility of a surprise attack by three or four divisions against the Portuguese, and that night Haig wrote Foch: "All information points to the enemy's intention to continue his efforts to destroy the British Army. With this object in view he appears to be preparing a force of 25 to 35 Divisions to deliver a heavy blow on the Bethune-Arras front." Haig wanted the French to either start a vigorous offensive in the next few days or send four more French divisions to relieve British troops south of the Somme.

The two met the next day, and the best Foch would offer was a combined British-French counterattack in the Amiens area. Privately Haig did not believe that either Foch or Pétain had any intention of putting French divisions into the attack, and so wired General Wilson to come to France and try to get better arrangements with Foch. Wilson replied at once that he was coming. He had recently written in his diary: "I really think Haig is stupid up to danger point." This new trouble with Foch was only further proof that the field marshal did not "in the least understand the situation yet." Yet when Haig had recently offered to resign and

SECOND LUDENDORFF OFFENSIVE
-THE LYS-
APR. 9-29

▬▬▬ Front Line Apr. 9   ─── Front Line Apr. 10
──── Front Line Apr. 11   ▬▬▬ Front Line Apr. 29
▬▬▬ Army Boundaries
▨▨▨▨ Held by Portuguese Corps

BELGIAN ARMY.

Passchendaele

Ypres

BR. SECOND ARMY

BELGIUM FRANCE

MT. ROUGE

MT. NOIR

Wytschaete

Kemmel

MT. KEMMEL

Messines

MESSINES RIDGE

GER. FOURTH ARMY

BELGIUM FRANCE

LYS

Meteren   Bailleul

Neuve Eglise

Hazebrouck

BR. FIRST ARMY

Armentières

LYS

Merville

Estaires

PORT. CORPS

Neuve Chapelle

Lille

GER. SIXTH ARMY

Fournes

LILLE CANAL

La Bassée

Béthune

LA BASSÉE CANAL

N

MILES
0   6
0   KM   6

palacios

114

Lloyd George, who was looking for a good excuse to get rid of him, suggested the previous day that they take the field marshal at his word, Wilson replied: "Failing some readily outstanding personality—and we have none I think—we ought to wait for Haig's report."

Haig knew of the growing sentiment against him and on April 8 wrote his wife about the attempts to get rid of him. "But I won't trouble you with this. You will be prepared, however, for *me* to be attacked like anything by some of the Government to save themselves. But *my* case is an overwhelming one."

That night final preparations for Georgette were completed. Lieutenant Colonel Bruchmüller, the artillery expert, reported to Ludendorff that "all was in order." The Kaiser was at the front, prepared as usual to toast victory. At 4:15 on the morning of April 9 there was a tremendous roar along the front between Armentières and La Bassée Canal—a fitting salutation to Ludendorff on his fifty-third birthday. Gas and high explosive shells smashed into the three divisions defending this eleven-mile stretch. A heavy mist hung over the battlefield, but the sun soon broke through. At 7 the bombardment shifted to the trenches and strongpoints, and at 8:45 the infantry assault began. The leading waves of the four divisions converging on the Portuguese 2nd Division found most of the front-line trenches empty. Small groups could only put up brief if heroic resistance, and the storm troops plunged forward three miles. It was not that the Portuguese were cowards. They saw little reason to fight. Besides they were spread too thin. The result was panic flight. "Some even took their boots off to run the quicker," wrote Haig, "and others stole the bicycles of the Corps Cyclists who were sent forward to hold La Couture and vicinity."

Private W. A. Tucker was one of the XI Corps cyclists rushed into the breach. His company dug in near a church. The only shells falling now were from their own side. It was obvious that their gunners assumed that all friendly troops had long been overwhelmed "and if their shells hit anyone it would not be *us*." They stoically assembled their Lewis guns, placed the muzzles at the ready through the firing slots of their sandbagged little fort, and waited. "No officer mentioned who or what might come, where we were, or what we were to do in any given circumstances. No officer knew."

Suddenly someone shouted, "Look, Jerries!" Dim figures scrambled toward them through barbed wire, debris, and swampy shell holes. Through the mist and smoke of bursting shrapnel from friendly guns, Tucker could dimly make out unfamiliar helmets and uniforms.

"Let the bastards have it!" shouted a corporal, and six Lewis guns went into action. Every so often a figure out front would come forward and, drawing fire, disappear. It seemed a funny kind of attack. Then someone yelled, "Hold it, lads. They're not Jerries. They're bloody Portuguese."

115

No one had mentioned anything about Portuguese. Their uniforms were a bluish gray and their corrugated helmets resembled dustbin lids. Gas shells from trench mortars began to fall, but there was such a din that the cyclists did not notice their telltale dull thud and were caught without gas masks. It took all Tucker's instinct for self-preservation to swallow an anti-gas pill before slapping on his mask. Shelling came from several directions. Surrounded, they were being pounded to death.

Except for such pockets of resistance the Germans were finding no opposition. "The assault battalion stormed on," recalled Stephen Westman, a German front-line surgeon, "occasionally fired at by German guns, because a stupid artillery observer who ought to have been with the most forward troops lagged behind and thought that the soldiers he saw through his glasses were British or Portuguese." The doctor followed the most advanced wave with stretcher-bearers and two medical orderlies. There were few casualties, but after passing through a wood the advance stopped. Westman came upon Germans staggering about, drinking from bottles of whiskey, liqueur, or wine. "This was something Ludendorff and his staff officers had not foreseen."

The British troops to the left of the Portuguese were also under heavy attack. F. H. Hornsey's company had been roused from their camp before dawn, armed with grenades and ammunition and led by an officer into a large wheat field. They were ordered to dig individual holes. Hornsey wondered what it was all about. Then came the chatter of machine guns. The Lewis gunner near him fell over, a bullet through the heart. What had happened? "The awful truth dawned upon me. The enemy had broken through our lines, and we were here to try and turn the tide." Ahead on the skyline he could see enemy moving about.

"Do your best, boys," said Captain Kay. "The Germans have broken through; we have got to stop them here as long as we can." The men complained they hadn't eaten for two days. "Can't help it," said the captain. It was now too late. No one protested, for Kay had always done his best for the men, "and there was not one of us who would not have followed him through Hell if he had only said the word."

A German plane dropped flares for artillery range and in moments shells began falling onto their positions. Where were their own airmen? Had all British guns pulled back to safety? Hordes of storm troops assaulted Hornsey's position. Despite answering heavy rifle and machine-gun fire the gray wave drew nearer and nearer. By 10 A.M. all the British officers were dead or wounded. The only chance, and that appeared slim, was to hang on until dark.

At noon the Kaiser arrived at Avesnes, listened to Ludendorff's report, and stayed for lunch. After praising Ludendorff's two dead sons, he presented the general with an iron statuette of himself.

Foch arrived at Haig's headquarters about the same time. He

would not hear of taking over any part of the British line, determined as he was to place four French divisions in reserve just behind Amiens. He did not take the attack on the Lys very seriously and thought that Haig was merely imagining disaster. However anxious he was to restore Haig's confidence, he could not throw into action French troops that were just being assembled. Haig was thinking how selfish and obstinate Foch was. "I wonder if he is afraid to trust French Divisions in the battle front." He was also wondering why General Wilson, who had just arrived from England, wasn't more helpful. "His sympathies always seem to be with the French."

Once alone with Wilson, Foch confided that he thought Haig was tired. Wilson agreed. "There is no doubt in my mind," he noted in his diary, "that he has no drive, that he is almost a beaten man, that he is always turning to a Peace to get him out of his difficulties—he spoke to me of peace 2 or 3 times again to-day —and that I really begin to think that he had better be relieved."

As Foch was leaving, Hornsey's unit was being hard pressed by storm troops supported by a barrage of shell fire and machine guns. "It was just as if Hell's gates were opened to us." By 3:30 P.M. the left flank was gone and they were harassed from three sides. It was now or never. Hornsey leaped out of his hole. So did several hundred others. They ran, heads down, fearing to look behind, praying to reach nearby farm ruins in time. A bullet smashed into Hornsey's canteen. He thought he was hit. Comrades were falling on both sides. He reached the ruins and looked back. The ground was littered with British dead and wounded. Only a few had made it. He and another man stumbled through the farmyard where cattle stood, bewildered and frightened. Four or five sprawled on the ground.

In a minute Hornsey and his companion were back at the camp they had left in the morning. Everything was smashed. An officer was dead. The two men half ran, half walked "like madmen" with other survivors toward a road, their only thought to escape the cruel fire. At last they reached the highway. Many dead and wounded were strewn about. A French family was slowly walking with everything they could save—including two cows. Despair was written on their faces, but the bombardment did not seem to worry them. "The shells had already done their worst to them. Their home lay in ruins—everything lost!"

By the end of the day the entire Portuguese front had disintegrated. Six thousand were prisoners and thirteen thousand were scattering into the rear area. The gap they had left was only partly closed on each side. But Ludendorff was not completely satisfied. The attack had slowed down in the afternoon. The ground was still soft in places and it was taking too long to bring up guns and ammunition.

It had been a difficult day for Lloyd George. The news from the front was alarming and he had to make an important speech in the House of Commons introducing the new manpower bill, including compulsory military service for Ireland. Hankey went to the official gallery to hear the speech. It was obvious that his chief was "depressed and nervous and ill at ease." He could not help noticing that the Prime Minister had aged terribly in the past year and his hair had turned almost white. Hankey had hoped this speech would be the trumpet call of a leader to the nation in this critical moment. "The whole thing lacked crispness. The Irish part was interrupted constantly by declamations of the Irish party." And when he took advantage of the motion for wider powers of conscription to refute charges of his personal responsibility for the weakness of Haig's army, the house became sullen and unresponsive.

Never, he claimed, had the army been stronger than it was before the March offensive; and hadn't General Wilson accurately forecast the date and location of the attack? Both statements were far wide of the mark and gave the impression that Haig was the culprit. He then pointed out the enemy's numerical superiority without comparing them directly with the vast numbers he claimed were available to Haig.

No one objected when he followed with fulsome tribute to the gallantry of the troops. Then someone shouted, "What about the generals?"

"Until the circumstances which led to the retirement of the Fifth Army, and its failure to hold the Somme . . . are explained," he said, "it would be unfair to censure the general in command of the army—General Gough. But until these circumstances are cleared up, it would equally be unfair to the British Army to retain his services in the field."

"Is he to be court-martialled?" asked Member of Parliament T. M. Healy.

"It was necessary to recall him until the facts have been fully ascertained, and laid before the government by their military advisers."

He had failed to follow the straightforward, concise brief prepared for him by Hankey, and made a number of inaccurate statements. In his attempt to excuse the shifting of substantial forces to Palestine and Egypt, for example, he stated that all but three divisions sent there contained very few white soldiers. Incorrect also was his claim that General Carey on his own initiative had formed the pickup group that had helped save Gough from a complete rout. Gough had formed it himself while Carey was in England on leave. Another gross mistake was his claim that General Byng's Third Army had held, "never giving way a hundred yards to the attack of the enemy," retiring only to conform to Gough's retreat. It was apparent that the Prime Minister had not known of Byng's mistake in clinging too long to the salient in front of Bapaume.

The Prime Minister's enemies, along with adherents of Haig and Gough, filed out of the House seething with indignation.

Colonel Repington was not there but wrote that night in his diary: "I had written an article yesterday defending the 5th Army against their traducers, but the Press Bureau, under orders I suppose, took care that it should not appear today, so L.G. no doubt intends to place the blame on the soldiers in his opening speech when Parliament reassembles to-day, and does not wish the other side to be heard until he has manufactured an opinion in his favour." The ill-considered speech just delivered would undoubtedly give the crusty Repington an opportunity to present the other side.

Across the Channel, Haig's chief of staff, General Lawrence, was complaining about the attempts to oust Haig. He was writing General Maurice, Director of British Military Operations, who had recently informed him that the Lloyd George crowd were doing their utmost to replace Haig, to save their own skins. "For myself," wrote Lawrence, "I care nothing and am quite ready to make room for a better man and to take other employment or go if they don't want me—but I do care about D.H. and think it would be a national misfortune to change him now. As regards Clemenceau, he can send anyone he likes here and we will give him all he wants. The Boche is pushing the Portuguese heavily which is tiresome and makes calls upon our diminishing resources."

2.

At three the following morning the second phase of Georgette began with a tremendous bombardment in the north. Two and a half hours later storm troops appeared in the heavy mist at the foot of the Messines Ridge, five miles above Armentières. Other attacks were thrusting on both sides of the city. Again the weather was bad for flying, but British observation planes braved ground fire to skim over the area at 200 to 400 feet to report the main fluctuations of the battlefront.

In the south the Germans did little but consolidate their considerable gains of yesterday. Tucker and the other corps cyclists who had tried to plug the gap in the Portuguese lines were still surrounded. Shelled the whole night, they wearily and fearfully awaited a mass attack at dawn. There was nothing to eat or drink and they nursed their dwindling ammunition. All at once the shelling stopped, a sign that something was going to happen. Ten yards ahead Tucker saw a German helmet slowly rise from a trench. Everyone opened fire, riddling the helmet. It was a decoy hoisted to discover if their redoubt was still manned. The mortar shelling resumed with even more fury. Of the two hundred or so cyclists who had arrived twenty-four hours earlier, only a handful were alive, but all Lewis gun posts remained manned. It was now full daylight and a quarter of a mile ahead Tucker could see a horse-drawn enemy column coming down the road with drivers astride their horses as if they were on parade. Without a word of command the six Lewis guns blazed into action. In a minute the entire column was piled up in awful disarray. Tucker himself was horrified at the frightful havoc. That was the end of the ammunition except for a few rifle rounds. At 10 A.M. the enemy fire ceased and a German officer shouted in English to come out in two minutes. "You have no chance. We are all around you. Come out and save your lives."

"Give us half an hour, mate," shouted back a private from Birmingham. Others called out insults that brought another barrage. Half an hour later there was again quiet. "I ask now for the English commanding officer to come out to us and see the position you are in," shouted the same officer. "We do not want to kill any more of you." After a pause, the cyclists' commanding officer, haggard and ashen, came forward. He soon returned. "Our position is now quite hopeless," he explained wanly, "even if we had ammunition and food. I cannot allow you to die needlessly. I must now order you to surrender. It is my duty."

There were angry shouts of defiance, but in a few minutes the remaining corporals and sergeants persuaded the men to give up. Slowly, sullenly, they made their weapons useless and began ripping off the Lewis gun symbols from their shoulder sleeves; there was a rumor that the Boche literally crucified machine gunners.

Led by a few Portuguese who had taken refuge in their redoubt, the men filed through a farmyard and out an archway to the road. The Portuguese still had their guns and approached the enemy with rifle bolts drawn back. But the Germans did not understand and let loose with grenades and machine guns. The survivors bolted back through the archway, scrambling among the debris in the farmyard for weapons.

There was no more fire from ahead. Their own commander appeared, urging them to go out through the arch again. The German officer, he said, had apologized for the assault and guaranteed their safe transit. Slowly the survivors trekked through the archway. There they found one of their men groaning and bleeding from grenade wounds. Tucker and another man helped him forward. A German officer stuck a revolver in Tucker's stomach. "Why you not come out?" he growled. "Much kamerad dead because you not come. English good soldat but"—he tapped his head to imply that the English were lunatics—"no answer. Why?" Tucker wearily shrugged his shoulders.

The German grunted, withdrew the revolver, and told Tucker to take his wounded comrade to the gutted farmhouse which was being improvised into a dressing station.

General Wilson was in Paris listening to Clemenceau say, "Never, never, *never* will I make peace." Foch, he noticed, was upset by the retreat of the Portuguese and was doubtful if even the British troops were fighting well. "He seemed fairly content with Haig saying he was insufficient but we did not appear to have a better. He was much more severe on Pétain for whom all his old liking is disappearing." This pleased Wilson, who had previously warned him that Pétain was a peace general and not a war general and had made his name last year by not fighting.

They then discussed what the British should do in case of a serious withdrawal. "The Tiger said we should swing on over right and come back to the Somme, but I was very soon able to dispose of that, saying that it was death to uncover the ports, and so our right must fall back; and if the French would hold the left bank of the Somme we would never lose touch with them."

Wilson found Paris quite empty; 800,000, he heard, had already left. Many shops had closed and banks were beginning to send records and securities to safety. The ministries were also disposing of their documents, and the British Embassy was arranging for their nationals to be sent back home by barge if necessary.

Wilson left Paris for Versailles and was delighted to find that General Bliss, the American Representative at the Supreme War Council, was "entirely on our side, and against Pershing, as regards the employment of American batts [battalions], so we can count on the old boy." At midday he received an alarmist telegram from General Maurice in London that the position up north was very serious and "could only be saved by all the French and Americans coming to our assistance." Wilson immediately telephoned Foch with a request to hasten the movement of his troops over the Somme. The Frenchman replied that they were ready and had been for two days but wouldn't be able to move until tomorrow because of the roads. A few minutes later Lloyd George called to ask if he should send over Milner, but Wilson replied that it was not necessary.

As the Chief of Staff was setting out for the north, the Baroness de la Grange arrived at Supreme War Council headquarters with more advice. Earlier she had warned that the Germans would next strike at the area near her château which had been denuded of French and British troops. Now she heard that the Germans were attacking in that very sector. "I was received and reassured with kind words; in fact, the usual administration of opium to the unfortunate civilian! General Sackville-West, General Knox, and Captain Cazalet all insist that my alarm is unnecessary, but I am pretty sure of my information—namely, that the line has been broken, and on that very spot that I had indicated on the map!"

Early that evening Wilson arrived at Haig's headquarters, where he found the field marshal looking "brighter and better than yesterday." While they were talking, Foch arrived. He said he had carefully considered Haig's request for help and, according to the latter's diary, "agreed that the enemy's objective was the British Army, and that his main effort would be between Arras and the Somme. So he had decided to move up a large force of French troops ready to take part in the battle. I am glad that the French at last are beginning to realise the object of the Germans." But Haig still feared that Foch was unwilling to put French forces into the battle and wouldn't do so "until force of circumstances as a last resort compel him." Even so, Wilson was patently pleased. "This is, at last, *good*. Relations between Foch and Haig are quite good."

Their conference was interrupted at 10:30 P.M. by another telephone call for Wilson from the Prime Minister. The Chief of Staff soothed him by saying that a meeting with Foch was going on satisfactorily and that he would be returning by the morning boat. But Wilson's optimistic words were belied by more bad news the next day from the front. There were critical withdrawals above Armentières and in the south where two reserve divisions were being steadily pushed back. One of them, the British 51st, was in such precarious shape that only the arrival of another territorial division, the 61st, saved it from destruction.

The situation seemed so perilous to Haig that he drafted an uncharacteristic Order of the Day just short of alarm. Addressed to all ranks, it told of the German efforts to split the Allied armies.

There is no other course open to us but to fight it out! Every position must be held to the last man: there must be no retirement. With our backs to the wall, and believing in the justice of our cause, each one of us must fight on to the end. The safety of our homes and the freedom of mankind alike depend on the conduct of each of us at this critical moment.

He also sent his operations officer to Foch with a letter begging him to mass at least four French divisions in front of Dunkirk. Foch said he could only afford to send one cavalry corps and this would not arrive for six days.

In London, Henry Wilson, back from France and no longer sanguine, reflected Haig's anxiety in a talk to a War Committee "where I frightened them properly about this attack of the Boches, and I am frightened myself as I am afraid it will end in the loss of Dunkirk." Later that evening Lloyd George summoned him to Churchill's, where he was spending the evening. Wilson repeated his grave fears. It looked, he said, as if they would lose Hazebrouck and this would mean eventual loss of Dunkirk. Wilson then went to the War Office, where he sent a wire to Foch repeating his plea to prepare to flood the area in front of Dunkirk.

The news next morning, April 12, was worse. Merville and Hill 63 were gone, and Bailleul, which stood before strategic Hazebrouck, was threatened. If they lost Hazebrouck, Wilson realized, they would have to retire their whole left, and Dunkirk would surely be lost. The other danger was that "we cannot any longer make good our losses, and so we are a fast dwindling army. This is desperately serious."

Commanders at the front were aware that this was the most critical day. The first trainloads of Australian reinforcements were arriving in Hazebrouck and moving up by battalions to defense positions. But would they arrive in time? The British 33rd Division was already at strategic Bailleul, hurriedly digging in on the ridge just south of the town. The previous day the advance machine-gun battalion commanded by Lieutenant Colonel Graham Seton Hutchison had found masses of British infantry in headlong flight. At revolver point Hutchison halted one battalion, led in withdrawal by its commanding officer. He ordered the men to turn back and occupy Hoegenacker Ridge. They refused. Twice more he gave the order but the men would not budge. Several called out that they only followed orders of their own officers. Hutchison threatened to shoot their commander if he didn't give the order in two minutes. The two minutes passed and Hutchison punched the commander. "That's what I've been waiting for all day," said one sergeant, and led the reluctant battalion back up to the ridge.

But Hutchison could not stop the mainstream of retreat. It had turned into a rout. "They appeared like whipped curs: men in panic can be just so." He asked several where they were going. They didn't know but there were swarms of Germans just behind and most of their comrades had been killed or captured. He stopped a captain who said he was retiring to the hills beyond. Hutchison punched him, too.

From a meadow he could see gray uniforms a few hundred yards ahead. Machine-gun bullets sprayed Hutchison and his band of scouts. He turned and began a frantic search for men, at last locating an estaminet, the Belle Croix, crowded with British soldiers. "They had been filled with funk and now were filled with drink." He herded the men out toward the enemy. One was a large kilted Scot. "He was crazy with drink, fighting drunk, but with no fight in him. I saw his huge body lurch forward over the hilltop, and then the great torso, huge shoulders, and waving arms went limp and he disappeared from view."

By Friday morning eight guns were disposed on the crest of the hogback ridge, and two of Hutchison's companies were dug in over a three-mile front. He told the men that the ridge had to be held at all costs, since it was the only considerable rise in ground covering not only Hazebrouck but the approach to Mount Kemmel and other Belgian hills to the north.

The assault came late that morning, but Hutchison's machine guns swept the approaches from the south. The line held and at noon Hutchison went back to the Belle Croix estaminet for more men. Again he found it filled with drunken stragglers. "We routed them out, and, with a machine-gun trained on them, sent them forward to the enemy. They perished to a man." On the way back to the front he came upon the corpse of the huge Scot he had sent back the day before. "He was a filthy sight, the whole body churned with machine-gun bullets, the clotted pools of blood stinking with wine. So this pack at least was successful in drowning, once and for all, their sorrows in drink."

Throughout the day the Germans pressed forward, determined to take Hazebrouck, but the reinforcements from the 33rd Division held the line along with a mixed assortment of other troops and the gap was closed. From dawn to dusk the advancing enemy was subjected to relentless attacks from the air. Visibility was good and every British squadron was in action. Never since the war began had more hours been flown in a single day. Never had more bombs been dropped, more aerial photos taken.

Douglas Haig's "backs to the wall" appeal reached few of those who were fighting. "We to whom it was addressed," recalled one corporal, "the infantry of the front line, were too scattered, too busy trying to survive, to be called into any formation to listen to orders of the day." But such simple, emotional words coming from a stolid, cool figure had an inspiring effect on many of the reserve troops coming up to shore the lines. One young subaltern of the 1st Australian Division brought up to plug the gap below Bailleul was so inspired that he issued orders that their position would be held until relieved. "If the section cannot remain here alive it will remain here dead, but in any case it will remain here . . . If any man through shell shock or other cause attempts to surrender he will remain here dead."

Saturday, April 13, was another fine, warm day. Crown Prince Rupprecht wrote in his war diary that the ridge in front of Bailleul was of decisive importance and must be taken at once. Another obstacle to the drive on Hazebrouck was Neuve Eglise, four miles east of Bailleul. The village was being defended by the 2nd Worcestershire Battalion. Just as its commander, Lieutenant Colonel G. F. L. Stoney, was finishing breakfast in his headquarters at the local brewery, an orderly rushed down the steps. "The enemy are in the village, sir!" he said. "And are coming from three directions." Stoney and the chaplain, E. V. Tanner, snatched up what few articles of kit they had and ran into the street. The Boche were coming up both the main and the side streets. Signalers and runners hastily formed up across the road and began firing, while Stoney and Tanner scuttled across the square, past the church. The chaplain had never seen such excitement and confusion. This was the beginning of "one of the most thrilling days of my existence."

Field guns were rushing back at full speed to avoid capture and troops were retiring on all sides. To the right a panic-stricken group started to run for their lives until a sergeant, Tanner, and others shouted to keep their heads. "Panic spreads like measles, and if they had been allowed to go on the retirement would have developed into a disorderly rout." By this time Colonel Stoney had ordered C Company to counterattack immediately, and the chaplain had joined the medics. They set up a station a half mile behind the village in an old trench. The first patient's leg had been smashed by a shell. The doctor and Tanner dressed the wound, but it was obvious that the man could not live long. "Tell my mother I died painlessly," he told Tanner, and expired.

Firing in the village grew less and finally ceased. Then word came that there were no Germans in Neuve Eglise; apparently C Company had driven them out. The doctor decided to move back, and they found the road ahead littered with debris—branches of trees, bodies, the limbs of men hit directly. It was a gruesome sight. They cautiously made their way into the village. The streets were covered with push-bikes, packs, and other equipment which the Boche had abandoned in their hurried retreat. But in the short time they held the village they had broken into nearly every house. Front doors were forced open or smashed in. Tanner found Stoney and his adjutant back in the brewery cellar as if nothing had happened except an annoying interruption of breakfast.

A few miles to the rear the hogback ridge was still in British hands, but early that afternoon the enemy pressed forward courageously and the troops of the 1st Queens, which had come up to help Hutchison, were forced to retire half a mile to the north. Fearing an assault from the rear, Hutchison and his orderly, on two stray horses, rode into Bailleul. The streets were deserted as they galloped over the cobbles. Shells smashed into the wreckage, filling their eyes and nose with brick dust. "I was able to establish touch with a Brigade on our left and requested them to squeeze in to prevent the enemy from penetrating the village of Meteren." But as he rode back to his position, Hutchison felt it would be impossible to hold the line. They were running short of ammunition, and there was little hope of getting further reinforcements.

Hornsey, who had fled for his life after the Portuguese line caved in, was now in a unit of stragglers from twenty different battalions. They were to attack toward Bailleul. Their spirits were high. Although they were all practically strangers, they had at last a single purpose—to stem the tide. Hornsey grasped his Lewis gun tightly, waiting for the signal. It went up and they all jumped. It reminded Hornsey of an obstacle race at school. Once they reached those who had gone on ahead they threw themselves on the ground. The left flank went forward, drawing heavy machine-gun fire. Men began to fall but the advance continued. Hornsey jogged forward. Soon they were halfway to their objective, a building another quarter mile ahead.

They were losing men fast, but the survivors at last reached the building. Hornsey was weary but relieved to think the worst was probably over. Masses of Germans were retreating, but it seemed mad to try and hold the position against such overwhelming forces. "What would happen next? God only knew."

Gravely concerned, Clemenceau cabled Lloyd George to return to France for a consultation. This proposition disturbed Henry Wilson, who feared that the Tiger was about to interfere in military operations. What mischief might erupt if Lloyd George went over to help him meddle! Wilson told a colleague on the Army Council, Sir W. Furse, "I must go to him, Fuzz, but I'll be back in half an hour. I'm dammed if he, or I, goes back to France." He was back in that time, smiling. "We are not going, but it was the devil to get it home to him. After much talk I said"—and he began imitating Lloyd George, speaking very slowly with many pauses, in a deep sepulchral voice—" 'There are times—and seasons—when a

Prime Minister's presence is worth—his weight—in diamonds. There are other times—and seasons—especially when a decisive battle is in the fighting—when a Prime Minister's presence—is nothing but—an infernal nuisance.' "

"Did that settle it?"

"Yes! Arthur Balfour was the only other present, and when I said that he exploded with laughter, put his hand on my shoulder with a clap, and said, 'Quite right. Quite right.' "

Late that afternoon a sniper almost killed Chaplain Tanner, who was giving a dying German soldier a drink of water in Neuve Eglise. After waiting until men of another battalion silenced the sniper, he brought back three more wounded enemy to the new first-aid post near the brewery. By this time Colonel Stoney decided to move his headquarters to the *mairie,* the large town hall at the back of the village which commanded a good view. No sooner had they moved than a heavy enemy bombardment began. A Lewis gun was mounted in one of the top windows and snipers were posted at other windows. Heavy German machine-gun and rifle fire broke out all along the village. An attack apparently was imminent. As soon as it became dark a Very light was fired near the church. Other Very lights illuminated a party of a dozen Germans moving around the church. One machine gun opened up and the Germans withdrew, leaving one dead. Sporadic action continued until midnight, when another enemy party was seen approaching. The sentries opened fire and the Germans cleared off at once, leaving a sergeant lying on the road. He crawled to the *mairie.* "Who goes there?" challenged the sentry. "Voosters," he said. "I'll give you Voosters," said the sentry, and fired. They brought the wounded German, a sergeant major, into the first-aid post, where he was interrogated. In the sleeves of his greatcoat were many papers, including a map with dispositions. There was no sleep that night, for every so often "pineapple" bombs from a trench mortar fell onto the roof. Tanner was sure the building would be rushed any moment and they would all be captured.

At 4:30 A.M., Sunday morning, they were startled by heavy rifle and machine-gun fire. Soon after dawn they were completely surrounded. The Boche had occupied the barn behind the town hall and were firing at anyone standing in a window. Some crept forward to drop grenades into the cellar. British runners attempting to deliver messages were shot as soon as they stepped outside. Rifle-grenade fire was directed on the barn, the road, and adjacent houses. About sixty men, including Stoney and the chaplain, took turns sniping at the Germans from the top windows. Tanner could see many gray forms running along the hedges.

In this apparently hopeless situation, the young adjutant, 2nd Lieutenant Crowe, asked leave to make a sortie so as to clear an escape route to the rear. "Well, Crowe," said the colonel, "I'm not going to order you to go but if you do you're a very brave man." Crowe, with five men and another lieutenant named Poynton, crept through the barn at the rear and found a German machine-gun crew behind the hedge with barrel trained on the town hall side entrance. Another machine gun was twenty yards further on, commanding the length of the street. Crowe's party suddenly opened rapid fire, forcing the Germans to withdraw further up the hill. In a determined charge the seven men overran three machine-gun nests, pushing the enemy back to the line of houses. At the same time the men in the *mairie* joined in, catching the Germans in the open. Groups of enemy could be seen withdrawing to the center of the village.

Hope of reinforcements ended early that afternoon, and when Stoney learned that the Boche were massing in fours with packs on their backs only a hundred yards away, he gave the order to evacuate the building. "It was a case of *'Sauve qui peut,'*" recalled Chaplain Tanner. "We left in single file, diving across the small courtyard and out through the barn at the back. A Boche machine gun immediately opened fire on us and continued to do so for about 400 yards. However, by keeping low, we managed to escape without casualty, though bullets were hitting the ground all around us." They finally got to a row of trenches manned by star-tled infantrymen who had been under the impression that they were the front line.

That Sunday, April 14, Lord Milner and General Maurice crossed over to France in a bad storm. They had breakfast with Haig, whom they found tired and worried. Later they all drove to Abbeville for a conference with Foch. Once more Haig explained "the urgent need" for the French to take a more active role in the battle. The British divisions, he said, were fast disappearing; the men were exhausted.

Foch repeated his old arguments: relieving units during bat-tle "would immobilize both the relieving troops and those relieved during the time required for the operation"; furthermore, a power-ful German attack might readily take place on some other part of the front. The French divisions, he said, were distributed where they could best intervene actively at any endangered point.

Haig was exasperated. This, he thought, was all "a lot of non-sense." The British had borne the brunt of the fighting since March 21, exhausting their reserves. All he wanted was for Foch to move the small French reserve north of the Somme further north-ward to the La Bassée Canal or Vimy Ridge. Foch replied with familiar phrases: *"On fait ce qu'on peut," "Jamais reculer," "Jamais la relève pendant la bataille."* But what irked him most was Foch's frequent exclamation, *"Bon!"* Finally Haig exclaimed, *"Ce n'est bon du tout!"* This broke the tension and even Foch smiled. He promised to consider Haig's proposal. The latter also warned that Ludendorff was likely to continue his efforts to take Calais and Dunkirk. If these two ports fell, the British might be forced to come to terms. There was, therefore, a pressing need for help in the Hazebrouck sector. French cavalry divisions already sent north were indeed welcome but more were needed.

Foch said that he would see what the situation was once the present movement of troops was finished; but he thought that Haig was exaggerating the peril. How could the French engage their last remaining troops on a portion of the British front when other parts of their own long line were also under threat of attack? Haig left with misgivings. "Foch seems to me unmethodical and takes a 'short view' of the situation. For instance, he does not look ahead and make a forecast of what may be required in a week in a certain area and arrange accordingly. He only provides from day to day sufficient troops to keep the railway accommodation filled up. Also (as at Ypres in 1914), he is very disinclined to engage *French* troops in the battle." And how could a French commander assess the real condition of British troops?

For the first time General Maurice was seeing the situation from Haig's point of view, and he came to the disconcerting conclusion that those in France were more sensitive to the speeches of the Cabinet ministers than himself, a member of the inner circle in London. Until coming here, he had not been aware that those commanding the battle in France had been struck a blow by those at home. He felt guilty that he had not seen the truth until the officers at Haig's headquarters revealed it to him. Now he was as indignant as Haig that Lloyd George in his recent speech to the House of Commons had stated that the army in France was stronger in 1918 than it had been the year before. He had implied that through faulty leadership the British had been beaten by an enemy inferior in numbers. Maurice knew as well as Haig that the Prime Minister had refused to send more reserves from England before the March offensive and instead had insisted on a campaign in Palestine.

Maurice apologized to those who raised the question of the Prime Minister's gross exaggerations, on the grounds that he himself had not properly studied the speech in question. He promised to do so upon his return to London.

Hornsey and his mates from twenty different battalions had been withdrawn from their precarious position and sent back to Bailleul. The streets were covered with dead soldiers from both sides. As the new arrivals passed a building, a Tommy beckoned to them: "Hey, mate, do you want some grub? If so, be quick." It was a supply depot and the Royal Engineers were about to blow it up rather than let it fall into Jerry's hands. "We hurried inside and nearly fainted at the sight—I began to think it was all a dream. There were stacks and stacks of tinned fruit: strawberries, apricots, peaches, mixed fruit." There were also piles of tobacco, cigarettes, and good sweet biscuits. "Surely we must be in heaven."

Hornsey and a friend named Bill filled two sacks. One was so heavy the two men couldn't lift it, and it nearly broke their hearts to have to remove some of the tins. The building was packed with excited, starving troops. With nearly everyone puffing on a large cigar, the place reeked with smoke. "Who worried about 'Jerry' now? No one. Food was there in plenty, and that was all anyone seemed to care." They struggled with their booty to the cellar of a wrecked building which once was probably a church. Hundreds of others were there eating, smoking, and sleeping. Shells began to fall but no one was concerned. Then a tremendous explosion shook the ground. Still no one was worried. It was only the ammo dump going up.

During the day large gaps were made in the British lines on the hogback ridge in front of Bailleul. Hutchison's machine-gunners had suffered severe losses but his men held. He moved continually between posts, sometimes on foot, sometimes on horseback. Great piles of enemy lay on the slope. By early evening the situation was so critical that Hutchison felt obliged to issue orders to the gun teams to fire on any fleeing British troops. Later he was called back to report to General Mayne, commanding the 19th Brigade. Was it possible to hold any line south and east of Meteren? Yes, said Hutchison, and took over two platoons of the 2nd New Zealand Entrenching Battalion. Under his direction they trenched and wired a line eight hundred yards north of the ridge. Then he dispatched written orders to withdraw the guns to this line. "No finer retirement could have been carried out. In the face of great enemy opposition, and in the teeth of heavy machine-gun fire at its outset, it was carried out without loss to either personnel or material, and every gun was withdrawn . . . with irreproachable discipline to the line to which the Infantry had retired with some disorder, and which was now held firm by a few New Zealand marksmen."

3.

While the critical Battle of the Lys was at its height, secret negotiations between the Allies and Austria suddenly became public knowledge when the Austrian Foreign Minister, Count Ottokar Czernin, foolishly informed the Vienna Municipal Council that the French were so war-weary that Clemenceau had recently suggested they negotiate. Once this report was relayed to the Paris press, there was a public outcry. How dare Clemenceau open secret peace negotiations after pledging himself to uncompromising war! He indignantly retorted that Czernin was lying—then, to his chagrin, discovered that negotiations had indeed been initiated by a previous administration in 1917. Prince Sixtus, brother of the Bourbon wife of Karl of Austria, had conferred privately with President Poincaré, and later queried both Emperor Karl and Czernin on the possibility of peace. Sixtus brought back to Poincaré a signed letter from Karl acknowledging "the just claims of France to Alsace-Lorraine." At this point Lloyd George was brought into the secret discussions and he endorsed them, but the Italians protested. They had been promised Austrian territory under the Treaty of London.

And how could there be a separate accord between the Allies and Austria? So in June of 1917 the Sixtus negotiations had stalled.

Although Poincaré had given his vow of silence to Karl, Clemenceau now reluctantly decided that he had to do something drastic to quiet the outraged criticism against himself. He issued a communiqué referring cryptically to letters "addressed to Paris and London" by a personage of very high rank. Czernin knew, of course, that this was a reference to the indiscreet letter written by Karl, and he should have heeded the warning, but he continued the international debate to publicly retort, without consulting the Emperor, that he "unhesitatingly affirmed" that he did remember those other negotiations but they had failed, because France had refused to abandon her claim to Alsace-Lorraine.

Amazed at Czernin's foolhardiness, Clemenceau decided to bring everything into the open. On April 9 he denied that France's false claims to Alsace-Lorraine had ended hope of peace. "For it was actually the Emperor Karl who, in an autographed letter of March, 1917, gave his definite support to the just claims of France relative to Alsace-Lorraine. A later letter establishes the fact that the Emperor was in agreement with his minister. The only thing left for Count Czernin to do is to make a full admission of his error."

In consternation, Karl, who had also been secretly negotiating with President Wilson, telegraphed the Kaiser that all of Clemenceau's charges were lies, and ended with an emotional pledge of his personal loyalty to Germany: "At a time when Austro-Hungarian cannon are thundering alongside German guns on the Western Front proof is scarcely needed that I am fighting and will continue to fight for your provinces as though I were defending my own."

Appeased by these reassuring, if lying, words, the Kaiser replied that he had "never doubted for one moment" his ally's loyalty. But he began to have misgivings when Clemenceau published Karl's letter on April 12.

Czernin was indignant that the pledge of secrecy was broken. He was also frightened and charged that the letter was a forgery. Karl, he said, had merely written a personal letter to his brother-in-law that he would have supported French claims to Alsace-Lorraine *if* they had been just, "which in fact they were not."

That evening the Emperor had a heart attack, and when Czernin arrived in Baden on the thirteenth to see him, he was met by the Empress. While Karl rested in his bedroom, Zita and the Foreign Minister were alone together in the nearby study for more than one hour. "Czernin behaved like a madman," she recalled. He demanded that the Emperor sign a "Declaration of Honor" which swore that the letter to Sixtus was purely personal and that it had not contained the version about Alsace-Lorraine quoted by Clemenceau.

"Of course I know what really happened," said Czernin, according to her version, "but still I need the Emperor's signature on this oath. I know it is a false oath but I must have it. I need it for myself and for the honor of the family."

"But Count Czernin, do you realize what you are asking? You cannot expect the Emperor to sign and it would be more to the honor of you and your family if you do not want him to."

Czernin repeated his threats to Karl, promising he would lock the paper in his desk where nobody would ever see it. He only wanted it for his own personal security and honor. Though the Emperor thought there was only a faint hope of this, he felt that Czernin "must be pacified in case in his frenzied state of mind he really did sound the alarm in Berlin." After signing the document, he telephoned the Foreign Office to order that nothing be published without first consulting him. But Czernin managed to release the "Declaration of Honor" to the press. It was a rash move that promptly ended his career as Foreign Minister. He was forced to resign during a stormy cabinet meeting on the morning of April 14. At the same time Karl was discredited in the eyes of the world as an intriguer, a liar, and a traitor. More important, the Sixtus scandal scotched Austria's hope of a separate peace with the Allies. Until Karl's letter was published, President Wilson had supported all efforts to wean Austria from Germany, but he now realized that it was impossible to deal with a man whose own people regarded him as a traitor.

Most observers in the West presumed that the Germans would avenge themselves on Karl and put their ally under rigid control, but the Kaiser felt that he should support Karl and do everything possible to prevent his deposition—even though he could no longer trust him.

On April 15 the British War Cabinet took up the Sixtus case, finally deciding to avoid discussion on the subject in Parliament as long as possible. "Indeed," recalled Lord Milner, "it was feared that there might be an outburst in this country, particularly when it became known that Italy had stood in the way of our following up this matter."

After the meeting Wilson and Lloyd George discussed Lord Derby. It was high time they got rid of such a weakling, but who should succeed him as War Minister? "I plumped for Milner," wrote Wilson. ". . . I said that Robertson and Haig were chiefly responsible for the present disaster by never fore-seeing anything and by d—— stupidity and obstinacy. LG entirely agreed."

The average Briton was still shaken by Haig's "backs to the wall" message. The streets of cities were filled with girls; there were fewer civilians; long lines waited outside theaters. Outwardly all seemed normal, but everyone was thinking, "Is the line still holding? Has the tide turned?" There was a wearing anxiety, and each time a new edition of the papers was rushed to the streets, it was seized eagerly and probed for something hopeful.

The newspapers declared that Haig's call to his men was also one to the entire nation. "There is no other course open to us but to fight through," said the *Observer*. "The safety of our homes and freedom of mankind depend alike upon the conduct of each one of us at this critical moment." The *Herald* called for an end to class warfare. "There must be no strike during the present crisis." And so Labour postponed its demands. Even freedom of thought was postponed. A former member of Parliament, Arnold Lupton, was imprisoned for six months. He had some hundred copies of a peace pamphlet in his flat. He was seventy-one.

In Bailleul, Hornsey was wakened early that morning. In the uncertain light of flares he could see two officers going around the church cellar, kicking the men awake. "Get out, all of you, and line up in the street, and be quick. Jerry is in town!"

Hornsey and the others, still half awake but wise enough to hang onto their sacks of cigarettes and food, staggered outside. They were marched to another street and put in houses in small parties and told to be quiet. Jerry was somewhere in town. Hornsey, Bill, and a sergeant crawled into a bed covered with clean linen, their six muddy boots sticking out the bottom. No sooner had they fallen asleep than they were wakened by a spruce officer who looked as though he had never been up front before. "What regiment do you belong to?" he shouted angrily. "Do they allow you to sleep all day?"

"Blimey," said the sergeant, "when you've been out here as long as me, you'll want a sleep. That's about the first sleep I've had for over a week."

"Have you lost all your manners? I am entitled to 'Sir' when you address me. I have been out here a month now, and I think most of you fellows have forgotten what you learnt in England."

The spick-and-span officer ordered them outside where shells were dropping faster than ever. They huddled for cover and toward noon heard the rat-tat-tat of machine guns. Two Tommies dashed from around the corner. "There are thousands of them!" one shouted, and pointed behind. The noise of hand-to-hand fighting increased as British troops came running toward them. In moments Germans swooped around the corner. Hornsey and the others held them off for a few minutes with their rifles, then took to their heels. They went through a house, out the back door into a garden, and over a high wall. From the top of the wall Hornsey looked back to see Bill struggling with his sack of food and cigarettes. He leaned down and helped heave the bag over the wall. "We ran like madmen out of an asylum—there were hundreds of us, each one wondering whether we would get out of town alive or whether we would run right into the enemy again."

The Germans were swarming through Bailleul, but Hutchison's line north of the hogback ridge still held. He called for a volunteer to reconnoiter the entire position. His groom, riding the colonel's big black horse, Old Bill, traversed the length of the three-mile line under a heavy hail of fire. Hutchison observed him through his glasses, noting his trail upon a map. "As he rode past the front of the 1st Queen's, the men rose from the little trenches which they had dug and cheered him lustily, as they had done when the Transport wagons had galloped through their lines delivering ammunition to my posts."

Several hundred miles southwest, the director of the American Army Tank School was writing a friend about the great Ludendorff offensive. The Boche cavalry seemed to have been too cautious, said Lieutenant Colonel George Patton. "I believe that in their place I would have gone through. The tanks were caught with their pants down owing to their being in the act of changing equipment so did not do so well as could have been hoped. This proves my contention also that the big tank is like a very heavy gun and is also only good for a prepared assault. The light tank on the other hand with its mobility can act like field guns." The Americans had a great army and when it got into action Pershing would use it like another General Grant. "I hope to God that I will be in at that time. It will be a great day and some show . . . After the war I am never going to work for a month and then start getting ready for the next war."

The following morning, April 16, Henry Wilson left for France. Bailleul had just fallen, as well as Wytschaete, a town near Mount Kemmel. That afternoon he and Haig met with Foch, who no longer saw eye to eye with his old friend "Henri." Wilson supported Haig's request for genuine French assistance, but Foch brushed this aside. And when Haig raised the question of inundating the area in front of the Channel ports, Wilson chimed in to belittle Foch's efforts in that field. In plain terms he said that Foch must "inundate up to full at once." But nothing was settled.

After dinner Wilson had another long talk with Haig. "I told him that in my opinion the time had come when we should look into the future and decide whether we ought not to cut our losses and fall back with our left on the St. Omer inundations. We should lose Dunkirk, but it looked rather as though we would lose that in any case. What was certain was that our army would soon be reduced to impotence, if the French did not directly intervene and take some of our punishment off us."

Although Haig agreed completely, Wilson still had little regard for him. "Haig is very passive, and has *not* yet got full grip of the situation nor any life and drive." There was no doubt he ought to be removed, but who could replace him? On his part, Haig was changing his opinion of the Chief of Staff. He wrote his wife that Wilson "is doing good work, and means to play straight. Indeed in view of Foch being where he is, things are likely to go more smoothly with Wilson as CIGS than with old Robertson. Wilson and Foch get on together very well."

The Kaiser visited the front again that day, but upon return to his special train, spirits high, he found a sober entourage. They had learned that the offensive had come to a halt for replenishment of ammunition. "Obviously," wrote Admiral von Müller, "the hopes of the Supreme Command have not been fulfilled." There was also pessimism at the Reichstag, for the members had learned that the breakthrough promised by the Supreme Command had not materialized. When Deputy Hans Hanssen, of Danish descent, told two colleagues that the Scandinavian press just revealed that "it has lost hope in the possibility that the break will occur," he noticed that his listeners had already given up hope that the break could come. He talked to others. "The impression was the same. Germany has suffered fearful losses, and they are affecting opinion."

At the front there was still a spirit of triumph. That night Franz Seldte and his motion picture crew returned to their quarters after four days of filming the battle. They were caked with mud and their clothes were soaked. Exhausted and dog-tired, they were buoyed up by the exaltation of the foward sweep. They had seen the fall of Armentières and Bailleul and had taken part in the attack south of Mount Kemmel. What amazed Seldte was that his unit had come through without a single wound. What a terrific film! he thought. The storming up the bank of the River Lys, the attack on Armentières station, the storming of Bailleul and the village near Mount Kemmel. "That must have been something worth showing. With the pictures of the stormed trenches, the machine-gun nests so skilfully camouflaged by the British, the advanced dressing-stations, the bringing up of the captive balloons, and the laying of the long lines of duckboards through the impassable crater area could be made up a connected picture of the battle." Now he had to write out the titles and reports and send everything as quickly as possible to Berlin.

4.

That day the French began relieving units of the British troops holding strategic Mount Kemmel, unaware that the front line was in front of Kemmel. "Their commandant, on arriving at our headquarters," recalled H. Lloyd Williams, a British major, "expressed his amazement on finding us in so far advanced a position, and his disgust that the great gallantry of his regiment and himself in riding at their head as they charged through and captured the village behind had all been in vain." Williams found the French troops amazingly casual as they moved about in full exposure. They didn't seemed concerned when a number of them were hit by enemy snipers and shells. "It was courageous but to no purpose, and very costly. Even while we were in with them for an hour or so, they lost about 150 men—about the total strength of our Brigade at that time." What would happen when they were hit by a real attack?

To the south, the 1st Battlion of the King's Own Royal Lancaster Regiment, which included some fresh troops from England, was moving forward that evening to man the La Bassée Canal defense line. H. Howard Cooper, just turned nineteen, heard a sudden tearing noise in the air, nearer, nearer! a roar—crash! He fell instinctively as a great blast shivered on the right. In seconds clods of earth and pebbles descended like rain. Several newcomers turned to run but were checked by a few harsh, brutal sentences out of the darkness. It was their first German shell.

A year earlier Cooper had been called up from the sixth form of Sandringham, a school near Liverpool. He was, in a sense, a replacement for his older brother, Leslie, who had almost been killed a few weeks earlier in the bitter fighting at Péronne. Ahead he saw strange lights, like Roman candles. Very lights. Then came a knocking noise. "There's his bloody machine guns!" a voice said. The sweet country smell had gone, replaced by a faint burning odor, like that from a smoldering bonfire. Against the sky Cooper saw the ribbed laths of a roof, black and desolate. We must be near now, he thought. There was soon a queer stink and, upon passing an overturned car, he saw two dead horses at the side of the path, their legs sticking out and upward like the animal balloons he used to have.

They came to a canal, perhaps a hundred feet wide. It was La Bassée, but nobody knew it as they crossed the bridge. The burning smell came from barges set on fire a week earlier to prevent them from falling into the hands of the Boche, who had smashed through the Portuguese.

The King's Own fumbled their way through darkness past strange deserted gardens and a few gaunt, forlorn cottages. A half mile from the canal they halted near a hedge in what seemed to be a vegetable garden.

"No talking or noise, lads," whispered Corporal Tedder. "You're in the front line!"

A light flashed and a white ball shot up spluttering in the dark. This was followed by a deafening racket. Cooper fell flat; his brains yelled, "Machine gun!" Hugging the earth, he listened in awe to its venomous bullets split the air overhead, crackle and sting through the hedge.

"Must have heard a noise," whispered Tedder. "It's he who's got the wind up. Come on. we've got to relieve the Somersets." Tedder led them a few yards forward until Cooper heard muffled voices saying something about, "Who, you?" "K.O.s! Somersets?" "Yes, just dug in here yesterday." There were a few final words and the Somersets disappeared. The King's Own were now holding the front line.

Tedder spread out his section in shallow holes about six feet long. "How different from what I had imagined," recalled Cooper. "No trenches at all, trees here and there, hedges! And yet it all seems tense and weird. Germans, the enemy we had read of, imagined, talked about, only just the other side of the hedge, probably within shouting distance." As he settled down to the beginning of this new life, he realized that he was all alone. Then he heard a popping sound from the other side of the hedge, the whitish light again, and again the ear-piercing stutter of a machine gun. He cowered flat, thinking, *He must be almost on top of us.* He could vividly imagine the gray-uniformed figure huddled up to his machine gun in the darkness, trying to pour a stream of bullets into Cooper's little bit of trench. He felt unsafe and exposed in the shallow ditch. Supposing real shelling started! Or trench mortars! They'd had lectures on those things in camp; big bulbous sort of bombs that went up almost vertically and dropped like howitzer shells but with no shriek through the air, just a puffing sound. He began to dig.

"Foolishly I had a sort of thrill having to use this 'drill' implement for the first time in earnest, like a school boy who comes to the time when he really *has* to use those lovely shiny instruments in a set of geometical gadgets." But he soon found that the entrenching tool was not as useful as a spade and that the clay was getting sticky and soggy after six inches. In half an hour it was like dough. Every ten minutes the machine gun would burst out and each time it was terrifying and made Cooper cower as low as possible. "The row and swish of it all! I felt the bullets were only just skimming the top of my cover."

He was still frantically digging as the sky lightened in the east. "Hello, here we are." It was Tedder. "What's all this mess? You'll be getting trench feet, me lad." Cooper, standing in the mud, explained he was digging for cover. "To hell! They won't be able to see you behind this hedge. Besides I don't suppose Jerry knows where we bloody are. 'E don't know we're 'ere. Don't suppose he's got 'is guns up yet. We'll get no shells 'ere yet awhile."

It was almost daylight and gradually and strangely their whereabouts unfolded. They were in a barren garden belonging to a cottage, whose roof could be seen on the left. Beyond, said the corporal, was the village. Cooper could only see scattered houses in a group of trees. To the right was another hedge and beyond lay open ground. A half mile further lay an ominous, silent wood, half veiled in the morning mist. Pacaut Wood.

They sat on steel hats, brewed up tea, and ate boiled bacon, bread, bully beef, and jam. Cooper had not dared to imagine such luxuries in the line and drank his "char" with relish. "Well, laddie," said Tedder, "what do you think of this life?" "Better than I expected so far." "You'll be all right, stick to me, and I'll see you O.K. A few hints are always . . . Listen! Keep still, he's got one of his damned planes over." There came a drone. The plane was fairly high but Cooper noted its foreign "odd" look.

"Keep under cover and lay still!" shouted Tedder to the others as the plane maneuvered slowly like a great hawk. He disappeared through a gap in the hedge. There were rifle shots and someone shouted, "Sniper!" Tedder came running back through the gap. Another crack. Tedder knelt down. "He's got me, the bastard. He's got me!" His hand went to his leg, his face was pale, and sweat broke out on his forehead. Cooper saw a shining dark blob forming on the corporal's puttee. Then it broke and began trickling. "Stretcher-bearers!" shouted someone. "I suddenly realized that I hadn't known what to do. I suppose I just hadn't thought of such an eventuality." As they lifted Tedder on the stretcher, he said to Cooper, "This is a Blighty all right. Well, goodbye, laddie. Look after yourself now. Good luck!"

Cooper felt alone and exposed. "I could only liken the feeling to what I had experienced when, as a tiny boy, my Mother had been sitting with me after a nightmare and had then gone away saying, 'Now you'll be all right.' "

A few hours later as he and Acting Lance Corporal Hall were talking, an unfamiliar soft swishing sound passed overhead toward the village. Suddenly there was a great crash and earth, stones, and smoke flew upward. "Trench mortars!" said Hall. A wince went through Cooper's stomach. Another puffing sound. Crash! then another. "Oh, God!" said Cooper's brain. More and more puffings. The noise and detonation rent the air. Hell! They fell at the foot of the garden. Steel fragments hummed and shrieked over their heads. They were falling every second or two, shaking the earth till their tiny ditch shuddered and seemed to rock from side to side like a boat. Fumes, scattering earth, steel! In a brief respite Cooper looked up. They were still blasting the village. He saw trees falling as volleys of earth and shrubbery blew sky high. Nearer again! A blast and crash behind. Sh-sh-sh-bang! Another. To the right great columns of earth also rose.

"Look!" cried Hall. A man was hurled into the air. His steel hat shot above him. The barrage continued for a half hour. Cooper found he was shaking all over. "I wonder what that meant," said Hall. "Whether he's showing us he's here or whether it's a preliminary to something worse."

"It's enough for me. I never thought trench mortars would be so rotten. I mean I thought bombardments wouldn't matter much if the Germans didn't actually attack."

"Hm," replied Hall. "It puts the wind up everyone. Some more than others, of course. But you never get used to it. It scares you the more you see of it."

"I never knew it would make me shake like this," said Cooper. "I've heard of people trembling with fright but I never thought they really did. And I didn't realize I felt particularly windy. I don't know *why* I'm shaking. I just can't seem to help it and I'm not windy now and I wasn't dithering when it was actually on."

"I'm sort of shaking a bit, too," admitted Hall. "But it affects men differently. It's reaction you're feeling."

There was no attack, and as dusk slowly crept over the flat landscape, the air cooled and a damp grassy smell was wafted with the breeze to their nostrils. "It seemed to be a kind of curtain fall and to my mind it seemed to emphasize the feeling of loneliness and mystery. Once night fell here a certain protection seemed to melt away and be replaced by the sensation of brewing activity 'over there' and the knowledge that night was the signal for outbursts of machine guns and artillery."

The first day of battle was over, but toward midnight distant rifle fire sounded on the left and increased in violence like a huge crackling bonfire. "Too bloody Irish it is!" said Hall. "Good way off though. Look at the Very lights, hell! There's something doing there. He must be 'over.' " They were interrupted by the voice of their company commander, who was ordering the section to build a barricade in front of the hedges. "Get it done in quick time too!"

While they were frantically piling up a dirt barricade, a shell crashed like thunder into the village. Then another. "He's started," said Hall. Cooper hated him saying that; it seemed so sure and final as if he knew the sign. Now he heard more distant shrieks on the right. Bursts of machine guns rent the air. Shoo—ooo—ooo—crash! Shew-eee-oo-crash!

"Now they're coming, get down in!" A dreadful explosion drowned Hall's words. They had both fallen flat and felt the blast of air. Earth showered down. Shoo-oo-oo-ooa-shoo-ooo-crash! The guns thundered louder, the sky flickered. Amid the turmoil Cooper could hear a sort of churning rumble from behind the German lines. Explosion after explosion thundered in the village and to the rear. God help those behind! he thought. It was bad enough here. A shell crashed a few yards away—a hot blast, then a vile smell of explosives. Another and another. An officer shouted at them in an anxious, harsh voice, "Rapid fire to your front! Come on, rapid fire every one of you!"

Cooper breathlessly clapped the bolt of his rifle, pressed. There was a savage kick and a report that made his ears ring. Shouts couldn't be heard. "To the front," his brain repeated. Crack! Crack! He peered through the hedge into the darkness. Then looked up. His worst fear! There, hanging in the sky were three flaring lights—red, green, red! The S.O.S.! High up it hung, slowly drifting. Another rose. Instantly a chaotic rumble broke from behind his own lines. Hundreds of blue flashes lit the sky. Friendly artillery had opened its barrage. "Pandemonium! Shells shrieked in droves, like some gigantic host of devil's pigeons. My hands shook, rapid fire, rapid fire, the deafening crackle. The artillery let loose hell!" He looked up. Flickering sky, shrapnel exploding. "Now it was as though an unseen giant pressed the emergency pedal of some gargantuan machine of hell." The noise rose in a crescendo with the hammering thunder of both German and British guns, the frightful clattering of hundreds of rifles. Uncanny lights leaped into the sky, burst into green and red balls. Things like Roman candles and showers of golden sparks like rain hurtled into the dark sky from the German lines.

Cooper bolted cartridge after cartridge into his rifle, firing chest high as he imagined the gray horde advancing at him. The terrible clamor continued. Shells fell closer and something shouted at him, "The next'll come on us." Then he heard a real voice bawling in his ear, "Getting wind up? Keep on firing, you bloody fool. He's 'over' on the right." It was the officer again.

Time had no meaning but the noise seemed to slacken. Then there was more clamor and a crash nearby. Cooper shouted but his comrade couldn't hear. They fired through the hedge and each moment Cooper expected to see monster German forms breaking through. Abruptly, half an hour later, the thunder lowered, to his untold relief. His brain whirred. It had all been so new and strange. Then something worse happened, something he had not thought of till he heard cries of anguish—the wounded. Through the weird night air, still saturated with a faint odor of explosives, rang the shouts of those torn by shell fragments. It made him shudder. These were screams of agony unlike anything he had ever heard before.

Cooper was posted near a gap in the hedge and told to keep his eyes skinned for Jerries. As he sat there on this cold spring night, completely alone, he could hardly imagine he was part of the army in France. At last dawn broke, and as he was eating breakfast the captain hurriedly came through the gap and said, "Get ready to retire at once!" With two panniers of Lewis gun ammunition slung around his neck Cooper followed the single file crouching its way along the hedge. He couldn't understand why they were pulling back when everything was quiet—unaware that the enemy had broken through on both sides and was already in the village behind them. They entered a battered house through a huge hole. The inside was packed with men.

"Well, men," said Lieutenant Dobson of D Company, "I can't do much for you but any man who wishes, follow me." Cooper had no idea what he was talking about and watched as Dobson ran out the front door onto a narrow road. There were shots but the lieutenant continued in a zigzag crouch. A sergeant followed. "Snipers on all the roofs," said someone. A few had decided they would surrender. Cooper finally realized they were surrounded. He darted out after the sergeant. More shots. A spurt of dust ahead. He crouched and zigzagged. Cooper saw the sergeant run into the open and jump into a shell hole. Cooper followed. Here were several men with a Lewis gun. There were only two drums for the gun and Cooper felt guilty for having abandoned his two panniers in the race for the house.

"Now we've got to line that hedge," said Dobson. He climbed out, darted among the shell holes as shots cracked from the village. Another man followed. More cracks, suddenly he seemed to crumple. A third man left the trench and the others watched anxiously until he disappeared—probably in a shell hole. They saw their captain at the edge of the village. He threw both hands to his face and fell down. Two men ran to his aid. "It was all like a dream. People appeared in the wrong places. Canals turned around. Germans shouted and fired from where I thought was behind our lines."

Two others got to the hedge safely. It was Cooper's turn but he hung back. Another went. Cracks and the venomous crackle of a machine gun. Cooper watched as the preceding man's hands went up and he fell like a log. Gripping himself, Cooper jumped up, dodging and crouching between the new gaping shell holes. Shots rang out and he heard a "pth!" He fell into a shell hole, crawled out, jumped into another, and found two King's Own men there. Dead. He crawled out. More rifle shots and at last he was near the hedge. He fell flat in a slight depression by the side of a gaping shell hole. Inside were three machine-gunners. "Come in," shouted one. "If you lie there you'll be a dead 'un!" Cooper wriggled down with them. There was a fourth man, a sergeant, gazing with wide open glassy eyes into the sky. His skin was whitish and marble-like. Cooper smelled rum and blood. A breeze fluttered a curl of black hair on the sergeant's forehead. It seemed on a tailor's dummy.

From time to time, Cooper heard awful shouts from the desolate fields around them. Once or twice came the most blood-curdling screams and Cooper guessed that they were from wounded horses. What would happen now? He hadn't slept since Monday night. Now it was Thursday morning, April 18. There was no shellfire at last and Cooper felt drowsy. He surveyed the somber country: the village, quiet and grim; the dead shell-holed field; the murky sky. Smoke drifted up from the canal from coal barges set afire. It was silent now, but he heard the vicious machine guns shattering the slates of the uncanny little cottage; he smelled the blood and rum and glanced again at the glassy eyes of the sergeant. Then sleep overcame him.

When he opened his eyes it was dark. He drowsily wondered where he lay until the smell came to him—blood, rum, burning. In a flash it all poured back. Night! He must have slept for hours. He and two comrades had lain there lost to everyone. What if the Germans had attacked again! "No sound pierced the darkness but ahead of us a Very light rose and cast its shimmering white glare over all, twisting up curious contorted shadows as it fell slowly to earth, then blackness."

Soon they heard a voice coming nearer and nearer. "King's Own. Any King's Own there? Any 'A' Company there?" For a moment the three kept silent. What were they going to be dragged in for? They weren't A Company. Then their better judgment said, "Here!" A peering form came warily forward. "Who are you?" It was an officer of A Company. He told them they were now attached to him. "We're going to make a counterattack!" A barrage was to begin in ten minutes. Soon a clamor rumbled from behind. Blue flashes illuminated the sky and almost simultaneously there was the angry rush of shells skimming over to the German positions. Machine guns chattered. The officer came running along among their sparse ranks as the short barrage lifted. "Come on, lads," he called softly. "Now crawl forward! Don't make any bloody noise. Keep on your tummies!"

As they crawled forward the guns stopped. They passed through the orchard and beyond. "Stop," whispered the officer. Once the stragglers closed up he said, "Come on!" Suddenly there was an earsplitting rattle. Cooper and the others pressed to the ground as a stream of machine-gun bullets swept over them. The gun must be almost on them. It stopped. Cooper knew nothing. Where were they? What now? All seemed strange. Without any warning the officer scrambled up and shouted in a whisper, "At 'em, come on, give 'em hell!" They leaped to their feet and almost unconsciously rushed forward, rifles extended, yelling the lusty cries of Oswestry bayonet classes: "Urr! Arrr!"

"In a second and almost with a shock I saw we were upon 'them.' Dim German helmeted figures, head and shoulders above their post. Urr! Aaa! Grrr! I saw the fearsome machine gun, right at us. A demon leapt toward it, seized the handles. It was all momentary, then, the hesitation was fractional, we were almost upon them. The coal-scuttled demon threw up his hands, then the four others cried, 'Mercy, Kamerad! Oh, mercy, mercy!!!' Our bayonets were prodding them. Suddenly shots rang out right and left; machine guns spluttered. I knew not what happened there nor how far this counterattack extended. 'Oh, show mercy!' almost screamed the Germans. They did scream, even blubbered. I'll never forget that scene and sound—like pigs screaming."

When someone shouted, "Come out, you square-headed bastards!" the Germans began climbing out, hands still up. It seemed so strange to Cooper with these unfamiliar scuttle-helmeted men at his side, hearing the guttural foreign voices, looking upon the high boots and strange gas helmets. "Germans! How often we had talked of them in camp; imagined them! Even in the tumult of a few hours ago they had been distant and such very 'unknown,' mysterious, invisible beings. It seemed now we were looking upon creatures who had suddenly descended from the moon. One felt 'So this is the Enemy. These are the firers of those invisible shots, those venomous machine guns, all the way from Germany and here at last we meet. These are samples of the thousands, ever consciously present in the apparently flat landscape in front of us, the "other" mysterious, vacant yet impenetrable land, a land where for weeks guns might thunder, venomous bullets come flying to claim their victims, strange and meaningless lights might rise and yet the eye would look out and see, staring back, just a blank expanse, where never a living creature moved and yet be conscious that always the expanse concealed thousands of these grey waiting beings, eating, sleeping, seeing and not being seen. And further back; squatting by great newly oiled and shining monster guns.' Here on this cold dark April night I looked upon them."

5.

That noon the Kaiser lunched not far away at Fourth Army headquarters. Lieutenant Seldte was presented to him. Remembering him from Italy, His Majesty made polite inquiries about the doings of the film unit. Seldte told about the special film, *The Battle of the Lys*. That evening the lieutenant listened to staff officers discuss a new attack that should break the deadlock. They were to shift to the north and make another attempt to seize Mount Kemmel. Seldte and his crew were instructed to get acquainted with the area. The next two days the film makers, along with Intelligence officers, tramped around Kemmel, thoroughly surveying the ground. Preparations continued and spirits were high among the planners when some snow fell on the morning of April 20. The unseasonable cold would ensure secure footing not only for the Kemmel attack but for another try at the La Bassée Canal defense line.

April 21, a Sunday, was cold with bright intervals. There was a lull in the Lys battle, so air activity turned to the Somme Valley where the wind was blowing from the east, a quarter unfavorable to German pilots. Usually the winds in France were westerly, but this Sunday was one of those rare days with the wind favoring British and French fliers. When Baron Manfred von Richthofen awoke, he hoped it would be raining so he could get some sleep. He could see that it was an overcast sky, but there was no welcome patter of rain on the roof. His head ached from a wound received almost a year earlier and if he got to his feet too quickly he became giddy. His orderly laid out his uniform, but he donned a flying suit over his gray silk pajamas. Then if they were grounded he could go back to bed. Yesterday he had scored two kills, bringing his record to eighty. A very decent number and one that could not be topped for a long time. He could use a rest. After a light breakfast he left the officers' mess and again examined the sky. The sun was trying to break through. He noticed the wind was coming from the east. Not so good. It would blow them over enemy lines. The crash of a regimental band playing outside his quarters assaulted his head. It had been sent by a nearby division in honor of his eightieth victory. Too loud, he told a companion, and walked toward the hangar. Here his spirits lightened and he began to make jokes. He even tipped over a recent replacement who was lolling on a stretcher. Seldom had the other fliers seen him in such a gay mood.

He autographed a card that a mechanic nervously held out, and allowed his picture to be taken playing with his Danish hound, Moritz. A telephone operator interrupted with a message that several English planes were over the front. Richthofen donned his parachute, mounted his blood-red Fokker triplane. In moments he was in the air with his Circus, which included his cousin, Wolfram, a fledgling, and five experienced men, one of whom had but one hand. They were joined by a dozen other Tripes and Albatrosses.

A few minutes after flying over Bapaume at seven thousand feet, Richthofen spotted two British reconnaissance planes a thousand feet below. He signaled four of his men to follow him while the rest stayed above to watch for enemy fighters. The five dived, expecting a quick and easy victory, but the observation planes put up a gallant stand, knocking down one Fokker. Richthofen broke off the fight and while attempting to re-form his Circus swept down within range of British anti-aircraft guns which opened fire. The exploding puffs were seen by a formation of eight Camels. Led by

Captain Roy Brown, they dived down to save the observation planes.

Richthofen saw the cherry-nosed Camels swooping down, so he signaled his men to come about and fight the attackers head-on. He set out after his eighty-first victim. Above, Lieutenant Wilfrid May, a newcomer ordered by Brown to stay out of the fight, could not resist the beautiful target offered by one of the Tripes. He flung himself at the German plane, then found himself "in a regular beehive of enemy aircraft." They were coming from all sides and he headed for home. The next thing he knew someone was firing from behind. It was a red Fokker. "Had I known it was Richthofen, I should probably have passed out on the spot." May swooped down, zigzagging toward the west. Richthofen followed him over the British lines. It was only a question of seconds before he got the range.

Above, Brown saw what was happening and soon caught up with the two planes which were careening down the valley at five hundred feet. He got the red Fokker in his sights, fired, and watched it drop out of sight. Confident that he had scored, Brown headed for home.

But Richthofen had only disappeared behind a row of trees as he closed on May's tail. The novice had run out of sky and was hedgehopping. A moment later he cut over a hill. Now May was sure he was "a sitting duck." He was too low down between the banks of a river to turn away. "I felt he had me cold and I had to restrain myself from pushing the stick forward and disappearing into the river. Richthofen was thirty feet behind. One more burst and he'd have his eighty-first!" But one of his Spandau guns stopped. A broken firing pin. The other gun jammed. He broke off pursuit, then banked to the east just as Australian anti-aircraft fire smashed into the forward section of his plane. It staggered, swerved. Richthofen ripped off his glasses as the Fokker dropped into a sideslip. May happened to turn around just then and "saw Richthofen do a spin-and-a-half and hit the ground."

When May landed he rushed up to Brown, grabbed his hand. "Thank God, Brown. Did you get the red one? It looked bad. A second later and it would have been all over for me." A little later, the commandant telephoned. The chief engineer took the call and shouted, "Man, Brownie! Get ready for a medal." What for? "The old man says the red flier was Richthofen."

Brown almost fainted.

He and his commandant found the Red Baron's body near an aviation field hospital. "The sight of Richthofen as I walked closer gave me a start. He appeared so small to me, so delicate. He looked so friendly; his feet were slender, like those of a woman. They were set in his Uhlan boots, brightly polished." Blond, silky hair fell from his broad forehead. "His face, particularly peaceful, had an expression of gentleness and goodness, of refinement. Suddenly I felt miserable, desperately unhappy, as if I had committed an injustice."

Brown received credit for the kill, but death had come from the ground. He was shot down by Gunner Cedric Bassett Popkin and Gunner Rupert F. Weston of the 24th Machine-Gun Company, 4th Australian Division.*

The following afternoon, Richthofen was buried with military honors. Wreaths were placed around the plain wooden coffin. One read: "To our gallant and worthy foe." At the cemetery a chaplain of the Church of England preceded six captains carrying the coffin. After prayers and a eulogy, it was lowered. Then a fourteen-man squad fired three volleys. The next day a British plane flew over Richthofen's airdrome, dropping a metal container. Inside was a photograph of the ceremony and this message:

> To the German Flying Corps
>
> Rittmeister Baron von Richthofen was killed in aerial combat on April 21, 1918. He has been buried with all due military honors.
>
> From the British Royal Air Force †

No death in the war had caused such worldwide attention. He was eulogized by the British press. There was mourning throughout Germany. "Richthofen, we realize, was more to us than just a symbol," wrote Dr. Max Osborn in the *Berliner Zeitung am Mittag*. "He was the able and high-minded type of young man on which the nation must rely for its future progress and prosperity."

His mother received messages of condolence from the Kaiser and Hindenburg. At the front the news was learned with shock. "On the fatal day all the German armies were paralyzed with horror," recalled Hans Schröder. "But their inertia lasted only a brief while, then every one wanted to avenge Richthofen, and so the murder in the air went on with redoubled rage." Ernst Udet had the same reaction. Affected "profoundly," he bullied a doctor into passing him as fit to fly again so he could return to the front. Infantry officer Sulzbach, while shattered by the news, was grateful to the enemy. "The British are indeed truly chivalrous, and we must thank all of them for honoring our great airman." Pilots like Rudolpf Stark would not believe at first that Richthofen was dead. Then came confirmation. "Richthofen dead!" he wrote in his diary. "We whisper the dread tidings softly to one another; our laughter dies away in the mess. The hammers are silent in the workshops, the engine that was just being given its trial stands still. A gloomy silence broods over all. A great one has gone from us."

* The controversy over who downed Richthofen was settled, in this author's opinion, by P. J. Carisella, who, with James W. Ryan, wrote *Who Killed the Red Baron?* Carisella, a redoubtable researcher, devoted years to the solution of the Richthofen mystery.

† On April 1 the Royal Flying Corps had been reorganized as an air force entirely independent of the army and navy. Now it was a third service, the Royal Air Force.

Major action was at last approaching in Italy where the Austrians, hoping to emulate the Ludendorff victories, were mounting an offensive to be launched in late May. In Palestine attempts of the new German commander, General Liman von Sanders, to retake Jerusalem were being held off by Allenby.

Chapter Six

"ST. GEORGE FOR ENGLAND!"
APRIL 22–MAY 15

1.

WHILE most Englishmen on the morning of April 22 were absorbed with the account of Richthofen's death, the commander of the Dover Patrol, Admiral Roger Keyes, was making the final decision to attack Zeebrugge, Belgium, which was connected by canal to nearby Brugge. Every day two U-boats emerged from this seaport of Brugge to prey on Allied shipping, and ever since German occupation of the Flanders coast in 1914 there had been schemes to neutralize the troublesome nest.

The main objective was to bottle up the canal, which emptied into the English Channel at Zeebrugge. It seemed an impossible task, since the entrance was protected from the storms of the North Sea by a long solidly constructed mole that left the coast a half mile west of the canal mouth and curved out northeast in a great mile-and-a-half arc. The mole was eighty-one feet wide, with a thick sixteen-foot-high wall on its seaward side. A fortress with six naval guns and machine guns at the tip end, it was also protected by heavy shore batteries.

The attack could only be carried out under the best conditions of tide and moon, and that morning the meteorological report was not too bad. It could have been better, but Keyes was certain that if he failed to bring the operation off within the next week the Admiralty would cancel it for good. "My wife walked down to the pier with me to see me off, apparently quite unperturbed. She alone knew what a hell of a time I had been going through and her last words were that the next day was St. George's Day (which I had not realized), and that it was sure to be the best day for our enterprise, as St. George would bring good fortune to England, and she begged me to use St. George for England as our battle cry."

The Royal Marines, who were to storm the mole, were drilling on the quarterdeck of *Hindustan* when the signal came to prepare for the "stunt." The men boarded a tug which took them alongside *Vindictive*, an old cruiser converted into an assault ship. It would carry most of the storming parties.

145

As the invasion expedition set out early that evening, Keyes, from the battleship *Warwick*, sent out a general signal by semaphore: "St. George for England." Acting Captain A. F. B. Carpenter signaled back from *Vindictive*: "May we give the dragon's tail a dammed good twist." *

A Marine was writing in his diary: "We are doubtful that it will come off, but we all hope it will. We have taken up our stations and had tea, and we are on our way to the Mole. Everything seems certain as the wind is holding favorable. I do wish that it comes off, as the suspense is awful." The men were given their daily ration of rum a little after 8 P.M., and the platoon sergeants were made responsible that each man had only his share. They were all in good humor, laughing, joking, playing cards, and some were boasting of what they would give Jerry on the mole.

At about 10:30 P.M. four cruisers veered to the right toward Ostend. Two of the ships, *Sirius* and *Brilliant*, were scheduled to sink themselves in the entrance to Ostend harbor and thus ensure complete blockage of German raiders. The main force continued toward Zeebrugge. *Vindictive*, accompanied by two Merseyside ferries, *Daffodil* and *Iris*, headed for the mole. The two ferries drew a scant eleven feet of water and were to be used to land the Marines in case *Vindictive* encountered a shallow minefield. They were escorted by *Warwick* and two smaller ships. Then came *Trident* and *Mansfield*, towing two submarines, the bow of each packed with five tons of amatol. They would smash into the railway bridge connecting the mole with the shore. The explosions would tear a hole in the bridge, preventing German land reinforcements from coming to the aid of the mole garrison.

Behind came the sting of the invasion, the three blockships. They would swing around the mole, fight their way to the canal mouth, where they would scuttle themselves in interlocking positions. And this would effectively block all entrance of submarines to the Channel.

The entire procession was led by a flotilla of twenty-four motor launches and eight coastal motorboats. They would lay the smoke screen off the mole. Nine other coastal motorboats would attack with torpedoes. Soon after 11 P.M., an hour before *Vindictive* was scheduled to come alongside the mole, it became misty. Clouds obscured the moon and a light, cold rain began to fall. This was fortunate, since visibility was now limited and *Vindictive* could approach within several hundred yards of her objective before being sighted. It was unfortunate, since the rain would cancel out help from Handley-Page bombers scheduled to knock out the shore batteries.

At 11:20 P.M. the two monitors *Erebus* and *Terror* opened fire on Zeebrugge. They had done the same on the two previous nights, and the Germans thought it was just another harassing bombardment. They had no suspicion that a landing attack was

---

* Carpenter's signalman first substituted "darned" for "damned" and, when corrected, sent out "dammed" as a compromise.

ZEEBRUGGE, THE MOLE
APR. 22-23

NORTH SEA

LIGHTHOUSE

GUNS

INTENDED POSITION
OF VINDICTIVE
& FERRIES

NET BARRIER
ANCHORED
TO BARGES

IPHIGENIA

THETIS

SISTER

NETS BETWEEN
BUOYS

INTREPID

SANDBANK

U-BOAT
SHELTER

VINDICTIVE
DAFFODIL
IRIS

SEAPLANE
BASE

THE MOLE

SUBMARINES

DESTROYS
BRIDGE

LOW WATER LINE

VIADUCT

DUGOUTS & GUNS

RAILWAY
TO BRIDGE

8 GUNS

NETS
RUNS
AGROUND

IPHIGENIA
& INTREPID

GUN
EMPLACEMENTS

BASIN

GUN
EMPLACEMENTS

CANAL
ENTRANCE

TO CANAL
TO BRUGGE

4 NAVAL GUNS

GUN
EMPLACEMENTS

ZEEBRUGGE

0   500
YARDS

ZEEBRUGGE AND VICINITY

NORTH SEA

Zeebrugge

CANAL

MOLE

Blankenberge

U-BOAT BASE

Brugge

Ostend

CANAL

Torhout

N

0   5   10
MILES

0   5   10   15
KM

adcus

147

coming. Not a patrol boat was out and no defensive minefields had been laid. Three destroyers were moored on the inner side of the mole. Eleven submarines of the Flanders flotilla were at sea. The remaining seven were at their pens in nearby Brugge, ready to emerge from the canal mouth.

Twenty minutes later thirty-two small craft began laying smoke to hide *Vindictive*'s approach. A gentle northeast breeze blew it toward the mole. The Marines were ordered to fall in, fully rigged, on the upper deck. They hastily shook hands. Rifles were loaded, bayonets fixed. Nerves strained, everyone spoke in whispers. There was no movement, only the noise of propellers. "Ah, what was that?" exclaimed someone. A star shell floated just over the ship, lighting it up as if it were day. "They've seen us!" whispered someone. It was ten minutes before midnight.

Lieutenant Commander Hilton Young was at his station in *Vindictive*'s port battery. His two six-inch guns were ready for action. He noticed a few illicit cigarettes glowing in the corners, but this was no time to lay down the law. The battery deck was crowded with anxiously waiting men. Most of them were Marines preparing to go over the side. They were within a mile or two of the mole and should be there in ten minutes. Now he could see the flashes of the guns from the battery on the mole. Those flashes were to be his target. If the lighthouse out there at the tip end became visible, he was to shoot at that also. But they were not to fire until the guns topside opened up.

Searchlights from shore began probing the sea. Then came a roar like an express train as a huge shell passed over the invaders. Admiral Keyes felt intense relief. The battle was at last joined and there could be no turning back.

Suddenly the wind turned. The blanket of smoke was pushed back to sea and *Vindictive* was revealed, a perfect silhouetted target for the mole battery. She still had a quarter mile to run before reaching the sheltering wall.

Vindictive was pinned by a searchlight. Guns from the mole opened fire. From his dark bay, Lieutenant Commander Young saw their quick flashes on the port bow, then noticed a strange faint popping all around the ship. It was the noise of shells that had missed and were bursting in the sea. A moment later shells began to hit the antiquated cruiser. Young was eager to open fire and thought, "When is the top going to begin? Will it never begin?"

Then came a series of swift, shaking detonations close by, and one blinding flash of blue light in his eyes. Nearby the Marine commander, Lieutenant Colonel Elliot, was killed, along with his second-in-command, Major Cordner. Young was listening so impatiently for the first shot from the top that he hardly noticed what was going on. Looking out the embrasure, he did see a friendly motor craft dashing forward, "almost flying" across the waves as she spewed out smoke to hide the cruiser. "She swung across our bows, right between us and the batteries and under the very muzzles of their guns, and vanished into her own smoke unharmed. It was a gallant act, and glorious to see." Something went "Ponk!" just behind Young and he felt a sledgehammer blow on his right arm that sent him spinning down the narrow entry into a group of Marines on the battery deck. "Why, whatever's the matter with you?" said a comrade in a surprised voice, and stirred the wounded Young with his foot.

"The noise was terrific and the flashes of the Mole guns seemed to be within arm's length," recalled Captain Carpenter. It seemed impossible for the mole guns to miss their target, and he thought it was little short of criminal on the part of the mole battery that *Vindictive* was still afloat. From the flamethrower hut on the port side, Carpenter swung the ship to starboard, holding speed as she ran the gauntlet of guns. At one minute past midnight on St. George's Day the ship arrived alongside the mole into a field of fire of enemy machine guns that swept its length. Carpenter ordered engines immediately reversed at full speed, and *Vindictive* gently bumped the mole.

From the hut Carpenter could just see over the top of the wall, but the smoke, the intermittent glare and flashes, and the rain obscured his vision. The ship seemed to be westward of the desired position, so the engines were kept at full speed astern. Time was pressing. At all costs they must develop their main diversion before the blockships arrived at 12:20 A.M. Through the voice tube he gave the order to let go the starboard anchor. Nothing happened. It was jammed. Carpenter ordered the engines at full speed astern and full speed ahead alternately to keep the ship in position. The port anchor was dropped at the foot of the wall, the ship allowed to drop astern until a hundred yards of cable had been veered. As the cable was secured, *Vindictive* swung immediately out from the mole. No gangways could reach, and each time an officer tried to get ashore to make a grappling line fast he was picked off by machine-gun fire. At this desperate moment—it was 12:04—little *Daffodil* steamed out of the smoke. The skipper, Lieutenant Campbell, pushed the ferry's nose against *Vindictive* and shoved her bodily alongside the mole.

Instantly two gangways—the other sixteen had been destroyed—were lowered until they rested on the wall. Someone shouted, "Storm the mole!" and the word was passed. The surviving Marines began scrambling over the wildly swaying gangways, carrying ladders and ropes. The first man on the mole was Lieutenant Commander Bryan Adams. He saw no enemy and, after fruitless efforts to secure the mole anchors in position over the parapet, led the bluejackets to the left toward the batteries. They came to something that looked like a trench with stones heaped up in front. Adams collected his small party and led them forward with a rush. But a machine gun behind the trench abruptly opened fire. Germans rushed out, loosed a volley, and retired. Adams knew that he could not storm his way past this obstacle to reach the guns without reinforcements. He hurried back to get them.

Two Marine platoons led by Major Weller, now their acting commander, were slithering down ladders from *Vindictive* to the lower part of the mole. Originally there were forty-five men in each platoon. Now there were but a dozen. A few Germans rushed out with hand grenades but were quickly picked off. Sergeant H. Wright and thirteen men dashed forward, anxious to avenge their comrades lying dead and wounded on *Vindictive*. They found that the Germans had pulled back to concrete shelters further up the mole. Wright fired red Very lights to let those behind know his group had reached its position. In the meantime, *Daffodil* kept grittily pinning *Vindictive* to the mole with 160 pounds pressure to the square inch on boilers designed for 80 pounds. The engineers and stokers kept at their arduous task, ignoring explosions outside.

The two submarines, C1 and C3, were supposed to ram into the bridge connecting the mole to the beach, at 12:15 A.M. But the former's towline parted and she could not attack. The latter cast off from *Trident*, proceeding under her batteries at nine and a half knots. She was still more than a mile from the target when star shells revealed her to the Germans. Two searchlights found C3 and blinded her little crew. Shells almost immediately exploded on both sides, but Lieutenant Sandford kept on course, determined to ram the steel bridge at right angles. Miraculously the firing ceased. Sandford ordered smoke canisters turned on, but the smoke not only failed to hide the submarine but obscured the bridge. Sandford ordered them turned off.

A third searchlight caught C3 and she was a perfect target but still no shells came. She was a hundred yards from her objective. Now all Sandford had to do was set the gyro steering gear, light the fuse to the amatol, and abandon ship. This was so risky he decided to ram the bridge with the crew aboard. He made his last course correction, ordered the men to join him topside. Together they stood staring at the looming target, gripping the rail against the expected shock. They could see men on the bridge gesturing and laughing at the idea of catching an enemy submarine alive in the steel network beneath them. The submarine smashed into the target with a terrifying shriek. As Sandford lit a twelve-minute fuse that would set off the amatol, the crew was lowering a skiff into the water. Sandford leaped into the boat but its propeller was broken and it had to be slowly rowed away, drawing a storm of small-arms fire. Three of the six men were wounded, but the sound men managed to get the boat two hundred yards away. Then there came a tremendous roar. The bridge erupted, raining debris on the skiff. A column of smoke climbed into the sky.

Captain Carpenter aboard *Vindictive* saw "a huge tower of flame and debris and bodies" flung into the black sky. His men cheered like mad, for they knew what it meant. "I never saw such a column of flame! It seemed a mile high!" A picket boat emerged out of the dark to hail the skiff. The C3 crew was hauled aboard and Sandford, now twice wounded, realized that he had been saved by his older brother, skipper of the picket boat.

There was now a break in the bridge to the mole more than forty yards wide. This cut off all reinforcements, as planned. It also severed all communications, including telephone lines, and kept the batteries on shore from learning that the three ships escorted by three motor launches presently passing the mole extension were the British blockships. Assuming that these were their own destroyers, the shore guns were silent.

As *Thetis*, the first blockship, rounded the end of the mole at 12:25 A.M., her starboard guns opened upon the lighthouse. She headed straight for the southernmost of the barges which barred the channel. By now the 4.1-inch guns near the mole lighthouse began pouring shells into *Thetis* from a hundred yards. Caught by a strong tide, she swung to port, missed the barge, and tore through a heavy net, fouling both propellers and bringing the ship to a stop. The crew of *Thetis* managed to clear the net obstruction away while their captain signaled *Intrepid* and *Iphigenia*, the two other blockships, to pass to port. They did so as *Thetis*, still under heavy fire, grounded three hundred yards from the eastern canal pier. Finally the starboard engine was restarted and she limped into the dredged channel, where she was sunk.

As *Intrepid* passed *Thetis* she was undamaged. She could have rammed the lock gates, but her captain, Bonham Carter, following orders, went ahead full starboard upon reaching the narrow part of the channel entrance, and then backed full port. Carter waited for most of his crew to get into boats, but, fearing that the ship would swing into the channel, blew his charges before the engine room was cleared. Eighty men abandoned ship in three cutters.

The third blockship, *Iphigenia*, followed *Intrepid*. She had been hit only twice from the mole battery, and the captain, Lieutenant Billyard Leake, found the canal entrance obscured by smoke and got entangled with a barge. Once clear, Leake went ahead with both engines. Sighting *Intrepid* aground on the western bank with a wide gap between her bow and the eastern bank, he tried to close this breach. He collided with *Intrepid* while turning. Since his own ship was not completely blocking the channel, Leake maneuvered her to the eastern bank. He abandoned ship, fired his charges. The entire ship's company left in one cutter. Although subjected to heavy machine-gun fire, most of the crew managed to transfer to a motor launch and safety.

Those standing on the compass platform of *Warwick* could see clearly over the mole's parapet. All three blockships were in the canal entrance! Admiral Keyes was not sure whether or not they had successfully blocked the canal, but there was nothing more *Vindictive* could do to help them. Her captain, Carpenter, had already decided it was time to leave. It was 12:50 A.M. and the blockships had had almost a half hour to accomplish their mission. *Vindictive*'s two sirens had been shot away, so Carpenter ordered *Daffodil* to sound the retirement signal. The ferryboat's siren spluttered, gurgled, and shot up a veritable shower bath. Finally it went from a low groan to a shriek. The Marines on the mole who

151

heard the four blasts returned to the ship with their wounded and as many dead comrades as they could carry. The gangways were still heaving convulsively. One Marine hauled a wounded comrade aboard and gently lowered him to the deck. "I wasn't going to leave you, Bill," he was heard to say.

The *Vindictive* crew cast off the hawser from *Iris*, the other ferryboat. (She had arrived late with a load of Marines, but due to the swell had been unable to land them on the mole; although she danced like a cork, some of her assault group had managed to leap onto *Vindictive* and join the attack.) *Iris* had luckily escaped damage, but now she had to steam past the mole batteries. On *Vindictive*, Lieutenant Young, back at his post despite a badly wounded arm, watched the ferry with sinking heart, remembering how his ship had been pummeled coming the other way. A minute later there came a crash and bang from the mole's naval guns. "It was a terrible thing to watch. At that short range the light fabric of the little ship was hulled through and through, flames and smoke spurting from her far side in the darkness, enveloped in a thick cloud of smoke." Young thought *Iris* must be sinking. She was hit ten times by small shells and twice by large shells from the shore. Part of the bridge was blown away, killing two officers and severely wounding Lieutenant G. Spencer. But he continued to con the ship until relieved. Heroism on *Iris* was common that night. Commander Valentine Gibbs lost both legs but protested when medics started applying tourniquets. "Leave me alone," he said. "I want to get these men back home." His ship was saved by the daring efforts of Motor Launch 558, which darted out in front of her to lay down a dense smoke screen. But 77 officers and men were dead, with another 105 wounded.

While *Iris* was being pummeled, *Daffodil* gave a snort as if relieved from having to hold *Vindictive* in place, then backed away. Aided by the tide, *Vindictive* swung away from the mole. The two gangways slipped off the wall and fell overboard, fouling the port propeller. This was quickly cleared, and at 1:11 A.M. Carpenter ordered, "Full speed ahead." He gave instructions to turn on the artificial smoke apparatus and in less than a minute the ship was shrouded. She steamed northwest at utmost speed with flames pouring through the holes of the funnels. From the mole it looked as if *Vindictive* were on fire.

Carpenter had the sensation of the ship jumping at irregular but frequent intervals. He figured that heavy shells were striking the water near the ship. If any hit, no serious damage was done, and in twenty minutes *Vindictive* passed the light of Blankenberghe buoy. Ahead was the dark form of a vessel. It turned out to be one of their own destroyers, *Moorson*. With a pocket flashlight, an officer signaled her to guide *Vindictive*, whose compass was useless.

Back at the mole, Sergeant Wright and his platoon heard the siren but were told that it was not the proper retire signal, and went back to their post. Then to their consternation they saw *Vin-*

dictive move way. They were stranded. "It seemed cruelly hard to know we had come through that terrible experience unscathed, and now were left behind through no fault of our own."

Admiral Keye's flagship, *Warwick*, stood in toward Zeebrugge looking for stragglers. They met Motor Launch 282 coming out, packed with men. Keyes hailed Lieutenant P. T. Dean and asked how many he had picked up. About seventy, was the answer, including a good many wounded. These were the survivors of *Intrepid* and *Iphigenia* and all were transferred with difficulty to the battleship. The captains of the two blockships reported to the bridge. "Billyard Leake might have stepped out of a military tailor's shop," recalled Keyes, "equipped for the trenches, leather coat, shrapnel helmet all complete, very erect and absolutely unperturbed." Bonham Carter was in a dirty wet vest and trousers since he had been swimming in the canal. He reported that he had sunk *Intrepid* across the canal and thought that she filled the fairway.

At about 5 A.M., as *Warwick* was nearing Dover, she overhauled *Vindictive*, whose upper works looked very battered. Smoke and flame poured out of the holes in her funnels, but she was steaming at nearly seventeen knots. Keyes informed *Vindictive* that the blockships had been sunk in the canal, then signaled, "Operation successful. Well done, *Vindictive*." The crews of both ships cheered lustily as *Warwick* steamed past.

On reaching Dover, *Warwick* ran alongside the hospital yacht and discharged the wounded. Then Keyes sent a telegram to the Admiralty reporting that two of the blockships were, according to their captains, sunk in the correct positions. Soon after 8 A.M. *Vindictive* arrived. All the ships in the harbor mustered crews on the decks and they cheered the returning heroes to the echo.

The Marine battalion disembarked at 9:30 A.M., bade farewell to Captain Carpenter ("the hero of the hour and no one can describe what he has done") before entraining for Deal, where they marched through that town to their barracks.

Admiral Keyes had breakfast with his wife, who related how she had spent an anxious night listening to the guns on the Flanders coast which rattled her windows. She had sat up until 3 A.M., and then experienced a strong feeling that all was well and that her husband was on his way home. Their triumph was somewhat diminished by bad news from Dunkirk. The blocking attempt at Ostend had failed, since the Germans had moved the light buoy that was guiding the two blockships, which, consequently, were sunk far from the canal mouth.

Yet the great success at Zeebrugge, a feat worthy of Horatio Hornblower, more than compensated for this disappointment. The people of Britain were thrilled by an enterprise in the great tradition of Drake and Nelson. No incident had so moved British popular imagination. In *Punch* a cartoon showed Drake's ghost telling Keyes, "Bravo, Sir! Tradition holds. My men singed a King's beard, and yours have singed a Kaiser's mustache."

That morning the Kaiser visted Zeebrugge to congratulate those heroes who had repelled the British assault. Sergeant Wright, captured during the night, got a brief glimpse of him. His Majesty complimented a British officer on the pluck shown by all ranks, and gave orders that all those captured in the raid should be treated well. He then offered to shake hands with the Briton, who stood at rigid attention ignoring the royal hand.

After inspecting the mole and the harbor, His Majesty telegraphed the General Staff that the British attack had been frustrated. Three light cruisers, he said, had managed to enter the Zeebrugge harbor and scuttle themselves, but to no avail.

This was correct. The blocking of the canal had failed. Submarines and destroyers were already bypassing the scuttled vessels. Materially little was accomplished by the raid, but the morale effects were tremendous. "It's done more for the honour and reputation of the Navy than anything in the war," said Admiral Sir Walter Cowan. Winston Churchill declared that the raid had given back the Navy "the panache that was lost at Jutland." There was rejoicing throughout the Allied world, for it proved that the British were not cowed by the great retreats on the Western Front. Englishmen knew how to fight and how to die. The gallantry at Zeebrugge was an inspiration to all those now trying to stem the German tide. And the eight who won the Victoria Cross along with all the others who fought at Zeebrugge deserved the plaudits they were receiving from a grateful nation.

2.

Lieutenant Seldte had been wakened by the guns of Zeebrugge. The windows of his bedroom were quivering. He thought at first that the thundering came from Mount Kemmel, but discovered that it was from the coast. He ordered his film crew to prepare for an emergency and hastened to the Intelligence officer for information. Hearing that it was a naval attack, Seldte said that at all costs he had to film what was going on. He was given permission to go but warned to return by evening. The attack on Kemmel was starting in two days.

The film unit's automobile raced through the dark to Brugge, where the Navy Corps insisted on sending along an artillery officer as their escort to the scene of the battle. The intensity of gunfire increased as their Benz speeded on the road parallel to the canal. As they approached the harbor, the first light of day appeared. The mole was covered by dense sea fog. Furious gunfire was in progress: heavy and light artillery, punctuated by rifle and machine-gun fire.

Seldte insisted on getting out to the action and commandeered a small motorboat. On the right he made out two half-sunk ships. On their decks he was surprised to see a large number of barrels. On the left was the mole. The connecting bridge had somehow been blown up. Further on sailors were lying inert or running about the mole. This must have been where the British had tried to land their assault party. Out in the mist to seaward the fire of the British warships was diminishing. It was an unaccustomed sight for an infantryman. Smoke, fumes, and fog prevented any filming. Seldte ordered the boat to proceed slowly. He surveyed the scene on both sides. Flashes from the shore batteries were spurting out. From the sea the British were still returning the fire. Shells dropped far to the right of his boat. As they struck, great fountains of water spewed up. When they hit the dunes, they raised what looked like gray-black trees.

Finally the sun came out and Seldte and his crew began to take pictures. They came alongside one of the British blockships. The barrels were filled with cement. He climbed onto the deck, which was awash. All over the deck lay crowbars, cordage, large shell cartridges lashed together in threes. What boldness and determination it had taken to carry out such an operation! He made his way across the slippery deck and, with two officers, climbed up to the bridge to silently survey the strange scene. He couldn't help admiring the boldness and determination of the Englishmen who had navigated these ships. A notable feat even if it had failed. Stout devils, those British bluejackets! "Wasn't it after all idiotic that we should be trying to smash in each other's skulls and tear out each other's throats and entrails? . . . If we fought not against one another, but side by side, couldn't we together smash the whole world, or rule and lead in co-operation?"

The next day his film unit drove to a village at the base of Mount Kemmel. As they walked through the empty, ruined streets, shells began to fall, and in minutes they were enshrouded in black fumes and clouds of red brick dust. Behind them lay the long ridge of Kemmel, which was alive with brown, black, and white shell bursts. Tomorrow it would be theirs.

At 2:30 A.M., April 25, Seldte was wakened. Outside he could see flashes from the slopes of Kemmel. It was normal. So far the enemy apparently had no suspicion what was coming. All at once there was a terrific crash and from hundreds of big guns gas shells began falling on French and British batteries and the rear areas. Shells exploded "like some terrific firework" and the ridge loomed out of the night as if floodlit. Fiery rockets shot up "as from the crater of a volcano."

At 4:30 A.M. the bombardment stopped for a half hour and, upon resumption, the front-line trenches became the main target. For almost an hour shells fell on the French positions "far worse," recalled one veteran, "than anything ever experienced at Verdun." By 6 A.M. practically all the French batteries were silenced or neutralized by gas. Only six French regiments held Kemmel and at this moment they were being assaulted by three and a half German divisions with the burden of the attack falling on the Alpine Corps (a division despite its name), which had failed to take the ridge near Bailleul on April 14. These troops were eager to atone for Bailleul and were only stopped by their own creeping barrage.

White flares shot up out of the smoke: shift fire forward! Almost instantly came a roaring, howling onslaught of shells.

As the film crew followed the onrushing Alpine troops, the silhouette of Kemmel was sharp against the morning sky. Ahead they could see Germans attacking through the undergrowth. Machine guns chattered; rifles crackled angrily; hand grenades exploded with dull thuds. Behind, field guns already were being dragged up the slope by gunners and infantrymen. As men ahead fell, fresh waves of infantrymen filled the gaps. They disappeared behind a rise, emerging like shadows against the nearest slope. Wounded started drifting back—German, French, English. A supporting battery was firing its guns rhythmically, without pause. The men were in high spirits, singing the gunner's fighting song: "'Wenn einer wüsst, Wie einem ist!'" Seldte saluted the officer in charge, who excitedly waved his arms and pointed to the crest of Kemmel. "Forward, forward!"

In minutes the film unit reached the first captured machine-gun nest. Camouflage nets had been torn aside, revealing evidence of grim hand-to-hand fighting. The enemy positions rose like terraces. Everywhere was a crashing, roaring din. The infantry worked its way higher and higher just behind the terrifying barrage. Seldte did his best to keep up with the advance and still film the amazing scenes around him. Just ahead the barrage was concentrated on the long slope of the hill. The top of Kemmel abruptly emerged and he saw silver flares darting up triumphantly. Mount Kemmel was German!

By 7:10 the Alpine Corps reached the summit. In half an hour it was secured and 800 prisoners taken. To the right, ten minutes later, a regiment of the 56th Division swarmed into Kemmel village and took 1,600 prisoners.

French infantry were already streaming down the other side of the hill, fleeing to the northwest. British troops coming up to join in the battle asked what had happened. The answer was one word, *"Gaz!"* The rush had put the Germans two thousand yards behind the British right flank positions held by the Royal Scots.

At 9:07 General von Lossberg, chief of staff of the Fourth Army, telephoned Ludendorff that everything was going well and he intended to develop the attack. Lossberg's enthusiasm was not shared by his superior, who stressed "the very possible delivery of counterattacks by the enemy and the necessity of keeping reserves well forward."

But Lossberg was so eager to extend the advance he telephoned the chief of staff of the Guard Corps that matters were developing successfully. Lossberg ordered him "to be ready to follow up if the British abandoned the Ypres salient."

Seldte's crew was filming the slope which was littered with dead. Throngs of prisoners streamed down from captured positions. This would make another wonderful picture to show the war-weary people back home what German soldiers could do. The pride and intoxication of being at such a historic scene overwhelmed the cameramen. They were dripping wet from exertion and excitement as they struggled up the last few hundred yards to the devastated crest of Kemmel. Before them lay a magnificent panorama: the smoke and fumes of battle and the fountains of earth as shells exploded. To the right they could see the towers of Ypres and a string of villages. To the left, out of sight, lay Calais and Dunkirk—and the English Channel.

A few hours later the Germans deciphered a British wireless message announcing the loss of Kemmel and the necessity of holding the line to the north. After consulting with subordinate commanders, Lossberg decided to resume the offensive the next morning.

In London that day there seemed to be more interest in their internal battles than in the grave loss of Mount Kemmel. Enemies of Lloyd George were charging that he, not Haig or Gough, was personally responsible for the debacle of March 21. And there was much gossip in high circles about "feather-headed" Lord Derby, who had been fired as War Minister and sent in semi-disgrace to Paris as Ambassador. Lloyd George was grumbling about Ireland. The day before, he had abused that unhappy land to Henry Wilson: "I wish your damned country was put at the bottom of the sea." Wilson chaffed that this was simply because the Prime Minister would not, or could not, govern Ireland. "Altogether," he noted in his diary, "Lloyd George's Government is in a rather rocky condition."

About the time the Germans were securing the summit of Kemmel, Wilson told Lord Milner, Derby's replacement, that if a Home Rule Bill was brought in putting Northern Ireland under Dublin there would be civil war; and there weren't enough troops in Ireland to cope with such a situation.

At the House of Commons, Churchill did talk about the military crisis and munitions production. The present problem, he said, was manpower. After appealing for men to enroll as war munitions volunteers, he praised working men and women for their great work. They certainly didn't deserve the "carping and croaking which goes on about the attitude of labour towards the War." He particularly commended the nearly three quarters of a million women employed by his Ministry of Munitions. They were responsible for 90 percent of "the shells which constitute the foundations of the power and terror of the British Artillery." He ended his hour-and-a-half address with a ringing tribute to the people of Britain. "No demand is too novel or too sudden to be met. No need is too unexpected to be supplied. No strain is too prolonged for the patience of our people. No suffering or peril daunt their hearts. Instead of quarreling, giving way as we do from time to time to moods of pessimism and of irritation, we ought to be thankful that if such trials and dangers were destined for our country we are here to share them, and to see them slowly and surely overcome." These last words could have been taken as criticism of those running the country, who were busy snapping at each other instead of inspiring the people.

Surprisingly, Lord Derby was assuming his new responsibilities as Ambassador to France with good humor. Haig found him "a different man! In such good spirits and eating well." At dinner he even slyly joked about his predicament. "Bad lot, these politicians, aren't they?" "I don't know," said Haig with a chuckle. "I haven't had much experience with them." Everyone laughed at this. "You are a qualified diplomat yourself," said Derby. "We shall yet see you as Our Honored Representative." Derby enjoyed dealing with the French and was getting along well with Clemenceau. On the day Kemmel fell, he wrote his close friend, Foreign Secretary Balfour: "What amuses me is Clemenceau's open contempt of our P.M. He evidently thinks he can do what he wants with him."

The next day Henry Wilson made another trip to France. Unlike most passengers he enjoyed the trip across the Channel and always made his way to the bridge no matter how rough the weather. He first visited Haig's headquarters at Montreuil, where he learned that the French had given up Kemmel after several hours' bombardment without much of a fight. "How they managed to leave it," Haig had just written his wife, "I don't know."

Early that afternoon Haig himself visited that area for two reasons. He wanted a firsthand look at the critical situation and he also wished to confer with Admiral Keyes. They met at Second Army headquarters. With General Plumer they watched British guns blasting the top of Mount Kemmel. Later Haig told Keyes that, since it was essential to keep contact with the left flank of the French Army, Dunkirk might have to be abandoned before long.

Keyes protested. Dunkirk was vital to safeguard communications across the Channel. Haig replied that "it was a choice of evils, and we simply could not afford to lose touch with the French left, and heaven only knew where that would be before long."

Keyes returned to Dunkirk feeling rather depressed, while Haig arrived back at his headquarters still fuming over the French retreat. In his diary he wrote that cavalry had to "collect French fugitives from Kemmel, and prevent a rout. What Allies to fight with!"

The following morning, April 27, Haig met with Clemenceau, Foch, Milner, and Wilson at Abbeville. Tempers flared during a discussion of Kemmel. Foch used the French losses as an excuse to deny any support to the British, who were fighting off heavy attacks in the Amiens area. Wilson pointed out that in the past month the sixty British divisions had suffered 300,000 casualties while Foch's hundred divisions only had lost between 60,000 and 70,000. "If this goes on," he said, "and we start a *roulement*, the British Army will disappear and we shall lose the war." He proposed that the French take some of the punishment, but Foch stubbornly refused to relieve during a battle.

After the meeting broke up Wilson went for a walk with Clemenceau. "I then tried to find out whether Foch favoured covering the ports or retiring behind the Somme. I tried hard, but he absolutely refused to consider the problem. He said that he would not go back a yard, that he would stop the Boche, etc., etc. Of course, this must not rest here, and I mean to have it out. The attitudes of Foch and Tiger were difficult, and it is clear to me that we must assert ourselves much more."

The attacks in the Kemmel area continued and on the morning of April 29 a report was received at Haig's headquarters that the Germans had pushed on to capture those hills beyond Kemmel, the Scherpenberg, along with the whole range of the Mount Rouge-Mount Noir heights. "The news was so serious, so unexpected, and so unaccountable," recalled one of Haig's staff officers, George Dewar, "that it was received with a gasp of incredulous laughter." Even the French couldn't have collapsed so completely! The loss was confirmed by General Plumer, who had been in direct communication with the French corps concerned. "Incredulity gave place to acute anxiety and redoubled activity." Plumer's entire Second Army was in desperate danger.

"My experience is that the situation is never so bad, nor so good as first reports indicate," Haig told his chief of staff, but he left for the north as fast as his car could take him. An hour later a third report came in: the entire story was a mistake started by an overexcited French artillery observer.

While Haig was up north he talked first with Plumer and then General Godley of XXII Corps, who was very disgusted with the action, or rather inaction, of the French. "They produce excellent orders, talk about organisation 'en profondeur' but nothing ever happens."

The French debacle at Mount Kemmel was the main topic of discussion in Paris. "I am quite certain the French are letting us down—and bady too," wrote Derby, whose reputation for weakness was not altogether justified. Admittedly of a wavering nature, and an inveterate gossip, the new ambassador was a shrewd observer of human nature and his lengthy informal letters to the Foreign Secretary were revealing if a bit malicious. "Their one idea is to cover Paris and I am sure they look upon keeping the Channel ports as being quite of a secondary matter. The division that was detached to defend Kemmel was a division which had been taken out of the line further south because it had fought badly! They made no attempt to defend the place. There is apparently not only a bitter feeling between French and English—but in our army. I am afraid there is a feeling with regard to Robertson's resignation —or whatever it was—and they are inclined especially in the higher ranks to put a lot of blame on Wilson for all our troubles." He repeated his conviction that Clemenceau was anti-Lloyd George, only, he stressed, to put Balfour on guard. "I can't trust the P.M.

He never believes anything which is not in accordance with his own views! and Henry Wilson is *too* French."

Fortunately for the Allies, the bad feeling between French and British, as well as their own internal feuds, was not accompanied by a vigorous German attack. Ludendorff's troops had run out of supplies and energy. Their assault groups were exhausted and becoming dispirited. At dinner that night General Butler of III Corps told Haig that the enemy was not fighting with the same determination he showed at the beginning of the battle. "The prisoners too seem now to be careless as to who wins as long as the war ends."

Next day Lieutenant Heinrich Lamm's company near Mount Kemmel was attacked and he crawled out to the forward positions to see what had happened. Finding the first guard "sleeping like a sack," he smacked him with a broom. The man cleared his throat and fell back to sleep. The next guard was also asleep. Lamm did nothing, for he saw this was not normal sleep, but almost like death. These men were utterly exhausted by continual battle. He hurried to the next guard, who was half awake. "Seventh Company?" asked Lamm. The other man only said, "Mm," in a daze and didn't even know there had been an attack. My God, he must have slept through it! Lamm crawled along with his broom, looking for his missing company. He found empty trenches, deserted shelters. He kept calling, "Seventh Company!" Silence. "Can't you at least answer me?" he shouted. "Must you sleep the whole night!" Peng! Peng! Bullets whistled past his ears. "It's me, you jokers!" he shouted. He crawled into a dark shelter, touched something soft. It was a comrade, asleep. He shook the man. No answer. Then he felt the face. Ice cold! An electric shock went through his body. The helmet was English. It was an enemy. Something rustled. "Seventh Company?" No answer. "A nice company," he said. "Can't you answer at all? Where is the corporal?"

Suddenly shouting men in kilts charged at him with bayonets. All Lamm could do was exclaim, "I'm lost!" A Highlander fingered the German's shoulder strap and said, "One officer!" The fierce-looking enemy all at once became friendly. Everyone offered him a drink. Lamm thanked them but refused. One fat Highlander who smelled strongly of alcohol kept pushing a bottle at him. "Drink, Comrade!" Another offered him a piece of bread. In appreciation Lamm handed over his pistol.

It was the end of the war for him; and the end of the second German offensive. Bitterly disappointed, Ludendorff called off the battle. Twice he had come close to victory, but this time several German divisions had been reluctant to attack and others had looted and drunk themselves senseless after success. He blamed all this on the Reichstag for weakening military discipline.

In each offensive he had won tactical success and had scored a breakthrough. But each time he had failed to reach his strategic aim. Perhaps that aim was impossible to realize. For each of the two great attacks had ended in a battle of attrition. The modern battle of material seemed to defy Schlieffen's postulate of "the decisive battle."

3.

On May Day the Supreme War Council met again, this time under no pressure of imminent disaster, but with the usual sharp differences of opinion. Clemenceau began by berating both the Americans and British. He opposed the recent agreement between Pershing and Lord Milner to let the British have the entire May allotment of 100,000 American troops. "The French have not been consulted," he said with some petulance. "We might suppose that in compensation the Americans troops arriving in June would be given to France. But it now appears they are also to join the British. I wish to protest that this is unsatisfactory."

Ordinarily calm, Milner was incensed. "M. Clemenceau has intimated there was something mysterious about the London agreement." He and Pershing had no intention of depriving France of any American troops. "I do not know that anything has been said regarding their allotment on arrival in France. We simply wanted to hasten their coming."

Pershing was just as irritated as Milner. "There is no agreement between my Government and anyone else that a single American soldier shall be sent to either the British or French." He pointed out that Clemenceau himself had approved that six divisions should go to the beleaguered British.

Clemenceau tried to brush this aside. "Well, I won't argue about that," he said, and grumbled that when four are in alliance two of them can't act independently. "I accept what has been done for May, but I want to know what is intended for June."

With supreme tact, Lloyd George restored harmony. "I am of M. Clemenceau's opinion. The interests of the Allies are identical; we must not lost sight of that, otherwise the unity of command has no meaning." He reminded the French that ten British divisions had been so severely handled since March 21 that they could not be reconstituted.

While admitting this, Foch pointed out France's recent serious losses. "So American aid is now needed almost as much for France as for Great Britain." The long-drawn argument continued to the obvious distaste of Haig. What a waste of time! Most annoying was Pershing's insistence on America having its own army. "I must insist on its being recognized," he had announced. "The principle of unity must prevail in our army. It must be completely under its own command. I should like to have a date fixed when this will be realized." How very obstinate and stupid, thought Haig. Pershing did not seem to realize the urgency of the situation. "He hankers after a *great self-contained American Army*' but seeing that he has neither Commanders of Divisions, of Corps, nor of Armies, nor Staffs for same, it is ridiculous to think such an Army could function unaided in less than two years' time." Henry Wilson agreed heartily. Pershing, he wrote in his diary, was "maddeningly mulish."

During the day Clemenceau protested to Derby that there were a million trained soldiers in England, kept there only for home defense. Derby tried to explain that these were invalids, sick and wounded, prison guards, troops manning forts and anti-aircraft stations. "Rest assured," he said, "that whatever men we have who are fit for service will be sent to France." But it was apparent, Derby wrote Balfour, that Clemenceau didn't believe a word he said. "And I am sure," he added, "that the feeling of doubt that he expressed on the subject is one that is shared by both Clemenceau and Foch . . . As I have told you before, there is no doubt a strong undercurrent of feeling existing in this country against us, and it is based on the idea that we are not doing all that we can or ought to do in the way of man power."

The next morning a secret meeting between the French and English was held at a private home in Abbeville to discuss the military crisis. In the event of unavoidable retirement, asked General Wilson, should they fall back on the Channel ports or retire behind the Somme? *"Ni l'un ni l'autre* [Neither one nor the other]!" persisted Foch. To Wilson this was no answer and he repeated the question.

Haig cut in to say that it was vital to hold on to the French. Separation from the French lines, he said, would mean absolute disaster, as both army and ports would be lost. Cornered, Foch said that if the ports were lost he would fall back to the south. But that would never happen—*"Jamais, jamais, jamais!"* He kept repeating the phrase in half-bantering tones along with such phrases as *"Ne bougez pas, ne bougez pas; jamais, jamais, jamais."* Through all this Lloyd George, Milner, and Clemenceau sat in wondering silence.

"It was a remarkable scene," recalled Hankey, "Henry Wilson, Haig and Pétain arguing for withdrawal behind the Somme, Foch half-chaffing, half-contemptuous, rejecting the whole thesis, the statesmen listening for once instead of talking most of the time and vastly intrigued at the experience." Foch won his way and it was decided unanimously that the British would hold on to the French first, and the ports second.

Although Lloyd George had played little part in this hot discussion, Haig wrote his wife after the Prime Minister's departure for England: "I must say that I am not sorry to see the back of Lloyd George; he strikes me as such a thorough humbug. Always most civil to me, personally, and very entertaining at dinner, but I fear only thinks of what will pay himself and is thoroughly dishonest."

4.

Ever since Lloyd George's unwise and false remarks in Commons on April 9, his opponents had been sniping at his claim that the British Army was stronger on March 21 than it had been for a year. His unjustified slur on Haig and Gough came back to haunt him a few days before the Germans took Mount Kemmel. On April 22, the War Office reported in its Weekly Summary that the German infantry had outnumbered the Allies in the great offensive by 330,000 men. Lloyd George was outraged—and caught off balance. "Alas!" he later wrote. "All of a sudden our superiority disappeared in a weekend! . . . The disaster that tore such a yawning chasm in the Allied battalions occurred not on the blood-stained fields of France but in a carpeted chamber of the War Office. The devastation of our ranks was not wrought by German artillery but by a British fountain pen." These new figures, he reasoned, had been suddenly produced only to embarrass him. "I realised that the battle had been transferred to the Home Front."

His fury was turned on the new War Minister, Lord Milner, who had permitted the new figures to be published by his department. Was it a blunder by an old, exhausted man? An oversight? Or part of the conspiracy to drive him out of office? He wrote Milner a scorching note challenging the new figures as "extraordinarily slipshod," and called for a thorough investigation of those responsible for issuing the dastardly document.

He also brought up the subject before the Cabinet. Wilson could not explain the discrepancy between the figures and disclaimed all responsibility. Nor did the Director of Military Intelligence know anything of the fresh estimate. The culprit was evidently General Frederick Maurice, who had that day been relieved of his duties as Director of Military Operations. Lloyd George had done so out of suspicion that Maurice—a close friend and confidant of former Chief of Staff Robertson—was now openly working against the Government. Release of the embarrassing report, he was sure, had been Maurice's revenge.

It was true that Maurice had stoutly supported Robertson, Haig, and others detested by Lloyd George, but he had nothing to do with the report. The son of a distinguished soldier and the grandson of F. D. Maurice, the Christian Socialist, he was described by the *Manchester Guardian* as "the most dry, reserved and punctilious man in the War Office." He had not even read Lloyd George's April 9 speech until the twentieth. It had shocked him, for he considered it "clearly an attempt to shovel off responsibility on the soldiers while appearing to treat them generously."

Two days later Maurice left for a week's leave in the country, where he finally had time to study the Prime Minister's speech. "Simultaneously," he wrote afterward, "I learned that a scheme for removing Haig from the supreme command in France was rapidly coming to a head." This was part of the Prime Minister's assault on the Army: first Robertson, then Gough and Haig.* Moreover

* Recently Gough had written Sergeant Maze: "As for myself I am quite unmoved by my so-called evil fortune, as my own conscience is clear and I know the 5th Army fought and was fought out, magnificently. But I am anxious about the general situation, it is not too good anyhow and to add to it, we have these vile and rotten politicians surrounded with their intrigues, at the head of the Government. They are our real danger."

he was seriously concerned by the constant slurs cast upon the Army and by the effect all this was having on morale in the armed forces.

Maurice felt that something should be done and he should do it, regardless of the cost to himself. He told his wife of the personal crisis he was facing and of his growing conviction that if Lloyd George's vendetta against the Army succeeded the war would be lost. He also told her that the truth was being withheld from the people and could only come to light if Parliament discovered the facts. A devoutly religious woman, she supported his resolve.

On the last day of April he wrote Henry Wilson, calling his attention to the incorrect statements made by the Prime Minister and Bonar Law, his Chancellor of the Exchequer. "The general effect has been, I am told, to produce a feeling of distrust and lack of confidence in France." There being no reply, on May 5 Maurice wrote his children, Nancy and Frederick:

> I have decided to take a very important step which may make a great difference to our lives, and I want you to know about it before it happens; but you must not tell a soul before you hear it in the papers.
>
> You know that for some time past, the Government has not been telling the truth about the War. Their object is to show that they did everything possible and that the blame rests with the Generals. This is absolutely untrue, and I am one of the few people who know the facts. I am, in fact, the only soldier who knows them and is not actually employed. I have therefore decided to write the letter, which I enclose, to the papers, and I hope it will appear on Tuesday. This is, of course, a breach of military discipline; but there are occasionally—not often, thank God!—times when duty as a citizen comes before duty as a soldier; and after long and careful thought, I am convinced this is one of them. They may turn me out of the Army and you may suffer in consequence, though I will do my best to see that you don't. I hope you will think that I am right. Mother has never wavered since I told her, and that has been a great support to me.
>
> I am persuaded that I am doing what is right, and once that is so, nothing else matters to a man. This is, I believe, what Christ meant when he told us to forsake father and mother and children and wife for His sake. It has been a difficult decision, for, as you know I love the Army and I have you all and Mother to think of, but it is made now, and you must help me to make the best of it.
>
> > Your loving
> > Father.

His own integrity, as well as the tradition of social conscience inherited from his family, made it impossible for him to do otherwise. "I knew that I was sacrificing a career of some promise and

164

giving up my means of livelihood," he later wrote, "but I believed that I was acting rightly, and that if I was right, I would not suffer materially."

The following day he took the letter to Colonel Repington of the *Morning Post*. In it Maurice flatly said that statements made by Lloyd George on April 9 formed part "of a series of misstatements which have been made recently in the House of Commons by the present government." He then assured the public that "this letter is not the result of a military conspiracy" but was written "in the hope that Parliament may see fit to order an investigation into the statements I have made." Repington's superior agreed to publish the letter the following day. Maurice also sent copies to *The Times, Daily News, Daily Chronicle* and *Daily Telegraph*, then left for the country, resolved that he would not take a personal role in the controversy that was certain to erupt in the morning.

On May 7, all of the newspapers printed the letter except the *Daily Telegraph*. The charge that Lloyd George's statement that the Army had been stronger in 1918 than a year earlier was false created even more of a sensation than Maurice envisaged. The *Morning Post* lauded the former Director of Military Operations for his "chivalry" and attacked the Prime Minister for failing to keep the Western Front up to its proper strength, and now "not even his Press will be able to save him." The loyal papers, the *Daily Express* and the *Daily Mail*, predictably assaulted Maurice and were even more violent against Asquith, the opposition leader, who was calling for an inquiry into the allegations. But the *Manchester Guardian*, usually friendly to the Government, declared that Maurice's statements "went to the heart of the responsibility for our recent reverses."

As soon as Henry Wilson got to his office, he asked the Adjutant General to write an official letter to Maurice asking why he had written such a letter. Then the Chief of Staff went to Downing Street, where the Cabinet held "a long argument and wrangle," finally agreeing to set up a Court of Honour, consisting of two judges of the High Court, "to enquire into the charge of misstatements alleged to have been made" by Lloyd George and Bonar Law.

But at 5 P.M. Lloyd George called Hankey to say that he had decided to resist Asquith's proposal for an inquiry. Instead he would "make a great speech" to Parliament "in which he would tell as much as possible, and perhaps more than he would have wished." He gave Hankey the task of preparing the brief for such an address. Hankey had already been writing "an immense précis of the whole affair" since lunch. Working with relays of stenographers, he completed the brief at 9:30 P.M. and brought it to Lloyd George. "I had to do the whole thing myself because much of it was in the proceedings of international conferences and minutes of especially 'hush' meetings of the War Cabinet and some in this diary even. Of course the issue is immensely wider than the small

165

charges in Maurice's letter." The fate of the Government hung in the balance.

That evening the lobbies of Parliament were in a hubbub. The entire country was extremely excited, for the Maurice scandal was being supported or damned in countless homes, public meetings, bars, boardrooms, and pubs.

Reuter's reports to France were read eagerly by everyone at Haig's headquarters. They admired Freddy Maurice's pluck in publishing the letter, "and whatever other effects it may have," wrote General John Charteris in his diary, "it should go far to bring about a more wholesome atmosphere in the Cabinet and Parliament. There are strange rumours here that L.G. had intended to remove D.H. [Douglas Haig] to succeed Lord French as Commander-in-Chief at home, and that Maurice's letter has at least stopped that scheme, and D.H. remains here for the time being. General —— came to see me today, full of admiration for Maurice, and anxious to write himself and endorse Maurice's facts. ——'s letter would of course be authoritative, for he deals with the side of the question here; but it would bring D.H. into it, and unless L.G. fails, that would inevitably mean D.H.'s removal. I am afraid Maurice will have to stand alone."

Haig, however, let it be known that he believed the Maurice letter was very ill-advised since it offended his ideas of discipline. All the same he admired Maurice for writing it. "It will be a salutary check on the Cabinet's fixed belief that they can publish any misstatement they like without any contradiction from the Services."

In Paris, Lord Derby was enjoying the fracas from afar. In another long letter to London, this congenial gossip couldn't conceive why Maurice had taken such a drastic step. "Of course he is a great friend of Robertson and a bitter foe of Henry Wilson and he may want to bring the latter down together with the P.M. in revenge for the treatment of Robertson. Here the whole place is buzzing and the result is disastrous. They are always arguing here that we give them false figures about our man power. It is apparently Clemenceau's favorite topic and here, they say, is justification for all we have said because I must tell you that Maurice speaks the truth and not our beloved P.M. or melancholy Bonar! Of course amongst the French soldiers there is I am told only one feeling—of blank astonishment at such a thing being possible—for an officer of high standing to give the lie direct to the Government of the day is to him an unheard of—and undreamt of —— [this word undecipherable in original manuscript] and they are wondering how soon he will be shot. I suppose the P.M. will be able—in his own sweet way—to reconcile his figures with facts . . ."

Next morning, May 8, the *Daily Mirror* headline read:

PREMIER TO ASK HOUSE TO JUDGE MAURICE
Mr. Lloyd George to Give Facts and Figures
in Open Session To-Morrow
TO STAND OR FALL BY THE DECISION

The *Express* countered, quoting the Prime Minister's sarcastic reference to the coming debate as "Maurice's dance." The paper scathingly pointed to the strange bedfellows in the Maurice camp. "Pacifists and placemen are reinforced by the ultra-Tories, who have not yet discovered that we are in the twentieth century and that the war has caused every social arrangement to suffer a sea change, and by the extreme militarists, who resent civilian control and would have us governed by a junta of generals." Most of Labour and the trade union movement also vigorously supported Lloyd George. One group of workers at Woolwich Arsenal telegraphed him: HOLD FAST. WE ARE WITH YOU, BECAUSE YOU ARE THE PEOPLE'S PRIME MINISTER AND OUR SYMBOL OF VICTORY. THE GERMANS WANT YOU TO GO: BUT WE THE WORKERS, DO NOT WANT YOU TO GO. YOUR ENEMIES ARE OUR ENEMIES! DAMN THEM ALL! GOD SAVE ENGLAND!

During the Cabinet meeting, Lloyd George told his colleagues what he intended to say the next day and at 6 P.M. rehearsed his speech for Milner, Chamberlain, and Hankey, who "cut it about a good deal." The Prime Minister was confident and in good spirits.

The day of the debate, Thursday, May 9, was fine and bright. There was no Cabinet meeting and at 1 P.M. Hankey was at 10 Downing Street, checking the notes of Lloyd George's speech and making some alterations. In fighting trim, the Prime Minister was on the terrace walking up and down with Bonar Law. The latter felt insulted by Maurice and was nervous. "The case," he fretted, "seems so strong that I cannot help feeling that Maurice, who is a clever man, has something up his sleeve." He need not have worried. The leader of the opposition, Asquith, was preparing his own speech without the help of Maurice, who had unwisely kept his resolve to remain in the country. This fatalistic, almost masochistic attitude was characteristic of Maurice. From the beginning he had predicted, as if from presentiment, that he would have to suffer for his action.

Hankey lunched alone with the Prime Minister as he always did before a major speech. Though cheerful the latter was in a chastened mood. "He admitted that speeches dealing with facts and figures were not his strong point, and that his Celtic temperament made him unable to resist stretching them to their entire limits." Since we was in "a much less truculent frame of mind than usual," Hankey took the opportunity of urging Lloyd George to let the new Viceroy of Ireland form an Irish Cabinet as preparation for Home Rule and to try voluntary recruiting before enforcing conscription. To Hankey's delight, the Prime Minister agreed.

By the time Lloyd George reached the House of Commons he was as fit and bouncing as a champion boxer entering the ring. Asquith opened the debate with a suave, highly polished and ineffective speech calling for a Select Committee to investigate the Maurice charges. He barely mentioned the Maurice letter itself, and his verbose comments were finally interrupted by a minor MP who shouted, "Get on with the war!"

167

Within moments after Lloyd George took the floor, he had the House in hand, thanks to a brilliant concoction of truth, half-truth, and misstatement that crushed the Maurice charges. The killing blow came when he categorically stated, "The figures I gave were taken from the official records of the War Office, for which I sent before I made the statement. If they were incorrect, General Maurice was as responsible as anyone else . . . There is absolutely no doubt that there was a very considerable addition to the man-power of the Army in France at the beginning of 1918 as compared with the man-power at the beginning of 1917." He expressed regret that Mr. Asquith had failed to deprecate General Maurice's grave breach of discipline, which set a most subversive example to the Army at large, and conluded with a plea to the Members to rally behind the Government in this worst crisis of the war. "I really beg and implore, for our common country, the fate of which is in the balance now and in the next few weeks, that there should be an end of this sniping."

Opposition was crushed and Walter Runciman, who was to have wound up for the opposition, looked utterly miserable. He never rose. The vote was an anticlimax, with the Government defeating the opposition by 293–106. A pretty girl sitting next to the wife of the leader of the opposition said, "I suppose, Mrs. Asquith, my poor father's case will never be heard."

"Is your father General Maurice?" It was. "No, my dear, the Government will take good care of that."

The man who had written the brief, Hankey, thought that the speech was a superb parliamentary effort. "Nevertheless I felt all the time that it was not the speech of a man who tells 'the truth; the whole truth; and nothing but the truth.' For example, while he had figures from the D.M.O.'s Dept. showing that the fighting strength of the army had increased from 1st Jan. 1917 to 1918, he had the Adjutant-General's figures saying the precise contrary, but was discreetly silent about them. This knowledge embarrassed me a little when M.P.s of all complexions kept coming to the official gallery to ask me what was the 'real truth.' " *

Most of the press hailed Lloyd George's great victory as an end to any further serious opposition. "Maurice was apparently crushed," wrote Wilson in his diary, "and he ought to be. I think he is mad for vanity."

In Paris, there was little sympathy for Maurice. That day Derby wrote Balfour that the affair was creating the very worst impression. "Quite apart from the extraordinary lack of discipline it shows and which has shocked the French people, both soldiers and civilians, it is looked upon as an attack on the Supreme War Council and as such is bitterly resented. Asquith having taken the question up has made them even more suspicious." At luncheon with American Ambassador William Sharp and French Foreign

---

* This passage was deleted from Hankey's own account of the debate, apparently out of loyalty to his employer. Fortunately Hankey's able biographer, Stephen Roskill, had loyalty only to the facts.

Minister Pichon, Derby took it upon himself "to state definitely that the question of the Supreme War Council was in no danger, especially emphasising the loyalty of Haig to Foch and saying that was symbolical of the loyalty of the whole country and the Army to this Supreme Command." This comment pleased both listeners, and Derby concluded his letter with the hope that he had done some good.

While Haig remained loyal and still decried Maurice's action, he wrote his wife: "Poor Maurice! How terrible to see the House of Commons so easily taken in by a clap-trap speech by Lloyd George. The House is really losing its reputation as an assmbly of common-sense Britishers. However, I don't suppose that Maurice has done with L.G. yet."

"Soldiers are so stupid," Lord Esher, a man of sound sense and sly malice, wrote to Hankey. "They never understand that politics is not a battle. Maurice will be let down by all those who have used him." Clemenceau's comment was, "Why do soldiers try to fence with politicians?"

On May 11 General Maurice was retired on the half pay of a major—£225 a year. It was a spiteful piece of vengeance that was resented by many military men. And those in the War Office who knew that Lloyd George had used false figures were so indignant they passed this information on to their chief, Lord Milner. This strictly honorable man brought it up at a meeting on May 15 after everyone was dismissed except Lloyd George, Hankey, Wilson, and himself. He revealed that a mistake had been discovered about the figures of the British fighting strength. Of course, the Prime Minister already knew this but, pretending innocence, replied that he could not be held responsible for an error which had been made in General Maurice's department—and that ended the whole matter.

Colonel Walter Kirke, responsible for issuing the first incorrect figures, had expected that the House of Commons would be informed of the mistake and so rectify the injustice done Maurice. Indignant, he wrote a minute to the Director of Military Operations, Maurice's successor, requesting that the correction be made without delay. General P. deB. Radcliffe replied that it was not in the interests of the Service to take further action. "I consider that you have done all that is necessary or desirable in the matter, and I will take the responsibility for it."

Although Maurice was officially discredited, he accepted a handsome offer to write for the *Daily Chronicle*. This brought an admonitory but friendly letter from Lord Milner impressing on him the importance of not giving information to the enemy in his articles. Maurice politely replied that he "would not indulge in any recriminations nor attempt to open the case until I am asked authoritatively to do so." He added: "I shall regard the Censor as a help and not as an enemy, as it is always possible that I may quite inadvertently hint at something which it is not in the public interests to have published."

On that same day, May 17, General Robertson also wrote Milner assuring him that the rumors being circulated that he was conspiring with Maurice, Asquith, and others to bring down the Lloyd George Government were utterly false. Milner replied that he had heard the rumors but never credited them. "As you say, there is 'much mischief and intrigue in the air.' I am doing all I possibly can to put a stop to a most poisonous controversy, which threatens not only to sow distrust of the civil authorities in the Army, but, on the other hand, to excite public opinion against some of our leading soldiers, and again to create factions within the Army itself. All this is thoroughly bad, and every man, who has the country's interest at heart, must leave no stone unturned to put a stop to it. I feel confident that you will help in this, and I can assure you that I on my side will continue to do what lies in my power in the same direction. Whether it is the 'Morning Post' abusing the Government, or the 'Daily Mail' abusing what it calls 'the old gang'—it is *all equally detestable*. And with the enemy at our gates we simply must close our ranks and put an end to this eternal discord."

This was advice sorely needed by all the Allies, but unfortunately Lord Milner now had little influence with Lloyd George, who pettishly excluded him from meetings of the War Cabinet on the grounds that "the old man's" health was failing. Nor was there any sign that the Prime Minister's bitter feud with his generals was ending.* It was tragic that two such extraordinary and able men as Haig and Lloyd George were at odds. Despite faults, Haig was the best man to lead the army and Lloyd George the best to lead the nation. They disagreed only on one major point: Haig felt the war could only be won on the Western Front, while the Prime Minister wanted a victory that cost fewer lives. Both were dedicated to defeating Germany, but to gain it they would have to work in tandem. "There are upon the side of the Allies only two fighters," Lord Esher wrote Haig, "you and Lloyd George. I apologize for the bracket but it is a hard fact." It is difficult to imagine two men more unlike in appearance, size, demeanor, temperament, and character. But both had proved plucky in adversity, and the winning of the war would probably depend on their working in harmony.

Though the second German offensive had been stopped, Ludendorff was already planning two more. There remained doubt that sufficient Americans could be properly trained in time to help stop these new attacks. And it was obvious to those behind the scenes that the French Army was far from the formidable force it was before the 1917 mutinies. Their people were also war-weary, and

---

* A few days earlier Haig wrote his wife: "I hope you are not troubling your little head over the idle gossip which is passed on to you regarding me and the possibility of my being appointed Commander in Chief at home. I have every confidence in Milner as S of S for War. He is not mixed up in Politics, and I am convinced he is an honest man and means to do his best for the Army and the Country, without considering his own personal interests."

170

many French workers, inflamed by left-wing pacifists, were disgruntled. Recently four cavalry divisions had to be held in the interior to handle disorders. Strikes in the Loire could only be quelled by force, and another major strike had just broken out in the Paris Renault factory. These workers were protesting the draft, the use of foreigners in the plant, and the rejection of the enemy's peace offers made in 1917. Derby summed it up: "I think this period of tension in waiting for the great attack is having rather a bad effect on people's nerves, and their confidence is a little oozing out."

The fate of the world was still at stake in mid-May and victory for the Allies would have to be won at home, as well as on the battlefield.

Chapter Seven

INTERVENTION I
MARCH 18–MAY 26

1.

ON March 18, three days before Ludendorff had launched Operation Michael, a message from Foreign Secretary Balfour was delivered to President Wilson, warning him that the danger in the East was now "great and imminent." The new Bolshevist nation was at the mercy of German exploitation and only Allied intervention from Siberia and the northern ports would save the day. He stressed that Japan would send troops to Vladivostok only as a friend of Russia, and under the mandate of the Allies. This was the only solution, concluded Balfour, but it could not be effected without American support.

Even so President Wilson could not be persuaded to abandon his "hands-off" policy, and it took unexpected events in Vladivostok to change stalemate into crisis. On March 24 Bolsheviks seized the telegraph office. Rumors began to spread of a combined German-Bolshevik attack on Allied war stores in the port. Two days later, Admiral Knight, commander of the American Asiatic Fleet, telegraphed that there was marked unrest in the city "with danger of conflict between Soviet . . . and conservatives." Forty-eight hours later he reported that the danger the supplies would be commandeered was such that it "may compel us to land."

On the morning of April 4, several men in Bolshevik uniforms entered a Japanese shop with a demand for money. After the staff refused, the raiders opened fire, wounding three clerks. One died. Early the next morning the Japanese naval commander, Admiral

171

Kato, on his own initiative landed five hundred marines "to safeguard the lives and property of Japanese citizens." They were followed shortly by fifty marines from the British cruiser *Suffolk*, with orders to guard the consulate. British involvement had come because of a snap judgment by a Japanese officer and without any consultation between the two countries. The American, Admiral Knight, merely watched the operation. The Bolsheviks were taken by surprise and there was no resistance as the foreigners took up positions throughout the city.

There was instant alarm in Moscow. Lenin telegraphed Vladivostok: IT IS PROBABLE, IN FACT ALMOST INEVITABLE, THAT THE JAPANESE WILL ADVANCE. UNDOUBTEDLY, THE ALLIES WILL HELP THEM. WE MUST PREPARE OURSELVES IMMEDIATELY, STRAINING ALL ENERGIES TO THIS END.

With Trotsky now Commissar for War, a statement was issued by Georgi Chicherin, the new Foreign Commissar. It denied any knowledge of the murder of the merchant and charged that the Japanese imperialists only wished "to strangle the Soviet revolution, to cut Russia off from the Pacific Ocean, to seize the rich territories of Siberia, and to enslave the Siberian workers and peasants." And what were the plans of the Allies? "The American Government, it seems, was against the Japanese invasion. But now the situation can no longer remain indefinite. England intends to act hand in hand with Japan in working Russia's ruin."

That evening Chicherin summoned representatives of the Allies for an explanation and in the morning sent them notes demanding immediate withdrawal of those troops which had landed. A special memorandum was dispatched to Colonel Raymond Robins, the amateur diplomat in charge of the American Red Cross, asking for "a full and definite immediate statement of the attitude of your Government towards the occurrence which has taken place at Vladivostok." Robins himself was indignant. "Stupid and vicious," he described the Japanese-English intervention in his diary. "War or a war policy. How full of the evil such plans are."

He replied guardedly to Chicherin, urging that the Vladivostok incident be treated as local and could be "settled by friendly diplomacy." Robins reported all this to American Ambassador Francis, adding a warning that if further intervention took place the Russians would declare war on Japan and their resentment against Germany would be transferred to the Allies. "We are now at most dangerous crisis in Russian situation, and if colossal blunder of hostile Japanese intervention takes place all American advantages are confiscated." Should the Japanese advance, he said, the Soviets would take this to mean that America agreed to it.

Lord Balfour's first reaction was simultaneously to reassure and scold the Bolsheviks. He instructed Lockhart to assure Trotsky that marines had landed only to protect British property; then to imply that Bolshevik disorders in Vladivostok were the real cause of the landings.

The peril of foreign invasion, in the name of friendly intervention, was accompanied by a crumbling of control from within Russia. And the growing strength of the right-wing Whites was accompanied by dangerous assaults from the far left. The large cities themselves were under a sort of siege from anarchists. They had established clubs in expropriated homes and buildings and were applying the Bolshevik slogan "Loot the looters." Many of these clubs were truly anarchistic, but some were run by criminals and others by White officers posing as revolutionaries to mask their anti-Red activities. The anarchists had their own big daily newspaper in Moscow, *Anarkhiya*, which was both idealistic and demagogic with little grounding in reality. In a city stricken by famine, the sincere demagoguery of these libertarian anarchists appealed to the less educated. Although there were only several thousand activists, these were directed by a "Black General Staff" and constituted an irresponsible, uncontrollable armed State within the State.

At last on April 11—the same day Haig issued his dramatic "Backs to the wall" communiqué—the Bolsheviks decided to disarm the robber bands. A detailed plan was worked for liquidating the anarchist centers by detachments of Red Army troops and the Cheka, the secret police. The action began at midnight. Armored cars surrounded twenty-six anarchist houses which were protected by machine guns. The anarchists were asked to surrender their arms immediately, and given five minutes for reflection. Most complied and some five hundred people were arrested. But those who resisted fought bitterly with more than a hundred being wounded or killed. Afterward, at the invitation of the Cheka commander, Raymond Robins and Bruce Lockhart, the British agent, toured the fighting areas with a Cheka guide, Jakob Peters, who had lived so long in England he had a Cockney accent. Lockhart was appalled as they entered house after house. "The filth was indescribable. Broken bottles littered the floors. The magnificent ceilings were perforated with bullet-holes. Wine stains and human excrement blotched the Aubusson carpets. Priceless pictures had been slashed to strips. The dead still lay where they had fallen. They included officers in guards' uniforms, students—young boys of twenty and men who belonged obviously to the criminal class and whom the revolution had released from prison. In the luxurious drawing room of the House Gracheva the Anarchists had been surprised in the middle of an orgy. The long table which had supported the feast had been overturned, and broken plates, glasses, champagne bottles, made unsavoury islands in a pool of blood and spilt wine. On the floor lay a young woman face downwards. Peters turned her over. Her hair was dishevelled. She had been shot through the neck, and the blood had congealed in a sinister purple clump. She could not have been more than twenty. Peters shrugged his shoulders. '*Prostitutka*,' he said. 'Perhaps it is for the best.' It was an unforgettable scene. The Bolsheviks had taken their first step towards the establishment of discipline."

Two days later Lockhart discussed intervention with Commissar for War Trotsky, who admitted that the Bolsheviks had to choose between some agreement with the Allies or a forced intervention that would either bring them down or drive them into the Germans' arms. Impressed by Lockhart's assurance that the Allies would guarantee Russia's territorial integrity, he made a statement which he authorized Lockhart to wire Lord Balfour: REALIZING THAT RUSSIA MUST SOONER OR LATER FIGHT GERMANY IN ORDER TO RID HERSELF OF THE YOKE OF AN UNFAIR PEACE AND THAT IN THESE CIRCUMSTANCES ALLIED HELP WOULD BE MOST DESIRABLE, HE INVITES THE ALLIED GOVERNMENTS TO SUBMIT TO HIM AT THE EARLIEST OPPORTUNITY FULL AND PROPER STATEMENT OF HELP WHICH THEY COULD FURNISH AND OF GUARANTEES THEY ARE PREPARED TO GIVE. IF CONDITIONS ARE (?SATISFACTORY) HE CONSIDERS CONCLUSION OF AN AGREEMENT BOTH NECESSARY AND DESIRABLE.

The statement committed the Bolsheviks to nothing and probably was only a ruse to give them more breathing space. If so, it worked. Until he read Trotsky's proposal, Balfour was convinced, as he had recently wired Washington, that the Bolsheviks lacked the ability to fight Germany and that, moreover, their goal was "to produce a world wide social revolution, not to gain a military victory." But the Trotsky statement so changed Balfour's mind that he wired his ambassador in Washington: PLEASE EXPLAIN TO COLONEL HOUSE THAT IN MY VIEW SITUATION IS ENTIRELY ALTERED BY APPARENT WILLINGNESS OF TROTSKY TO INVITE ALLIED ASSISTANCE AGAINST GERMAN AGGRESSION.

In Russia, the Government newspapers were busy lauding the resolute and bloody liquidation of anarchist centers. Robins also was delighted, convinced that he personally had persuaded the Bolsheviks to stablize their power and demonstrate their freedom from German control. But Lockhart was beginning to have second thoughts about intervention. On April 21 he cabled London that perhaps the Allies should, after a short wait, flatly inform the Bolsheviks that intervention was coming whether they agreed to it or not.

Lockhart did not explain this rather abrupt reversal of opinion. Perhaps he had been influenced by a young and fascinating Russian aristocrat, Moura Budberg. "Her vitality, due perhaps to an iron constitution, was immense and invigorated everyone with whom she came into contact." So he wrote when he first met Moura and by now he was deeply in love. "Into my life something had entered which was stronger than any other tie, stronger than life itself." All he revealed to the Foreign Office was that in the past fortnight he had been in contact with all the anti-Bolshevik groups of any importance in Moscow; supporters of the former monarchy as well as Cadets, Right Social Revolutionaries, and

Mensheviks. All of these groups, he said, would welcome Allied intervention as long as it didn't mean occupation of Siberia.

If Lockhart's faith in the new regime appeared to be weakening, that of Albert Rhys Williams, an American Presbyterian minister turned radical, was unshaken. He was distressed, however, to learn, as he was preparing to go home, that most of the Bolsheviks to whom he bade farewell suspected that their tenure of power was about over. "We'll meet again, old man," said Peters of the Cheka with his Cockney accent. "That is if we aren't all hanging on lampposts within a few days." He said this somewhat cheerfully, but another acquaintance, Lunacharsky, was grim. "We may have to abandon Moscow. But if we slam the door and get out, we shall be back again."

During his year-long stay in Petrograd as a correspondent for the New York *Evening Post*, Williams had become intimate with Lenin, who corrected his Russian and even offered him instruction in Marxism. Williams never took advantage of this rare proposal; he was too busy helping organize a Foreign Legion to fight in the Red Guard.

Lenin took time out to see Williams on the morning of his departure. Switching from English to Russian and occasionally to German, he spoke frankly of the problem of hunger and unemployment in the cities. Life itself, Lenin added, would force the Bolsheviks to do now what they should have done earlier—organize committees of poor peasants. "Iron detachments" of workers would go to the villages. These same people had defeated the Czarist army and would now have to vanquish the kulaks while establishing self-confidence and vanquishing their own vices.

Greed, he explained, was not limited to the bourgeoisie. The sudden gain of power had also corrupted the workers, who selfishly grabbed grain and bread only for themselves and their friends. Like those they despised, the workers were becoming hoarders. Those who enforced the great socialist principle, "He who does not work neither shall he eat," must now learn to produce for the community.

Lenin seemed as excited as if he were going to make the trip east himself. With enthusiasm he pointed out the route on a map. "I envy you," he said, and in his enthusiasm over the wonders of Siberia reminded Williams of an eager travel agent "proposing a ticket for the most distant spot within the reach of our pocketbooks."

He asked if Williams had everything he needed for the trip. Was he taking many mementos with him? Williams said he had a truckful of diaries, notes, documents, newspapers, and a motion picture reel showing the creative and artistic life of the Revolution. Enough material, Williams hoped, for a book.

Lenin stroked his bald head. "I'm afraid they won't allow all your literature and films to get into America," he said, then warned that Williams would encounter in Vladivostok "the first point of the Allied invasion." "The Japanese and British are there to greet you already. It would be unfortunate if you did not get there ahead of the American forces. I suggest you make all haste possible."

Williams blurted out that Lenin surely couldn't be serious. "Why when I told Colonel Robins goodbye he still seemed fairly hopeful of United States recognition, or some sort of support."

"Yes," said Lenin, "but Robins represents the liberal bourgeoisie of America. The liberal bourgeoisie does not decide the policy of America. Finance capital does. And finance capital wants control of Siberia." He spoke with confidence of the socialist future, envisioning electrification of Petrograd industries and development of the mines of the Urals along the most modern lines. On the map he pointed out where canals, dams, and hydroelectric stations would be built, just as though there was no famine throughout the country and her very existence was not being threatened. He had utter faith in the people and refused to believe that Russia's plight was hopeless. "Lenin was now unsmiling," recalled Williams, "but neither was he mournful. He repeated more or less what I heard him say before, that the Soviets faced a situation unlike anything Marx had foreseen. Nevertheless, there would be resistance to intervention, not only within the Socialist Republic, but within the capitalist countries by the working class, depending on their developments."

That, said Williams, was why he was going home: to mobilize protest against such policies. Hitching his chair closer to Williams, Lenin began questioning him about American engineers and scientists. "We need thousands of them," he said. And how was socialism developing in America? What factors in American society would affect relations between the classes?

The dictatorship of the proletariat, Lenin admitted, would be unlike any other dictatorship. Bourgeois resistance had to be crushed at once. A classless society, communism, was far away. Its advent was not dependent on Russia alone. "We will triumph—if we survive meantime; but this means we will have to make a few concessions *for the moment* to get the productive machine going enough to survive. And, if we triumph, or even if we do not, our example will be the inspiration of revolutions in far-off Asian, South American, and African countries."

Before long the European proletariat would join them. He refused to say when. "But I will tell you this much. The Kaiser's downfall will come within the year. That is absolutely certain." And with the same assurance he added, "In the end, countries will coalesce into a great socialist federation or commonwealth—seventy-five or one hundred years."

The five minutes Williams had expected had turned out to be far more and he realized he should end the interview with a final question. "But all you say about the future—if intervention is a reality, if my country puts no brake on it but aids it, what then?"

"Then it means all-out defense on our part. We are going on

that assumption now. It will take priority over all else. In that event, the Revolution might be slowed or even temporarily distorted in form; its purpose, its goals would remain the same, their achievement only postponed. Under foreign invasion our war-weary people will find a new stimulus to fight, and the peasants to defend their land. They will learn that, just as it did with the Germans, the coming in of the Japanese, British, French, *or* Americans will mean the return of the landlords. For any invader must have a base, and the only one he can find among the people will be the White officer class. So who knows? The Revolution may be hastened by your imperialistic government. If so, it will be a great mistake—for your people and for mine."

3.

Raymond Robins was also thinking of returning to America. Ever since coming to Moscow he was vigorously opposed by Consul General Maddin Summers, an esteemed consular professional who, married to a Russian of good family, was dedicated to the Czarist regime. The two men were sending in conflicting reports. Summers was convinced that the Bolsheviks were losing power, while Robins contended that it was being strengthened. He also recommended Allied military collaboration with the Soviets, while Summers ridiculed the idea. Their opposing views turned Summers into a bitter personal enemy. Robins never stooped to personal attack, but in his diary he described Summers as evil.

Tension between the two men was becoming intolerable. Both were well-meaning, but instead of consolidating their various sources of information each insisted that his own view was the only valid one.

Convinced that Robins was acting as a Bolshevik agent, Summers decided that something must be done. He cabled the State Department a formal request to be transferred from Moscow. "There can be no cooperation between Robins and myself."

It soon became obvious to Robins that he was *persona non grata* with the State Department and on April 22 he philosophically wrote in his diary: "The great drama draws towards the last act." Three days later he cabled the Red Cross that liquidation of relief work was practically complete. "Recommend return all members mission America. Planning departure about May fifteenth." Despite disappointments, he still had faith in the Bolshevik dream and had not lost his idealistic ardor; and on Russian Palm Sunday, April 28, wrote ecstatically: "Moscow Russia the first in the greatest proletarian revolution the world has ever known. Lenin in the Kremlin! What an hour. The dauntless close of the April hour!"

Summers was greatly relieved that his nemesis was leaving and the following day cabled the Secretary of State he was convinced Lenin, in accord with the newly arrived German Ambassador, Count Mirbach, was conducting a diplomatic offensive against America with intent of weakening her alliance with Japan.

He recommended a joint Allied statement expressing friendship for the Russian people and hostility to the "adventurers now in power" who had delivered Russia to the Germans. At the same time he warned that recognition of the Bolsheviks as the legitimate Government would mean recognition of the Treaty of Brest-Litovsk.

On the Western Front, Mount Kemmel had just fallen to the Germans, but Ludendoff's second offensive was already lagging, and by the first of May the danger was over.

In Moscow, May Day was cloudy and cool and Robins felt that a strange quiet lay over the city. "Is it ominous of the coming hour?" Would the anarchists attempt to break up the scheduled parade or stage some armed protest against Count Mirbach's presence in the city? More than forty thousand people marched nine miles through Moscow, which teemed with dissident groups, yet not a shot was fired. The vast parade marched past the reviewing stand in Red Square, just outside the Kremlin. Each detachment paid honor to bodies lying in a long trench, patriots who had died for the Soviet Revolution.

Robins watched intently from his car until he became conscious of a stir. Something was breaking through the crowd. It was an automobile, flying a red flag on each side of the hood. Soliders, grasping bayoneted rifles, stood on the running boards. In the back seat was Count Mirbach. He smiled and chatted as he watched the passing columns, completely at ease despite a stinging personal attack in *Pravda* a few days earlier: "He comes as the representative of a military clique which kills and robs and violates whatever its bloody imperialistic bayonets can reach."

Then something did disturb Mirbach. He stood up in the car to watch a huge banner with a socialist slogan—in German. WORKINGMEN OF ALL COUNTRIES, UNITE! GERMAN COMRADES, THROW OFF YOUR KAISER, AS THE RUSSIAN COMRADES HAVE THROWN OFF THEIR CZAR.

Behind the banner was another detachment of Red Army troops —in German uniforms. Some carried pictures of Karl Marx. Mirbach watched stolidly and, upon returning to his embassy, dispatched a stiff protest. The Bolsheviks apologized, promising to cease enlistment of foreign nationals in the Red Army, explaining that they had merely conferred Soviet nationality on new recruits from Germany and Austria.

This abject apology alarmed Ambassador Francis, who swung over to Summers' side. "In my judgment," he cabled Washington on May 2, "time for Allied intervention has arrived." He had come to this grave conclusion, he added, because Mirbach was already dominating the Soviet Government and was "practically dictator in Moscow."

Robins' fight against intervention was ended. Summers was victorious, but a few days later he died of a brain hemorrhage, brought on by overwork and worry.

178

In London, three days after Summers' funeral on May 8, the Cabinet held a long discussion on Russia. Should they occupy Archangel, Murmansk, and Vladivostok? Should they blow up the Russian Baltic Fleet? "I have a simple rule," commented Henry Wilson, "which is to help my friends and down my enemies."

During the meeting, the Japanese Military Attaché arrived to tell Wilson that the time was ripe for Japanese intervention. Did Wilson agree? "Later in the afternoon I wrote a note for him, which I read to Milner, Smuts and Wemyss, saying that from a military point of view the Japanese Army could not intervene too soon nor go too far, and that I was always impressing this on my Government, and hoped that the Japanese G.S. [General Staff] would do the same to their Government."

Lockhart was not aware of this during the farewell dinner with Robins on the evening of May 13. The American was leaving Moscow the next day and still felt that, once in Washington, he could persuade President Wilson to favor collaboration with the Bolsheviks. Robins seemed as enthusiastic and spirited as ever. "He was a great personality and a man of sterling character and iron determination," wrote Lockhart. "His departure was a great loss to me. In the almost lone hand I was playing his moral courage had been an immense support."

The next day Robins said goodbye to Trotsky and Lenin, and each gave him a signed photograph. The latter also handed over an amazing document suggesting possibilities for trade with America. Attached was a personal handwritten note to Robins: "I enclose the preliminary plan of our economic relations with America . . ."

Robins exulted. This could be the material he needed to sway opinion in the United States! The document, entitled "Russian-American Commercial Relations," frankly revealed the decline in Russian production and imports as well as the pathetic state of Soviet economy. It then presented statistics indicating how greatly the American share in Russian trade had increased just before the Revolution. Other statistics showed what a tremendous advantage American capitalists would have after the war. "With the inability of Germany to exploit the Russian market for German industry, it will be very difficult for her in the future to regain the leading part, if during that time America succeeds in taking advantage of the favorable circumstances created for her by events and establishes a working apparatus of commerce between the two countries."

The document continued, in the style of an alluring Wall Street prospectus, to suggest valuable concessions to those getting in on the ground floor. The United States could, it prophesied, "participate actively in the exploitation of the marine riches of the Eastern Siberia, of coal and other mines, as well as in the railroad and marine transportation construction in Siberia and northern European Russia."

When Robins read this, he could see how it would appeal to visionary American capitalists. Those who had been too late to profit by the expansion of their own west would have an even greater and richer territory of exploitation. This was also implicit in Lenin's suggestion that security for payment for American economic aid could come from U.S. participation in the "development of the water routes of the Donets Basin and the Volga-Don Canal," as well as that of coal mines, lumber, and railway construction.

Robins walked out of the Kremlin in an exalted daze. With such an offer in his pocket he could bring together the two nations he loved. The next morning, May 14, he had a final breakfast with Lockhart. That evening he boarded his special car, attached to the train for Vologda, bearing a special pass signed by Lenin: "I beg you to give every kind of assistance to Colonel Robins and other members of the American Red Cross Mission for an unhindered and speediest journey from Moscow to Vladivostok."

"The tide runs flood," wrote Robins in his diary as the train headed toward Vladivostok. The letter from Trotsky and the documents from Lenin "made the final road all clear . . . The great experience! We thank Thee, our Father, Jesus Christ Savior and Lord! Blessed Holy Spirit comforter and Guide! The final hour—faith and [illegible word] power Amen!"

In Moscow, Lenin was making a major foreign policy speech at a combined session of the All-Russian Central Executive Committee and the Moscow Soviet. While acknowledging that the Bolshevik state was "an oasis amid the raging sea of imperialist rapaciousness," it would survive because of conflicts among the capitalists. The great war in the west was hopelessly dividing the Germans and British. And in the east, Japan and America, though presently allies, were fated to be bitter enemies. "The economic development of these countries over the course of several decades," he prophesied, "has stored up a great mass of inflammable material which renders inevitable a desperate conflict between these two powers for mastery of the Pacific Ocean and its shores."

Eventually, he continued, the imperialists would launch a final attack on the Soviet state. "We will do everything in order to prolong this short and unstable breathing-space which we gained in March, because we are firmly convinced that we have behind us tens of millions of workers and peasants who know that with every week and with every month that this breathing-space lasts they are gaining new strength. We say to ourselves . . . everything that our diplomacy can give to delay the moment of war, to prolong the intermission, we are obliged to do."

All these words revealed why Lenin had given the document to Robins. He hoped to entice the American capitalists to keep their trade rivals, the Japanese, out of Siberia. The hinted-at concessions were a lure to Wall Street to protest any Japanese intervention. America was not the only one being wooed. At the same time

Francis Lindley, the British diplomatic representative, was being urged to send a British economic mission to Moscow to establish economic relations between the two nations.

At the short stopover in Vologda, Robins took the opportunity of revealing to an Associated Press correspondent that he was carrying an unusual proposition from Lenin to the American Government. "I have the goods on my person," he said. That was why he was hurrying to America, but he would return very soon.

At the same time Ambassador Mirbach was advising Berlin that it would best serve German interests "to continue to provide the Bolsheviks with a minimum of essential goods and to maintain them in power. In spite of all their decrees, something can probably be achieved with the Bolsheviks for the present time, for they are now all of a sudden much more cooperative again in economic affairs, and at least some preparations can be made for future economic infiltration."

This Bolshevik gesture had come on the same day Lenin handed over his alluring proposition to Robins. In a nearby office Foreign Commissar Chicherin had been assuring the Germans that the Soviets were ready to set up the economic commission mentioned in the Treaty of Brest-Litovsk. And on the fifteenth, as Robins was telling the Associated Press man that he had the goods on his person, Russian-German negotiations for a renewal of commercial negotiations opened in Berlin.

The Soviet carrot was being offered to three powers. That was one reason Lenin had given Robins the special pass urging all officials to give his party the speediest possible passage to Vladivostok. Another reason for speed was to delay Japanese intervention in Siberia. Even a few more weeks of breathing space might keep the Soviet regime afloat. Every day and hour counted.

5.

Survival of the new nation suffered a serious blow the day Robins left Moscow. That morning a troop train from Vladivostok had pulled into the station at Chelyabinsk, an unimportant town some fifteen hundred miles from Moscow. It was loaded with Austrian and Hungarian prisoners of war as well as civilian refugees, all of whom were being repatriated under the Brest-Litovsk treaty. Here they met several trains carrying Czech soldiers to Vladivostok. These stateless men, whose land still formed part of the Habsburg Empire, had fought against the Germans at the side of Czarist troops. They were still eager to continue to fight on the Western Front, which desperately needed such dedicated and experienced soldiers. Other Czech trains were strung out at wide intervals along five thousand miles of the Trans-Siberian Railroad, and the leading *échelons* (Russian jargon for a train of forty cars) were already in Vladivostok. Those to the rear were moving slowly, erratically, due to misunderstandings with the Bolsheviks.

There was some tension between the newcomers from the east (who regarded the Czechs as traitors) and the Czechs, who in turn looked upon the Austro-Hungarians as toadies of the Habsburgs. Despite their differences, a number of Czech soldiers lined the track to say farewell as the westbound train slowly pulled out of the station. Suddenly a prisoner leaned out of a coach, shouting insults at the Czechs. In fury he hurled a large piece of cast iron from a broken stove. It struck a Czech on the head. He fell dead.

Infuriated, Czechs leaped onto the locomotive and stopped it. Others swarmed into the train and threatened to shoot everyone if the murderer wasn't handed over. At first the Austro-Hungarians refused, but seeing that the angry Czechs meant business they turned over the assailant, a soldier named Malik, a Czech renegade. Malik was dragged outside and lynched.

Following an all night party with friends on May 25, Bruce Lockhart drove his beloved Moura out to the Sparrow Hills to watch the sun rise over the Kremlin. "It came up like an angry ball of fire heralding destruction. No joy was to come in the morning." For he had learned that British Major General F. C. Poole, commander of Allied Forces in Northern Russia, was to arrive in Archangel that evening. Hostile intervention was bound to follow soon. It was also obvious that Ambassador von Mirbach was exerting more and more influence on the Bolsheviks and, when the British agent was invited to go to Vologda to "find a common formula" with Ambassador Francis and French Ambassador Noulens, he felt obliged to comply. On May 28 he dined with Francis, whom he found amusing and charming though there was little serious talk. "As soon as dinner was over," wrote Lockhart, "Francis began to fidget like a child who wishes to return to its toys. His rattle, however, was a deck of cards, and without loss of time they were produced. The old gentleman was no child at poker. We played late, and, as usually happens when I play with Americans, he took my money."

But the following day's lunch with the French Ambassador had an all-important influence on Lockhart's career. "There was nothing childish about M. Noulens. If he played poker, he played without cards. Politics—and politics viewed from the narrow, logical angle of a Frenchman—was his only game." Noulens flattered the younger man while pointing out how wrong were his views on intervention. We must intervene even without Bolshevik consent, he said, and advanced many arguments in favor of this new formula. The war would be won or lost on the Western Front and the situation there was critical. Some diversion in Russia would prevent the Germans from transferring more troops from the East. Unity among the Allies, he said, was essential. Dissension in policy had already grievously harmed the Allied cause. He urged Lockhart to join him. "I was alone," recalled Lockhart. "Robins had left. Sadoul, the French Robins, had been side-tracked . . . Feverishly I tried to summarise my own position in my mind. Perhaps I could still pull off a coup with Trotsky. Perhaps M.

Noulens was cleverer than I realised. I was in a corner. If I refused to agree, M. Noulens would go ahead with his own policy. He would carry the Italians, the Japanese, and even Francis with him. If I consented, at least I should escape the stigma of having stood out against the united opinion of all the other Allied representations. I capitulated." He sent a telegram to London recommending intervention with or without Bolshevik approval.

A few days earlier, during the formal opening ceremonies at New York's Metropolitan Opera House, President Wilson had spoken extemporaneously on peace feelers from the Central Powers. Wilson assured the audience that he would "not be diverted from the grim purpose of winning the war by any insincere approaches upon the subject of peace." He would not approve of a peace that gave Germany "a free hand, particularly in the East, to carry out the purposes of conquest and exploitation."

His audience listened with sympathy and when, on the spur of the moment, he exclaimed, "Now, as far as I am concerned, I intend to stand by Russia as well as France," there was a burst of applause and a standing ovation that amazed Wilson. How could such a prosperous audience react so enthusiastically? "It was," he later said, "rather too well dressed. It was not an audience, in other words, made of the class of people whom you would suppose to have the most intimate feeling for the sufferings of the ordinary man in Russia."

"How Wilsonian all this was, and how reminiscent of the Fourteen Points Speech!" commented noted Russian expert George Kennan. "Here, in this impromptu statement, was still the favored image of the Russians as a simple people, clothed in a peculiar virtue compiled of poverty, helplessness, and remoteness from worldly success—a mass of mute, suppressed idealists, languishing beneath the boot of the German captor, yearning for justice, freedom, and union with the spiritual brothers in the West—sure to respond to the distant voice of sympathy and understanding."

Wilson seemed to feel that American aid could pass directly to the noble Russian people rather than go through the Bolshevik Government. He was sincere in his bold words about supporting Russia, but all his sympathy meant little unless it was also clearly extended to the Bolsheviks.

Officially, America still opposed any hostile intervention in Russia, but there were whispers of a change in the wind. Several weeks earlier Secretary of State Robert Lansing had discussed with the Japanese the possibility of an American expedition to Siberia. And two days after his inspiring talk at the Metropolitan Opera House, Wilson personally typed a note to Lansing asking for his comments and judgment on a recommendation for the establishment of an Allied commission "to reconstruct Siberia." That same day he also asked Lansing to "follow very attentively what Semenov [the White Russian general fighting against the Bolsheviks in

Siberia] is accomplishing and whether there is any legitimate way in which we can assist."

Though he had not yet met the persuasive Professor Thomas Masaryk, who had come to America to plead the cause of the Czechs, Wilson had heard his praises from those who had. That he was a professor and the spokesman for a small freedom-loving people already made Wilson sympathetic; and the possibility now loomed that the battle between Bolsheviks and Czechs along the Trans-Siberian Railroad could tip the precariously balanced scales to intervention.

Chapter Eight

"THE YANKS ARE COMING!"
MAY 20–JUNE 13

1.

ON the Western Front, the Allies had been uneasy early in May, but as two weeks passed with little action, the feeling grew that the Germans must be exhausted. Such optimism was not shared by Haig and Pétain. Why would the Germans cease attacking after driving two great salients in the British lines? They still had a large number of divisions in reserve and vast numbers of men remained in the east. Both front-line commanders feared another major Ludendorff offensive, each positive it would fall in his sector. A young American intelligence officer, Captain Samuel T. Hubbard, Jr., predicted that it would come just south of Laon, where the Big Bertha guns were still emplaced. Such a brash prophecy was politely ignored at the Supreme War Council, since this meant a direct attack on the Chemin des Dames ridge. This had been a quiet sector since the Germans had lost it the previous autumn, and both Haig and Foch regarded the area as safe enough to transfer four tired British divisions there for rest and regrouping.

Hubbard's reasoning that an attack in this direction offered a direct route to Paris and would be an extremely difficult area for the Allies to reinforce was ridiculed by the French. The American was obviously unaware of the rugged terrain. The Chemin des Dames, a ridge running from east to west, was named for the almost straight carriage road that had been hacked along its crest for the convenience of ladies of the court. The German lines lay to the north, the French to the south. In between spread a mile-wide No Man's Land covered with stumps and bushes. The French felt supremely confident. The enemy would not only have to climb up the ridge but then attack down slopes cut by numerous valleys whose sides were often so steep that one had to clamber about on hands and knees.

For more than a month the Germans had been secretly planning to break across the Chemin des Dames and continue south toward the Marne. But it was only to be a diversionary attack—a ruse. Once German troops broke across the ridge toward the Marne, Ludendorff guessed that the French would panic, since it would look like a threat to Paris, which lay only forty miles beyond that strategic river. Consequently the Allies would hastily transfer all their reserves from Flanders. Then Ludendorff would launch his main attack against Haig with Rupprecht's group of armies. This would be the decisive blow to end the war and, curiously, was code-named Hagen, the slayer of Siegfried.

Early in May the four battle-weary British divisions occupied the eastern end of the Chemin des Dames. The French called this area the "Californie Plateau," but to the Germans it was the *Winterberg,* since the bare white limestone on its sides looked from the distance like snow. To the battered Britons the area indeed seemed like a rest area. Everything was peaceful. Trim, prosperous villages nestled in quiet hollows only two miles behind the front line and the farmers toiled away as if there were no war.

"All the houses are standing, roofs on, shutters up," recollected Private R. H. Kiernan. "There is Trigny, too, where business is as usual. It is all a scream to us—you can't find a shell hole anywhere . . . Our fellows are always joking about the French Front. There is never any strafing here, and if there is a Boche 'plane, it is umpteen thousand feet up, and is quickly plastered with anti-aircraft shells for miles around it." There was never any sound; no machine guns, no artillery. "The atmosphere on this front is wonderful. From a road nearby I can see the towers of Reims Cathedral, as though it were only a hundred yards away, yet it is some kilometres." Here everything was green and blue and bright, not like Flanders with its frightfulness, dullness, rain, mud, stench, and dead bodies. This place made war a pleasure. Kiernan did not know that a French officer had remarked as the British 50th Division took up its position, "You are like rats in a trap."

On noon of May 20, Ludendorff instructed Rupprecht to start the diversionary attack in exactly one week. Long-range plans for Hagen, the main offensive in Flanders, were already being drawn up, and positions were being unobtrusively strengthened from La Bassée Canal to Kemmel.

For the past few days the men in Private Howard Cooper's area just above the canal had been under attack. Only the day before, several hours before dawn, Captain Carr had ordered Cooper and three others to bury German dead out front. "They're smelling like hell!" The quartet worked cautiously in the pitch dark since the slightest clang of a shovel would surely bring on a sweep of machine-gun fire. Cooper put on his gas mask to combat the overpowering smell, and by 4 A.M. that awful task was done. They

then started on another, the burial of a great bloated cow at the side of the road.

From behind the hedge Captain Bentley Meadows of the adjoining unit, D Company, warned them to return to their trench. The first light of day was about to break. On their way back to the support line they ran into their own captain. Upon learning they hadn't finished burying the cow, Carr became livid. "Then what the hell are you disobeying orders for? Get back, the lot of you, and don't return till the job's finished!"

They started back but were stopped by Meadows, a kindly, impetuous officer. "Give my compliments to Captain Carr," he said, "and tell him it would be impossible for anyone to go and work in that position after dawn." They gratefully returned to their trench, passed on the message to Carr, who grunted and told them to get to their sections. No sooner had they finished breakfast than they were ordered to bury bodies in the orchard, a few yards to the rear. Fortunately it was just out of sight of the Germans, but working in the daylight made their task doubly unsavory. They found four Germans and two English, all blown up like balloons, their hands and distended features jet black. Cooper and another man started with a fallen comrade from the Machine Gun Corps. "As we lifted the body by levering with our spades, the back of the scalp came away a seething mass of maggots. We levered the heavy weight towards a shell hole which it eventually rolled into with the sound of a football bladder." They took the man's identity disc and a letter. Obviously from his sweetheart, it asked why he had overstayed his leave as he would only be punished. How incongruous, thought Cooper, to think that this bloated, black, abhorrent thing could recently have been reading that letter and living the life of a young machine-gunner.

There was absolute silence in their sector while they worked. Neither shot nor explosion disturbed the quiet of the hot, sunny spring day. As Cooper returned to his trench the awful stench of the dead clung to him. "Everything I ate, drank, or touched seemed permeated with that nauseous odor for the rest of the day." With darkness, the silence ended. The drone of shells and wild bursts of machine-gun fire sounded almost continuously all through the night. After delivering rations, Cooper and his party were sent forward with barbed wire and corkscrew wire posts. They struggled over the dark shell-holed ground toward the front-line trenches, ever alert for oncoming shells. As the party squatted down to rest behind a hedge, Captain Meadows, the pleasant chap who had earlier saved their necks, crawled to meet them. "All you men have been on a wiring party, haven't you?" he whispered. "That's done it," guessed Cooper with foreboding. They were going to have to go out front! "Now Jerry seems to be on the lookout tonight," said Meadows, "and he's got a few machine-gun posts just opposite and you're not to make any sound—understand?"

Feeling that someone had removed part of his insides, Cooper said, "Yes, sir." Meadows warned them "to keep on the alert, dead still when the Very lights go up and flat down if there's time," then disappeared into the darkness. The party crawled through a gap in the straggly hedge into No Man's Land. Some carried heavy rolls of barbed wire. Others, like Cooper, brought four corkscrew stakes. Once in position, the party began screwing the stakes into the ground. These were a welcome invention. Formerly heavy wooden stakes had to be thumped into place. Cooper was crawling back for his fourth load of stakes when he heard a splutter—a light going up! He flopped before it broke into flare. Flat on his face he could see the area flooded with a shimmering silver glare. Abruptly the "viper" struck: tat-tat-tat-tat-tat, sweeping in an arc, searching for its prey. Then silence. They kept working cautiously until another light and a hail of fire overhead. Silence. A figure came from the right. Their corporal. "Make no noise here," he whispered. "Captain Meadows and Corporal Bridson have just been killed ten yards from you. It was that last burst of fire. They've got a machine gun just on the road in front."

Just as they finished the wiring at 3 A.M., four men appeared in the gloom carrying a limp sagging body—Meadows. Others brought Bridson. Stretchers were produced and Cooper was one of the four selected to carry out Meadows. They wound their way, twisting and turning, expecting any moment to hear the deadly chatter. After passing the support line, they picked their way over obstructions and around gaping shell holes. Dawn was breaking as they tramped on. The body pressed the hard stretcher handles relentlessly on the bones of Cooper's thin shoulders. To relieve the aching, he would bring his other hand over and with both raise the handle from his shoulder. Then his rifle, slung by its strap on the right shoulder, would slither down to his elbow and he would have to let go again with an "Oh, hell!" He sweated and stumbled out of breath, no match for the other burly bearers.

Meadows' lifeless arm kept falling off the stretcher and swinging. Time and again, Cooper lifted it back. He didn't know why he didn't let it keep swinging. He wondered what the captain's parents would feel when they heard the bad news. They would be sleeping now and probably spend the day enjoying a lunch or tea, unaware of the swinging lifeless arm and riddled body. "I then suddenly hoped my turn wouldn't come."

Finally they reached the canal and a small cottage, brigade headquarters. A sleepy orderly came out, followed by two figures, the colonel and adjutant. "Captain Meadows and Corporal Bridson have been killed, sir," said young Cooper. "Oh, I am sorry," said the colonel. "Poor old Meadows, dear, dear."

Cooper and his mates made their way back across the fields. It was light by the time they reached the reserve line, and as they crossed to the supports, two echoing shots rang out in the crisp morning air. Sniper probably. They passed some stubby willows and reached their trench, just in time to "stand to"—but too late, of course, to think of a bit of sleep.

* * *

This had been just another quiet day on the south Flanders front, according to the communiqué, but Haig was not fooled by the deceptive calm. He knew that Ludendorff's main objective was to beat the British Army. To hold back the Boche, he needed reinforcements and he hoped to find them among the mass of Americans that were streaming into France, 120,000 or more a month; already more than 600,000 had landed. The next day, May 21, he visited their 77th Division at training near Eperlecques. The divisional commander was away but Haig talked with General Wittenneger, who commanded a brigade. A regular officer with thirty years' service, he seemed to Haig "very old for his years both physically and mentally. At first he spoke to me as if he felt that he was being hurried in the training and pressed to go into the battle before his men were adequately trained. But after I had been with him half an hour he saw that I did not want him to do impossibilities." Wittenneger said he was ready to do whatever Haig thought right but begged him to leave the British officers and noncoms who were helping his troops, otherwise "it would be little short of murder to send *his* men into the trenches in their present ignorant state, *without them*." Haig inspected the troops, appalled to find all ranks ignorant of their duties. The staff had only theoretical knowledge and no concept of how to supply their men. The noncoms were good material but had "no idea of how to command and get things done. They and men all live together. This must be changed." He noted that the Americans were lugging enormous packs: " . . . one man carried 83 pounds; another had 12 bars of soap in his pack!"

While Haig was preparing to be attacked in Flanders, German batteries received orders to set up a creeping barrage for the assault on the Chemin des Dames. That night Lieutenant Herbert Sulzbach and his captain rode off on reconnaissance through the weird ruins of a village, then onto the "Snake Road." It was hot and thousands of nightingales were singing as if it were high summer. They were so near the front the two men had to dismount and stumble around on foot until four in the morning in search of the command post allocated to them. This was almost the exact position their battery had held last year. There was just a little sweeping fire from the French. "They seem not to be noticing anything, in spite of all the columns of ammunition being trundled up to the front; many batteries will be moving into positions partly in advance of the infantry lines. The croaking of the frogs in the Ailette area is so powerful that it drowns the rattle of ammunition columns; so the frogs are what you might call our latest allies. I daresay that after this the French will be saying that the Boche have been bribing the frogs to do it."

The next day Sulzbach tackled a huge pile of administrative and tactical orders. "This work of deploying troops for action is enormously exciting, and this time it is on just as great a scale as the preparations for 21 March." Everything was being worked out, conceived and calculated down to the smallest detail. The barrage would be laid down on the very second, and would last for seven hours. "The transformation from static to mobile warfare demands unbelievable accuracy and farsightedness, and I'm kept at work until 3 o'clock in the morning."

On May 24 orders swamped him. The new offensive was given the code name *Turnstunde*—Physical Training Period. He was triumphant: "Everything has been marvelously well worked out, and it's going to succeed!" His battery would be stationed close to the front and, after laying down the barrage, would follow up as second-line infantry troops. And by the second and third days they would have the grand job of chasing the enemy, who should be in full flight.

In Paris, Lord Derby was writing Balfour that if by any chance there was any serious reverse on the Western Front and the Allies had to retire any considerable distance, Clemenceau would fall. "He is absolutely omnipotent and nobody can call their soul their own under his rule and they have a slight resentment at his tigerish attitude." Later in the day Derby commented about the next German attack. "I think everybody is puzzled as to why the offensive has not begun and M. Klotz who was here the other day seemed to think it is just possible that no offensive will take place and that Germany will simply sit down where she is now and make some peace proposal. Personally I do not believe in that."

There were, in truth, influential Germans seeking an early end to war. One was Max, Prince of Baden, who a week earlier had gone up front to appeal personally to Hindenburg and Ludendorff. Unaware that two more major offensives were already being mounted, Max urged Ludendorff to promise him one thing. Would he enlighten the Government before Germany's last offensive strength had been thrown in? Negotiations must go to the conference table with an army still capable of striking. "Before you take your last horse out of the stable," he said, "make an end." Ludendorff absentmindedly agreed and there was no more Max could say. But he wondered why the general was so preoccupied.

On the morning of May 25 three exhausted men appeared at the front lines held by the British on the right flank of the Chemin des Dames. They were French poilus, escaped from a German prison camp. Interrogators were concerned by their report of activity on the enemy side of the ridge. Masses of troops, it seemed, were moving up while guns were being emplaced far to the front.

The British reported all these portents to the French, who replied: "In our opinion there are no indications that the enemy has made preparations which would enable him to attack tomorrow." It was ridiculous to think that any significant attack would be launched against the formidable barrier which had already cost so many German lives.

The following morning a British intelligence officer noticed blackboards raised in the enemy lines. These were apparently direction signs to guide tanks and transport. More definite information came from two prisoners captured near dawn, who admitted that an attack was coming an hour after midnight. But the interrogators were so skeptical that this warning was not sent to the French Sixth Army until midafternoon. General Duchêne's Sixth Army headquarters took it even more lightly: it was just another of the trench rumors that kept recurring.

It was not until 3:45 P.M. that the British 23rd Brigade received the same warning. "Oh, well, it can't be helped," Major Howard Millis told Sidney Rogerson, his dogsbody, who did anything not covered by others on the staff. "We're for it again." He set off to inform his general and prepare for the worst. Several hours later a signal officer from Duchêne's army arrived to inspect communications and, seeing the bustle, smiled. The enemy attack the Californie Plateau? Nonsense. Those rumors had been going on for months. "They are wiser than that. They could never break through here." All looked so peaceful up front that an attack did seem unlikely, but with darkness an uncanny silence settled over the countryside, and there was not a single answering shot by the enemy to the nightly harassing fire on German communications and assembly points.

On the Italian front, preparations for the Austrian offensive still lagged and the launching date was put off until mid-June. The Italians themselves were in no condition to go on the offensive, remaining content to hold their positions.

In Palestine, Liman von Sanders' Turkish army was melting away, with the number of deserters now exceeding that of effectives. Moreover, the military clique in Constantinople had lost all interest in Palestine in favor of adventures in the Caucasus and Persia.

2.

Some of the German troops on the other side of the ridge also looked upon the Chemin des Dames as a rest area. They too had come from Flanders and were as battle-weary as the British. Many were almost totally exhausted and unfit for combat. For the past few days Captain Fritz Wiedemann had been sent out front to listen to the enlisted men's complaints. Their regimental commander pleaded with Wiedemann to tell division headquarters the plain facts and not try to make things sound better than they were. The front-line troops needed time for recovery before going back into action.

In the presence of the regimental commander, that evening, Wiedemann reported all this to their division commander. After listening quietly, the latter announced that the regiment was to attack across the Chemin des Dames in the morning.

"But that is utterly impossible!" exclaimed the regimental commander. "Haven't you heard what Wiedemann has just reported?"

"The attack must be carried out nevertheless," said the division commander coldly. "If we don't do it, then we must all request transfer to a quieter front. And, in that case we'll be 'depreciated' for the rest of the war." He thought for a moment, then added, "Perhaps we could change the order to read that the attack should be *attempted.*"

Someone protested that there was no such order to "attempt" an attack. One either did or did not! But the division commander instructed the order to be written, and after signing it, casually asked his operations officer, "Do you think the regiments will attack tomorrow?"

"By no means, General! Out of the question!"

Wiedemann was completely confused. Speechless, he left the dugout and tried to calm himself. "So we had come to the point where one played with orders which could cost the lives of thousands." He would not have believed the whole incident if he had not been present.

There were similar reports from other units, but the majority of men being brought into position were eager to attack. There were many like Corporal Adolf Hitler, who had earlier served under Wiedemann. He certainly had lost none of the fervor he had taken to battle in 1914. He still volunteered for every hazardous mission; like so many other Austrians, he was more Pan-Germanic than the Germans.

Lieutenant Sulzbach was also caught up in the excitement as he watched the final state of deployment. Battery after battery rumbled by, then came long columns of infantrymen. For the first time he saw chasseurs and mountain machine-gun battalions brought up for this hilly terrain. French harassing fire began falling on the road, but he and his companions galloped through it without losses. They dismounted and climbed up a ridge to their command post. The soldiers were in splendid spirit and as they marched by would shout, "Make a good job of it!"

Telephone lines were rapidly laid from the command dugout to all the batteries. Then came the weather report, which enabled them to work out the exterior ballistics. By midnight, 1,321 batteries stood ready. There was no moon and in the silence the assault groups of thirty divisions moved into position to wait for the opening barrage. At exactly 1 A.M., May 27, it began. Moments later the enemy harassing fire began to slacken. Sulzbach saw dozens of Very lights shoot up as the batteries—again under the master, Bruchmüller—loosed Blue Cross and Green Cross gas shells. "It all works marvelously, there isn't silence for a moment, it just went on uninterruptedly, rumbling and banging away; rapid fire of every calibre was rattling down on the French, and we hoped they still had no notion of what was coming. Not a single battery had done any range-firing, but our shooting was a masterpiece of accuracy, all worked out and plotted according to the latest principles of ballistics."

Unlike the other massive Bruchmüller bombardments, guns and trench mortars used gas ammunition on all targets for the first ten minutes. This was designed to create confusion and break down morale from the start. There followed more than an hour of mixed gas and high-explosive shells from the main batteries on the Allied artillery, while mortars systematically began knocking out all front defenses including barbed wire.

While the greatest concentration was on the center, held by the French, the British positions were also savagely punished. At 23rd Brigade headquarters, Sidney Rogerson was drinking a whiskey and soda when there was a sudden whizz-plop! whizz-plop! Two gas shells burst nearby. A moment later came a thunderous roar as hundreds of enemy guns roared in unison. "The night was rent with sheets of flame. The earth shuddered under the avalanche of missiles: leapt skywards in dust and tumult. Ever above the din screamed the fierce crescendo of approaching shells, ear-splitting crashes as they burst: all the time the dull thud, thud, thud of detonations—drumfire." The dugouts rocked and were filled with acrid fumes of cordite mixed with the sickly sweet tang of gas. The men scrambled for gas masks, grabbed their kits, weapons, message pads, and dived for deeper shelter. "It was a descent into hell. Crowded with jostling, sweating humanity, the deep dugouts reeked and to make matters worse we had no sooner got below than gas began to filter down." The entrances were hastily blocked with saturated blankets. This excluded the gas but also the air and Rogerson, with a clip on his nostrils and gag between his teeth, had to heave to get a breath of oxygen through his mask. "At first my heart thumped and my head swam distressingly, but I found if I kept still I could just bear it."

Down forty feet, the clamor of the bombardment was muted, yet every so often a shell would burst overhead, causing the walls to shiver. They were in touch by wire and phone with the brigades on right and left. One was getting similar punishment, but the West Yorkshires cheerily reported, "We're all right. You're getting the worse of it. It's going over us." Then their line went dead.

At 3:35 A.M. the Bruchmüller Concerto began a new movement. All batteries abruptly concentrated on the Allied front lines. Five minutes later shells began to creep forward steadily, and masses of German infantry, rising from cover, advanced. In a few minutes the first light of day appeared but a thick mist gradually formed. This was made more dense by smoke shells, and the storm troops were almost across the wide No Man's Land before they were sighted. Both the French and British were taken by surprise as their front-line trenches were quickly overrun. Now it was up to the support lines.

"They have advanced two kilometers during the night," a support company commander of the 8th Leicestershires told his officers. "We will have the opportunity I know you have been waiting for, to get at close grips with the Boche."

Overhearing this, Private Kiernan brought the news to his dugout. "He has come over and advanced two kilos. We are going to stop him." No one said anything. Someone began singing:

"I want to go home, I want to go home,
  I don't want to go in the trenches no more . . ."

As they filed from the dugout and up a steep road to the top of a hill, they could hear a German machine gun slowly firing in the distance. Shells began to fall but their officer shouted, "Keep moving there!" From the crest Kiernan could see that the plain below was covered with drifting smoke. They hurried down to shallow trenches shielded by low shrubbery. A small shell hit near his foot and slithered along. Thank God, a dud.

An officer, a corporal, and two men went through the shrubbery to reconnoiter. Looking through it, Kiernan could make out hundreds of front-line comrades scurrying back toward him "like a football crowd running for the trams. Jerry's machine guns were going and they were dropping a score at a time and lying in heaps, khaki heaps."

The officer was coming back, helping drag the corporal, whose face and body were covered with blood. He was gray and yellow. "Good luck, corporal," said Kiernan.

"It's you as wants the good luck," he whispered. "I'm out of it."

They all retreated along a woody lane where they found an artillery captain, listlessly holding the bridle of a chestnut horse. A colonel asked, "Where is your battery?" The captain pointed to his horse. "Here it is, sir."

Back at 23rd Brigade headquarters word came that the enemy had turned both flanks and was closing in. Their own position was no longer a stronghold but a deathtrap, just as the French officer had predicted. Orders came to fall back across the Aisne River and everyone scrambled up the steep stairs, abandoning everything except the confidential dispatch box. "What a scene met us as we floundered into the light of the young day!" recalled Rogerson. "Everywhere was ruin, desolation thinly veiled by mist and smoke."

"Rogerson!" shouted Brigadier W. G. St. G. Grogan. "You know the way by the trench, don't you? Well, lead on!"

Rogerson put his head down and dashed down the trench, but the goggles of his mask soon fogged and he collided into the trench wall. He turned to urge the others on, to find himself alone. He was petrified. At any second one of those shells would smash him. His greatest fear was not death but disablement. "To share danger with others was bearable, to be alone was terrifying." As he stumbled back he ran into two gunnery officers. What merciful relief! No one knew the way, so all three started blindly toward the Aisne across shell holes, through barbed wire brambles and the shattered remains of shelters and gun pits. Rogerson stumbled, picked himself up, and hurried on, weighed down by the heavy pack on his back, his steel helmet bobbing rhythmically. He gasped openmouthed into the mask, whose clip pinched his nostrils. Finally the three reached the river along which a steady barrage of large-caliber shells was sending up tall geysers of black mud.

They searched vainly for a bridge until they heard the ominous slow rattle of German machine guns just behind. The other two men, tearing off helmets and jackets, plunged into the Aisne. Still burdened by helmet, pack, and mask, Rogerson tried to swim, then realized that he had a signal book in his right hand. Holding this out of water, he tried to stay afloat but the weight dragged him under. Water filled his mask, flooding into his nose and throat. He turned around and just made it back to the bank. He ripped off the mask and tried again. He sank, again barely made it back. Next time he dumped his pack first but the sacrifice was in vain. He was too exhausted and returned to locate a bridge. Plunging through nettles, rushes, and shell bursts, he found it not two hundred yards away. He staggered onto the bridge, stunned to see Brigadier Grogan calmly standing there, crook-handled stick in hand. He was quietly directing the walking wounded and collecting the stragglers.

The French, taking the main force of the onslaught, were falling back even faster. By 5:30 A.M. they had been driven off the Chemin des Dames and before 9 were almost back to the Aisne. Now that the sun had cleared away the mist, German artillerymen from the ridge were watching the advance with wonder. "From the right, from the left, from behind, everyone was going forward followed by the artillery," wrote Albert Sagewitz to his family in Wählitz. "My God, where have all these people come from? It looks like the migration of a nation with the hills and valleys crowded with men, horses, cannons, and wagons. All run forward like a wide river. Everywhere is activity but not only around us but above us. There are our airplanes, 8, 10, 12, no 15 and more, all headed toward the enemy. You can't see an enemy plane anymore."

From a hill on the other side of the river, Rogerson was also watching with fascination. "The Aisne and its attendant canal glittered like silver ribbons in the sun, but in the vacated trench area beyond hung a pall of haze and dust, which lifting at intervals revealed the roads thick with marching regiments in field grey, with guns, lorries, and wagons. Above, like great unwinking eyes, rode observation balloons, towed along by motor transport." Never before in the war had he seen the Boche so rapidly follow up an assault. Battalions were advancing in fours across the British trenches despite clusters of defenders. "What a target the whole scene presented! What havoc even a few eighteen-pounders would have worked on those crowded roads!" But the divisional artillery had not been able to get across the river. There was nothing to fire.

By noon pontoon bridges had been flung across both the Aisne and the canal which was just south of it, and gray infantrymen poured to the other side, regrouping for an assault against the Allied Green Line, which lay beyond.

The sensational advance, coming as a surprise to Hindenburg, caused consternation at Pétain's headquarters. Jean de Pierrefeu, who prepared the daily communiqué, was horrified to see the new pencil marks on the situation map. There was no news of one entire division, which must have been taken prisoner to a man. The only rampart between the Aisne and the Vesle was the remains of units fighting a retreating action. "What were we to say in the communiqué? We could not very well admit, at the first mention of the battle, the loss of the Chemin des Dames and the crossing of the Aisne, which was the bitter truth, without the risk of striking panic into the public. But unless we prepared the way, what arrears might we not have to make up? Besides, if the enemy communiqué announced the true position, we should forfeit all faith in our veracity." It was decided, after much discussion, to follow the usual habit of making no mention of happenings between dawn and 9 A.M. By dealing only with the events of the previous night, it would be natural to mention only the artillery preparation and state simply, "The battle is in progress."

The people of Paris were already in a state of apprehension. Since early morning they could hear the distant rumble of guns. It was louder than that on March 21, and, coming from the east, more ominous. It concerned them far more than that morning's shower of fifteen shells from Big Bertha, silent for twenty-seven days.

As soon as the news reached England, the King sent for General Wilson, who, "much upset," began railing at the "brutes of French" and how the British Army was going to disappear. "This is really rather an amazing business as all that country is so naturally strong," Wilson wrote in his diary. "I don't like this sort of thing at all."

That afternoon, the Germans pushed all the way to the Vesle. Great numbers of French and British were captured and General von Unruh noticed that the latter were fraternizing with his troops. Cigarettes, bread, and flasks were exchanged. As the British marched past the automobile of Crown Prince Wilhelm, several saluted him. His aides, in turn, passed out cigarettes to the prisoners.

The Kaiser was also up front. He returned to Trélon at 11 P.M., still excited by the events of the day. "Gentlemen," he told his entourage, "a great victory, 10,000 prisoners taken, a host of guns captured including the heavy howitzers which had constantly shelled Laon."

It was an astounding success. Ludendorff had driven a twenty-five-mile-wide salient almost twelve miles into the Allied lines. His troops had destroyed four divisions and nearly wiped out four others. Such a sweeping victory presented an unexpected opportunity to Ludendorff. The primary goal had been accomplished, since Allied reserves were already being drawn away from Flanders. Why not exploit the success and convert this diversionary attack into a genuine breakthrough? His troops were steam-rolling south and could easily reach the Marne. Then, turning west toward Paris, they might possibly take the capital itself and end the war. It was a temptation he could not resist. On to Paris!

3.

The offensive resumed two hours after midnight. Sulzbach was excited. Yesterday, after the barrage, his troops had been in the second line. Today they would be in the front. As adjutant, he was busy all morning taking messages from Brigade to the infantry commanders and back to the batteries "and all of a sudden we are right in the middle of a proper battle command; you can see how the individual attacks develop and how everything is thought out and prepared to the tiniest detail." The right wing of his corps turned southward toward Soissons while the adjoining corps, led by General Larisch, assaulted that key town head-on. The latter was slowed down, but Sulzbach's brigade swept forward, taking many prisoners including the commander of a battalion of French Chasseurs who wore the Cross of the Legion of Honor. Sulzbach attempted to interrogate him but he just stood "proud, serious-faced, not saying a word, bent in body and broken in spirit."

To the right the British front-line troops were slowly falling back to the Vesle, while all their vehicles and the remaining guns were hustled across the river and onto the high ground overlooking the valley behind. The exhausted drivers unyoked their weary horses, gave them their nose bags, and tried to get some sleep under the wagons.

There were only ten left in Private Kiernan's platoon, and they found themselves fifty yards behind a French unit which was holding back the enemy with light machine guns. Many of the French looked quite old. They were stout with long black beards, but they ran like children as they dashed from one side of the woods to the other, firing brief bursts to give the impression of greater numbers.

At 9 A.M. Pétain issued orders calling upon General Duchêne to "reestablish the integrity of the line of the Vesle, driving the enemy back to the north of Mont Notre Dame, with a view to recapturing the heights between Vesle and Aisne." By the time this order reached Duchêne an hour later, the French were already south of the Vesle River and only too glad to escape, let alone launch a counterattack.

While Pétain remained at his headquarters, Clemenceau left Paris early that morning of May 28 to find out what was happening. First he visited Foch, who blamed Duchêne for sending almost all of the French 137th Division, "which was back on the Aisne, to the support of the first position, thus leaving along a wide front the important position of security offered by the Aisne almost wholly unguarded. By a fatal chance the Germans made their main effort in this direction and they thus reached the river without striking a blow."

Clemenceau went forward to see General Duchêne for himself and was told that the Germans were pushing on without pause, and there was nothing to oppose them but *"de la poussière"*—mere dust. Duchêne added without complaint that no *"grand chef"* had yet been to visit him.

At his headquarters Foch was writing Haig that the new offensive would force him to greatly reduce the French forces in the north. He warned the field marshal that the British might be entirely thrown on their own resources and suggested that he form a general reserve. Haig did not protest, convinced that the Germans would give him a breather while diverting all their energy and divisions to exploiting the success on the Aisne front.

Back in London, General Wilson was more concerned than Haig. He was praying that the present German attack *was* the main one. "I hope so. This would be good." He also wrote in his diary that Lord Milner, just returned from Versailles, was convinced that the French could not stand a disaster, and kept on saying, "I wish we had our army back in England." "But," noted Wilson, "we can't, so what is the use of saying it?"

By noon the situation worsened. The two German corps were closing in on Soissons and the British were being pushed across the Vesle. The Kaiser, along with the Crown Prince, Hindenburg, and General von Böhn, arrived early in the afternoon at the Californie Plateau, where General von Conta reported that all objectives south of the Vesle had just been gained. While General von Unruh was explaining the new position to His Majesty, an order came in by telephone from Ludendorff: "Pursuit to be continued at once. Forward to the Marne!" Exuberant, the Kaiser dispatched Unruh immediately to the front "to convey his thanks to the troops and their commanders and to give orders on the spot for a rapid prosecution of the offensive." By dark Soissons was captured and in the center German troops were only four miles from Fère-en-Tardenois—an ancient town only eight air miles from the Marne.

Just as the French in front of Private Kiernan's platoon fell back, an officer announced that this was now the front line. A few exhausted Durhams arrived. "Ould Jerry's swarming," said one of them. "Thousands of the bastards." This panicked the Kiernan group into retreat and they fell back another six kilometers, finally settling in a trench near a long black wood. It was dark, without moon. No one spoke. "Suddenly in the wood in front there began a shouting and screaming, high screams of warning and fear and hate, and the crack of bombs, and the clashing of steel, the most horrible sound there is to hear." Their officer led them out of the trench up to the wood, rifles ready to fire. The clash of steel and screams continued. Then from the dark came French stretcher-bearers carrying men wringing wet with blood. "It dripped through the stretchers on the bearers, oldish men who were trembling but grinned when they saw we were English. One man was groaning and crying and muttering words in a deep voice of agony. He was like a large piece of raw meat, so covered with blood." The wood grew quiet as Kiernan's platoon crept back to their trench.

By evening the people of France knew the extent of the defeat and, according to one observer, "there was a feeling that a most serious blow had been struck both to French prestige and to French armed forces—and perhaps a mortal blow to the Entente." Ambassador Derby wrote that many were leaving the capital "and really except for officials Paris is a City of the Dead. All this I think is rather demoralising to the people who cannot get away and I am afraid the result will be a reaction against Clemenceau. Meanwhile the fact that it was our Divisions—poor tired fellows who had been both in the retreat from the Somme and at Mount Kemmel—who had to bear the brunt of the fighting [not true; it was the French this time] and gave way owing to force of numbers, will mean a restarting of recrimination between French and English which was very bad when I came here though to a great extent had died down." He told of his long talk that day with Albert Thomas, the Socialist. "Many people want peace. They are War weary to a degree which we do not understand and that if we were now to have a reverse especially if that reverse falls on French troops, he is very doubtful whether it would be possible to really go on with the war. He thinks Clemenceau would fall and be replaced by somebody else who might be in favour of making the best Peace possible."

Already Clemenceau was under attack, with certain members of the Chambers of Deputies evidencing "an absolutely incredible fury against the Commander-in-Chief of the French Army." Late that same evening Pétain was visited by Foch. The latter got a hostile reception from the general's staff, who regarded him as the real villain of the rout. Why had he taken away all their reserves and sent them up to Haig? Pétain greeted his superior icily, yet they could agree on some points. Both were not only shocked at the size of the new Ludendorff attack but puzzled that it should be launched against the Chemin des Dames. Why had he committed such a force in this unlikely area? And how long would he maintain the pressure?

They also agreed on the defense. The shoulders of the salient must be held. True, Soissons was now in German hands, but the plateau to the south could possibly be held. Pétain was confident he could do this if he were given the Tenth Army in reserve behind Haig's center as well as four French divisions in Flanders. Foch reluctantly agreed to let Pétain have the Tenth Army but flatly turned down the second radical proposal.

Foch returned to his own headquarters at Sarcus, where he received another visit from Clemenceau. He tried to calm the excitable Tiger. This was not a genuine offensive, he said, only a diversionary attack to mask Ludendorff's real intentions. Clemenceau insisted on knowing what Foch intended to do about stopping the German steamroller. Nothing, at the moment, he calmly replied. The advance over the Aisne, he explained, was not as perilous as it seemed to those in Paris. Even if the enemy crossed the Marne and turned west toward Paris, the city was in no real danger for this would place the French Tenth Army on the German flank. Couldn't Clemenceau see that Ludendorff was only trying to divert Allied reserves from some "strategically sensitive" point—such as Flanders?

Although Foch had perfectly read Ludendorff's intentions, Clemenceau didn't believe it and was not at all reassured. Still, he promised to do his best to quiet the critics in the Chamber of Deputies. Stop the Boche tomorrow, he said, and I will be able to handle the Chamber.

At 11 P.M. Pétain issued a new directive, designed to limit the German attack by vigorous resistance on the wings. "It is the duty of all," he ordered, "to maintain their positions without troubling about the thrust of the enemy's advanced units." The Marne bridges were to be guarded to prevent raiding parties from crossing. On the east the hills of Reims were to be held, and on the west the so-called "Paris Line" was also to be maintained as far as a point five miles south-southwest of Soissons.

That evening an important conference was going on at Crown Prince Wilhelm's château in Charleville. Hindenburg and Ludendorff came from Avesnes. The Kaiser, flushed from his trip to the front, was on hand to make sure that his son would be allowed to carry his victory to its conclusion. He remembered the first battle of the Marne, when the Crown Prince's Fifth Army had been forced to break off a successful assault and retreat. Both he and his son felt that had been a grievous mistake.

Siding with royalty, Hindenburg voted to continue the attack, but Ludendorff, who now wondered if it was wise to exploit their success further, reminded them that this was planned as a mere diversion and the real target was the English front. But he did not press the argument, privately fearing that if the drive were stopped now the French would simply patch up their lines and keep their reserves in Flanders. Then the whole point of the assault would be lost. He also was aware that time was growing short. The Americans were landing in hordes. Only that morning their 1st Division had successfully assaulted a village in Picardy fifty-five miles northeast of Paris. Within thirty-five minutes the doughboys had taken the village and then, despite grievous casualties, turned back several counterattacks. While the encounter was of no consequence strategically, it was historic. For the first time Americans had taken offensive action in France—and succeeded. They had exhibited such enthusiasm, vigor, and reckless valor that it was a warning what would happen when Pershing finally got his entire army into action. German victory had to come before then. And so

Ludendorff added his vote to continue the attack. Once they crossed the Marne and the Paris Gun continued its bombardment, the feisty Clemenceau would surely fall from power and the French would seek a peace.

The Germans directing the battle were not as sanguine as their superiors. They had punched a huge salient into the Allied lines, but their own flanks were hanging back. It was a "strangulated hernia," a most undesirable situation, since the only railway communications into the salient ran through Reims and Soissons, the former still held by the enemy and the latter under Allied guns. But they followed orders and, on the third day of the offensive, May 29, kept pushing south toward the Marne.

The attackers knew only that they were advancing as never before. Lieutenant Sulzbach smelled final success. Everyone around him shared the feeling of triumph. The morale was as high as in August 1914. "It's wonderful to see the present look on the faces of our valiant regiments as they advance in an assault; they are almost laughing for joy, and all they can see is victory. If you people at home could only see it!"

The Crown Prince could restrain his own impatience no longer. "I simply had to go forward and see with my own eyes how things were shaping. I wanted to visit the Staffs, view the battlefield and greet as many as possible of my brave soldiers." First he thanked General von Böhn for his brilliant arrangement of the operation, then drove to the Chemin des Dames. "What streams of blood had already flowed in fighting for this ridge!" These thoughts flashed through his mind as he viewed the battlefield. "The only road leading over the ridge looked as if a nation of ants were busy on it—transports, batteries, and infantry simply poured along it. It was a wonderful picture of war!" With difficulty his car was pushed and pulled along a shattered road. "Everywhere I met with a warm reception. How nice it was to be once more among my brave troops, with my finger on their pulse, so to speak, instead of sitting in the office at Headquarters and waiting with uncontrollable impatience for every telephone or aeroplane report. The commander of modern times is denied the part assigned to a Frederick or a Napoleon on the battlefield."

Standing on a knoll with General von Winkler, he saw before him a vast panorama. It was like maneuvers. The headquarters flag fluttered in the wind as runners and motorcyclists dashed in and out. The little party continued down into the valley and along the canal to a small mill where he had a moving reunion with his brother, Eitel Friedrich. They were both exalted by the victory, and two enemy bombs dropping close by "helped to raise our spirits even higher."

Captain Fritz Matthaei, a battalion commander in the 36th Division, was experiencing the same rapture. He had just rejoined his unit after a leave. "Everywhere was battle joy, battle enthusiasm," he wrote home. "Victory called from every corner, prisoners and booty were brought past, and the shining May sun smiled success.

The days of 1914 seemed to have returned." On his way to the front his driver suddenly braked the car and Matthaei watched in awe as two gray figures drove past, stiffly erect: the Kaiser and Hindenburg. He jerked his hand to his cap and His Majesty returned a gesture of thanks.

The indomitable Clemenceau was also up front with his troops. Just as his car reached one end of Fère-en-Tardenois, German troops were entering the other end. The car spun around just in time to avoid capture. Undeterred, he and the chief of his Military Cabinet, General Mordacq, continued on to XXI Corps. Its commander, General Degoutte, told of his divisions being flung into the battle one after another, without artillery. "A tragic sight," recalled Clemenceau, "to see the General weeping over a tattered remnant of a map, and all the while a continuous stream of motorcyclists arriving with reports of the enemy's approach. I left him with no hope of ever seeing him again. For me this is one of the most poignant memories of the War."

By noon Pétain began to wonder if he could hold the Marne and requested Foch to bring their Tenth Army back south at once. Ignoring his earlier promise, Foch refused. There were still sufficient enemy troops to launch another attack up north, and it would be premature to remove them. At the same time he warned Haig that he might have to recall the Tenth Army. In fact, he might even have to call on the British general reserves.

The desperation of the French increased as reports of new setbacks arrived. "The French are bothering the life out of us trying to persuade us to put our half-trained divisions on the front line," Colonel Fox Conner, Pershing's chief of operations, told Major Lloyd Griscom that afternoon. "They say it's the greatest emergency of the war. I don't know when to believe 'em. One minute they're on the crest of the wave and the next at the bottom of the lowest trough."

Suddenly, without a knock, two French officers rushed in. *"C'est terrible! C'est affreux!"* exclaimed General Ragueneau of the French Military Mission. *"Les Boches sont arrivés au Marne. Au secours!"* "We'll send busses, we'll send lorries, we'll send trains. Only give us men!"

Conner calmed the Frenchmen as if they were children. "We'll help you out," he said. "That's what we're here for. We'll send you our 2nd Division."

"Fine!" said Ragueneau. "But it's not nearly enough. We must have more."

Conner studied his map. "Well, General, we hate to put an untrained division into the battle line, but if it really is a crisis we'll go ahead." He decided to send another less experienced division.

"It couldn't be worse," said Ragueneau, and Griscom noticed tears welling in his eyes.

Conner went to the telephone, asked for 3rd Division headquarters. "Hell, Bob, that you?" he said after a minute. "Can you have your division ready tomorrow morning to go into the line?" Apparently the staff officer at the other end was gasping. "Yes, I know you haven't had any trench training . . . Yes, it's an emergency. The French will get you there. How about it?" Conner turned to the French general for confirmation, then said, "Everything is arranged."

Every available French unit was also being rushed to the Marne to form a defensive line, reminiscent to some of the desperate cavalcade of taxicabs in 1914.

Kiernan's platoon had fallen back to a valley, and their officer was indicating targets on the skyline. "There you are," he told Kiernan, pointing up at a big German standing sideways so his pack showed clear and square. As Kiernan took aim, the officer pushed his rifle down with his stick. "Don't aim high." Kiernan looked along the sights and thought, "He has come through all this fighting," and could imagine the German's mother receiving a telegram. Something gripped Kiernan and he thought, "I cannot do it." His officer was down the trench, so Kiernan hurriedly fired straight but high over the German's head. He must have heard it whistle past, for he trotted along the skyline to hide behind a tree.

Late that afternoon it was unbearably hot and there was no water. The Kiernan group filed out of the reeds following a captain who led them at least to their own battalion. Their brigadier galloped up, shouting, "Fix bayonets!" He was big, young, and handsome. "Jerry is just over the hill," he shouted as he gestured with his whip. "Go at him and he'll run, simply run. He's a lot more frightened than you are of him." He wheeled his horse dramatically and galloped off. Two officers conferred, walked up to the brow of the hill for a look, then trotted back. "Unfix," said one, and the men gratefully followed him to the rear. Fear at last had come to Kiernan. He had not known it during the hell of Ypres. "I do not want to go back to the line. When I think of it my stomach turns sick," he recalled. While he was at Ypres his mother had written him: "I know you will be a man and face it." He had done so for many nights despite the cold and heat, misery, pain, and agony. "But I cannot feel the strength of that letter now. I am afraid of going up to the Front again. I am afraid."

Nothing could stop the Germans. In the east they approached Ville-en-Tardenois the next morning, May 30, and for the first time threatened to encircle Reims. In the west they were approaching the Marne.

In Paris there was a growing demand for the heads of Duchêne, Pétain, and Foch. Although Clemenceau had his own doubts about Foch, he felt obliged to support Foch's authority and sent a reassuring telegram to the Allies: . . . WE CONSIDER THAT GENERAL FOCH, WHO IS CONDUCTING THE PRESENT CAMPAIGN WITH CONSUMMATE SKILL, AND WHOSE MILITARY JUDGMENT INSPIRES US WITH

Clemenceau also visited President Poincaré at 11 A.M., urging him not to hector Duchêne while the battle was raging. "Yesterday I saw him only two kilometres from the enemy, near Fère-en-Tardenois. He is very courageous and never ceases exposing himself." Pétain, he added, was preparing an operation to stop the enemy and he begged the President to be patient. He should not listen to those criticizing the conduct of the war. "I know very well that you don't wish to shoot me in the back. I also know very well that you have friends." He was referring to former Premier Aristide Briand and others who not only bitterly criticized Clemenceau's dictatorial methods but railed at Pétain. Poincaré denied that there was any such cabal. It was only Foch's imagination. "I remain convinced," said the President, "that it is not necessary to disturb either Foch or Pétain."

"Then, we are in agreement," said Clemenceau.

"That is what I myself wrote you some time ago, and I have not changed my mind."

"Then, all goes well."

Poincaré thought: "Yes, all goes well. But one more time Clemenceau has listened to gossip and acts suspicious and defiant."

The Tiger hurried back to the battlefield with General Mordacq. Everywhere the news was bad. There was no artillery to stop the Boche and, as Mordacq recorded, the troops were starting to get discouraged "because, as at the beginning of the war, they were being bombarded with heavy stuff, and could only reply with rifles and machine guns: the game was all one-sided." The roads were crowded with despondent refugees hurrying to safety with their pitiful belongings stacked on carts; and to many Frenchmen it seemed as though Clemenceau was leading the nation to defeat—despite the so-called unity of command, American aid, and the heroism of the poilus. "Soissons taken," despairingly wrote Aristide Briand that day. "We are back where we were at the end of 1914."

Poincaré was despondently strolling in his garden when a liaison officer rushed up to announce that the Germans were approaching Château-Thierry, a strategic town on the Marne some fifty air miles from Paris. To his further consternation Poincaré learned that tomorrow's offensive aimed at the enemy's right flank was already being openly discussed in the corridors of the Chamber of Deputies. It was *"une indiscrétion criminelle."* Critics of the Government were also demanding a conference with Clemenceau to find out what was being done to stop the German advance. If the enemy came much further, he would have Paris under direct fire. Then what should they do? Remain in a city being constantly bombarded? How could the Chamber meet? Could they even continue the war under such circumstances?

By evening the Germans were at the banks of the Marne just

east of Château-Thierry. In some parts it was so narrow that a baseball player could throw a ball to the other bank. It did not seem possible that the few troops on the other side could stop them. The German commanders had high hopes. Already they had captured more than 50,000 prisoners and some 800 big guns. Further, "the main object of the attack had been accomplished: that is the drawing away of French reserves stationed behind the British front" and "favorable conditions for the decisive blow planned against the British were developing."

An American observer, Frederick Palmer, was appalled. "It was nothing less than a rout. Among the French soldiers in disorganized retreat and along the lines of communication, and among the people, I noted an attitude of nervous despair far more than their attitude when the German drive of 1914 was at full tide." A little more pressure from the enemy, he thought, would bring defeat, for it was obvious that the French were "now very near the breaking point."

Early the next morning, the last day of May, a German assault group prepared to cross the Marne. Wagons heavily loaded with half-pontoons moved toward the bank amid shot and shell bursts. Captain Matthaei led his battalion to sedge near the river. Suddenly machine-gun bullets from a castle on the other side whipped into the bank. There were cries of "Medic!" then silence. Engineers were hit. The wounded and dead were dragged up the bank as a single boat started across carrying a guide rope.

"Third company up!" shouted a lieutenant who sprang into another boat, quickly followed by thirty men. They whispered jokes and bantered with the engineers. Once on the south bank the little group seized the bridge abutment. Their report came back: south bank clear of enemy, all quiet.

By 4:45 A.M. Matthaei's entire battalion was across the river. The sun was just creeping over the eastern horizon. Ahead lay a broad road. On both sides were wheat fields and meadows. Beyond, the castle of Varennes, shinning in the bright sunlight, stood in ominous silence.

Matthaei gave the command to attack. "A proud picture. The riflemen plunged into the high waves of the wheatfields. The railroad, the castle must be ours. Then from every floor burst fire thick as hail towards the shock troops. Many fell in the wheat, yet the attackers did not stop." All at once from the other side of the hills to the south came a dull rolling. French shells began to fall among the Germans and into the barges. Too late. "We have the Marne, and our bridgehead is secure; but an advance is now no longer possible. We are cut off from the other bank. Nothing moves; we are alone and hold the conquered south bank with clenched teeth."

Later that morning, Clemenceau assured Poincaré that Château-Thierry would not be taken, and the Boche would not cross the Marne. Pétain was going to attack on that flank.

"Today?"

"The operation has been delayed a few hours but will surely start today."

What about the vexatious indiscretions in the matter? asked Poincaré tartly. "They came, it appears, from your Cabinet." He hoped it wouldn't compromise the attack. Clemenceau changed the subject, warning Poincaré of such advisers as Briand. "I am a bit suspicious," admitted the President.

"Be a good deal suspicious."

The Tiger proceeded to the front, meeting with Foch and Pétain at Trilport, the new headquarters of Sixth Army, twenty miles east of Paris. Although he had been urged by his staff to put the blame on Foch, Pétain refused to stoop to such tactics, for he was convinced that the Generalissimo was necessary for victory. Usually he had been the pessimistic one, seeing dangers on all sides, but in this crisis he appeared the one least concerned. He assured Clemenceau that the Germans could be contained and the worst was already over. If the Allies could hold out until July, victory was a certainy. Foch also believed the Germans could be stopped.

Clemenceau left not quite convinced. He never had liked Foch and suspected that the Generalissimo might have made a fatal mistake, but on the motor trip back to Paris, Mordacq supported Foch. It was still odd that the Germans were attacking in the Champagne area. They would have to mount an entirely new offensive if they wanted to march on Paris, said Mordacq. And even the fall of that city would not mean defeat.

Such stout talk roused Clemenceau. "Yes, the Germans may take Paris," he said, "but that would not stop me from fighting. We will fight on the Loire, on the Garonne, if we must even in the Pyrenees . . . but as to making peace, never."

At lunch Foch's guest was Haig. The Generalissimo said that Pétain desperately wanted American divisions, "no matter how untrained," to hold the long front on the Swiss frontier. That would release French troops. Haig gave "some good reasons against the proposal, but said he would consider it and reply tomorrow." While they were talking, a message arrived from Pétain: the situation was critical; the reserves sent out to stop the Germans had "melted away very quickly." Foch looked more anxious than Haig had ever seen him.

American aid was already on the way. A fourteen-mile cavalcade of French camions "driven by little, yellow, dumb-looking Annamites," was moving the 2nd Division out of Normandy and Picardy; and the 3rd Division was already approaching Château-Thierry. Two newsmen, Junius Wood of the Chicago *Daily News* and Ray Carroll of the Philadelphia *Ledger*, were ahead of them. They had learned there was a breakthrough and wanted a scoop. They passed Château-Thierry and a few miles later ran into the German bridgehead near Varennes. Narrowly escaping capture, they raced back to Château-Thierry, where they were stirred to see troops and trucks with American insignia. It looked like a machine-gun company deploying on the outskirts of the town. Thank God, there was at last something to stop the Germans!

It was the spearhead of the 3rd Division. The first to come were fifteen doughboys carrying two Hotchkiss guns which had never been fired in combat. They were led by Lieutenant John Bissell, a recent graduate of West Point. While he was shifting his two guns from house to house, elements of the 7th Machine Gun Battalion began digging in across the Marne. By the time Major James Taylor arrived at dusk, eight Hotchkiss guns had been emplaced on the south bank covering the wagon bridge leading to Château-Thierry.

At Versailles a large contingent of British dignitaries had just arrived for tomorrow's Supreme War Council meeting. On the trip across the Channel, Henry Wilson had told Milner, Lloyd George, and Balfour that Foch was trying to hold too long a line with the troops at his disposal and that either he must shorten it or he would crack. Upon arrival in Versailles, Wilson was told that Château-Thierry and Villers-Cotterêts had been lost. "This last must mean they are not fighting. If this is so, we are done."

Thirteen sat down to dinner, but apparently Cabinet Secretary Hankey was the only one who noticed it or was superstitious enough to note it in a diary. Afterward he had an important conversation with Lieutenant General Sir John Du Cane, head of the British Mission at French Headquarters. Du Cane took a gloomy view of the future "and was very anxious at the idea of our having two and a half million hostages on the Continent in the event of a French defeat. He envisages the possibility of the French Army being smashed and cut off from us, the enemy demanding as a condition of peace the handing over of all the ports from Rouen and Havre to Dunkirk, and, in the event of a refusal, the remorseless hammering of our Army by the whole German Army. He does not think we could get our Army away and considers that, if we wanted to go on with the war, we should have to face the prospect of over a million prisoners in France. He evidently thinks a situation of this kind might develop quite soon." Du Cane also told of the disagreement between Foch and Lawrence, Haig's chief of staff, who wanted to abandon the Channel ports and fall back behind the Somme while it was still possible.

Hankey promptly reported this to Milner and Lloyd George. The latter was furious at the thought of sacrificing the Channel ports in order to shorten the line. "I am sure," Hankey added in his diary, "he means to get rid of Haig as soon as there is a lull in the fighting." *

Lloyd George, Wilson, and Haig stayed up late discussing the holding of Dunkirk until the last was "thoroughly tired of them!

---

* In his own book, Hankey records the entire day's entry except for this telling sentence.

Fortunately an air raid started and the lights went out." Wilson went to bed in an anxious frame of mind. "Tomorrow," he wrote, "will be a critical day. If Rupprecht now attacks south from Montdidier to Noyon and takes Compiègne the French Army is beaten. It is not easy to follow what would happen after that."

4.

The British Chief of Staff awoke on Saturday, June 1, in the same frame of mind. "Writing now, before breakfast, I find it difficult to realize that there is a possibility, perhaps a probability, of the French Army being beaten! What would this mean? The destruction of our army in France? In Italy? In Salonika? What of Palestine and Mesopotamia, India, Siberia, and the sea? What of Archangel and America?" Would they be able to answer any of these questions at the Versailles conference that afternoon?

Lord Milner was even more depressed. For more than six months his object had been to conclude a "tolerable" peace for the Empire and the Allies. Was this the moment? He was prepared to negotiate with the Germans but not to give way to them. He was not the only one thinking in these terms. A few weeks earlier, during the April crisis, the Prime Minister had privately discussed with some of his Cabinet, ex-ministers, and members of the Labour Party the possibility of ending the war in the west by giving the enemy a free hand in the east.

Lloyd George was still shocked at the incredible ineptitude of the French generals. First they had been swept out of Mount Kemmel, a position well behind the British front line for years. And now the disaster on the Aisne. Was their principal ally about to crack? "If the French had so readily given up elaborate entrenchments when the Germans were advancing on their capital, what reason was there to expect that they would hold on to positions when there was no time to prepare adequate defences?" He, like other British, was forgetting that their own troops on the Chemin des Dames had fallen back as quickly and as far as the French.

Even though he had been warned by Lord Derby of the wave of pessimism sweeping Paris, Lloyd George was surprised to find general despondency in France. "I did not anticipate it. I did not share it. I thought it was unjustified. I was convinced we had got over the worst."

After breakfast he went for a stroll in the park with Milner, Du Cane, and Wilson. It was "a really glorious morning," he said to Hankey, who accompanied them, notebook in hand. They discussed the line to be taken with Haig, who was due to arrive soon, and agreed that if he would not use the Americans the French should have them.

Upon return to their quarters, the Villa Romaine, they found Haig, and the group proceeded to the balcony on the shady side of the house. Hankey slipped away, feeling it was wiser to leave them to talk freely without notes being taken. The field marshal was as "wooden" as usual, thought Wilson. First they discussed the size of the American Army and agreed that President Wilson should be asked to aim for one hundred divisions. By when? As soon as possible. Haig suggested that the Americans be allowed to have "a definite *organized force*" within a year. He also hoped to quicken their training so that four divisions would be fit for the line in two weeks. Most important, said Haig, was to find out whether the French Army was fighting or not. From what he had heard their reserves in the recent attack just "melted away," and this, according to Haig, was "due to coddling them last summer, and to want of discipline and to the lack of reliable officers and N.C.O.s." In view of all this, he concluded that it would be "a waste of good troops" to send Americans to the French. The British would make much better use of the doughboys. So spoke the "wooden" soldier.

In Paris, Clemenceau was preparing for the momentous conference by conferring with Poincaré. Looking gray, the Tiger reported that last night he had found a very somber Pétain who envisaged the evacuation from Paris by the Government.

"I will not leave Paris!" said Poincaré.

"I don't want to risk the fate of France in one battle," said Clemenceau. "We must endure and wait for the Americans." Poincaré protested that it was necessary, once more, to stop the Germans at the Marne and so save Paris. Clemenceau agreed but pointed out that their reserves could not get to the front any quicker. All the roads were jammed and railroads could be cut off. "It appears certain to me that the Germans will come close enough to bombard Paris."

"That is not reason for leaving," said Poincaré, suspecting that the Tiger wanted him out of the capital so he could reap all the glory in case of a siege. And so both decided to stay in the city to the end.

Clemenceau went on to the Trianon Park Hotel in Versailles, where a preliminary meeting was held in his office with Lloyd George, Wilson, Haig, and Foch. The two Frenchmen began accusing the British of failing to bring enough men to France. Lloyd George stoutly denied this, insisting that his Government had made great efforts to get men across the Channel before the March 21 offensive. Foch insisted that Haig keep up the total of divisions promised, adding bluntly that, if he did not, the war was lost. "And so," confided Haig to his diary, "these people went on wrangling and wasting time." Finally Lloyd George agreed to let Foch send to England an expert to examine the British manpower figures. And this appeared, at last, to satisfy Clemenceau.

It was almost two hours past the scheduled opening of the Supreme War Council. The large waiting room was crammed to overflowing with Italians and Americans, secretaries and interpreters. "Not a single window was opened!" observed Haig as he entered the meeting room. "The place was stifling."

It turned out that the only subject discussed by this impressive gathering was the appointment of a supreme commander to control all the Allied fleets in the Mediterranean. The British and French somehow managed to agree, but the Italians protested. "Their object seemed to be to stay in port and keep their fleet safe," noted Haig. "I was disgusted with their attitude." Nothing, of course, was settled, and after two and a half deadly hours Haig left for a walk in the garden with Balfour. Later he wrote his wife: "I spent all day at Versailles listening to much talk. There is no doubt that a democratic form of Government is a bad one as compared with the Germans for controlling a war!"

The important business of the day was discussed by Pershing, Foch, and Milner in Clemenceau's office. Foch began by painting a desperate picture of the military situation. He proposed that the Americans send nothing but infantry and machine-gun units in June and July, 250,000 each month. "The battle, the battle, nothing else counts!" he exclaimed, waving his arms.

Pershing was just as positive. America had to build up its army as a unit to carry on the battle to the end. Already the program had been seriously interrupted by concessions. The French railway system, moreover, was breaking down and the ports would be hopelessly blocked unless they were improved. Furthermore, the restriction of shipments to infantry and machine-gun units would be a dangerous and shortsighted policy. Foch seemed to be paying little attention and impatiently insisted that all these things could be postponed. The argument went on without anything being accomplished until Pershing proposed that they adjourn for the day.

In the meantime the Germans continued to advance. The railway stations in Paris were filled with those escaping the city. Baggage was piled, haphazardly, on the platforms since there was no room left in the baggage rooms, and travelers had to pick their way through the stacks to find an exit.

The Kaiser returned to his headquarters, dust-stained from a long trip to the front, but in good spirits. "He is quite intoxicated by the successes of the Army," wrote the exasperated Admiral von Müller in his diary, "and makes marginal notes on the despatches with such comments as 'The victors of Craonne.' Pity that he should thus lose all sense of proportion!"

His Majesty would have been particularly proud of one of his corporals, Adolf Hitler, who had single-handedly captured four French soldiers. Armed only with a pistol, he had shouted so commandingly that the poilus thought he was leading at least a company. Hitler delivered his four prisoners to his regimental commander, Colonel von Tubeuf, and was commended. "There was no circumstance or situation," recalled Tubeuf, "that would have prevented him from volunteering for the most difficult, arduous and dangerous tasks and he was always ready to sacrifice life and tranquility for his Fatherland and for others." A little later Hitler was awarded the Iron Cross, First Class, for former achievements and not this outstanding feat. The coveted medal was presented to him by the battalion adjutant, who had initiated the award, a Jew named Hugo Gutmann.

The next morning, Sunday, Clemenceau again called on Poincaré. After discussing at length the peril that Paris was facing, he unexpectedly turned emotional. "If I had died before the war, I would have died convinced that my country was lost. The vices of the parliamentary regime, the intrigues, the shortcomings, the idiosyncrasies, all made me believe we were decadent. But this war has revealed to the entire world a France so beautiful, so admirable, that now I am full of confidence." Poincaré was thinking that although this display was genuine it unhappily seemed more sentimental than rational. "And if," continued the Tiger, "it is our bad fortune to die, I wish, at least, that my country die battling for its independence and that it dies in beauty." Sentimentality became bitterness by the time the mercurial Clemenceau met with Pershing and the British early in the afternoon. He had since learned that the British had received an option on the 120,000 American troops sent in May. Why shouldn't half these reinforcements be assigned to French divisions? he accused rather than asked. If not that, would the Americans let the French have 120,000 men from the June allotment?

Pershing stiffly declined to commit his Government on this point. An acrimonious debate ensued until Clemenceau finally agreed to postpone the question until a later meeting, then he began to berate the British. How strange, he said sarcastically, that the Germans, with a population of 68,000,000, could put 204 divisions in the field, while the British, with 46,000,000, could only assemble 43. This sparked another long wrangle, with Foch reiterating rudely, according to Hankey, that he could not conduct the war unless the British maintained their divisions.

Everyone seemed at odds. Pershing obstinately refused to consider the British proposal to make Haig the authority for deciding when Americans were to go into the lines. And both the British and French were annoyed because Pershing stoutly resisted their demand for exclusive shipments of American infantry and machine-gunners. Lloyd George became so frustrated that he dejectedly admitted that the Allies were in a sense in the hands of the United States. All they could do was call on President Wilson to come to their aid in this crisis.

It appeared as if nothing would be accomplished for the second day in a row until it was suggested that Pershing, Milner, and Foch get together and draw up an agreement. What eighteen could not accomplish, the three did in short order. They agreed that of the 250,000 Americans sent to France in June, 170,000 would be combatant troops, 25,400 would service the railroads, and the rest would be determined by Pershing. For July 140,000 would be combatant troops and the rest designated by Pershing.

During the lunch break, Foch and Lord Balfour strolled in the garden. The elderly Foreign Secretary deferentially asked the Generalissimo how he was going to stop the Germans. "I will hit here," he said, kicking with one foot. "Then hit there," kicking with the other foot. He repeated the footwork, adding arm gesticulations to the delight of Lloyd George and others watching from a distance who had no idea what all these pugilistic gestures meant.

The entire group walked back to the conference chamber to discuss the Mediterranean once more. The little they had settled yesterday—appointing Admiral Jellicoe as over-all commander—was undone by the Italians, who now demanded that one of their own officers, Admiral de Revel, be in charge. Revel, noted Hankey, "distinguished himself by boasting that the Italian fleet had not been to sea for 18 months and consequently, had not lost a ship!" The argument dragged on for hours until everyone began shouting at once. "What is going on in there?" someone in the corridor asked. "I guess," remarked the quick-witted General Bliss, "they are all at sea except the Italian admiral who won't go there!" Lloyd George became so annoyed he bellowed that they wanted to make the appointment a sham! He wouldn't think of asking a man of Jellicoe's eminence to accept it. Whereupon he withdrew the original suggestion.

Wilson was disgusted. "There was terrible waste of time all day, what with Foch and his inaccurate figures, with Pershing, and with the Italian admiral. And all the time the Boches are gaining ground below Château-Thierry, and towards Villers-Cotterêts, and west of Soissons, and south of Noyon. A council is a pathetic and maddening thing."

On Monday, June 3, the final session of the Supreme War Council ended with comparative amicability but little accomplished. Afterward Hankey went shopping with Lloyd George for souvenirs to take to his family. The Prime Minister, Hankey noted, was attracted to the pretty girl waiting on them. Like Clemenceau, Lloyd George was known for his partiality to women, particularly favoring his secretary, Frances Stevenson, to whom he was sending almost daily passionate notes, usually addressed to "My Darling Pussy."

The next day, Clemenceau was tried for his political life in a heading of the Chamber of Deputies at the Palais Bourbon. If he fell, his successor would surely dismiss Foch and Pétain—and seek a negotiated peace with Germany. From the beginning it was obvious that the opposition was after Clemenceau's blood. He was greeted with noisy derision, and two demands: to negotiate for peace and to fire Pétain and Foch.

Controlling himself, the Tiger maintained his poise as Deputy Frédéric Brunet charged that the recent fighting proved that France's leaders were incapable. "When we saw the first onrush of the Germans on the Somme not a soul faltered in the entire country; we all said with you, 'They shall not pass.' But when we have seen the debacle at the Chemin des Dames, along which so many of our men have fallen in order to keep it in French hands, we could not but feel a momentary pang, and ask ourselves if those in command had really done their whole duty . . . and if the law comes down with crushing force upon the soldier who fails to do his duty it ought to deal still more drastically with the leader who through negligence or lack of foresight may well be the cause of irretrievable defeats."

After a demand for a secret session, the Tiger mounted the tribune to do battle. "What would we achieve by an immediate discussion?" he said. "Sow doubt in anxious minds. Add further misapprehensions to those already established. I cannot lend myself to this." There were hoots and jeers, but Clemenceau ignored them. "If, to win the approbation of certain persons who judge in rash haste," he continued scathingly, "I must abandon chiefs who have deserved well of their country, that is a piece of contemptible baseness of which I am incapable, and it must not be expected of me. If we are to raise doubts in the minds of the troops as to the competence of certain of their leaders, perhaps among the best, that would be a crime for which I should never accept responsibility."

He admitted that mistakes had been made and it was his duty to correct them. "That is what I am devoting my energies to. And in that task I have the support of two great soldiers whose names are General Foch and General Pétain." This brought another storm of boos. "Our Allies have such high confidence in General Foch that yesterday at the Conference of Versailles, it was their wish that the communiqué should contain reference to that confidence."

"It was you that made them do it!" shouted someone, and after Clemenceau continued imperturbably to describe the battle they were waging near the Marne, he was interrupted again and again. "Is it for us, because of some mistake that occurred in this place or that, or even never occurred, to ask for, to extort explanations before we know the facts, while the battle is still raging, from a man exhausted with fatigue, whose head droops over maps, as I have seen with my own eyes in hours of dreadful stress? Is this the man we are going to ask to tell us whether on such and such a day he did thus or thus?"

There were as many cheers as jeers, for he was beginning to speak with inspiration, but the opposition made such an uproar that, at one point, Clemenceau was literally driven from the podium. Once the riot stopped he was back again. "Turn me out of the tribune, if that is what you want, for I will never do it." He caught fire as he began to rouse the chamber to a pitch of enthusiasm. The words seemed torn from him and there was "such painful appraisal of tragic truths, such a heavy sense of his responsibilities and grim determination to fulfill them," observed Geoffrey Brunn, "that lesser minds were awed and silenced."

In moving terms he told of the heavy odds the poilus were fighting against and the enormous losses sustained. "Yet we shall not surrender." And they were not fighting alone. "French and English effectives are becoming exhausted, but the Americans are coming." This brought a spontaneous cheer. "We are giving ground but we shall never surrender." They would surely be victorious if only the public authorities were equal to the task. "I myself am fighting before Paris. I shall fight in Paris. I shall fight behind Paris." This brought more shouts of approval. "Dismiss me if I have been a bad servant, drive me out, condemn me, but at least take the trouble to put your criticisms into plain words. For my part I claim that up till now the French people, and every section of it, has done its duty to the full. Those who have fallen have not fallen in vain, for they have found a way to add to the greatness of French history. It remains for the living to finish the glorious work of the dead."

Although the opposition still clamored, they were drowned out by those who approved. And by the lopsided count of 337 to 110, the Chamber voted down the proposal for further explanations. The Tiger had won despite a strong and well-armed opposition. "Not reason and logic alone," commented Brunn, "but reason and logic stated with contagious courage and honesty, enabled him to compel assent even when he failed to convince."

"This is a very good thing," Haig wrote his wife, "because if Clemenceau were to go there would be a Government of all sorts of scoundrels. Clemenceau is a good strong patriot who only thinks of winning the war."

While General Wilson undoubtedly agreed, he still questioned Foch's ability to stop the Germans. The following day, June 5, he came to 10 Downing Street with Milner to discuss the question of the reserves and the proposed evacuation of Ypres and Dunkirk. Foch could not see beyond his nose, said Wilson, and would surely lose the war unless he shortened his line up north and made greater use of saltwater inundations in the Dunkirk region. "It is simply d—— * nonsense saying he won't 'lacher un pied' [turn tail] and then run from the Chemin des Dames to Château-Thierry." They then discussed the possibility of withdrawing the entire British Army from France if the French should crack. "It was a very gloomy meeting," recalled Hankey. In the end it was decided that Wilson and Milner would return to Versailles the next day to see Foch and Clemenceau. "This will be a delicate business," glumly commented Wilson. "Foch will lose this war."

Just before he and Milner left for France, Wilson told Lloyd George flatly "that if Foch would not agree to our proposals, viz. either to take four of his French divisions from the north and to leave us our Americans, or else to shorten the line in the north, and in any case to allow Haig to fight his line in any way he may choose, then Lloyd George would get a letter from me to say the British Army would be lost."

* This is Wilson's own truncation, not Callwell's.

The vaunted principle of unity of command was tottering and would probably fall unless the Marne line held. The hinge was a pretty little wooded area some five miles northwest of Château-Thierry. It was known as Belleau Wood. Germans infested most of it and were driving south to take the rest so they could reach the village of Lucy-le-Bocage. From there they would only be forty-five miles from the Eiffel Tower.

It was not a large wood. The trees were about six inches thick and so densely planted that one could scarcely see twenty feet ahead except where ax or shell had cut a swath. Unlike American forests it had been constantly under care of a forester who cleared out the underbrush and those trees ready for timbering. Despite the lack of undergrowth there was ample shelter in the high, rocky ground which was scarred with gullies and crags. It was an irregular area not much more than a square mile that from the air reminded some of a sea horse, some of a twisted kidney. It had once been the hunting preserve for the ancient Château of Belleau, which was a half mile north of the wood and was connected to Lucy-le-Bocage by a farm road. At the southeast corner of the wood was another small village, Bouresches. This was held by the Germans and had to be retaken before the Allies could clear the wood.

By June 5, the U.S. 2nd Division was stretched out below Belleau Wood, eager to show the world that Americans could fight as well as talk. It was a hybrid division with 1,063 officers and 25,602 men in two brigades, one Army and one Marine. The Leathernecks were commanded by a Regular Army officer, Brigadier General James Harbord, former chief of staff to Pershing, who had told him that he was getting the best troops in France and if he failed he'd know whom to blame.

Their race to Belleau Wood had been a hectic one. "We rode day and all night—it was an awful cold and dirty trip," 2nd Lieutenant Clifton Cates wrote his mother and sister. "If you can imagine about one thousand trucks lined up one behind the other and running as fast as possible. We passed through the outskirts of gay Paree and on thru numerous towns." All along the way he saw refugees "plodding their way back and old men, women, and children: some walking and others on carts trying to carry their valuables back—it was the most pitiful sight I have ever seen, and there is not a man in our bunch that didn't grit his teeth, and say 'Vive la France.' 'Do or die' is our motto—and the mother that can furnish a boy should say—'America—here's my boy, God grant that he may come back, if not, I am glad he died for a noble cause, and I am willing to give him to you.'"

The French cheered these outlandish, boisterous young men from overseas who stuck their legs out of the trucks and acted as if they were going to a party. The sight of their cheery, cocky faces gave new spirit to the people. The Yanks were finally coming and now there was hope that the Boche could be stopped. "Striking was the contrast in appearance between the Americans and the French regiments, whose men, in torn uniforms, hungry and hollow-eyed, were scarcely able to hold themselves erect," recalled Jean de Pierrefeu. "New life had come to bring a fresh, surging vigor to the body of France, bled almost to death. Thus it came to pass that in those crucial days when the enemy stood for a second time on the Marne, thinking us disheartened, then, contrary to all expectation, an ineffable confidence filled the hearts of all Frenchmen."

The 2nd Division, ordered "to hold the line at all hazards," had already stopped the Germans in the wheat fields five miles west of where the Marne dipped abruptly south. Now the Americans were eager to attack and that night they got their wish. Major General Jean Degoutte of the XXI French Corps ordered them to drive into Belleau Wood the next morning.

At 3:45 A.M., June 6, the commander of the 1st Battalion of the Fifth Marine Regiment arrived at the front-line trenches. He found some of the men had already gone over the top and were twenty-five yards out front, so he gave the word to advance. Heavy machine-gun fire from the wood killed some and sent the rest to the ground for cover, and the attack would have stopped but for Captain George Hamilton, commander of the 49th Company. Realizing they were up against something unusual, he ran along the line getting the men onto their feet, urging them to attack the wood. Back and forth he went, inspiring his troops to follow—and they did. They rushed forward, bayonets fixed, thrusting themselves at the gray-clad enemy. Some Germans threw up their hands with a scream of *"Kamerad"* and were saved, but most were not spared and some Marines remembered that they squealed in an undignified way.

Hamilton, an outstanding athlete, was everywhere. "I have vague recollections of urging the whole line on, faster, perhaps, than they should have gone—of grouping prisoners and sending them to the rear under *one* man instead of several—of snatching an iron cross ribbon off the first officer I got—and of shooting wildly at several rapidly retreating Boches." He was carrying a rifle and using it to good advantage. "Farther on, we came to an open field—a wheat-field full of red poppies—and here we caught hell. Again it was a case of rushing across the open and getting into the woods." Three machine-gun companies were holding the wood, but Hamilton and his men plunged forward to take the position. Then Hamilton realized that they had come too far. The crest of the hill they had just rushed over was his objective. They had to get back, reorganize, and dig in. "It was a case of every man for himself. I crawled back through a drainage ditch filled with cold water and shiny reeds." Machine-gun bullets were grazing his back and, since he was six hundred yards too far to the front, friendly shells were falling dangerously close. At last he got back and began reorganizing the survivors. He had lost all five of his junior officers, so, with no thought for his own life, he ran from group to group setting up a defensive line.

The company behind Hamilton was also advancing to its objective against heavy rifle and machine-gun fire. The situation was critical all morning, but by noon counterattacks had been beaten off and at 2:15 P.M. General Harbord ordered another attack, this one a two-phase assault, the first to seize the eastern edge of Belleau Wood and the second to take the strategic village of Bouresches. Zero hour would be five o'clock.

An enterprising correspondent was on the way to the scene of the action. Floyd Gibbons of the Chicago *Tribune* had motored down from Paris that morning with Lieutenant Oscar Hartzell, formerly of the New York *Times*, in hopes of seeing the Americans in their first major engagement. Gibbons reached Fifth Marine headquarters at 4 P.M. and told its commander, Colonel Neville, that he wanted to get out to the front line.

"Go wherever you like," said Neville. "Go as far as you like but I want to tell you it's damn hot up there."

It took Gibbons and Hartzell almost an hour to reach Lucy-le-Bocage. Shells were falling. Farmhouses were in flames. The ground under the trees was covered with tiny bits of paper. Gibbons examined several and saw that they were letters from American mothers and wives which the weary Marines had removed from their packs and destroyed so the enemy could make no use of them. He came upon a pit containing two machine guns and their crews. Out front was a field sloping gently down two hundred yards to another cluster of trees. Part of it, apparently, was held by the enemy.

At 4:55 a young platoon commander arrived with the order to advance. "What are you doing here?" he asked Gibbons, looking at the green brassard and red "C" on Gibbons' left arm.

"Looking for the big story."

"If I were you I'd be about forty miles south of this place," said the officer, "but if you want to see the fun stick around. We are going forward in five minutes."

The Marines waited, stripped for action—no extra clothes or blankets and only twenty pounds on their packs. Colonel Albertus Catlin, commander of the Sixth Marine Regiment, came up to find his men cool and in good spirits. "Give 'em hell, boys!" he told several of them.

At exactly five o'clock everyone leaped up simultaneously and started forward. There was a sickening rattle of machine-gun fire. German artillery increased the fury of its attack. The 3rd Battalion of Major Berry faced a large open field of wheat, all green but about two feet tall. It was swept by machine-gun bullets. The wheat bowed and waved in the metal storm. The advancing lines wavered until someone shouted, "Come on, you sons of bitches! Do you want to live forever." It was the legendary Gunnery Sergeant Dan Daly, recipient of the Medal of Honor, whose voice had been striking terror in recruits for the past twenty-five years. The line moved forward, but a hundred yards from the wood the enemy fire was so brutal that the men had to fling themselves down. Many died trying to crawl back. A few got safely into the woods. The rest hugged the ground and waited for dark.

Floyd Gibbons and Hartzell were just behind Major Berry when he turned and shouted, "Get down, everybody!" They fell on their faces. Withering volleys of lead scissored the top of the wheat. It was not coming from the woods but from the left. Up ahead came a shout. Gibbons lifted his head cautiously and saw the major trying to struggle to his feet. He was grasping his left wrist in pain. "My hand's gone!" he exclaimed. "Get down. Flatten out, Major!" shouted Gibbons. "We've got to get out of here," said Berry. "They'll start shelling this open field in a few minutes."

Gibbons looked around cautiously. "You're about twenty yards from the trees," he called to Berry, and said he was coming to help. The correspondent crawled forward, keeping as flat as possible. Suddenly it felt as if a lighted edge of a cigarette touched his upper left arm. It felt like a minor burn. There was no pain. A bullet had gone clean through his bicep muscle without even leaving a hole in his sleeve. Then something nicked the top of his left shoulder. Again the burning sensation but he was surprised to find he could still move his arm.

It wasn't anywhere near as painful as a dentist's drill. He continued moving, occasionally shouting words of encouragement. As he swung his chin to the right to keep close to the ground, he moved his helmet over. Then came a crash like a bottle dropped in a bathtub. Sergeant M. K. McHenry was so close he saw Gibbons get hit in the face. To Gibbons it seemed as if a barrel of whitewash had tipped over and everything in the world turned white. He didn't know where he had been hit but surely not the head; if so, everything was supposed to turn black. He began taking mental notes. "Am I dead?" It wasn't a joke. He wanted to know. He tried to move the fingers of his left hand. They moved. Now the left foot moved. He knew he was alive. He brought his hand to his nose. Something soft and wet. He found his hand covered with blood. There was a pain in the entire left side of his face so he closed his right eye. Dark! He tried to open his left eye. Still dark. Something must have struck him in the eye and closed it. He didn't guess that a bullet had gone through his eye and crashed through his forehead. He could not reach the major now. But moments later he saw Berry rise and, in a hail of lead, rush forward and out of his vision.

Merwin Silverthorn, a rather small, energetic, and bright sergeant, was just to the left with his platoon commander, an Army lieutenant named Coppinger. They had set off in approved trench warfare formation, holding rifles at high port and moving at a slow steady cadence. They started down a ravine and near the bottom were raked by machine-gun fire. They hid behind a pile of wood. After five minutes Coppinger shouted, "Follow me!" and ran bent over up the other side of the ravine. At the top he looked back and said in wonder, "Where the hell is my platoon?" They had started with fifty-two and now there were six. "I'm going back," he told Silverthorn, who thought, "Here's where you and I part company, because we just got across that place, and that's the last thing I'm going to do—go back."

Silverthorn figured that in the military no one ever got into trouble for advancing toward the enemy, so he kept going until he found the remnants of another platoon, led by Sergeant Gay. They finally reached the wheat field. And there Silverthorn saw one of the most magnificent sights of his life—Major Sibley's battalion marching across the field in slow cadence under terrific fire. As Gay's platoon started up toward the field, he was hit in the back. Silverthorn bound the wound; told him it wasn't too bad. "You stay here and I'll come back after dark to get you." He took charge of the few men left and they all went forward in rushes. The din was deafening. As Silverthorn hit the ground on the second rush, he thought he'd struck a rock. He looked down. There was no rock. It felt as if someone had swung a baseball bat across the knee cap. Yet there was no pain. He told the only man left, an automatic rifleman, to move on into woods where they probably needed him. "I'm going to stay right where I am until it's dark and can get out under cover." He thought of his father, who had been shot in the lung at Gettysburg, yet lived to be ninety-six.

On the right, Major Berton Sibley's battalion was having better luck and Colonel Catlin watched with admiration as the battalion pivoted on its right with the left sweeping the open field in four waves, as steadily as though on parade. It was "one of the most beautiful sights I have ever witnessed." There was no yell or rush but a deliberate march with lines at right dress. Catlin's hands were clenched, all his muscles taut as he watched the Marines march in the face of machine-gun sweeps. Men fell but fortunately Sibley's men had slightly better cover than Berry's and the rest plodded on stolidly, listening for orders. Closer and closer they came to the wood and it must have been a terrifying sight to those holding it.

Catlin had no field telephone. He hurried to a little rise so he could see what was going on ahead. Through his glasses he watched Sibley's men plunge into the wood. Captain Tribot-Laspierre, a French liaison officer, begged Catlin to get to a safer place, but the colonel ignored the bullets whipping around him until one hit him in the chest. "It felt exactly as though some one had struck me heavily with a sledge. It swung me clear around and toppled me over on the ground." When he tried to get up he realized his right side was paralyzed. Captain Tribot-Laspierre rushed to Catlin's side, and dragged the big man to a shelter trench—no simple matter since he was so small. The bullet had gone through Catlin's lung, but he felt little pain and never lost consciousness. The bleeding was internal and there was little to be done for him as he lay in the trench, waiting for first-aid treatment.

In the meantime Major Thomas Holcomb of the 2nd Battalion

had instructed Sergeant Don Paradise of the 80th Company to take Private Slack across the wheat field. They were to locate the 80th Company commander, Captain Coffenberg, as well as Major Sibley, the adjoining battalion commander, and get their map locations and any other information. Paradise, followed by Slack, safely crossed the deadly field and soon found Sibley. "For God's sake," said Sibley, "tell Major Holcomb not to take Captain Coffenberg and the 80th Company away from me! We've lost at least half our battalion."

"Come on, Slack, let's get back," said Paradise, but the other man was horrified. "You aren't going the same way we came?" It was the shortest route, said Paradise, and headed back alone. Sometimes the shell smoke was so thick he couldn't see where he was going and wounded men kept calling for help, but a runner couldn't stop to be a medic. He finally found Holcomb on the side of a hill and lay down beside his hole to give him the message. He then asked permission to go back to help the wounded, but Holcomb said he'd have to carry more messages, so he crawled into a nearby hole until needed. He could see Bouresches and, figuring that the Germans could see him, crawled over to a hedge where other runners were digging in. A moment later a shell exploded directly in his evacuated hole.

Sergeant Silverthorn was still lying in the wheat field. It felt as though machine-gun bullets were passing only an inch or two over him. Every so often a speck of dirt flicked up nearby. He guessed a sniper was zeroing in on him. Then shells began falling and he decided to get up and run whether he had one leg or not. It was about two hundred yards to the woods. He dashed across plowed ground into tall grass hip high. Here he found a friend named Pilcher, who was weeping and moaning. He had been hit in the stomach. Silverthorn repeated what he had told Gay—"I'll come back after dark and get you"—then he crept through the grass, which hid him until he could lunge safely into Belleau Wood. Here it was quiet, peaceful, deserted. It was eerie and for the first time he was frightened. He was alone yet he knew that the Germans were near. He limped along and was lucky enough to find a dressing station where he was tagged to go to a hospital. But he located a stretcher and convinced someone to go back to the wheat field with him. On the way he looked for Sergeant Gay but couldn't find him, so he started for Pilcher. He looked for the wheat field in the dark, at last finding it by instinct. He softly began calling Pilcher's name. "Of all the screwy situations," he told himself. "Here you get out of this thing once and you're right back where you started from." He felt his way until he stumbled upon Pilcher. He was motionless. "Pilcher, we're here," he said, shaking his friend. "I've got a stretcher. We're going to take care of you now." But he was dead. Silverthorn was a religious man and finding the stiff body of Pilcher intensified his Christianity. "It convinced me that the Lord had something for me to do."

Gibbons was still waiting in the field for a medic. Lieutenant

Hartzell, hiding nearby, called, "I don't think they can see us now. Let's start to crawl back." Gibbons had no idea where he was and crept toward the voice. They met halfway. "Hold your head up a little," said Hartzell. "I want to see where it hit you."

Gibbons lifted his head, painfully opened his right eye, and looked directly into Hartzell's face. "I saw the look of horror in it as he looked into mine." Twenty minutes later they reached the edge of the woods and safety.

In the meantime, Lieutenant Clifton Cates of Holcomb's 2nd Battalion was leading his platoon across the wheat field toward Bouresches. Men were falling on both sides. A machine-gun bullet knocked off Cates's helmet. He dropped, stunned. A few minutes later Cates came to. He tried to don his helmet, but it wouldn't go on at first because of a dent the size of a fist. "The machine gun bullets were hitting around and it looked like hail. My first thought was to run to the rear. I hate to admit it, but that was it." Glimpsing four Marines in a ravine, he staggered toward them and fell at their feet. One took off the dented helmet and poured wine from his canteen over the lump on Cates's head. "God damn it," said the lieutenant, "don't pour that wine over my head, give me a drink of it." This revived him. He then grabbed a French rifle and led the quartet into Bouresches.

Several miles to the west, Major Wise's battalion was in reserve. About midnight a runner from General Harbord brought an order to go into the line to the left of Berry. "This was the damnedest order I ever got in my life—or anyone else ever got," Wise wrote. "It went on the calm assumption that all the objectives of the First and Third Battalion had been secured . . . I was between the devil and the deep sea. If I didn't move, I knew I'd catch hell. If I did move, I knew I was going right down into Germany."

They set out at 2 A.M., June 7. It was "black as pitch—impossible to see even one foot ahead"—as Wise led the battalion in single file along a road which led to "sloping grain fields like a bottleneck opening into a bottle." Wise had a hunch and stopped the column. It was too deadly quiet. He led several squads forward about two hundred yards until sharp rifle fire burst out on the left. Wise recognized the sharp bark of Springfield rifles and shouted out to hold fire. From the dark someone shouted, "Look out. The Germans are on your right in the Bois de Belleau."

Wise went back, shouted to his men, "About face to the rear—on the double!" Like everyone else Lieutenant Lemuel C. Shepherd, Jr., was confused. He had been taught never to obey such an order without saying, "By whose command?" This word went back up the line and was answered with, "By orders of Major Wise—we're in the wrong spot."

Those in the rear decided that if a major said it was time to run it was time to move fast. "We picked up our feet," recalled Lieutenant E. D. Cooke, "and galloped back in the direction from which we had been going." Those behind could not go as fast. They would take a few steps, then halt before taking a few more.

This continued until the first light of day as they were emerging from woods into an open field at the point where the road made a sharp curve to the left. Wise gave orders to take cover on both sides of the road and dig in. The 55th Company of Captain Blanchfield was in the lead and Lieutenant Shepherd led his platoon to the left, distributing them along the edge of the woods facing the clearing. All at once firing broke out.

In the light of dawn Shepherd could see Germans moving in the clump of woods up ahead and on the right. What Major Wise had unwittingly done was lead his battalion into an open field at the left of Belleau Wood—and this was heavily defended by the enemy. A fierce fire fight erupted. Mortar shells began falling on all sides, landing with dull thuds and then exploding "with a tremendous concussion which was truly frightening."

A breathless runner told Shepherd that Captain Blanchfield had been seriously wounded and ordered him to command the company. As Shepherd headed along the edge of the wood, his orderly went down. While trying to help him, something struck Shepherd in his left thigh. It felt like the kick of a mule. He crumpled in a heap, not realizing in the excitement of the moment that he had been hit. "As I lay there unable to move, I glanced down and what should I see on the ground beside me but the bullet which had struck me." Blood was oozing from his britches. Close beside him with his head on Shepherd's leg was his little dog, Ki-Ki, who had tagged along behind him all night. He was so quiet Shepherd thought he was dead. "Damn it, they shot little Ki-Ki too," he said, and pushed him to one side. But Ki-Ki jumped up and placed his head again on Shepherd's leg, apparently sensing something had happened to his master.

Later that day newspapers throughout the United States headlined the attack. OUR MARINES ATTACK, GAIN MILE AT VEUILLY, RESUME DRIVE AT NIGHT, FOE LOSING HEAVILY announced the New York *Times*. And in Chicago the *Daily Tribune*: MARINES WIN HOT BATTLE SWEEP ENEMY FROM HEIGHTS NEAR THIERRY.

At last America had something to cheer about and the Marines were lauded incessantly. "Everywhere one went in the cars, on the streets, in hotel or skyscrapers, the one topic was the Marines who are fighting with such glorious success in France." So commented the New York *Times*. Reports received at their recruiting headquarters in New York indicated that applications had increased more than a hundred percent.

To read these papers, one would have thought it was the most important battle of the war. The wounding of Floyd Gibbons had much to do with the spate of publicity. Before the attack he had sent to the censor in Paris a skeleton dispatch, intending to fill in the details afterward. When it was rumored that he had been killed, the Paris censor, a friend, said, "This is the last thing I can ever do for poor old Floyd," and released the dispatch. Later Gibbons' detailed story added more luster, not only to himself but to the Marines. All this was to the detriment of doughboys who were fighting in the same division, as well as those in the 3rd Divsion holding the Marne River line west of Château-Thierry. Everything accomplished near that city was now assumed to be done by the Marines.

Small as the action was at Belleau Wood, it put new spirit in the French and deeply impressed the German soldiers who had faced the Americans. The dash and raw courage of the Leathernecks struck terror in those defending the wood and word was passed to beware of the wild Americans.* To their officers, the reckless display at Belleau was even more ominous. They saw the charge over the wheat fields multiplied many times. There were already about 700,000 Americans in France and more than a million others were on the way. And these were not worn and dispirited but strong, young, and brazenly confident.

6.

In the excitement of the American fight at Belleau Wood, the most important event of the day was ignored: the German High Command decided to end the third Ludendorff offensive. Serious offensive action along the Marne was halted.

Paris was saved but didn't yet know it, and there was still talk of getting rid of Foch and Pétain. The Allied leaders had no idea the Germans had abandoned their drive, and that same afternoon again met in Versailles in an atmosphere of anxiety. Lord Milner started by revealing that Lloyd George was quite concerned by the constant withdrawal of troops from Haig's command in view of the large numbers of German reserves still available for action against the British. Haig then read a memo stating that he fully agreed with Foch as to the necessity of making all preparations for supporting the French in an emergency, then asked that he should be consulted "before a definite order to move any Divisions from the British area were given."

Perturbed, Foch finally made a threat of sorts: unless the British kept up the strength of their army he could not carry on. Moreover, if the British attacked on a wide front from the Somme to the Marne he would have to take *all* of Haig's reserves.

At this Haig bristled and Milner tried to calm him by explaining that Foch had only said "if" such an attack as he suggested took place. Surely Foch did not intend withdrawing any more American divisions from Haig? When Foch replied, "No," Haig promptly reminded him querulously that the Generalissimo had previously withdrawn both the American and the French divisions without informing him. "I never saw old Foch so non-plussed," wrote Wilson in his diary. "He simply had not a word to say." Despite the wrangling and display of nerves both Foch and Haig returned to their headquarters free to concentrate on their own problems:

---

* The bitter fight at Belleau, which continued through the month, produced renowned fighters who would lead the Marines in World War II. Among the future generals were Cates, Holcomb, Shepherd, and Silverthorn.

Haig's on the growing evidence of yet another large offensive on his front, and Foch's on the threat at the Marne. "This meeting has done a vast deal of good and has been well worth the trouble," concluded Wilson.

The French still dreaded a German breakthrough to Paris. Ambassador Sharp reported to Washington that plans for evacuation of women and children were under way but could not be made public. A good many Americans had already left the capital, and arrangements had been made for orderly evacuation of others if it should be necessary. "This exodus has been without doubt very much hastened by the almost nightly raids of hostile aeroplanes and the daily visitation of the shells from the long-range guns."

After two days without alarms, a terrifying report came on the morning of June 9 that the Germans were launching still another mass attack, less than sixty miles northeast of Paris. And this time there was no formidable Chemin des Dames ridge to bar the way, only two small rivers and nine worn French divisions.

Major Lloyd Griscom was preparing to leave the capital for London on a special mission for Pershing and stopped at the French War Ministry for the latest information. He found utter despondency, and the Chief of Staff, a perfect stranger, began pouring out his despair. "France is on the brink of catastrophe," he exclaimed. "She is exhausted. Every bayonet is on the front line, we've drained our factories of their best workmen, we've crippled our service of supply, our railroads can hardly operate." He continued in this vein for almost an hour, then looked questioningly at Griscom, a consular officer before enlisting in the army. "If you will you can render us a great service. You see, the British take the war differently than we do. Their able-bodied men by the thousands are mining coal to sell at a profit all over the world. In their munition factories they have far more healthy sound men than they need. It is well known the number who can go on their fighting fleet is limited, yet their navy is crowded. Now is the moment for forcing the *embusqués* [soldiers not at the front line] into the battle lines of France. But we cannot make them comprehend our desperate straits."

He picked up a thick report, a comparative study of the utilization of French and British manpower. Would Griscom please give it to the British War Office? "Do, I beg you, bring home to them the urgency of putting more men into the fighting line."

Griscom was impressed, for the document was indeed a most damning indictment of the British Government—if the figures were correct. He left Paris for Pétain's headquarters at Chantilly. The general was away but his chief of staff, General Anthoine, spoke openly. "All is lost!" he told Griscom. "Nothing can save Paris! Nothing!" Griscom tried to calm him by saying that Pershing felt quite the reverse and that Anthoine's own superior at the War Ministry wasn't that gloomy. "What do they know about it? It is we who are fighting the war who know. You as a stranger can have no idea of what losing Paris means. Paris is not only our capital, but also our greatest manufacturing city. Without it we are lost." Every Frenchman realized that.

Griscom spent an hour trying to reassure him, "all the time aware of the absurdity of an American major, just two months over from the United States, consoling a French veteran who had headed armies in the field." As Griscom was leaving, Anthoine shook his hand warmly. "You Americans are giving us *du courage!*"

Back in Paris, Griscom's chief, General Pershing, was asking Clemenceau what would happen if Paris should fall under the new offensive. The Tiger said he had discussed this possibility with Lloyd George and they had both concluded that even so they would keep on fighting, for "above Paris is France, and above France is civilization." Just before his departure Pershing said, "Well it may not look encouraging just now but we are certain to win in the end."

Clemenceau clung to his hand and in a tone of utmost solicitude said, "Do you really think that? I am glad to hear you say it."

The general motored to Foch's new headqaurters at Bombon, arriving in time for luncheon, and asked the same question. Foch's tone was so positive that Pershing sprang to his feet, vigorously shaking his hand. Then he made an offer that surprised and delighted Foch. Taking it upon himself to speak for the entire United States, Pershing gave positive assurance that the American Government and people would stick with France to the last.

By this time the new Ludendorff offensive northeast of the capital, consisting of fifteen divisions, had already driven well into the French lines along the valley of the Matz River. This advance continued during the afternoon, and by dusk General von Hutier's Eighteenth Army had taken over eight thousand prisoners and smashed three French divisions. The Germans had not only driven "an important bulge in the French line," to quote Foch, but had crossed the Matz River and now threatened Compiègne, which lay little more than forty air miles from the capital. Once this strategic town fell, a second road to Paris was virtually open.

Similar panic was also spreading among the British leaders in London. That day Lord Milner wrote Lloyd George:

. . . We must be prepared for France and Italy both being beaten to their knees. In that case the Germans-Austro-Turks-Bulgar bloc will be master of all Europe and Northern and Central Asia up to the point at which Japan steps in to bar the way, *if* she does step in . . .

In any case it is clear that, unless the remaining free peoples of the world, America, this country, and the Dominions, are knit together in the closest conceivable alliance and prepared for the maximum sacrifice, the Central Bloc . . . will control not only Europe and most of Asia but the whole world.

In such a case the whole aspect of the war would change and the fight would be for southern Asia and above all for Africa.

All this is assuming the worst and looking far ahead. Perhaps I should not say "far" . . .

Last year we discussed the terms of peace. If this year *we were seriously* to consider the necessities of the New War, it would be more to the purpose.

One thing more—intimately connected with the above. Of course all this depends on what America may do. . . . Unless he [President Wilson] can be shaken out of his aloofness and drops "co-belligerency" or whatever halfway house he loves to shelter himself in, for out and out alliance— . . . I don't see how the new combination can have sufficient cohesion and inner strength. Moreover, he will have to be made to see—*and so will the Dominions*—who are just as stupid about this—that he must wholly alter his attitude to Japan, if that country is to be part of the New Alliance . . .

Across the Channel, not far above Compiègne, the French 53rd Division collapsed the next day, June 10, dragging back with it the division on its left. This exposed the entire right wing of General Humbert's Third Army, leaving Compiègne in dire danger. In this emergency, General Fayolle, commander of the Reserve Army Group, placed his troops, as well as the XXXV Corps, under General Charles Mangin, who was momentarily without a command. Perhaps the most dynamic and ruthless commander in the French Army, he had been relieved in disgrace after his infantry suffered 60 percent casualties in the Nivelle debacle of 1917. But Clemenceau had such faith in Mangin that he now placed the fate of France in his hands. At 4 P.M. he was ordered to re-establish the crumbling line to his left by attacking the Germans in the flank. As if it were a play, Foch abruptly appeared at Mangin's field headquarters to deliver a stirring speech calling upon the general to launch his assault "like a thunderbolt."

It was not until after midnight that all the commanders of the assembling force arrived at Mangin's headquarters. Then, with Foch, Fayolle, and Humbert silently watching, the man who had finished at the bottom of his class at St. Cyr issued his orders. The counterattack near Compiègne, said Mangin, would begin the following morning. Some of his subordinates begged for more time while others protested they were asked to do the impossible. His hard face expressionless, Mangin listened without comment, then in a quiet but menacing voice said, "You will do exactly what I have ordered you to do." Zero hour would be an hour before noon. "There will be no preliminary artillery bombardment. The attack will be ruthlessly pressed to the limit." This would be the end of all the defensive battles waged since March. "From now on we attack. We must succeed. Go back to your men and tell them just this."

Fayolle protested. They should postpone the attack for forty-eight hours to set up a proper artillery barrage. But Foch backed Mangin and for once that spring the weather favored the Allies. At dawn a thick mist hid Mangin's deploying troops. It held until 10:30 A.M., when a pitiful artillery barrage opened up on German positions, but it was so feeble that many of the poilus didn't even hear it. An hour later four French divisions in the front line advanced with friendly aeroplanes hovering overhead.

Battalion commander Henri Desagneaux couldn't understand an attack under such conditions. No artillery and the terrain out front as flat as a billiard table! They would be in full view of the enemy, for the sun was now shining brightly and their uniforms were already getting soaked with sweat. It was utter madness. To make it worse, there would be no tank support until they reached Courcelles, four kilometers distant. Almost immediately German shells began to blossom all over the plain. "We think we must be dreaming. Is it possible that they have ordered the division to attack under such conditions?"

But Desagneaux's unit plodded on silently despite clods of earth flying in all directions. They advanced under the burning sun and the fierce enemy fire, pushing their way through a cornfield, stumbling over bodies. Finally Courcelles appeared in a swirl of smoke, in a hurricane of fire. "This day seems crazier and crazier. Yet we advance, frightened and worn-out as we are, hastening on, with the idea that the quicker we go the sooner we shall reach our goal. Goal? Who knows what it is? Do the big chiefs alone know what we are supposed to be doing?" There was a reason. These troops were being sacrificed to create a diversion while the other divisions assaulted Ressons-sur-Matz.

Mangin's daring plan worked. The Germans were caught in the open, for there had come no warning artillery preparation and no tanks were in sight. And who would have guessed that such a considerable attack would unexpectedly develop just before noon? The villages of Méry and Belloy were rapidly seized and the entire valley of the Aronde cleared. Finally, about 4 P.M. the advance was stopped but Mangin had turned the tide, stalling Ludendorff's Compiègne offensive.

The following noon the Kaiser was in very low spirits at lunch and would eat nothing but chocolate mousse. "Those in the know," Admiral von Müller commented in his diary, "maintain that the repulse of yesterday's attack was the reason." The next day, June 13, Ludendorff ordered the offensive stopped, and at last all was quiet along the entire French front. The crisis was over.

And the future was bright. Haig wrote his wife on the fourteenth after inspecting two American divisions. "When they appear in the front I am sure it will be a great surprise for the Enemy and I doubt whether he will be keen to go on with the war in view of the tremendous resources and the determination of the American people. But we shall see!"

Part 3

THE ROAD BACK

Chapter Nine

INTERVENTION II
JUNE–JULY 17

1.

IN the meantime, under continued British pressure, President Wilson had withdrawn his objections to a limited operation in northern Russia. It had been made official early that June, at the Supreme War Council by the American representative, General Bliss. "The President," he said, "is in sympathy with any practical military effort which can be made at and from Murmansk and Archangel, but such efforts should proceed, if at all, upon the sure sympathy of the Russian people and should not have as the ultimate objects any restoration of the ancient regime or any interference with the political liberty of the Russian people." While the words were grudging and camouflaged by democratic phrases, it opened the door—and the council members quickly approved a program for occupation of northern Russia, advocating seizure first of Murmansk, then Archangel. Czech detachments, supposed to be moving in that direction, would shore up the Allied force.

But the Czechs were trying to fight their way east to Vladivostok at the other end of Russia, and there were still local conflicts all along the Trans-Siberian Railroad. Perhaps local negotiators could have brought the Czechs to Vladivostok without bloodshed. They had already found an amicable settlement at Chelyabinsk, but this had been disrupted by interference from Moscow in the form of an inflammatory Trotsky telegram. Foreign interference came later in the day, the Allied diplomats vastly irritating the Bolsheviks by sending a delegation to the People's Commissariat of Foreign Affairs with expressions of sympathy for the

Czechs. The attempted disarming of Czechs, they said, was causing the Allied representatives "great concern." Leader in the protest was Bruce Lockhart, who was now in Moscow. It was a shock to the Bolsheviks, who had always found him so tractable. "I told the two Commissars that for months I had done my best to bring about an understanding with the Allies, but that they had always put me off with evasions. Now, after promising a free exit to the Czechs, who had fought for the Slav cause and who were going to France to continue the fight against a foe, who was still the Bolshevik enemy as well as ours, they had yielded to German threats and had wantonly attacked those who had always been their friends."

Lockhart noticed that Foreign Commissar Chicherin looked more like a drowned rat than ever and stared with mournful eyes, while his assistant seemed stupidly bewildered. After a painful silence, Chicherin coughed and said, "Gentlemen, I have taken note of what you said." The Allied representatives shook hands awkwardly with the Russians and filed out of the room.

"I must explain the motives which had driven me into this illogical situation," wrote Lockhart. He had gone to Russia with no special sympathy for the Bolsheviks but grew to admire men who "were obviously inspired by the same spirit of self sacrifice and abnegation of worldly pleasure which animated the Puritans and the early Jesuits . . ." Now that he had reversed himself, he felt that he should have resigned and come home but did not for two reasons. He was unwilling to leave Russia because of the woman he loved, Moura Budberg. "The other motive—and it was the all-compelling one, of which I was fully conscious—was that I lacked the moral courage to resign and to take a stand which would have exposed me to the odium of the vast majority of my countrymen." There was perhaps, he added, a third, more creditable motive. "In my conceit I imagined that if the Allies were bent on a military intervention in Russia my special knowledge of the Russian situation would be of some value in aiding them to avoid pitfalls." He knew the Bolsheviks more intimately than any other Englishman. "The clamjamfery of military experts, who from outside were screaming for intervention and who regarded the Bolsheviks as a rabble to be swept away with a whiff of grape shot, was deprived by its geographical situation of that knowledge. Having gone over to intervention, I did my best to ensure that it would have at least some chance of success." In doing so, he had fallen between two stools. To the Bolsheviks he was now the incarnation of counterrevolution. To the interventionists he remained the obdurate pro-Bolshevik doing his best to wreck their plans. It would have been humiliating had Raymond Robins remained in Moscow to see the *volte-face*. One consolation: he still had the love of his Moura.

During his long trip across Siberia to Vladivostok, Raymond Robins had lost neither his enthusiasm for the young Soviet regime nor hope that America would not intervene. At the same time what he had seen on the long railroad trip made him wonder if the Siberian Soviets could win. A fellow American, even more pro-Bolshevik, saw him off for home at the pier on June 21. Albert Rhys Williams had preceded him to Vladivostok and intended to stay longer. "Look, Williams," said Robins sternly, "don't you *want* to get away from Vladivostok?" They said little about the possibility of American intervention, and Robins mentioned none of his plans, but there was no mistaking Robins' gloom as he told Williams, off the record, that there was small chance the Siberian Soviets could make a comeback without help. "Was he still hoping for American rejection of intervention?" recalled Williams. "I could not tell . . . Robins only said that it was ironic he had been blamed for acting unofficially when everything he did was with the full knowledge of Francis, and now he was being rushed away 'because certain Americans are aching to act fast, *before* authorization—in case it does not come.' "

Williams noticed that Robins' face, as he climbed the gangplank, was sad and set, with jaw thrust out grimly. "For as long as we could see him he stood at the rail looking back at the city that was so many thousands of miles distant from the 'iron battalions' of the new Red Army."

After dinner Robins went out on deck. "Sunset," he wrote emotionally in his diary, "and the flame dies in the western sky—and the headlands of Asia fade from view—the only sound the sweep of the surging sea—the stars shine out the sea ahead is blue black and the Russian tale is told and I have had my day!!! Our Father I thank Thee. O how I thank Thee. Amen and Amen Forever."

The next day, Sunday, he spent reading *Ivanhoe* in his dirty cabin. "Sabbath and rest. Rebecca Rowena Ivanhoe and the Black Knight all so clear. Youth and the call of Quest. How it surges again and again . . . Help us our father Amen. The sunset and Margaret and beauty and love of life." It was the end of his diary, the end of his great Russian adventure.

On June 8, while Americans were exulting over the action at Belleau Wood, their consul in Moscow, DeWitt Poole, cabled Washington that the immediate future in Russia depended on whether Germany acted before the Allies did and in what manner. German influence in the capital was becoming much stronger. "Specific evidence accumulates daily to show that, the Allies having failed to act, liberal and conservative elements alike are finally prepared to accept German support." He was convinced more thoroughly if possible that the Soviet Government was only a shell: "Industrial leaders including bankers, professional men, landed proprietors, commercial men, generally, have formed combinations regardless of party to appeal again to redeem Russia before industry ruined by Bolshevism. This combination with headquarters Moscow, rapidly extending throughout Russia, favors Allies but will treat with Germany for establishment of strong government if Allies support Soviet Government or fail to show responsiveness or to manifest disposition to assist in restoration order and any longer delay by Allies is dangerous."

Bruce Lockhart was also continuing to urge intervention, and with the same vigor he had formerly urged the opposite. He wired Balfour that all Russians, even the Bolsheviks, now expected intervention momentarily. The Czech uprising had created the perfect opportunity for decisive action. Never would the Allies have so favorable an opportunity. "I feel it is my duty to state that I must be freed from my responsibility in the event of any further delay."

Balfour's answer on June 11 was a gentlemanly scolding. "You need not fear that your work is unappreciated here or that you have in any way lost the confidence of His Majesty's Government. I fully understand the difficulties of your situation." Then he added with a touch of sarcasm that Lockhart's telegrams of the past five months doubtlessly "faithfully reflected" the variation of opinions as well as "the constantly changing aspects of the present transitional period of Russian History." But he was not sure that Lockhart equally comprehended the difficulties as seen from the Allies' viewpoint. "You constantly complain of indecision, as if all that was required was that His Majesty's Government should make up their minds. But there has been no indecision on the part of the particular members of the Alliance."

The various governments, he painstakingly explained, had not failed to make decisions. They had disagreed. "Britain, France, and Italy have thought the dangers of intervention less than its advantages; America has thought the advantages less than the dangers; Japan will do nothing on a grand scale until she receives an invitation from her co-belligerents. The only thing on which everybody agrees is that without the active participation of America nothing effective can be accomplished in Siberia; and the active participation of America has been so far refused. . . . We can therefore do no more at the moment than press our views on the Administration at Washington and hope that by the time the necessity for intervention is universally admitted and common action becomes for the first time possible it may not prove too late."

2.

American military leaders were making a concerted effort to persuade President Wilson to halt any intervention. "If I had my own way about Russia and had the power to have my own way," Secretary of War Newton Baker told the President on June 19, "I would like to take everybody out of Russia except the Russians, including diplomatic representatives, political agents, propagandists, military representatives and casual visitors, and let the Russians settle down and settle their own affairs."

Similar advice came from General Bliss at Versailles the following day. In a long letter to General Peyton March, the Army Chief of Staff, Bliss agreed with Colonel House that intervention would undermine American prestige abroad even though there was increasing bitterness in Europe toward the Soviets. March needed no convincing. Like others in the War Department in Washington he felt that intervention would only strengthen Germany's hand in Russia.

Ambassador Francis completely disagreed. "I have recommended Allied intervention and the Government at Washington has it under consideration," he wrote his son on the twentieth. "We have no forces, however, to send to Russia as we are sending all of our available men to France. The only country that can send a formidable army into Russia at this time is Japan, against which there is a strong prejudice among the Russians, who fear that Japan will have a covetous eye towards Siberia."

Trotsky issued a statement on that very issue two days later. There was no difference, he said, between a German offensive and a "friendly" intervention by Allied armies. "To think that a Japanese army would enter Russian territory in order to help the Allies and to liberate Russia from the Germans, would be foolish. Japan could intervene in Russian affairs only in order to enslave Russia, and upon meeting German troops would stretch to them a hand of friendship."

And so Russia was put in a nutcracker, with little to choose between friend or foe. In the meantime the Czechs were scoring victories along the Trans-Siberian Railroad. And those seventeen thousand Czechs who had already reached Vladivostok, infuriated that their comrades en route were still having to fight their way east, finally took action on June 29 by demanding the immediate and unconditional surrender of the local Soviet. The chairman of the Soviet Executive Committee was arrested, along with any other Bolshevik leaders who could be located. All this was done so quietly that Albert Rhys Williams was unaware of the takeover until he met a commissar having his shoes shined near the Red Fleet Building. "In a few minutes I may be dangling from a lamppost," he said nonchalantly, "and I want to be as nice looking a corpse as possible." Williams stared at him in wonder. "Our days are done for," the commissar explained with a smile. "The Czechs are taking over the city."

Their troops were already filling the streets. Launches from British, Japanese, and American battleships landed soldiers and marines. The Japanese seized the powder magazine while the British occupied the railroad station. American Marines were throwing a cordon around their consulate. "I felt sick and sick through," wrote Williams. "Was intervention, then, all decided even on the part of my country?" He watched Czechs converge on the Soviet headquarters. With loud shouts, they crashed through the doors. The Red Flag was pulled down, and the banner of the Czar run up. "The Soviet has fallen!" someone shouted, and the call was passed from street to street. People rushed out of cafes, yelling and flinging their hats in the air in joy at the fall of the Bolsheviks. By evening all Vladivostok belonged to the Czechs.

Three days later the Allied Supreme War Council gathered for its seventh session in Versailles and immediately took up the Japanese agreement to intervene in Vladivostok if America approved. The council did approve and prepared a memorandum to gain President Wilson's support, indicating that its members felt "bound to point out that in their judgment failure to intervene immediately must inevitably cause effects which can only be described as disastrous to the Allied cause." The council also argued that unless the Allies acted immediately the gallant Czechs would be placed in dire peril. Moreover, there was such widespread sympathy in America for the Czech Legion that its presence in Siberia would lessen home opposition to the proposed expedition. Large-scale intervention by the Japanese would relieve the pressure on the Western Front by forcing the Germans to transfer troops to the east. Adding force to the document were the signatures of the prime ministers of Britain, France, and Italy.

The proposal reached Washington on the afternoon of July 3, shortly after word arrived of the Czech seizure of Vladivostok. It was met with mixed reactions, but the State Department, supported by Colonel House, had been so affected by the gallant Czech anabasis as well as other developments in June that it now leaned toward some form of intervention. Wilson himself, moved by the council's arguments, concluded that his policy of absolute opposition to intervention was obsolete. At the same time how could he condone what he had so forcefully and eloquently denounced to the world? "In short," commented one observer, "President Wilson hoped to maintain his own policy while seeming to accept the Entente proposal."

The next day, the Fourth of July, was extremely hot and the President took an excursion on his yacht, *The Mayflower*, to Mount Vernon. He discussed the crisis with his Secretary of State and sometime, during or after the trip on the Potomac, Robert Lansing had time to draw up a memorandum for the President. It declared that the seizure of Vladivostok and other Czech successes had "materially changed the situation by introducing a sentimental element into the question of our duty." It was America's responsibility to aid the Czechs with arms and "some" troops to assist in guarding the Trans-Siberian Railroad and in "disarmng and dispersing" German and Austrian prisoners of war.

After reading Lansing's memorandum the following day, a Friday, the President telephoned the Secretary of State, asking him to come to the White House on Saturday at 2 P.M. along with General March, and the Secretaries of War and Navy, Newton Baker and Josephus Daniels.

They arrived and were escorted to an upper room. After seating themselves, "somewhat in order of rank," as March put it, "Wilson entered, pad in hand, and taking a position standing and facing us, somewhat in the manner of a school teacher addressing a class of pupils, read from his pad his views on the matter at issue." The present situation of the Czechs, he said, required this Government and others to make an effort to help the Czechs. Since the

United States could not provide any considerable force within a short time, the Japanese would furnish small arms, machine guns, and ammunition to the Czechs at Vladivostok with America sharing the expense and supplementing the supplies as rapidly as possible. In addition, a military force of some seven thousand Americans would be assembled to guard the line of communications of these Czechs proceeding toward Vladivostok. In the meantime, a similar force of seven thousand Japanese would be sent to Siberia at once.

All this, Wilson concluded, would be announced publicly with the explanation that it was being done only to aid the Czechs against German and Austrian prisoners of war and there was "no purpose to interfere with internal affairs of Russia," whose political and territorial sovereignty would be guaranteed.

Wilson turned to Lansing, who commended the paper. So did Secretaries Baker and Daniels. But March shook his head vigorously. "Why are you shaking your head, General?" the President asked with some asperity. "You are opposed to this because you do not think Japan will limit herself to 7000 men, and that this decision will further her schemes for territorial aggrandizement."

"Just that," said March, "and for other military reasons which I have already told you."

"Well," said Wilson, "we will have to take that chance."

America at last was bound on the course of intervention. And those who felt that the President had betrayed his principles in coldhearted disregard of the Russian people did not realize that his icy exterior masked warm sentiment. When Mme. Botchkarova, a Russian introduced to him that summer by Mrs. J. Borden Harriman, told of the terrible privations of her countrymen in the revolution, tears streamed down his face. He was, in fact, possessed of the idea that it was his God-given mission to ameliorate the misery of all people ravaged by war, and was now convinced that his new policy in Russia could help do so.

His conscience was driving him in his endeavor to save mankind and become the peacemaker of the world. He truly burned with religious zeal. A man of genius, he was burdened at times with crippling, temperamental defects. Compulsive and impatient of delay he demanded instant solutions and too often would make no compromises.

Wilson himself was aware that this compulsive, insatiable ambition was dangerous. He confided to House that he had nightmares reliving his struggles at Princeton where his failures almost equalled his triumphs. He feared, he said, that this same pattern might repeat itself while he was President of the United States.

3.

Undaunted by defeat at the All-Russian Congress of Soviets, which had opened on the Fourth of July, the Left Social Revolutionaries were still bent on rekindling war with Germany and bringing down the Bolshevik regime. The best way to do this, they decided, was to assassinate the German Ambassador. On July 6 two executioners, posing as Cheka agents, called on Count Mirbach at the German Embassy in Moscow. One, named Blumkin, revealed that there was a terrorist plot to murder the Ambassador and they had brought papers giving particulars. Blumkin put his hand into his briefcase and suddenly drew out a pistol. He fired three shots but all went wide. To avoid the other assassin, Mirbach ran behind Blumkin, but the second man shot him.

This was the signal for uprising. Moscow's central post office was seized by surprise and 'legrams were hastily dispatched all over Russia revoking any Bolshevik decisions. With sixty machine guns, a half-dozen field guns, three armored cars, and no more than 1,500 men, the Left Social Revolutionaries were attempting to take over the capital. Some anarchists and Black Sea sailors joined them and the citizens watched with indifference.

The Bolsheviks could only depend on the Latvian Praetorian Guard, which had already done such yeoman service, a few detachments of the young Red Army, and an international brigade comprised principally of Hungarian prisoners of war led by Béla Kun, a Communist. But by the following noon the uprising was crushed. Almost three hundred Left SRs were arrested and several executed. It was not only the death of their party, but the end, apparently, of Allied hopes to bring Russia back into the war against Germany.

4.

In Washington, President Wilson was "sweating blood" over his recent decision to intervene in Russia. He had done this in opposition to his generals—then had outraged his allies by failing to inform them of his decision until the morning of July 9. The British Ambassador, Lord Reading, was astounded, particularly upon learning that the Japanese had known the day before. He was also disturbed at the ambiguous part America would play. His displeasure was made plain to the Secretary of State, who reported it to the President. This in turn irritated both Wilson and Lansing, and the matter was aggravated in the afternoon by Reading's appearance at Lansing's office with the French and Italian envoys. Speaking for all three, Reading demanded to know "whether the Allied Governments were not to take part in the initial landings of troops at Vladivostok or whether it was [the American] purpose to confine the enterprise to Japanese and American troops."

For months the Allies had begged the United States to join in a Siberian venture, and now the Americans were so determined to act quickly that they couldn't wait forty-eight hours. It was an insulting attitude which George Kennan put down to wartime strain and weariness. "Wilson and his Secretary of State had both now worked themselves into a high state of suspicion of British motives and resentment of British pressures in the Siberian problem."

"I know exactly what the President had in mind," commented Colonel House in his diary. "He knows what the French and English want, therefore he thinks it essential to work out a plan with the Japanese. When he does this he will undoubtedly advise the other Powers, but until then he considers it unnecessary. In this he is mistaken. The better way—the diplomatic way, and the way to keep from offending sensibilities, would be to have them all cognizant of everything that is going on."

Lord Reading, a consummate diplomat himself, allowed none of his personal pique to color his cable to London. After summarizing the American decision without comment, he suggested that, with all its shortcomings, it was "a distinct advance in the direction of the policy advocated by the Supreme War Council."

Hankey happened to walk in the next day as Lloyd George got the news, and found him "furious with Wilson and most sarcastic, comparing him to Gladstone and the inadequate Gordon relief expedition." The Prime Minister shot off a long reply to Reading marked "Private and Secret." The American proposal, he said, was "really preposterous," and he again compared it to the "fatal error" of the Khartoum expedition to relieve Chinese Gordon. It was obvious, he added, that the Bolsheviks were going over to the side of the Germans and it was "now really a race between the Germans and ourselves" for control of Siberia. The Allies "should send a force which can make sure that the Czecho-Slovaks will not have their throats cut by German and Austrian prisoners" as well as "definitely secure Siberia to the Urals against German-Bolshevist attack." He feared that American insistence on having as many troops in Siberia as the Japanese would deeply injure the latter's national pride and drive them into resentful neutrality. "I am sure that the proper way to deal with Japanese is to ask them to undertake same obligations towards Russia as rest of Allies and to make expedition part and parcel of Allied plan of campaign against Germany and in future to agree to trust them completely."

He concluded with the hope that these personal observations might aid Reading in convincing the President of the "total inadequacy of his present proposals" and "induce him to amend them" in line with the Supreme War Council's resolution. "Of course if we can get this expedition and cannot get more we must accept it and press on with it as fast as we can for essential thing is that we should get movement started without delay. We have only a few months before Russian harbours freeze and if we are to save Russia from becoming a German province we must have firmly established ourselves before the winter arrives."

Like his Ambassador in Washington, Lloyd George knew how unwise it was to take umbrage at an ally's bad manners and limited vision. He had not yet come to share the patience of those like Lord Milner who felt that any American intervention was better than none, but at least he had not provoked American feelings with a show of temper.

President Wilson was still being bombarded from all sides and finally, without consulting any advisers, he typed out an *aide-mémoire* on intervention in Russia. Presented to the Allied ambassadors on July 17, it preached idealism and disinterestedness while ignoring reality. After opening with superficial friendliness, Wilson abruptly announced that it was "the clear and fixed judgment of the Government of the United States . . . that military intervention there would add to the present sad confusion in Russia rather than cure it, injure her rather than help her, and that it would be of no advantage in the prosecution of our main design, to win the war against Germany. It cannot, therefore, take part in such intervention or sanction it in principle." Apparently he had heeded his military advisers and civilians like Raymond Robins. Yet this forthright statement was immediately followed by ambiguity.

> Military action is admissible in Russia, as the Government of the United States sees the circumstances, only to help the Czecho-Slovaks consolidate their forces and get into successful cooperation with their Slavic kinsmen and to steady any efforts at self-government or self defense in which the Russians themselves may be willing to accept assistance . . .

The next minute Wilson compounded ambiguity with outright confusion by agreeing to establish a small American force in Murmansk "to guard military stores at Kola and to make it safe for Russian forces to come together in organized bodies in the north." Did he mean White Russian or Bolshevik forces? Not in the entire document had he mentioned the apparently unmentionable word Bolshevik. "But it owes it to frank counsel to say that it can go no further than these modest and experimental plans. It is not in a position, and has no expectation of being in a position, to take part in organized intervention in adequate force from either Vladivostok or Murmansk or Archangel." A little bit of intervention, like a little lack of virtue, seemed to be acceptable.

To soften the blow to Anglo-French hopes and sensibilities, Wilson then stressed that none of the above sentiments were meant as any criticism of the Allies or Japan. "All that is intended is a perfectly frank and definite statement of policy which the United States feels obliged to adopt for herself and in the use of her military forces." She had no intention at all of limiting the action or defining the policies of her associates.

But such pious protestation could not hide the fact that the *aide-mémoire* would probably bring about the very thing it professed to renounce. At the same time it was a flat rebuff of the Supreme War Council and the Allies. What the President had belatedly offered on July 9 with his right hand he was now taking away with his left. Although he had bowed to powerful Allied pressure momentarily, he appeared to be back to his original Fourteen Points. Or did he really know where he was? The British Military Representative in Washington perceptively cabled London that he thought it probable that the President would be forced into full-fledged intervention by events and, until then, Britain "should accept the situation and make no further representations" until the troops were "on the spot."

Chapter Ten

THE TURNING POINT
JULY

1.

IT was not until late June that an Austrian offensive was finally launced across the Piave. But within a week the attackers were forced to retreat across the river in disorder. It was a major victory proving that the Italian Army was at last superior to the Austrian. This meant that Ludendorff could now hope for little help from his strongest ally.

By this time the planning for his new offensive was completed and it had an uninspiring code name: Operation Road Construction. It was another attack on the French, even though Ludendorff still intended launching the main blow, Operation Hagen, against the English in Flanders. That would have to be postponed for several weeks. In the meantime he thought the time was ripe to strike again from the great bulge they had just driven into the Champagne area. Here the prospect of massive captures of prisoners and war material was too tempting to resist. It would also enable him to wipe out the baneful Reims salient.

And so attacks on both sides of that city were planned for July 12. The one to the west of it was designed to cross the Marne on a broad front all the way up to Château-Thierry. This would so endanger Paris that the French would insist on help from the British. "Immediately following this operation," wrote Ludendorff, "we meant to concentrate artillery, trench mortars, and flying squadrons on the Flanders Front, and possibly attack that a fortnight later."

There was considerable opposition to Ludendorff's plan, and he complained that these pessimists were so depressed that he had to carry the whole burden. "They were advising him not to continue the offensive," a colonel at headquarters wrote in his diary, "saying that he was overdrawing the bow, but he must risk it, he thought." Ludendorff felt they had to strike before the Americans became a decisive factor. Admittedly battalion strength was reduced "but

238

was still high enough to allow us to strike one more blow that should make the enemy ready for peace. There was no other way."

By the beginning of July the army group of Crown Prince Wilhelm was already covertly moving into position and the date had been postponed until the fourteenth. Advising him on the opening artillery barrage was the redoubtable Colonel Bruchmüller, and it promised to be as effective as the others. The utmost secrecy was demanded. All reconnaissances, marches, and ammunition deliveries were to be made "without any noise whatever." The wheels of vehicles were wrapped and a guard line established.

The preparations took a little longer than anticipated, and on July 3 Ludendorff sent a coded telephone message to the Crown Prince: "Y day has been set back one day." This meant that the offensive would definitely start on the fifteenth.

In the previous offensives, the Allies had been surprised, but this time both the French and Americans were sure of an imminent strike in the Reims area. Even so, Foch felt that the moment was propitious to launch his own attack on the Champagne bulge from the woods just east of Villers-Cotterêts. "Why not wait until the enemy has involved himself in his own attack?" asked Pétain. "That will facilitate our offensive, seeing that we now have the advantage of superior numbers." Foch conceded that the idea was tempting, but he was determined to cease adapting Allied movements to those of the enemy. Pershing had complained there had been too much of that already and was urging an attack to catch the enemy off guard. This eagerness for a rush against the enemy amazed the French because of the Americans' lack of artillery, but their willingness to risk everything upon a single action apparently made a convert of Foch. When Colonel Hellé, Mangin's chief of staff, ventured to advise Foch that he was certain Crown Prince Wilhelm would attack soon, Foch said simply, "Our plan will go through."

"A general offensive?"

Foch nodded gravely. They would attack west of the bulge while staying on the defensive along the Marne.

"Who will lead?" asked Hellé, expecting that two commanders had been selected.

"General Pétain will conduct both battles."

Mangin's army would spearhead the attack. He was to emerge from the forest of Villers-Cotterêts and strike east across the plateau of Soissons toward the strategic Soissons–Château-Thierry highway—and so strangle the German pocket in Champagne by cutting off its supply lines. The date was set for July 18, and would come, therefore, three days after the Ludendorff offensive.

On the seventh, the order went out from the German Seventh Army that from now on all marching by day, "even by headquarters, small units or single vehicles, is strictly prohibited." Having no suspicion of the French trap, the confident Ludendorff was tirelessly pressing his own offensive. "This energy," recalled Colonel Mertz von Quirnheim, "was all the more astonishing since in so doing he had to override so many different considerations put forward by his colleagues." It was telling on Ludendorff's nerves and he was becoming increasingly irritable with anyone who dared to have a contrary opinion.

By this time, Pétain was positive that Ludendorff was going to attack not only along the Marne but at Reims, and he convinced Foch to seek help from the British. Since Haig was on leave in London, Foch summoned General Lawrence to his headquarters on July 12 and asked him to move two British divisions south of the Somme and another two astride the river. This would enable Foch to transfer four French divisions to the threatened Champagne area. Lawrence sent off one division immediately with another to follow. But, sharing Haig's belief that the main German offensive would be aimed at Flanders, held back the other two so the field marshal could make that decision upon his return.

That same day German regiments were finally given attack orders. The 5th Grenadier Regiment, for instance, was told that they were to cross the Marne just east of Château-Thierry on the fifteenth. It came as no surprise to the men. Those on leave had come back with the same information. It seemed everyone in the homeland, despite Ludendorff's strict order for secrecy, knew when and where the attack was coming. This concerned many front-line veterans who feared the enemy might also know what was coming.

Their premonitions were justified. All French army commanders had been warned that the German attack would come within forty-eight hours. And after that had been turned back, General Mangin would launch his own offensive.

But the German commanders remained supremely confident. "The picture we have gained of the enemy," read the Seventh Army War Diary of July 14, "induces us to believe that our offensive intentions have been kept hidden from him—that we may expect to take him by surprise." By this time Operation Road Construction had a more dramatic if still misleading name: *Friedensturm*, Peace Assault.

In Paris it was drizzling at dawn, but the sun finally came out to shine upon the Bastille Day celebration. One would have thought that the war had just been won as troops of a dozen nationalities paraded from the Arc de Triomphe to the Place de la Concorde. In the van was the Garde Républicaine, in shining helmets, and astride spirited horses. Then came detachments from all the Allies, each led by a band playing its national anthem. There were French Chasseurs Alpins sporting berets and black tunics, British Life-Guards, Italian Bersaglieri in rooster-tail hats. Portuguese with their dishpan helmets, anti-Bolshevik Cossacks wearing astrakhans. There were Poles, Romanians, Slavs, Montenegrins, Greeks in stiff white skirts, Bohemians, and Slovaks. And when the Americans in battle-stained uniforms, soiled but trim knapsacks, and battered "tin hats" appeared the onlookers spontaneously shouted, *"Vivent les Américains!" "Vivent nos alliés!"*

"I thought then," recalled Mildred Aldrich, an American living in France, "that the kind of crowd which was gathered that day could not make any more noise than they made for the Americans, who, with their guns on their shoulders, marched as steadily as veterans, though their faces were the faces of boys. But I was mistaken, for, with a fine spirit that I loved, they had justly reserved their most ardent acclamations for their own war-torn troops, and the shouts of *'Vivent nos poilus,' 'Vive la France,'* were as near hysterical as anything I have seen in France since the war began. I saw women laughing and crying at the same time, and only able to wave their hands in greeting."

Probably no one enjoyed the pageantry of Allied unity more than Clemenceau. He good-naturedly joked with Lord Derby, who was about to leave for London. "I suppose you will get back to England and talk of those damned Frenchmen. That is what many of your colleagues do." He asked Derby to carry out two commissions. "The first is to tell Lord Milner that they are quite mistaken in thinking that I want to interfere in their Home Affairs. I have not the least intention of doing it; nor have I the least intention of stopping what they are doing now, interfering in my own. They may do that as much as they like and the more of my work they wish to do for me the better I shall be pleased." All this was said in the most friendly, chaffing manner "but like everything with Clemenceau," observed Derby in a letter to Balfour, "there is something at the back of it and there is no doubt he is very resentful against LG and Milner." Clemenceau's second commission to Derby was to bring back an Aberdeen terrier. His own had just died, "and he says he cannot live without one."

The gaiety of Bastille Day was marred by the death of Quentin Roosevelt, son of the former President, who had been such an ardent advocate of military aid to France. His plane went down in flames over the German lines in a dogfight north of Château-Thierry. His death, wrote America's leading ace, Lieutenant Eddie Rickenbacker, was a sad blow to his comrades. "Everyone who met him for the first time expected him to have the airs and superciliousness of a spoiled boy. This notion was erased after the first glimpse one had of Quentin. Gay, hearty, and absolutely square in everything he said or did, Quentin Roosevelt was one of the most popular fellows in the group. We loved him for his own natural self." His father's brief statement was typically Rooseveltian: "Quentin's mother and I are very glad he got to the front, and had a chance to render some service to his country and to show the stuff that was in him before his fate befell him."

Upon his return to France that day, Field Marshal Haig sought an interview for the morrow with Foch with the request that the dispatch of further British divisions to the Champagne be delayed until then. After informing General Wilson of the dangers which would be run by lending his reserves, Haig wrote a memorandum reminding Foch that he had promised that the British reserves should only be used to support the French if the enemy decidedly concentrated his forces in the direction of Paris. "Such a situation has not yet arisen, nor can it be truly said that the enemy has begun a concentration with this object."

In England, Lloyd George was equally concerned and sent for Milner, who was at his home in Surrey. After dinner there was a long conference. "The Prime Minster was very strong (almost violent) about the withdrawal of divisions," recalled Hankey. "He evidently suspected Clemenceau of using unfair political influence on Foch to save the French Army and Paris at all costs." But Milner and Wilson were so inclined to support Foch that they managed to persuade Lloyd George merely to send Haig a telegram reminding him of the Beauvais agreement, which authorized him to appeal if he thought the safety of the British Army was endangered.

2.

Under cover of darkness, German assault units were already moving into position in a snakelike line from the outskirts of Château-Thierry, along the Marne to Dormans, then northeast to Reims, around that salient and east for another twenty miles. Their Supreme Command still had no suspicion that the French were ready. General Gouraud, commander of the French Fourth Army defending the west flank, was so positive the attack was about to come that he had just ordered a patrol in depth to "capture live prisoners at all costs." Sergeant Joseph Darnaud and his squad left at 7:55 P.M., creeping all the way to the German fourth line. There they fell upon a group of enemy and, after a savage knife and bayonet fight, captured nineteen prisoners. They were turned over to Gouraud's Intelligence Section, which shortly learned that the German artillery bombardment was to start at ten minutes past midnight.

Gouraud decided to take a chance and unmask all his batteries on the chance that the prisoners' information was correct. He ordered his own artillery to start counterbattery fire at 11:30 P.M. It caught the German troops massed along the line of departure in the Reims area completely by surprise. Where was their own artillery?

Gouraud's own chief of staff was wondering the same thing. He entered the commander's room, watch in hand. "They have not begun!" he said. "It is past zero. We have been betrayed by the prisoners." But the red-bearded Gouraud was not at all perturbed. His exploits in Algeria had won him the nickname *le lion d'Afrique,* and he was still that despite the loss of one arm and half a leg. "There are still minutes," he said, also watch in hand. They waited breathlessly for the German barrage and finally there was a roar like a railway train passing overhead, followed by a deafening explosion. All the lights went out. Gouraud had not risked his guns in vain.

Crown Prince Wilhelm had been driving forward in his Protos automobile. He noted what a lovely summer night it was, but as he neared the front he heard the irregular thunder of guns. His ear was so well trained after four years of trench warfare that he realized it was harassing enemy fire, "a conclusion which filled me with a certain anxiety." At last he reached his destination, an artillery observation post near Pont Faverger. He climbed up to the little wooden platform to receive the report of the artillery commander there: "Moderate harassing fire. In general the enemy is quiet." The Crown Prince said he could not accept that view. It seemed to him that the French were keeping up a very lively fire on the German rear areas. Many explosions were now heard and they could see several ammunition dumps on fire. Wilhelm's doubts increased as they all waited, "keyed up to the highest pitch," for their own bombardment. An officer counted off the last seconds: *fifty, forty, thirty, twenty, ten.* "And then," recalled the Crown Prince, "there was a thunderous roar, as if the end of the world had come." The whole front vomited fire and flame. "More than two thousand batteries of all calibres hurled their iron hail at the foe. It was an overwhelming scene, the pitch-black sky stabbed by quivering flashes of lightning, bursts of flame, a scene from the Inferno, an apocalyptic symphony of destruction."

Colonel Billy Mitchell, commander of the American Air Service, was enjoying a late snack in a Paris restaurant with a Red Cross friend, Donald Brown, when they heard a rumbling sound. Mitchell looked at his watch. It was exactly ten minutes past midnight. From the street they could see tremendous flashes in the sky. Mitchell guessed the main attack of the Germans had begun. If Brown wanted to see the greatest battle in history he could come along. They leaped into Mitchell's fastest staff car and sped toward his headquarters.

The continuing rumble wakened Parisians. Housewives hurried to see that gas meters were turned off; bridge players shaded their lamps. Those awake waited for the warning sirens. But none came. It was no air raid but something worse. The noise first reminded Pearl Adams, an Englishwoman living in Paris, of an immense symphony, then like a funeral march, finally like a heavy truck a half mile away. People whispered to each other fearfully, *The Front.* "This noise we had only heard vaguely before, and those of us who had heard it were laughed at by those who heard it not; these lights we had never seen. It meant the long waited-for offensive, the new attempt of Polyphemus to catch the valiant and undaunted Ulysses."

Like his son, the Kaiser wanted to watch the artillery softening-up. But he didn't arrive at his observation post north of Reims until 1 A.M., July 15. It was the thirtieth anniversary of his accession to the throne, a fitting day for the offensive that could crush the enemy. Already he had issued a message describing the war as "a conflict between the two approaches to the world. Either the

Prussian-Germanic approach—Right, Freedom, Honor, Morality—is to remain respected or the Anglo-Saxon, which would mean enthroning the worship of gold." Like Ludendorff, he saw England as the main enemy, not the French.

For the first time, the Allies were not significantly outmanned. The opposing forces were about even with forty-eight German divisions against forty-three, all French except for three American and two Italian divisions.

The French bombardment had caught the 5th Grenadier Regiment just east of Château-Thierry by surprise. Points of assembly for the assault across the Marne were hit so badly that two companies were completely routed and others were crippled. The impact of the incessant artillery fire, recalled Lieutenant Hesse, shattered the nerves. "Men, panic-stricken, run this way and that, seeking only one thing, to get under cover. And again the shells whistle all around us; the explosions are now dull gas-shells." Before, they could hardly see anything. Now the darkness was complete. "A sombre discouragement seizes many. If only daylight would come!" At last a company commander shouted, "Form ranks! Has everyone his rifle?" And they advanced down the narrow shell-ravaged ravines to the river.

At 4:30 A.M. the 5th Grenadiers and others in the 36th Division began launching pontoons, hidden by reeds and bushes. The gas and smoke of both friendly and enemy bombardments had mixed with the morning mist to form a dense fog, and under this cover the Germans were halfway across the Marne before the Americans of the 3rd Division sighted craft loaded to the gunwales with infantry and machine-gunners.

The doughboys of the 38th Infantry Regiment promptly opened up with rifle and automatic weapon fire. "Scores of these boats," recalled an American lieutenant, "were shattered or sunk or else disabled and sent drifting harmlessly down the river. Hundreds of Huns jumped into the water and were drowned. Those who reached our side by swimming were either killed or wounded."

But in other places the Germans swarmed over the south bank of the river to overwhelm American advance posts and clamber up the hill toward the main defense line behind the embankment of the Paris–Metz railroad. Here the Americans held despite heavy casualties. The French on both sides began to fall back, but the 38th Infantry would not budge.

By this time Colonel Mitchell had taken off to find out what was happening. The ceiling was quite low in places, but he saw no German planes or movement of ground troops. There was artillery fire all along the front. He passed Château-Thierry and started up the Marne, flying low on account of the fog and clouds. "Suddenly as I rounded a turn of the river east of Dormans, I saw a great mass of artillery fire hitting the south bank, and, spanning the river, five bridges filled with German troops marching over." He looked around for enemy planes but saw none. No one was paying any attention to him, although he was flying within five hundred feet of the bridges. "Looking down on the men, marching so splendidly, I thought to myself, what a shame to spoil such fine infantry." He continued a few minutes, then followed the front lines northeast along the river toward Reims. A fierce battle was going on there with the air full of German planes, so he came back to the Marne. "By that time, a terrible combat was taking place on top of the hill just south of the bridges. The opposing troops were almost together. This was the nearest to hand-to-hand combat than anything I had ever seen so far." He guessed he was seeing Americans in action and he was right. It was the 38th Infantry, making its gallant stand.

Some fifty miles east, beyond Reims, the chief of staff of the American Rainbow Division, Colonel Douglas MacArthur, was watching the battle from the main line of defense. As the Germans stormed the abandoned front-line trenches, he saw the American barrage descend on them like an avalanche. But they came on, emboldened by the easy conquest of the first trenches. And by the time the enemy troops reached the real line, they looked exhausted, uncoordinated and scattered. "Their legs are broken!" MacArthur told his sweating cannoneers. The legs of the Germans in this area were indeed broken. Although they managed to pierce through in a few spots, they were thrown back.

The enemy was making some progress west of Reims, where some six divisions smashed into the line held by the Italian 8th Division and drove it back to its second line. To the left the French also felt the weight of the assault and were being pressed back. By 9:30 A.M. the enemy had driven a dangerous salient into Allied lines from Dormans on the Marne up to the heights of Reims. Help was needed and Pétain telephoned General Fayolle, commander of the French reserves, to rush up the 168th Division and the II Cavalry Corps. He also sent orders to temporarily suspend preparation of the Mangin offensive.

A little later Foch met Fayolle on the doorstep of his headquarters. Sixty years ago they had been schoolmates. "How's your attack? Is it going ahead all right?" he asked.

"No, it isn't," said the troubled Fayolle. "General Pétain has just ordered me to suspend the counter-offensive because he needs the troops to support the defensive battle."

"Let Gouraud take care of himself!" exclaimed Foch, and rushed into the office. Hurriedly he dictated an order to be telephoned to Pétain: "It must be understood that until there are new developments that you let me know about, there can be no question in any way of slowing up, much less stopping, the Mangin preparations. In case of urgent and absolute need, you will take from there troops absolutely indispensable, informing me at once." His message, sent without even consulting Pétain, was insulting. But it was gleefully welcomed by Fayolle and his staff. "We were delighted, after having been consternated by Pétain's decision. At heart, the latter is very timorous. It was evident that the counter-offensive should be allowed to go forward, since on the right Gouraud's line had held."

Although the Germans had succeeded by now in driving substantial bridgeheads across the Marne on either side of Dormans, Crown Prince Wilhelm was unhappy. He had seen reports that the enemy had evacuated his front line according to plan and there was little forward progress. "This had a discouraging sound and I saw my first doubts in the way of being confirmed." He decided to see his father and arrived at the observation tower while the Kaiser was in the middle of his victory breakfast. A General Staff officer came to meet the Crown Prince in the expectation of good news. "He was horrified when I told him my impression that we should probably be held up after taking the first line."

The Kaiser awaited his son eagerly and it grieved the latter "to have to say that I regarded the situation as unpromising." They rang up the Crown Prince's chief of staff for confirmation to learn that their troops were being held up before the enemy's second line. The Crown Prince ordered this line prepared for assault by a fresh bombardment, "but in my heart of hearts I had to admit the bitter truth that the offensive had failed." In deep and anxious thought he returned to Charleville. "Here I found grave and resolute men. My Chief of Staff confirmed on the map what I already knew, that the French plan had been to evade our blow, so that our artillery preparation had destroyed a trench system which had been almost entirely evacuated."

Soon after noon, Foch was having lunch with Haig. In the best of spirits now, he listened to the Scotsman's objections to giving up reserves, and then said he only wanted the British divisions in case of necessity and would return them at once if the British front were threatened. Under these circumstances, Haig agreed. It was a grave responsibility, particularly knowing of Lloyd George's hostility, but this was the moment to help an ally.

At his headquarters, Pétain read Foch's telephone message with care. By now the urgency of midmorning had somewhat abated. The thrust across the Marne was slowing, and it was now evident that Gouraud had the situation well in hand east of Reims. At 1 P.M. he ordered Fayolle to continue the Mangin attack, news that, of course, came as no surprise to Fayolle.

3.

Ludendorff still hoped they could break through, and told a staff officer, "If my blow at Reims succeeds now, we have won the war." Dissatisfied with the progress of the Third Army, held up east of Reims, he telephoned its chief of staff. "Why isn't the attack getting any further?" he stormed. "It must be pressed home at once."

Lieutenant Colonel W. J. von Klewitz calmly replied, "The Army Commander has ordered it to be discontinued because the prerequisites of the Chemin des Dames are not in evidence here. The French have pulled their artillery back a long way and the present French positions are laughing at the withering fire."

Such common sense brought Ludendorff back to earth. "I quite agree about the discontinuation of the attack," he said. "I am the last man to order an attack that merely costs blood."

The battle raged in the afternoon with the intense heat adding to the torture of combat. Georg Bucher, who had fought as a private for almost four years, had gone into the fray that morning with enthusiasm. He had fought across the Marne, which ran red with blood, and then continued up the hill watching the company ahead get mowed down. Undeterred, his company followed, shouting madly. But the murderous fire forced them to hide in the corn. "If only fresh storm-divisions had been with us during these hours we should have broken right through, even without artillery for support, for the devil was in us." But by late afternoon they had to dig in across that same cornfield after a disappointing advance of only three miles. "We lay there exhausted and dispirited. They had asked us for more than we could give—we had given all we could, our strength, our eagerness, our courage. For us the end had come." It wasn't the intense shellfire that unnerved him and his comrades, but the helplessness of exhaustion, the consciousness that they could do no more. "I almost envied those who had fallen in the advance—they at least had escaped the agony of that trench." What good was there hanging on to that tiny bridgehead across the Marne with almost no ammunition? "Were we, I asked myself, really a nation's hope? I dared not believe it for we were at our very last gasp."

The carnage was even worse on the other side of the river, where Allied artillery throughout the day had blasted the reserve units. "Never had I seen so many dead," wrote Lieutenant Hesse, "never contemplated a spectacle of war so frightful as on the northern slopes of the Marne. On the southern side the Americans in a hand-to-hand fight had completely wiped out two of our companies. Hidden in the wheat in a semicircle, they had let our men advance, then had annihilated them with a fire at thirty or forty feet away. This enemy has coolness, one must acknowledge, but he also gave proof that day of a bestial brutality. 'The Americans are killing everyone!' Such was the terrifying word that spread through all our ranks on the 15th of July."

Lieutenant Rudolf Binding was writing in his diary: "I have lived through the most disheartening day of the whole War." His unit had only advanced two miles before seeking refuge in a trench. He had pointed out the absurd exposure of the position to Division, but no one listened and a few minutes later a shell burst a few yards from him. "I was simply mad. How could one expect to put one's heart into such a business? It was no courage to behave as these people did; at the most it could amuse a few irresponsibles who were prepared to gamble with their own and other people's lives." Worse was to follow. All telephone wires were cut, so no orders could be carried out. "Everything seemed to go wrong. My own work was useless."

But Pétain still had qualms and at 4:45 P.M. sent a message directly to Foch, again requesting permission to postpone the Mangin offensive for twenty-four hours. A little later good news came from Gouraud: "At 1700 hours the first parallel of the position of resistance is in our possession on the entire front of attack." In other words, the entire right wing of the line was safe. Moments later the French Sixth Army announced that they had repulsed the enemy which had crossed the Marne near Château-Thierry. Even the French Fifth Army, which had taken the hardest blow, reported that the Germans showed signs of tiring. At last it was evident even to Pétain that a great victory had been scored; he telephoned Foch that he felt the Mangin attack could proceed as planned.

The Kaiser returned to his headquarters at 7 P.M. "His mood," wrote Admiral von Müller, "was slightly less ebullient than usual. I have the impression that the day's objectives have not been reached." Ludendorff, telephoning General von Kuhl, sounded very depressed about the poor outcome of the attack. Kuhl advised him to continue the assault and mentioned March 21, when the Second Army had made no progress either. At first Ludendorff felt they could not risk the losses, then he ordered the Crown Prince to resume the attack in the morning. But the feeling at Supreme Headquarters on July 16, so wrote Colonel Mertz von Quirnheim in his diary, was depressed. "Difficult question what to do next." Heavy fighting continued along the Marne front, and some minor successes were achieved, but by afternoon the situation of the six German divisions in the bridgehead was becoming precarious because of gun and air attacks on their bridges.

The Crown Prince got no orders from Supreme Headquarters, so that evening he stopped not only the assault across the Marne but that east of Reims. Only the two corps between the Marne and Reims were to attack on the morrow. When the Kaiser returned after another day at the front, he told his courtiers that fifteen thousand prisoners had been taken and that Châlons-sur-Marne had been successfully shelled. Then he read aloud a report from Vienna. "It was very pessimistic and forecast a catastrophe in the autumn." The mood that evening was "low," particularly since Müller and the others had heard by the grapevine that the entire Champagne offensive was about to be abandoned.

It dragged on through July 17, although any chance of a breakthrough seemed hopeless. "I am so convinced," wrote Mertz von Quirnheim, "that neither Wetzell [head of the Operations Section of the General Staff] nor Ludendorff know what they must do next." Ludendorff had managed to convince himself that the main object of the offensive had been attained because the French reserves were irretrievably committed to the Champagne front;

Operation Michael, Western Front trench system just before the attack, March 21, 1918.

The Kaiser, a frequent front-line visitor, was convinced of victory by the end of March. "The battle is won," he said, "the English have been utterly defeated!"

The hard-fought road between Amiens and St. Quentin.

Operation Georgette, April 9, 1918.

At Estaires, to the north halfway to Armentieres, British troops blinded by tear gas that same day.

The remains of Béthune's clock tower in the background.

The Germans seize Mount Kemmel, but their hospital unit was almost wiped out by Allied shells.

After the battle Brigadier J. C. Campbell addresses men of the 137th Staffordshire Brigade, 46th Division, at the same place they crossed the St. Quentin canal on September 29th.

Opposite, above left: Infantry commander Brigadier General Douglas MacArthur.

Opposite, above right: Tank specialist Lieutenant Colonel George S. Patton, Jr. During the battle he encountered MacArthur, who was personally supervising an infantry assault. They were caught in a creeping barrage. "I think each one wanted to leave but hated to do so," recalled Patton, "so we let it come over us."

Opposite, below: The German Big Three: Hindenburg, Kaiser Wilhelm, and Ludendorff.

Personalities
THE GERMANS

General John Pershing with Marshal Foch, the Supreme Allied Commander.

The War in the Air

Opposite, above: Early in the war this unique German plane was designed to land upright or upside down.

Opposite, below left: "The Black Swallow of Death," Eugene Bullard, the world's first black pilot, was the only black flier in the Great War. Born in Columbus, Georgia, he joined the French Foreign Legion shortly after the outbreak of war. He transferred to the French 170th Infantry Regiment, nicknamed "The Swallows of Death" for their daring bayonet attacks. After being wounded twice at Verdun, he learned to fly on a bet, then joined the Lafayette Flying Corps. As a fighter pilot, he was aggressive to the point of recklessness and would often take on several adversaries at once. When the U.S. entered the war, all American pilots were transferred to the U.S. Air Service with an advancement in rank as commissioned officers—all, that is, except Bullard, a recipient of the Croix de Guerre, who was grounded. It was not until 1943 that a black flying officer was finally commissioned.

Opposite, below right: America's leading ace, Eddie Rickenbacker.

Germany's leading ace, Baron Manfred von Richthofen after his sixty-second victory.

What Price Glory?

and he could now, with easy mind, unleash Hagen in Flanders. He was gambling that this offensive would surely succeed and end the war. That evening he drove up north to the headquarters of the Army Group of Rupprecht, Crown Prince of Bavaria, to review the state of their preparations for the crucial blow against the British.

Mangin's troops were assembling at the east end of the Champagne bulge in the great forest just northwest of Villers-Cotterêts. He had twenty-four divisions against eleven German, and Mangin's troops were of first quality, four being American with their complement of 17,000 men each, as compared to an average of 7,000 in a German division. Crown Prince Wilhelm's troops in this area were of low grade; many had been transferred from Russia and had no experience with tanks, which Mangin planned to use in masses. The main assault was to be made by the tough Moroccan Division, which included the legendary Foreign Legion, flanked on each side by a big American unit, the 1st Division on the left and on the right the 2nd, which had fought so courageously and recklessly in Belleau Wood through the month of June.

It was midafternoon of July 17 before the American units reached the depths of the forest. The doughboys and Marines marveled at the great number of camouflaged tanks. There were big ones that looked like prehistoric monsters and tiny ones that seemed like windup toys. They all rattled, roared, and snorted and sent up clouds of noxious fumes. The roads were jammed with rolling kitchens and mule-drawn water wagons, as well as thousands of cavalrymen carrying long lances like King Arthur's knights. The greatest menace to the marching infantrymen was the endless line of artillery: howitzers towed by tractors; the deadly 75s hauled by six-horse teams, and the larger field guns each by eight dray horses. The traffic reminded Marine Sergeant Gerald Thomas of a turgid stream, flowing slowly, irresistibly forward. "It was much as though we were moving through a tunnel as everywhere the bows of the great trees reached out well over the roadway." And the foot soldier had small chance for a piece of the road. Drenched by several showers on the day's march, their uniforms steamed in the sunlight and the forest was like a great Turkish bath. There was little water, and thirst became a torture.

In the meantime Mangin and his staff were working industriously, but it was not until 4 P.M. that the plan of attack was finished and instructions relayed to the artillery and infantry commanders. The infantry was to charge out of the eastern edge of the forest at 4:35 the next morning.

The foot soldiers trudged single file along a ditch. There were dark Moroccans in khaki, black Senegalese, and French in their blue carrying pots and pans that jangled. The Americans hadn't eaten for more than a day and there was no hope of food till next morning. With the twilight lasting for hours, it didn't become dark until almost eleven. There was no moon and the forest was suddenly pitch black. This was the hideout of the fifteenth-century monster Gilles de Rais, the original, according to some scholars, of the infamous Bluebeard. With darkness came a fearful rumble. Thunder. Rain began pelting down. The marching men were protected at first by the leafy roof of the forest, but within minutes the clay roads were mud. Vehicles slipped into the ditches; horses stumbled and the men, already exhausted, found the footing miserable.

In the downpour maps became indistinct or worthless and the rest of the night was spent by staff officers frantically trying to gather up scattered remnants and searching for lost platoons and companies. "As we grope in single file," Private McCord wrote in his diary, "we cling each man to a packstrap of the man in front, as blindly, doggedly on we go, in spite of the mud, the heavy packs and the rain that comes down in torrents . . . Blindly feeling our way, with the help of God and our own intuition, we the lousy infantry, s.o.l. [shit out of luck] as always, until they get us to where they need us, managed to miraculously accomplish the impossible by getting from the right to the left side of this dark, seething, confusing stream of traffic to follow other lousy troopers, men like ourselves, the other battalions and companies of our regiment, in single file off through the woods to our left."

Wherever General Harbord, now commander of the entire 2nd Division, went he found the same story: no information, no maps, no guides, no orders. And they had to get in place in time for the early morning attack. "All realized that the task was almost superhuman, but the honor not only of our Division but of the American name was at stake." At 4 A.M. on July 18 his two regiments, the Fifth Marines and the doughboys of the 9th Infantry, were pressing hard to arrive in time. Exhausted and hungry, they began to hustle, double-timing, arriving at the point of departure almost out of breath.

Floyd Gibbons, only a month out of the hospital, was with the Marines again, a black patch over his destroyed eye. He was worried that the Germans might guess that an attack was coming and pour gas shells into the forest. It would be a massacre. But there was no noise, no confusion, no shouting of commands or waving of swords. Officers whispered their orders and the only noise was the roll of thunder and the eternal dropping of water from wet leaves, and an occasional ear-splitting crash of lightning.

At 4:35 A.M., with the first light of July 18, silence was broken by the bark of a 75. Almost instantly there was a tremendous roar as the Allied barrage opened up. To Marine Sergeant R. M. Ganoe it was "a grand, glorious, terrific, ear-gouging explosion." The earth shook up and down and sideways. Once he had heard 1,600 guns discharged simultaneously and thought it the peak of din. "But this barrage! It shook the leaves off the trees. The heavens came down and the earth went up; I can't describe it." He and the others forgot their hunger and thirst, blistered feet, aching joints, and wet clothes. "Our eyes shone like a zealot's and our hearts filled with the glory and splendor of that mighty thunder. O, man! What a grand and glorious feeling that was!" Ganoe heard someone nearby say, "I never want to have a grander feeling or I'd just naturally die of joy." The enemy was completely taken by surprise. The racket of the tanks was terrifying and so were the battle cries of the Americans. The Germans fell back in disorder. All along Mangin's line there was little resistance. Some German units, out in the fields harvesting the crops the farmers had abandoned, took to their heels in panic.

The Allied barrage roared on steadily and occasional German shells exploded between the first and second waves of advancing Marines. One group captured a four-inch gun, a telephone station, and several prisoners. They found hot coffee and German war bread "which the men devoured after making the prisoners first sample it." Other Marines liberated a barrel of sauerkraut and continued attacking through a wheat field carrying rifle in one hand and a fistful of sauerkraut in the other.

Germans in the front lines were holding up their hands in blank astonishment, and those in the second lines were still shocked by the Allied barrage, which was creeping forward to allow their own tanks and men to mop up.

Ganoe's battalion in the second wave was plunging through a huge wheat field. Someone shouted, "Here they come!" Ganoe looked ahead at a column of men marching toward him, four abreast. Germans! But they were prisoners. "At least twenty officers were at the head of the column. They were the happiest prisoners alive, I believe." The ones who spoke English cheered on the Americans. One shouted, "Give 'em hell, boys. It won't last long." Those who spoke French shouted out, *"Fini la guerre!"* Ganoe made a rough count. There were at least 1,300 and most of them were young. "It made one's heart ache to think of how recently they had been dragged from their mother's hearth by the Kaiser's mailed fist. Nothing but rosy-cheeked, red-lipped, bright-eyed boys!"

For miles to left and right across the rolling fields could be seen successive waves of assault with small and large tanks rumbling on ahead. Just behind were Marines, doughboys, Senegalese, Foreign Legionnaires, and poilus. As they advanced through the wheat, the German lines wavered, then broke. Here and there stubborn groups held out, but these were soon bypassed or overwhelmed. Some Germans died fighting, others threw down their rifles and shouted, *"Kameraden!"* at the sight of any attackers.

The heat was punishing and there was almost no water to quench parched throats; the canteens of dead Germans were avidly drained, their leather packs searched for food. Even moldy bread was gulped down and occasionally someone would find a real treasure, a comb of honey.

To the left of the 2nd Division, the Moroccans, the best assault and shock troops of the French Army, were living up to their reputation. Perhaps they were fighting so courageously to show that men of a different race and color could fight as fiercely as the white man. There were coal black Senegalese as well as Moroccans, and they all were battling with desperate bravery. To their left were the doughboys of the American 1st Division. Private First Class James Rose's unit walked into sheer hell. A shell exploded in the midst of a dozen men to his left. "We were transfixed as we watched the holocaust. Some of them fell and never moved again, some flew through the air and miraculously walked away, others just disintegrated before our eyes. Pvt. Lewis got it behind the ear and Oleson in the hip. Lewis went wild and I had to tussle trying to head him to the rear. Many were dazed but still on their feet." By a freak of chance Rose wasn't scratched. But his machine gun was disabled and he gave his ammunition to the loader of another crew. Their gunner suddenly went berserk and turned his gun on the French in the trench ahead, thinking they were the enemy. "They are Germans!" he kept shouting. Rose couldn't make the gunner understand in the din of battle, so pushed his gun muzzle up in the air. The French piled over the parapet and began smothering the embarrassed Rose with kisses "and I believe they would have decorated me then and there with the Croix-de-Guerre if they could have."

The doughboys leapfrogged the French line, continuing into a vast wheat field, hip high in grain. Rose abruptly realized that he and Sergeant Manning were alone. Those who had fallen were hidden in the wheat. All of a sudden the two came upon a young enemy officer, horribly mangled. He screamed to them in German, pointing to their rifles and his heart. "Rose, can you do it?" said Manning. "I can't." Neither could Rose and they both cursed their lack of guts as they continued forward.

Watching the battle was Pierre Teilhard de Chardin, a stretcher-bearer who was also a priest. He had no specific duties—except to observe. "You can imagine the vast uplands of the Soissons country dotted with groups of men advancing in single file—then halting and taking cover," he wrote his sister. "On all sides, great bursts of smoke appeared, white, black, and dirty grey, in the air and on the ground. Over all this there rose the sound of a continuous light crackling and it was a shock to see among the ripening crops little blotches that lay still, for ever. Here and there a tank slowly made its way through the tall corn, followed by a group of supporters, like a ship sailing the sea. Too often, you'd see that it had been hit, and was burning in a thick cloud of black smoke."

From above this turmoil, groups of planes would suddenly sweep low to machine-gun, seemingly at random. "There was something implacable about all this, above all; it seemed *inanimate*. You could see nothing of the agony and passion that gave each little moving human dot its own individual character and made them all so many worlds. All you saw was the material development of a clash between two huge material forces." He had a close-up view of the neighboring Americans. "Everyone says the

FOURTH LUDENDORFF OFFENSIVE, JULY 15, AND
FRENCH-AMERICAN COUNTER-ATTACK, JULY 18 – AUG. 6

FR.TENTH ARMY
MANGIN

U.S.2ND DIV.
FOREST OF RETZ
Villers Cotterêts

MOROCCAN DIV.

U.S.1ST DIV.

(½) U.S. 4TH DIV.

(½) U.S. 4TH DIV.

Aisne

Soissons

Vierzy

Berzy-le-Sec

FR.SIXTH ARMY
DEGOUTTE

MARNE

Belleau

U.S.26TH DIV. AND BELLEAU WOOD

Bouresches

Château-Thierry

U.S. 3RD DIV.

Lucy-on-Bocage

Vaux

Torcy

Fère-en-Tardenois

Vesle

FR.NINTH ARMY
MITRY

Jaulgonne

Dormans

Ville-en-Tardenois

Fismes

Brogle

FR.FIFTH ARMY
BERTHELOT

IT. 3RD DIV.

HILLS OF REIMS

Vesle

Trigny

Reims

Vesle

Epernay

MARNE

N

Front Line July 15
Front Line July 18
Front Line Aug. 6
Army Boundaries

MILES
0   5   10
KM
0   5   10

prlacia

253

same: they're first-rate troops, fighting with intense *individual* passion (concentrated on the enemy) and wonderful courage. The only complaint one would make about them is that they don't take sufficient care; they're too apt to get themselves killed." Their wounded walked back erect, almost stiff, impassive and never complaining. "I don't think I've ever seen such pride and dignity in suffering. There's complete comradeship between them and us, born fully-fledged under fire."

From above, a Canadian in command of the 1st Pursuit Group, U. S. Air Service, had a "grandstand seat" of the battle. Lieutenant Colonel Harold Hartney's sixteen planes were several miles high when the barrage opened up, and he could see the ground being churned to powder, the air full of smoke and dust. "No man ever saw a more magnificent or, rather, a more significant sight. Here was the tide of a world war involving twenty million men actually turning before my very eyes." There were the Americans, fresh, vigorous and engaging in their first major battle, sweeping across the wide fields along with the French and Moroccans.

Floyd Gibbons, despite his condition, was following the advance. He too saw the great line of prisoners, four abreast. The first eight Germans were carrying a wounded American on one litter and a Frenchman on the other. These two were half-sitting, half-reclining, smoking cigarettes and chatting gaily as they rode high on the shoulders of their captives. The prisoners told Gibbons that the British were in the war because they hated Germany; France because the battling was in their country; the Yanks only to collect souvenirs.

Gibbons stopped one of these collectors bound for the rear. He was one of the shortest men he had ever seen in U.S. uniform and he was herding two huge prisoners who towered above him. A white bandage ran around his forehead and there were blood-stained strips of cotton gauze on cheek and neck. He carried a huge chunk of German black bread; dangling from his right hip were five holsters containing Lugers. Suspended from his right shoulder by straps to his left hip were six pairs of expensive field glasses. His filthy face was wreathed in a remarkable smile.

The reporter asked a German officer what he thought of the fighting capacities of the Americans. "I do not know," he said as if talking to an inferior. "I have never seen him fight." He had been in a dugout when the terrible bombardment landed. Once it stopped he looked up the stairs to behold his first American soldier. "I did not like his carriage or his bearing. He wore his helmet far back on his head. And he did not have his coat on." Nor was his collar even buttoned. His sleeves were rolled up to his elbows and he held a grenade in each hand. "Just then he looked down the stairs and saw me—saw me standing there—saw me, a major—and he shouted roughly, 'Come out of there, you big Dutch bastard, or I'll spill a basketful of these on you.'"

At 10:54 A.M. Crown Prince Wilhelm realized that the divisions on the right flank had been pushed back and even supporting divisions were already engaged. He ordered resistance organized on the general line from Soissons to Château-Thierry, pointing out that the fighting divisions should not retire back to this line at present. If they did, however, they must hold this rear line to the last. At the same time he ordered preparation of a second line of resistance five miles behind the first. This unique command indicated that the Crown Prince had little faith in his men's ability to stem the tide. If further proof were needed, it was his next order: evacuation of the bridgehead south of the Marne.

His superior, Ludendorff, was far away in Flanders conferring with the army group of Crown Prince Rupprecht. "Ludendorff was confident and eager to attack," recalled General Fritz von Lossberg, chief of staff of the Fourth Army, "and to the joy of us all still held to the intention of carrying out an attack in Flanders." While discussing the date to launch Operation Hagen, a telephone message was brought into the room. An unexpected tank assault had pierced the German line southwest of Soissons. There was consternation among the conferees and Ludendorff himself was "naturally in a state of the greatest tension" to learn that all local reserves had been committed as well as all those of Crown Prince Wilhelm's army group, which had been about to launch another all-out attack on Reims. This meant that his cherished hope of capturing that key city and thus forcing Haig to send further reinforcement from Flanders was dashed. In the space of three days all his hopes in Champagne had dissipated and the enemy was threatening *him*. It was an incredible turnabout. He immediately ordered the 5th Division to proceed by train from St. Quentin to Soissons.

Lossberg counseled him to adopt a systematic policy of defense in the Soissons area by yielding ground. Ludendorff was impressed but after a long pause said, "I think your proposals are pertinent, but I cannot follow them for political reasons." What political reasons? "I must think of the impression on the enemy, on our own army, and on the home front."

Lossberg protested that, when military necessity was sacrificed to political expediency, trouble always followed. Despairingly, Ludendorff said that he would have to resign, then ended the conference and started back to Avesnes. On the way he was deeply disturbed and disgusted. His own grand offensive of July 15 had failed because the French knew exactly what was coming. He had been victimized by his own men! "While the commanders were doing their utmost to keep these secrets, the love of talking and boasting that is inborn in Germans betrayed to the world and to our enemies matter of the greatest weight and significance." Now he must devise means of stopping the surprise French attack.

As his train pulled into Avesnes at 2 P.M. (1 P.M. Allied time),

Hindenburg was waiting with veiled impatience on the platform. En route to the red brick house that was headquarters, Hindenburg brought him up to date. Apparently a dozen German divisions had already been destroyed or seriously damaged. The 5th Division coming by rail was being held up by enemy artillery fire, and those divisions being rushed to the critical area by trucks could not get there for hours. The discussion continued at lunch, but Ludendorff, apparently under no strain at all, said little until Hindenburg turned to Colonel Mertz von Quirnheim and said, "The simplest and most complete solution of the present crisis is, in my opinion, to summon up all troops immediately, including those from Flanders, and to start an offensive across the high ground north of Soissons in a southerly direction against the left flank of the enemy's attack."

This instantly brought Ludendorff to life. "He declared that anything of that sort was utterly unfeasible and must therefore be forgotten, as he thought he had already made abundantly clear to the Field-Marshal." At these insulting words, Hindenburg left the table without a word. Ludendorff, annoyed and scarlet of face, followed. He was faced with a difficult decision. Should he send south those precious reserves he had been collecting for Operation Hagen? Finally he concluded there was no alternative. He ordered the 50th Division sent to Soissons immediately with the 24th to be held in readiness.

By early afternoon the Americans were pinned down by a murderous crossfire of machine guns near the Vierzy ravine, a precipitous and wooded gash in the earth. They watched in wonder as French cavalrymen abruptly emerged from a nearby woods and began spreading out in preparation for a mass attack. It was like something from a movie with the prancing horses and the beautifully uniformed dragoons, lancers, and armored cuirassiers. Shells began falling. Gunnery Sergeant Paradise watched in horror as men on horseback tumbled down but others galloped by unharmed and began mopping up isolated positions of Germans bypassed by the Marines.

Less than a mile away, doughboys were also enthralled witnesses. "As those precision riders moved out, it was the most inspiring sight my hillbilly eyes had ever beheld," recalled Pfc. Rose. "So brave, so proud and so beautiful." It was just as he had pictured Napoleon's armies. Then the shells fell and the slaughter was horrible. "Horses, men, gore. My God, only a handful survived. I shall never forget that sight."

Still shaken, Rose and his mates advanced with the French Foreign Legion until they came to a huge cave with four machine guns guarding its mouth. They were pointed at the open fields Rose had just crossed. But the doughboys and the Foreign Legion rushed inside and in a few minutes some 1,200 prisoners marched out in columns of four.

At another cave-fortress, which was holding up the 1st Division advance, a French tank waddled up to the entrance "like a huge turtle," as machine-gun pellets rattled off its armor. With its own guns roaring away, it trundled into the cave and disappeared. Minutes later it backed out, followed by about 600 prisoners including a colonel.

As soon as the Kaiser learned of the breakthrough, he rushed to Avesnes. It was late afternoon by the time he mounted the steps to Hindenburg's headquarters. Coming out to meet him was the old field marshal, dignified, stately, and unhurried. Wilhelm stretched out his hand and nodded vigorously. His lips moved and his personal news reporter, Karl Rosner, was close enough to notice that he could not speak.

"Your Majesty has seen much in these hard days," said Hindenburg with understanding. "The war has shown a hard face."

Wanting to be alone with Hindenburg and know the truth, the Kaiser hurried into the red brick villa. At his desk, poring over papers, Ludendorff looked up. The monocle fell from his eye. He quickly rose and advanced.

"You have had a strenuous tour, Excellency," said Wilhelm.

Hindenburg interrupted. "I believe that Your Majesty may desire first of all our opinion as to how we got into the critical position in which we are at present."

The Kaiser nodded, closing his eyes as Hindenburg briefly explained that the troops had given way and many Germans taken prisoner. He told of the French use of small whippet tanks and the consequent breakthrough at several points. But a new line of defense had been organized.

Wilhelm nodded, said nothing, finally tugged at his coat and asked abruptly, "Will the new line hold?"

"That really can't be foretold, Your Majesty." The enemy offensive might continue for days.

Wilhelm was excited and perturbed, yet eager to appear deliberate. But he could not control his voice and the words came tumbling out rudely: "So we shall retire still farther—give up more ground?" He checked himself and almost apologetically added that they had to consider the restive sentiment back home and in the rest of the world. "The significance of this opposition cannot be overestimated—in the interest of the throne."

Hindenburg quietly replied that he had to be first occupied with purely military responsibility. He paused, then turned to Ludendorff. "Perhaps my comrade—?"

The Quartermaster General cleared his voice and stiffened slightly. "I beg to impress on Your Majesty that I received news that the enemy had broken our line only this morning, while discussing our new Flanders' offensive. This painful surprise—"

Wilhelm interrupted. "Then we were all thoroughly taken by surprise?" He was angry, threatening, but Ludendorff continued unperturbed. The surprise, he said, was not in there being an attack but in the failure of the front line to hold and the extent of the enemy's initial success. He stepped to the chart table and, adjusting his monocle, began explaining what had to be done. "Unless we can be certain of our western flank, we cannot undertake operations around Reims, or withdraw in an orderly way from the south bank of the Marne." They must erect a new front before resuming the initiative. "Here is where we have got to settle things. Here we must decide our further plan of campaign."

It was obvious to Rosner that the Kaiser was furious at the thought of any further withdrawal. The blood rushed to his face. He tapped his foot. "No!" he at last blurted out. "I trust we shall not give up a single foot of the soil we have won!"

As they were leaving the room, a young officer handed a paper to be approved by Ludendorff. It was the text of the evening announcement of the Wolff Telegraph Agency. The Kaiser took the paper and read the official notice: "The French attacked with heavy forces and tanks between the Aisne and the Marne and made some gains. Our reserves have been brought into action."

How harmless it all sounded, thought Rosner. "And yet," he concluded, "unless God works a miracle, this is the turning of the tide!"

At almost that moment, Mangin's chief of staff, Colonel Hellé, telephoned that Generals Pétain and Fayolle were on their way to Mangin's forward command post. He had heard Pétain remark, "It is good, it is very good, it is almost too good . . . but it is necessary to stop." There were no more divisions to throw into the attack.

Half an hour later the two generals arrived at Mangin's observation tower in the Forest of Retz. It was about sixty feet high and all day had afforded Mangin a bird's-eye view of the most important part of the battleground. Pétain congratulated Mangin but decried his unconventional notion of such a forward headquarters. "Here you don't command anything," he said. Mangin explained that he had his staff at the foot of the tower ready to gallop forward with orders. Then he impatiently asked for more reserves. "I don't have any," said Pétain. "I know that you are very persuasive but this time I am very strong, for having absolutely nothing myself, I can give you nothing."

Mangin acidly protested that one should not stop an attack of such importance at the moment it could lead to decisive results. Otherwise, it would have been better not to have started it in the first place. But Pétain repeated that he had no reserves—and he himself regretted it. "Besides, I am obliged to assume that the Germans are south of the Marne. That is what concerns me particularly and that is what I must prevent. Here I must adopt a defense in depth and, in a pinch, adjust the actual line."

Mangin argued that it was easier to force the Germans to evacuate the bridgehead south of the Marne, and even the Château-Thierry pocket, by following the present attack than in trying to patch up the Marne breakthrough. But Pétain insisted that he could not possibly give Mangin another division, and he left with Fayolle. Mangin thought a moment. Setting his aggressive jaw, he finally told his chief of staff, "In short, General Pétain says that he will give me nothing yet has not really ordered me to stop the attack. So we will continue with what we have and the attack will resume tomorrow."

Late that afternoon two U. S. Marine battalions attempted to take Vierzy. Three companies started down the ravine in two waves, but were riddled by the machine guns emplaced on its other side. While the Americans were trying to destroy these emplacements, six French tanks headed back through their lines, drawing intense enemy artillery fire. Many Marines were killed or wounded and four of the tanks were knocked out.

The Marines tried again at 6:30 P.M. This time, after re-forming their lines, they attacked with fifteen tanks and were supported by machine guns and a powerful artillery concentration. They swept through Vierzy with amazing rapidity as doughboys came in from another direction, and by 8 P.M. the deadly ravine was taken and it would be possible to push forward the next morning.

By nightfall of the eighteenth the Allies had pushed forward almost six miles but at appalling cost. General Harbord moved 2nd Division headquarters up near Vierzy to a large farm that had been wrested from the Germans. "It was an advanced dressing station and a very distressing scene," he wrote in his diary. "The congestion on the one country road prevented ambulances from getting to the front and the men had lain there in the yard of farm buildings all day, and were to continue to lie there twelve or fourteen hours longer. Water was unobtainable, the buildings were in ruins from shellfire, and the boche still dropped an occasional bomb as they circled over. But from these wounded there was no word of complaint, nothing but patience in suffering. There were wounded Germans, Americans, and darkskinned Moroccans side by side on the ground, blood over everything, clothes cut away, some were dead, and a ceaseless stream of traffic still pouring to the front with ambulances and supplies for fighting." Harbord's division had outrun its communications and there were no wire connections at all to the rear. But finally a corps order was brought by a French officer. The division was to attack in the morning.

The men tried to get some sleep. Most of them had eaten little or nothing but they suffered far more from thirst. All the springs and wells for miles around had been almost drunk dry and long lines stood with empty canteens at the few remaining water holes.

Lieutenant Sulzbach's artillery unit was on the road hoping to get into position before dawn so they could help stop the Allied advance. "So we are moving along behind the front; it looks as though we are being thrown into the largest enemy offensive of all time—and it was supposed to be *our* offensive! We couldn't even have dreamed this would happen—never. We seem to be coming to the exact site of our offensive of 27 May, or else into the battlefield of early June. But in spite of everything it was a lovely night, cloudless and warm." Although the roads were packed they were making good progress. Troops in trucks continuously passed and would be soon thrown into the new critical position before the artillerymen. And what was the present situation? "We are all in the grip of incredible tension, and can hardly speak for excitement and anticipation."

The Kaiser was back at his camp. He told Admiral von Müller that operations had been abandoned on the right flank, then blamed the failure of their own attack on one of their own engineer officers who had swum over the Marne to betray their plans. Müllr permitted himself to observe that it was highly unlikely that an engineer officer would have any real knowledge of the plans. But the Kaiser said, "It must have been someone who had to do with the pontoon bridge."

His son and heir was still reflecting on the situation with his own chief of staff. They were both "a prey to a great fear" that their Seventh Army was heading straight for catastrophe unless the wings at Soissons and in the hill region of Reims held. "It was certainly the most critical situation I had found myself in as Commander during the whole war."

At Avesnes, Hindenburg was waving his left hand over a map at the high ground northwest of Soissons. In a subdued but clear voice he said, "This is how we must direct the counterattack, that would solve the crisis at once!"

At these words Ludendorff straightened up sharply. His face flushed with rage and he started for the door exclaiming, "Madness!" Hindenburg took after him. "I should like a word with you," he said. Both of them disappeared into Ludendorff's study. Later that night Hindenburg wrote his wife that if the war were lost it would not be his fault but Germany's lack of spiritual strength.

5.

There could be no surprise on the second day of attack, so the Allies found themselves faced by a stubborn enemy reinforced during the night and now hidden in the wheat and corn fields. At 4:30 A.M., July 19, the doughboys of the 1st Division were rousted out and told they were going over the top in an hour. Private Rose's unit started up a small ridge. At the summit they were met by a solid sheet of machine-gun fire. He saw his major fall, then the first sergeant. Soon there were no officers and Sergeant Manning took charge. He was hit and as he sank, strangling in his own blood, he gasped, "Follow Rose!" Now a private first class was in command of the remnants of the company and for some strange reason Rose was not the least bit frightened. All he could hear in the din of battle were the dying words of his sergeant, "Follow Rose." He motioned the others to follow, but by the time he reached the Paris–Soissons road he had lost all but one man. He knew they had to cross the highway to a trench on the other side. The other grabbed his arm. "My God, man, we can't cross that road. We'll get killed." Rose jerked away from him and started but slipped halfway across, falling flat on his face. It was providential for a hellish crossfire began ripping just over his body. He'd lost a piece of a front tooth but otherwise was untouched. He scrambled to the trench just as a spray of machine-gun bullets buried itself in the mud behind him. He had advanced five hundred yards and was all alone. The shooting stopped all at once and the lull was unbearable, for he could now hear the heartrending cries of his buddies in the rear. As he watched the sun rise he felt he was the last person left alive on earth. He wondered if he would see that sun set.

To his right, Harbord's division was moving up for its attack. The Sixth Marine Regiment, not used the day before, was to make the infantry attack. Lieutenant Clifton Cates led his platoon down the ravine to Vierzy. Just as he was getting his men into position outside the town, shells and machine-gun bullets came over the hill. Something hit the back of Cates's shoulder. A rock, he thought. It was a red-hot bullet. He pulled it out and called to Major Holcomb, "Well I got the first blessé. Here's the first wound." He handed the bullet to Holcomb, but it was still hot and the major dropped it.

Others were hit, and Lieutenant John Overton shouted to a friend to send his Skull and Cross Bones pin to his mother if he were killed. At last the French tanks they were waiting for arrived and the attack began with the lumbering vehicles in the lead. It was about a thousand yards to the German lines, and enemy shellfire was concentrated several hundred yards in front. It looked to Sergeant Paradise like a great black curtain as Major Holcomb led them toward the blackest and thickest part of the German line. Men were going down on all sides. Someone behind him yelled, "Paradise, help me!" Paradise looked back, saw a friend grab his stomach and fall. He started back but Holcomb yelled, "Let the medics take care of him!"

Paradise was wondering how the new commander of their company, Captain Lloyd, would do in action. The men had little confidence in him, for he came from a desk job. But now Lloyd was out front brandishing his cane, urging them forward. Fire was getting hotter and the dust of battle thicker, as the four lines of Marines advanced "straight as a die," with their bayonets shining in the bright sunlight. It was a picture that Major Robert Denig would never forget. He yelled to an officer that each gun in the enemy barrage was working from right to left. Then he noticed a rabbit darting ahead and wondered if it would get him. "Good rabbit, he took my mind off of the carnage." He shouted to a friend that he had a hundred dollars on him and to be sure and get it. The friend yelled back that his own chances of living that long could be bought for a nickel.

There were eight waves of men moving across the open wheat

fields with the big tanks out in front. Shells were bursting all around and Cates called to a sergeant, "Look at Captains Woodsworth and Robinson getting right together there! That's bad business." Just then a shell hit and they both went down. Two other lieutenants were also wounded, and that left Cates the only officer in the company.

A shell burst to the right and a fragment ripped Cates's breeches, hitting his knee. But he led the men toward the German trenches. The enemy leaped out, streaking to the rear "like wild deer." The Marines swarmed after them shooting and yelling like cowboys. "It was too funny for words," Cates wrote his mother and sister. "We ran off and left the tanks far in the rear." But he could never reorganize his men in the bedlam and after less than a mile the attack petered out. He gathered what men he could, about twenty of them, took refuge in trenches near an old sugar mill, and waited for an enemy counterattack.

The man next to Private Carl Brannen was killed in that same charge by a shell, but he himself only suffered powder burns. He left his comrade writhing and groaning on the ground, and to continue the attack he caught up with Lieutenant Overton, who was walking backward, shouting something. The din was so terrific that Brannen had no idea what Overton was saying, but from his expression Brannen figured he was encouraging the men. Then Overton was killed and so was the gunnery sergeant. Brannen leaped barbed wire just as a shell hit to the left. By this time all the tanks had been crippled or stopped and everyone near him was down. He found refuge at last in an old sunken road. Bullets kept passing over him. In less than an hour his regiment had been almost annihilated. The field he had just crossed was strewn with the dead and dying, and he could hear their cries for water and help weaken as the hot July sun got stronger. Here he was almost in the enemy lines, all alone. When German enemy planes flew low he lay still, feigning death. The sun made his thirst almost unbearable.

Nearby his friend Lieutenant Cates was becoming very annoyed with the strafing planes. One came down so close that Cates saw the gunner's eyes. He fired three shots with his pistol and saw fabric fly from the plane. "I would have given a million dollars if I could have downed that guy with my pistol."

Those Marines still alive were also dug in, praying for darkness so they could get back to safety. Major Denig was in a beet field desperately digging with a spade he had picked up, while shrapnel rained about him. Holcomb asked if he could borrow it awhile. Denig said yes, when his hole was deep enough. It was as hot as a furnace, there was no water, and the Germans had their range. The Marines lay there all that torrid afternoon. Denig wound his watch, smoked, drew pictures, and wrote the names of his sons on the clay walls of his hole. When shells landed nearby he could feel himself bouncing in the air. He lay on his back, visualizing pictures in the clouds. Finally, near twilight, he saw Captain Lloyd walking toward them with the aid of a long staff. He looked like a shepherd. Lloyd reported that he was occupying some trenches near a sugar mill. He only had six men and with more he could easily hold the place. There were none to give him, so he walked sadly back. "He bore a charmed life and stuff was bursting all about him."

Water parties came back with tales of dead Marines all over the place, so Denig set out in the dusk on a reconnaissance. In a shallow trench nearby he found three men blown to bits, another had lost his legs, a fifth his head. At the end of the trench an insane man looked at Denig. With a shrill laugh, he pointed and said repeatedly, "Dead men."

Sulzbach's artillery unit had finally arrived near Soissons. They found mattresses and dropped off to sleep in the broiling sun until evening. "So here, near Soissons, the bastards are at it on a large scale!" the German lieutenant wrote in his diary. "The fact that they are driving us back at such a pace must mean that the situation has really got ticklish. Let us hope that this may be the final display of strength by a desperate adversary!" Lieutenant Binding was writing in his diary: "Since our experiences of July 16 I know that we are finished. My thoughts oppress me. How are we to recover ourselves? *Kultur*, as it will be known after the war, will be of no use; mankind itself will probably be of still less use. We must get away out of ourselves, away from folly, away from delusion, from stupidity, shallowness, lower pleasures, and from the commonplace."

Ludendorff was irritable and short-tempered, and when General von Lossberg arrived for a conference, he found the Quartermaster General "in a really agitated and nervous state. To my regret, he made some very unjustified remonstrances against the Chief of the Operations Section and others of his colleagues who, he implied, had 'failed' in their assessment of the fighting forces. The scene was a really painful one. The Chief of the Operations Section, Wetzell, said nothing, like a good soldier, but he obviously found these rebukes hard to take. His eyes grew wet from inward emotion which he otherwise fought down bravely."

After his reconnaissance Major Denig reported to Holcomb. They wondered if they would get relieved. At 9 P.M. a welcome message was received. Algerians would take over at midnight. The two began collecting the wounded in the dark. A Marine who had lost his eyes asked Denig to hold his hand. Another with his back ripped up wanted his head patted. One youngster struggled to his hands and knees. "Mother, look at the full moon," he said, then collapsed, dead.

By the light of the moon they buried their comrades even as bullets snarled by, but there was no shelling and Denig prayed it would hold off while the wounded were being evacuated. "The dead and wounded were covered with clotted blood and having laid all day in the boiling sun the odor from them made me sick in the stomach. Such signs as these show you what a sordid affair a battle is."

Since Captain David Bellamy knew a little French, he was sent back to guide the troops relieving Major Holcomb's battalion. He figured that the French would not come in if they knew they were relieving a front-line unit, so he told the newcomers that they would be in reserve. "They were disgusted when they saw their place, and one company refused to take over the sector occupied by one of our companies." But by midnight, all problems were solved. Holcomb and Denig showed the relieving officers the extent of the battalion front, where the Germans were, wished them good luck, and pushed on out. In the relative quiet of the night they could hear German commands, the crack of whips, and the rattle of artillery wheels as the enemy got guns into position for the next day's battle.

The Marines walked out under German flares and the light of burning houses. They tramped through the gully to Vierzy, now in ruins. Private Brannen and two others were carrying a comrade in a blanket. They lost their hold several times, letting him slip to the ground. Each time he groaned. Finally they got to a well and Brannen drank almost a gallon of water within twenty minutes. Paradise and seven others were carrying out the last wounded Marine. This man had a broken leg and Paradise put one belt (his own) around the knees and another (a dead comrade's) around the ankles. There was no stretcher and they sat him on a rifle held by two men. Two others kept his back upright. It was so tiring they had to be relieved after a hundred yards by another four men. It was daylight by the time they reached the aid station and deposited their burden. Scattered artillery was falling, so the eight men headed for the rear as fast as they could. Coming upon Major Holcomb sitting on a stump, Paradise asked if he needed any help. "No, thanks. Just get yourself out of here as fast as possible." A very weary and dejected man, if Paradise ever saw one.

The remnants of the battalion finally reached their starting place, the Forest of Retz. Of the 726 men who had gone into battle, 146 came out. "They just melted away," Denig recalled. Throughout Harbord's 2nd Division it was the same story. In forty-eight hours they had suffered 4,925 casualties.

"To picture a fight," Denig wrote his wife, "mix up a lot of hungry, dirty, tired and bloody men with dust, noise, and smoke. Forget the clean swords, prancing horses and flapping flags. At night, a gas-filled woods, falling trees and bright, blinding flashes—you can't see your neighbor—that is war . . . We advanced ten kilometers, with prisoners and guns, and the bells rang in New York for the victory, while well dressed girls and white-shirted men, no doubt, drank our health in many a lobster palace."

The 1st Division was still in the line, and at nine that morning they followed the edge of a ravine, advancing a mile across a wheat field before heavy artillery began firing point blank. Private Rose and a comrade found refuge behind an embankment. As they were peering over to locate the big gun that was harassing them, a huge shell plowed through the embankment between them. Petrified, they watched in fascination as it skidded about seventy-five yards before coming to a stop. A dud! Rose looked at his buddy. His eyes were like saucers; he was white as a sheet. "On audibly knocking knees, we left that spot toot sweet and, with the rest of our outfit, we continued on toward Berzy-le-Sec." Within an hour they had captured the village. The Germans appeared to be in confused retreat, and Rose could see smoke and flames rising from Soissons. The Boche must be putting the torch to their supplies.

Field artillery units were moving forward behind the advancing American infantry. "When the Huns retreated," Eldon Canright of Wauwatosa, Wisconsin, wrote home, "they threw away some of their equipment—the woods are full of German ammunition of all kinds, hand grenades, rifles, bayonets, steel helmets, mess kits, canteens, and even clothes! So at last the 'souvenir hunting' Americans can get all the souvenirs they want. The Huns must have stolen everything they could from the towns they captured as there is everything from baby carriages to sewing machines lying around in the woods and all kinds of civilian clothes, dishes, etc., and even tables and chairs."

News of the French-American counteroffensive stunned the Germans. Princess Blücher, the Englishwoman in Berlin, wrote in her diary: "People here may well look grave; the meaning of America is coming home to them at last. They comprehend now that it means an increase of the French reserves at the rate of 300,000 fresh, well-equipped men per month, whilst Germany can bring up no fresh reserves." In four days General Foch had completely transformed the situation in the west, and the German blow at Paris had failed. "It is sadly tragic to look on and see the slow fate of Germany overtaking her. I, who have watched the people struggling, and seen their unheard-of sacrifices and stolid resignation, cannot but pity them from my heart. In spite of their odious officialdom, which makes the Prussians so disliked everywhere, the whole world must admire them for the plucky way they have held out, and even the enemy says how pathetic it is to see the poor, half-starved, half-clothed German soldiers going bravely forward to meet all those fresh well-fed Americans."

She was by no means alone in realizing the desperation of the German situation. At the beginning of the month Chancellor Georg von Hertling had felt sure that the enemy would send peace proposals before September. But on July 18 "even the most optimistic among us knew that all was lost. The history of the world was played out in three days." The Kaiser was in a state of depression and his wife suffered a stroke.

On July 20 Ludendorff was forced to telegraph Prince Rupprecht that in view of the critical situation of Crown Prince

Wilhelm's group of armies, "which, as far as can be foreseen, will absorb a still greater amount of troops, and in view of the possibility of a British offensive action, the *Hagen* operation will probably never come to execution." Abandonment of this cherished operation meant that he was giving up hope of winning the war. The best he could do now was not lose it.

During the next forty-eight hours the German defense stiffened to such a degree that Hindenburg proposed a counterattack west of Soissons against Mangin's left flank. But Ludendorff was more influenced by Crown Prince Wilhelm, who felt that his troops were too exhausted and should fall back at once to the Aisne and Vesle rivers. And so, the afternoon of July 22, Ludendorff confided to Colonel Mertz von Quirnheim that he was going to withdraw from the Marne. He outlined the military necessity for doing so. "I am not superstitious or rather, yes, I am," he said. "You know, I had no confidence in July 15." He opened the right-hand drawer of his writing table to remove his tattered prayer book. Then he read the text for July 15. "He interpreted it," noted the colonel, "in contrast to the texts in our other days of attack, as unfavorable. Then he read me the texts for March 21, April 9, May 27, and June 9. Afterwards, we talked long and seriously. I was really inwardly moved."

Ludendorff finally bade him farewell. "The good Lord will, I hope, not forsake us."

That afternoon the Kaiser came to Avesnes, where he was told "the bitter truth which conflicts with the optimistic communiqués." Hindenburg admitted total failure, putting the burden of blame on betrayal of their offensive plans. The dazed monarch asked what he should now do. The field marshal advised him to return to Spa. After dinner the Kaiser admitted to Admiral von Müller and three others in the inner circle that he himself was "a defeated War Lord for whom we must show consideration." He could not sleep, and at lunch on the train he revealed to Müller that he had "seen visions of the English and Russian relatives and all the ministers and generals of his own reign marching past and mocking him. Only the little Queen of Norway had been friendly to him."

Two days later, Mertz von Quirnheim's diary revealed that Ludendorff's "nervousness and disjointedness" were having an adverse effect on his work. "His Excellency is working himself to death, worrying too much about details. The situation is really grave." And on July 25 he recorded that General Count Schwerin, Chief of the General Staff of the Balkan Army Group, was very much disturbed by the appearance and nervousness of the Quartermaster General. "It really does give the impression that His Excellency has lost all confidence. The army chiefs are suffering terribly as a result of it. Hence telephone conversations lasting one and a half hours on the day's agenda." Others noticed Ludendorff's intense internal stress and loss of appetite, and staff officers were embarrassed the next day by a quarrel between Ludendorff and Hindenburg over orders.

By this time the Supreme Command's efforts were concentrated on withdrawing the troops trapped in the Champagne to a new defense line. Hans Zöberlein's unit had started pulling out long before dawn on July 26. "We leave the ruined glade, climbing over the numerous shell holes in the underbrush. Here and there rises a sandy mound in which a rifle is stuck, a steel helmet over its butt. There they lie buried, those who would never come back from the battle of the Marne. . . . Along the road back to Romigny the column passes, rattling artillery, the riders in the blowing rain bent over in their saddles, the cannoneers hanging on the limber of the guns. Between slouched the dispersed fragments of infantry, the remnants of companies, guns slung around necks, tarpaulins over heads against the rain, the knapsacks underneath bulging with the effect of comic hunchbacks. Wagons stand waiting to take away supplies. . . . The long lines of infantry file in the grey morning out of the woods, over the open field, without haste. . . . Behind us thunder the engineer's demolitions. The engineers soon come running down the slope, followed by the infantry rearguard. . . . Our dead alone remain behind." Only other survivors of such a retreat, like the men of Gough's Fifth Army, could comprehend their bitterness, terror, and utter exhaustion.

Richard Arndt's regiment also started its withdrawal on the twenty-sixth, and the pitiful remnants of his company were ordered to cover the rear—eight men with five light machine guns. Arndt, only eighteen, was a hardened veteran, for he had been fighting since '14. He emplaced his guns and waited. There were no friendly troops to his right and he was alone. But he was going to hold on as long as possible.

Georg Bucher, another veteran of '14, was one of those who had left the Marne area to head north for safety. "We marched on and on through the night, past tens of thousands of troops; we took back with us our equipment, our rifles, our memories and our weary souls." They trudged on and on, through hilly country to the Chemin des Dames ridge. "We felt certain, though we did not express our thought, that the whole army would soon be in retreat. We had ceased to believe in our fighting power and felt that not we ourselves but the homeland must bear the blame."

The following day the order was issued for a general withdrawal behind the Aisne and Vesle in two stages. Young Arndt and his men were still waiting for a French attack, but it didn't come until noon of the twenty-seventh. They waited until the blue uniforms crossed a field and were fifty meters away before opening up with machine guns. The slaughter was great and the survivors fled back to a clump of woods. But they returned in two hours with Americans. This time the attack was pressed and in the midst of the melee, Arndt's only remaining gun jammed. The gunner cursed as he tried in vain to tear out the cartridge belt. Hearing the firing stop, the Americans jumped up and ran forward. From behind

Arndt could hear voices and the clump of marching feet on the road running into the forest. He turned to see a long column of French approaching. He cut the cartridge belt with his knife. Now the gun could fire. The gunner grabbed the gun but dropped it because it was hot; he wrapped a handkerchief around the barrel and with Arndt escaped into the forest. The two finally reached the rest of their company. The thin line held in a grim rearguard action until the night of the twenty-ninth. Then the order came to fall back and Arndt packed the few treasures he had left. At midnight he shot three white flares into the air to celebrate his birthday, the fourth in battle. He was nineteen years old.

That midnight Lieutenant Sulzbach was told to report to the regimental commander. "There, we adjutants were given grave and disagreeable news; the front is being withdrawn in this sector, it will be the same here as in the case of the Siegfried withdrawal, it's the Marne down there, yes, the Marne, that's done this to us once again! It began down there with the loss of Château-Thierry, then it moved up to Fère-en-Tardenois, and now here. We feel terribly depressed and filled with pain at having to give up all that ground which was so dearly paid for, all the more since we held the line so brilliantly. My God, we thought July was going to be different! But we've got to pull ourselves together; you can't be lucky every time, and even a decision like that, taken by the Supreme Army Command, can be great, in fact magnificent, since it only proves our strength and our ability to cope with any circumstances." And so the grim withdrawal went on, but not in rout. The Germans were successfully breaking away from a cautious enemy. Not yet defeated, they were preparing for the next battle.

By now Crown Prince Wilhelm feared that victory was no longer possible and he wrote a lengthy memorandum which he handed to his father, suggesting that they try again to reach a negotiated peace through neutral channels. In order to do so a clear statement of Germany's war aims had to be drawn up. "Of course we want to keep Alsace-Lorraine," he wrote, "and we also want back our colonies. Perhaps we may also demand the Briey basin. But on the other hand we should agree to renounce a war indemnity and to restore Belgium." Holding that country would only mean increasing the number of unreliable foreign minorities within their boundaries. Besides, Britain would never let them keep the Flanders coast. It was of little use to Germany, however, since its ports were not suitable for naval bases. "In addition," he concluded, "the coast would force us to maintain a fleet at least equal to that of England, which we would hardly be able to do. We therefore better agree that Belgium will remain independent, neither pay nor receive an indemnity, may not keep an army, and recognize Germany's economic equality with the states of the Entente."

But his father was not yet in a mood to give up Belgium, for he knew the military would never accept such a sacrifice. And yet on the last day of the month, in a new appeal to his subjects, he made it appear as if he had done his utmost to end the war equitably. "We have neglected nothing in an effort to bring peace back to a destroyed war!" he said. "But the voice of humanity is still not heard in the enemy camp. Whenever we spoke words of conciliation, we were met with mockery and hatred. Our enemies still do not want peace. They are shamelessly polluting the clean German name with new libels."

Even though the tide had definitely turned in Italy after the Austrian defeat at the Piave, the Italian High Command was reluctant to start a counter-offensive. But in Palestine, General Allenby was drawing up plans to launch a major campaign. Unaware of this, the Turks were continuing their marauding in the Caucasus.

Chapter Eleven

BLACK DAY
AUGUST 1–27

1.

By the beginning of August the German troops in the Champagne were in new positions after a remarkably orderly withdrawal —and Ludendorff's confidence had returned. On the second he issued to his four army group commanders on the Western Front a strategic directive that gave each of them renewed hope. "The situation demands that on the one hand we should place ourselves on the defensive, but on the other that we should go back to the attack again as soon as possible. . . . In these attacks of ours . . . it is of less importance to conquer more ground than to inflict loss on the enemy and gain better positions." They must adhere to surprise attacks, he said, and, recalling the July 15 debacle, added that these should be prepared in the utmost secrecy. The utter gloom of Supreme Headquarters was at last dispelled. This was the old Ludendorff. At Spa the Kaiser was even more aggressively confident, and he subjected Admiral von Müller and others in his circle to "a very unpleasant evening" by picturing "our defeat on the Marne as the greatest defeat the enemy has ever suffered. Piles of American corpses, etc."

But some of the more thoughtful officers at the front felt that the end was near despite their own successful evacuation. "I have got a bad opinion of the situation," Lieutenant Binding wrote in his diary on the fourth, "but when I express it I find that people shut their minds rather than their ears to what I say. The German officer cannot realize that things are as they are. Here are the indications. Everybody is tired of the war. One hears men say, 'Why not give them this bloody Alsace-Lorraine?' (This from men who are by no means the worst, even from the strongest fighting-men.) Their manhood has been sapped in such a way that there is no stiffening it . . . Here is the stupidest war of position starting afresh. It is necessary because it is forced upon us, and from the military point of view it may yet prove justified; in the end it may lead to something which can be called peace. But I am not convinced that it is reasonable for me personally, and therefore I feel it is unreasonable for me to go on."

Ludendorff was well aware of such defeatism as well as the fears in many quarters that another enemy offensive would crush them. "There is nothing to justify this apprehension," he said, "provided our troops are vigilant and do their duty." The enemy success on July 18 was only due to surprise. "At the present moment we occupy everywhere positions which have been very strongly fortified, and we have, I am convinced, effected a judicious organization in depth of the infantry and artillery. Henceforth, we can await every hostile attack with the greater confidence. As I have already explained, we should wish for nothing better than to see the enemy launch an offensive, which can but hasten the disintegration of his forces."

No one knew better than he how disintegrating and enfeebling offensives could be, and no one knew better than Haig how close the Ludendorff assaults had come to success. The field marshal was the only Allied military leader who believed that the war could be won in 1918. But victory could come only with a series of offensives, and early in July he was determined to launch a major one as soon as possible. Foch, equally aggressive even though he could not see victory until 1919, suggested on July 12 that the British launch an attack near La Bassée Canal. Haig replied a week later that, rather than push forward over flat, wet country, they should attack the enemy still threatening the key rail center, Amiens. This was of the greatest importance, he argued, and should be carried out as early as possible by a combined French-British operation. On July 24 the two men met at Foch's headquarters at Bombon, thirty miles southeast of Paris. After agreeing that the Amiens operations should start on August 10, they held a formal meeting with Pershing and Pétain. First a memorandum prepared by Foch was read, stating that the German defeat at Soissons must be exploited to the full. "The moment has arrived to abandon the generally defensive attitude forced on us hitherto by numerical inferiority, and to pass to the offensive." He proposed a series of offensives, the first in front of Amiens. Haig, of course, heartily agreed with the Foch plan. So did Pershing, who would take no part in the Amiens operation since he was already involved in planning a major American offensive against the troublesome St. Mihiel salient below Verdun. Pétain was also agreeable but asked for time to consider the possibilities.

Four days later Foch decided that the French First Army should take part in the initial attack, and he placed it under Haig's orders to ensure unity of command. Anxious to take advantage of the German withdrawal from the Marne, he updated the offensive by forty-eight hours to August 8.

All these preparations were made in the strictest secrecy and were withheld even from Lloyd George. He was becoming disenchanted with General Wilson, who, now working harmoniously with Haig, had recently had the audacity to send a memorandum strongly urging concentration on the Western Front. Lloyd George, needless to say, was furious. He told Hankey that he was "bitterly disappointed with its purely 'Western Front' attitude and described it as simply 'Wully redivivus.' " Wilson had turned into another Robertson. Most of the Empire's prime ministers agreed with Lloyd George at a meeting on the first day of August. "Practically all the Prime Ministers, i.e., Lloyd George, Borden, Hughes (but not so much), Smuts, Massey and Milner," noted Wilson in his diary, "are of the opinion that we cannot beat the Boche on the Western Front, and so they go wandering about looking for laurels.* Hughes sees clearer than the others, and sees that we must beat the Boche if we want a real peace. However, we all ended peacefully."

Across the Channel, secrecy was the watchword. General Henry Rawlinson, who would lead the British attack as commander of the Fourth Army, printed a small notice that read, "Keep Your Mouth Shut," and ordered it pasted into the paybooks carried by every man and officer. From now on any unusual movement was made by night, and paved roads were sanded to cut down noise. In all orders the word "offensive" was never used, only "raid."

On August 3, Haig met Foch at a village near Beauvais. After they discussed last-minute changes, the latter said he thought the Germans were breaking up. When Haig returned to his own headquarters, he found a cipher telegram from General Wilson marked "personal." It suggested that they exchange views by telegrams similarly marked so that others in the War Office couldn't read them. To Haig, unaware of Lloyd George's disenchantment with Wilson, this was "an extraordinary proposal." How could a chief of the Imperial General Staff and a commander in the field exchange opinions on military matters in personal telegrams?

On August 5, King George arrived by destroyer to begin a strenuous tour of France and Belgium. On the following day zero day was formally set at August 8 with zero hour to be 4:20 A.M., more than an hour before sunrise, so that Rawlinson's 534 tanks could close up while the infantry battalions were breaking the first line of German defenses under cover of darkness.

General Debeney, commanding the French First Army, secretly ordered his XXXI Corps to start their attack forty mintues *after* the British zero hour, and only advance two miles so as to protect the right flank of XXXI Corps. This, disregarding Foch's direc-

---

* W. M. Hughes, Australia; Sir Robert Borden, Canada; W. F. Massey, New Zealand; General Jan Smuts, Minister of Defence, South Africa.

tion, made his army only a flank guard and put the burden of attack on the British.

By dawn of August 7, the main assault units were fully assembled within two or three miles of the Germans, while the tanks were hidden in clumps of trees or destroyed farmhouses several miles behind the line. Ludendorff still had no idea that a massive infantry and tank assault was about to descend on his Second and Eighteenth armies in the very area where General Gough's army had been so savaged in March. Despite a show of confidence, the Quartermaster General was deeply disturbed by the increasing defeatism in the ranks, and that day he issued a secret order to his staff that underlined his own inner fears:

> Whether rightly or wrongly, each member of the OHL [*Oberste Heeresleitung*—Supreme Army Command] is looked upon as being well informed and corresponding value is placed on all he says. For this reason every member must even outside the OHL remain conscious of his responsibility. . . . The OHL is free from despondency. Sustained by what has previously been achieved on the front and at home, it prepares stoutheartedly to meet the challenges that are to come. No member of OHL may think and act in a manner other than this.

Haig, lunching with the King, noticed that he looked very cheery. "So different to his frame of mind on the occasion of his last visit in March." His Majesty brought a message from Lloyd George, who, he said, now talked about "poor Haig" and "the excessive length of line which he had to hold." The Prime Minister seemed now determined to support Haig against the French and wanted him "to insist strongly on having our front reduced before the autumn comes, so that men can be given leave and troops be rested and trained." If Haig was amused he gave no sign, only remarking that the British front would be much further forward before winter arrived. Then he explained in detail on a map the operation that would begin next morning.

He had selected the Canadians and Australians to carry the burden, since they were both in better condition than the other British units. Besides they were the elite of the British team. On the whole their officers and NCOs were probably the best leaders, for they had been chosen "for their practical experience and power over men and not for theoretical proficiency and general education." Later in the afternoon Haig visited Rawlinson. Everything was going without a hitch and the enemy apparently still was ignorant of the coming blow.

Rawlinson was a tall, gangling man with a striking resemblance to General Wilson and, like him, was brilliant as well as witty. An aristocrat brought up in the grand Victorian tradition, he was a learned orientalist. Some of his colleagues therefore regarded him as "too clever by half," while other, meaner ones nicknamed him "the cad." More discerning military men realized that he was not only an able commander but far-seeing. A polo player with a love for the cavalry, he was one of the few leading Allied generals who saw the potentialities of the tank. And his assault for the morrow depended on these rackety, unconventional behemoths.

Haig proceeded to the Canadian Corps, whose commander, General Sir Arthur Currie, reported that it had been a hustle to be ready on time, but everything was in place except two long-range guns and they would be set on their platforms after dark. The Australians were also primed for battle. Although General Monash's men had not yet received any orders, they knew that a big push was coming. All roads leading forward were jammed with troops, tanks, and artillery. While the Australians were lying "doggo" in villages and other cover that afternoon, a Special Order of the Day from Monash was read aloud: For the first time in the history of the corps, all five Australian divisions would tomorrow engage in the largest and most important battle operation ever undertaken by the corps. This battle, he said, "will be one of the most memorable of the whole war; we shall inflict blows upon the enemy which will make him stagger, which will bring the end appreciably nearer." The work tomorrow would make heavy demands on their staying power, "but I am confident that, in spite of excitement, fatigue, and physical strain, every man will carry on to the utmost of his powers until his goal is won; for the sake of AUSTRALIA, the Empire and our cause." One might have expected that the Australians, notorious for their poor discipline, would ridicule such an appeal. But they were eager to fight. They liked Monash and he could always count on them in a battle. Their rugged defense in the Nieppe Forest in the March offensive had helped halt the German advance, and since then their successful raids on the Somme had done much to keep the Germans off balance.

Soon after dusk, the movement forward proceeded with planes flying overhead to mask the traffic noise. Never before had a British attack been preceded by such a vast parade of men and supplies, not only of the assault forces but of those divisions in reserve which would keep pace behind them and carry on any advance. Horses as well as tanks would be used, and the Cavalry Corps, concentrated just west of Amiens, began marching through the almost deserted streets of a city whose population had been evacuated. To one Canadian observer it was an inspiring sight. "The British cavalry columns were paired off exactly as in a review, always precisely abreast. If there was a cart beside us, then there was a cart beside it, paired off almost wheel for wheel—two carts, two waggons, twenty pairs of waggons, twenty pairs of guns, two streams of horsemen—all streaming the same way on the pale, clean cobblestones through the dark, winding streets."

Two battalions of Whippets—small tanks capable of traveling at thirty miles an hour—joined the column as it passed. The cavalry moved forward with remarkable precision until it neared the crowded front, where it veered onto a special track which had been hastily constructed by engineers of the Cavalry Corps and a battalion of American engineers. Now the horsemen could advance without interfering with the infantry or masking the artillery.

Tapes were laid out to guide the leading infantry units in their predawn attack. Behind were other tapes for the tanks. Tanker A. W. Bacon's company was mustered at dark and formed into a hollow square. From the center their commander said they were attacking before dawn. Everything depended on it. Every man was to make the greatest sacrifice tomorrow to conclude the terrible war. "With what mixed feelings did we listen to this exhortation! We had heard similar speeches before and what had been the outcome?—the ordeal of seeing crowds of men, amongst them our own pals, shot down to gain a few hundred yards of lousy field, which the enemy recaptured shortly afterwards." Yes, they were sick of it, but now the Yanks were pouring into France so tonight perhaps this show might turn out to be different after all.

They loaded the tanks with petrol and then had a good hot meal of soup and bread. Cigarettes were issued and the men were grouped by sections to hear details of the coming fracas. They were going into battle with the largest number of tanks ever gathered for one scrap. Bacon's company was to lead the Canadians, with the Anzacs on their left and the French on the right. Then they were told to get some rest until midnight.

Captain D. E. Hickey's tank section was already moving up to the forward area. Finally it was halted and tea, stiffly laced with rum, was handed around. The tankers waited in darkness and silence as machine-gun crews began leaving the cover of trenches to move stealthily forward.

That night Sergeant Paul Maze, the artist, was dining with the 17th Lancers in bivouac outside Amiens. General Gough had passed him on to his successor, Rawlinson, for whom he was providing similar service. But it wasn't the same. Rawlinson was blunt, stiff, and quite impersonal. At dinner Maze observed how excited the cavalry officers were. They were going to have their chance to gallop at last! At 10 P.M. orderlies cleared the tables and their gay party disbanded. Outside it was pitch dark. Troops and cavalry were passing through a cloud of coal dust rising from the road. Maze set out on his motorcycle to meet a staff officer of the Fourth Army. He overtook long lines of troops and tanks moving forward in weird masses in the dark. Finally he reached the Gentelles Plateau, where the ground was taped and pegged. Boards indicated directions for each unit. "The whole area might have been the scene of a gymkhana. Aeroplanes were droning loudly overhead so as to drown out the noise of the approaching tanks. Every object looming in the darkness hid something—the woods sheltered hundreds of silent guns awaiting their signal."

He found the staff officer at a hole dug on the slope of a spur a thousand yards from the front line. The two squatted between four narrow earth walls with a mackintosh sheet for a roof. They had a direct wire laid on to General Rawlinson and were to give an eyewitness report of the attack. Both felt increasing tension, though neither would admit it. Every so often the purring of tank engines or the report of a single gun broke the silence. "I got up and looked into the night. The atmosphere had grown hazy, the ground felt clammy. I had a hint of troops through the mist moving down the slope to their assembly position like long shadows, darker than the night. All I could see of them were their fumbling feet. Every hour had increased the conglomeration of troops on the plateau. It seemed too marvelous that so far the enemy had not fired a shot. Could he know anything?" Their buzzer squeaked like a tiny kitten. It was Rawlinson. What was the situation out there? All quiet, they answered.

Along the entire front men were praying they wouldn't be discovered until zero hour. Their supreme commander, Douglas Haig, was pleased. Troops, guns, and tanks were in place. "Last night was our most critical moment," he was noting in his diary. "If the Germans had bombarded the Canadian zone, we could not have retaliated last night. To-night the situation is quite different, and we are ready." He also wrote his wife that one corps had been attacked the previous morning, "and at first I thought it might upset our plans, and perhaps the enemy might have taken some prisoners who knew of the intended attack and might have given information away. But so far the enemy seems quite in ignorance of our intentions."

From Haig down to privates, men were anxiously waiting. C. E. Montague, a gifted author, lay on his back in a meadow gazing at a fresco of winking stars. "Could it be coming at last, I thought as I went to sleep—the battle unlike other battles? . . . Was it to be only Loos and the Somme and Arras and Flanders and Cambrai, all over again?" He was wakened by the squeak of a bird. A quilt of white mist, about a foot thick, was spread over the meadow. "Good! Let it thicken away and be shoes of silence and armour of darkness at dawn for our men." An owl hooted, then came the low buzz of a passing enemy plane. "In the east, the low, slow grumbling sound of a few guns from fifty miles of front seemed, in its approach to quietude, like the audible breath of a sleeper. The war was taking its rest." It was long past midnight and the enemy still gave no sign of knowing what was coming.

2.

At 3 A.M., August 8, H. R. Williams' infantry unit was roused. The men hastily ate a hot meal at the cookers by the light of flickering candles. Cigarettes glowed in the dark just before the whistle blew for fall-in. They paraded; platoons were checked; and the men stood waiting for the battle to begin. The morning mist thickened and by 3:30 AM. it was difficult to see twenty yards away. "It was getting too foggy to be pleasant," recalled the commander of an Australian battalion. Just then German shells began to fall near the Villers-Bretonneux railway, and the men figured the enemy had heard the racket just to their rear where tanks were assembling. The officers quickly pushed their men into trenches or shell holes. "They're having their fun now," said someone, "but wait till our barrage begins."

Although this bombardment lasted for some time, there were only about twenty-five Australian casualties, and the Canadians and French to the south didn't even hear it. Nor did Maze. Then about 3:40 came the whistle of a German 5.9, followed by a crash. Others came in quick succession, but it was only a local action. A German battery had a report that Tommy in fighting kit was lying out in front of their battalion. But there was not much ammunition to spare and after about five minutes orders came to cease firing unless the infantry's demand was repeated. It was not, and quiet returned to Maze's area. "I looked at the drawings which in my nervousness I had carved on the walls, shivering with excitement and cold, for the air had grown chilly with the early morning."

By that time the mist was so thick that the Australians feared it might have prevented British planes from coming over again to drown out the noise of the droves of tanks that were about to begin their final move to the front. But at 3:50 they heard a distant engine—either tank or airplane. It was a plane, thank God! Then another and another. The RAF was back and through the buzz of aircraft the purr of throttled-down tank engines was inaudible even to the waiting Australians.

There were 430 tanks, including 96 Whippets, in position, motors running. Bacon was getting cramped in his seat. He left the motor gently ticking over and climbed out to get some fresh air and a good stretch. It was so quiet it was eerie. Knowing what was to happen probably helped to emphasize the silence. The mist seemed to envelop the front in mystery. Every so often a star shell shot into the air, the phut of its dull report distinct in the quiet. A rifle shot broke the silence. Then the staccato cough of a machine gun. On the left there was a low rumbling like distant thunder—artillery. Officers kept peering at their wristwatches as if fearing they had stopped. Bacon clambered up, fitting himself into the driving seat. He fixed his gas mask at the alert and hung his steel helmet on the handle of a loophole plate.

Now 4:18. How the time dragged. Bacon broke his Webley to see if it was loaded. It was, of course. 4:19. One minute to go! "Now the silence was painful; I wanted to shout. I wondered if I was in the throes of a vivid dream. How was it possible that this silence could be changed to chaos from one second to another? Someone behind me was drinking from a water bottle."

"Get ready," said an officer. It was 4:20 A.M.

There was a terrible roar as the British barrage opened up. "Hell was let loose, the heavens seemed to fall. The noise was like a colony of giants slamming iron doors as fast as they could go." Bacon's tank crept forward on the tail of the one ahead. Just as he neared the deploying point a blinding flash knocked him backward. He was thrown violently forward against the front plate as his tank collided with the one in front and began climbing it. Bacon threw out the clutch and rubbed dirt and muck from his eyes. There was another crash that shook the whole bus. Peering forward, Bacon saw smoke rising from the tank ahead and its left trackband was rearing into the air like a cobra about to strike. The officer of that tank ran over. "Swing out and pass us! My driver's killed. Got a direct hit."

The main guns of Rawlinson's Fourth Army, two thousand of them, had started almost with a single crash. It was an astonishing outburst to both sides. In some places the men cheered the welcome thunder, and nearly every Australian infantryman lit a cigarette as he started to follow the tanks. These cumbersome machines started out in formation but not for long in the mist, which was thickened by the dust of the barrage and the artificial fog of smoke shells. Sections in each line could not see their neighbors and in the confusion many tanks did not even reach the foremost infantry.

Some infantrymen found themselves in their own barrage. "I had a feeling," recalled Lieutenant H. A. L. Binder, "of being behind a curtain of rushing noise." Scattered into small groups, the men were led by a noncom or some natural leader who took responsibility. Many just pushed on blindly and would blunder every so often into terrified German machine-gunners. Usually the crew would throw up hands, but some brave ones kept their guns firing until rushed from the flank or rear. The mist was far more terrifying to these defenders. Apparitions would suddenly come out of nowhere; monsters of tanks would loom up through the shifting vapor causing panic and rout.

Bacon's tank was crushing the German wire defenses like so much paper, leaving a clear path for the Canadian infantrymen to follow. As his tank broke through the thick mist to straddle the enemy front line, another huge object collided with him head-on. A friendly tank! The other machine backed away and Bacon pushed on to an orchard where a noisy machine gun attracted his attention. Just as they reached the gun, a grenade exploded under his front window. He swung quickly to the left. One German darted away. Another was not so fast and the tank crushed him along with his machine gun. Apparently the enemy had abandoned his front line and was manning the supports. Bacon started forward through the mist. It was uncanny driving at speed toward an invisible objective with only a compass as guide.

Soon he reached the support line and straddled his machine across the main trench so his machine-gunners could get busy on both sides. After they had cleared out the trench, Bacon drove his bus forward blindly, several times coming across Canadian infantrymen who had forged ahead. Another Boche machine gun was firing from close range so he swung toward the noise. Suddenly a brick wall loomed up ahead. He stepped on the gas and charged through. There was a terrific rumble of masonry and when the

BRITISH COUNTEROFFENSIVE
AUGUST 8

N

ANCRE

Bray

SOMME

SOMME
CANAL

BR. FOURTH
ARMY

AUST.
3RD DIV.

BR. III CORPS

AUST.
4TH
DIV.

AUSTRALIAN CORPS

AUST. 5TH DIV.

Warfusée

Marcourt

6 M. TO
AMIENS

SOMME

ROMAN ROAD

Villers-Bretonneux

AUST.
2ND DIV.

CAN. 1ST
CAV. DIV.

Bayonvillers

GENTELLES
PLATEAU

CANADIAN CORPS

Hangard

MORGEMONT
WOOD

Harbonnières

GER. SECOND
ARMY

CAN. 3RD
CAV. DIV.

LUCE

MOREUIL
WOOD

Moreuil

FR. FIRST
ARMY

AVRE

FR. XXI CORPS

AVRE

GER. EIGHTEENTH
ARMY

3 M. TO
ROYE

AVRE

0   MILES   3

0   KM   3

2½ M. TO
MONTDIDIER

Front Line 4:20 A.M. Aug. 8
Front Line 9:00 P.M. Aug. 8
Army Boundaries

278

tank regained level keel he opened the window to peer out. "Gosh, we were inside a church, and had routed a machine-gun nest!"

By 6:30 A.M. both the Canadian and Australian corps reached their first objective. The German front system was completely broken and most of the enemy field artillery had been overrun and captured. Now the British creeping barrage was halted and a protective barrage was put down to allow the troops destined for the next advance to get into position to attack at 8:20. Mark V tanks not engaged in the first stage closed in on the attacking brigades, ready to move forward to the third objective as soon as the second objective was reached. Also moving up was the 1st Cavalry Brigade, accompanied by sixteen Whippets, ready to dash forward the moment their opportunity came. Just behind them were a dozen armored cars.

Sergeant Maze had left his observation post at dawn, since the mist was too thick to see more than a hundred yards. He headed for the 3rd Canadian Division headquarters, which had a report center. Upon learning here that the advance was progressing favorably he was anxious to get back to his motorbike. It was almost time for the cavalry to move and he didn't want to miss seeing them start off. No enemy shells were falling and the anxiety of the reserve troops had changed to excitement. Fritz was on the run! Then he saw something that would remain engraved on his mind. The commander of the 3rd Cavalry, Major General A. E. W. Harman, was riding quietly down a slope followed by his trumpeter. Maze hurried up to give him the news. "He greeted me cheerfully, gave a sigh of satisfaction, then put his horse into a trot to meet the return of the patrols that had gone forward with the infantry to report whether the cavalry could cross the river. As he moved off the leading squadrons of his divisions appeared, surging forward out of the mist from the brow of the hill as in a shifting mirage. In a moment the slopes were moving with cavalry and tanks rolling down like a cascade. The tanks were zigzagging along, backfiring as they went like jumping crackers. A yellow balloon was ascending in the sky, and now, visible above the disappearing mist, aeroplanes were buzzing above us. Something kept saying to me: 'Look, for you will never see such a sight again.'" Maze noticed that others felt the same exhilaration. "I was swept off my feet. I waved to passing friends in the cavalcade and longed to be with them." He ran to where he had left his bike, and glimpsed General Sir Charles Kavanagh standing beneath his corps pennant surrounded by his staff, taking the salute of his passing cavalry regiments. The din of the British artillery, the vibration of the air, the rattle of machine-gun cases on the packhorses, and the roar of the tanks were deafening.

From the heights to the west C. E. Montague, the author, was watching through glasses as the mist dramatically lifted just before eight. "It rolled right up into the sky in one piece, like a theater curtain, almost suddenly taking its white quilted thickness away from between our eyes and the vision so much longed for during four years. Beyond the river a miracle—*the* miracle—had begun. It was going on fast. . . . Across the level Santerre, which the sun was beginning to fill with a mist-filtered lustre, two endless columns of British guns, wagons, and troops were marching steadily east, unshelled, over ground that the Germans had held until dawn. . . . For a moment, the object of all dream and desire seemed to have come; the flaming sword was gone, and the gate of the garden open."

Momentarily all eyes on the battlefield took in the astounding sight: hordes of British infantrymen moving forward in formation accompanied by tanks that resembled elephants in an oriental army. Then came battery after battery of field guns drawn by spirited teams, chains jingling, heads and manes tossing. In streams across the fields rolled countless wagons carrying water, ammunition, and tank replacement parts.

A van of the sixteen armored cars was entering demolished Warfusée. Here tanks towed them across the hurriedly cleared debris. On both sides of the village, the Australian 5th Division was drawn up in deep artillery formation; and behind impatiently waited the 1st Cavalry Brigade with about a hundred tanks, most of them Whippets. They would have their turn in the third and final stage. Light field batteries arrived at a gallop, and like a scene from a film, in efficient haste, the gunners were loading and firing to the glee of Australian onlookers who broke into a cheer.

From the other side, Württemberg artillerymen watched in distress as the mist fell at one stroke into the steaming meadows. "The southern slope of the Somme valley gradually rising to the commanding Roman road was teeming with enemy columns which, hurrying forward under the protection of the slowly vanishing ground mist, had already passed the alignment of the German trenches on this (the northern) side. The German lines appeared to have been wiped away." Halfway up a slope crept four enemy tanks in echelon. "Next to them a light English battery had unlimbered under cover of the mist. With the glass each man could be clearly seen at the guns. All this in impetuous, hurried forward movement. . . . It was a bit of luck that immediately over the low ground a light mist still lay, which wrapped its cloak over the foreground so far as all things in the valley were concerned." Thus the German gunners standing on the hill at the northern end of the valley could make out the shadowy columns hastening with all speed toward the east. Their first long shell burst into a march column of Australians. The gunners were exuberant. "The immediate danger from the left was first removed. Now targets offered in confusing plenty. First came, in their turn, the tanks, which in their clumsiness had not managed to get much further forward. After five or six shots all four flamed up, providing a dreadful end for their crews."

The most forward Canadian tanks were also being punished. Young Bacon suddenly was aware of a German field gun firing from a thicket almost in front of him. "Driving the bus on a zigzag course I made for the gun, and was within twenty yards of it when CRASH!—a flash—and merciful oblivion." But the infantry of both the Canadians and Australians flowed on past the flaming tanks and relentlessly overran the German guns. The Anzac 4th Division, for instance, rushed their second objective, the valley at Marcourt, to capture hundreds of German support and reserve troops along with stores and canteens.

In Bayonvillers, a village just behind their front, Germans of the 6th Battery of the 58th Artillery Regiment heard the tumult of battle. It looked as though they might be cut off. Someone shouted, "Tank on the right!" A large tank rumbled toward them, opening up murderous fire at two hundred yards. It knocked out one of the battery's remaining two guns; the other's shield and sights were seriously damaged, but its crew crouched behind the steel shield and revolved the gun carriage. The pointer coolly took aim and just as the tank plunged into the sunken path ahead a shell crashed through its side. The gun crew could only see dense smoke and flying pieces of iron. Now it was high time to fall back, for the Allied assault troops behind the tanks were surging in small groups from all directions. Bullets whizzed from all sides. "We dashed from shell hole to shell hole." This group escaped but others strayed too far to the right and were made prisoners.

The wildest rumors began spreading in the German lines. "It was said that masses of English cavalry were already far rear of the foremost German lines," wrote Hindenburg. "Some of the men lost their nerve, left positions from which they had only just beaten off strong enemy attack and tried to get in touch with the rear again. Imagination conjured up all kinds of phantoms and translated them into real dangers." On that eighth of August panic was spreading on all sides.

Maze was heading forward on his motorbike to watch the cavalry in action. In the distance he could see the Scots Greys, their gray horses pressing on. He came upon a mass in the road. Germans! Prisoners, thankfully. He stopped to watch them pass. They looked still dazed with surprise. Maze continued to the reserve trenches, which showed the passage of the attack; the pegs and tape lines were in a tangle. Many machine guns lay about, and here and there derelict tanks sent up black smoke. Some still burned. In his haste, Maze mired his motorbike in a deep hole. Finally he emerged and raced on, at last catching up to the cavalry as it was trekking through Morgemont Wood. Groups of captured Germans were being collected, and he could see by tank tracks how they had been rounded up. Some, run over, lay flattened out like pancakes.

It was now nine and the light was still slightly diffused. The moment had come, thought Maze. The cavalry was about to realize its dream. Regiments were waiting echeloned down the slopes; large groups of horses gathered here and there. Thank God, the enemy wasn't shelling. Flushed with excitement, the men restrained their nervous mounts. At last word came that the Whippets were safely across the river and the Canadian Cavalry Brigade set the pace over a bridge, followed by the rest. It was like a hunting field pressing to get through a narrow gate all at once. The cavalry squirted out into the open to catch up with infantry a thousand yards ahead.

Maze found it too difficult to follow, so he turned down the first ridable path which brought him to a road. Behind came the clopping of hooves, and in moments he was overtaken by a cavalry regiment which he then could not resist following down a serpentine road through a thickly wooded gully. "It thrilled me to see the leading horses taking the turns below me at a gallop, some of the horses rearing wildly. The distant outbreak of machine-gun-fire sounded as exciting as a hunting cry."

They swept through a German headquarters which resembled a beer garden with ingeniously constructed huts and tables made of branches. Maze caught a glimpse of plates filled with food. "We passed some infantry waving excitedly, and then, as the squadrons were rounding the elbow of a hillside, I saw them disperse after victory."

Just to the left the 1st Cavalry Brigade was also meeting with success. A squadron of the Queen's Bays led the way. Swinging past tanks and Australian infantrymen, they overtook a transport column trying to escape, capturing it intact. The squadron then charged on Harbonnières but were driven back by heavy fire. After the Bays took cover, Whippets speeded to their aid. They too were held up and it took the infantrymen to finally break into the town. As they were preparing to raise the Dominion flag from a church tower, a squadron of the 5th Dragoon Guards galloped past Harbonnières to reach the second objective. It was 10 A.M. and the dragoons had penetrated six miles in five hours and forty minutes.

By eleven there were similar advances all along the Australian and Canadian lines. Never had the British or Dominion forces attained such success in a half day; and the victors themselves were dazed. Never had casualties been lighter in such an action, never the seizure of prisoners and guns greater. It was a success brought about by a remarkable marriage of tanks, cavalry, infantrymen, and artillery. Having reached the two forward objectives, there was now the task to fortify them against counterattack. On their right, the French had made little progress. Starting forty minutes after the Fourth Army, they began well but their tanks did not come up in time and they now lagged far behind their allies.

By this time Ludendorff had "already gained a complete impression of the situation. It was a very gloomy one." He immediately dispatched Colonel Mertz von Quirnheim to the battlefield to ascertain the condition of the troops. From reports it appeared that six or seven divisions had been completely broken and the situation was "uncommonly serious. If the enemy continued to attack with even ordinary vigor, we should no longer be able to maintain ourselves west of the Somme."

Earlier that morning Haig thought there was an "autumn feel" in the air. After going through the German dispositions, his intelligence officer said, "Well, sir, *au revoir* until tomorrow." "Good luck to me," said the field marshal, pulling a branch of white heather from his roll-top desk and extending a piece. "Good luck to all of us and here's a piece for you. It was sent by my wife this morning."

About eleven he learned of the success and sent an officer to General Debeney, commander of the French First Army, informing him of the situation with a request to send forward all his mounted troops on the right of the British cavalry. The French should extend the break in the enemy's front southward by operating in the rear of those Germans holding Montdidier. But the French commander replied that the roads were blocked by infantry and his cavalry couldn't get through until the next morning.

Haig restrained any sarcastic remark and set off to see Rawlinson in a pleased frame of mind. The situation was developing "more favourably for us than I, optimist though I am, had dared even to hope! *The enemy was completely surprised,* two reliefs of Divisions were in progress, very little resistance was offered, and our troops got their objectives quickly with very little loss." He told Rawlinson to organize his left strongly and, if opportunity offered, to advance it to the line from Albert to Bray-sur-Somme.

He returned to his train for lunch before setting out to see Debeney. He found him "much distressed and almost in tears" because three of his Colonial Infantry battalions had bolted before a single German machine gun. Haig assured him that the British advance would automatically clear his front. In the meantime, would Debeney do his utmost to join hands with the British at Roye and send his cavalry forward as soon as possible to cooperate with the British who had already pierced the German line of defense? These must have been bitter words for Debeney's ears.

The afternoon was relatively quiet, but the ferocious attacks of the morning by Rawlinson's Fourth Army had driven a hole in the German line twelve miles wide and up to seven miles deep. The Allied loss in tanks and horses was costly: a hundred of the first and about a thousand of the second. On paper that seemed like too dear a price for a few miles, but the victory of the day was not in gain of territory but in the way it was won and the panic it was spreading throughout the German Army. It was also a knockout blow to Ludendorff, whose confidence had been so badly shaken on July 15 and 18. "As the sun set on the 8th of August on the battlefield," read the official German report, "the greatest defeat which the German Army had suffered since the beginning of the War was an accomplished fact. The positions between the Avre and the Somme, which had been struck by the enemy attack were nearly completely annihilated."

That evening Crown Prince Rupprecht received a curt message from the OHL: "Today, for the second time, our troops have allowed themselves to be surprised by an enemy attack. It is absolutely necessary to urge each man that the greatest alertness is demanded henceforth."

The Kaiser was in extremely low spirits at dinner. "It's very strange," he complained, "that our men cannot get used to tanks."

Maze was watching a solemn ceremony for the dead, attended by both British and Germans. "Near-by brigades of cavalry which had been withdrawn made a large square in the middle of the plain. All the horses had their heads down and looked tired." Exhausted as he was, Maze was buoyed by the thought that in one day they had won back what it had taken the enemy four days to gain in the fearful retreat of March. Hostile aircraft murmured overhead, but he was too tired to care and he wouldn't have moved a yard to get out of the way of a bomb.

Tank driver Bacon, knocked unconscious that morning by a field gun, came out of his oblivion to find stars gleaming above him. For as far as he could see, hundreds of men were lying on the grass. Some were groaning, others crying out for water. A strange voice next to him kept calling, *"Mutter, O Mutter!"* Bacon's throat and guts were burning. He called for water but to no avail. A plane droned overhead. Bombs crashed. Once more oblivion.

Haig was writing his wife: "How much easier it is to attack than stand and await an enemy's attack! As you well know I am only the instrument of the Divine Power who watches over each of us, so all the Honour must be HIS." Attack, attack! That would be his watchword from this day on. Then the war could be won before the end of the year.

According to a story attributed to Haig's private secretary, there was a strange reaction when General Wilson announced to the War Cabinet, "Gentlemen, there was an attack this morning and many prisoners and guns have been taken." With one accord they reportedly said, *"There,* I told you so, I *knew* we'd be surprised again!!"* After Wilson had informed them it was a British, not a German assault, he was asked why the attack had been launched in the first place. He fliply replied, "So that the R.A.F. pilots may have supper with their young ladies, in peace, in Amiens." If the irrepressible Wilson did not say this, he surely would have liked to.

3.

The Canadian Corps was supposed to resume the general attack the next morning at ten, but lack of communications forced a delay of an hour, and some brigades did not get under way for another three hours. To make matters worse, the Australians were also unable to reach their assembly position in time to cooperate with the Canadian advance. Consequently the Fourth Army was unable to develop or exploit the initial success as General von Hutier had done so brilliantly on March 22.

It turned out to be a day of hesitation and missed chances, but even so three miles were gained. More important, the panic at German Supreme Command continued with incessant telephone calls and tense visits heightening the turbulence. Although General von der Marwitz, commander of the battered Second Army, managed to plug up the gaps in the morning, he asked permission to withdraw behind the Somme in the afternoon. Ludendorff exploded! The Second Army had lost its nerve! He telephoned Crown Prince Rupprecht personally. The Second Army was to hold its line at all costs. Rupprecht protested that this was risky because of lack of reserves. But Ludendorff could think of nothing except holding the front. General von Kuhl, Rupprecht's chief of staff, joined his chief in protesting that this would leave them naked of all resources. In desperation Kuhl asked one of his staff officers to read aloud a detailed report of Second Army's plight, but Ludendorff broke in to demand that the position be held. "Ludendorff is continually insisting on having a say in all the particulars," wrote the harried Kuhl, "talking to all the armies and their chiefs, arranging details often quite contrary to his orders to me. Then when one talks to the army commanders, one hears they are doing something entirely different from what we ordered. This makes everything terribly difficult. At the same time he is extremely restless and does not listen to a single suggestion."

Adding to Ludendorff's woes was the return of Mertz von Quirnheim with a devastating report of the collapse of morale at the front. Ludendorff was crushed, although reports had been coming in for months of disorder on troop and leave trains: shots were fired from the windows of the trains; the men left at every chance, many disappearing at stations; officers trying to maintain discipline were stoned; even hand grenades were tossed out of train windows, and the sides of the trains were scrawled with slogans such as: "We're not fighting for Germany's honor, but for the millionaires."

Today's report of men breaking for the rear in mobs infuriated Ludendorff. He issued a directive calling for prompt and energetic reprisals for all commanders to "save us from the grave danger resulting from a *constantly increasing lack of discipline.*" He also summoned divisional commanders and officers from the line to discuss the problem. Their firsthand reports completely unsettled the Quartermaster General. "I was told of glorious valor but also of behavior which, I openly confess, I should not have thought possible in the German Army; whole bodies of men had surrendered to a single trooper, or isolated squadrons. Retiring troops, meeting with a fresh division going bravely into action, had shouted out things like, 'Blackleg,' and 'You're prolonging the war.'" Most appalling were those numerous officers who had lost their influence and allowed themselves to be swept along with the rest. "All that I had feared, all that I had endlessly and repeatedly warned against, had here at one place become an actuality. Our fighting machine was no longer of real value. Our capacity for war had suffered harm even if the far greater majority of our divisions fought bravely. August 8 marked the decline of our military power and took from me the hope, with the replacement situation that existed, of discovering some strategic expedient that should restore the situation in our favor." The conduct of the war hereafter would only take on "the character of an irresponsible gamble, one that I always looked on as dangerous. The fate of the German people was too valuable for that game. The war had to be ended."

Now, forty-eight hours after the opening debacle, Ludendorff came to his famous conclusion that August 8 had been "the black day of the German Army." He decided to arrange conferences as soon as possible with the Chancellor and Foreign Minister. Before this could be done, the Kaiser arrived to find out what had happened. Ludendorff offered his resignation, but both His Majesty and Hindenburg refused to accept it. Ludendorff blamed the defeat on lack of discipline, but the Kaiser, echoing the Crown Prince, replied that too much had been required of the troops.

After Ludendorff confessed that he could no longer guarantee a military victory, Wilhelm was silent for a moment. Then he said calmly, "I see that I must balance accounts. We are at the end of our ability to do anything. The war must be ended." While inevitable, these words were shocking to Ludendorff and Hindenburg. "I will expect you, gentlemen, at Spa in the next few days." There and then the matter could be settled. For once it was the Kaiser who was cool and in complete command of himself. This, despite a telegram just received that Austria was near the end of her endurance; food was almost gone; and Emperor Karl had felt obliged to declare categorically "that peace must be concluded during the course of the year 1918, and that, if no general peace were negotiated, he would have to conclude a separate peace."

While the German leaders at last faced the possibility, if not the probability, of utter defeat, the Allies were advancing slowly, while wrangling over who should get credit for the victory. The French claimed it should be Foch; the British were divided, with some naming Haig, some Rawlinson, some Monash, and some Lloyd George. The world's praise was being heaped largely on Foch with little mention of Haig, who, with Rawlinson, had conceived the assault. There was much indignation not only in British but American headquarters, for the latter were also piqued at Pershing's lack of recognition. "Don't ever forget," a wise British general warned Lloyd Griscom, "that the history of the war that is accepted by posterity will be written by Foch and his entourage. When all's said and done, he's the supreme commander."

No word of congratulations had yet come to Haig from his Prime Minister. But Winston Churchill, who had been touring the front the past two days, realized what Haig and his generals had accomplished and he was lavish in praise. He also wrote a private letter to Lloyd George. "There is no doubt Haig has won a very great success which may well be the precursor of further extremely important events . . . It seems to me this is the greatest British victory that has been won in the whole war, and the worst defeat that the German army has yet sustained. How thankful you must be after all the anxieties through which we have passed."

Lloyd George felt no need to issue congratulations. Instead he felt that the field marshal had bungled a good thing. "Had Haig flung his army into the gap created and pursued the broken and demoralised Germans without respite an even greater victory was within his grasp. When the enemy was scattered and unnerved, and their reserves were not yet up, Haig did not press forward with relentless drive and the Germans were given time to recover and reform their lines."

Lloyd George *did* find time to write another of his ardent love letters to "My Darling Pussy":

> When I woke up at 6 my first thought was of the loving little face engraved on my heart & I had a fierce impulse to go there & then to cover it with kisses. But darling I am jealous once more. I know your thoughts are on roast mutton & partridge & chicken & potatoes & that you are longing to pass them through the lips which are wine & to bite them with luscious joy with the dazzling white teeth that I love to press. I know that today I am a little out of it & that your heart is throbbing for other thrills. . . .
>
> > Your very jealous old
> > Lover

On August 10, Foch, recently promoted to marshal, told Haig that he believed the enemy was demoralized. Haig agreed that some German divisions were, "but not *all* yet!" The next day proved this was right. Enemy counterattacks prevented any further Allied progress, indicating beyond a doubt that German resistance was stiffening. But mutiny was spreading in the homeland among recruits bound for the front. That day a battalion of five hundred staged a riot in the station at Neuss, and when men of the *Landsturm* (Home Guard) intervened the mutineers threatened to fire. Another rebellion occurred in Graudenz after troops bound for the railroad station refused to obey the order "Shoulder arms." Officers reminding the men of the severe punishment they faced were greeted with a unanimous shout: "We won't go to the front!" A crowd of soldiers appeared at the windows of the caserne to encourage the rebels by shouting out, "Bravo!" "We are hungry!" and singing seditious songs.

Lieutenant Binding wrote in his diary that he shuddered to think of going through the Somme wilderness for the fourth time. "It will be the same all over again, but without any confidence. Our troops will be thinner and worse; for days the horses have not had a grain of oats; the men are being given barley-bread which will not rise in the oven, and we have taken some knocks. Against us we shall have thousands of tanks, tens of thousands of airmen, hundreds of thousands of hearty young men, behind whom there will be an American Army which may number a million. I can see and feel mysterious powers rising out of the deep which are not governed by any man's brains but by uncontrollable movements and forces. . . . Last night I dreamed I saw the Kaiser entering what seemed to be the gateway of a camp, bareheaded and on foot, forced by his people to give himself up to their mercy. I don't know whether he ended on the scaffold, but I should not be surprised." Binding had seen too much in these last days. "This generation has no future, and deserves none. Anyone who belongs to it lives no more. It is almost a consolation to realize this. All that an individual can do to get out of the wrack is to find some way of hewing out blocks of stone wherewith to found a new structure which to this generation will be nothing, and leave it as a legacy to others."

Early on the morning of August 13 Ludendorff and Hindenburg headed toward Spa for a meeting that was to decide the course of Germany. The field marshal's spirit was not broken and he still felt they could overcome future military crises. But, according to gossip in Berlin, the Quartermaster General was "a completely broken man." Many were now repeating the acid words that former Chancellor von Bethmann-Hollweg once said about him: "You don't know Ludendorff, who is only great at a time of success. If things go badly, he loses his nerve. I've seen this happen in the Eastern campaign."

Upon arrival at Spa at 8 A.M. the two commanders went directly to their rear headquarters at the Hôtel Britannique to confer with the new Foreign Minister, Rear Admiral Paul von Hintze. He expected to see "a completely broken man" and was surprised to find Ludendorff in control of himself. "He took me aside," recalled Hintze, "and admitted that although he had told me in July he had been certain of breaking the enemy's fighting mettle and of compelling him to accept peace by the offensive that was then in progress, he was no longer sure of it." Yet when Hintze asked what he thought of the future conduct of the war, Ludendorff said—and stressed that his next words were given in confidence—"We should be able through a strategic defensive to weaken the enemy's spirit and gradually bring him to terms." Hintze was overwhelmed.

At 10 A.M. the formal meeting with Chancellor von Hertling began. Both Hindenburg and Ludendorff admitted that the military situation had changed for the worse, but they were convinced they could break the enemy's will to continue the war and compel him to sue for peace. Ludendorff stressed morale as of the first importance and was concerned by enemy propaganda aimed at the civilians. Hinderburg was more optimistic. The problem of morale at home was not that serious and he reminded everyone that they were "still standing deep in the enemy's territory."

Hintze was more interested in discussing those subjects which, he said, "required a new definition in view of the necessity of diplomatic peace overtures." He was referring to war aims and the fate of Belgium and Poland in particular. "Why bring up Belgium?" exclaimed Ludendorff. "That question has been settled and is laid down in black and white." Deciding not to make an issue of Belgium, Hintze gave a frank appraisal of their deteriorating political position. Austria, he said, was close to collapse; Bulgaria seemed about ready to desert the Central Powers; and Turkey was going her own way. Ludendorff was patently impatient with such gloomy talk. To him it was morbidly pessimistic.

The meeting broke up without any show of bad feeling, but Hintze was deeply concerned and, upon waking the next morning, the Supreme Command's optimism regarding the military situation, far from reassuring him, only made him more pessimistic. The Crown Council meeting was to start at 10 A.M., so he hurriedly called on Hertling to reveal that he was going to ask the Kaiser for permission to begin peace overtures. Would the Chancellor support him? If he could not get His Majesty's approval he would have to resign.

"I am an old man," said Hertling. "Let me go first."

They proceeded to the meeting, where the Kaiser took the chair. Also present were three of his suite, Crown Prince Wilhelm and the two military leaders. Hertling began with a review of the internal situation. The people were weary of war; there was inadequate food and clothing. Ludendorff brusquely countered by demanding stricter civilian discipline. "We must gather together all our strength at home with the utmost energy."

Admiral von Hintze took the floor. His voice broke with emotion and tears dimmed his eyes as he said, "The enemy is more confident of victory and more willing to fight than ever." This came not only from their recent victories but mainly the ever-growing conviction that they were superior in manpower, raw material, and manufactured goods. "Moreover, time is working in their favor." The longer the war lasted the sooner the resources of the Central Powers would give out. The neutrals, by now thoroughly tired of the war, were beginning to think the Central Powers were doomed to defeat by time alone. And most of them favored the enemy for sentimental reasons. "As regards our allies, Austria declares—and our own information confirms her opinion—that she has reached the end of her resources, that she cannot hold out another winter . . ." Bulgaria was rapidly weakening and Turkey was plunging into a campaign of murder and rapine in the Caucasus, contrary to German interests.

Hindenburg, he said, had admitted they could no longer hope to break the will of the enemy by military force and all military efforts must now be gradually to paralyze the determination of their enemies by a strategic defensive. "The political authorities," he concluded, "accept this view of the great military leaders who have fought this war, and draw the inference that in a political sense also we are no longer in a position to break the will of our enemies, and are therefore compelled to bear the military situation in mind in deciding upon the political course we should take."

Crown Prince Wilhelm, who had already seen the writing on the wall, agreed with everything Hintze said, while insisting that the home front be kept together by stronger discipline. Then the Kaiser spoke. He also called for better order at home, pointing out that the enemy too was suffering. "The harvest in England is bad this year. Tonnage is getting less all the time and it is possible that England will gradually begin to think of peace as the result of these difficulties." At the same time he agreed with Hintze's view of the deteriorating political situation. "We must find a suitable moment in which to come to an understanding with the enemy." He suggested going through the King of Spain or the Queen of the Netherlands.

The old Chancellor had his say, and it was brief. Diplomatic feelers, he said, should be thrown out at the most opportune time. "Such a moment might present itself after the next successes in the west." Hintze, who was keeping minutes of the conference, must have winced at such unfounded optimism as well as the last words of the morning spoken by a stern-faced Hindenberg: "I hope, in spite of everything, that we will be able to stay on French soil and thus eventually enforce our will upon the enemy."

As soon as Hintze wrote down these last words, Ludendorff seized the pen from him and struck out the word "hope" and wrote in "will see to it." * Tears filled the admiral's eyes. It was a time for weeping. The leaders of a great country all knew that peace had to be bought and yet agreed that it should only be done after another military success on the Western Front. This, when the will of the German soldier was fast ebbing.

That afternoon the Emperor Karl arrived at Spa and asked for immediate diplomatic steps to end the war, since Austria could continue fighting only until December. But Ludendorff argued against any peace move until "the favorable moment" came and the Germans were "firmly established on a new line or until some military success should cause a reaction among our enemies." The Austrians suggested that they approach the enemy directly, but the Germans insisted on mediating through neutrals.

Haig was puzzled by the actions of Rupprecht's army group. How strange that the enemy should begin his retirement and then reinforce his line! The enemy should have counterattacked in keeping with traditional German views and strategy. "But has he the necessary force? and will they fight?" he wrote on August 17. "In any case we cannot expect the Germans to own defeat, until they have played their last card! So we ought to be prepared for numerous counter-attacks."

The next day he gave a luncheon for Clemenceau, Marshal

---

* At one point in the meeting Ludendorff excitedly interrupted Hindenburg to again demand stricter discipline at home. "There must be more vigorous conscription of the young Jews, hitherto left pretty much alone."

Foch, Rawlinson, Derby, and a dozen others. It was a harmonious affair. Haig was presented with the French Médaille Militaire, and the conflict between him and Foch, both of whom wanted to attack but in different places, was held in abeyance.

When they were alone, the inveterate gossip, Lord Derby, revealed to Haig that Lloyd George remained extremely jealous of Clemenceau and the two were squabbling a good deal. Derby himself had become a pet of the Tiger's, partly because he had recently brought back from England an Aberdeen terrier as replacement for Clemenceau's which had died. Derby claimed that the dog had saved the bad situation between their two countries, and now the Tiger talked to him "fully and very frankly but, as he said, as man to man and not as Minister to Ambassador." Perhaps it pleased Haig almost as much to know that the dog was Scottish as that his old enemy Lloyd George was still detested and distrusted by Clemenceau.

The peace offensive advocated by Admiral von Hintze opened on August 20 with a speech to the press by Colonial Minister Wilhelm Solf. "Last month," he said, "the Chancellor declared in the Reichstag to all who had ears to hear that 'we do not intend to retain Belgium in any shape or form.' Belgium was to be set up again after the war as an independent state, under vassalage to none. Gentlemen! Nothing stands in the way of the restoration of Belgium but the war will of our enemies."

There was nothing really new in it that would attract the Allies to the peace table and it ended in a stinging denunciation: "Once more a wave of arrogance is passing through their peoples as happened after Italy and after Rumania entered the war and as happens after every passing political or military success. Once more the old war aims, laid down so clearly in the secret treaties which have never been denounced, are held in readiness. The war is once more being fought by the Entente for plunder and prestige." It was a peculiar way of extending the olive branch and yet perfectly understandable to a German regime which, after the reassurances of Hindenburg and Ludendorff, still felt it could bargain.

At the same time German troops were still retreating in Flanders, some in panic. During a tank attack on August 23, an artillery officer, Lieutenant R. von Dechend, could see "masses" of gray forms heading toward him out of the fog. "This was not an orderly retreat, this was a wild escape. We are their officers and why couldn't they be stopped and turned around in a counter-attack?" When the fog cleared he could see that only a half-dozen tanks had caused the panicked flight. "Not understandable. I tried to comfort myself that these men were probably just young recruits who hadn't even completed training. Surely other companies will resist the enemy." But old as well as new soldiers were trying to escape. Lieutenant von Dechend stopped a sergeant with a bandaged arm. "But he could not give a reasonable answer to what had happened and why. They had been encircled, he said. His company had been captured and only a few had escaped. That's all he knew."

A sense of depression was now spreading over the entire front. The following day, a second lieutenant of the German 197th Division wrote home: "At present I have the impression that we are approaching the end at a giant's pace; the blind are gradually beginning to see; it is the coming of dawn. The beast affected with the folly of grandeur will soon be obliged to face the reality entirely nude."

The next day General von der Marwitz, whose Second Army was being driven relentlessly backward by Haig, issued an order: "The unreasonable rumors lately circulated in the rear by men who have lost their heads surpass all imagination. These men with troubled conscience see squadrons of tanks, masses of cavalry and dense lines of infantry everywhere. It is indeed high time that our war-hardened soldiers speak to these pusillanimous and cowardly persons and relate to them the truth about the front." Corporal Adolf Hitler was already doing this. According to a comrade, "he became furious and shouted in a terrible voice that pacifists and shirkers were losing the war." He even attacked a new noncom who said it was stupid to keep fighting. They had a fistfight and Hitler won. From then on, his comrade recalled, "the new ones despised him but we old comrades liked him more than ever." But the *alten Kämpfer* were outnumbered by the recruits and those who had lost their nerve, and the number of stragglers and deserters roaming about the rear was increasing "in a startling manner."

Crown Prince Wilhelm felt that Ludendorff's attempt to resist withdrawal would lead to disaster, and wrote him on the twenty-sixth that the enemy was obviously trying to destroy their reserves. "We can only prevent his doing so by adopting the principle that battle is not to be accepted except where the conditions for defense are favorable. Where these conditions do not exist, we must withdraw by sectors according to plan, until an opportunity for a counter-attack or a favorable defense, e.g., on some strong line, presents itself. The enemy's initiative makes this course inevitable." Retreat was bound to lower morale, so whenever possible they should deal a shrewd blow at an enemy following incautiously. Losses then would be less than in a rigid defense. "Systematic withdrawal remains but a temporary expedient. It must end in the occupation of a strong permanent line favorable for defense over a long period, and giving us a chance of creating a large reserve by a substantial shortening of our front. This permanent line must be so far from the present battlefield that even if the fluctuating actions now in progress continue for weeks we shall have ample room for a systematic retirement."

But Ludendorff wrote back that he would withdraw only to the jumping-off line of March. In no mood for wise advice, he was like a gambler who desperately tries to win back all his losses in a single throw. At the same time his soldiers were openly writing home that they believed it was useless to fight: "The men did not fire a shot. When Tommy advanced, the company commander gathered up his men and they surrendered in march column." "Many were taken prisoner that day. I should have preferred to be among them." "I would also like to see us pushed back to the frontier. Then Michel [one of the defense lines] would have somewhat shorter teeth and peace would be nearer." "The enemy is superior to us in almost everything. . . . I no longer believe in our victory, there will again be bad days."

On August 27 Haig wrote his wife: "We have given the Germans a severe blow. I suppose we have gained the greatest victory which a British Army ever gained. This is already represented by some 47,000 prisoners, 6 to 700 guns, and great gain in territory as well. But we have not done with the Germans yet, as I expect soon to get more prisoners, as the German Army is thoroughly war weary, and our attacks will still go on!"

Lieutenant von Dechend could testify to that. It had been another frustrating day. He couldn't telephone back to his battery because of continually broken lines and the troops out front were scarcely putting up any resisance. "I saw our infantry keep coming down the hill in masses without making any attempt to stop the enemy; they fired not a single shot and there was not even drumfire from the artillery that would have forced the enemy to move back. A little later a few khaki figures appeared on the hill, then more and more. Calmly, walking upright, rifles under arms, they come on in groups. No battle, no rush. They just drive the Germans in front of them like a shepherd his sheep. A few hung back and were encircled, and then calmly captured as if it were a dance."

By this time Ludendorff had lost the spirits regained briefly at the Crown Council. "I must recognize for the first time," wrote Colonel Nicolai, Chief of Military Intelligence, in his diary, "that [Ludendorff] seems to have reached the end of his strength." The Quartermaster General's slogan, "Where we are, we stand," was a miserable failure. If this policy continued much longer there was no chance for Germany.

Part 4

THE HINGE OF FATE

Chapter Twelve

THE RED TERROR
JULY 16–SEPTEMBER

1.

IN the meantime civil war was ravaging Russia. Brutal White beatings and murders (begun after Baron Gustav Mannerheim, with the help of the Germans, had defeated the Red Guards in Finland in May) were now being answered by equally savage reprisals. In addition there was the continuing running battle with the Czechs along the Trans-Siberian Railroad. This and the Left Social Revolutionary uprisings following the Mirbach assassination, together with the growing threat of Allied intervention in the north, so terrified Bolsheviks that they began responding with brutality.

This policy of desperation was climaxed with a mass murder that horrified the world the day before Wilson presented his ill-conceived *aide-mémoire*. In early spring the Ural Regional Soviet had insisted that the Czar be transferred to Ekaterinburg, less than two hundred miles north of Chelyabinsk. During the trip the Ural Regional Congress of the Communist Party met in Ekaterinburg to demand his death, and by the time the entire royal entourage was installed in the mansion of a wealthy engineer, the Ural Soviet also demanded his execution. But the Cheka insisted on trying Nicholas before the proletarians. The trial was to start late in July and, with the flamboyant Trotsky as public prosecutor, it promised to be a historic and memorable event.

But the approach of the Czechs from both sides and the uncovering of an officers' plot to rescue the Romanovs caused a change in plan. By mid-July it was obvious that the Czechs would take Ekaterinburg within a week, so it was decided to execute the Romanovs without delay and destroy their remains so that no relics could be used by Whites to inspire a counterrevolution.

Near midnight on July 16 Nicholas, the Czarina, their son Alexis, Anastasia, and the three other daughters were told to gather downstairs with their loyal attendants. All thought they were being transferred, but as they stood in a row a sentence of death in the name of the Ural Soviet was read out. In surprise the Czar said, "So we're not being transferred to another place?" They were shot and reportedly taken to an abandoned mine nearby where their bodies were burned and the ashes buried in a swamp. The following night seven other members of the royal house—four grand dukes, Prince Palei, the widow of the Grand Duke Sergei, and Princess Helena of Serbia—were shot in the factory town of Alapayevsk, 250 miles to the northeast. Their bodies were flung down a mine shaft.

Apparently the well-coordinated assassinations were supervised from Moscow by one of the highest Soviet officials, Jacob Sverdlov, the chairman of the Central Executive Committee. Being Lenin's closest confidant, he was probably acting with his leader's authorization. Lately Lenin had been asking his comrades, "Do you really think that we can emerge victoriously from the Revolution without rabid terrorism?" He even ignored the protests of his friend Maxim Gorky. "What would you have? Is humanity possible in such a furious struggle? Can we allow ourselves to be softhearted and magnanimous, when Europe is blockading us and the hoped-for assistance from the European proletariat has failed, and counter-revolution is rising against us on every side? No, excuse me, we are not imbeciles." Pointing to children at play, he said their lives would be happier than their fathers'. "Circumstances have compelled us to be cruel, but later ages will justify us; then everything will be understood, everything."

Lenin didn't learn about the assassinations until July 18 during a session of the All-Russian Central Executive Committee, where a draft decree on public health was being debated. Sverdlov walked in, sat down behind Lenin, and whispered something. "Comrade Sverdlov," said Lenin, "requests to make a communication." Whereupon Sverdlov, a former pharmacist apprentice, stated evenly that the Czar had been shot at Ekaterinburg by order of the Regional Soviet. "Nicholas wanted to escape. The Czechoslovaks were approaching. The Bureau of Vee-Tsik [Cheka] approves." After a brief silence, Lenin said calmly, "We will pass to the examination of the public health draft." *

* There is no official record of any notification of the murders to the Allies, but Norman Armour, secretary of the American Embassy at Vologda, recalls Ambassador Francis receiving a "cold-blooded" note from Foreign Commissar Chicherin on either July 17 or 18, "boasting" of the Czar's assassination and explaining that the approach of the Czechs to Ekaterinburg had forced the Soviets to execute him. Upon reading the note, Armour immediately drafted a bitter reply, but Francis instructed him not to send it.

On July 19 the Moscow press disclosed that the Czar had been executed but that the rest of the family had been "sent to a safe place." However, the truth of the other deaths emerged and when it was learned that the Czarina, little Alexis, and the four daughters had also been murdered, many who had previously sympathized with the Bolsheviks became hostile.*

The increasing savagery of the civil war impelled Ambassador Francis to urge his fellow diplomats in Vologda to be prepared to leave for Archangel on short notice without asking the consent of the Bolsheviks. Foreign Commissar Chicherin also advised the diplomats to leave Vologda—but for Moscow. He telegraphed Francis on July 23: "COME HERE. DANGER APPROACHING. TOMORROW CAN BE TOO LATE. WHEN BATTLE RAGES, DISTINCTION OF HOUSES CANNOT BE MADE. WHY BRING ABOUT CATASTROPHE WHICH YOU CAN AVERT?"

After consulting his colleagues, Francis wired back that they all appreciated Chicherin's uninterrupted interest in their personal safety and therefore decided to follow his advice and leave Vologda. He didn't add that they were going to Archangel, nor that they planned to leave that evening by special train.

But Chicherin learned of their destination and pleaded with Francis to reconsider, adding persuasively that "in the expectation of a siege Archangel cannot be a residence fit for ambassadors," and then pointing out like a high-powered real estate agent how superior the quarters were in Moscow with "its peaceful gay suburbs" and splendid villas. The city was now the official center of Russia and "a friendly reception awaits you."

There was a certain charm in the invitation, but the Allies preferred the presence of friendly troops in Archangel to the gay life of Moscow, and Francis was delegated to reply that they were going north. All the missions and staff had been living in the special train for twenty-four hours awaiting authorization from Moscow for use of a locomotive.

The harried Chicherin bowed to the inevitable and late that evening telegraphed that a locomotive would be put at the Allies' disposal and a boat prepared for them in Archangel; then, like a host, who fears he has offended the guests, added: ONCE MORE WE EMPHASIZE THAT WE DO NOT ASCRIBE A POLITICAL MEANING TO THIS INDIVIDUAL LEAVING OF DIPLOMATIC REPRESENTATIVES, WHICH WE PROFOUNDLY REGRET AND WHICH WAS CAUSED BY SORROWFUL CONJUNCTURE OF CIRCUMSTANCES, INDEPENDENT OF OUR WILL.

After midnight the special train finally pulled away from the Vologda station. At Archangel the Allied party was met by a dele-

---

* In the ensuing months there were persistent rumors that not all the Romanovs were dead. Through the years the most enduring mystery has been that of Anastasia, the Czar's youngest daughter. A number of women have claimed to be Anastasia, with the most likely candidate Anna Anderson. But even she has been discredited by most authorities. An unpublished manuscript by an industrious researcher, Brien Horan, disclosed information which, in my opinion, gives credence to her claim.

gation of local Bolsheviks and a Moscow representative who asked them to board a small ship on the Dvina River. Francis refused, explaining that they did not intend to leave Russia before communicating with their governments. Guards were stationed around the train and the officials left, still in a state of perplexity.

Back in Vologda, Norman Armour, left behind to take care of the last few Americans in town, was informed that there was fighting nearby and everyone should be taken at once to Moscow for safety. When Armour refused, he was told that the Americans would be taken there by force. As he packed the last papers, the sight of the yawning, empty safe gave him an inspiration. He found Francis' top hat, the symbol of everything the Bolsheviks detested, and put it in the safe. Next to it he placed a note with one word, *"Dosvidanye* [goodbye]." Then he locked the safe, sealed it ostentatiously on three sides with red tape and wax, and took the train to Moscow.*

The departure of the Allied diplomats was acknowledged that day, July 26, in a bitter article in *Pravda* by Karl Radek, an influential Bolshevik; it belied the pleasant words of Chicherin and clearly revealed Soviet policy, aims, and fears. Ever since the Revolution, claimed the author, the Allies had been "wildly persecuting Russia by supporting every movement directed against it." But the Soviets tolerated this since they did not wish "to break the ties with the people's masses of the Allied countries" and needed "the economic assistance of the more developed countries."

The sarcastic diatribe concluded with an aggressive olive branch: "The Russian Government," Radek said, "aims to maintain friendly relations with the Allied people; but it cannot allow the agents of the Allied Governments to organize rebellions on Russian territory. . . . The time is nearing when the Allies will be compelled to say whether they are with us or against us."

Francis was still negotiating for proper vessels to take the diplomats to Murmansk, and at last, early in the morning of July 28, the entire group along with about seventy British and French residents boarded two small steamers.

But their departure only aggravated the situation of fellow diplomats in Moscow. The Bolsheviks by now were convinced that full-scale intervention was being plotted. On the night of the twenty-ninth Lenin personally sounded the warning in a speech at a joint session of the Moscow Soviet and city labor unions. He charged the British and French with inciting the Czech uprising and exaggerated the scale of British military operations in Murmansk. The Allies, he said, were attempting to involve Russia in their imperialist war by fomenting civil war throughout the land. "We have again gotten into war, we *are* at war, and this war is not only a civil war—it is now Anglo-French imperialism which op-

---

* After trying in vain to open the safe, the Bolsheviks had to resort to dynamite. They were so furious at finding that it contained only a top hat, the housekeeper later told Armour, that if they had caught him "they'd have shot you on the spot."

poses us; it is not yet in a position to launch its legions against Russia; geographic conditions stand in the way; but it gives all that it can—all its millions, all its diplomatic connections and forces—to the support of our enemies."

The Allied diplomats in Moscow were deeply distressed. Was this a declaration of war? Were they now hostages on enemy territory? They called on Foreign Commissar Chicherin the next morning to ask these questions. In embarrassment, he insisted that there was no state of war, only "a state of defense," which did not necessarily mean a rupture of relations. While they were talking a message was handed to Chicherin. Field Marshal von Eichhorn, German commander in the Ukraine, had been assassinated by a young Left Social Revolutionary student. Chicherin, ordinarily impassive, leaped to his feet and began dancing gleefully around the room waving the message. "You see what happens when foreigners intervene against the wishes of the people!"

2.

On the morning of August 1, an Allied flotilla intent on landing a small military force in Archangel approached the fortified island of Mudyung, which was protecting the harbor. If the Allied warships advanced further they would be fired upon, but they had no intention of doing so. Secret agents had arranged a *coup d'état*, and that night an adventurous young White naval officer, Captain Georgi Ermolaevich Chaplin, a former Czarist naval officer, led an assault on the fortress. It was so well organized that only two men were wounded.

The next day the Allied warships steamed peacefully into the harbor to be greeted by a large, enthusiastic crowd. Twelve hundred men were landed—a French battalion, a detachment of Royal Marines, and fifty American Marines from the cruiser *Olympia*. There were no Soviet troops in town. They had been put to rout by the Whites in an almost bloodless occupation of the city, and there was now a new government headed by N. V. Chaikovsky, a well-known Populist and Socialist.

Although the Reds had been driven out of the city, they remained in the vicinity, and the British commander of the operation, Major General F. C. Poole, began setting up a defensive perimeter. The fifty American Marines, commanded by a navy ensign, joined in with enthusiasm. Bored by inactivity, they commandeered an ancient wood-burning locomotive with a funnel-shaped smokestack, hitched on several flatcars, and set out after the retreating Reds. As in a movie serial they chased the Bolsheviks for some thirty miles before the pursued managed to burn up a bridge. Here a brief machine-gun and rifle skirmish broke out. About the only blood shed was by the ensign, who was hit in the leg. And so America entered the conflict against the Soviets despite Wilson's announcement that he did not want his troops to be involved in any organized intervention. His ambiguous policy had brought him to undeclared war with the Bolsheviks and, being a halfhearted one, it also infuriated his own allies.

"As to the future the real security against what the President fears lies in the President himself," Lloyd George had recently cabled his ambassador in Washington, empowering Reading to tell Wilson that, provided he "really" acted, Britain would give him full support. "What I am frightened of, however, is that we shall drift along until it is too late to save Russia from falling under German domination . . . If we don't act decisively now I greatly fear that the Germans will find ways and means through pro-German elements in Russia to beat down the truly liberal elements, to round out the Czecho-Slovaks or drive them out of Siberia, and so reduce Russia to such impotence that she will become a negligible quantity for the rest of the war. I am an interventionalist just as much because I am a democrat as because I want to win the war." Unfortunately the pragmatic Llyod George had as little concept as the idealist Wilson of the dynamic forces and ultimate aims of the struggling Soviet republic. He regarded it as merely another pawn in the greater game of the war against Germany.

At the same time, the Bolsheviks so overestimated the puny Allied forces in the north that Chicherin was instructed to seek German military aid. On August 2, hat in hand, he visited Mirbach's replacement, Karl Helfferich. An open military alliance, said Chicherin, was still impossible and German troops could not be allowed to enter Petrograd, but he begged for a military operation against the British in the north without delay. He also asked for an offensive against the White Cossack Army. The mouse was asking to be rescued from a cat by another cat.

Helfferich reported to Berlin that "this move" proved the great weakness of the Soviets, and he urged his superior to "pretend to fall in with the Russian request for intervention and to make all feasible military preparations for it, but at the last moment to form a common front with the Cossack leaders against the Bolsheviks." The German Foreign Minister, Admiral von Hintze, opposed overthrowing the Bolsheviks, and Helfferich was promptly ordered to return to Berlin at once. This, in turn, angered Ludendorff, who felt that he had enough troops in the east to drive out the British as well as wipe out the Bolsheviks. He informed Hintze that the German Army could readily advance into Russia and set up a new government "which would have the people behind it."

Hintze demolished this shortsighted view with a brilliant analysis of German relations with the Russians. A Russian Government that had the people behind it, he telegraphed, didn't need their support. "We do not have any friends worth mentioning in Russia; whoever informs Your Excellency to the contrary is deceiving himself." Although the Bolsheviks were losing popular support, there was no likelihood they would be overturned in the near future. Nor would a rapid end of their power be to Germany's advantage. "Whether or not we like the idea of working with them is unimportant as long as it is useful to do so. History shows that to introduce feelings into politics is a costly luxury . . . To this day and for a long time to come, politics are utilitarian." After all, what did they want in the east? "The military paralysis of Russia. The Bolsheviks are doing a better and more thorough job than any other Russian party, and without our devoting a single man or one mark to the task. We cannot expect them or other Russians to love us for milking their country dry. Let us be content with Russia's impotence."

After reading copies of this telegram, Chancellor von Hertling and the Kaiser informed Hintze that they were "in complete agreement" with his policy. And Ludendorff for once was forced to submit but not before stating that he still wanted "to fight against the British on the Murmansk coast, if we can occupy Petrograd." Ironically, the next day was August 8, and this "black day" ended any hope of moving against the Allies in Russia. All available forces in the east now had to be transferred to the west.

Four days earlier Moscow had first learned of the Archangel landings and the initial reports were grossly exaggerated. One source claimed that 100,000 Allied soldiers had arrived. The capital, according to Lockhart, "went wild with excitement." This alarm was closely followed by another. The Japanese were sending seven divisions through Siberia to help the Czechs. "Even the Bolsheviks lost their heads and, in despair, began to pack their archives." Chicherin's assistant told the British agent that the Bolsheviks were lost but would never surrender. They were going underground and would fight to the end.

In despair Chicherin wrote a letter to American Consul DeWitt Poole, implying that the British were behind all the interventions. "Seeing that you have declared that your people does not wish to overthrow the Soviets, we ask you whether you cannot make it clear to us what Britain really wants from us. Is it Britain's aim to destroy the most popular government that the world has ever known, the Soviets of the poor and the peasants? Is its aim counter-revolution? . . . I must assume that this is so. We must assume that Great Britain intends to restore the worst tyranny in the world, odious Tsarism. Or does it intend to seize certain towns, or a part of our territory?"

Panic in Moscow, recalled Lockhart, was indescribable. The next morning, while visiting the British Consul General at Yusupov Palace, the building was surrounded by agents of the Cheka. While they were cross-examining consular officials downstairs, upstairs British Intelligence officers were hastily burning ciphers and compromising documents. Clouds of smoke belched from the chimneys and polluted the corridors, but the Cheka agents, even though it was a torrid day, never became suspicious. Everyone in the building was put under arrest except Lockhart and his assistant, who were left alone because of a pass from Trotsky.

When Consul Poole learned that about two hundred British

and French had also been arrested, including consular officials, he wondered how he could carry on with no one to consult. Ambassador Francis was in Murmansk and all communications to Washington were cut. In desperation, he decided this was the end and the next day burned his codes, closed his office, and placed himself and other Americans under the protection of the Norwegians.

On August 9 the Bolshevik panic abruptly ended upon learning how few Allied forces had landed in Archangel. The relieved Soviets released the consulate officials. Even so, the Allied diplomats realized that their position was helpless. A new crisis could erupt at any moment. They all lowered their flags and, like Poole, turned over representation of their interests to neutral colleagues.

Relieved of immediate concern over foreign invasion, the Bolsheviks concentrated on the internal menace. That same day Lenin ordered "a ruthless mass terror against kulaks, priests, and White guards." The campaign was accelerated a week later by an article in *Izvestya*, calling for slaughter of all White wounded. "In civil war there must be no trials for the enemy. If you don't break him, the enemy will break you. So smash him before he smashes you."

It was a declaration of terrorism aimed not only at the White menace but at those who were trying to overthrow the Bolsheviks by conspiracy. The most dangerous of the myriad conspiracies was being plotted by the Right Social Revolutionary Party. At their recent Eighth National Council meeting they had passed a resolution that the Bolshevik policies threatened the very independence of Russia and that "this danger can be removed only by the liquidation of the Bolshevik Government." The task of "removing" the Bolshevik leaders, Lenin and Trotsky, was turned over to a compact "Battle Organization" in Petrograd. There were about ten in this group and they had been in Moscow all July, placing Lenin under surveillance. He had discontinued his walks in the streets and would wander within the confines of the Kremlin, which was guarded by Latvian soldiers. The only times he could be shot were while making speeches in public. The group learned that he might address the workers of the Mikhelson factory on the night of August 30, and Fanya (familiarly called Dora) Kaplan was selected to be on hand just in case. She was one of four executioners. The twenty-eight-year-old daughter of a Jewish teacher, she had spent eleven years at hard labor under the Czar. Now she felt impelled to kill Lenin since he was a "traitor to the Revolution," and his very existence "discredited socialism."

Lenin did make his speech at the factory, a bitter denunciation of the Allies. In conclusion he exclaimed that the battle lines were at last drawn between the parasitic banditry of the bourgeoisie and the British and French Allies ("masquerading under the slogans of freedom and equality") and the proletariat. "There is only one of two ways out for us: either victory or death!"

As he walked out of the building toward his car, adulatory

workers pressed around him. In the excitement, Fanya Kaplan squirmed her way up to Lenin and fired twice. One bullet struck his left shoulder. The other pierced his neck, grazing the left lung before lodging near the right collarbone. Kaplan was captured.

Refusing to be taken to a hospital, Lenin ordered his chauffeur to drive him back to his apartment in the Kremlin and, according to Communist legend, he walked the two floors up to his lodging. General Bonch-Bruyevich put iodine on his shoulder wound and a few minutes later the general's wife, a physician, treated him.

He complained of pains in his heart but was told that he was only wounded in the arm. He fell asleep, then suddenly wakened and said, "Why are they tormenting me? Why didn't they kill me right away?" He was convinced he was dying and kept repeating, "When will the end come?" He was given morphine.

A surgeon found the second wound in his neck. By this time Lenin's lungs were filled with blood, and, in great pain, he began to cough and spit. His wife sat near him all through the night, though she herself was ill.

3.

By morning numerous messages, resolutions, and telegrams poured into the Kremlin. German Foreign Secretary von Hintze expressed his sympathy and the hope that Lenin would recover quickly. The Eastern Front telegraphed that the wounds of Vladimir Ilitch were their wounds. Red Army Socialists adopted a resolution calling for death to the counterrevolutionaries. "To your white terror, we will reply by a blood red terror. Blood for blood!" Scores of similar resolutions came in from peasant and worker organizations. An Extraordinary Commission for Combating Counter Revolution was hastily organized and within hours it was announced that they had "shot over 500 people from the hostages."

All during August 31 the headquarters of the Moscow Soviet was besieged by representatives of labor organizations seeking hopeful news of Lenin's condition, and even when a council of doctors discovered that his wounds were not serious, the anger against the counterrevolutionaries continued. Newspapers throughout the land expressed the common outrage in unbridled terms. "Each drop of Lenin's blood must be paid by the bourgeoisie and the Whites in hundreds of deaths" declared the *Krasnaya Gazeta* of Petrograd. The interests of the revolution demanded the physical extermination of the bourgeoisie. "They have no pity: it is time for us to be pitiless."

Putting such words into action, an armed Petrograd mob led by Cheka agents stormed into the British Embassy at 5 P.M. The naval attaché, Captain F. N. A. Cromie, the senior official in the building, courageously barred the way. Stand aside or be killed "like a dog," someone shouted. He drew his pistol, killing one Cheka agent and wounding two others before bullets killed him almost instantly. In fury the marauders horribly mutilated Cromie's body, then marched off the entire staff of the consulate and missions, along with a few civilians who happened to be there, to Cheka headquarters. Later they were all imprisoned in the Fortress of Peter and Paul, already crowded with Russian prisoners twenty to a small cell.

Bruce Lockhart was another target of the Cheka, which had recently uncovered a harebrained plot by another British agent, Sidney Reilly, to bribe members of the famed Latvian bodyguard to kidnap Lenin. The Cheka was convinced that Lockhart was the real brains of the conspiracy, and orders were issued for his immediate arrest.

He was sleeping soundly at his flat in Moscow when he was wakened by a rough voice at 3:30 A.M., September 1. He opened his eyes to see the barrel of a revolver. About ten armed men were in the room. Recognizing the man in charge, Lockhart asked what this outrage meant.

"No questions. Get dressed at once. You are to go to Loubianka No. 11."

Lockhard was taken to Cheka headquarters, and after a long wait in a small room was led into a long, dark room lit only by a hand lamp on a table. Behind the table in white Russian shirt was Jakob Peters. Better known as Jake, he was a slight curly-haired young Latvian with a snub nose who, while living in political exile in London, had married an English girl and acquired a Cockney accent. After the revolution he left her in England and returned to Russia to become assistant to the Cheka chief.

"I am sorry to see you in this position," said Peters sympathetically. "It is a grave matter."

Lockhart demanded to speak to Chicherin, but Peters ignored this request and asked, "Do you know the Kaplan woman?" Lockhart did not but protested as calmly as possible that Peters had no right to question him. "Where is Reilly?" asked Peters. Lockhart repeated his protest and, after Peters brought out a piece of paper, Lockhart knew that he was in trouble. It was a pass he had recently given to two Latvian soldiers who wanted to surrender to the British. He had then put them in touch with Sidney Reilly.

"Is that your writing?" asked Peters. Once more Lockhart politely insisted that he could answer no questions. Peters made no attempt to bully the prisoner. "It will be better for you if you speak the truth."

Lockhart said nothing. Obviously the Cheka was trying to link him to the attempt on Lenin. He had nothing to do with it, but the mention of Reilly's name and the pass did concern him. Perhaps the two Latvians were *agents-provocateurs*. Although Lockhart knew that Reilly wanted to stage a counterrevolution in Moscow, he himself had turned down the wild idea.

At 6 A.M. a woman was brought into his room. Her hair was black; her eyes, set in a fixed stare, had great dark shadows under them. He guessed that she was the would-be assassin, Kaplan, and the Cheka had put her in the room hoping she would recognize him. "Her composure was unnatural. She went to the window and, leaning her chin upon her hand, looked out into the daylight. And there she remained, motionless, speechless, apparently resigned to her fate, until presently the sentries came and took her away." Three hours later Peters told Lockhart he could leave. It was a rainy Sunday morning. He took a droshky home and found the flat in chaos. The servants had disappeared. Moura had been taken to the Cheka.

He was greatly agitated and with a sinking feeling sought out Robins' replacement at the Red Cross. This man promised to try to secure the release of Moura and the servants, and Chicherin, he said, had promised to see him the next day. "As I walked back to my flat," Lockhart recalled, "I was struck by the emptiness of the streets. Such people as went about their business did so with quick steps and furtive glances. The street corners were guarded by little groups of soldiers. A new fear was abroad. In forty-eight hours the whole atmosphere of the city had changed."

The next day a proclamation was issued by the Cheka, virtually converting Russia into an armed camp whose defense was entrusted to a Revolutionary Council of the Army headed by Trotsky. Cheka reprisals were spreading through Russia. Their weekly bulletin listed 105 executed in Moscow, nine in Archangel, twelve in Kimry, seventeen in Zebezh, fourteen in Vologda, nine in Kursh, thirty-one in Potchekhoni (including entire families), eight in Penza, three men who happened to be in jail for embezzlement in Chernij, eight in Valanoanovsk, eight in Novgorod, thirty-four in Smolensk, and so on and on.

The Moscow papers were full of the shameless, base "Lockhart Conspiracy," and much was made of his pass to the two Latvians, who were described as vicious counterrevolutionaries. An official statement was released boasting that the conspiracy was liquidated, and charged that it had been "led by Anglo-French diplomats, at the head of which was the Chief of the British Mission, Lockhart, the French consul, General Grenard, French General Lavergne and others."

American Consul Poole informed Washington of the wave of terror, recommending that the Allies and neutral nations jointly condemn "the present inhuman and purposeless slaughter" and threaten to deny all members of the Government future asylum unless the executions ceased. "The other and truly efficacious course is a rapid military advance from the north. Our present halfway action is cruel in the extreme. Our landing has set up the Bolshevik death agony. It is now our moral duty to shield the numberless innocents who are exposed to its hateful reprisals."

As he was sending off this advice, a decree was signed by Petrovsky, People's Commissar of the Interior, accelerating the Terror. It called for widespread arrests and mass shooting.

The measures even repelled some Bolsheviks, and it was whispered that if Lenin were not still recovering from his wounds he would have stopped this legalization of the Red Terror.

Once put into motion, it could not be controlled, and the peasants, whom Lenin truly loved, suffered. In some villages the Cheka imprisoned them in cold warehouses, stripped them, and beat them with gun butts to get confessions for crimes they knew nothing of. Local officials excused such brutality. "They told us at headquarters: better to oversalt than not to salt enough."

On the evening of September 3, the diplomatic corps in Petrograd met to discuss a united protest of the unprecedented actions taken against foreign subjects. Surprisingly the German and Austrian consuls general appeared and marched with them to the residence of Grigori Zinoviev, an old comrade of Lenin and currently chairman of the Council of People's Commissars of the Northern Commune. After a wait, Zinoviev reluctantly listened to the diplomats' protests and a demand that a neutral representative be present at the examination of any accused foreigner. Zinoviev said that he had to consult his colleagues and then was astounded by the German Consul General's protest "in the name of humanity against the terrorism now entered upon by Bolsheviks." He also vigorously condemned the "sanguinary" speech that Zinoviev had recently made, adding that even though the "French and English arrested belonged to nations at war with Germany yet it was impossible not to unite with neutral representatives in a strong protest against the course now adopted by Bolsheviks."

The next day international unity at Petrograd was dramatized by the state funeral of Captain Cromie. As the impressive procession, which included the German and Austrian officials, slowly crossed the bridge across the Neva, Red sailors loafing on the decks of destroyers rose in respect. In Moscow the indignant Poole was writing a personal letter to Chicherin. "It is impossible for me to believe that you approve of the mad career into which the Bolshevik Government has now plunged. Your cause totters on the verge of complete moral bankruptcy. There is only one possible means of redemption. Words and discussions will no longer avail. You must stop at once the barbarous oppression of your own people."

The Dutch Minister, Oudendijk, felt that such appeals were useless. He informed his superiors that the entire Soviet Government had sunk to the level of a criminal organization. He had warned Chicherin, he said, that the moment would soon come "when the Soviet authorities, man by man, would have to pay for all the acts of terrorism which they committed. But in spite of persistence with which I drove these facts home, I could not obtain any definite promises from Chicherin but only a few evasive replies and some lies. Bolsheviks have burnt their boats and are now ready for any wickedness."

Lockhart was still trying to free Moura. At the Foreign Ministry he found Karakhan in a friendly mood. He laughed good-humoredly at Lockhart's protest that the story in the Soviet press about the so-called Lockhart Conspiracy was a tissue of lies. "Now you know," he said, "what we have to put up with from your newspapers." But he was not hopeful about releasing Moura. In despair Lockhart decided to approach Peters, who had shown some sympathy. He walked to Loubianka Prison, formerly an insurance company's office, where his appearance caused a stir among the guards. After a long wait, Peters received him. Lockhart swore that the conspiracy story was a fake and, even if it were true, Moura knew nothing about it. He begged for her release.

Peters listened patiently and politely, promising that he would consider Lockhart's assurance of her innocence. "You have saved me some trouble," he said. "My men have been looking for you for the last hour. I have a warrant for your arrest. Your French and English colleagues are already under lock and key."

4.

Despite participation by Americans in the Archangel landings, Moscow still hoped that they would not play a major role, and Chicherin had explained the previous day to the Central Committee that Americans citizens were not being interned with those of the other Allies "because although the United States Government was compelled by its allies to agree to participation in intervention, so far only formally, its decision is not regarded by us as irrevocable."

No sooner had these words been broadcast to party members through *Pravda* than three British transports began landing 4,500 American troops at Archangel. Many of the men came from Detroit and Milwaukee with no idea why they had been issued skis and snowshoes. Were they going on some sort of vacation? Twenty-four hours later, on August 5, one combat battalion of Americans was packed into boxcars and sent off to Obozerskaya, seventy-five miles to the south, where British and French troops were battling the Soviets. Another battalion, along with a battalion of Royal Scots, was loaded on riverboats to sail up the Dvina a hundred miles and join a small British force. Together they would try and seize Bereznik for a winter camp.

Perhaps the Soviets had not yet heard of the landing of the Americans. When orders were issued on September 6 for the arrest of the Allied officials in Moscow, again no United States officials were included. The Cheka did not even force their way into the former American Consulate, where Allied officials happened to be meeting with Poole. Their agents merely waited on the street to seize the visiting officials as soon as they left. Poole rushed out, dragged his colleagues back through the gate, and ordered the Cheka not to enter. They obeyed but set up a guard, cut off water and electricity, and prepared for the siege. Fortunately the basement was filled with Red Cross supplies and had one faucet which, for some reason, still flowed. To fool the guards, the besieged officials would tote bathtubs into the courtyard whenever it stormed to catch rainwater.

While Lockhart was reading in his cell at Loubianka that afternoon, the Cheka's second-in-command, Peters, came to chat. They talked about England and the girl he had married there, the war, capitalism, and revolution. "He told me that he suffered physical pain every time he signed a death sentence. I believe it was true. There was a strong streak of sentimentality in his nature, but . . . he pursued his Bolshevik aims with a sense of duty which was relentless."

That day Chicherin finally felt the cold fury of British reaction to the killing of Captain Cromie. Balfour demanded immediate and severe punishment of those responsible.

> Should the Russian Soviet Government fail to give complete satisfaction or should any further acts of violence be committed against a British subject His Majesty's Government will hold the members of the Soviet Government individually responsible and will make every endeavour to secure that they shall be treated as outlaws by the governments of all civilized nations and that no place of refuge shall be left to them.

This was no mere threat. The British had recently decided, as a gesture of goodwill, to send home twenty-five Russians selected by Maxim Litvinov, the Soviet Plenipotentiary in London. Now they not only canceled this order but placed Litvinov and his staff in preventive arrest until all British representatives left Russia.

Chicherin retorted by issuing a statement the following day accusing the chief of the British Mission, Lockhart, of conspiracy and declaring that the British Embassy in Petrograd "was practically turned into conspirative headquarters of conspirators." Behind the blustering language was the offer to return all Allied prisoners, including Lockhart, once Russian citizens were allowed to leave England and France.

5.

Early in that month, General William S. Graves, at the Kansas City railway station, had been given a ten-minute briefing of a new assignment. Secretary of War Baker explained that Graves was to lead an American expedition to Siberia, then he handed over the President's *aide-mémoire* of July 17 in a sealed envelope. "This contains the policy of the United States in Russia which you are to follow," he said. ""Watch your step; you will be walking on eggs loaded with dynamite. God bless you and goodbye!" Graves was an intelligent officer but knew almost nothing about Russia. He set off with misgivings.

He arrived in Vladivostok on Labor Day with the first contingent of an eventual force of nine thousand men. Forty-eight hours earlier the Czech relief force from Vladivostok had joined with the main body of the Legion, which was fighting its way east, thus eliminating Graves's primary task of rescuing the embattled Czechs. Now his only legitimate object, according to Wilson's instructions, was to guard military stores which might subsequently be needed by Russian forces. But which Russian forces? The Bolsheviks or the Whites? "I could not give a Russian a shirt without being subjected to the charge of trying to help the side to which the recipient of the shirt belonged."

A few days later Major General Alfred Knox, head of the British Military Mission, arrived. He spoke Russian and, as military attaché, had followed the fate of the Czar's armies from the Battle of Tannenberg to the Red Revolution. He had seen so many Russian friends butchered that he detested the Bolshevik regime and from the beginning had urged Allied intervention. He vigorously favored backing the White forces of Admiral Aleksandr Kolchak, former commander of the Czar's Black Sea Fleet, against the Siberian Bolsheviks. Graves just as violently opposed setting up a reactionary regime in Siberia. How could he cooperate with his allies, who were so eager to fight the Bolsheviks, and still carry out the President's instructions? "I have often thought that it was unfortunate I did not know more of the conditions in Siberia than I did when I was pitch-forked into the melee in Vladivostok. At other times I have thought that ignorance was not only bliss in such a situation but was advisable." Despite British pressure and pleadings he refused to go beyond the limits of Wilson's *aide-mémoire*, following to the letter a neutral position. American military intervention would not come in the east unless Graves got definite orders from Washington.

On the other side of Russia, Ambassador Francis had returned to Archangel once the Bolsheviks were driven out. He had received the same vague instruction as Graves to guard military stores, but interpreted this as an invitation to intervention. "In default of instructions," he wrote Washington a few days before the attempt on Lenin's life, "I shall . . . encourage American troops . . . to proceed to such points in the interior as Kotlas, Sukhona, and Vologda, as at those places, as well as in Petrograd and Moscow, are stored war supplies which the Soviet Government, in violation of its promises and agreements, transferred from Archangel." In other words, he took Wilson's words to mean not only sending American troops into battle against the Reds several hundred miles along the Trans-Siberian Railroad, but mounting a drive on Moscow and Petrograd.

The reply to all this from Secretary of State Lansing started reassuringly and ended by confusing Francis. "Department approves your action fully. Determine your future course by careful compliance with policy communicated to you in Department's No. 253, September 9, 6 P.M." Practically a paraphrase of Wilson's *aide-mémoire*, this directive was even clearer about limiting the use of American troops, for it stated that the Government "had no reasonable expectation of being in a position to take part in organized intervention in adequate forces from either Vladivostok or Murmansk and Archangel." This clear-cut admonition drew the line against intervention. Yet Lansing's instructions to Francis continued with a sentence that could be taken to mean just the opposite.

"You appreciate of course that in military matters Colonel Stewart is under the command of General Poole." In other words, the American military commander in northern Russia was required to obey instructions of the British commander to intervene. It was not surprising that the bewildered Francis concluded that Lansing wanted him to keep supporting intervention as usual, no matter what was said for the record.

Sporadic action except on the Western Front. But in the Balkans, where the Allies had done little except suffer boredom and die of various diseases, combined British-French-Serbian-Greek armies were about to launch an offensive designed at knocking the Bulgarians out of the war. Allenby's forces were also poised for their all-out attack in Palestine.

Chapter Thirteen

"AND WE WON'T BE BACK TILL IT'S OVER OVER THERE" AUGUST 27–OCTOBER 5

1.

ON August 27 Haig sent Foch a letter urging him to put the 1,400,000 Americans now in France into the battle "*at once* in order to enable an important advance to be made without delay." He also wrote Pershing, who had just thanked him for turning over so promptly five American divisions which had been training with the British. Haig had bitterly opposed losing soldiers who could have been so useful in his present drive, and noted somewhat caustically that he hoped events would justify Pershing's decision to withdraw over 150,000 men at the height of the battle. "For the present," he wrote in his diary, "I am convinced that if they had taken part in this battle, they would, owing to the present tired and demoralised state of the Germans on this front, have enabled the Allies to obtain immediate and decisive results." Pershing, of course, was anxious to launch his own attack against the St. Mihiel salient—the first true test of American leadership.

Two days later Haig saw Foch, who had been pressing him to attack a position the British commander felt could only be taken with heavy casualties in men and tanks. "I am responsible to my Government and fellow citizens for the handling of the British forces," Haig had declared so categorically that Foch wisely backed down; and by the time they met on August 29 they were on better personal terms. But there was still tension between the two men and Haig noted in his diary, with a slight shade of satisfaction, that the French attack on his left was not progressing well. "Very few French Divisions are said to be in good heart now, but most are 'war weary.'"

Haig's problem with his allies was soon aggravated by one with his own superiors. On September 1, the day after the attempt on Lenin's life, he received a personal telegram from General Wilson cautioning him to avoid "heavy losses" in the coming attacks on the Hindenburg Line lest the War Cabinet become anxious.

General Davidson had brought in the message, half-expecting some sign of disgust. Haig merely laid aside the dispatch, raised his eyes, and calmly asked what the devil Davidson was waiting for. Inwardly the field marshal was boiling. How could Wilson, as Chief of Staff, possibly send a telegram like this to a commander-in-chief in the field as a *personal* one? The Cabinet were ready to meddle and interfere in an underhanded way, but dared not say openly that they would take no responsibility for any failure, only credit for every success! "The object of this telegram is, no doubt, to save the Prime Minister [Lloyd George] in case of any failure." If his attack on the Hindenburg Line were successful, Haig would remain as commander-in-chief. "If I fail, or our losses are excessive, I can hope for no mercy! . . . What a wretched lot of weaklings we have in high places at the present time."

Despite all the wrangling, Haig's troops were still attacking and the Germans were slowly falling back toward the Hindenburg Line. During the day the Australians captured Mont St. Quentin, thus turning the enemy line along the Somme. After dark the Anzacs moved most of their field and heavy artillery over the river while an entire division crossed by the causeway south of Péronne to support their 14th Brigade, which was in the town. While the Australian artillery was getting into position for a morning barrage, further north, east of Arras, the British First Army and the Canadians were preparing an assault on the Drocourt-Quéant position, a northern extension of the Hindenburg Line. Private Howard Cooper's unit had been trucked down to this area in London buses. He was now a runner. Even at 2:30 A.M. no one knew definitely when the attack would begin. No guns were firing except some big German howitzer which, about every four minutes, sent a shell into the nearby village of Eterpigny. "Now there was a great silence over everything, a horrible silence, men's dark forms showing up in the moonlight, men in suppressed excitement gathered nearby dishing out rum . . . All spoke in hushed hurried voices, like those a sick man hears outside his bedroom in the night. Men came here quickly, took several boxes of bombs, and disappeared into the night. Then as though objecting to the hush the great on-coming roar of this howitzer shell followed by a tremendous explosion in Eterpigny, echoing and re-echoing with a hollow sound."

By 4 A.M. everyone had disappeared to take up positions in the line. All was ready by the time word finally came that the barrage would commence just before dawn on the stroke of 5 A.M., September 2. The men would go over ten minutes later behind the creeping curtain of fire.

At quarter to five everything was still and Cooper comforted himself by thinking he would be safe in the runners' dugout. Then the adjutant told him to take some men to a trench mortar section. He glanced at his watch. Five to five. A thrill went through him. If he wasted a second he would be out in the open just as the British barrage started. He winced at the realization that a German counterbarrage would surely reply. Some friendly shells might also fall short. Cooper led the newcomers. Their officer seemed frightfully excited. "How far is it?" he asked nervously. "The bloody barrage will open in a minute." Seeing crouching forms in mackintosh capes at the post, he exclaimed in a whisper, "They're Boche!" and drew his revolver. "No," said Cooper. "Ours."

A gun fired from behind. The signal! "At that moment the intense barrage awoke, a thing of dreadful clamour and violent lightning. The sky was filled with a blaze of shimmering blue flashes behind us—north to south, hundreds of shells screamed and roared over my head." Explosions broke as one roar as Cooper started to run. Towers of smoke hung in the air, shrapnel shells flashed like stars and from over the ridge enemy rockets shot up summoning German reserves and artillery support. "I was deafened and lost as I ran on towards the dugout in the open. Crash! Earth flew over me, our own shells! Hell had broken, our guns thundered more relentlessly. 'I cannot stop it—it won't stop,' my brain rang. Shrieks and rushes of shells, deafening explosions, the glaring showers of uncanny lights. The thunder was deafening. Still the sky was aglare with the flashing of hundreds of guns; the crackling of machine guns was incessant; streams of bullets were swishing overhead. I ducked, fell flat, got up again as shells burst only yards from me. At last I reached the dugout, how I don't know. From inside I heard the frightful boiling and thundering barrage. German guns were answering, soon big shells crashed outside the dugout entrance, blasts of hot air coming on our faces."

Dawn was just breaking and he could see the officer he had just led to the post come slowly toward him. One eye was out. An arm wounded. Suddenly some two hundred captured Germans came over the ridge escorted by a few Tommies. More shells crashed down and Cooper heard his colonel shout, "Runner!" then order two men to take a message to A Company. Cooper and Burbidge set out just after another shell landed outside. They dove over the bank. Sloping bare ground lay ahead. Planes screeched overhead toward the Germans. Shells boomed and burst all over the plain ahead where four great tanks lumbered forward. A bullet pinged past. Sniper. They leaped into a shell hole and found four Tommies in firing position on their stomachs—all dead in a row.

"Let's get out," said Burbidge. They scrambled out, flopping down as a machine-gun burst swept overhead.

"Keep away from the tanks!" Cooper shouted as he saw the

black bursts of shells creep closer to them. "Our poor dead men lay every few yards in horrible positions, their white faces staring glassily to the sky. We passed the German posts; in one two Germans lay on the edge, as though they had been trying to escape; one had the whole of his chest out, the other his head off. Later I passed just the naked back of a man—no other limb—and even now it was steaming."

They finally found A Company and were sent on to D Company. "As we passed the dead lying about on this desolate plain I thought of their poor mothers who would have the news soon. At a gap in the great barbed wire-entanglements six men lay in a line dead, all caught by a machine gun I should think." The huddled gray forms of Germans also bespattered the ground. The two runners picked up a badly wounded comrade in a shell hole and helped him back. The man's trousers were soaked with his own blood.

It was now about 11 A.M. with the two main lines of the Drocourt-Quéant position overrun, but Cooper heard the colonel remark that the limit of the planned advance had not been reached and they must keep on the attack. He and Burbidge were sent out to C Company and again were bedeviled by a sniper. Just as they thought they had escaped, they heard the boom of a gun, a swish, then the crash of a small shell as it landed just behind them. "The sniper could not down us so they were trying a 'whiz-bang' gun." Again they heard a shriek that seemed to skim over their heads, and almost simultaneously the crash of a shell several yards past their prostrate bodies. Burbidge shouted, "They're going to get us."

Cooper could only silently repeat a prayer to be kept safe. Again and again the "whiz-bang" shells burst in front of them. As the two runners zigzagged, the constant shelling unnerved and tired them. Finally they reached B Company's trench, where several German bodies sprawled. It was the first main trench of their second line. No one knew where C Company was. Burbidge was too tired to go on, so Cooper kept moving out front by himself. He came to a blown-up light railway track that looked like the skeleton of some prehistoric animal. Beyond was an empty Jerry trench. Were they still holding it? Hurriedly he got rid of German buttons, badges, coins, and other souvenirs in case he was captured. He followed the trench but found no one. Coming to a roadway which blocked the trench, he jumped out and rushed across the road. A machine gun spat furiously but he leaped safely into a continuation of the trench. "I had been luckier than others, for here lay a veritable 'pile' of dead khaki figures, just on top of each other as they had fallen in, after being caught by the gun. There must have been eight or nine, long ways, upside down; their deathly faces and hands sticking out in various directions; small drying scarlet rivers of blood showed the bullet had done its work. I paused to look at them a minute and realized I might have now been with them. Even their very legs looked dead. I cannot explain but a dead man's very limbs somehow look like models dressed in clothes. On the soles of their boots was the mud and chalk on which they had so recently trodden. Their wide open eyes seemed to stare into 'the beyond.' The hands, so white, were soiled with the work which I could hardly imagine they had done even an hour or so ago."

At least he knew he was not in a German-occupied trench and, after hurrying a minute, came to Company C. Just outside a dugout lay five dead Boche, some only half out of the entrance. One young boy was still grasping a black and white kitten. It looked up at Cooper. "A man standing there said that when they took the trench they called down the dugout for the Germans to come up and waited for them with bayonets at the top. This un-British cold-blooded act turned me. They said the captain had told them, 'Stick all the bastards.' At the bottom of the next dugout I found the captain in a crude bunk and he seemed half drunk."

The crucial Drocourt-Quéant position was at last broken. And this meant that the Hindenburg Line to its south was seriously compromised. This, along with the Australians' conquest of Mont St. Quentin, further south, meant that the Germans would have to make a general withdrawal. The whole great salient won by Ludendorff in March would have to be abandoned. Upon learning that many Germans were surrendering without putting up a fight and many others would not obey their officers, Haig wrote in his diary: "If this is true, then the end cannot be far off, I think. Today's battle has truly been a great and glorious success."

2.

The German Supreme Command was already preparing the nation for the worst, and that day of September 2 a manifesto from Hindenburg was being relayed to the people by newspapers and placards posted in every city and village. "We are engaged in a severe battle with our enemies," it began. "If numerical superiority alone were to guarantee victory then Germany would long since have lain crushed to the ground. The enemy knows however, that Germany and her allies are not to be vanquished by arms alone." Therefore, the enemy was trying to break the will of the civilians. "He wants to poison our spirit, and believes that the German arms will be blunted if the German spirit is corroded." Hindenburg told of the pamphlets that Allied planes were showering onto the troops along with bombs. Hundreds of thousands of these "poisoned arrows" were telling lies about the course of the battle. Many of these enemy pamphlets were making their way into the homeland itself and were being passed from hand to hand. "It is discussed at the beer table, in families, in workrooms, in factories, and in the streets." The enemy was also attacking the home spirit with the most insane rumors sent out from Switzerland, Holland, and Denmark. These were spreading in waves through the land. "This poison takes effect on men on leave and flies in letters to the front, and again our enemies rub their hands. . . . Therefore, German Army and German Home, if one of these poisoned morsels in the form of leaflet or rumor comes to your ears or eyes, remember it comes from the enemy and that nothing coming from the enemy is of any service to Germany . . . Be on your guard, German Army and German Home."

The news of the British breach of the Drocourt line that day could not be kept from Schloss Wilhelmshöhe. That evening the Kaiser slammed his fist on the table. "Now we have lost the war!" he exclaimed. "Poor Fatherland!" He rushed into the dining room to tell his guests that he had serious, shattering news. "The Seventeenth Army has suffered a heavy defeat and is being harassed on both flanks. The salient has had to be smoothed out. The political effect of such a defeat and the loss of so much ground is disastrous." Distraught, he began carping at his generals over past defeats. "I don't know what they are doing at Avesnes! When the offensive on the Marne began on July 15th I was assured that the French had no more than 8 divisions in reserve and the English perhaps 13. Instead the enemy assembled a number of divisions unobserved by us in the Villers-Cotterêts forest, attacked and forced us to retire after piercing our right flank. Since then we have suffered defeat after defeat. Our army is at the end of its tether. The senior officers have all gone." He was almost hysterical. "It means nothing more or less than that we have lost the war!"

The company was stunned. There was a deathly silence. A few tried to console him. Admiral von Müller, believing little of what he had heard, mentioned that they had been in far worse positions. For example in the autumn of '14 they had no ammunition and the Dardanelles was about to fall at any minute. But His Majesty sat down glumly. He tried to eat but could swallow scarcely a mouthful and, what was even more unusual, could utter hardly a word. The next morning he stayed in bed.

Although the people did not yet know the extent of the defeats on the Western Front, rumors were circulating of widespread collapse. To counteract public distrust, Crown Prince Wilhelm issued a statement to the press on September 4. "The war is one of annihilation only for the enemy, not for us. We want to annihilate none of our enemies. We mean, however, to hold our own. . . . The word victory must not be understood to mean that we want to annihilate the enemy, but only that we mean to hold our own and not let ourselves be vanquished."

At Schloss Wilhelmshöhe, the Kaiser was suffering a nervous collapse and fears were voiced that he might decide to abdicate. Although the Empress Augusta Victoria had scarcely recovered from her own breakdown, she rushed to his bedside and succeeded in reviving his strength and confidence. On the morning of September 6, His Majesty was well enough to go out for a walk with Admiral von Müller, just returned from Berlin. "I have had a slight nervous breakdown as the result of the Empress's illness and the news from the Western Front," he said. "But I retired to bed, slept for 24 hours and am a new man once more."

Three days later he felt well enough to visit the Krupp Works in

Essen and address 1,500 steel workers. His adjutant, Captain Sigurd von Ilsemann, handed him a speech, but he ignored it and began to talk extemporaneously. His first mistake was wearing a field-gray uniform, the symbol of all that the workers detested; his second was to address them as "My Dear Friends." On their glum faces was the question: "Since when?" For the next thirty minutes he spoke so excitedly that his brow became wet with perspiration. Ilsemann squirmed. "How much better it would have been if he had not said some of the things he did." He talked of the suffering and starvation of the people, but it was obvious that he knew nothing of such suffering and when he said, "To every single one of us his task is given—to you your hammer, to you at your lathe, to me upon my throne!" the adjutant noticed sarcastic smiles. The Kaiser went on and on about the courage of the men at the front, the noble cause of Germany, the Bible, and even tried to squeeze some sympathy by mentioning the grave illness of "my dearly loved wife and mother of you, her people."

The workers' scorn became embarrassingly obvious when he chided those who doubted the outcome of the war. "Doubt is the greatest ingratitude toward the Lord. And now I ask you all quite simply and honestly—have we then really ground for doubt? Just look at the four years' war. What immense achievements we have behind us!" He called upon them to be as hard as steel, then passionately asked all of those present determined to fight to the last to shout out "Yes!" According to the printed speech the assembly answered with "a loud 'Yes!'" but those present heard only a few "Ayes," a number of furtive laughs, and a general embarrassing silence.

3.

Haig was so convinced that victory was within grasp that he wrote General Wilson on the seventh that he wanted to come to London in a few days "to explain the sudden change in the military situation in our favour as this must alter the arrangements for providing men and material for the future." He was franker in a note to his wife: "Too many men are being sent to Air Service, Tanks and such fancy jobs, and not enough to Infantry who can win the war!"

The next day Churchill, who delighted in spending as much time as possible at the front, arrived at Haig's headquarters during a rainstorm. The field marshal told him bluntly that the Allies should aim at getting a decision as soon as possible. "This month or next, not next spring or summer as the Cabinet proposed." Predictably Minister of Munitions Churchill agreed and in his enthusiasm suggested that they set men free from his own munitions factories. Later in the day after a meeting with Foch, Haig motored to Calais, where he boarded the destroyer *Douglas*. In fifty minutes, despite heavy weather, the ship crossed to Folkestone.

But it was not until Tuesday morning, September 10, that he had his important talk at the War Office with Lord Milner. His presentation was vigorous and impassioned. The Cabinet must reconsider all their plans and methods after the astounding victories of the past four weeks. 77,000 prisoners and nearly 800 guns captured! There had never been such a victory in the annals of Britain. He assured Milner that the discipline of the German Army was fast deteriorating. "It seems to me to be the beginning of the end." The character of the war had changed and what he needed now were the means to exploit their successes to the full. All reserves in England should be rushed to France at once. "If we act with energy now, a decision can be obtained *in the very near future.*" Fully agreeing, Milner promised to do his best.

General Pershing was still preparing his offensive at the other end of the long, twisting front line. Since 1914 the St. Mihiel salient, some twenty-five miles south of Verdun, had been a blunt-headed spearhead pointing toward Paris. It remained an affront to French military prestige as well as a hindrance to all communications in that area; and that July, Foch had suggested that the Americans try to eliminate it. From the beginning Haig objected to wasting so much energy in that area. Victory, he argued, would come from a series of converging attacks launched from Flanders to the river Meuse. But Pershing was as stubborn as Haig and insisted that his troops operate independently. The field marshal was overridden.

On August 30, Pershing assumed command of the entire St. Mihiel sector and met with Foch, who presented a master plan for operations all along the front. *"Tout le monde à la bataille!"* he exclaimed. Everybody fights! The Germans were in disorder on the British front and weak in the Aisne area. They were on the run and the Allies must exploit their successes: the French at Mesnil and the British in Cambrai and St. Quentin. Gesturing dramatically, he spoke of the wonderful prospects if these drives went well, then to Pershing's consternation proposed limiting drastically the St. Mihiel attack. Pershing should hit only the southern face, pinch it quickly, then switch some of his divisions to the French Second Army between the Meuse and the Argonne. At the same time an American army could form between the French Second and Fourth Armies for a combined assault through the Argonne.

Pershing could not hide his distress and Foch quickly said, "I realize that I am presenting a number of new ideas and that you will probably need time to think them over, but I should like your first impressions."

"Well, Marshal, this is a very sudden change. We are going forward as already recommended to you and approved by you, and I cannot understand why you want these changes." All that he had been fighting for—an American army operating independently—was at stake. Foch argued that the fate of the 1918 campaign would be decided in the Aisne region. Pershing bristled. "But, Marshal Foch, here on the very day that you turn over a sector to the American army, and almost on the eve of an offensive, you ask me to reduce the operation so that you can take away several of my divisions and assign them to the French Second Army and use others to form an American army to operate in the Aisne in conjunction with the French Fourth Army, leaving me little to do except hold what will become a quiet sector after the St. Mihiel offensive. This virtually destroys the American army that we have been trying so long to form."

Responding sympathetically, Foch said that he would agree to anything as long as the new operations were executed. He sincerely wished there were some way to keep the Americans together. Did Pershing have a better solution? Neither man could reach the other. To Foch the American seemed blind to reason; after all he was in supreme command and was insisting on a concentric attack for the good of the cause. Pershing simply had to agree. On his part, Pershing was furious at the idea of splitting his forces. Why, he asked, couldn't the Americans simply replace the French Second Army? "I don't want to appear difficult," he said, controlling himself, "but the American people and the American Government expect that the American army shall act as such and shall not be dispersed here and there along the Western Front." Outwardly courteous, he boiled inside. Every time he had pointed this out, some proposition had been put forward to prevent it.

Foch became livid. *"Voulez-vous aller à la bataille?"* he asked sarcastically. It was an insult to ask another general if he wished to take part in a battle, and the French translator was embarrassed to put it into English.

"Most assuredly," said Pershing, who had understood it in French, "but as an American army and in no other way."

"That means it will take a month!"

"If you will assign me a sector I will take it at once," was the polite but firm answer. And, after Foch asked a bit testily *what* sector, Pershing quickly replied, "Whatever you say."

At Foch's protest that the Americans lacked artillery and auxiliary troops, Pershing reminded him that the French had insisted on the United States only shipping over infantry and machine-gun units with the promise that auxiliary troops would be supplied by their allies. The American insisted that these promises be kept.

"It is now August 30th," protested Foch, "and the attack must begin on September 15th; it is a question of time." Again he pressed for shifting American units into the French Second Army. Again Pershing resisted and, when Foch persisted, lost his temper. "Marshal Foch," he said, "you have no authority as Allied Commander-in-Chief to call upon me to yield up my command of the American Army and have it scattered among the Allied forces where it will not be an American army at all."

Taken aback to see the usually controlled Pershing speak so sharply, Foch rose from the table and said angrily, "I must insist upon the arrangement."

Pershing also stood up. "Marshal Foch, you may insist all you please, but I decline absolutely to agree to your plan. While our

317

army will fight wherever you may decide, it will not fight except as an independent American army." Foch knew as well as he how the critics back in the United States had been carping about the parceling out of American troops here and there. And, added Pershing. President Wilson's message to the embassies in Washington stated specifically that the American Army should fight as a unit.

As he picked up his maps and papers, Foch muttered that he would do what he could for an American army. Pale and exhausted, he started to leave, then turned and handed Pershing a memorandum of his earlier proposal. Study it carefully, he urged. If so, Pershing would surely agree with it. The American promised to reply quickly, and the next day he sent a long, courteous rejection of the Foch plan. That same afternoon he sought out Pétain at his headquarters train. The two field commanders were beginning to like each other and the Frenchman sympathized with Pershing's predicament. He admitted that Foch had no right to interfere in tactical arrangements by an army commander. It was Foch's job to order the strategy, theirs to carry it out. He suggested that Pershing take over the front from the Moselle to the Argonne, leaving the French Second Army in place but under Pershing's command for logistical and staff help. Later an American Second Army could drive west toward the Argonne and a Third toward Reims. Foch should be made to understand that the American divisions would fight only under their own commanders.

The three met on September 2 at Bombon. This time there was harmony, for Foch had become resigned to American rigidity. Did Pershing mean to cancel the St. Mihiel operation? he asked. No. Pershing was confident that he would wipe out the salient and move his main force without much delay to the Argonne and be ready to attack there on September 25.

After thanking Pershing for his "splendid expression of good will," Foch expressed the hope that the Americans could hit the St. Mihiel salient on September 10. Then there would be time for both complicated operations.

This gave Pershing only eight days to launch the first and he faced, in his own words, "a gigantic task." After St. Mihiel he would have to extract some 300,000 men and shift them to the Meuse-Argonne sector along with another 300,000 men and 2,700 guns. "In other words, we had undertaken to launch with practically the same army, within the next twenty-four days, two great attacks on battlefields sixty miles apart."

4.

It was impossible for the American commander to begin on September 10, so H Hour was set at 5 A.M. on the twelfth. After dinner on the eve of the battle, twenty-five American correspondents were ushered into a room of the Hôtel Angleterre in Paris. They sat on beds, on a table, on the windowsill to hear General Dennis Nolan describe the St. Mihiel operation. He warned the newsmen that this was only a limited push but it was an all-American show.

Secretary of War Baker had arrived for the occasion and would watch the rolling barrage from old Fort Gironville. It might even be possible for correspondents to see some of it from the roof of the Angleterre. The newsmen, still a little dazed to have been taken so fully into the army's confidence, left at midnight.

At the front the artillery was in place and doughboys and a regiment of Marines were marching in the pitch dark through drenching rain. Before midnight most of the infantrymen reached the jump-off trenches, which had been abandoned for a year and were in bad condition due to lack of care and to shells and rain. The men sloshed through the mud and, even though the Americans put up flares, it was raining so hard the Germans never saw them.

At 1 A.M. the rain turned into a savage storm. Almost at the same moment the preparatory artillery barrage of almost 2,800 guns began. The Germans were caught by surprise although they had been expecting a major attack for days and intended evacuating the salient once it came. Two divisions, in fact, were already in the process of moving to the rear.

Wherever George Tomek, of the 33rd Division Field Artillery, looked, all he could see were lurid flashes. "It was indeed a spectacle to behold!" he wrote his parents. "And some miles in back of our lines were stationed the big French railroad guns of tremendous caliber and when each of them fired at about 10 minute intervals and although they were miles behind us, we could plainly hear and see the thunderous booming and the lightning-like flashes of these monstrous guns which alone lit up the entire sky."

Lieutenant Colonel George Patton, commander of 144 American and 33 French tanks, was watching from a hill in front of the main line. "When the shelling first started I had some doubts about the advisability of sticking my head over the parapet, but it is just like taking a cold bath, once you get in it is all right. And I soon got out and sat on the parapet."

Sergeant William L. Langer, of the 1st Gas Regiment, had been carrying heavy loads of ammunition up front for hours and didn't return to his dugout in town until 4 A.M. Just as Langer, a young instructor of modern languages in a New England boarding school, was about to start back to the trenches, the Germans began to bombard the town. For a moment he and his mates were undecided, then set out on the run, reaching the trenches without mishap. The first wave was about to go over the top and friendly machine guns had just opened a rolling barrage to precede it. "For green men it was a novel experience—the stuttering breathless chatter of the machine guns behind one. The trenches were in places so congested that to get through would have been impossible had we not struck on a rather clever idea. 'Heads up, men, high explosives, watch these sacks'—shouting words to that effect worked like magic and we secured an easy passage." He watched the infantry go over, following each other through the fields of barbed wire, over the enemy trenches and toward woods where the Germans had artillery.

Pershing was at a high outlook on Fort Gironville, but the rain and mist prevented a clear view. He could follow the progress, of the troops only by the barrage that preceded them. There was a chill breeze blowing and he couldn't hear the artillery in his immediate front, although the more distant artillery bombardment on the western face was distinct. The sky over the battlefield, aflame with exploding shells, star signals, burning supply dumps and villages, was a scene picturesque but terrible. "The exultation in our minds that here, at last, after seventeen months of effort, an American army was fighting under its own flag was tempered by the realization of the sacrifice of life on both sides, and yet fate willed it thus and we must carry through."

From the top of the Hôtel Angleterre in Paris, Fred Ferguson was watching with other correspondents. They could see flashes on the northwest horizon and hear the low growl and grumble of guns. Most of them wanted to hurry up front and get the story firsthand.

As dawn broke, Douglas MacArthur, now a brigadier general, led his infantry brigade of the Rainbow Division forward. They were followed by a squadron of tanks which soon bogged down in the mud. From his vantage point Colonel George Patton could see his tanks getting stuck in the trenches. "It was a most irritating sight." He started forward on foot, passing dead and wounded. "I saw one fellow in a shell hole holding his rifle and sitting down. I thought he was hiding and went to cuss him out, he had a bullet over his right eye and was dead."

The Marines followed the 23rd Infantry. It was a sight that Major Denig would never forget. Shells were bursting in front, phosphorus fire blazing on all sides, the edge of the wood they would have to cross was on fire. The ruins of a village ahead reminded him of decayed teeth. He was hit in the left hand by a piece of shell which cut his cigar in two just as he was taking it from his mouth. His adjutant, Willard Smith, found the lighted half and returned it to Denig with a great flourish. Moments later they got their first prisoners: five gray figures, resembling big rats in their gas masks, emerged from a shelter in the village. The Marines kept moving, and before long Denig's adjutant, walking ten feet ahead, was killed. Denig jumped to his side, yelling, "Willard!" but saw his brains pouring out. Denig covered the adjutant's face and led his men into the wood.

To those Marines who like Captain David Bellamy had fought at Belleau Wood and Soissons it was "a walk away," with slight casualties and very little opposition. Up ahead the Rainbow Division and other doughboy units were advancing without pause. "As far as the eye could reach," recalled Major Walter Wolf, "west and east, the waves of assault rolled steadily forward with a power and irresistibleness that made this scene more resemble an especially staged spectacle than an important operation. It was just like a picture."

By 7:45 A.M. Major Denig's men had cleared the Bois de Four, reorganized, and set out across an open field, a hundred yards behind their own shellfire. Machine-gunners holding them up were wiped out. The Marines found huge shell holes every hundred feet. Suddenly a gray hunter dashed across the open field and Denig sent his orderly to catch the horse. Others had the same idea, but the orderly, claiming him on the grounds of seniority, brought him back proudly. The hunter turned out to be a gold mine. He carried two good blankets, a raincoat, butter, a box of cigars, a dozen compasses, cigarettes, sugar, a porcelain pipe, and other gear.

American airmen were ready to take off at dawn, but the weather was almost impossible with solid clouds and mist at less than a hundred feet. Even so, a dozen planes in Harold Buckley's squadron went out, patrolling as low as fifty feet. "No enemy aircraft were encountered but we had an exciting day flying just over the heads of Germans, shooting into trenches, at retreating columns on the roads, troop trains, and whatever targets we could find."

At 9 A.M. Pershing, back at his headquarters, began getting reports. All along the twenty-five-mile battle line "everything was going well, with losses light." War Secretary Baker, returning from his observation point, was elated at the success of the Americans. It was a proud day for him to realize that his directing hand had led to such results.

George Patton was still looking for his tanks. "We passed through several towns under shell fire but none did more than throw dust at us. I admit that I wanted to duck and probably did at first but soon saw the futility of dodging fate, besides I was the only officer around who had left on his shoulder straps and I had to live up to them. It was much easier than you would think and the feeling, foolish probably, of being admired by the men lying down is a great stimulus." They came to St. Baussant, where he found one of his French units stuck in a pass under shellfire. He talked to their major, who was working on a disabled tank, and went on. Before he had gone twenty feet a large shell struck the French tank killing fifteen men. Patton continued toward Essey, in front of which infantrymen were pinned down. But he strolled on ahead puffing his pipe as shells flew by. Everyone was huddled in shell holes except one man standing on a rise. It was his old friend, Douglas MacArthur. "I joined him and the creeping barrage came along toward us, but it was very thin and not dangerous. I think each one wanted to leave but hated to say so, so we let it come over us." They stood and talked, but neither was interested in what the other said "as we could not get our minds off the shells."

As Patton continued on to Essey, five of his tanks came up from behind. He told their commander to cross the bridge ahead and enter the town. "Some damned Frenchman at the bridge told them to go back as there were too many shells in the town. The Lt

AMERICAN FIRST ARMY OFFENSIVE
AT ST. MIHIEL SEPT. 12-16

Front Line Sept.12
Front Line Sept.16

METZ

MOSELLE

Pont-à-
Mousson

U.S. 82ND
DIV.

U.S. 90TH
DIV.

U.S. 5TH
DIV.

Thiaucourt

U.S. 2ND
DIV.

U.S. 89TH
DIV.

Jaulny

Pannes

Essey

U.S. I CORPS
LIGGETT

U.S. 42ND
DIV.

St. Benoit

U.S. 1ST
DIV.

St.
Baussant

FR. 39TH
DIV.

Vigneulles-
lès-Hattonchâtel

Woël

MEUSE

FR. 2ND
DIV.

FR. 26TH
DIV.

Apremont

St. Mihiel

U.S. IV CORPS
DICKMAN

Hattonville

FRESNES

U.S. 4TH
DIV.

U.S. V CORPS
CAMERON

VERDUN

MEUSE

N

Palacios

MILES
0   10
KM
0   10   20   30

322

in command obeyed. This made me mad so I led them through on foot . . ." Both he and MacArthur crossed the bridge even though it was supposed to be mined. In the town some Germans came out of their dugouts to surrender personally to MacArthur. Others were surrendering to Patton, who then asked his friend if he could attack the next town, Pannes. The answer was affirmative.

The road to Pannes was so strewn with dead men and horses that Patton could not induce infantrymen to enter the town. The sergeant commanding the only tank nearby was also reluctant. "He was nearvous [sic] at being alone so I said I will sit on the roof." Patton climbed on top of the tank. "This reassured him and we entered the town."

At 11 A.M. General Hunter Liggett, commander of I Corps, got a message by carrier pigeon that his divisions had already reached their final objective of the day. A little later they were at their second day's objective. Apparently the dazed enemy was offering little resistance, since his men were close to the base of the salient and approaching the last German defense position, the Michel Line.

At noon the German commander, Lieutenant General Fuchs, ordered the complete evacuation of the St. Mihiel salient. He did this not only to save the remaining German troops from capture but because the American 2nd Division was already dangerously close to a weak point in the Michel Line, and Fuchs feared "there was danger of a break-through."

After directing the seizure of Pannes, Patton walked along the battlefront to see how Major Brett, commander of the left battalion, was doing. Having lost his sack containing food and brandy, Patton took crackers from a dead German and pressed on until he found Brett. He was crying because he had no more gas. "He was very tired and had a bullet through his nose. I comforted him and started home alone to get some gas." Tired and thirsty as he was, Patton was entranced by the trip back over the battlefield. "Like the books but much less dramatic. The dead were about mostly hit in the head. There were a lot of our men stripping off buttons and other things but they always covered the face of the dead in a nice way." Then he saw something he would have liked to photograph. "Right in the middle of a large field where there had never been a trench was a shell hole from a 9.7 gun. The hole was at least 8 feet deep and 15 across. On the edge of it was a dead rat, not a large healthy rat but a small field rat not over twice the size of a mouse. No wonder the war costs so much."

That afternoon Pershing, upon learning that the roads leading out of the salient were filled with retreating enemy troops and artillery, seized a field telephone and urged the commanders of the IV and V Corps to move forward faster. By dusk the salient was all but wiped out. For four years it had been a great thorn in the flank of France. At last it had been removed—and in a single day. "I have experienced a good many things in the five years of war and have not been poor in successes," recalled General von Gallwitz, "but I must count the 12th of September among my few black days."

A colleague told Admiral von Müller that, upon being informed of the American-French breakthrough at St. Mihiel, Ludendorff was stunned. This rout, coming on the heels of the August debacle, had transformed him into "a completely broken man."

Friday the thirteenth was another lucky day for the Americans, and by noon the bulk of the defenders had already fled. The victory was a fitting birthday present for Pershing.

By dusk of the next day the main action was over. The Americans had taken 16,000 prisoners, 443 guns, and great stocks of material. More important, they had given notice to the Germans that they were at last ready to fight as an army—fresh, spirited, and in overwhelming numbers. Even their inexperienced style of combat was unsettling. They would rush in where wiser troops feared to tread, willing to take heavy losses to gain an objective. American airmen were fighting with the same daring. Eddie Rickenbacker, commander of the Hat-in-the-Ring Squadron and now a captain, shot down one of the Richthofen Circus, commanded by Hermann Göring; and Frank Luke, having learned the knack of exploding enemy balloons, had destroyed three in three days. Billy Mitchell's bombers were also wreaking havoc behind enemy lines.

The first task of the American Army was completed, and Pershing now had the task of disengaging front-line troops and swinging them, along with new units, to the east across the Meuse, then northward for the main operation in the Argonne. The problem was to get the mass of men and supplies into position in eleven days.

5.

The coordinated attacks on the Western Front were at last joined by operations in Macedonia and the Middle East. On September 15 the British-French-Serbian-Greek forces on the dreary Salonika front in northeastern Greece launched their assault on the Bulgarians. It easily smashed through their lines, for the German troops strengthening them had been withdrawn to the west. Left to their own resources, the Bulgarians put up little resistance since they were already convinced that Germany's cause was doomed. Within four days they were in full flight.

Disaster also faced the Germans in Palestine on September 15. Early that morning Allenby opened his assault on the Turks commanded by Liman von Sanders. A thousand shells a minute shattered the Turkish positions and the infantry assault by French and British troops smashed through the defenders' first lines. Surprised and dazed, the Turks put up little fight; many prisoners were taken. By noon remnants of Sanders' forces were retreating in confusion as the R.A.F. bombed and machine-gunned the jammed roads. The next dawn the 13th Cavalry Brigade, under Brigadier P. J. V. Kelly, an Arabic scholar, climbed up to Nazareth to catch

Sanders' headquarters completely by surprise. His staff and clerks fought courageously in the streets, allowing the general to escape. In the meantime the 4th Cavalry Division and the Australian Mounted Division cut off the Turkish retreat except for one road over the Jordan. They might have escaped as well, except for British airmen who espied the long column. There followed four gory hours of bombing and strafing which reduced the Seventh and Eighth Turkish Armies to scattered fugitives who were rounded up like cattle. There now remained only the Fourth Army, east of the Jordan; and there was little likelihood that these troops would last very long.

Deep depression was settling over Germany. On the morning of September 19 someone asked the Kaiser if he had slept well. "Very badly," he replied. "I haven't had a wink of sleep since I left Wilhelmshöhe. I'm gradually cracking up." And when someone else asked what news there was from the front, he said, "The troops continue to retreat. I have lost all confidence in them."

By now there was a "chancellor crisis" in Germany. It became so acute the next day that the Government unofficially sounded out the Majority Socialists on their willingness to join a coalition. The matter was discussed two days later at a joint conference of the Socialist deputies in the Reichstag and the party's executive committee. They decided to abandon the cardinal tenet of their party, voting four to one to participate in a coalition because of the unprecedented crisis facing the Empire. But conditions were laid down: the new Government must be willing to enter a League of Nations which would peacefully adjust all future conflicts; Belgium must be rehabilitated as well as Serbia and Montenegro; autonomy must be granted to Alsace-Lorraine; all occupied territories must be evacuated; equal, secret, and direct right of franchise must be granted in all German federal states; all decrees limiting the right of assembly or freedom of the press must be abrogated; and all military institutions serving to exert political influence must be abolished. Most Germans would welcome such a program even though the Conservatives and one wing of the National Liberals would surely oppose it bitterly.

On September 24, at a committee meeting in the Reichstag, Chancellor von Hertling revealed the desperate situation facing the nation. He frankly admitted that there had been serious reverses on the Western Front, but there was no need to lose heart. Their soldiers continued to show spirit and the enemy had suffered frightful losses. "The American armies need not frighten us," he said. "We shall take care of them." His attempts to inspire some hope were unconvincing and elicited no applause.

Once he began to talk about the Belgium question, a National Liberal deputy shouted, "We have not come here to listen to that kind of thing!" Someone else called out, "Grandfather is telling stories." As the weary Hertling continued there were many shouts of *"Olle Kamellen"* (old stuff), and an indignant Social Democrat deputy named Landsberg urged everyone to leave. "That's the only right answer to the speech."

The heckling increased when Hertling spoke of Germany's policy toward the border states; and the army representative, General von Wrisberg, describing the German retreat as a defeat of the enemy, was met by a storm of derisive laughter and mocking shouts. Ironical jeers drowned out the navy representative who said, "Our case is favorable." And as he tried to finish a sentence beginning, "Submarine warfare is the best means . . ." someone added angrily, ". . . to bring America into the war."

"All in all," recalled Deputy Hans Hanssen, "it was a bad day for the Government. Dissatisfaction and misunderstanding are widespread within the ranks of the majority parties. After the meeting, criticism at the tables in the restaurant were merciless."

The following day General von Wrisberg, seeking to justify the War Ministry's criticism of the Left's peace resolutions, was again greeted with laughter and catcalls, and there was vigorous resentment voiced against the entrance of the military into politics. The Government bench was in a state of confusion and many of the deputies, bored with the speeches, began to collect in groups to discuss the situation. "We will experience a complete military collapse in November and December," a colleague confided to Hanssen. "If the whole thing were not so tragic, we might rejoice because our predictions are approaching fulfillment."

That day the Kaiser assured all U-boat officers at Kiel that Germany would bring the Allies to their knees. "We know our goal, our rifles cocked, and traitors to the wall." Admiral von Müller gave instructions that the address was not for publication. Three hours later on the train carrying the retinue to Wilhelmshöhe, news arrived that the Bulgarian Army had completely collapsed and their king was requesting an armistice. The Kaiser's warlike manner evaporated. "This can bring the war to an end," he said, "but not in the way we wanted it."

6.

In Russia the relations between the United States and the Bolsheviks were still ambiguous. A few days earlier American Consul Poole, ordered to abandon his post in Moscow, had crossed the border into Finland ten minutes before orders for his arrest arrived. And from Archangel, a very confused Ambassador Francis cabled Washington: "Can Department advise me whether a state of war exists between the United States and the Bolshevik Government?"

This question was resolved forty-eight hours later, on September 25, at a meeting in the White House of the President, Secretary Lansing, and General March. They decided to announce definitely to the Allies that America would send no more troops to any part of Russia. Among the first to get the news was Francis. The next day Lansing cabled him that all military effort in northern Russia would be given up "except the guarding of the ports themselves and

326

as much of the country round about them as may develop threatening conditions." That ended the problem of American intervention. Or did it? Could those American troops already at both ends of Russia carry out simple guard duty while their allies were bent on overthrowing the Bolsheviks by force of arms?

By this time Bruce Lockhart was a prisoner in the Kremlin, ensconced in an apartment that once housed a czarist lady-in-waiting. The British secret agent was treated well and Moura was even allowed to visit him occasionally. Within a few days he was set free and allowed to return to England—without Moura.

And so the last of a long line of fascinating innocents from the west left the Russian scene. Of a colorful gallery including Ambassador Francis, Albert Rhys Williams, and Raymond Robins, Lockhart was perhaps the most interesting and enigmatic. Each was intelligent, well meaning, vital. Flung into the birth pangs of a new philosophy, religion, and way of life, not one could comprehend clearly the complexities, diversities, and problems of Bolshevism; any more than brilliant men like Lenin and Trotsky could fully understand the complexities and problems of capitalism. The western innocents often opposed each other in the struggle for intervention; Lockhart fought on both sides, and, at times, on neither.

It had been a year of lost opportunities and now the Allies, including the reluctant, idealist Americans, were at war with the new regime. It was an undeclared war and the Americans, in their continued naïveté, imagined they were well out of it. Hadn't they announced as much? But it is far easier to announce that you are really a neutral in the midst of a brawl than to make a peaceable exit. Particularly with your allies grasping your coattails.

7.

Pershing's operations officers estimated that they would need nine divisions in line with four in corps reserve for the Meuse-Argonne offensive. The burden of the planning was assigned to Colonel George Marshall, who not only had to place 600,000 American soldiers into the attack sector but to remove 220,000 French troops. The problem of transporting ammunition, gasoline, and oil, as well as signal, medical, motor, and tank supplies, seemed insurmountable. While Marshall's plans were shrewd and practical, they broke down almost from the beginning. Thousands of the 90,000 horses that were hauling supplies through the waterlogged country near the Meuse collapsed or died in their traces, causing monumental traffic jams. In the almost constant drizzle, engineers worked tirelessly with rocks and gravel, mud and logs to repair mired roads.

American road discipline was so bad that staff officers had to constantly patrol the lines urging division and brigade commanders to untangle the chaos and keep their men moving. Marshall himself roamed the roads as did Pershing, who persistently barged into division headquarters demanding organization. Somehow the traffic was kept moving and on D-Day minus one the line divisions were almost at their positions.

They were to attack along a twenty-four-mile front between the Meuse and the western edge of the rugged Argonne Forest. Few places along the Western Front afforded greater advantages to a defender. On the right were the heights of Montfaucon, Cunel, Romagne, and Barricourt, rising to a thousand feet and providing natural strongpoints as well as all-around observation. On the left the Argonne Forest, itself a thousand feet above sea level, was thickly wooded and marshy in wet weather. Only three roads led into an area replete with deep ravines and dense thickets. And the Germans in the past four years had not only emplaced many concrete machine-gun posts but sited thick entanglements of barbed wire.

This was the nightmare that Pershing faced, and Pétain thought the Americans would do well to take strategic Montfaucon before winter halted the fighting. Only five German divisions held the entire twenty-four-mile line, but these could be reinforced by fifteen more within three days. Pershing's plan was to swamp the enemy front-line troops with a quarter million assault troops before these enemy reinforcements could come into action. So he set as the first day's objective the entire formidable rocky ridge defenses centering on Montfaucon.

Colonel T. Bentley Mott, the American representative at Foch's headquarters, met the marshal returning from daily Mass. As Mott saluted, Foch unexpectedly stopped and stared at the American, who, in embarrassment, mumbled something about how well things were going. Weren't they? Seizing the colonel's belt with his left hand, Foch dug his right fist into Mott's rib, then quickly followed with a feigned cross to the chin and a punch on the ear. It was a pantomime of his theory of battle. Then, still without a word, the ebullient marshal brought his stick to shoulder arms and marched off triumphantly.

To ensure surprise, the French held the front-line positions until the night of September 25. All American reconnaissances had been carried out by officers wearing the helmets and blue overcoats of the French. Fortunately there was no rain that night and the last of the American assault troops moved up into place before midnight. Probably only Pershing among Allied commanders would have dared to take the risks he faced. Since the operation was mounted so hurriedly, his most seasoned troops were still tied up at St. Mihiel and the majority of Americans were going into action for the first time. Only four of the assault divisions had seen any fighting at all, and many men, drafted in July, had spent their six weeks in the Army mainly in traveling. Some newcomers did not even know how to insert rifle clips. Enterprising old-timers were getting five dollars apiece to instruct them. "They at least had no prejudices to overcome," recalled one company commander about his seventy-two replacements.

After Major General Robert Alexander, commander of the 77th Division, briefed his officers, a French liaison officer asked permission to make an observation. "Sir, I have no doubt that your men are brave and that you have made every preparation that will give them a chance for victory tomorrow, but permit me to say that, in my opinion, the line in your front *will not move*. It has been in place for four years, is solidly established, well wired in, and the Boche is a good soldier. I fear that you will not be able to make the advance you hope for." The commander assured the Frenchman that the line *would move*.

George Patton was impatient for the battle to begin. "Just a word to you before I leave to play a part in what promises to be the biggest battle of the war or world so far," he wrote his wife, Beatrice. "I will have two Battalions and a group of French tanks in the show in all about 140 Tanks. . . . I am always nearvous [sic] about this time just as at Polo or at Foot ball before the game starts but so far I have been all right after that. I hope I keep on that way it is more pleasant."

At 2 A.M., September 26, General Alexander was wakened. He mounted a little knoll near his dugout to watch the bombardment. A half hour later 3,800 guns ranging from 75 mm. to enormous American-made 14-inch railroad guns opened fire with a crash. More ammunition was expended during this preparation fire than was used by both sides during the entire Civil War—and at a cost estimated at a million dollars a minute. The infantry, awed and expectant, waited in their jumping-off trenches. In three hours they would go over the top, an exciting, terrifying, new experience for almost all of them.

At four Captain Eddie Rickenbacker was wakened by his orderly who told him that the weather was good. They would need it. Mitchell had ordered all squadrons to attack enemy observation balloons along the entire front. "The safety of thousands of our attacking soldiers depended upon our success in eliminating these eyes of the enemy." Attacking a balloon hanging only 1,500 feet above anti-aircraft was a terrifying business.

Rickenbacker routed out five of his best pilots. Their squadron was assigned two balloons, and at early breakfast he explained that three men would go after each target. Day would break at 6 and the six fliers took off at 5:20 so they could attack at first light. Once they lifted into the darkness, the airfield ground flares were extinguished. And then Rickenbacker beheld the most marvelous sight that his eyes had ever seen. "Through the darkness the whole western horizon was illumined with one mass of jagged flashes." Millions of guns seemed to be shooting along the entire front, for the French were also attacking on both American flanks. "The picture made me think of a giant switchboard which emitted thousands of electric flashes as invisible hands manipulated the plugs." He was so fascinated by the fireworks that he was startled to peer over the side and discover Verdun below. He set his course above the dim outline of the Meuse and followed its windings downstream, occasionally taking short cuts across little peninsulas, since this route was as familiar as the path to his own home.

At 5:30 the preparation shelling stopped and the rolling barrage opened up. The doughboys started forward through heavy mist. Special units slung chicken wire bridges over enemy barbed wire and those behind recklessly plunged toward the German front line. At first the defenders were so stunned that only a few machine guns opened up, and there was good progress all along the line except in the center, which was dominated by the heights of Montfaucon.

By now Rickenbacker's men had destroyed their two gas bags and he was searching for another one. Glancing to the right, he was almost startled out of his senses to see a Fokker flying alongside him not a hundred yards away. The next instant he saw the German was heading straight at him. They both began firing and it was still so dark that their four streams of tracer bullets cut brilliant lines of fire through the sky. "For a moment it looked as though our two machines were tied together with four ropes of fire." Rickenbacker's ammunition was incendiary; the German's part tracer, part incendiary, and part plain lead. As they drew closer Rickenbacker wondered if they were going to collide, but the Fokker abruptly dipped under him. Rickenbacker made a *renversement* which put him directly behind the enemy. He pressed both triggers. The Fokker fell over on one wing and plunged down.

Rickenbacker's own engine began to vibrate violently. One blade of his propeller had been shot in two. He throttled down to reduce the pounding and, being only a thousand feet above ground, he just cleared the German lines and made it to the Verdun airdrome. He soon had a new propeller on his Spad and was back at his own field. There was great news. Their group had shot down ten balloons in addition to his Fokker—eleven victories in an hour without the loss of a single pilot.

At about 6:30 A.M. George Patton was walking behind his tanks accompanied by a signal officer and a dozen runners, some carrying field phones and others pigeons. They were heading up the east side of the Aire River toward Montfaucon. He stopped several groups of disorganized infantrymen heading for the rear who explained that they had been separated from their units by the fog and machine-gun fire. Ordering them to join his group, Patton led them to the reverse slope of a hill. He ordered everyone to spread out and lie down just before machine-gun fire swept the area. Moments later he learned that his tanks were being held up by a French Schneider which had become bogged down trying to cross two enormous trenches. Its crew had started to dig away the banks until shells and bullets drove them into a trench.

In a fury, Patton started down the slope. He ordered the French crew to get back to work, then went to the blocked American

MEUSE-ARGONNE OFFENSIVE SEPT. 26–OCT. 15

Front Line Sept. 26
Front Line Oct. 1
Front Line Oct. 15

tanks, removed the shovels and picks strapped to their sides, and routed out the tankers from inside to help tear down the sides of the trenches. He stood on the parapet directing the work although warned periodically to find shelter. Each time he yelled back, "To Hell with them—they can't hit me."

Once a passage was dug between the two trenches, Patton and another officer chained several tanks together for better traction in the mud. Ignoring the storm of bullets, the two men gave hand signals to help the drivers cross the quagmire. At last all but the French tank were across. Waving his walking stick, Patton shouted, "Let's go get them, who's with me!" and started forward, followed by a hundred men. As the group came over the crest of the hill, they were met by heavy machine-gun fire. Patton flung himself to the ground. It was undoubtedly at this moment that he had the vision he later described in a letter to his father:

> Once in the Argonne just before I was wounded I felt a great desire to run, I was trembling with fear when suddenly I thought of my progenitors and seemed to see them in a cloud over the German lines looking at me. I became calm at once and saying aloud "It is time for another Patton to die" called for volunteers and went forward to what I honestly believed to be certain death.

Waving his stick and shouting, "Let's go, let's go," he started forward. Six men followed. Five were felled. "We are alone," said the sixth, Pfc. Joseph Angelo.

"Come on anyway," said Patton. Something drove him onward. Seconds later he felt something strike his leg. He tried to keep going but crumpled to the ground. Angelo helped him into a small shell hole and bandaged his bleeding wound. The battle was over for Patton, but his tankers had taken both Varennes and Cheppy and were waiting for infantrymen to come up and support them so they could assault Montfaucon.

As soon as the infantry arrived, they pushed on toward the day's final objective with the remaining tanks. To Americans used to real mountains, the ridge on top of which nestled the village of Montfaucon seemed puny from a distance. But the closer they came to the base the more awesome it became, and as they dug into the sides of its ravines at dusk the infantrymen realized they would be lucky to take it the next morning.

To their left the infantry slogging through the Argonne Forest did reach their objective, a point five kilometers north of the jump-off line; and to their right the three divisions nearest the Meuse River, after overcoming stiff resistance, penetrated the enemy's second position, then beat off counterattacks. Despite the failure to take Montfaucon, it was a good day's work for Pershing's men. But by now the Germans were alerted and support units were being rushed to the area.

At Schloss Wilhelmshöhe the Franco-American attack was the

least of the Kaiser's worries that day. He sent a telegram to the King of Bulgaria saying that five German divisions were on the way to help his retreating troops. There was no reply. Then came news from Spa, Belgium, that depression reigned at the new Supreme Command Headquarters. The only straw that Ludendorff could clutch at was the influenza epidemic ravaging France.

The next morning Rickenbacker again set out in the dark to destroy balloons. At 5:30 he caught a panoramic view of the great battlefield. From both sides came a horizontal line of flashes. As far as he could see there was a dark space outlined between the lines of living fire. "It was a most spectacular sight." Finding no balloons, he decided to fly a bit lower. "Perhaps I might meet a general in his automobile and it would be fun to see him jump for the ditch and throw himself on his face at the bottom." Ahead was a truck moving in his direction. "Here goes for the first one!" he said to himself. He tipped down the nose of his machine and reached for the triggers. Over the top wing he saw something that took away his breath. Directly in his path swaying in the breeze was an enemy balloon, towed by the moving truck. It was being put into position for observation. Flattening out, he opened fire at the swaying monster. He was so close he only had time to loose a burst of fifty rounds before making a vertical bank to avoid crashing through it.

Underneath he heard the rat-tat-tat-tat of a machine gun. It came from the truck and one explosive bullet zipped past his head to crash into the tail of his plane. He barely cleared the side of the gas bag and, as he passed, glanced behind. An observer was leaping from the balloon, which obviously was about to explode. As he wondered whether the poor devil's chute would open in time, the interior of the bag ignited, and there was a great burst of fire. "I couldn't resist one shout of exultation at the magnificent display of fireworks I had thus set off, hoping in the meantime that its dull glare would reach the eyes of some of our own balloon observers across the line who would thus be in a position to give me confirmation of my eleventh victory."

Down below doughboys of the 27th Division were starting up the Montfaucon slopes. Foch had not thought it could be taken until early 1919, since the village was fortified and there were numerous camouflaged machine-gun posts on platforms in the trees. It was considered impregnable to infantry attack. After the first assault was halted by machine-gun fire, two patrols were sent out to clean out the nests. One patrol was wiped out, the other pinned down. But Lieutenant Fred Kochli of Alliance, Ohio, volunteered to crawl out and get it moving. He found a dozen uninjured men and spread them out, then led them on their bellies in a search of the slope. He finally located the enemy battery. Gathering his men, he rushed the position so unexpectedly that not an American was killed. The little patrol captured fourteen machine guns, killed many of the crew, and took twenty-six prisoners.

Lieutenant Kochli detailed four men to take back the prisoners before leading the rest to the western part of the town. Again his assault was so sudden that the enemy was taken by surprise. Three fieldpieces were seized along with their crews, and still not an American was hit. Kochli couldn't afford to weaken his patrol by sending back the new prisoners, so he herded them toward the observation post where, in 1916, the Crown Prince had witnessed the bloody battle of Verdun through a periscope.

When the Americans were about twenty yards from the post, a burst of fire cut down all of the prisoners and five doughboys. Kochli and his two unwounded men flung themselves in a shell hole where they were pinned down from three sides. But comrades from the 79th Division were already advancing toward the town in strength, backed up by machine guns and tanks.

These attackers were also met by machine-gun fire and a shower of grenades, but they pushed ahead despite heavy casualties, clearing the village before noon. It was a remarkable feat and the way to the north seemed open.

But there was little more progress that day as the Germans stiffened their defenses all along the front. By nightfall the American lines were disorganized. Officers couldn't follow the maps in such broken countryside and numerous units became lost. Messages were missent; artillery pieces foundered in the mud; supply trucks could not get through. Such utter confusion meant postponement of the drive until the farrago could be straightened out. Pershing's critics were already calling for his dismissal. "Those Americans will lose us our chance for a big victory before winter," Clemenceau bitterly complained to Foch. "They are all tangled up with themselves. You have tried to make Pershing see. Now let's put it up to President Wilson." It was unfair, disregarding the achievements of the Americans who had advanced far ahead of the neighboring French forces. Foch was more understanding. "The Americans have got to learn sometime. They are learning now, rapidly."

On that same day a far more important drive was launched by Haig's First and Third Armies against the most formidable defense system on the Western Front, the Hindenburg Line. Compared to the five German divisions faced by the Americans, Haig had to deal with fifty-seven. Success against such a force would have a crushing effect. Since the August 8 debacle, the British had pushed the enemy back nearly twenty-five miles on a forty-mile front over an area pocked with trenches, shell holes, and wire of both old and new battlefields. The cost had been great—180,000 casualties—but now that they had at last reached the Hindenburg Line, Haig smelled complete victory before winter and judged that there would be fewer casualties in the long run with a determined series of assaults. It was extraordinary that he had advanced so far with 50 percent of his infantry under nineteen years of age. These adolescents fresh from England were only partially trained and were led largely by junior officers who had only experienced static warfare but, with the valor of ignorance, were fighting well against an experienced, tough-minded enemy.

Perhaps the novices were inspired by Haig, who was experiencing his finest hour. He now lived in a train and closely supervised every operation. For a man reputed to be rigid he was showing remarkable elasticity, urging corps commanders to show initiative and seize every opportunity to knock the enemy off balance.

Zero hour for the attack was 5:20 on the morning of September 27. At last the whispered order was given to fix bayonets. It was almost a relief to do something, thought F. E. Noakes, of the 3rd Coldstream Guards. A few minutes later he glanced at the luminous dial of his watch. It was exactly 5:20. Three big guns spoke out in regular sequence from far in the rear. "The scream of their shells hardly ceased to vibrate in our ears when, with a tremendous simultaneous crash, as though the vault of heaven had burst and was falling upon us, the Barrage opened." It was as if some devilish force had been unchained, the power of hell let loose. At first there seemed to be chaos in the German lines with Very lights of every color shooting up in the air as if fired in panic. But soon the enemy recovered and their machine guns swept the ground. The parapet just above Noakes's head spurted with jets of earth.

At 5:30 the barrage moved forward. The moment had come. Officers dropped arms in signal. Men swarmed over the parapets. Noakes scrambled upright as soon as possible. It was safer standing for the bullets were sweeping low. A noncom near him was killed, but Noakes was untouched as he half-trotted through broken wire and shell holes illuminated by the flickering lights of the explosions.

Deneys Reitz of the 1st Royal Scots Fusiliers saw men ahead of him clubbing and bayoneting Germans who had risen from behind their breastworks to meet the attackers. He quickly rushed across No Man's Land and dropped into the great Hindenburg trench. Here comrades, flushed with victory, were rounding up prisoners and shouting down the dugout staircases for others to come up. The Germans had fought manfully and the floor of the trench was thick with their dead and wounded. Beside almost each machine gun lay its crew, struck down by the barrage.

By this time the British guns had lifted their range to the next German trench, four hundred yards beyond, and the 7th Shropshires began coming through the Scots. With no excitement or haste the newcomers walked forward behind the creeping barrage, rifles aslant. Even when they entered the German counterbarrage, and many fell, the rest of the Shropshires continued on steadily until they took the next trench. It was such an inspiring sight that the Scots cheered.

Soon after dawn the 3rd Coldstream Guards were at the Canal du Nord, which was like a gigantic trench across their path. The steeply sloping sides were badly broken by shellfire, so the descent for Noakes and his mates was comparatively easy. They slithered to the bottom, which was almost dry, and crossed piles of rubble and pools of mud and water. Then came the long, arduous scramble up the other bank. Near the top Captain Frisby was waiting, disdainful of the hail of bullets still sweeping the ground just overhead. He gave each man a helping hand along with a cheerful word.

It was now quite light and Noakes could see his immediate surroundings plainly, but the various attacking groups were now so mixed up that he found himself with a Lewis gun section of another platoon. He accompanied them along a trench leading to the left. They stepped over many corpses, flinging hand grenades into every dugout they passed. Noakes stayed with the crew until it was full daylight, then set off to find his own platoon. To his relief, he came upon them after a quarter mile. They were in the first of the double line of trenches which formed the Hindenburg Line. To their right Noakes could see the second main wave advancing in open order through fairly heavy shelling. They seemed to be successful, for the battle receded out of Noake's sight beyond the skyline.

By afternoon the First Army had advanced well beyond the canal toward Cambrai. Through glasses, Deneys Reitz could make out a group of German officers standing atop the round tower of a Cambrai brewery. Tall pillars of smoke rose from the houses as though the city was being put to the torch. On the outskirts he could see black masses of German infantry in reserve. To the left the advance was being held up before the village of Graincourt, but strong reinforcements of the Guards Brigade came up and Reitz watched them attack. Many fell but the men pushed on, soon disappearing among the wrecked houses. In moments enemy machine guns fell silent, and he could see batches of prisoners being marched out.

Reitz walked to the right, passing enemy guns which had fired a barrage that morning. He counted more than fifty abandoned pieces. The First Army had bitten three miles into the main German defensive system, and almost everywhere the final objective of the battle plan had been reached. Further to the right the Third Army was also enjoying success, having reached the line of the St. Quentin Canal only two miles southwest of Cambrai.

Reitz started back in the growing dusk after taking a last look at Cambrai, which was still fiercely burning. On his way to the rear he passed more dead men of both sides than he had yet seen in the war. The cost was dear, but in one day Haig's two armies had taken 10,000 prisoners and 200 guns. More important, they had blasted their way through the northern section of the Hindenburg Line and emerged into open country; "and from then onward," thought Reitz with relief, "the evil of the old trench warfare was a thing of the past and a new phase had begun."

There still remained, however, the titanic task facing Rawlinson's Fourth Army on the extreme British right flank. The southern segment of the Hindenburg Line they were scheduled to breach in forty-eight hours was even more hazardous and difficult.

8.

While Rawlinson was making last-minute preparations for his assault the following day, the envoys of the Bulgarian Government arrived at Salonika to sue for an armistice. And in Berlin, Foreign Minister von Hintze, although knowing nothing of this imminent capitulation, had concluded that a general peace must be sought. He ordered his ministry to devise an entirely new domestic and foreign policy for Germany. They drew up an extraordinary document which opened explosively: "A vital condition precedent to the opening of peace negotiations is the immediate formation of a new Government on a broad national basis on the unfettered initiative of His Majesty the Kaiser." The new regime was to approach President Wilson with a request to initiate steps for peace. "Our suggestion to Mr. Wilson will be accompanied by a declaration that Germany, and if need be the Quadruple Alliance, would be ready to accept the programme of the President's well-known fourteen points as the basis of negotiations." *

Hintze himself called this proposal "a revolution from above," and while it did not propose a truly democratic government it implied that Socialists were to enter the Government. While he was preparing to travel to Spa and find out exactly what the military situation was, Ludendorff at his room in the Hôtel Britannique was receiving the bad news that the Hindenburg Line had been breached in front of Cambrai. Lurching to his feet in a rage, he began to curse—not the enemy but his Kaiser, the navy, the home front, and particularly the Reichstag. An aide hastily shut the door.

It was 6 P.M. when, still pale and trembling, he went down to Hindenburg's room on the next floor. The two men looked at each other silently. Hindenburg remembered: "I could see in his face what had brought him to me." Then Ludendorff haltingly said that they must ask for an immediate armistice. Tears came to Hindenburg's eyes but he nodded in agreement. He said he had intended to propose the same thing that evening. They both agreed that it would be necessary to evacuate all occupied land in the west. The two men parted with a firm handshake and with no. recriminations on either side. "Our hardest resolve," the field marshal wrote, "was based on convictions we shared in common." He knew that he would now be "abused and held responsible for every misfortune," but he had to do his duty. Ludendorff was experiencing similar emotions. He and Hindenburg would be forced

---

* Wilson's Fourteen Points (see pages 129-30) were far more reasonable than any terms that could be expected from England, France, and Italy; and it was generally felt by the German Government that the President could undoubtedly persuade his allies to accept them since the horde of Americans already in France was now the controlling military factor.

"to sacrifice our names to ensure the step being taken that we had done everything humanly possible to avoid." The Quartermaster General at last accepted the bitter truth. "The war is now lost. Nothing could alter that. If we had the strength to reverse the situation in the West, then of course nothing would yet have been lost. But we had no means for that. After the way in which our troops on the Western Front had been used up, we had to count on being beaten back again and again. Our sitaution could only get worse, never better. There was no hope of further reinforcements for the time being from home."

There was little talk of capitulation at the front lines. The Germans were retreating, but slowly, methodically, and those who manned that portion of the Hindenburg Line opposite Rawlinson's Fourth Army felt secure behind its barriers.

The most formidable section was the northern half where the St. Quentin Canal ran through a tunnel three and a half miles long. Here the main defenses were sited on the western side of the canal. These consisted of two or three strong lines of trenches, each protected by thick belts of barbed wire. The tunnel itself added greatly to the strength of the position. It was lit by an extensive electric system and housed numerous barges for quartering reserve troops. There were many bombproof exits and lateral approach galleries from the rear as well as numerous underground passageways connecting the tunnel with the main defense system. This permitted any part of the line to be easily reinforced under the heaviest fire. In addition to the main defenses were numerous trenches constructed to take advantage of the lie of the land and give good fields of fire. The villages in the area, such as Bellicourt and Bony, were also heavily fortified.

The Australian-American Corps was assigned the difficult task of breaking through this section. The U.S. 27th and 30th Divisions were to spearhead the attack and their corps commander, General Monash, was apprehensive not only because these troops had little battle experience but because some had not yet reached the jump-off line. He pleaded with Haig to postpone the assault to give the Americans a chance to catch up, and confessed that he was "in a state of despair." But Haig, assuring him that it was "not a serious matter," ordered Monash to "attack to-morrow morning in force as arranged."

Young Pat Campbell's Field Artillery Brigade, now attached to the Australians, was also preparing to take part in the action. There was a new battery commander, for his hero, the redoubtable Major John, was dead. Recently the camouflage over one of their guns had caught fire from the heat of its own firing. Since there were stacks of ammunition by the side of the gun, John ordered everyone to leave. He stayed, fighting the fire single-handed until the ammunition blew up.

The new commander was Major Cecil, a selfish man who cared more for his black and white setter than any of his men. She was always in the way. "Everyone in the battery was waiting for the day when she would get in the way of a shell, but Betty, like her master, knew how to look after herself."

They had been taken over by an Australian battery, and Cecil's main hope was they would not have to participate in the assault on the Hindenburg Line, but there they were, unhappily surprised to find the American 30th Division, never in action before, holding the line in front of them. Campbell spent the day at an observation post examining the future battlefield. He could see where the canal came out of the tunnel near Bellicourt, a deep chasm between steep banks. In front were white scars against the hillside— German trenches. The wire out front was disconcerting. There was so much of it. "I could see the strength of the position, it was enough to daunt anyone. How could any troops cross that canal under heavy fire and scale the bank on the other side! An English division to our right was to make the attack opposite the canal, but it looked an impossible task. And how could the Americans get through the wire!" He could also see unspoiled country beyond the Hindenburg Line, undulating hills, villages, little woods, and a hillside without shell holes. "It was like a Promised Land. But it had not been promised to us, it would be ours only if we succeeded in storming the canal and capturing the trenches on the other side of the wire. If! Cherry had said we should succeed, but it was easy for an adjutant, planning battles but taking no part in them himself, it was easy for him to be optimistic. I hardly dared to hope."

By late morning of September 28 it began to rain and soon mist obliterated the green unspoiled country. Only the white scars of the trenches remained, and the lines of wire, and the deep gash on the right which was the emerging canal. At dusk Campbell's battery moved forward to its battle position. News from all fronts was stupendous. The Bulgarians were asking for peace, the Turks were being driven out of Palestine, and the whole Western Front was on the move. And tomorrow they would join in. "We shall go through them like a knife through butter," said their brigade commander. "We shall be eating our Christmas dinner in Berlin." This convinced Campbell, and that night he did believe they were about to enter the Promised Land.

But the next morning was cold and unpromising. They opened fire at zero hour, five minutes to six. Daylight came, but the fog was so thick Campbell could hardly see from one gun to the next. No one seemed to know anything about what was happening out front. Someone said, "It doesn't smell like victory." Then came word to advance. There still was no news and no prisoners were coming back. Perhaps they had gone by in the fog. After proceeding about a half mile the fog cleared enough so they could distinguish other guns and wagons ahead. The column didn't look like it was moving very fast. In fact, nobody was moving at all. By this time Campbell could see five hundred yards up to a crest. Wagons and guns were stalled all the way to the top. Nothing was going over. This meant that the enemy was still holding the Hindenburg Line.

On Campbell's right British troops of IX Corps—using lifeboats, rafts, mats, and portable bridges—crossed the canal and took the village of Bellenglise. But on his left the American 27th Division was in trouble. Tanks allotted to it had been quickly put out of action, and only two battalions had managed to catch up with and follow the barrage. The rest could not even get as far forward as the artillery start line.

Paul Maze, the French artist in khaki, was now attached to these troops. The first intimation that they were encountering stiff opposition was the sight of the knocked-out tanks. He entered the dugout of one regiment to find an American colonel and two staff officers facing a map. "Waal," drawled the colonel, adjusting his tortoise-shell glasses, "I have no news as yet of how the boys have gotten on, but they went over at skeduled time, and I am confident that they have done their dooty."

Maze suggested that perhaps someone should go forward and find out how things were. At the steps of the dugout, Maze saw men in the distance coming down the sloping ground and asked who they were. "Waal," answered the colonel, "I guess it's some of the boys coming back." While he was ordering a lieutenant to see what it was all about, Maze leaped on his motorcycle and hurried up the crest as far as he could. He ran the rest of the way and found that the men were retreating simply because they were not in touch with anybody. They had no news and most of their officers were killed. Maze ordered some to stay where they were and set up their machine guns. The rest he told to rejoin their comrades out front, which they did. "They were not in any sort of panic, but had merely sauntered back for want of instructions." Returning to the American headquarters, he found it shattered as if by an earthquake. Three bodies lay partly covered by a sack; the sentry and two of the officers he had just been talking to. The colonel sat alone mopping his brow. "Say," he told Maze, "this certainly is war." The Americans, in their eagerness to catch up, had advanced too fast in the fog. Failing to mop up, they had been attacked from the rear by Germans emerging from dugouts and tunnels.

It was not until 2 P.M. that General Monash gathered enough reliable information to make a decision. With the failure of the American 27th Division to reach its objective, the Australian 3rd Division had only managed to get obliquely astride the line of the tunnel. At least the American 30th Division had managed to seize Bellicourt and control the southern entrance of the tunnel. This enabled the Australian 5th Division to cross the tunnel line in force. Since Monash only held one end of the tunnel, he had to abandon his original plan until he could secure the gains of the day. He would have to organize a continuation of the battle next day on totally different lines.

It had been a frustrating and somewhat revolting day for

STORMING THE HINDENBURG LINE
SEPT. 29 – OCT. 2

Front Line Morning Sept. 29
Front Line Night Sept. 29
Front Line Oct. 2
Corps Boundaries

ST. QUENTIN CANAL
HINDENBURG LINE

BR. III CORPS

U.S.

U.S.
AUST.

U.S. 27TH DIV.
AUST. 3RD DIV.

AUST.

AUSTRALIAN-AMERICAN CORPS

AUST.

U.S.

U.S.

U.S. 30TH DIV.
AUST. 5TH DIV.

AUST.

S. END OF TUNNEL

BR. 32ND DIV.   BR. 46TH DIV.

BR. IX CORPS

BR. 1ST DIV.

N. END OF TUNNEL

Le Catelet

Beaurevoir

ST. QUENTIN CANAL
(UNDERGROUND)

Bellicourt

Estrées

Levergies

Bellenglise

ST. QUENTIN CANAL

HINDENBURG LINE

N

MILES
0   2
0   KM   .2

palacios

341

Campbell. The battery had been forced to pull back several times, and finally Major Cecil put Campbell in charge of the wagon lines. "Don't go a bloody yard back," was his departing order. As some gas as well as high-explosive shells began to fall among his teams, Campbell galloped back to tell Cecil that they would have no horses left to make an advance unless he allowed them taken further back.

"It's always the same," growled Cecil, who had washed down his lunch with a good deal of whiskey. "Put a man in charge of the wagon lines and he's never happy till he's taken them back to the sea." With ill grace he allowed Campbell to move them a half mile further back. It was cold and rainy. Summer had gone and winter come in a day. Campbell was kept awake all night by German shells as well as by the cold and restlessness of the horses which he had tethered close so they couldn't kick one another. "I was afraid they might break free or that a shell might burst in the middle of them, and the Major would certainly say it was my fault." He could have endured the loneliness and cold, the shells and responsibility, if only today's attack had succeeded. "It was the failure of all our hopes, that was what I could not bear. The Promised Land! We were practically in the same place where we had started. The Hindenburg Line was impregnable, we should never get through."

This temporary setback was not taken seriously in London, particularly since British troops to the south were across the canal in force and other troops in the north were closing in on Cambrai. Lloyd George, who had suffered from flu most of the month, was so gleeful on hearing all this that he began to dance a hornpipe.

It had been a harrowing day at Spa for the German Supreme Command. In the morning Ludendorff, Hindenburg, and Hintze had conferred with the Kaiser. After the Foreign Minister explained the political situation, Hindenburg revealed that the Western Front was about to collapse and the army needed an immediate armistice. The only way to save Germany, he said, was to appeal to President Wilson at once. Ludendorff broke in, demanding that an armistice be arranged within twenty-four hours.

Hintze protested that such a demand would be tantamount to unconditional surrender, and would mean revolution and overthrow of the imperial dynasty. He begged for a few days' delay. The Kaiser, listening calmly to all this, was the most contained man in the room. With no show of emotion he sided with Hintze, who promised that a note to Wilson would be dispatched by October 1 at the latest.

After Hintze said that His Majesty was faced with two choices: to democratize the Government or to establish a dictatorship to suppress a revolution, the Kaiser replied, "Nonsense," to the second and declared himself in favor of the first, "with suppressed emotion, with kingly dignity."

Early in the afternoon Chancellor von Hertling arrived. Upon learning from Hintze what had happened, he came out of the room and exclaimed to his son, "It's absolutely terrible! The Army Supreme Command demands that *as soon as it can possibly be done*, a request for peace be sent to the Entente!" At a conference a little later with the Kaiser, Hertling refused to remain Chancellor with a democratic, parliamentary Government, and tendered his resignation. The Kaiser accepted it but then told Hintze that he could see no danger of an imminent revolution. "We can afford, therefore," he said, "to postpone for awhile the formation of a new Government and the question of peace." Two weeks should be taken to quietly consider the matter.

The Foreign Minister reminded the Kaiser that His Majesty himself had promised Ludendorff to send a note to Wilson in two days; and a new Government that would be acceptable to the enemy must be formed before an offer of peace and armistice could be made. The Kaiser, he said, must sign the decree lying on the desk which provided for a change in Government. Wilhelm wearily turned, walked to the table, and affixed his name, then hurried off to dress for dinner.

Admiral von Hintze was one of the guests that evening at His Majesty's invitation. He told the company that Chancelor von Hertling had to quit immediately even if there was no successor in view. After the meal Hintze instructed his undersecretary to "inform Vienna and Constantinople that I propose to suggest peace to President Wilson on the basis of the Fourteen Points and to invite him to call an immediate cessation of hostilities." With Austria-Hungary and Turkey informed of the intended peace move there could be no step backward. Hintze set out for Berlin on a special train to carry out his mission.

As Deputy Hanssen walked toward Unter den Linden after a depressing, nerve-racking day at the Reichstag, he felt a "mysteriously heavy and oppressive atmosphere was hovering over the large cafés. A dense crowd was pressed together outside the telegraph room of *Lokal Anzeiger* to read the latest telegrams. 'How pitiful it is,' an unknown man said to me as I walked into the hall. Morale was below zero."

At 10:50 P.M. Bulgaria signed an armistice agreeing to every one of the Allied commander's conditions. Hostilities would cease at noon the following day. With less than one percent of its country occupied by invaders, Bulgaria had surrendered. With her collapse, the back door to Austria-Hungary as well as to Turkey and to Germany herself was ajar.

The next morning, the last day of September, news of Bulgaria's ignominious capitulation brought further gloom to the Reichstag. "The war will end in four months," one member told Hanssen, "it cannot continue longer because the states will collapse." Another, just arriving from Switzerland, said that everyone there was convinced of Germany's approaching collapse.

During the day the Australians manfully struggled to seize the northern half of the canal tunnel and so break the entire Hindenburg Line. The American 27th Division also pushed forward. Maze stayed with them and early in the afternoon had come upon a battalion of Australians on the right who were coming to their aid. The Anzac colonel asked Maze to take a message back to brigade headquarters, and he started walking down the road to Bony. As shots flew past him he dropped into a shell hole. He peered over the edge and saw not two hundred yards away the tops of German helmets. "I raised my field-glasses to have a look at them, and as I did so my left arm dropped in excruciating pain with a bullet in the wrist." He crawled out of the hole and finally reached some Australians waiting in reserve. They dressed his wound and he walked to the rear, his left hand and wrist throbbing. On the way he registered everything he saw, "for, half unconsciously I was taking leave of the war." He was thankful that it was not his painting hand. He reported to Rawlinson's chief of staff, General Montgomery, whose genial welcoming smile was refreshing. That evening Maze was in a hospital train riding slowly away from the battle. "I could still hear the guns making a thundering row, and as I looked out at the desolation gliding past the windows and saw all the reinforcements coming up to finish the assault on the Hindenburg Line . . . I thought of the comment of the mother of a French friend of mine who had succeeded in reaching her soldier son in a village immediately behind the line during a battle. She had sent word and was waiting for him, a tall black figure in the middle of the road; as she spied him coming toward her down the shattered street she called out: 'My dear child, why all this noise? What is it all about?'"

Little ground was won on that last day of September, but Rawlinson's men were in good position to seize the rest of the Hindenburg Line on the morrow. Marshal Foch was in his glory, for at last his grand coordinated attack was being realized. Everyone was fighting from Flanders to Verdun. In the far north the Belgians were attacking under their king; at Ypres, General Plumer was pushing forward with his usual vigor; and to his right four more British armies were either through or approaching the Hindenburg Line; then to their right four of Foch's own armies were also progressing, if with little dash except for the irrepressible Mangin; finally came the Americans, who, with frantic energy, were reorganizing for another major push in the Meuse-Argonne. To Foch it was a dream come true and he was beginning to think that Haig was right after all. Victory could come in 1918.

In London that evening Lloyd George may not have executed another hornpipe, but he surely felt like it upon learning that three of General Allenby's cavalry divisions had reached the outskirts of Damascus. Within the city Turkish rule had already ceased and flags were flying in the streets to welcome the conquerors. What was left of the Turkish Army was in flight. The collapse of the Ottoman Empire was only a matter of time. At dawn of October 1, Colonel T. E. Lawrence, already a legend, entered

Damascus with his Arab forces to receive a frenzied welcome from the people. Simultaneously detachments of the Australian 10th Light Horse entered from the north as the 14th Cavalry Brigade from the south reached the "Street that is called Straight."

At the Hindenburg Line the rain finally stopped just before dawn. By 10 A.M. Australian patrols reached the northern mouth of the canal tunnel. Rawlinson's Fourth Army had completed the task of breaching Ludendorff's formidable barrier and Lieutenant Campbell's Promised Land was now open for the taking.

9.

Although the Supreme Command had reluctantly agreed to accept Prince Max of Baden, a leading member of the liberal community with an ardent desire for peace, as the new Chancellor, he had not had time to form a new Government by the morning of October 1. This was the day Hintze had promised to send his peace offer to President Wilson, but there was no official chancellor yet to sign it. This mattered little to the frenzied Ludendorff at Spa, who was insisting that pressure be put on Berlin to send the offer immediately no matter who signed it. The enemy, he warned, might break through his lines at any moment. The Kaiser's Foreign Office representative was so shaken by Ludendorff's hysterical arguments that he sent a message to Berlin urging Hintze to dispatch the message at once, come what may. The military, he added, seemed "to have completely lost their nerve here."

Prince Max was already on his way to Berlin to form the new Government but did not arrive until midafternoon. Informed that the Supreme Command demanded an immediate armistice because of the desperate military situation, he balked. Although he had been striving for peace and was now willing to make "large concessions," he was determined to fight to the death if the Allies insisted on dishonorable conditions.

"If the situation is as serious as this," he said, "it can no longer be saved by an armistice offer, and we must simply risk the catastrophe; a precipitate peace offer, above all a precipitate armistice offer—must have disastrous political consequences." He refused to put his name to such a document and went at once to see the Chief of the Cabinet, F. W. B. von Berg. "The armistice offer," he said, "is a fatal mistake and I will not sign it." Therefore, he could not accept the chancellorship.

"You were certainly not my candidate," said Berg testily, "but I have no other."

"I do not shrink from the sacrifice," the Prince heatedly retorted, "but it must not be a senseless sacrifice, which it would be if my first step as Chancellor was to be an appeal to the enemy." How could Berg, as the Kaiser's closest adviser, wait until matters had reached this state of bankruptcy before summoning him? "I am now to throw away my good name and my reputation to save anything that can be saved. No man ought to be put in such a position, and no nation either."

"You see," interrupted Berg, "you are already getting nervy!"

"I have good reason to get excited over the news I've just faced upon arrival."

Prince Max realized that there were only two courses open to him: either to leave Berlin or attempt to form a Government and carry on the fight against the peace offer. His departure, he felt, would result in an immediate signature by the Vice-Chancellor of the old Government. And so he decided to remain and become Chancellor.

His cousin, the Kaiser, was in a very depressed mood but he still clutched the hope of the influenza epidemic in France. Yet it must have been as obvious to him as to his courtiers that the Western Front could crumble at any moment. At seven that evening he and his party left Spa. "Shall we ever see it again?" wrote a disconsolate Admiral von Müller in his diary.

Twenty minutes later a telegram from Hintze arrived at Supreme Command Headquarters: NEW GOVERNMENT WILL PROBABLY BE FORMED TONIGHT, OCTOBER 1. SO THE PROPOSAL CAN ALSO GO OUT TONIGHT, MILITARY SITUATION IS STRONGEST MEANS OF PRESSURE ON UNREASONABLE AND ARROGANT PARTIES.

Hintze was laboring under the illusion that the "unreasonable and arrogant" Prince Max was about to sign the peace offer; and his message heartened Ludendorff, who immediately appointed an armistice committee, then requested the Foreign Ministry to let him know as soon as possible the exact time the peace proposal would go to Wilson. Ludendorff's growing hysteria was evident in a midnight message to Hintze stating that the army could not wait another forty-eight hours. The general again begged the Foreign Minister "most urgently to make every effort to have the proposal issued in the quickest possible manner." Everything, he insisted, "depended on the proposal being in the hands of the Entente by Wednesday night or early Thursday morning at the latest," and he begged Hintze "to leave no stone unturned to that end." This frantic telegram was followed shortly by a Ludendorff telephone call personally urging Colonel Hans von Haeften, the army representative of the Foreign Ministry, to get Prince Max out of bed so he could sign the note. Haeften said the best he could do was see the Prince in the morning, but he doubted whether he would sign it until the new Government was actually formed.

At 8 A.M., October 2, Colonel von Haeften was at Prince Max's door. As predicted, the Prince refused to sign and set to work forming a coalition Government. Ludendorff kept applying pressure throughout the morning, going so far as to instruct his emissary in Berlin, Major Count Hilmar von dem Bussche, to gather representatives of all the political parties and reveal to them the frank details of the military collapse. For the first time Ludendorff was going to be completely honest with the civilian leaders, but only because he desperately needed an immediate armistice. Bussche's revelations left the party members pale and utterly crushed. Social Democrat Friedrich Ebert, leader of the reformist wing, for one, "went as white as death and could not utter a word," and Gustav Stresemann, a National Liberal deputy, "looked as if he had been struck." The Prussian Minister reportedly said, "There is only one thing left now, and that is to put a bullet through one's head."

Prince Max was stunned. This frantic effort of Ludendorff's to force immediate action had dealt his own plan a mortal blow. "Up to this moment the home front had stood unbroken. It had been held together by the overwhelming force of suggestion, which went out from the two commanders in the field—the suggestion: 'You must hold out! Don't give in!' Now the spark of panic leapt across to the people at home."

Early that afternoon the Kaiser and Hindenberg arrived in Berlin, and at 3 P.M. Prince Max and his advisers held their first conference with the latter, who strode in with such unruffled assurance and talked so calmly that the Chancellor had a flutter of hope. But once the field marshal said, "Give me a breathing space of ten, eight, or even four days, before I appeal to the enemy," it was evident that he shared Ludendorff's position. A moment later he went even further by admitting that the military situation was so grave there should be "no delay."

Prince Max took Hindenburg aside to ask privately if the state of the front really necessitated such precipitate action. "We have so far survived this attack," was the answer. "I am expecting a new mass attack within a week and I cannot guarantee that there will not be a catastrophe." No sooner was this unspeakable word out of his mouth than he corrected it, " . . . or at least the most serious consequences." The meeting was interrupted by the announcement that the Kaiser wanted to hold an immediate Crown Council meeting.

The Kaiser greeted everyone almost lightly. "What a state of nerves Berlin is in, to be sure!" but after Prince Max said that he was still opposed to making the peace offer, His Majesty interrupted sharply. "The Supreme Command considers it necessary," he said. "And you have not been brought here to make difficulties for the Supreme Command."

But the Prince was not to be intimidated and the next morning again told Hindenburg that an immediate armistice offer, besides being ineffective and dangerous, would be treated all over the world as a confession of German defeat. "All the favorable effects of the new Government in furthering the cause of peace would be lost in the sensation which the offer would make." He proposed that instead he proclaim in his first speech new war aims that would correspond to Wilson's Fourteen Points.

But when Hindenburg stubbornly insisted on an immediate peace offer, Prince Max promised to authorize the offer—on one condition "that the Supreme Command states in writing—so that

I may be in the position to communicate their statement to the Cabinet today, and eventually to publish it—that the military situation on the Western Front does not allow delaying the note till my speech is made . . ." After they parted, Prince Max telegraphed Hindenburg questions he had to have answered before sending a peace offer: How long could the army keep the enemy from crossing the German border? Did the Supreme Command expect a military collapse, and would this mean the end of the power to defend the nation? Was the military situation so critical that an armistice and peace must be inaugurated at once?

Hindenburg replied that the army "is still firm and in good order, and is victoriously repulsing all attacks," but the situation was "daily growing more acute" and the German people should be spared useless sacrifice. "Every day's delay costs the lives of thousands of brave soldiers."

These were scarcely the hard answers the Prince sought, so he still objected to sending any note until he had addressed the Reichstag. This body was then in an uproar. "Tomorrow will be a great day in the German Reichstag," one member called out to Deputy Hanssen, *"then for the first time it will hear the half truth from the Government bench."* Hanssen asked what the news was from Austria. "Everybody in Vienna is crying for peace. Everything is collapsing. Agitation for peace is in full swing."

In the cloakroom he met Dr. Rudolf Hilferding, a Socialist deputy, who confirmed that everything in Austria was in dissolution. "Bulgaria has given up, and Turkey is played out. Everything will soon collapse. The Entente will certainly not accept the peace conditions which Germany offers." He predicted that peace might come in November. "If not, the war will continue throughout the winter, and peace will come next summer. In the meantime, we may consider it as settled that the Four Power Alliance has lost the war." Another revealed that Hindenburg had remarked in the Crown Council that the continuation of the war was *zwecklos,* aimless. "Everything will soon collapse."

Hanssen went down to Unter den Linden and found the exchange of S. Bleichroder crowded. Many customers were standing in line with bundles of war loan certificates, but the bank clerk refused to accept them. "But you bought a large bundle from me yesterday," protested a well-dressed gentlemen.

"Yes, that was a great mistake."

"But why won't you buy them?" asked the customer tearfully.

"Because we cannot dispose of them."

By evening Prince Max yielded to the inevitable. At the first session of the new cabinet he agreed with the others to send the note to Wilson immediately. It was a question of that or resigning. He signed a note asking President Wilson "to take steps for the restoration of peace." Germany was willing to negotiate on the basis of the Fourteen Points, he said, and requested an immediate armistice.

He wakened on the morning of October 4 feeling "like a man

who has been condemned to death, and has forgotten it in his sleep." He spent the day in completing his Government and composing the speech he would make to the Reichstag the next day. It took so long that it was not until 11 P.M. that he was ready to read the draft to intimate friends gathered in his hotel room. It contained a detailed analysis of Wilson's points and made them the basis for Germany's war aims. He even called for an international investigation of the question of war guilt. His listeners were so moved it was clear they heartily approved. Colonel von Haeften was instructed to bring the manuscript, as an act of courtesy, to the new cabinet members.

He returned at midnight "pale as death," and Prince Max thought he must be bringing news of some catastrophe at the front. Haeften reported that the ministers and the Foreign Ministry members unanimously opposed making such a speech. Its consequences abroad would be disastrous and Wilson would be offended at the attempt to interpret his mind. "I looked around the assembled company," wrote Prince Max, "and saw the light fade away from their eyes. . . I asked the company to leave me alone. Instinct told me to stick to the speech, but logic seemed to favor the other side." He decided to give up his speech and write another.

That night he and several friends began a new draft. They were still working the next morning, October 5, so the opening of the Reichstag was postponed until 5 P.M. The members, arriving for the one o'clock session, heard a rumor that there would be a postponement since "new, important information had arrived from abroad." The lobby seethed with rumors. A fellow deputy assured Hanssen that a second note was being sent to Wilson which went much further and even offered capitulation.

"Who told you that?" asked Hanssen.

"That I can't say, for I am bound to a promise of secrecy. I am telling you this in the deepest confidence, but I repeat I believe my source to be thoroughly reliable." He also had inside information from "a most trustworthy and well-informed source" that the military situation was steadily becoming worse. "The situation is untenable. The army has no more reserves. Everything will quickly collapse."

In the plenary room, Hanssen congratulated the new Secretary of Labor, who thanked him, then added a bit dolefully, "Actually one does not know but that he should be consoled rather than congratulated." Another colleague had good news. He attributed postponement of the session to Wilson's last speech, which had just been published in Germany. It was most promising. "He is obviously afraid that England and France, now that military fortune favors them, will demand too much. I hope, therefore, that we shall conclude a peace we can endure." Another member said, "We are facing a collapse. But do you know," he added with a grin that disgusted Hanssen, "I am glad of it!"

The hours passed slowly and Hanssen returned to the lobby to chat with the Social Democrat deputies from Alsace-Lorraine. "If Wilson does not accept our last peace offer," said one, "Prince Max has primarily one duty: He must go to Wilhelm immediately and say: 'Your Majesty, here is your stove-pipe hat, take it and go!'"

The Kaiser, laid up with arthritis, was complaining of rheumatic pains. His main task of the day was to sign a proclamation to the army and navy informing them both that he had decided to offer the enemy peace. "Whether there will be a cessation of hostilities is still uncertain. Until then we must not flag. We must, as hitherto, do our utmost to hold our own untiringly against the enemy assault. The hour is grave. However, in reliance on our strength and on God's gracious help, we feel ourselves strong enough to defend our beloved country."

The hour of five was near and the approaches to the Reichstag building had been crowded for almost an hour. The galleries and lodges were filled to overflowing. Hanssen pushed his way to the plenary room, where he counted over three hundred representatives of the Government, high officials, and military leaders. The court loges were jammed. Without fanfare the tall, slender Chancellor quickly entered and the secretaries of state clustered around him. At 5:15 President Konstantin Fehrenbach opened the meeting. Then Prince Max took the floor amid breathless silence. Slowly and clearly he began reading his speech. In a monotonous voice he outlined his program of reform and peace and, while most of the audience was surprised by its liberal, almost radical character, there was little reaction. Despite his uninspiring manner, pulses quickened when he told about the note to President Wilson. "I have taken this step toward the salvation not only of Germany and her allies but of all humanity, which has been suffering for years through the war, because the thoughts regarding the future well-being of the peoples which were proclaimed by Mr. Wilson are in accord with general ideas cherished by the new German Government and by the overwhelming majority of our nation." His words, uttered in monotones, were effective since all his hearers knew of his long, sincere fight for peace. "And so, with an inner calm, which my clear conscience as a man and as a servant of the people gives me, and which rests at the same time upon firm faith in this great and true people, this people capable of every devotion, and upon their glorious armed power, I await the outcome of the first action which I have taken as directing statesman of the Empire."

President Fehrenbach feared there would be "an hysterical outburst" from the deputies, but there was only polite applause. Nor did there even follow debate on Prince Max's program, and, once the meeting was adjourned, the members of the new Government congratulated each other that a crisis had been averted. There had been little drama in the hall, and now there was only an orderly hubbub in the corridors as groups gathered to discuss the situation. "How strange it is that there is no more excitement," a friend remarked to Hanssen. "Apparently the Reichstag does not realize the significance of what has taken place."

"The war has, for the most part, benumbed the feelings," said Hanssen. "War weariness and the longing for peace are great. Joy over domestic reforms is evident. The Germans yield to power and find themselves facing the inevitable. But even so, it is remarkable that passions do not break loose, that there is not more agitation, even here where we are facing a turning point in the history of Germany."

Few people realized that it was the army which had forced Prince Max to make the peace move, and his popularity in the streets was expressed in a catchy phrase, "Max means Pax." Princess Blücher could see "peace" smiles in the eyes of every shopgirl in a baker's or grocer's. "For the wealthier classes and the militarists things bear a different aspect," she wrote in her diary. "They could very well support another year or so of the war materially, as they are not half-starved and overworked like the greater mass of the people. For them the metamorphosis from rosy dreams of world-power and expansion and increased wealth to the gloomy realities of an impoverished, humiliated Germany is all too overpowering." In the meantime all Germans were in an agony of suspense to know what President Wilson's answer would be. "Will he prove himself great enough to bear the huge responsibility of the destiny of almost the whole world, which fate has placed in his hands? Will he recognize himself as the instrument of a divine will, or show himself to be but the puppet of party strifes and short-sightedness?"

The note had still not reached Washington, although it had been forwarded from Berne the previous day. Wilson would not receive it for another forty-eight hours, but Clemenceau was already reading its terms, for the note had been intercepted and decoded by French Intelligence. Clemenceau was alarmed, not knowing what to expect from an idealist like Wilson. He also feared that the German offer was some sort of trap and that Prince Max was a puppet of the military, who were trying somehow to escape defeat on the battlefield. In this mood of distrust the French began to work on armistice conditions.

Four bitter years of war made it easier to offer peace than to accept it.

Part 5

WAR AND PEACE

Chapter Fourteen

"I AM DEALING IN HUMAN LIVES— NOT IN POLITICS."
Woodrow Wilson

OCTOBER 1–26

1.

DESPITE the victorious advance all along the Western Front, Foch was displeased and on the first of October sent a disconcerting message to Pershing. Resistance, he said, was apparently very strong in front of the Americans in the Meuse-Argonne, and he proposed inserting another French army between Pershing and the French Fourth Army. This new force, naturally, would absorb some American divisions.

This was the same old August plan to break up U.S. forces, and Pershing correctly guessed that Clemenceau was behind it. The answer to the carrier of the message, General Weygand, was a resounding rejection. Such a change, said Pershing, would retard rather than increase Allied progress. "General Weygand, I believe, left thoroughly convinced that my arguments were sound," he wrote in his diary. In any event Pershing was determined to continue with the attack planned for the following day in the rugged Argonne Forest. He ordered the 77th Division, the left wing of the American First Army, to move forward even though the French lagged behind and there was already a gap between them. There was no use trying to maintain communications in the forest, decided Pershing, and the best policy was for each unit to push ahead "without regard of losses and without regard to the exposed conditions of the flanks."

As soon as these orders filtered down to Major Charles Whittlesey, commander of the 1st Battalion, 308th Infantry, he held a glum conference with Captain George McMurtry, the acting commander of the 2nd Battalion, which was to support Whittlesey's attack. Being a stern, upright New Englander, a graduate of Williams College and a Wall Street lawyer, Whittlesey could not accept such an illogical mission without argument. Constant combat in the forest had cut his battalion to half strength and the survivors were exhausted. Moreover his left flank hung in the air and he feared the Germans would infiltrate behind him as they had done two days earlier. A tall, slim, bespectacled man, he bore a resemblance to Woodrow Wilson both in appearance and manner. While McMurtry was also a Wall Street lawyer, he was as outgoing as Whittlesey was introverted. A man of action, he had seen action with Teddy Roosevelt's Rough Riders at San Juan Hill. But Whittlesey's logic convinced him, that they should protest jointly. Their regimental commander, Colonel Stacey, seeing some merit in Whittlesey's complaints, passed them on to the brigade commander, who in turn brought them to the division commander. But General Alexander, a do-or-die type who had been pushing his men hard ever since September 26, had no intention of bucking an order from Pershing.

"All right," the studious Whittlesey told Colonel Stacey, "I'll attack, but whether you ever hear from me again I don't know."

The attack began at 6:30 A.M., October 2, in the fog and light rain. The 1st Battalion led the way with Whittlesey just behind the forward scouts carrying a pistol and a pair of barbed wire cutters. He wanted to make sure they were heading in the right direction with units maintaining constant contact in the tangle of bushes and trees.

With McMurtry on his right, Whittlesey advanced into the Charlevaux Valley, but by 10 A.M. the entire force was pinned down by heavy fire from a hill to the left which should have been occupied by the French. Since there was surprisingly little fire from the right early that afternoon, Whittlesey headed in that direction. He broke through the German line with McMurtry right behind. After pushing on to their objective, Whittlesey sent runners back to Colonel Stacey with a request for reinforcements. Ninety men had been lost and two of nine companies were missing.

Alexander was pleased with Whittlesey's progress, for it was the only successful assault that day in the entire Argonne. With visions of scoring a major breakthrough, the general ordered another infantry battalion to move up during the night to support Whittlesey. The major was far from happy. There was limited ammunition, almost no rations—and Germans were now on all sides. While he and McMurtry hastily set up a defense perimeter, enemy artillery and mortar shells began straddling the area. With no equipment for digging deep trenches, the men were exposed to the barrage and could do little during the pitch-black night except remain alert.

Of the rifle companies sent out to reinforce Whittlesey, only Captain Nelson Holderman's Company K managed to find its way through the dark woods to the beleaguered battalion. It was a welcome sight and Whittlesey asked Holderman to take his company and find out if the hill that his company had just crossed had been retaken by the Germans. Once Holderman's men started up the hill, they were met by heavy machine-gun fire on both flanks as well as sniper fire from the woods behind. The enemy not only held Hill 198 but had rewired it and set up machine-gun nests. Holderman had to fight his way back to the pocket.

In the meantime Whittlesey had sent off Lieutenant Karl Wilhelm with fifty men to find the two lost companies. They ran into a strong force of Germans and only twenty survivors managed to crawl back. By morning of the third there was no doubt. They were surrounded completely, and there were only 550 men left. McMurtry scribbled a message to all company commanders and showed it to Whittlesey: "Our mission is to hold this position at all costs. No falling back. Have this understood by every man in your command." Whittlesey approved, then dispatched a message to Alexander stating his position and requesting reinforcements. It was placed in a metal capsule attached to one of eight pigeons brought up by Private Omer Richards.

The pigeon arrived safely at division headquarters, but Alexander did nothing; all of his reserve troops were in combat. Disturbed, he set out that afternoon for a corps conference, but before he could bring up the crisis of the two surrounded battalions, General Liggett announced there would be a full-dress attack by the entire American First Army the next morning. The main thrust would come to the right of the 77th Division up the Aire Valley. The French to the left of Alexander promised to knock a hole in the German line and the twin drive would pinch out all the Germans on the 77th Division front. Since this should bring quick relief to Whittlesey, Alexander left the meeting relieved. He decided to throw the weight of his division toward the left, alongside the French.

In the pocket the last food was parceled out and a German infantry attack was turned back. Whittlesey sent another pigeon message requesting food and ammunition be dropped by planes. One third of his men were dead or seriously wounded and all medical supplies used up. That night McMurtry crawled from one company to another whispering, "Everything is practically okay." When one soldier, shot in the stomach, groaned, McMurtry begged him to be quiet lest he draw another machine-gun burst. "It pains like hell, Captain," he said, "but I'll keep as quiet as I can." He made no sound and died half an hour later.

As scheduled, the second phase of the Meuse-Argonne battle began at 5:30 A.M., October 4. This time, in hopes of catching the enemy napping, there was no artillery preparation. Mist and fog mixed to hide the infantrymen as they scrambled forward. At the right edge of the Argonne Forest Pfc. James Rose of the 1st Division, which had helped win the great victory in the Champagne bridge, started across the narrow open field. "Everything was fairly quiet until we came to within 50 yards of the German trenches, then the air about us became a solid sheet of machine-gun and heavy artillery fire. No words could possibly describe the horror of it. Body stacked upon body in waves and piles, and the whole bloody massacre was made vividly clear to the rest of us by continuous flashes of gun-fire from the entrenched line of German machine guns. Our boys never faltered, they came, wave on wave, climbing over the bodies of their fallen comrades with one obsession in their minds, to reach and destroy every machine gun which was mowing down our advance. Heroes all of them." The German positions were well camouflaged but finally all except one gun were silenced. This was holding up the entire advance. Lieutenant Parker screamed something at Rose before slipping to the ground. "Oh, my God, they've got him!" thought Rose. But Parker scrambled to his feet, grabbed the Pfc.'s arm and yelled in his ear, "Let's smother them, Rose, let's smother them!" The two men raced toward the last machine gun. One German left the gun in panic but the gunner kept firing at the two Americans. The lieutenant grabbed the red-hot barrel and flung it and its trailing ammunition twenty feet into the woods. This performance "so thrilled and inspired the rest of us that we felt invincible." They swept through the woods unchallenged up toward the village of Exermont. There in a deep trench about seventy-five Germans stood at attention with their rifles across their chests. While offering no resistance, they refused to lay down their arms. Rose, inspired by Parker's heroics "and maybe a little unhinged at the horrors I had just been through," called to the others to cover him. He leaped into the trench and began jerking rifles from the Germans' hands. Soon several other men joined Rose. "It took some guts to do that, Rose," said Parker, slapping him on the back. Rose didn't remind him that a few weeks earlier the lieutenant had sentenced him to six months without relief in the front lines for going AWOL.

After Exermont was seized, Rose started across a shell-pocked cemetery with another lieutenant named Carter. All at once the enemy opened fire. Instinctively everyone leaped for the nearest grave or shell hole. Rose saw what he thought was a slit trench and hit it feet first instead of his usual head-first dive. His feet kept sinking and then a stink told him that he was knee deep in a latrine —and still sinking. "All thought of being killed departed from my mind—I looked wildly around and glory be, I could see a stream of water running from the Chateau wall into a stone trough some 75 yards ahead of me." His one obsession was to reach that water. He scrambled out of the cesspool yelling, for some inexplicable reason, "Follow me!" Twenty others, scared and confused, but used to obeying orders, chased after him. He was peeling clothes all the way and by the time he reached the trough he was almost naked. After scrubbing himself and getting clean clothes from a dead body, he was congratulated by Lieutenant Carter. "Rose," he said with a straight face, "I don't believe we could have made it if you hadn't led that charge." That afternoon Rose was hit in the foot by a machine-gun bullet and his war was over.

All along the front the Americans were advancing—except on the extreme left flank where Whittlesey's men remained surrounded. That morning he used two of the remaining piegons to report that his two companies were still missing and he still needed medical supplies and food. "Situation is cutting into our strength rapidly," he concluded. "Men are suffering from hunger and exposure; and the wounded are in very bad condition. Cannot support be sent at once?"

By noon General Alexander realized that his own attack had failed. But what worried him was the pocket. The loss of so many men would not only be a black mark against him but could set back the entire offensive. He ordered artillery to hit the Germans surrounding Whittlesey. When a plane flew over the pocket a few hours later and its pilot fired a rocket, the trapped men were elated. They'd been found. In minutes shells began to explode nearby. "It's ours!" someone shouted, and there were cheers until the explosions began to move toward them—and then fell directly into the pocket. To quiet their panic, Galloping Charley, as Whittlesey was nicknamed, calmly stalked in the open, while McMurtry kept shouting assurances: "Take it easy! This won't last long."

But the shells kept pouring into the pocket. One hit Whittlesey's orderly and the 1st Battalion sergeant major, Ben Gaedeke, whose body was blown apart and all his comrades could find were his helmet and pistol. Whittlesey wrote another message: "Our own artillery is dropping barrages directly on us. For heaven's sake, stop it." While Private Richards was taking a pigeon out of its cage, it escaped his grasp. This left only Cher Ami, a black checker cock. Despite his name, he was one of six hundred birds sent by British pigeon fanciers to the American Army. Richards clipped the message to Cher Ami's leg and tossed him into the air. After flying in circles, he landed on a nearby tree and began preening his feathers. The major and Richards waved their helmets to no avail. "Boo!" shouted Whittlesey, but the stubborn bird still refused to move. They threw sticks and stones but their target only hopped to another branch. Richards muttered, "What the hell," and began shinnying up the tree. He shook the branch until Cher Ami took off and again began circling above them. As Richards shouted instructions, the Germans began shooting at the pigeon. Cher Ami made several tentative circles before finally sailing away.

It seemed a miracle that he made it through the storm of shrapnel. Once he staggered and fluttered helplessly before gathering himself and resuming his flight. One leg was shot but he continued on his mission. Somehow he made it home. Dropping down like a stone, he struck his left breast first. He staggered, swayed from side to side, and finally began hopping on one bloody leg to the entrance board, where he was grasped by a trainer. The capsule bearing the message hung by the ligaments of the wounded leg and there was a hole through his breastbone from the same bullet.*

Thanks to Cher Ami the artillery barrage was lifted, but this did not end the travail of the two battalions. The Germans launched another infantry assault. After this was repulsed, volunteers resumed the deadly mission of getting water from a muddy stream running along the ravine. The wounded were made as comfortable as possible and the men settled for some needed rest. But a chilly rain began to fall, making sleep impossible. About 9 P.M. flares began shooting up around the pocket illuminating it like a stage. Grenades and potato mashers fell from several points. In an abrupt silence a German voice shouted, *"Kamerad,* vil you?" "Try and make us, you Dutch bastards!" someone retorted. This brought more grenades, followed by an infantry assault that was turned back only by stubborn small-arms fire. The Germans fled over the hill in confusion, and silence once more settled over the pocket except for the half-muffled moans of the wounded.

Upon learning that eighty men, including two captains, had been killed or wounded in the friendly barrage, Whittlesey conferred briefly with McMurtry. Should they change positions? But every possibility was vetoed. Division now had their exact coordinates and there probably would be more American artillery fire. The odds were it would come exactly where they moved. And there were no more pigeons to notify Division of any change.

The next day, Saturday the fifth, Allied planes passed overhead and dropped the desperately needed supplies. They landed just out of reach. Whittlesey kept ambling around the pocket, giving encouragement. One man asked if they'd ever get out. "We'll get relief all right," he said. Hadn't he heard the distinctive sound of American automatic rifles the night before? "There are two million American soldiers coming for us." By now those who had ridiculed him for looking like a crane began calling him "Bird Legs" with respect and affection. At last he was one of them.

Sergeant Tuite, a Catholic, noticed Lieutenant Gordon Schenck reading *Science and Health,* by Mary Baker Eddy. "This is food and drink to me," said the lieutenant, "a wonderful comfort."

"This is my comfort," said Tuite, pulling out his rosary.

That afternoon the Germans again rained down potato mashers with a half dozen wired together. One explosion blew the legs off a man in one of the center foxholes. Those nearby heard him cry out in fright, "Mama, mama, mama." Then his voice grew weaker and his final words were, "Goodbye, everybody. I forgive all."

*   *   *

* Cher Ami became a national hero. He died a year after being taken back to the United States; he was stuffed and displayed at the Smithsonian Institution, where he is today.

To the right, the 1st Division was still advancing up the Aire Valley. In their wake came Eddie Rickenbacker, who was driving up front to inspect a German plane he had shot down beyond Montfaucon. He·was impressed by the endless lines of cheerful doughboys marching into battle. All of them were smiling, making jokes, whistling or singing as they hiked along at route step. He found the plane, a Hanover, in remarkably good condition. It was nosed over and a few ribs in the wings were broken, but these could easily be repaired. A newly dug grave marked the last resting place of the observer killed by one of Rickenbacker's bullets.

While his mechanics were taking the Hanover apart for loading onto a truck, he went to an observation post to get a close-up of the war on the ground. "It was a spectacle never to be forgotten!" Through periscopes he could see the German trenches behind which American shells were dropping. "Our shells were creeping back nearer and nearer to the open ditches in which the German troops were crouching. I watched the gradual approach of this deadly storm in complete fascination. Some gigantic hand seemed to be tearing up the earth in huge handfuls, opening ugly yellow holes from which sprang a whirling mass of dirt, sticks, and dust. And nearer and nearer to the line of trenches this devastating annihilation was coming. To know that human beings were lying there without means of escape—waiting there while the pitiless hailstorm of shrapnel drew slowly closer to their hiding places—seemed such a diabolical method of torture that I wondered why men in the trenches did not go utterly mad with terror." All at once a shell fell directly in the enemy trenches. One German sprang out and, throwing aside his rifle, began running to the rear. Another shell landed in front of him, and he flung his arms over his head. "Next instant he was simply swept away in dust and disappeared, as the explosion took effect. Not a vestige of him remained when the dust had settled and the smoke had cleared away."

By now the world knew of the plight of the "Lost Battalion," and Pershing was embarrassed by publicized failure to come to its rescue. He ordered Alexander to make "a vigorous attempt" that afternoon to relieve Whittlesey. The order was relayed to Colonel Stacey, who was leading an attack in the ravine behind the pocket. Stacey was a good officer with two citations for gallantry, but almost constant combat for ten days had frazzled his nerves. He refused to advance up to the pocket without fresh troops. When the brigade commander, General Evan Johnson, reported this to Alexander, he shouted angrily, "Relieve him! You should have done that without reporting to me." Johnson protested that relieving Stacey would leave the regiment under the command of an emergency captain. "I don't care if it leaves the regiment in command of an emergency corporal, as long as he'll fight. Relieve that man at once and send him back to headquarters and relieve any other officer who talks in that way. You will take personal command of the attack." The fifty-seven-year-old Johnson led a company of eighty-five riflemen up the ravine, but he was wounded in the leg and after ninety minutes of fighting had to turn back.

The next day was the most harrowing for the survivors of the pocket. In the afternoon several Germans advanced with flame-throwers. Jets of flame licking out a hundred feet started a panic. One man raced back to Whittlesey shouting, "Liquid fire!"

The major rarely resorted to profanity but now he said, "Liquid hell! Get back there where you belong."

Other men were falling back in terror. Captain Holderman, who loved a fight and wouldn't have wanted to be anywhere except in the pocket, had a grenade fragment in his back, but using two rifles for crutches he directed a counterattack that killed all the flame operators and turned back the enemy infantrymen. Even so, two more American machine guns were captured, and there was still no food except for the packages air-dropped outside the pocket. The thought of this food so near and yet so far lured nine of McMurtry's men to crawl out at dawn on the seventh. They ran into an enemy patrol. Five were killed; the others were captured and interrogated by Lieutenant Fritz Prinz, who had sold tungsten in Seattle for six years. He asked Private Lowell Hollingshead to take a message back to his commander. Hollingshead, eighteen years old, balked. "All I want you to do is take them a message stating the case and giving them a chance to surrender." Another flame attack was scheduled for the afternoon. Convinced that he would be saving the lives of his comrades, Hollingshead, support-ing himself with a cane, approached the pocket that afternoon car-rying a white flag and a note.

Whittlesey and McMurtry were discussing how they could beat off another attack; Lieutenant Schenck, a tower of strength, had just been killed and few were left with the capacity to lead. Then Hollingshead appeared with the note. It stated that Hollingshead was delivering it under protest and it was useless to resist anymore. "The suffering of your men can be heard over here in the German lines and we are appealing to your human sentiments. A white [he spelled it "withe"] flag shown by one of your men will tell us that you agree with these conditions. Please treat the Lowell R. Hol-lingshead as an honourable man. He is quite a soldier we envy you."

Whittlesey handed the letter to McMurtry, who passed it on to Holderman. The three officers looked at each other and smiled. "They're begging us to quit," said McMurtry. "They're more worried than we are."

After reprimanding Hollingshead for having left his post to find food, Whittlesey told him to get back where he belonged. Then he ordered the white sheets that had been spread out as a marker for friendly aircraft rolled up. He did not want them mistaken for a white surrender signal. As word of the surrender appeal passed from foxhole to foxhole, the men reacted as McMurtry had. One shouted, "You Heinie bastards, come and get us!" Others joined in a chorus of obscenities.

The Germans retorted with a fierce attack. In the thick of the assault was Holderman, hobbling around on his rifle crutches and enjoying himself. Blazing away with his pistol, he whooped with delight every time he hit an enemy. Just as he shot his fifth German, he got his fifth wound. But he managed to stay on his feet and, with the help of a sergeant, broke up the assault on his flank.

It was the final attack. Another advance by the 1st Division in the Aire Valley had weakened the enemy's position in the Argonne Forest and by sunset the German lieutenant from Seattle and the other besiegers began silently withdrawing to the north in the rain.

It was dark at 7 P.M. by the time a patrol of riflemen led by Lieutenant Richard Tillman reached the pocket without drawing a single shot. The five-day siege was over.

The next morning Whittlesey walked back through the valley with 194 comrades. Another 190 seriously wounded had to be carried out. There were 107 dead and 63 missing. Whittlesey was met on the old Roman road leading to the pocket by General Alexander, who was swinging his malacca cane and smoking a cigarette as if strolling down Fifth Avenue. The lanky major looked worn and dilapidated. Alexander greeted him with a warm, "How do you do?" Then he said, "From now on you're Lieutenant Colonel Whittlesey." Whittlesey mumbled something that showed little enthusiasm.*

2.

As soon as President Wilson learned of the German peace offer, he telephoned House for his advice. The colonel immediately telegraphed from New York City not to make a direct reply. Later on that Sunday, October 6, he wrote Wilson: "It is stirring news that comes to-day. An armistice such as the Germans and Austrians ask for seems to me impossible, and yet a refusal should be couched in such terms as to leave the advantage with you . . . With Foch hammering in the West and you driving the diplomatic wedge deeper, it is within the range of possibilities that the war may be over by the end of the year." The New York *Times* was already ad-

---

* Whittlesey, McMurtry, and Holderman were all awarded the Medal of Honor. Whittlesey was uneasy in the role of hero and avoided publicity. He undoubtedly cherished the honorary degree given him by Williams College in 1919 more than his medals. In November of 1921 he asked one of his best friends, Robert Little, an associate in the law firm of White and Case, to draw up a will leaving all his property to his mother. He also made minute notes on twelve pending cases in banking law. On Thanksgiving Day he boarded a ship bound for Havana. He wrote nine letters to relatives and friends and a note to the ship's captain regarding disposition of his luggage. He spent the evening in the saloon talking about the war to a man from Puerto Rico. After a single drink he "most abruptly" announced he was going to bed and left. He jumped overboard.

"He was a victim engulfed in a sea of woe," Little told reporters. "His last work as chairman of the Red Cross Roll Call this month was all based on the suffering of the wounded. He would go to two or three funerals every week, and visit the wounded in the hospitals, and try to comfort the relatives of the dead."

vising the President to first make Germany depose of her "irresponsible, braggart Kaiser and speak by a government of her own people." Others were warning that the offer was simply a trap to catch Wilson in a "negotiated peace" and thus save the enemy from a crushing defeat.

On Monday the colonel was summoned by telephone and he arrived at the White House as the clock was striking 9 P.M. The President took him to his study. A few minutes later Secretary of State Lansing arrived and Wilson read aloud his reply to Prince Max. House was disappointed, since it was "mild in tone and did not emphasize the needs of guarantees providing for thoroughgoing acceptance of Wilson's peace conditions." The President seemed much disturbed at House's decided disapproval. The two argued for a half hour before the President told him to write something embodying what he had in mind.

Henry Wilson was already extremely annoyed with his "Cousin Woodrow." He looked upon Prince Max's offer as a "pretty piece of impertinence. As I have always said, let the Boches get behind the Rhine and then we can discuss." Only yesterday he had written in his diary, "I agree with LG, and am certain that a few good *straight* home truths would do *that vain ass* of a President good." British irritation with Wilson was aggravated by their conviction that Pershing was botching things in the Argonne with *his* arrogance. "The state of chaos the fool has got his troops into down in the Argonne is indescribable."

One of the few high-ranking Britons urging a less emotional approach to their problems with the United States was the man his peers described as featherbrained. That Monday, Lord Derby counseled Lord Balfour to work in close cooperation with the Americans to avoid more misunderstandings. "At present, the absence of any authoritative representative of the President makes any close co-operation difficult, if not impossible. . . . In my view the only satisfactory remedy would be for the President himself to come here. If he could not come, at least let him send Colonel House." Derby urged the Foreign Secretary to "send a private wire to House suggesting the above course."

The Paris papers were becoming increasingly hostile to the German offer, some accusing Prince Max of being a liar. "Must we conclude a *disastrous* peace?" editorialized *Le Temps. Intransigeant* demanded harsh conditions including occupation of strategic points in Germany. *Le Petit Parisien*'s leading article was entitled "The trickery of the armistice"; and *La République Française* demanded that they "advance beyond the Rhine." The papers shared Clemenceau's dread that President Wilson would compromise the Allied position, thus forcing France to accept a lenient peace without annexations or indemnities, and this would seal the fate of the nation for a generation. Both Clemenceau and Poincaré also feared that talk of an imminent armistice would relax the people's war spirit. Then if the peace offer proved to be a trap, French morale would collapse.

Completely disregarding his allies, the President was amending his reply to Germany. He worked until late Monday night and the next morning, the eighth, instead of playing golf as scheduled, asked House to go with him into his study for more work. House found to his pleasure that the President's viewpoint had changed overnight "and he had come around to mine. He did not seem to realize before the nearly unanimous sentiment in the country against anything but unconditional surrender. He did not realize how war-mad our people have become. This had to be taken into consideration, but not, of course, to the extent of meeting it where it was wrong."

The message, which was to be signed by Secretary Lansing, stated that the President "deems it necessary to assure himself of the exact meaning of the note of the Imperial Chancellor." Did Prince Max mean that Germany accepted the terms laid down by Wilson's Fourteen Points? Regarding an armistice, the President could not possibly propose one to his allies so long as the armies of the Central Powers "are upon their soil." Finally, the President had to know if Prince Max was "speaking merely for the constituted authorities of the Empire who have so far conducted the war."

Not altogether happy with the note, the President turned it over to Lansing, who distributed it to newsmen at 4 P.M. "It is not a reply," he explained, "but an inquiry." The note was sent to Germany through the Swiss Chargé in Washington.

In Berlin, Prince Max had just learned from the evening bulletin that the danger of an Allied penetration or encirclement of the front lines seemed over momentarily. Only then did Colonel von Haeften confess that the peace offer had been, from a military point of view, unnecessary. The Chancellor was stunned. "I can hardly describe what a blow this admission was to me. Why had not the Supreme Command grabbed at the life-line which I threw them? Why did they not grant me the eight days' delay which I demanded and which would have sufficed for reflection?" The Kaiser was still in bed with arthritis and complaints of rheumatic pains. He was also in a black mood because of the new Chancellor's recent demand that he dismiss the chief of his civil cabinet as well as the Minister of War.

The next morning Prince Max was cheered by Wilson's reply. Evacuation was demanded, as feared, and the Fourteen Points would have to be accepted as *conditions,* not as mere basis for negotiations. Despite that "the note spoke in a different tone from the howl of rage to which the yellow press of the Allies had given vent. Wilson did not refuse and was ready to undertake mediation."

A meeting was called to discuss a reply, and Ludendorff came from Spa to assure the conferees that the Western Front could be protected "for a long time yet" and the danger was past if the Allied attacks should cease. Not at all reassured, Prince Max asked if the war could be carried on until spring. "We need a breathing-space," fenced Ludendorff. "After that we can re-form."

But Colonel Heye, recently attached to the OHL as head of operations, spoke out more openly. "It will be gambling with fate on the part of the Army Supreme Command, if it does not hurry on the peace move. We *may* be able to hold out until spring. But a turn for the worse may come any day. Yesterday the question of a break through our lines hung on a thread." It was impossible to foresee whether the troops would hold out or not. "There are new surprises every day. I do not fear a catastrophe, but I want to save the army, so that we can use it as a means of pressure during the peace negotiations." The essential thing was to give the troops a rest.

After the long conference finally ended, Prince Max was left with the obvious conclusion that the military wanted the armistice continued even at the cost of assenting in principle to evacuation. But before he could draft a second note to Wilson he had to counter considerable pressure to break off the negotiations at once. Conservatives strenuously opposed evacuating any territory while Pan-Germans and other rightists were shouting that pacifists were instigating the peace offer.

The Germans were not the only ones arguing over Wilson's note. At a meeting of Allied leaders in Paris, Clemenceau urged that they ignore it, since they had not been consulted. Lloyd George was even more incensed. How dare the President make his precious Fourteen Points conditions for an armistice! If the Boche accepted them, that would put England in a most difficult position. How could she possibly agree to Point 2, "Freedom of the Seas"? He insisted that they tell Wilson plainly that evacuation of occupied territory was a necessary preliminary to any armistice. After a long argument, he got his way and a joint note to this effect was signed by the Prime Ministers of Britain, France, and Italy. It was dispatched at 8 P.M.

The British Prime Minister returned to London the next day, October 10, and was in such good spirits that he stayed up late with Lord Riddell and intimates exulting over the Allied victories. The talk turned to President Wilson and his conceit. "Yes," said Lloyd George. "Clemenceau calls him Jupiter. Wilson is adopting a dangerous line. He wants to pose as the great arbiter of the war."

Riddell then brought up a subject that was causing repercussions. That day, in the Prime Minister's message congratulating the army for having just driven the Germans out of their defensive positions behind the St. Quentin Canal, Lloyd George had stated that he had learned of the battle from Foch.

"That was quite an accident," explained the Prime Minister. "Foch came rushing in with the news, and I said quite naturally and truly that I had heard it from Foch."

The message congratulating the First, Third, and Fourth Armies for gains "during the past two days" was the first public praise he had issued to the victorious British forces. The reference to "the past two days" was an insult. There was no mention of the momentous advances in August and September, no mention even of the breaking of the Hindenburg Line.

The day was also notable for a biting article in *Pravda* by Karl Radek on peace negotiations. Wilson's program, he wrote, "means nothing else but an English landing on the north, the appearance of Czecho-Slovak bands in the east, who are to assist the Russian bourgeoisie in the organizing of the lives of the workers and peasants according to the will of the bourgeoisie." A reconsideration by the Allies of the Brest-Litovsk Treaty, he charged, would only "mean a substitution of one violator, a German violator, by another violator, an Anglo-American violator."

The linkage of America with Britain and France was not merely for home consumption. By now the United States, despite Wilson's protestations, was regarded by the Soviets as an enemy. Since the beginning of the month "the Anglo-French, American and Japanese imperialist robbers" had been grouped together under a single banner. What Wilson had always wanted to avoid was now a reality. Ameirca was irrevocably bound in the undeclared war against Bolshevism.

The Bolsheviks, in turn, were planning an assult of a different nature on both the Allies and Germany. The Russian proletariat, Lenin recently announced, would soon have to make the greatest sacrifices in the name of internationalism. "The time is approaching when circumstances may require us to confront British and French imperialism and come to the aid of the German workers, who are struggling against the yoke of their own imperialism." To do this they needed a powerful Red Army of three million men. "We can have it. And we shall have it." It was a declaration of ideological war.

3.

In Berlin, Prince Max and his associates were trying to frame an answer to Wilson. With Ludendorff absent, the civilians felt free to criticize him. Was he even competent to judge the military situation? His statements must be confirmed by such generals as Kuhl and Lossberg.

The new Foreign Minister, Wilhelm Solf, suggested that they telegraph Wilson an acceptance of his Fourteen Points and agree to evacuation. This was approved and the Foreign Ministry began drafting the reply. It was ready the next day, October 11, and approved by the army on the twelfth at 2:05 P.M. Its final sentence was the answer to the President's last question: "The Chancellor is supported in all his actions by the will of the majority, and speaks in the name of the German people." It also absolved the Supreme Command from the shame of surrender.

In America it was Columbus Day, which had a new name, Liberty Day, and the President marched at the head of a great parade in New York City. According to a New York *Times* reporter he was in rare good humor. "The Wilson smile was in evidence from start to finish, and his arm worked with the regularity of a piston doffing his tall hat to the cheering throngs."

Late that night London crowds in the Strand learned of Germany's note; there was cheering and singing. In the East End the people marched about till three in the morning, playing a variety of musical instruments and waving flags. "Soldiers of the King" was sung boisterously and the general shout was, "It's over now!"

Later that Monday morning Lloyd George at his country home was denouncing Wilson's rash actions as he led a walk to the top of a hill. "The Germans have accepted the terms as I prophesied they would. We are in serious difficulty. Wilson has put us in the cart and he will have to get us out." The time was coming when they would have to speak out, he said grimly. "We have borne the heat and burden of the day and we are entitled to be consulted."

General Wilson joined them for lunch and they all discussed what they should say to the President and the press. "As regards Wilson," the general wrote in his diary, "we agreed that we would wire to say that he must make it clear to the Boches that his 14 Points (with which we do not agree) were not a basis for an armistice, which is what the Boches pretend they are. As regards the Press, we agreed they should be told that Wilson is acting on his own, that the war is *not* over, that the 14 Points are *not* an armistice, and that an armistice is *not* a peace. It was a very interesting afternoon. Everyone angry and contemptuous of Wilson. A vain ignorant weak ASS." *

News of the German note did not reach President Wilson until early evening. Just before the Wilsons and Houses sat down to dinner at the Waldorf Hotel Joseph Tumulty burst in with an unofficial report that Germany had accepted the President's terms. As Wilson walked to the dinner table with House, he handed his adviser a little note signed W.W.: "Tell Mrs. W." It was curious why the President didn't tell her himself, and one wonders if Edith Wilson appreciated getting such important news from a man she considered an enemy. Since her marriage to Wilson in 1915 after the death of his first wife, she was deeply resentful of his dependence upon House. The colonel had tried to form an alliance with her, but, this failing, they were reduced to an uncomfortable truce. In the past months, however, hostility had broken through the polite pretense and she was openly expressing her distrust of House to her husband. "It seems to me that it is im-

---

* The last sentence is deleted from the Wilson diaries given in the Callwell biography of the general.

possible for two persons *always* to think alike," she recently had pointedly remarked, "and while I like Colonel House immensely, I find him absolutely colorless and a 'yes, yes' man."

After dinner they all went to the concert at the Metropolitan Opera sponsored by the Wilsons for the benefit of blind Italian soldiers. An overflow audience, excited by the news of the German offer, cheered the President. House was so stirred he could not listen to the music and, before the concert was over, left for home. "I did not try to sleep for a long while, for it seemed to me that the war was finished if we have the judgment to garner victory."

The Wilsons were equally excited and talked with Tumulty in their hotel room until long past midnight.

Early the following evening the Wilsons and House returned to Washington. The President went immediately to his study to read the newspapers and learned with some dismay that most senators held that the German note was not sincere and its terms too general. "If we agree to an armistice now, the war is lost," said Senator Lodge. And Borah still felt that Prince Max only represented the Kaiser: ". . . we must either insist upon dealing with a Government responsible to the German people or go on with the war."

4.

The tension between America and her Allies was brought to a head by Clemenceau's insistence that Pershing be dismissed for bungling the Meuse-Argonne campaign. He was almost as irritated with Foch and had already shown President Poincaré a letter he wanted to send the marshal demanding that he force Pershing to get his troops into action.

Poincaré advised him not to send the strongly worded missive. "I don't believe that things can ever be kept secret," he said. "If that letter is sent its contents will become known to the Marshal's entourage, and without a doubt to Pershing's as well. It might easily mean seriously wounded susceptibilities. At all events, I think some of its phrases ought to be softened."

Foch, in fact, was taking action on his own initiative. On Sunday, October 13, he had sent General Weygand to Pershing with a message the general was very reluctant to deliver. While Weygand was upstairs with Pershing, his aide showed a copy of the message to Colonel Jacques de Chambrun, who was the liaison officer at American headquarters. Chambrun, a descendant of Lafayette, was shocked to see that it was an order relieving Pershing from command of the First Army and placing him in charge of a quiet sector. This was "a great mistake in policy," said Chambrun, and could not possibly be obeyed.

In a few minutes Weygand came downstairs. He asked if Chambrun had read the order. Yes. "It is all off!" said Weygand curtly, and left. With some trepidation Chambrun went up to Pershing's office to find him seated quietly at his desk. What did Chambrun think of the order? "It would never do," replied the liaison officer, "it would be a fatal blunder and would forever obliterate the part America had taken in the war."

Pershing had heard rumors that Clemenceau was plotting against him, and he decided to force Foch's hand. On Sunday he drove to Bombon. He was ushered into Foch's drawing room, where Weygand observed that the man who had been weary and sallow yesterday was now alert and walked forcefully.

To Foch's question on how matters were progressing on the American front, Pershing replied equably, "We have met with very hard fighting. The Germans are putting up a very determined resistance."

This irritated Foch. "On all other parts of the front," he said tartly, "the advances are very marked. The Americans are not progressing as rapidly."

"No army in our place," Pershing observed icily, "would have advanced farther than the Americans."

"Every general is disposed to say the fighting on his front is the hardest." Foch waved at the map. "I myself only consider results."

"Results? In seventeen days we have engaged twenty-six German divisions."

This was an exaggeration and Foch said, "Shall I show you *my* figures on this?"

"No," was the crisp answer.

"I will continue my attacks until the Germans give way," said Pershing, before adding sarcastically, ". . . provided, of course, that this is Marshal Foch's desire."

"By all means," Foch said, and then, to Pershing's justified irritation, began lecturing. "In order to have an attack succeed, a commander must go considerably into details, so far as corps, division, brigade, even regimental commanders are concerned." Orders should be in writing, otherwise, how would the commander know they are ever written?

Pershing replied that this was the way it was done in his army. "We are not advancing rapidly because the Germans are fighting by echeloning machine guns in depth." Foch's silent but superior manner made Pershing lose his temper. "The Germans could hold up any troops Marshal Foch has at his command."

"Ah, I judge only by results," said Foch, and resumed the manner of the lectern. A *well-planned* attack, he said, could succeed with small losses.

"True only to a certain extent," retorted Pershing. What about the difficult terrain the Americans were fighting over?

"I am aware of the terrain," was the cold reply. "You chose the ground of the Argonne, and I allowed you to attack there."

This was not true and Pershing protested. "I had not understood it that way. In the first place, you proposed to split my army in half, fighting one force west of the Argonne, the other in the east, with the French between the halves. I said I was obliged to fight them as a whole and wherever the Marshal indicated."

Foch had had enough of this stubborn man. "Oh, well, it is a matter of no consequence now," he said wearily. "The only thing that matters is results."

In hopes of conciliating the two Weygand interrupted. "Here is General Pershing's plan for the formation of two armies," he said. Hunter Liggett and Robert Bullard were to be promoted to lieutenant general and each put in charge of an American army with Pershing as over-all commander.

But Foch did not even look at the plans. "Ah, yes," he said cheerfully. "I am inclined to grant your request." Then he added unnecessarily that Pershing was not to construe this as a plan to withdraw his headquarters to Chaumont.

Pershing fought to control his anger at what he considered an insult. He had always been up as far front as possible. "As usual," he said, "my headquarters train will remain in the woods at Souilly. I will visit Army, Corps, Division, and Brigade as often as possible."

Foch stood up. "Very good. General Pétain is agreeable to your plan."

But Pershing was not finished. Now that he commanded an army group, he demanded equal footing with Pétain and Haig. The marshal was either too weary to argue or knew it would be useless. He grudgingly agreed and the two men parted with frigid courtesy.

On Tuesday, the Paris papers resumed their attack on Prince Max's offer to accept Wilson's terms. "The Germans intend to deceive us," said *L'Echo de Paris*. "No armistice! This is not the end of the war!" It was no concern of Wilson's. It was time for the guns to speak.

But in London, the peace offer brought joy to the people and there was a rise in the stock market except in armament shares.

It was also "one of the stirring days" of House's life. He and the President went to work on the reply to Germany directly after breakfast. "I never saw him more disturbed. He said he did not know where to make the entrance in order to reach the heart of the thing. He wanted to make his reply final so there would be no exchange of notes. It reminded him, he said, of a maze. If one went in at the right entrance, he reached the center, but if one took the wrong turning, it was necessary to go out again and do it over. He confessed that many times in making extemporaneous speeches he had gone into the wrong entrance and had to flounder out as best he could."

House encouraged him. It could be done and they must get at it. The colonel thought they should refuse to discuss any armistice until the Germans immediately ceased atrocities such as the recent torpedoing of the Irish mail steamer *Leinster*, running between Ireland and England. Of the 450 lives lost, 130 were women and children. While agreeing, Wilson insisted this should be no vengeful peace. "Neither did he desire to have the Allied armies ravage Germany as Germany has ravaged the countries she has invaded. The President was especially insistent that no stain of this sort should rest upon the Allied arms. He is very fine in this feeling and I am sorry he is hampered in any way by the Allies and the vociferous outcry in this country. It is difficult to do the right thing in the right way with people like Roosevelt, Lodge, Poindexter, and other clamoring for the undesirable and the impossible."

Henry Cabot Lodge, for instance, had just introduced a resolution in the Senate calling for no further communication with the Germans except a demand for unconditional surrender, while his fellow Republican, Senator Miles Poindexter, was labeling Wilson's efforts "a crime against civilization" and only that morning the New York *Times* had printed a message to the public by Teddy Roosevelt regretting Wilson's entrance into the negotiations. "I hope the President will instantly send back word that we demand an unconditional surrender and that we refuse to compound felony by discussing terms with the felons." He hoped the Senate would repudiate the Fourteen Points, some of which were too vague to have any but rhetorical value "while others were absolutely mischievous. To do as the President has done in this case . . . becomes dangerously near to being treacherous diplomacy."

At last the note was composed and that afternoon it was dispatched. No armistice would be granted unless it provided "absolutely satisfactory safeguards and guarantees of the maintenance of the present military supremacy of the armies of the United States and of the Allies in the field." The note included House's suggestion concerning cessation of atrocities: "The nations associated against Germany cannot be expected to agree to a cessation of arms while acts of inhumanity, spoliation, and desolation are being continued which they justly look upon with horror and with burning hearts." It also demanded an end to an arbitrary type of government which could separately, secretly, and of its single choice disturb the peace of the world. "The power which has hitherto controlled the German Nation is of the sort here described. It is within the choice of the German Nation to alter it."

Wilson's next task was to send House off to Paris, a course already suggested by the British. The colonel's only credentials consisted of a note penned by Wilson "To Whom It May Concern," making House his personal representative while commending him to the confidence of all Allied representatives. As House was about to leave that evening, Wilson said, "I have not given you any instructions because I feel you will know what to do!" The colonel had been thinking of this and wondered at the strange situation their relationship had brought about. "I am going on one of the most important missions anyone ever undertook, and yet there is no word of direction, advice or discussion between us. He knows that our minds run parallel, and he also knows that where they diverge, I will follow his bent rather than my own." House felt that until the two were together again he would meet in none of the capitals of Europe a mind so sympathetic with his own. "He has his weaknesses, his prejudices and his limitations like other men, but all in all Woodrow Wilson will probably go down in history as the great figure of his time, and I hope, of all time." He went home to prepare for the long trip across the Atlantic. Edith Wilson must have experienced mixed emotions. Now her husband would be free from his alter ego's baneful influence, yet a House in Paris could damage the noble Wilson program.

It was already close to dawn in England, Tuesday, October 15. Later that morning Hankey found Lloyd George on the terrace at Downing Street with Lord Reading. In moments General Wilson arrived with Lord Milner, and there was lively discussion on the President's reply. "All were very sarcastic about the note," recalled Hankey, "which seems a complete *volte face*, flying from excessive leniency to austere strictness." The Chief of Staff, particularly infuriated with his "cousin," wrote in his diary: "It really is a disgraceful usurpation of negotiation. He practically ignores us and the French. He won't treat with the Hohenzollerns—thus making sure of Bolshevism. He won't treat as long as the Boches sink ships and have other frightfulness. And he is sending a separate letter to Austria. All this without consultation with his Allies. He *is* a B. [bloody] fool and a vain ass." * The Chief of Staff was strongly of the opinion that they should go to Paris immediately "and register a note to Wilson putting him in his proper place; but I was not able to persuade Lloyd George, and after lunch he went off to Walton Heath. Either he is seedy or is meditating a speech. I am certain we (British, French, Italians) ought to get together and put the truth baldly before Wilson. He is now taking charge in a way that terrifies me, as he is only a super-Gladstone—and a dangerous visionary at that."

5.

Prince Max could not sleep that evening and got up to write his cousin, the Grand Duke of Baden. Only on his arrival in Berlin, he said, had he realized how completely the old Prussian system had broken down. He was horrified to find that there was no military force to back his policy. "I believed that I had been summoned at five minutes to twelve, and find out that it is already five minutes past." They were in the midst of a widespread rebellion. If he succeeded in suppressing it peacefully, "our continued existence as a state after the conclusion of peace is assured. If I do not succeed, the revolution of force and ruin is at hand." He still hoped to save the Hohenzollern dynasty. "Thank God, I have in the Social Democrats allies on whose loyalty towards me at least I can entirely rely. With their help I hope to save the Kaiser. Such is the irony of fate." Germany's last hope of salvation could lie "in Wil-

* The last sentence is missing in Callwell's version of the diary. He also changed "disgraceful usurpation of negotiation" to "complete usurpation," etc., and omitted another telling sentence: "This fool Wilson frightens me by his complacency, self sufficiency, vanity *and* ignorance."

son's desire to play a big part in the world, and his theory for promoting world-happiness."

A few hours later, at 5:20 A.M. on October 16, the President's note arrived and brought Prince Max to despair. It was a "terrible document" that fundamentally changed the whole situation. The longing for peace throughout Germany had become the ruling passion of the masses. And once word spread of Wilson's demands most Germans were both shocked and alarmed. "Now," recalled Prince Max, "their disillusionment was like the bursting of a dam." "A black day," Admiral von Müller wrote in his diary. "All prospects for peace have been ruined. There remains a life and death struggle. Perhaps a revolution!"

The Kaiser showed the dispatch to his aide. "Read it! It aims directly at the overthrow of my house, at the complete overthrow of the monarchy." His son, the Crown Prince, thought that its tone was "arrogant and implacable" and that the "spirit of Foch" was overpowering the President.

Many of those who had enthusiastically supported peace now urged Prince Max to take a stand, and the Conservative party, which had opposed him, demanded a fight to the bitter end lest "for generations to come every German citizen and peasant, every man of business and of property, and, above all, every employee and laborer would be the wage-slave of our enemies. . . . No enemy shall put a foot on the soil of the Fatherland."

The Social Democrats, disappointed as they were, tried to counter this with an appeal supported by the faculty of the University of Berlin. "We are on the way to peace and democracy. All rebellious agitation blocks this way and serves the counter-revolution." The first priorities were peace and a government by the people. "Then we want to institute all the socialist reforms for which we have won the support of the people. Every intelligent Social Democrat must warn workers against following the mad counsels of irresponsible agitators."

Princess Blücher returned to Berlin to find "a terrible state of depression and gloom, portentous of the breakdown which we have been expecting for so long. One hears the wildest rumors as to what is going on, and every moment some one keeps coming in with a fresh account of what is supposed to be taking place." Ludendorff had a nervous breakdown and the army was said to be practically in a state of mutiny with soldiers turning on their officers. People in Frankfurt were being privately advised in whispers to leave, since the enemy might be there in a fortnight. "In any case, exaggerated as these reports may be, the universal demoralization of the people is very great, and one has sometimes the impression of a flock of sheep who have lost their leader and are going about in a dazed sort of manner, looking about for a loophole of escape from the impending evil." She wondered why the Kaiser had not already abdicated instead of waiting until he was forced out. Even as an Englishwoman she felt pity for His Majesty —but more so for his subjects. "It is a pitiful sight to watch the death-throes of a great nation. It reminds me of a great ship slowly sinking before one's eyes, and being swallowed up by storm-driven waves. I feel intensely for Germany and her brave long-suffering people, who have made such terrific sacrifices and gone through so much woe, only to see their idols shattered and to realize that their sufferings have all been caused by the blundering mistakes and overweening ambition of a class of 'supermen.' "

On the afternoon of October 17—as Colonel House was setting sail for Brest on the *Northern Pacific*—the German Cabinet met to determine the fate of the Fatherland. Their reply to Wilson would depend largely on the answers that Ludendorff had come from Spa to give them. "The situation in which we find ourselves is the result of the move we made on October 5," said Prince Max acidly. "At that time the Army Supreme Command urgently requested that we send the peace note and the appeal for an armistice to President Wilson." Then followed an interrogation of the Quartermaster General which Ludendorff turned into a display of confidence, and surprise that his simple request for an armistice several weeks earlier had been regarded as a cry of distress. Morale at the front, he said, was much better and he was doing everything possible to improve it, but unfortunately "these armistice negotiations are having very bad consequences, since my soldiers can't see why they should continue fighting if they have to give up Belgium and Alsace-Lorraine." It was almost as if Ludendorff himself had had nothing to do with the peace offer. He talked quietly, reassuringly about the front, even while admitting the situation was dangerous. How safe things would be if only they would send him replacements! "If we had battalions of full strength, the situation would be saved."

At this point he was supported by Lieutenant General Heinrich Scheüch, Minister of War, who predicted that he could raise 600,000 new troops during the coming months. "I am willing to promise that I will bend every effort toward enlisting the number stated; so now we will not waste a day in getting to work."

As the civilian members of the Cabinet sat stunned at the abrupt turnabout by the military, Ludendorff began to talk of defeat as if it were victory. "I should like to paint for you gentlemen a picture of the situation. Yesterday we had a battle at Ypres. The English and the French attacked us with very strong forces. We knew that, and we wanted to hold our own. We were driven back, but it came out well. It is true that gaps of four kilometers were broken in our front, but the enemy did not push through, and we held the front. How much reinforcements from home would have meant to us then!"

As if they had rehearsed, Minister of War Scheüch chimed in, "If I understand His Excellency Ludendorff correctly, he says that if he gets reinforcements all at once, the situation will be materially altered?"

"Yes," he said decisively, and reassured his listeners that they need not worry too much about the Americans. "They make a difference to the relative number, it is true, but our men do not worry about the Americans; it is the English. Our army must be relieved of the feeling of isolation."

He made it sound as if the problem was not his but that of the people back home. "If the army can get over the next four weeks and winter begins to come on, we are on safe ground." To do so, civilian morale *must* be raised for at least four weeks. "It would be preferable to have it longer. In any case after that period the crisis on the western front will be at an end, even if we have to retire still farther."

His newborn optimism was supported by the naval representative in the Cabinet, who said that the enemy was feeling the submarine war very acutely. "But if we accept the terms that are offered us, we throw all this away." The enemy's position was going to get worse.

"It is my impression," broke in Ludendorff, "that, before accepting the conditions of this note, which are too severe, we must tell the enemy: Win these terms by fighting for them."

"And when he has won them," asked the Chancellor, "will he not then impose worse conditions?"

"There are no worse conditions," was the proud retort.

One listener not taken in by Ludendorff's sleight of hand was Foreign Minister Solf. With sarcasm he remarked that it was his responsibility to advise Prince Max about the text and tone of the message they must send Wilson. "For this task I am scarcely better prepared by the explanations of His Excellency Ludendorff than I was before." He reminded the general that early in the month the OHL had insisted that they beg the enemy for an armistice. And Prince Max, against his own will and convictions, had been forced to accept responsibility for sending the peace offer. "Now an answer from Wilson has arrived which puts us face to face with the most serious of decisions, and at once the picture undergoes a change—showing that now we can hold our own; that if we can survive the next four weeks, we shall be in even a much better position than before. This seems to me an absolute riddle. What is the real reason that a thing can be done now which a short while ago was declared to be impossible?"

Ludendorff stiffly replied that today was the first time he heard he could get 600,000 replacements. "If I can get them now, the isolation of the army will come to an end." He still believed they should negotiate. "But we should only enter upon such armistice negotiations as will permit an orderly evacuation of the country—consequently a respite of at least two or three months. Further we should not accept any conditions that would appear to make the resumption of hostilities impossible. That this is the intention, we cannot fail to see from the note. The terms are meant to put us out of the fight." The enemy must now state what his terms actually were. "We should not break off with Wilson abruptly. On the contrary say, 'Just tell us what are we to do, anyway? If you demand anything that is contrary to our national honor, if you want to render us incapable of fighting, then the answer is certainly, No.'" He denied that he had changed his previous stand, then promised that if he got the 600,000 reserves, "we do not need to accept all the terms."

Not reassured by Ludendorff's sophistry, Prince Max still was relieved that the panic of early October had vanished. After the conference he took the Quartermaster General aside. "Do you believe that next year we should be able to conclude the war on better terms than we can get today?"

"Yes!"

"You would then look with equanimity on a rupture of relations with Wilson?"

"Yes."

Prince Max was not convinced. "The statement of the military, stripped of its embroideries," he wrote in his diary, "revealed the following situation: A reversal of fortunes in our favor is inconceivable. The submarine war cannot bring it about. We have lost the initiative." Even the combing out of 600,000 more recruits would be useless without an improvement of morale in the army and at home. "We had no right to fly the white flag on 5th October; we had no reason to do so even today. But it is clear that the situation will certainly be desperate in a few months." His own path was clear. "The negotiations with Wilson must go on." But if they were asked "to accept dishonorable conditions to get an armistice, then the people must be called out to make a last stand." If so, the Quartermaster General was not fit to lead such a desperate struggle. "In the course of the meeting I had lost confidence in Ludendorff as a man. He ought to have looked the situation ruthlessly in the face, without any regard for his own prestige."

Ludendorff showed to no better advantage at another Cabinet meeting later in the afternoon. He admitted that there might be further withdrawals but did no fear any collapse. To Solf's question whether they should take a stronger line in their reply even at the risk of breaking relations with Wilson, the Quartermaster General declared decisively, "We should take this risk. Our note should test whether Wilson's intentions are honorable or not."

There were still arguments about the note to Wilson, but the Cabinet could agree on two things: Wilson should not be given any pretext for breaking off negotiations, and it would therefore be necessary to make concessions on the submarine question. Second: "We cannot accept dishonorable conditions without being ruined forever. 'Rather utter defeat than a surrender' must be the fundamental idea of the note."

Prince Max spent the following day with his legal adviser drafting the reply. After agreeing to evacuate occupied land, the German Government promised to send instructions to all submarine commanders to cease torpedoing passenger ships. Army commanders would also be ordered to protect civilians to the best of their ability and prevent destruction of private property and seizure of booty. There was even a paragraph calling for a neutral investigation of every charge of atrocities and violations of international law committed by both sides.

Regarding Wilson's demand of a cessation of arbitrary government in Germany, it was admitted that until now the Government had been based on authority, but "this was not due to any arbitrary action on the part of the legal authorities, but to the fact that the great mass of the people accepted them, without feeling any desire for full responsibility of its own. The war has changed all this." All questions vital to the nation rested today with the Reichstag, and this answer to the President was being made "in the name of a Government which is responsible to the people." The assurance that the new system will not be revoked, "lies in the declared will and the inner conviction of the great majority of the German people which stands behind it."

Pleased with his reply, Prince Max felt that his colleagues and the Supreme Command would concur. Early on the nineteenth Solf did approve, but its submission to the Cabinet brought universal dismay. Count Roedern declared the note was undignified; Scheidemann feared its challenging tone; many protested the clause demanding a neutral investigation of atrocities on the ground that "if we demand this investigation, we shall get the whole reparation bill thrown at our heads." The Minister of Marine and Admiral Reinhard Scheer were appalled at the submarine restrictions and warned that this meant abandoning all use of submarines. On this point the other members supported the Chancellor, but Scheer would not yield and appealed to the OHL and the Kaiser.

The first repercussion came early the next morning when Colonel von Haeften delivered a telephone message from Hindenburg that read as if it had been drafted by Ludendorff. "There is no alteration in the situation," it began. "Turkey has opened separate negotiations. Austria-Hungary will follow suit. We shall soon stand alone in Europe." Although the Western Front was in "a state of the greatest tension," the struggle there could be prolonged with the promised reinforcements. Even if they were beaten, they should not be seriously worse off than if they yielded everything now. "The question must be faced, whether the German people is ready to fight to the last man for its honor, not only in words, and so to secure itself the chance of a revival later, or whether it will let itself be driven to capitulation and extinction *without* having put out its last ounce of strength?" To abandon the submarine war, concluded Hindenburg, would be to take the latter course. Such abandonment would also have extremely unfavorable effects upon army morale.

Prince Max was dumbfounded at the tone of the message. How could such words be used by men who had begged him to hoist the white flag a few weeks ago. He had Haeften telephone Ludendorff that unless the reply included the concession that passenger ships be spared, Wilson would surely break off negotiations. The President needed that card in his hand to play against the demands of the French for a dishonorable capitulation of the German Army.

But Ludendorff was adamant; and his stubbornness incensed the Cabinet, which was meeting that morning without the Chancellor. "Now we are to be made responsible for losing the already lost war," complained Vice-Chancellor Friedrich von Payer. Matthias Erzberger, Centrist leader in the Reichstag, insisted that the public be told that the OHL had forced the request for an armistice; otherwise, soldiers would accuse the civil government of sacrificing them to American shells. "The Cabinet," said Erzberger, "must demand that the Supreme Command accept the note without reservation."

At noon Prince Max was assailed from another quarter, a messenger arriving from the Kaiser to inform him that His Majesty supported the navy on submarine warfare and intended to convene a Crown Council at Potsdam that afternoon "should the Chancellor persist in his view." The Prince ordered a messenger to inform the Kaiser verbally that previously arranged meetings prevented him from coming to Potsdam. He therefore begged His Majesty to be graciously pleased to come to Berlin and receive his report, adding that he would resign before changing his mind about the submarine question. "It gives me no pleasure to have to say so," he concluded, "but I am completely convinced that if I go, the Cabinet will fall to pieces, and then comes the revolution."

"Shall I repeat this to His Majesty?" asked the astounded messenger.

"Yes, that is my wish."

A few hours later an indignant Kaiser arrived in Berlin, only to be further annoyed at finding that his old friend, Count Lerchenfeld, the Bavarian Minister, had been asked to be present at the conversation with Prince Max. "I was not aware that *you* were an expert on naval affairs!" said His Majesty tartly, and then explained why he so strenuously opposed abandoning the intensified submarine war. The Chancellor presented his arguments, adding that he could not remain in office unless the Kaiser changed his mind. At last the latter reluctantly gave his consent.

Count Lerchenfeld pointed out the dangerous currents of opinion in the Empire which were directed expressly against the monarchy. "I am well aware of this," interrupted the Kaiser. He also knew that many were demanding his abdication, and added emphatically, "A successor of Frederick the Great does not abdicate."

As far as Prince Max was concerned, this settled the submarine question. With the Kaiser's consent, Ludendorff would surely bow. But the Quartermaster General was in no mood to surrender and he parried all the arguments passed on from the Cabinet through Colonel von Haeften. The War Minister then took the telephone and after half an hour exclaimed, "If you want to negotiate, give up the intensified submarine war; if you want to carry on this war, then break off the negotiations." Ludendorff refused to believe that it had to be "either-or." The War Minister was even more persistent and finally Ludendorff capitulated.

But this victory was balanced by an unpleasant surprise late in the evening. Prince Max was informed that his ministers had had an attack of pessimism because of three recent developments: the fall of Lille, the capitulation of Turkey, and particularly the President's belated answer to Austria's request for an armistice in which he demanded that the nationalistic aspirations of the Czechs and Yugoslavs be recognized. This not only sounded the doom of the Dual Monarchy but indicated that Wilson did not regard himself completely beholden to his own Fourteen Points. The ministers consequently were now afraid to include two passages in the reply: one protesting the imposition by the Allies of dishonorable conditions and the other a reminder to the Americans that many Germans had suffered from the hunger blockade imposed by Britain. The Chancellor was so indignant that he immediately wrote a bitter letter to his colleagues which succeeded only in the retention of the first passage.

With all the changes and delays, it was not until twenty minutes after midnight that the third German note was at last sent off to Washington.

In London, on October 20, General Wilson was once more venting his fury on the President, for he had just learned of Wilson's reply to the Austrians demanding recognition of the Czechs and Yugoslavs. "This makes a fair pie of things, and he does this without consulting Lloyd George or Clemenceau." He was also upset with Haig, who had come across the Channel to advise Lloyd George not to demand unconditional surrender. The Germans, argued the field marshal, were still strong, and the British would have to carry the burden of battle since the French Army was "worn out and has not been really fighting latterly" while the Americans were "not yet organized." To Wilson's disgust, the Prime Minister and Milner "rather agreed" with Haig. The next morning, the twenty-first, the Cabinet met again at 10 Downing Street. Admiral Sir David Beatty, commander of the Grand Fleet, argued that the terms of the armistice should almost be terms of peace and practically all the Boche fleet and submarines must be handed over. While Wilson thought this was "very sound reasoning," both Lloyd George and Milner argued that such terms were too stiff.

Just after lunch a copy of Prince Max's reply to the President was received. To Wilson it was quite adroit. "No mention of Alsace-Lorraine, nor any mention of the salt water. My fool of a Cousin is trapped. My own opinion is that, unless Lloyd George and Tiger catch a hold, my Cousin will cart us all."

By the time the meeting ended at 6:15 P.M., Hankey, who had been taking notes single-handed, was exhausted. "The less said about the discussion on the German note the better, as it was long and desultory, but it resulted in a fairly good telegram to President

Wilson, warning him of the dangers of the situation, and asking him not to act without consulting us."

In Paris the understanding between the French and Americans reached by Foch and Pershing after their tempestuous argument was already being threatened by Clemenceau.* Ignoring Poincaré's advice, the Tiger finally did send his sarcastic letter to Foch that day. "You have watched at close range the development of General Pershing's exactions," it read. "Unfortunately, thanks to his invincible obstinacy, he has won out against you as well as against your immediate subordinates." The French and British armies, Clemenceau continued, were pressing back the enemy with ardor "but our worthy American allies, who thirst to get into action and who are unanimously acknowledged to be great soldiers, have been marking time ever since their forward jump on the first day; and in spite of heavy losses, they have failed to conquer the ground assigned them as their objective. Nobody can maintain that these fine troops are unusable; they are merely unused."

The Tiger was aware of all the efforts Foch had made to overcome Pershing's resistance, but the time had come, he insisted, to change methods. "When General Pershing refused to obey your orders, you could have appealed to President Wilson. For reasons which you considered more important, you put off this solution of the conflict, fearing that it would bring reactions of a magnitude which you thought it difficult to gauge." There should be no further hesitation. It was "certainly high time to tell President Wilson the truth and the whole truth concerning the situation of the American troops."

This was, in effect, a demand to relieve Pershing from command. But Foch refused to appeal to the President and in his reply explained that all improvised armies suffered the difficulties now being experienced by the Americans. Since the start of the American attack in the Argonne they had lost 54,158 men "in exchange for small gains on a narrow front, it is true, but over particularly difficult terrain and in the face of serious resistance by the enemy." The feud with Pershing, as far as Foch was concerned, was over.

In Spa, Ludendorff and Hindenburg were already preparing instructions for the German Armistice Commission, making it appear that the army was not at all responsible for the humiliating submission to Wilson. It was Prince Max's Government, not the military, which had accepted Wilson's Fourteen Points without

---

* Lord Derby had noted the increasingly bad relationships between France and the United States several days earlier in a letter to Lord Balfour. "It is extraordinary what a revulsion of feeling there is in this country on the part of the French against the Americans and the enthusiasm of the 4th of July has completely died out, whereas at that time everything that the Americans did was preceded by huge headlines in the papers; now they are hardly mentioned, and I hear on the other hand that the Americans are very much disillusioned with the French who they say are trying to make as much money as they can out of them."

reservations and was offering now to evacuate all occupied territory unconditionally.

After a long speech in the Reichstag on the twenty-second defending his actions, the worn Chancellor was stricken with influenza and confined to his bedroom. For the first time the left-wing press printed a demand for the Kaiser's abdication. It was a great shock to the Kaiserin, who was celebrating her birthday.

The third German note caught President Wilson by surprise and, unable to consult with House, who was in mid-Atlantic, he went to his Cabinet. "I do not know what to do," he confessed. "What do you think should be done?" After a long silence Secretary of the Interior Franklin Lane advised him not to negotiate until German troops were "across the Rhine." The Agriculture Secretary doubted the sincerity of Germany's political reformation. Secretary of the Treasury William McAdoo insisted that terms be set by the military. Albert Burleson, the Postmaster General, fearing that Foch, Haig, and Pershing might be too lenient, demanded an unconditional surrender.

Concerned as he was over public opinion, Wilson feared the hysteria of the diehards might make him take to a "cyclone cellar" for forty-eight hours. At the same time labor didn't want Americans to keep on fighting for the imperialist aims of the Europeans. After considering all sides, he typed out a reply to Germany stating that he was asking his allies to submit their terms of an armistice, then added that he did not feel that the principle of a government responsible to the German people had yet been fully worked out. "It may be that future wars have been brought under the control of the German people, but the present war has not been; and it is with the present war that we are dealing." It was evident that the people did not control the military, nor had the power of the Kaiser been impaired, and that "the determining initiative still remains with those who have hitherto been the masters of Germany." If America, he concluded, had to deal with "the military masters and monarchical autocrats of Germany . . . it must demand, not peace negotiations, but surrender."

The next afternoon Wilson again summoned his War Cabinet, and every man was asked for his opinion. He calmly listened to each opinion and the discussion that followed, then drew from his coat a typewritten memorandum. "Gentlemen," he said, "I have here the tentative draft of the note that I think I should send to Germany. I should like to read it, and since it is the consensus of your opinion that we should accept the proposal for an armistice, I shall be happy to receive your suggestions regarding any changes that you think should be made in the document."

He began to read his reply slowly and deliberately, pausing momentarily at the end of each sentence to let it sink in. "Not a man present," recalled E. N. Hurley of the Supreme Economic Council, "failed to realize that in that note Woodrow Wilson had written a declaration that would end the great World War."

The President laid the sheet on the table and asked for suggestions. Hurley expressed enthusiastic approval. Others were equally warm with only one member suggesting that it would be politically helpful if one expression were changed. But Wilson shook his head. "No," he said decisively, " I am dealing in human lives—not in politics."

Without a word altered, the note was cabled that day not only to Germany but to the nineteen Allies. Lansing added a note to the latter that they were not being forced by the President into a premature armistice; he only hoped they would "acquiesce and take part" in the negotiations. Wilson, he said, had endeavored to safeguard carefully the interests of every ally and sincerely hoped that each "will think that he has succeeded, and will be willing to cooperate in the steps which he has suggested."

It was natural that those Americans who had objected to Wilson's foreign policy previously would attack the latest note. "There is no German Government in existence with which I would discuss anything," charged Senator Lodge. Even more vociferous, Theodore Roosevelt sent identical telegrams to Senators Lodge, Poindexter, and Hiram Johnson urging the Senate to demand unconditional surrender and repudiate the Fourteen Points as a basis for negotiations. "Let us dictate peace by the hammering guns and not chat about peace to the clicking of typewriters."

Colonel House, preparing to land at Brest the next day, was also disturbed by the note but for a different reason. If he had been at home, the colonel wrote in his diary, he would have advised the President to have done nothing further than say he would immediately confer with the Allies regarding the German reply. "The Germans have accepted his terms and he could go on the theory that they intend to accept them in good faith." Then he would have communicated with the Allies and gotten their agreement. "Instead of doing this he has gone into a long and offensive discussion which may have the effect of stiffening German resistance and welding the people together back of their military leaders . . . He has taken, what seems to me, a reckless and unnecessary gamble. It might cost him the leadership in the peace negotiations."

The British War Cabinet was puzzled by the note. "We could not understand what it meant," wrote General Wilson, "but on the whole we were relieved by the fool's wire as it might have been worse." At least they had finally been invited to participate in the negotiations. Much of the British press was still demanding revenge instead of armistice. The reigning mood in the country on October 24 was, in fact, one of impassioned hate. Rudyard Kipling expressed what the majority felt in a poem entitled "Justice," which appeared in *The Times* and the *Daily Telegraph*. "If we have parley with the foe," he wrote, "The load our souls must bear." It was the terrible accumulation of casualties that brought the usually temperate British to such hatred and agreement with Kipling, who himself had lost a son.

The commander of the British armies in the field was less blood-thirsty. Haig wanted a peace on more generous terms than the public and politicians, since he knew that the German Army had not yet been destroyed. He strenuously disagreed with Foch, who insisted on having bridgeheads over the Rhine and occupying all German territory on the left bank. "On the whole," he was writing in his diary, "Foch's reasons were political, not military." Haig was also becoming increasingly disgusted "at the almost underhand way" in which Foch and Weygand were still trying to get hold of a part of his troops. "I told them a few 'home truths' for, when all is said and done, *the British Army has defeated the Germans this year,* and I alone am responsible to the British Government for the handling of the British troops, *not* Foch."

6.

When the Kaiser read the President's words refusing to deal with the military masters and the monarchical autocrats of Germany, he exclaimed, "The hypocritical Wilson has at last thrown off his mask! The object of this is to bring down my house, to set the monarchy aside." His empress was equally furious, labeling Wilson a "parvenu" who had the effrontery "to humiliate a princely house which can look back on centuries of service to people and country."

The note reached the Reichstag while Prince Max's opponents were attacking his policies and were, in turn, being assailed. In the "dejected, heavy and depressed atmosphere," Wilson's reply was circulated in the corridors. It was a moment for unity but the news only intensified the wrangling.

The ailing Prince Max, still confined to his room, wondered: Was Wilson sincere in his promise to negotiate with justice or would he demand capitulation? Was he actually demanding abdication of the Kaiser? "I kept putting this question again and again to myself, worried my head for hours with niceties of interpretation, and finally came back to the conclusion that, according to the meaning of the words, the constitutional changes already introduced and planned would provide the basis for the negotiations." The Chancellor could not face reality. The Allies, of course, would insist on dethroning Wilhelm; so would many Germans.

Prince Max instructed his legal adviser to draft a reply that would not "break off the thread of our negotiations with Wilson." He should be advised "not to expect any Government with a conscience to adopt—from tactical considerations and in order to influence a foreign country—measures, which are not supported by the declared will and the innermost convictions of the German people."

That afternoon an excited Colonel von Haeften rushed from the Reichstag to the Chancellor's bedside with an alarming report that some Social Democrats were convinced that if only the Kaiser were thrown out they would get "a decent peace." Haeften begged

Prince Max to withhold official publication of the Wilson note so the Kaiser could abdicate of his own free will. "But if His Majesty does not make up his mind at once, the only thing to do is break with Wilson. And all we can do then is remove our helmets and pray."

But the Chancellor would not listen to the distraught colonel, who then hurried to a telephone and reported to Ludendorff at Spa. The Quartermaster General, naturally, denounced Wilson's demand. Abdication was out of the question. There was only one solution: break with Wilson and fight to the last. The army, he said, was ready to fight to the finish for its Supreme Warlord. The colonel persuaded him to come at once to Berlin with Hindenburg, then reported all this to the Chancellor, who insisted that the two military leaders be urged to postpone their trip to the capital. Otherwise it would still look as though the military was running the nation. Haeften passed on this request, but Ludendorff refused. He would be in the capital the next day to see the Kaiser.

That evening the Cabinet met without Prince Max. Upon learning that Hindenburg and Ludendorff were coming to Berlin, Vice-Chancellor von Payer insisted that other authorities be asked if the war should be continued. "We need not heed Ludendorff's objections. He has shown symptoms of inner uncertainty."

Erzberger thought the time had passed to listen to *any* military authorities. "We alone must now bear the responsibility. The question today is no longer military, but political. If we call in the Supreme Command, Wilson will again have an excuse for asserting that the military commanders are still in control."

Others felt that they needed military experts' judgment for their own peace of mind. Then Foreign Minister Solf gave his interpretation of the Wilson note. The President, he said, did not demand abdication but was himself in serious trouble. He had to take into account the American public and the Allied military commanders, particularly Foch. "That is why the second part of the note contains the request that Germany give him facts which can reassure him. Among these are (1) Ludendorff's removal and (2) civilian control over the army. If we can guarantee both, we will have a favorable armistice, and a good peace."

Erzberger thought it was doubtful that Ludendorff could be persuaded to resign but perhaps would come to that conclusion by himself.

"We should, however," said Conrad Haussmann, a Democrat deputy in the Reichstag, "avoid provoking a crisis in the army and forcing Hindenburg's resignation." It was obvious that none of the ministers wanted to take the initiative in ousting Ludendorff. They decided to let events take their natural course.

Their indecision was not reflected at Spa. Hindenburg had only one answer for Wilson: a fight to the end. He had already sent off a letter to Prince Max trying to rouse his fighting spirit. "I had hoped," he warned, "that the new Government would call on the whole nation for all its strength to defend our Fatherland. That has not happened." Instead the only talk was of reconciliation. This was having a depressing effect on the troops. "For leadership in the defense of the country the army needs not only men but a conviction that it is necessary to fight and the moral energy for the great task. . . . I earnestly beg Your Grand-Ducal Highness, as head of the new Government, to rise to the height of this holy task."

Just before leaving Spa that evening for the capital, the field marshal issued a proclamation to his soldiers. "Wilson's answer," he said, "is a demand for unconditional surrender. It is thus unacceptable to us soldiers . . . When our enemies know that no sacrifice will achieve the rupture of the German front, then they will be ready for a peace which will make the future of our country safe for the great masses of our people." Although sounding as if it had been drafted by Ludendorff, it was Hindenburg's own work. It was probably the only critical order he had ever signed before submitting it to the Quartermaster General.

As soon as Colonel Heye, head of operations at OHL, saw the proclamation which virtually decreed that negotiations be broken off, he ordered it withdrawn. But a telephone operator in Lovno, who chanced to be an Independent Socialist, had copied it down word for word. Fearing that the generals were trying to keep the war going forever, the operator put a call through the military switchboard to Berlin and managed to reveal the facts to a representative of his party.

Appearance of the story in the press the following noon brought a storm of protest in the Reichstag against military interference. By this time the newspapers had abandoned their self-imposed restraint and were openly discussing the abdication of the Kaiser. The *Frankfurter Zeitung* not only demanded that Wilhelm step down but that the Crown Prince renounce the throne as a democratic guarantee to Wilson's demands.

That afternoon Ludendorff and Hindenburg arrived in Berlin and went directly to Schloss Bellevue with a request that His Majesty break off negotiations. Ludendorff argued that little could be expected of the new Government, but the Kaiser refused to make a decision, referring them to Prince Max.

The Chancellor refused to admit the two military leaders to his bedroom, insisting that they see Vice-Chancellor von Payer instead. A meeting was set up for that evening at the Ministry of the Interior. In the meantime Prince Max received two important documents that forced him to face a problem he had been avoiding—abdication. The first was a wire from his cousin, Prince Ernst zu Hohenlohe-Langenburg, who had been negotiating in Switzerland with American delegates on prisoners of war. I HAVE JUST LEARNED FROM A RELIABLE SOURCE THAT THE CONCLUSION OF WILSON'S NOTE CAN REALLY MEAN ONLY THAT THE ONLY WAY TO ANYTHING LIKE A TOLERABLE PEACE IS THROUGH THE RESIGNATION OF THE KAISER. . . .

Prince Ernst's informant believed that such a step would enable

383

Wilson to influence the United States Senate, which was demanding unconditional surrender, in favor of his more liberal peace plans. It would also strengthen peace sentiment in Britain and France.

The telegram continued: THE MAINTENANCE OF THE DYNASTY WOULD THUS BE ASSURED, OTHERWISE IT, AND ULTIMATELY ALL OTHER GERMAN DYNASTIES, WOULD RE ENDANGERED, IF ONCE THE BELIEF GOT ABOUT—WHICH THE ENTENTE WOULD DOUBTLESS MANIPULATE—THAT ONLY THE KAISER'S PERSON STANDS IN THE WAY OF PEACE.

He concluded with a warning that any attempt to prolong the final struggle would be taken as fresh proof of the predominant influence of the military and strengthen American suspicions that they could place no reliance on any of Germany's constitutional reforms.

A few hours later Prince Max received a similar telegram, this from the Prussian Minister in Munich: IT IS MY PAINFUL DUTY TO REPORT TO YOUR GRAND DUCAL HIGHNESS THAT WILSON'S ANSWER, PUBLISHED HERE YESTERDAY, IS INTERPRETED BY AUTHORITIES IN BAVARIA TO MEAN THAT THE LAST PARAGRAPH IS DIRECTED AGAINST THE PERSON OF OUR KAISER. . . .

The Bavarian Prime Minister and Minister of War, he continued, therefore urged that the Kaiser be candidly informed that the enemy will approve of no acceptable peace unless His Majesty lays down the imperial crown. HIS FIGURE WOULD LIVE ON IN HISTORY AS THE NOBLEST, THE MOST HIGH-MINDED AND THE MOST SELF-SACRIFICING OF THE GERMAN PEOPLES BENEFACTORS.

Faced with reality, Prince Max had only one course. He transmitted the two messages to the Kaiser without comment.

On his way to dinner Alexander, Prince Münster von Derneburg, a member of the Prussian Upper House, was bemoaning the universal agreement among friends at lunch that Germany should break off negotiations and stand by the monarchy—or at least leave the decision up to Hindenburg. Impulsively, the Prince decided to do something about it and went straight to Hindenburg's quarters. He was at dinner but came out a few minutes later. Taking Münster by both hands, he shook them warmly and insisted he come into the dining room. There Münster explained to the gathering that he had heard of the intention of breaking off negotiations in order to save the Kaiser. He entreated the field marshal to reconsider this decision, or in any case to take time to reconsider committing a step which must inevitably imperil the Fatherland.

Hindenburg only replied gloomily, "I stand or fall with my Kaiser."

Prince Münster continued to argue. If the field marshal as well as the Kaiser went, there would be no central figure for the people to look up to. The nation had to have someone to trust or chaos and anarchy would inevitably ensue.

"Hear, hear!" the others at the table cried.

If Hindenburg stayed on, continued the Prince, they might still save the Kaiser. But negotiations must be continued. Then if the conditions imposed were incompatible with the honor of the nation, an appeal could be made to the country to make a last stand.

Troubled but unmoved, Hindenburg left for his meeting with Vice-Chancellor von Payer at the Ministry of the Interior. It was 9 P.M. by the time he and Ludendorff greeted Payer. The Quartermaster General was agitated, exclaiming that Wilson's terms were insulting and dishonorable. Negotiations should be broken off. "We can't answer that sort of man!" Hindenburg concurred. The army still stood unconquered on enemy soil. It must not be forced to capitulate. Both men insisted that the Kaiser make an appeal to the people, the Government, the German states, the armed forces, and the Reichstag to gather strength and continue the war.

But talk of "soldier's honor," "shameful challenges," "inspiring the morale of the nation," and "rallying the country's last resources" made no impression on Payer. The hardheaded Swabian quietly observed that a great nation should not be driven into a last desperate adventure with so little hope of success. He could not accept "soldier's honor" as a political motive. "I am a plain ordinary citizen and civilian. All I can see is people who are starving."

Ludendorff was incensed. "In that case, Your Excellency, I fling the shame of it on you and your colleagues in the name of the Fatherland. And I warn you, if you let things go like this, you will have Bolshevism in the country in a few weeks. Then think of me!"

"Come now, Your Excellency," replied Payer calmly. "I'm not afraid of that. Moreover, you must leave the interpretation of such matters to me. I understand them better."

"There is no sense in talking further with you." Ludendorff glared at the civilian with utter contempt. "Neither of us understands the other and will never do so. We could never get together. We live in different worlds. I am through talking with you." He stalked off, irate and disappointed. Downstairs, Colonel von Haeften was waiting. In deep anguish Ludendorff muttered, "There is no hope. Germany is lost."

7.

He could not sleep and early on the morning of October 26 was at the red brick building on the Königsplatz which housed the Prussian General Staff. The sentries at the entrance clicked to attention, and the Quartermaster General went up to the first floor to his office. He began writing out his resignation. He had done so many times before, but never with the intention that it would be accepted. "In it I proceeded from the feeling that, in the talk of the day before with von Payer, I had become convinced that the Government would not bestir itself to any action, that His Majesty, the country and the army were thus put in an untenable position, that I was regarded as one who would prolong the war, and that, given the policy of the Government toward Wilson, my departure might perhaps make things easier for Germany in the future. For these reasons I asked His Majesty to accept my resignation."

But even after the letter was finished he must have still hoped it would not be necessary to submit it. As soon as Hindenburg walked in at 9 A.M. and glimpsed the letter, he guessed its contents and begged Ludendorff not to send it. He must not leave the Kaiser and the army.

"After a rather long inward struggle I gave in. I became convinced that I must retain my office and proposed to the Field-Marshal that we should try again to see Prince Max. But he would not receive us; he was still sick."

A little later Colonel von Haeften burst in with news overheard in the lobby of the Chancellery: at the insistence of Prince Max, the Kaiser was proposing to dismiss Ludendorff. He had hurried over to warn the Quartermaster General "so that the final scene might be played in as dignified form as possible."

Before Ludendorff could recover from the shock, official word came that he and Hindenburg were to report at once to Bellevue Castle. Ludendorff's hands shook so that he had difficulty buttoning his uniform, and he was still virtually beside himself as he reported to His Majesty. In a manner wholly changed from yesterday, the Kaiser complained about the army order of the twenty-fourth calling on all troops to fight rather than bow to Wilson's demands. "There followed," wrote Ludendorff, "some of the bitterest moments of my life. I said respectfully to His Majesty that I had gained the painful impression that I no longer enjoyed his confidence, and that I accordingly begged most humbly to be relieved of my office."

According to Hindenburg, the scene was tempestuous. Ludendorff responded to the Kaiser's complaint of abrupt changes in the OHL position with vehement accusations against Prince Max for not siding with the General Staff when it was unfairly attacked. His tone became so sharp that the Kaiser said, "You seem to forget that you are addressing your monarch." Ludendorff retorted with a demand to be relieved and, upon being offered command of an army group, brusquely refused it. This infuriated the Kaiser, who said it was to himself as Supreme Warlord to decide when and whether Ludendorff was to go. Once more Ludendorff offered his resignation and this time it was ungraciously accepted.

The bitterest blow to Ludendorff was Hindenburg's silence. He never came to his subordinate's support; only, at the end, offered his own resignation. "You will stay," said the Kaiser tartly, and the field marshal bowed from the waist. After the two officers left, the Kaiser remarked with satisfaction, "The operation is over. I have separated the Siamese twins."

Outside the castle Ludendorff accused Hindenburg of treachery and refused to ride in the same car. Margarethe Ludendorff was standing at the window as her husband's car arrived. "I was surprised that he had come back so soon from this important interview, and felt a strange sense of depression." He looked pale as death as he entered the room. "The Kaiser has sacked me," he said almost without expression. "I have been dismissed." She tried in vain to comfort him and asked who would be his successor. He replied that he had suggested Kuhl, then jumped up abruptly exclaiming, "In a fortnight we shall have no Empire and no Emperor left, you will see."

As Prince Max was listening to Payer's account of the last evening's conference, Haeften rushed in, excitedly exclaiming, "General Ludendorff is dismissed!"

"And Hindenburg?"

"He is to stay."

"Thank God!" everyone chorused.

A little later the Foreign Ministry's representative at the OHL telephoned. "The Supreme Command is furious," reported Baron Kurt von Lersner, "but in view of my long experience with it, I must, with the utmost emphasis, put you on your guard against placing any trust in its promises and must recommend you not to allow yourself to be turned aside from the peace proposals which are in view. The military situation is as bad as it was three weeks ago. An improvement is not to be expected and the invasion of our territory is only a question of weeks or at most of a few months."

There now remained for Prince Max the task of answering Wilson's note, and it was made no easier to learn late in the afternoon that the President's recent reply to Austria had been "the signal to the various nationalities for the concerted break-up of the Danube Monarchy. The Emperor Karl saw his only hope in cutting loose from Germany." A few hours later the Austrian Ambassador, Prince Hohenlohe, visited the Chancellor. "People will spit at me," he said with utter dejection. "I can show my face no longer in the streets of Berlin." Painfully he brought out a copy of the letter Karl had written to the Kaiser. "It is my painful duty to inform you that my people is neither able nor willing to carry on the war any longer," it began. Karl went on to say that he had no right to oppose the popular will now that there was no chance of winning the war. "I must therefore acquaint you with my irrevocable decision to issue within forty-eight hours a request for a separate peace and an immediate armistice."

There was nothing for Prince Max to do now but send the note to Wilson. It was brief and concise, promising that the peace negotiations would be conducted by a people's government which had all decision powers. "The German Government therefore expects proposals for an armistice and not for a surrender. Only then can the armistice lead to a peace of justice, such as the President outlined in his various public utterances."

While the note was being encoded, Foreign Minister Solf, who was to sign it, was informing his dinner partners of its context.

This group, which included federal councilors, ex-ministers, and a leading industrialist, protested unanimously that the proud tone of the note was quite impossible for either home or foreign consumption. Germany could not afford offending Wilson and if he broke off negotiations the German people could not stand it. On his own responsibility Solf held up transmission of the message and next day informed the Cabinet of what he had done. Since most of them approved of Solf's decision to reconsider, the note was revised to eliminate the demand of armistice rather than surrender. In its place was written: "The German Government now awaits proposals for an armistice which shall be a first step towards a just peace such as the President has outlined in his proclamations." The revised message was brought to Prince Max's bed. He approved and it was dispatched at 4:35 P.M.

Chapter Fifteen

THE FALSE ARMISTICE
OCTOBER 26–NOVEMBER 7

1.

As Ludendorff was preparing to see the Kaiser for the last time, Colonel House finally arrived in Paris to find the French intent upon a hard peace and the British divided. "I don't know how I lived through the day," he wrote in his diary on that memorable Saturday, the twenty-sixth of October. First had come interviews with the press and brief meetings with distinguished Americans and foreigners. Lunch followed with Haig and Milner. "It was a delightful and important meeting." To his surprise he found the former moderate on armistice terms. "He does not consider the Germany military situation warrants their complete surrender." House did much of the talking. "I desired to frame the case as the President and I wish; and wanted to convince both Milner and Haig we were right, in order that we might have the benefit of their support on Tuesday." That was the day set to draft the surrender document, and he needed all the help he could get to prevent vindictive terms.

At six o'clock he saw Clemenceau, who greeted him with open arms. "We passed all kinds of compliments. He seems genuinely fond of me. He spoke in acrimonious terms of Lloyd George and of the English generally. He said they did not tell the truth and remarked that 'Lloyd George sends his orders to me from time to time.' He also said, 'I wonder how I keep my temper!' It was news to me that he did."

Clemenceau handed over "in gravest confidence" Foch's terms

for an armistice. No one except himself had seen the document, not even President Poincaré, and he asked that it be kept in confidence except for the President. The Germans were to evacuate all territory west of the Rhine and there would be a substantial neutral zone set up on the right bank. They would also surrender 150 submarines and the surface fleet would withdraw to Baltic ports.

Clemenceau then let it be known that both he and Foch felt Germany was so thoroughly defeated that she would accept any terms. Apparently Lloyd George did too, for he had sent a rather peremptory letter to the Tiger under the impression that he was weakening and inclined to give the Germans better terms than the British thought should be offered. "If George has anything worse in his mind than Clemenceau," wrote House, "God help Germany."

The meeting ended with Clemenceau's criticism that Pershing had not advanced as far as he should have in the Argonne. Foch had offered to lend one of his best generals to untangle the mess, but Pershing had refused to take him. This same general was then offered to the Belgians. "You see the results," exclaimed Clemenceau, "the Belgians are advancing!" He liked Pershing but it was like going up against granite to get him to accept Foch's advice. "I replied," recorded House, "that it was Foch's fault if Pershing did not do, in a general way, what he, Foch, advised since he was generalissimo and had the authority."

The next morning, Sunday, House, who had set up offices in an old gray mansion on the Left Bank, asked to see Pershing, only to learn he was in bed with the flu. During the day the colonel briefed his new aide and interpreter, Stephen Bonsal, on their mission. "I will follow the President's instructions and give you no definite instructions but just a hazy idea of what I shall expect of you. I think I can handle Lloyd George and the Tiger without much help, but into your hands I commit all the mighty men of the rest of the world. I shall expect you to call at least once a day and my door will always be open to you. From time to time, if inconvenient to call, send a memo—or better still, leave it with the sailors who will guard my gate." After a moment's reflection he added, "You have seen all these strange people with whom Paris now is swarming on their native heaths. Most of them you knew and appraised before they were built up by war propaganda and nationalistic inflation. The war that has destroyed cities has puffed up some little men until they find their hats and boots too small, much too small for them. I shall count on you to present them to me in their original proportions."

Later in the day Sir William Wiseman, a close friend whose advice he often took, revealed to House that the British Cabinet had had "stormy sessions over the President's peace terms." The members particularly rebelled against the Freedom of the Seas and insisted on reparations for losses suffered at sea. Perhaps House was unaware that Wiseman was also covertly in British Intelligence, for he replied that "if the British were not careful they would bring upon themselves the dislike of the world," and that "the United States and other countries would not willingly submit to Great Britain's complete domination of the seas any more than to Germany's domination of the land, and the sooner the English recognized this fact, the better is would be for them." And if challenged, he added resolutely, the United States "would build a navy and maintain an army greater than theirs."

In Berlin the Kaiser was having trouble with his principal ally. Less than an hour after the fourth note to Wilson was dispatched, he wrote the Emperor Karl, who had just confessed he was going to have to ask for a separate armistice: "By carrying out this intention you would open the way for the plan of our enemy aiming at the separation of our countries in order the more easily to subject our lands to their will and to put into effect their antimonarchical purposes." Negotiations were already going on to bring about an armistice, but once the enemy learned that their alliance was broken, the conditions would become much more severe. "I therefore urgently beg You to refrain from any step that must give the impression that we are not united."

Along with the note, which had been drafted by Foreign Minister Solf, went a promise to send enough grain to supply Vienna and German Austria bread for several weeks. But it was not likely that either entreaty or food would keep Karl from surrendering. His sixty divisions on the Italian front had been pushed back to the Piave and there was little chance they could keep the resurgent Italians from soon crossing that river and scoring a crushing victory.

During the day the ailing Chancellor was subjected to a harrowing visit from two emissaries sent by his cousin, Prince Hohenlohe-Langenburg. They brought a letter explaining the Prince's recent telegram. Wilson's allies would never agree to negotiating a peace with the Kaiser, the Crown Prince, or Ludendorff. All three must go or Wilson would break off negotiations.

The two emissaries implored the Chancellor to make his decision quickly. It was only a question of days or even hours before the Americans would be forced to accept Foch's armistice terms, which were bound to be harsh.

The visit greatly disturbed Prince Max, but he still was determined to withhold any action until he had more information. The following afternoon, Monday, he was subjected to another plea for the Kaiser's abdication. This came from a surprising source: General von Chelius, who had been His Majesty's special aide-de-camp for many years. He had information from Belgium that unless the Kaiser abdicated Germany would have to expect terrible terms of armistice and as terrible a peace. His Majesty must make the great sacrifice to save dynasty and country.

Prince Max was distraught. "I begged the General to go at once to the Minister of the Royal Household, Count August Eulenburg, and through his mediation and if possible with his support to lay this view before His Majesty. It seemed important to me that men whom the Kaiser regarded as his personal friends and as pillars of the throne should first show him the honorable solution."

Chelius accepted the chore and brought with him the letter of Prince Hohenlohe, but the Minister of the Royal Household refused to be the bearer of such tidings. He refused to show the letter to His Majesty, who had no intention of stepping down, and had just sent Prince Max the text of a decree instituting the new constitutional reforms, as if he himself had thought of them. "I, together with My August Confederates, give My assent to these resolutions of the Representative Assembly, in the firm will to do My best to cooperate in putting them into full execution, convinced that I am thereby furthering the welfare of the people. The Kaiser is now the Servant of the People."

Such was his insensitive answer to the clamorous demands for abdication in the face of another military disaster. The Italians had crossed the Piave and Austrian resistance was crumbling. At six o'clock the next morning, October 29, an Austrian General Staff officer appeared at a railway embankment north of Serravalle accompanied by a man carrying a white flag. Two trumpeters blasted out "General March." The six-day battle of Vittorio Veneto was over: 30,000 Austrians were dead and 427,000 were about to be taken prisoner.

Germany's last ally had succumbed and there were two and a half million Americans in France. Prince Max knew he must act at once. Someone had to persuade His Majesty to renounce the crown without delay. It had to be someone close. Already Eulenburg and the court chaplain, Herr von Drysander, had refused, so the Chancellor's spirits were raised when General von Chelius was announced. Perhaps he could be persuaded to try again. But the general declared tersely that the Kaiser should, under no circumstances, abdicate. It would mean the dissolution of army and empire. Stunned by this complete change of attitude, Prince Max asked for an explanation. Yesterday, replied Chelius, he had been a victim of the Chancellor's suggestive influence and had not really expressed his real opinion. "Was it you or I," exclaimed the indignant Prince, "who came from Brussels to Berlin to demand the Kaiser's abdication as Germany's last hope, and brought along documents to support this demand?" He was in a quandary. "To whom could I now turn, who would be willing and fitted to speak to the Kaiser as a friend? I knew of no one in Berlin." No one except himself.

At the new palace in Potsdam the Kaiserin was urging her husband to go to Spa. She knew how easily he might change his mind and accede to the growing demand for abdication. But there in the Belgian resort town the Supreme Command, and particularly Hindenburg, could protect him from himself and the pernicious influence of Prince Max.

391

Admiral von Müller found the Kaiser wan and hollow-eyed, despite an outward mood of gaiety and confidence. "The English are at loggerheads with the Americans," he said. "The Landsdowne Clique has coalesced with the Labour Party to obtain a swift acceptable peace for Germany." Then His Majesty read aloud a confidential letter from an agent in Holland who recommended that Germany make peace overtures to England, not America, since the former was obviously perturbed by the latter's numerical superiority. Moreover, England was in a difficult situation and the workers in Scotland were causing great trouble. "The Kaiser painted a very bold picture in conclusion: An agreement with England, to include a treaty with Japan to fling the Americans out of Europe . . . The Kaiser already envisaged Japanese divisions arriving via Serbia on the Western Front to help throw out the Americans. In this way we could obtain a good peace, for the English have no interest in weakening us and would gladly see us in possession of a strong fleet and an even stronger submarine force." After spinning out this fantasy, the Kaiser spoke a few personal words, remarking that the two of them had lived through a very interesting era. He sent his regards to the admiral's family, then dismissed him from further service without revealing that he was about to leave Berlin.

Late that afternoon, Baron Kurt von Grünau, the Kaiser's representative at the Foreign Ministry, appeared at Prince Max's quarters to announce that His Majesty was going to Spa. "Is that a bad joke?" asked the amazed Chancellor. Grünau said that he himself had just learned of the trip a half hour earlier from the Kaiser's adjutant, Major Niemann. He had warned the major that such a sudden departure would excite public opinion and be taken to mean that the Kaiser was seeking refuge with the army. Niemann replied that Hindenburg regarded it of extreme importance, after the political turmoil of the past few weeks, to bring His Majesty once more into touch with the army.

Prince Max immediately sent Solf to persuade Count Eulenburg or the new head of the Civil Cabinet to prevent the journey, then telephoned the Minister of War, who knew nothing about the trip but assured Prince Max that if His Majesty did so he would soon return to Berlin. This did not satisfy the Chancellor. He telephoned the Kaiser directly, expressing painful surprise that such an important decision had been taken so abruptly without his knowledge. "I urgently begged for a postponement of the journey, which at the moment must make the worst possible impression. Questions of the greatest importance would have to be settled in the next few days—questions which we could not possibly settle on the telephone."

"You got rid of Ludendorff," said the Kaiser. Now he would personally have to replace him as Quartermaster General by General Wilhelm Groener, who had distinguished himself at the front and was also coordinator of wartime production.

The field marshal could surely do that by himself, replied Prince Max, and begged for a personal audience.

But the Kaiser said his doctors feared he would catch the Chancellor's influenza. "Besides you must take care of your own health."

Prince Max once more begged that he be allowed to come to Potsdam, but was refused. "We are now entering the most difficult time of all," he argued. "At such a time Your Majesty cannot be absent."

"If you do all I have told you to do, all may still be well," said Wilhelm in reference to his recent advice to base the peace action on England, not America. That evening His Majesty and entourage left for Spa. He was needed there, he explained in a telegram to the Chancellor, to settle the question of Ludendorff's successor, and to thank his brave troops for their superhuman efforts. "To make the situation easier for you, Ludendorff had to go. His going is from a military point of view a severe loss to the army. It is My duty to make good this loss; and it is necessary for Me to introduce his successor; that is why I am leaving this evening."

2.

House was suffering from indigestion on that morning of the twenty-ninth. He rested on a couch, covered by a blanket, sorting his thoughts for the important afternoon meeting of the Supreme War Council. "It seems to me of the utmost importance," he had written yesterday in his diary, "to have the Allies accept the Fourteen Points and the subsequent terms of the President. If this is done the basis of a peace will already have been made. Germany began negotiations on the basis of these terms, and the Allies have tentatively accepted them, but as Germany shows signs of defeat it is becoming every day more apparent that they desire to get from under the obligations these terms will impose upon them in the making of peace."

Pershing's personal representative, Lloyd Griscom, now a lieutenant colonel, arrived on his morning rounds to find House "white and frail." While they were discussing the afternoon meeting, one of House's secretaries, Joseph Grew, rushed in excitedly waving a telegram. It was Austria's answer to Wilson's note. All of the President's harsh conditions were accepted! "The Austro-Hungarian Government declares it is, in consequence, prepared, without awaiting the result of other negotiations, to enter into pourparlers regarding peace . . ." It was practically unconditional surrender and House, forgetting his misery, sat up full of fire. "That ends it!" he said. "The war's over!"

At luncheon with British leaders the rejuvenated House learned from Lloyd George that the second of Wilson's Fourteen Points, dealing with the freedom of the seas, "could not be accepted without qualifications, unless it were incorporated into the constitution of a league of nations satisfactory to the British."

Afterward they all went to the Quai d'Orsay to meet with Clemenceau and Italian Foreign Minister Sonnino, representing Premier Orlando, who had not yet arrived in France. The first question placed before the Supreme War Council was how to deal with the German request for armistice. After some argument, House suggested that the terms be communicated to Wilson for his endorsement, and that *he* should inform the Germans that their request for armistice would be granted. The terms in detail, however, would be given directly to Germany by the Allies. While Lloyd George readily agreed, Clemenceau objected to inviting the Germans to an armistice. "I find the arguments of Mr. Lloyd George excellent," he said, "and I cannot refute them. But there is one objection to his proposition: it is impossible. If we follow it out, it will be necessary for Marshal Foch to send a parliamentary to go to the German lines with a white flag to ask for an armistice. Marshal Foch would never do this and I would never permit him to do it."

Lloyd George explained that this was not the case at all. The Germans would be asked to send a parliamentary to Foch. This satisfied Clemenceau, but Sonnino raised another objection. What if the Germans accepted and Austria refused? That would leave Italy to fight Austria all by herself.

House patiently pointed out that Austria had just agreed to make a separate peace and to accept Wilson's conditions whatever they might be. Austria was certainly in a state of exhaustion and her army near collapse.

Sonnino's concern was ludicrous to Clemenceau and Lloyd George, who both assured him that proper steps would be taken to prevent such an impasse—and then they began wrangling with each other as to whether a French or British admiral should accept the Turks' surrender. To House it was a childish waste of time. "They bandied words like fishwives, at least George did. Clemenceau was more moderate. One thing Lloyd George told him was that the British were compelled to do all the fighting in Turkey and had several hundred thousand men there, while the French had a few 'nigger policemen around to keep the British from stealing the Holy Sepulchre.' There was much more like this. It would have been humorous if it had not been such a tragic waste of time. Clemenceau appears to better advantage than Lloyd George. They both have courage and are equally quick at repartee. The trouble with Clemenceau is that he thinks in terms of the Second Empire. He does not know what all this new thought is about and frankly says that his task is done with the winning of the war. I take it he will occupy a secure place in French history for he deserves it. There is but one master in France and that is Georges Clemenceau. His rule is almost absolute—temporary though it may be."

A much more serious argument broke out upon resumption of discussion of the German armistice, and Lloyd George openly assailed Wilson's terms. "Should we not," he asked, "make it clear to the German Government that we are not going in on the Fourteen Points of peace?" Clemenceau added that Wilson had never asked him whether *he* accepted the Fourteen Points. "I have not been asked either," exclaimed Lloyd George. Both, with some justification, regarded these terms as little more than propaganda with an appeal for justice that was woefully vague. Neither felt he could ratify nebulous precepts that seemed destined to make difficulties later not only with the President but with the Germans, who might very well claim that the peace terms violated the Fourteen Points.

Lloyd George turned aggressively to House. "What is your view? Do you think that if we agree to an armistice we accept the President's peace terms?"

"That is my view," said House.

There was such electricity between the two men that French Foreign Minister Pichon tired to smooth over matters. "We can say to Germany that we are only stating terms of an armistice, not terms of peace."

But the British were not to be assuaged so easily. "What we are afraid of," said Lord Balfour, "is that we cannot say that we are merely interested in the terms of an armistice. For the moment, unquestionably, we are not bound by President Wilson's terms; but if we assent to an armistice without making our position clear, we shall certainly be so bound."

"Then," spoke up Clemenceau, "I want to hear the Fourteen Points." As the first point ("Open covenants of peace, openly arrived at . . .") was read aloud it was obvious the Tiger was unhappy. "I cannot agree never to make a private or secret diplomatic agreement of any kind."

"I do not think it possible so to limit oneself," chimed in Lloyd George.

House explained that the proposal did not mean open conferences but merely publicity of results and he was supported by a Briton, Balfour, who argued that the intent was merely to prohibit secret treaties. But the American got no help from anyone on the second point, Freedom of the Seas.

Lloyd George reacted heatedly. "This point," he almost shouted, "we cannot accept under any conditions; it means that the power of blockade goes; Germany has been broken as much by the blockade as by military methods; if this power is to be handed over to the League of Nations and Great Britain were fighting for her life, no league of nations would prevent her from defending herself. This power has prevented Germany from getting rubber, cotton, and food through Holland and the Scandinavian countries." Until the League of Nations was a reality he would never let this power go.

House was not intimidated. The term Freedom of the Seas, he said, did not mean abolition of the principle of blockade but only immunity of private property at sea in time of war. British interference with American trade during a future war might throw the United States into the arms of Britain's enemy, whoever that might be.

The French and Italians then joined in the argument, not because of any concern over the issue of freedom of the seas but because they objected to almost everything in the Fourteen Points. Sonnino, for instance, demanded that Wilson be informed categorically that his points could not be accepted since it was impossible to agree upon a peace program while making an armistice. Settle the military and naval terms of the armistice, he said. The bases of peace must be left until later.

This was exactly what House was determined to avoid. He could not have Wilson's principles postponed. If the Allies persisted in their refusal to accept the Fourteen Points, he said, President Wilson would be forced to tell the enemy, "The Allies do not agree to the conditions of peace proposed by me and accordingly the present negotiations are at an end." Then, House added, the President would be "free to consider the question afresh and to determine whether the United States should continue to fight for the principles laid down by the Allies."

His quietly spoken warning, as he later told the President, "had a very exciting effect on those present."

"Do you mean that you will make a separate peace?" asked the astounded Clemenceau.

"It might amount to that—it depends on how far your criticisms go."

Lloyd George would not back down. "If the United States made a separate peace, we shall be very sorry. But we could not give up the blockade, the power which enabled us to live. As far as the British public is concerned, we will fight on."

"Yes," interjected Clemenceau, "I cannot understand the meaning of the doctrine. War would not be war if there was freedom of the seas."

House, who looked very sick to Hankey, was anxious to give the others the chance to reconsider the consequences of a refusal to accept Wilson's conditions. He also wanted time to exert persuasion on individuals. "It is for France, England, and Italy," he said, "to get together to limit their acceptance of the fourteen conditions; that would be the first preliminary to working out the armistice." Lord Balfour, ever the diplomat, quickly seconded the motion and graciously remarked that with few exceptions the Allies would probably find the Wilson program acceptable. And on those issues, some compromise might be arranged. It was obviously the intent of Germany, he said pointedly, "to drive a wedge between the Associated Powers," and urged them all to avoid this trap.

The dangerous tension eased and Lloyd George demonstrated his talent for calming waters he himself had stirred by intimating Britain only objected to Point 2. "Let us all of us," he intoned, "go on with the terms of the armistice, and in the meantime each of us, France, Great Britain, and Italy, make a draft of our reservations of the Fourteen Points and see tomorrow whether we cannot agree upon a common draft."

The French and Italians were unhappy with this British effort to conciliate the Americans. Sonnino was concerned with the point regarding Italian frontiers, while Clemenceau worried about reparations. But peace prevailed. The British suggestion to draft reservations was adopted and the conference adjourned quietly, if in a mood of uncertainty.

The frail House returned home depressed and still suffering from indigestion. After fretting all evening over the problem, he took it to bed. He slept fitfully and was awakened around 3 A.M., Wednesday, the thirtieth, by the clamor of motorcycles leaving with dispatches for Washington. He again fell to thinking of his dilemma with the Allies. "It then occured to me there was a way out of the difficulty." He was going to tell the prime ministers that, if their conditions for peace were essentially different from the Fourteen Points, he would have to advise the President to go before Congress and ask its advice as to whether America should go on fighting for the aims of Britain, France, and Italy. "I turned over and went to sleep, knowing I had found a solution of a very troublesome problem."

Upon waking, he cabled all this to Wilson, adding that the last thing the other Allies wanted was publicity. "Unless we deal with these people with a firm hand everything we have been fighting for will be lost." He suggested quietly diminishing the transport of troops to France, giving as an excuse the influenza that was indeed felling thousands of Americans at the front. "I would also suggest a little later that you begin to gently shut down upon money, food and raw material. I feel confident that we must play a very strong hand and if it meets with your approval I will do it in the gentlest and friendliest way possible."

With renewed hope, House set off late that morning for a meeting with the British and French prime ministers at the latter's office. In the anteroom, he had a chance for a few words alone with Lloyd George, who was in a friendly mood. He handed over the draft of Britain's objections. Although the Freedom of the Seas clause could still not be accepted and Germany had to pay reparations for damage done to civilian property, House was pleased by the temperate tone of the draft. He remarked that he was afraid the Prime Minister had "lifted the floodgates" yesterday and Clemenceau would not be willing to accept such moderate terms.

A few minutes later this prediction became reality. The Tiger had prepared an elaborate memorandum with many exceptions to the Fourteen Points. House promptly pointed out that Sonnino was undoubtedly preparing a similar memorandum. This was going to make it necessary, he announced, for the President to go to the Congress and ask whether Americans should continue fighting.

His calm words caused a sensation. Clemenceau and Lloyd George looked at each other significantly and the Tiger immediately accepted the British version without further protest. It was a notable victory for House, and at that afternoon's meeting, Premier Orlando and Foreign Minister Sonnino were the ones in the minority. Disregarding objections, Sonnino insisted upon reading his own tendentious draft claiming extensive territory on the Adriatic. This set off a heated argument, abruptly ended by Clemenceau. "Are we agreed respecting the reply to Germany?" he said bluntly. "I accept. Lloyd George accepts." He turned to Orlando. "Do you accept?"

"Yes," said Orlando, settling what could have become a contentious scene.

3.

The Kaiser's arrival in Spa that morning of the thirtieth took the Supreme Command by surprise. His presence, in fact, was a source of embarrassment. "Prince Max's Government," he announced to Admiral von Hintze, "is trying to throw me out. At Berlin I should be less able to oppose them than in the midst of my troops."

In the capital the Chancellor had just received information from two American diplomats in Denmark that Wilson was "still sticking to his peace of justice and is fighting an up-hill battle against the Entente chauvinists, who are at present in control in France and in England." Chauvinists were also strong in the United States, but Wilson "could easily dispose of them after the abdication of the Kaiser and the Crown Prince."

"Then I realized with horror," recalled Prince Max, "the extent of the mistake I had made in not compelling the Kaiser to remain in Berlin, cost what it might." He tried to rectify his "fatal omission" with a telegram stating he could not bring peace at home or abroad in the absence of His Majesty. He humbly begged the Kaiser to return as soon as possible. "I do not think I could answer for an absence beyond Thursday; at any hour we may be confronted with decisions on which the fate of Germany depends, decisions that only can be made through the cooperation of Crown, Chancellor and Government. In this situation I myself could not possibly leave Berlin."

A curt refusal soon arrived that by its tone indicated the Kaiser was deeply displeased and offended. Prince Max also was hurt that his liege now looked upon him as an adversary. "That was a very hard blow to me personally, and no less to the cause to which I was committed." He had always felt that His Majesty would see in him no mere chancellor of a democratic government but a friend and relative who was striving to save the House of Hohenzollern from collapse. "And now the Kaiser had hardened his heart against me, withdrawn himself and entrenched himself against me. I thus looked for allies who stood as near to him or nearer than I did." He telegraphed the Grand Duke of Hesse a request for his personal help.

Wilhelm was faced with a growing demand for his abdication. "What Will the Kaiser Do?" asked the Berlin *Vorwärts* the next day. "Nothing can still the whisperings and the mutterings of the people: 'What will the Kaiser do? When will he do it?'" Even men devoted to the monarch were asking the same question. And one thing was at last clear to Prince Max: the decision could not await the Kaiser's return; and he must fight for time. At a meeting of the Cabinet on that last day of October, the Chancellor said that he had been considering the question of abdication for some time. "But I declare expressly that any abdication of His Majesty the Kaiser can only and ought only to take place of his own free will. Only so can damage to empire and army be avoided, only so can Germany's dignity be preserved. I can only take action in this matter if my freedom is not impaired and if all attempts to exert pressure on me are avoided."

Scheidemann, a Social Democrat, replied that he had no wish to put pressure on the Kaiser, but it was their imperative duty to advise him to step down voluntarily. The demand for his abdication had not originated among workers but in middle-class circles. The peasants in South Germany also were clamoring for his abdication. "He must draw the consequences of defeat and withdraw voluntarily."

In the debate that followed, it soon became evident that the Cabinet was hopelessly divided, nor could it agree on what kind of Government should follow abdication. Even a private discussion with a select group in Prince Max's room failed to reach any consensus. The Chancellor was left with only one clear conviction: "that an abdication of His Majesty is possible only if it takes place voluntarily." His chief concern, he said, was not to let the situation degenerate until the people demanded abdication. "Such a situation would lead to civil war, since there are millions in the country who stand firmly by His Majesty." One man alone in the room, Bill Arnold Drews, the Prussian Minister of the Interior, spoke out with ruthless frankness, and he was so moved he could scarcely control himself. "Either the Kaiser goes," he said, "or we have to give up national defense."

After the meeting Prince Max took Drews aside and begged him to start that very evening for Spa to inform Wilhelm as King of Prussia in his own capacity as Prussian Minister of the Interior, of the widespread opinion throughout the nation that he should abdicate. "I was certainly doubtful as to the ability of this matter-of-fact official to hold his own in an atmosphere to which he was not accustomed." But there was no alternative. Drews accepted but on the way out was so moved that he almost collapsed on the stairs.

A sense of panic came over Berlin with the news that Austria had made a separate peace with Italy and that radicals had just turned Hungary into an independent republic. Facts were followed by a succession of rumors. Princess Blücher was told by her husband's man of business that Germany herself had practically accepted capitulation. Cologne was to be occupied by the English, Baden-Baden by the Swiss, Strassburg by the French, Metz by the Americans, Heligoland by the English, and so on. To prevent a catastrophe, German banks would allow no one to withdraw more than two hundred marks at one time. "Every moment the telephone brings us fresh tidings of foreboding for Germany. Its shrill call seems ominous of coming evil. The Austrians, they say, are helpless to prevent the enemy marching through their country, and the French and Italian troops are already approaching Germany. The former they expect through Dresden and the latter through Bavaria, while the Serbians will come through Silesia." Austrian troops were already returning in disorderly bands to plunder villages for food.

In addition to the unknown was the awful reality of influenza. Hardly a family in the country was spared. "From our housekeeper at Krieblowitz I hear that the whole village is stricken with it, and the wretched people are lying about on the floors of their cottages in woeful heaps, shivering with fever and with no medicaments or any one to attend them." In Hamburg four hundred were dying each day and furniture vans had to carry the bodies to the cemetery. "We are returning every day to the barbarism of the Middle Ages in every way. I am often astonished that there are no religious fanatics nowadays to run through the streets, dressed in sackcloth and ashes, and calling on the people to repent their sins."

At least 400,000 Germans would die of the so-called Spanish influenza which was ravaging both sides and striking down workers and leaders alike. In England, Lloyd George had been temporarily felled, and only after the recent death of Clemenceau's son-in-law was the scourge finally mentioned in the French press. By now 1,200 people in Paris alone were dying every week. In the United States the flu had spread like prairie fire and forty-six states were already affected.

It was difficult to maintain public services in London with so many policemen and firemen stricken. Deaths had risen in England and Wales by late October to 4,482 a week. "In trains and trams," recalled Caroline Playne, "the depression shown on travellers' faces was very noticeable and talk was all about specially sad cases of death from influenza. A sense of dread is very general. Some who, one knows, are anxious for peace, say they dread to think it may come."

The scourge had struck in two waves, the first reaching its peak that July. This was generally mild, with few fatalities and recovery usually coming within three days. The second wave in October was far deadlier. One out of ten of all sufferers became so ill that death resulted more often than recovery. The most tragic feature was its high quota among the young; about a quarter of those stricken were children, fifteen and under.

Nor could any effective remedy be found. Various vaccines were tried but without much success. About all doctors could do was recommend complete rest as soon as symptoms appeared. To the poor who had to work or starve this was impossible advice; and they continued at their jobs passing on the dread disease to others.

It spread with terrifying rapidity. One morning a school or factory would teem with the healthy, but by afternoon large numbers would be infected. "Barrack rooms which the day before had been full of bustle and life," wrote one witness, "would now be converted wholesale into one great sick room, the number of sick developing so rapidly that the hospitals were, within a day or two, so overfull that fresh admissions were impossible and the remainder of the sick had to be nursed and treated where they were."

Quarantine seemed the only means of stemming the disease. In Pittsburgh and other American cities movie houses and theaters were closed. Dance halls and other places of congregation were sometimes shut down temporarily. The healthy were advised not only to wear fine gauze masks over nose and mouth but to use disinfectants and sprays liberally. So many Australian troops in Britain were afflicted that special cemeteries had to be set up on Salisbury Plain. And in France, 70,000 American troops had to be hospitalized, nearly a third of them dying.

Before the pandemic ran its course 20,000,000 Americans would contract the disease and a half million of these would die. Throughout the world it was conservatively estimated that at least 27,000,000 perished—a toll far greater than that of all the battles of the Great War.

4.

On the morning of October 31, the three prime ministers and Foch came to House's residence on the Rue de l'Université to formulate the armistice terms for Austria. After Foch reviewed Germany's deteriorating military position, House asked if they should continue fighting or conclude an armistice. "I am not waging war for the sake of waging war," said the marshal. "If I obtain through the armistice the conditions that we wish to impose upon Germany, I am satisfied. Once the object is attained, nobody has the right to shed one drop more of blood."

House and Clemenceau wished to make protection of people and property one of the conditions for negotiations with both Austria and Germany. Lloyd George protested strenuously, claiming that this went without saying. "Clemenceau and I finally gave way in the interest of harmony," noted House, "for there was something to be said of Lloyd George's contention that such protection ought to be accepted without question. I afterwards told Clemenceau that I was proud of the position he took in behalf of France."

While they were in session, House was handed a cable from

401

Wilson in their private code.* It was so intemperate that "if I had read it to my colleagues, it may have led to serious trouble."

> I feel it my solemn duty to authorize you to say that I cannot consent to take part in the negotiation of a peace which does not include freedom of the seas because we are pledged to fight not only to do away with Prussian militarism but with militarism everywhere. Neither could I participate in a settlement which did not include league of nations because peace would be without any guarantee except universal armament which would be intolerable. I hope I shall not be obliged to make this decision public.

After his guests left House dispatched a reply to his impetuous chief informing him that everything was changing for the better and he hoped Wilson would not insist upon his showing the latest cable to the prime ministers.

> If you will give me a free hand in dealing with the immediate negotiations, I can assure you that nothing will be done to embarrass you or to compromise any of your peace principles. You will have as free a hand after the armistice is signed as you now have. It is exceedingly important that nothing be said or done at this time which may in any way halt the armistice which will save so many thousands of lives. Negotiations are now proceeding satisfactorily.

The next morning, November 1, there was another informal meeting at House's in preparation for a formal meeting of the Supreme War Council that afternoon. First they took up Foch's recommendations for the German armistice. "Rather stiff," commented Lloyd George, who felt the French were trying to occupy too much of western Germany.

House's main interest was still the Fourteen Points and he did not want to offend either side. He sympathized with the French yet saw the British point, and wound up by saying that "he was not disposed to take from Germany more than was absolutely necessary, but he was disposed to leave the matter in Marshal Foch's hands."

On that day Premier Orlando also acted as mediator. He suggested that they adopt a middle course: demand that the Germans return to the east bank of the Rhine and leave a neutral belt on the west bank. The argument went on until Lloyd George

---

* House would have been astounded if he had known that the British had broken this as well as the American diplomatic code. "We are intercepting all cablegrams from House to President Wilson and Lansing and Vice Versa," Henry Wilson would confide to his diary nine days later, "and they are the most amazing reding I believe Wilson to be an unscrupulous knave and a hater of England and House to be a poor miserable tool. Luckily I don't believe Wilson has any ability."

abruptly announced that he would abide by Foch's stern military terms.

The roles were reversed in the discussion on naval terms, Foch arguing that the Germans would never consent to the British demands. Why fear an enemy fleet that had not even left its home ports? "What will you do," he said, "if the Germans after having accepted the severe and ample conditions that I propose, refuse to subscribe to the additional humiliations you suggest? Will you on that account run the risk of a renewal of hostilities with the useless sacrifice of thousands of lives?"

After a British admiral protested that Foch had no idea what a serious factor the German fleet had been, Lloyd George again displayed his talent for negotiation. First he suggested a compromise, then proposed that the Allied Naval Council re-examine the question.

But the Welshman was not so agreeable at the afternoon session in Versailles, where he unexpectedly brought up the Fourteen Points. "This question," wrote House in his diary, "was definitely settled between George, Clemenceau and myself day before yesterday and was agreed to by the Italians later in the day, and yet he brought the matter up again this afternoon and would have precipitated an interminable discussion had I not refused to discuss it at this time."

Just before leaving Versailles, House got another cable from Wilson on that very subject. He "fully and sympathetically" understood Britain's dependence on the seas for survival. But the Freedom of the Seas was one of the essential American terms "and I cannot change what our troops are fighting for or consent to end with only European arrangements of peace." The matter must be clarified. "Blockade is one of the many things which will require redefinition in view of the many new circumstances of warfare developed by this war. There is no danger of its being abolished."

As soon as he returned to Paris, House sent for Sir William Wiseman and declared "that unless Lloyd George would make some reasonable concessions in his attitude upon the Freedom of the Seas, that all hope of Anglo-Saxon unity would be at an end. That the United States went to war with England in 1812 on the question of her rights at sea, and that she had gone to war with Germany in 1917 upon the same grounds. I did not believe that even if the President wished to do so he could avoid this issue, and if Lloyd George expressed the British viewpoint as he indicated, there would be greater feeling against Great Britain at the end of the war than there had been since the Civil War. I again repeated, with as much emphasis as I could, that our people would not consent to allow the British Government, or any other government determine upon what terms our ships should sail the seas, either in time of peace or in time of war." Wiseman promised to take up the matter with his people that evening and would give House the answer tomorrow.

*　　*　　*

403

By this time Prussian Minister of the Interior Drews had arrived in Spa to carry out his mission for Prince Max. It turned out to be even more distasteful than he feared. The Kaiser, after listening icily to Drew's self-conscious suggestion that he abdicate, surveyed him haughtily. "How comes it that you, a Prussian official, one of my subjects who have taken the oath of allegiance to me, have the insolence to appear before me with a request like this?"

Drews was flustered to silence. (*You should just have seen how that took the wind out of his sails,* the Kaiser wrote a friend. *It was the very last thing he expected, he made a deep bow on the spot.*)

As Drews stood mute in embarrassment, the Kaiser continued. "Very well then, supposing I did. What do you suppose would happen next, you, an administrative official? My sons have assured me that none of them will take my place. So the whole House of Hohenzollern would go along with me." (*You should have seen the fright that gave him, it again was the last thing he'd expected. He and the whole of that smart government in Berlin.*) "And who would then take on the regency for a twelve-year-old child? My grandson? The Imperial Chancellor perhaps? I gather from Munich that they haven't the least intention of recognizing him down there. So what would happen?"

Drews was able to say one word, "Chaos," then made another bow. (*You see, you only have to question such muddle-heads, and go on questioning them for all their confusion and empty-headedness to become obvious.*)

"All right, then," said the Kaiser, "let me tell you the form chaos would take. I abdicate. All the dynasties fall along with me, the army is left leaderless, the frontline troops disband and stream over the Rhine. The disaffected gang up together, hang, murder, plunder, assisted by the enemy. That is why I have no intention of abdicating."

Drews finally managed to get a word in to say he was there under orders of the Chancellor. Someone had to tell all this to the Kaiser. Wilhelm replied proudly that a descendant of Frederick the Great could not possibly abdicate. "I have no intention of quitting the throne because of a few hundred Jews and a thousand workmen. Tell that to your masters in Berlin!"

He summoned Hindenburg and Ludendorff's replacement, General Groener. The field marshal echoed His Majesty's warning, prophesying that the army would indeed disband after abdication and the men would stream home as a mob of plunderers. Groener, a blunt, good-natured Swabian, proceeded to violently criticize the Government for allowing the press to agitate. Germany's greatest danger was not the enemy but rebellion and collapse at home!

The concerted attacks stung Drews into spirited retaliation. He turned to Hindenburg: "Who asked for this Government?" he exclaimed. "You! Who telegraphed and telephoned incessantly [for an immediate armistice]? You!" He asked for permission to resign.

"No," said Wilhelm curtly, "nothing of the sort. We have only been explaining things to one another. Give my opinion to the gentlemen in Berlin." After dismissing Drews he went outside to regain his composure. There he told Major Niemann how Groener had championed him. "That it was actually a south German general who stood up for the German Emperor and the King of Prussia!" he said in wonderment. "That did my heart good."

Now that the Kaiser had withdrawn, Groener could express his true thoughts openly. "He should go to the front," he said, "not to review troops or confer decorations but to look on death. He should go to some trench which was under the full blast of war. If he were killed, it would be the finest death possible. If he were wounded, the feelings of the German people toward him would completely change."

Groener himself set out for the front. Word had just come that the American First Army had broken through the infantry and artillery lines in the Argonne and was driving toward Sedan with dash and power. The British and French were also advancing relentlessly, and it was evident even to Hindenburg that the end was near. "The strain had become almost intolerable," he recalled. "Convulsions anywhere, whether at home or in the Army, would make collapse inevitable."

One major convulsion came next day at the Baltic port of Kiel. The trouble had started a week earlier when Admiral Scheer ordered the fleet to proceed to sea. The crews of six battleships protested. They would defend the German coast but refused to fight a useless sea battle. With repetition of the senseless order by the Admiralty, open mutiny broke out, and most of the ships had to return to the home port, where a number of men were imprisoned. But this only inspired five hundred of their comrades, under the leadership of a stoker, Karl Artelt, to march to a large park where their emotions were brought to a boiling point by two Socialist speakers.

The following day, November 3, a Sunday, almost twenty thousand men, dock workers as well as sailors, crowded into the park to listen to Artelt and the same two Socialists demand the release of their comrades. The crowd roared approval and, torches aloft, marched toward the military prison singing the *Internationale*. A marine patrol refused to give ground. As the mob kept pressing forward, a volley of fire crackled. The sailors broke, leaving behind some twenty dead or wounded. But Artelt and the other ringleaders were not arrested and they set up what they called a Workers' and Sailors' Soviet. Besides release of their mates, they demanded recognition of Soviet Russia, abolition of the salute, equality of rations for enlisted men and officers, freedom of speech, and the abdication of the Kaiser. The mutiny was turning into a revolution.

It was drizzling in Paris that Sunday. House was still at odds with the British over the Freedom of the Seas issue. Saturday he had spent more than two hours with Wiseman and Reading but "got nowhere." "It is the most extraordinary attitude I have ever known and is sure to lead to trouble if not modified." The argument continued interminably. "I cornered him [Reading] so many times that it became tiresome. He could only go back and say again and again that Lloyd George had to consider his constituents at home and their opinion."

The colonel's frustration ended that afternoon at another meeting of prime ministers in his large parlor. Having gone into the meeting prepared to exert strong pressure, he began by reading a paraphrase of Wilson's stern telegram, omitting the President's threat to place the whole matter before Congress. Even so Lloyd George would not consider a change. "This is not merely a question for Great Britain, but also for France and Italy," he said, and turned expectantly to Clemenceau and Orlando. "We have all benefitted by the blockade which prevented steel, copper, rubber, and many other classes of goods from entering Germany. This has been a very important element in the defeat of the enemy."

"Yes," said House patiently, "but the President does not object to the principle of blockade. He merely asked that the principle of the Freedom of the Seas be accepted."

The Prime Minister would not budge. "On this point the nation is absolutely solid. It's no use for me to say that I can accept when I know that I am not speaking for the British nation."

If the principle itself could not be accepted at this time, asked House, were the British ready to discuss it freely at the peace conference? Or was the British reservation a peremptory challenge of Wilson's position?

"This formula does not in the least challenge the position of the United States," said Lloyd George. "All we say is that we reserve the freedom to discuss the point when we go to the Peace Conference. I don't despair of coming to an agreement."

House was relieved. "I wish you would write something I could send the President."

"Will he like something of this kind: 'We are quite willing to discuss the Freedom of the Seas and its application'?"

House was delighted. Although he had not succeeded in getting the flat declaration Wilson wanted, he had managed to avert a complete impasse. As the meeting was breaking up Orlando received a telegram confirming that Austria had accepted all the Allied armistice terms.

"Bravo, Italy!" House said to Orlando, who was close to tears. "I shall not easily forget the scene of enthusiasm," recalled Hankey. Everyone stood up and shook hands and "the utmost cordiality and jubilation prevailed." Noticing that Lloyd George was "curiously piano," Hankey wondered why, and was told "that as a Celt he was superstitious about so much success."

The Prime Minister was as good as his word and early that evening sent House the statement for Wilson: "We are quite willing to discuss the freedom of the seas in the light of the new conditions which have arisen in the course of the present war." At 9

P.M. House telegraphed this to the President along with a review of the momentous meeting. The colonel felt that he had won a distinct victory, but his President, upon reading Lloyd George's statement, was so disappointed he wired back demanding explicit acceptance of the Freedom of the Seas principle. If the British would not comply they could "count on the certainty of our using our present equipment to build up the strongest navy that our resources permit and as our people have long desired."

It was fortunate that House did not get this stiff reply before he hosted a meeting of the Supreme War Council on the morning of November 4. The mood was friendly and in short order they determined on the naval and military terms for Germany. Lloyd George left at 2 P.M. for England and so could not attend the afternoon session at Versailles. Long and tedious, it did result in an agreement to let Germany know that all the Allies accepted Wilson's Fourteen Points with two exceptions: compensation must be made by Germany for all damage done to Allied civilians and their property; and the Freedom of the Seas principle, being open to various interpretations, could not be settled until a peace conference.

If Wilson had been present he would undoubtedly have resisted the latter exception. House wired him in their private code that they had "won a great diplomatic victory" in getting the Allies to accept the Fourteen Points. "I doubt whether any other heads of the Governments with whom we have been dealing realize how far they are now committed to the American peace programme."

Others at the meeting were not so jubilant. Lord Balfour walked up to Colonel Griscom in a state of intense anxiety and said, "Griscom, the terms are too severe. It's the height of folly. The Germans will never consent." General Wilson joined them for tea and he too was convinced that the Germans would refuse such stiff conditions and make a counteroffer.

But House's exuberance extended to his diary that evening. "Wiseman and many other friends have been trying to make me believe that I have won one of the greatest diplomatic triumphs in history. That is as it may be. The facts are I came to Europe for the purpose of getting the Entente to subscribe to the President's peace terms. I left a hostile and influential group in the United States frankly saying they did not approve the President's terms . . . On this side I found the Entente Governments as directly hostile to the Fourteen Points as the people at home. The plain people generally are with the President . . . it is not with the plain people we have to deal . . . I have had to persuade, I have had to threaten, but the result is worth all my endeavours." He was even pleased with the two exceptions, for they emphasized the acceptance of the Fourteen Points. "If they had not dissented in any way, but had let the Armistice be made without protest, they would have been in better position at the Peace Conference to object to them."

His sense of triumph was justified. He had somehow managed

407

to retain the heart of Wilson's program without alienating their allies by stubbornly insisting on no exceptions as the President might well have done. The British and French had been impressed by House's common sense and impartiality, discretion and spirit of friendliness. He had never stooped to invective but gave the impression he was considering their side of the argument even while firmly trying to accomplish the task Wilson had given him.

That night the sky above the battlefields in Italy was lit up with a fireworks celebration of colored rockets and Very lights. And those at the front could hear in the village behind them the ringing of bells, singing, and cheering. The fighting at last was over!

5.

In the meantime the mutiny at Kiel was not only turning into revolution but was inspiring similar disturbances throughout Germany. That Monday morning the sailors had pillaged armories and small-arms lockers to take over most of Kiel. All but one of the ships still in port ran up the red flag of revolution. The men seized officers, tore off their insignia, and escorted them to prison.

Once the news reached Berlin, the Cabinet met to discuss this and other disturbances. Prince Max was still too ill to attend and it was up to them to take action. "Everything," said Count Roedern, "should be done to remove the Third Squadron from Kiel, irrespective of consequences, for the defense of the city."

Haussmann reported that the Berlin police feared riots might break out in hours. Then Scheidemann told about a report from a Munich newspaper. "It says that a large crowd marched to Stadelheim Prison and demanded the release of the inmates. It is very irresponsible of the paper to spread such news; but it is useless to issue orders to cease and desist."

Haussmann noted that the discussions in the press about the Kaiser's abdication were devastating, even confusing, in their effect on the navy mutineers. "The men say to themselves: if the Kaiser abdicates now, we are freed from our pledge of loyalty and need not obey the officers any more and may do what we please with them."

It was finally decided that Haussmann should go to Kiel to calm down the rioters. He would take with him Gustave Noske, a leading Social Democrat member of the Reichstag. No sooner did the two men arrive at the Kiel railroad station that evening than cheering sailors seized Noske, a burly former basket weaver and newspaper editor. He was hoisted onto their shoulders and shoved into the back seat of a car where he found himself next to the sailors' leader, Artelt. As they drove through crowds of sailors to a mass meeting at the Wilhelmsplatz, Artelt would occasionally lean out, wave a red flag, and shout, "Long live freedom!" At their destination, Artelt bounded to the speakers' platform to shout, "Noske is here!" The crowd cheered and waved red flags as Noske was hustled to Artelt's side. Someone shoved a sword into his hand; he hastily got rid of it and began to talk, but more like a negotiator than a revolutionary, for he considered his primary duty was to restore law and order.

Next morning, November 5, Noske went to the building where rebel dock workers and sailors were meeting. He found almost utter chaos. There were no arrangements to feed the men and it was obvious that if they weren't brought under control they would pillage the city. Since no one seemed to be in charge, he climbed to the hood of a car in the Wilhelmsplatz and shouted to the crowd that he was taking over. The crowd cheered. He was acclaimed military governor of Kiel. "I have been obliged to accept the post of governor," he telephoned Berlin, "and have already had some success." Even revolutionaries in Germany seemed to have retained a love of order. The mutineers turned over their weapons to Governor Noske and there was peace on the streets. The revolt had found its master.

General Groener had just arrived in the capital to report to Prince Max and the Cabinet. It was a bleak picture. Germany now stood alone and was rapidly being encircled by the Allies. His troops on the Western Front were so outnumbered that the Supreme Command could no longer put off the decision to retreat further. "Its first duty is and will be to avoid under all circumstances a decisive defeat of the army." But the critical problem was morale. The fighting spirit of his soldiers, he said bitterly, was being dangerously weakened. "How can this sacred fire be kept burning when ice-cold streams, enervating to the soldiers, are being poured out over the army by the cowardly and dissatisfied utterances of the press at home, by the men returning from home leave, and by returned prisoners from Russia who have again been put into the army?" If there were not a speedy change, the homeland would utterly destroy the army. "It is my duty to state that fact here. Likewise, the General Field Marshal has commanded me to state in so many words, with regard to the Kaiser's abdication, that he would look upon himself as a scoundrel if he deserted the Kaiser; and, gentlemen, so I think and all other honorable soldiers." If the fanatical attacks on the Kaiser did not cease, the fate of the army was sealed. "It will fall apart. The wild beast in man will break out in the bands of disorganized soldiers pouring back into their native land."

In conclusion he warned that the army could only resist the enemy for a brief period. It was for the people at home to say that the army must hold out until the finish. "If the army remains unbroken, we should be offered better terms and have a better foundation for reconstruction."

Later Prince Max privately attempted to convince Groener that His Majesty should abdicate, but the general retorted that the question showed a lack of feeling for the soldiers at the front, and then "stopped his ears to all reasoning."

In Washington, House's exuberant message had persuaded the President to abandon his Freedom of the Seas demand. He cabled his fourth and final note to Berlin. The Allies, he said, declared their willingness to make peace with Germany on the basis of the Fourteen Points except for the two reservations. Marshal Foch therefore "has been authorized by the Government of the United States and the Allied Governments to receive properly accredited representatives of the German Government and to communicate to them terms of an armistice."

During the day Wilson informed his Cabinet that Colonel House had forced the Allies to accept the Fourteen Points. To Secretary of the Interior Lane he appeared to be "in splendid humor and good trim—not worried a bit. And why should he be, for the world is at his feet eating out of his hand! No Caesar ever had such a triumph!" The Secretary of Agriculture also noted he looked well and happy. "He acted as if a load had been taken off his mind. He appeared to be less hurried and less under a strain than I had seen him for years."

But in the midst of victory from abroad came a resounding defeat at home. In the congressional elections that day the Republicans captured both Houses of Congress by narrow margins.

On Wednesday, November 6, Prince Max felt well enough to meet Groener in the garden of the Chancellery. The new Quartermaster General's forecast of the situation was even blacker than that of yesterday. He also reported that the Kaiser had just informed him that the army would now have to deal directly with Foch to ascertain what the armistice conditions would be. "We must now cross the lines with a white flag," said Groener grimly.

"But not for a week at least?" exclaimed the startled Chancellor.

"A week is too long a time."

"Anyway, not before Monday?"

"Even that is too late to wait. It must be Saturday at the latest."

Bowing to the inevitable, Prince Max summoned his Cabinet ministers to inform them that they could wait no longer. "Under any circumstances," Groener told them, "we must negotiate with Foch by Friday morning, November 8." The armistice delegation, he added, should leave that day. If no reply came from Wilson before then, they must raise the white flag and initiate negotiations for an armistice, perhaps even a surrender. The Cabinet approved without a dissenting voice.

At noon Friedrich Ebert and other leaders of the Social Democratic party, accompanied by Trade Union officials, arrived at the Chancellery to meet Groener. Rightly or wrongly, began Ebert, the people blamed the Kaiser for the collapse of the Fatherland. He should therefore announce his abdication the next morning at the latest. He could name one of his sons as deputy, either Oskar or Eitel. "The Crown Prince is now impossible; he is too hated by the masses."

"Abdication is out of the question," Groener replied sharply. "At a moment when the army is engaged in a fierce struggle with the enemy, it is impossible to deprive it of its Supreme Warlord."

The others pleaded with him. They had no objection to the monarchy itself, nor would this step abolish the monarchy. Many Social Democrats were perfectly content to have a monarch with social-reformist leanings as long as the Government was run on a parliamentary basis.

The argument turned into an academic discussion abruptly brought to an end by Scheidemann, who had returned from a telephone call, pale and excited. "Further discussion of the abdication is pointless," he said. "The revolution is in full swing! Sailors from Kiel have seized control in Hamburg and Hanover. Gentlemen, this is not the time for discussion. Now we must act. We cannot even be sure we shall be sitting in these chairs tomorrow."

Ebert alone remained calm. "Nothing decisive has happened yet," he said, and addressed Groener. "Once more, Herr General, I strongly advise you to seize your last opportunity of saving the monarchy and taking immediate steps to have one of the princes entrusted with the regency."

Other ministers, including one with tears in his eyes, joined in entreaty, but Groener stoutly maintained that all the Kaiser's sons had unanimously pledged not to accept the regency in case their father was forced to abdicate.

"Under these circumstances," said Ebert, "any further discussion is superfluous. Events must take their course." He turned to Groener. "We are grateful to you, Your Excellency, for this frank exchange of views, and shall always have pleasant recollections of our work with you during the war. We have reached the parting of the ways; who knows whether we shall ever see one another again."

With grave faces, the Cabinet quietly left the room. The silence was finally broken by Colonel von Haeften. "This means revolution. These leaders no longer can control the masses." It was indeed a critical day for the Fatherland. Insurgent sailors were already seizing power in Lübeck, Hamburg, Cuxhaven, Bremen, Bremerhaven, and Wilhelmshaven. They would enter each town by sea or rail, release confined sailors and political prisoners, then form councils in which workers were included. Even more important uprisings were brewing in Berlin and Munich, and it seemed certain that the red flag would soon wave over most of the nation.

Later in the afternoon the Chancellor and his Cabinet unofficially learned of Wilson's fourth note by wireless. The conditions were harsh but at least it gave them the protection of the Fourteen Points. Although the content and tone of the note strengthened their doubts as to Wilson's good intentions, there was a general feeling of relief. At least the army would not have to wait upon Foch.

Groener returned a little later with a suggestion that Prince Max appoint Matthias Erzberger, the Centrist leader, as the Government representative on the Armistice Commission. He would leave that night for Spa to join the military members for the journey into France. Prince Max suggested they publish the news that the Armistice Commission was on its way to negotiate. It would put the damper on the uprisings. Groener, "shaken to the depths," agreed. A statement was issued to the press stating that the Allies had agreed to accept Wilson's Fourteen Points, except for the Freedom of the Seas, and that the German armistice team had already left for the west. The Chancellor called upon the people to maintain order in the spirit of willing self-discipline. "May every citizen be conscious of the high responsibility he bears to his nation in the fulfillment of this obligation."

6.

Shortly after midnight a radio message was sent to Foch that the German Armistice Commission was ready to leave and wished to be informed by wireless where they could meet him. The commission would then proceed by automobile to the selected place. Within the hour Foch replied:

> If the German plenipotentiaries desire to meet Marshal Foch and ask for an armistice, they will present themselves to the French outpost by the Chimay-Fourmies-La Capelle-Guise road. Orders have been given to receive them and conduct them to the spot fixed for the meeting.

Erzberger did not reach Spa until eight o'clock that morning, November 7. To his surprise no preparations had been made for the other members and, after a phone call to Berlin, he was further surprised to find himself head of the commission. More than twenty-five officers were asked to accompany him, but he chose only two, General von Winterfeldt, former military attaché in Paris, and a Navy captain named Vanselow. The other member was Count Alfred von Oberndorff, German Minister to Bulgaria, a close friend of Erzberger's.

Hindenburg bade them farewell, observing that it was probably the first time politicians were concluding an armistice. But he did not object now that the OHL no longer ran the nation's policy. It must also have been some comfort to him that the military would not be responsible for what was going to happen. There were tears in his eyes as he grasped Erzberger's hand. "God go with you and try to get the best you can for our country."

After a quick lunch the delegation, which also included assistants, started for the front in five automobiles. The venture almost ended in catastrophe at the outskirts of Spa when the vehicle carrying Erzberger and the count flew off a curve, smashed into a house, and in turn was crashed into by the car behind. Luckily no one was injured but the two automobiles were so badly damaged the group had to crowd into the three remaining cars.

The streets of Berlin on that Thursday morning had looked warlike to Deputy Hanssen as he headed for the Reichstag. "Troops were marching in field equipment with shiny steel helmets. Street corners were occupied by strong military posts. Wherever it was possible to use a street strategically, windows in the upper stories of the buildings were dotted with machine guns. I passed several batteries. The artillery drove through the streets and made it plain that the cannon were ready for action, in order to show the citizens of Berlin what they may count on if they revolt. There is a foreshadowing of a bloody struggle."

During the night Prince Max had been forced to make a momentous decision. He would go to Spa and see the Kaiser while Ebert, a Social Democrat, kept things quiet in his rear. In the morning he met Ebert in the Chancellery garden to reveal his secret. "Unless the Kaiser abdicates," he said without hesitation, "the Social Revolution is inevitable. But I will have none of it. I hate it like sin." Once the Kaiser abdicated he hoped to bring around both his own party and the masses to the side of the Government. Reports from around the country were alarming. Although a certain degree of order had been restored in Kiel under Noske's leadership, things had worsened in Hamburg, Wilhelmshaven, and Hanover; and the Berlin Chief of Police had reported that insurgents were planning to seize the prisons and Police Headquarters during the day.

There was also apprehension in Munich, but so far there was an atmosphere of peaceful lethargy in the center of the city. It was pleasantly warm and would have reminded an American of Indian summer; here it was called *Altweibersommer,* Old Women's Summer. Ludwig III, King of Bavaria, was taking his daily constitutional in the English Garden.

But by 3 P.M. 100,000 protesters had thronged into the Theresian Field. Most of them were workers, but there were a number of students and intellectuals and at least a thousand sailors who had been detained in Munich because of the riots up north.

The crowd fanned out in front of the ninety-foot-high bronze statue, *Bavaria,* standing sword in hand, lion at her side—the symbol of that proud state. It was more like a country fair than a unified rally, with a dozen platforms from which orators of various political complexions were urging their listeners to stop the war.

Erhard Auer, a Social Democrat, held forth at the foot of *Bavaria.* As agreed with other speakers he spoke only twenty minutes, then called for a resolution. Across the spacious meadow, a convulsive waving of red flags was collecting an even larger crowd. On a podium stood a small elderly Jew wearing a black, floppy hat which, large as it was, couldn't contain a shock of wild hair. Epically untidy, Kurt Eisner was a living cartoon of the bomb-throwing Red. He had already spent almost nine months in prison for his wartime strike activities, but the Bavarian police regarded him as a little more than a coffeehouse intellectual. He passed most of his time at the Cafe Stephanie in the student section of Schwabing, writing theater reviews, playing chess, or talking politics in a grating monotone.

Now his monotonous voice, raised to an almost hysterical shriek by a faulty loudspeaker, was working the crowd to "a tremendous pitch of excitement." The time had come for action, shouted little Eisner. His lieutenant stepped forward waving a red flag and gestured toward the Guldein School, a nearby barracks. Linking arms, Eisner, his assistant, and two comrades marched forward, followed by vociferous sailors and a laughing, swearing mob of civilians. Eisner, gazing fixedly ahead "with passionate solemnity . . . half-anxious and half-bewildered," led the way to the barracks. Here the revolutionaries confiscated rifles before continuing across the Donnersberger Bridge to another barracks. A delegation forced its way in. A minute or so later a red flag fluttered from a window. Those inside had joined the revolution.

Ludwig III of the House of Wittelsbach was still strolling in the English Garden, unaware that revolution had erupted. A worker advised him to go home and by the time he arrived at his palace there was such a crowd at the front gate that he had to use the back entrance. In front the guards cowered under a barrage of shouts and insults, then went over to the rebels. All through the city it was the same. No one, it appears, was willing to fight for the Wittelsbachs.

At 8 P.M. two royal ministers advised Ludwig that his life might be in danger. Carrying a box of cigars and followed by his ailing queen and their four daughters, he made for the garage. Like the guards, the chauffeur had abandoned the sinking ship, taking with him all the royal gas. Cars were commandeered in a nearby garage and the regal procession escaped through streets filled with excited but controlled crowds. Just south of the city Ludwig's car, lost in a fog, ran off the road and mired itself in a potato field, an appropriate end to monarchy in Bavaria.

Back in the center of Munich—just off the "Stachus," the Karlsplatz—the revolution was being solidified in a large beer hall. In the ground-floor dining hall of the Mathäserbräu, Kurt Eisner was acclaimed First Chairman of the Workers' and Soldiers' Council. Without delay the council went into action. Trucks filled with occupants flourishing red flags rattled through the city. Eisner's men seized the main railroad station and government buildings. No one resisted. Police looked the other way as rebels set up machine guns at strategic corners.

In the meantime Eisner and his council marched out of the beer hall and, escorted by an armed guard of sixty men and a mob of adherents, straggled down the street to the darkened Parliament building. They roused the custodian and swarmed into the Lower House. Eisner stepped onto the president's podium at about 10:30 P.M., collar open, hair tangled, untidier than ever. "'Now we must proceed to building a new regime," he said. "'The one who speaks to you at this moment assumes that he is to function as the provisional prime minister." The spontaneous applause underlined the obvious—Kurt Eisner had replaced King Ludwig as head of Bavaria.

He wrote a proclamation announcing the creation of the Bavarian Republic, then, exhausted, curled up on a red plush sofa like a cat. As he slept the proclamation was hastily printed in bright red letters and dispatched to all parts of Bavaria. A few blocks away, a revolutionary ascended the steep staircase of the Frauenkirche to hoist a red flag atop one of its famed towers. ·

Revolution had come to Munich, German style, without too much fuss and without a single serious casualty. The people accepted their lot in the same spirit. There was no violent anti-revolutionary action. The people of Munich only grumbled and waited.

In Berlin, a delegation of Social Democrats arrived at the Chancellery with an ultimatum. They were neither threatening nor defiant, more like men "overwhelmed by a sudden panic" at the way power was slipped from their hands. "The Kaiser must abdicate at once or we shall have the Revolution," they said.

Prince Max replied bitterly that the foundation of his chancellorship had crumbled. Indignantly he cut short the discussion. There was now no use in his going to Spa. He dispatched a long telegraph to His Majesty telling of the pressure being put on him to ask for abdication. "In these circumstances it is impossible for me to preserve the unity of the present Government any longer." He begged the Kaiser "in the spirit of the deepest reverence most graciously to relieve me of my office as Imperial Chancellor."

By this time the German armistice delegation had finally arrived at Chimay, but here they were stopped by a German general who insisted that the roads ahead were impassable. Erzberger persisted and, after several phone calls to higher-ranking officers in Trélon, the party crossed the front line at 9:20 P.M. (an hour later than French time). A white flag flew from the back of the first car and a young lancer lieutenant stood on the running board blowing short blasts on a trumpet.

They had not gone much more than 150 yards before blue-clad soldiers halted the three cars. A French captain, recognizing the delegates, got into the lead vehicle as one of his buglers replaced the German trumpeter on the running board. The party was brought to the nearby town of La Capelle. As General von Winterfeldt was apologizing in excellent French to enemy officers for being so late, Erzberger was queried by several soldiers. *"Finie la guerre?"* they asked. There was applause and several cries of *"Vive la France,"* but otherwise the poilus were quiet.

Amid the flashing of magnesium flares from the press and newsreel photographers, the delegates transferred into French cars. *"Nach Paris!"* shouted someone from the crowd as the procession bumpily headed west.

7.

Not long after eleven on that morning of November 7 the French Deuxième Bureau (Intelligence) had received an erroneous report that the armistice was signed and all hostilities would cease at two that afternoon. The sensational news was passed on immediately by Captain de Cartusac to Captain Stanton, the representative of the American Liaison Service. He relayed it to his chief, Captain H. J. Whitehouse, in Paris. He, in turn, telephoned it to the American Army Intelligence representatives in Paris, who expressed both surprise and doubt. Whitehouse insisted that his news was "absolutely reliable and authentic," but Lieutenant Colonel Cabot Ward was convinced that it was physically impossible for the signing to have come so soon. Accordingly he telegraphed Pershing's headquarters that a rumor had been received from the French Ministry of War that the Germans had signed the armistice that morning. "This," he concluded, "is sent with all reserve."

In the meantime, Captain Stanton, believing that the rumor was fact, was already relaying it to various French officials, merely as news without stating it was official. It is the rare human who can resist broadcasting good tidings, and these recipients began spreading them around France.

The news reached Major Warburton, Military Attaché to the American Embassy, at 1 P.M. He cabled Washington while Captain Jackson, the Naval Intelligence officer in Paris, was telegraphing the rumor as authentic to Admiral Henry B. Wilson, the commander of American naval forces at Brest.*

By pure chance, the head of United Press, Roy Howard, was paying a courtesy call to the admiral before his boat left for America. His escort was the Brest A.E.F. adjutant, Major C. Fred Cook, formerly news editor of the Washington *Star*. While they were waiting in an outer office, Admiral Wilson came out, a paper in his hand. "Here's a telegram from Jackson, in Paris, saying the armistice was signed at eleven o'clock this morning, effective at two o'clock this afternoon."

There was a stunned silence of several seconds, then Howard blurted out, "May I use that, Admiral?" Wilson hesitated before replying hesitantly that he supposed so. "I'll see you later," said Howard, and together with Ensign James Sellards, who had volunteered to escort Howard to the cable office, raced down the stairway. "He must have touched only about every tenth step," recalled Cook.

The two first stopped off at the local newspaper, *La Dépêche*, whose leased wire was used by U.P. to transmit messages to America. The operator typed out the news flash on tape, then pasted it on a cable blank so that it looked like all other U.P. dispatches being relayed through Brest. Then, since William Philip Simms was the only U.P. executive authorized to send collect cable messages via Brest, Howard instructed the operator to add "Simms" to his own name.

* Several weeks later Captain Whitehouse was relieved from duty as liaison officer. No action was taken in the case of Captain Stanton.

It was now about 4:30 P.M. and an announcement of the armistice from Admiral Wilson had just been read out in French and English at an outdoor concert by the U. S. Navy Band in the Place du Président Wilson. As the band played "There'll Be a Hot Time in the Old Town Tonight," the joyous news spread and in minutes the streets were crowded with shouting celebrants. By the time Howard and Sellards reached the cable office with the dispatch, the censor's room was empty. Everyone had joined the festivities outside.

Howard waited in the outer office while the ensign took the message to the operations room. Having transmitted numerous U.P. dispatches from Paris, the operator assumed it had been censored there. He added a "Paris" dateline and sent it on to New York City. It reached the Western Union cable office at 16 Broad Street at 11:56 A.M. Eastern Standard Time. Three minutes later it was passed by the New York censor. A moment later it was relayed to the U.P. office on the third floor of the Pulitzer Building: UNIPRESS NEW YORK PARIS URGENT—ARMISTICE ALLIES SIGNED ELEVEN SMORNING [cablese contraction for "this morning"]— HOSTILITIES CEASED TWO SAFTERNOON—SEDAN TAKEN SMORNING BY AMERICANS   HOWARD—SIMMS

No one doubted the message's authenticity, since it carried the name of the president of U.P. and its chief European correspondent. With the Paris dateline it had to be censored by the French. In seconds the most important news in years was sent all over the nation.

New York went wild on that beautiful Indian summer day, November 7. There was a din of sirens, factory and ship whistles, automobile horns, and church bells. Crowds flooded onto the streets from offices, stores, and factories. Traffic was at a standstill. A storm of confetti and ticker tape descended from office windows. "The crowds resolved themselves into informal processions," wrote Mark Sullivan, "people forming arm to arm, no one cared who, no one cared where. A melting, exulting, half-sobbing, half-heart-lifting mood seized upon a whole city. Moist eyes looked out above ineradicable smiles. Here and there crowds formed little knots. In front of the Sub-Treasury cheers went up for the Allies. A crowd sang before the Waldorf. At Columbia University, students rushed out of class-rooms, snake-danced on the campus. The Stock Exchange closed at 2:30 instead of 3—the Curb perforce had stopped at 1. Between 1 and 3 the telephone company carried more calls than in any two hours of its history. The wave of feeling struck every one as it did the barber in Park Avenue who left a customer half-shaved, folded his razor, and exclaimed to his assistant, 'Finish him and then shut up the shop. Me? I'm going home to cry with my wife! That's where I'm going!' "

There were similar scenes all over America, in small towns and villages as well as in the great cities. In La Crosse, Wisconsin, home of many Germans, Ralph Toland took his two children downtown to witness a scene of unbridled joy. Free soda pop was passed out at Begun's Drug Store and at the newspaper office a straw effigy of Kaiser Bill was hung out a window and set afire. It was a sight that Toland's six-year-old son, who had spent much of the past year collecting peach pits for gas masks, could never forget.

But several hours later doubt began to spread at U.P. headquarters, since no other news service had the story. "It was too damned exclusive." Back in Brest, Roy Howard had learned to his chagrin that the report was "unconfirmable" and he hurriedly sent off an urgent cable to New York. It should have arrived at the U.P. office about 2 P.M., in time to warn afternoon newspapers to qualify the report, but the New York Navy censor had sent it instead to the Secretary of the Navy in Washington.

From exultation, America plunged to gloom. "One of the famous fakes of history," editorialized the New York *Tribune*. "A sky full of paper, parades, horns, madness! Well, in America it has been a people's war throughout. The people made it; they fought it. Why shouldn't they go mad at the thought of German surrender if they want to?" Later the same paper printed another editorial, "The Thief of Joy," and noted wistfully, "When the real news of peace arrives shall we have another celebration as good and joyous as those first hours? Hardly, we think. The edge has been taken off."

Chapter Sixteen

THE END OF THE BEGINNING
NOVEMBER 8–11

1.

IT was 9 A.M., November 8, by the time the Erzberger party was ushered into a railway car in the forest of Compiègne. The Germans stood at one side of a large table, behind chairs marked with their names. A few minutes later Foch entered with Weygand, Admiral Wemyss, and two other British naval officers. After a brief introduction and cool formal bows, the company took seats facing each other. Foch turned to his interpreter to say in a low, icy undertone, "Ask these gentlemen what they want."

Erzberger was surprised that there were no Americans, Belgians, or Italians present. In German he said, "We have come to receive the Allied Powers' proposals for an armistice on land and sea and in the air."

There were murmurs when the interpreters translated "proposals," and Foch abruptly interrupted. "Tell these gentlemen that I have no proposals to make," he said curtly, and half-rose from his chair as if to abandon the conference.

Count von Oberndorff leaned across the table. "Monsieur le Maréchal," he said urgently, "surely this is too serious a moment to quarrel over words. How would you like us to express ourselves? It is a matter of complete indifference to us."

"It is for you gentlemen to say what you want," Foch said brusquely.

"As you are aware, Monsieur le Maréchal," Oberndorff went on, "we are here as a result of a note from the President of the United States. If you will allow me I will read it." He read the note aloud, then said, after a pause, "If I understand this aright, it means that you will communicate to us the armistice terms."

Weygand began to read out the eighteen crushing clauses.* Foch noticed that General von Winterfeldt was very pale and sobbed several times. Tears welled in Captain Vanselow's eyes. "Gentlemen," said Foch, "I leave this text with you: you have seventy-two hours to reply to it. Meanwhile you may present observations on details to me."

"For God's sake, Monsieur le Maréchal," pleaded Erzberger, "do not wait for those seventy-two hours. Stop the hostilities this very day. Our armies are a prey to anarchy. Bolshevism threatens them: and Bolshevism may gain ground over the whole of Germany and threaten France herself."

"I do not know in what state your armies are," said Foch. "I only know in what situation mine are. Not only can I not stop the offensive, but I am giving orders to continue it with redoubled energy."

General von Winterfeldt, still distraught, intervened. "Monsieur le Maréchal, it will be necessary for our staffs to consult each other and to discuss the whole of the details of execution." He then read a prepared statement pointing out the large number of people who would die while the armistice terms was being studied.

But Foch was adamant. "The Governments have stated their conditions," he said. "Hostilities cannot cease before the armistice is signed."

Erzberger asked for permission to send radio messages in the clear to Prince Max and to Hindenburg, but Foch insisted nothing be transmitted except by code or special courier. He also refused Erzberger's request for an extra day to get the reply from Germany. The answer must come, he said, before 11 A.M., November 11.

After conferring, the Germans asked that a wireless to this effect be dispatched to both Berlin and Spa. Their request to send Cap-

* Their principal conditions were as follows: Evacuation of occupied territory including Alsace-Lorraine within fourteen days; surrender of all submarines; internment in neutral or Allied ports of ten battleships, six heavy cruisers, eight light cruisers, and fifty destroyers; renouncement of the Brest-Litovsk and Budapest treaties; reparations for damage as well as immediate return of all valuables and securities removed from the invaded regions.

tain von Helldorf to Spa was also granted. He was instructed to tell the OHL that it was not likely they would be allowed to make counterproposals on anything essential but that they would do their best to get what concessions they could. Helldorf set out at 1 P.M.

Throughout Germany the flames of orderly revolution were spreading. In Friedrichshafen, workers at the Zeppelin plant formed a council. The factory workers in the Stuttgart area, including the vast Daimler works, struck and, led by Socialists, made similar demands. Sailors engineered the revolt in Frankfurt am Main. Backed up by soldiers, they organized a council and forced the mayor to recognize their authority.

At Kassel the entire garrison, including the commanding officer, revolted without benefit of bullets. There were a few shots fired at Cologne once the garrison of forty-five thousand went Red, but order quickly settled over the city. A civilian revolt in Hanover succeeded even though authorities ordered troops to use force. Instead the soldiers joined the rebels. It was the same in Düsseldorf, Leipzig, and Magdeburg.

Regime after regime throughout Germany collapsed as workers' and sailors' or soldiers' councils took control. Berlin itself was practically under siege with communications so deteriorated that it was impossible to sort rumor from fact. Police were certain that a full-fledged revolution would soon break out in the capital, but officials could not agree on how to stem it. The military governor of the city, upon learning that trainloads of Red sailors were converging on the city, sent up planes to bomb them. The Minister of War hastily canceled this order and the governor resigned. Officers on leave were ordered to report to the Ministry of War; as they converged on the building with full field pack and side arms, the Government panicked, fearing that this congregation might be taken for a White counterrevolution. The confused officers milled around without orders before gradually dispersing.

Berliners thronged around the bulletin boards of various newspapers waiting for news from Spa. Would the Kaiser abdicate? At the Chancellery, Prince Max drafted a message for His Majesty which was telephoned to Spa. It was vital, he said, to keep the rebellious Social Democrats in the Government and prevent the masses from joining the extremists. The Kaiser, therefore, must at once announce that he would abdicate as soon as armistice negotiations allowed the election of a constitutional assembly. Until then His Majesty should appoint a deputy. But when the message was delivered to Wilhelm, he said evenly, "Tell the Imperial Chancellor that the Kaiser is not thinking of abdicating."

Prince Max agonized all that afternoon. Upon learning that the officer in charge of defending Berlin against the rebels had resigned and that other cities were succumbing to the Red revolution, he decided to make a personal plea to the Kaiser. "I must speak to you as a relative," he said over the telephone in the second person singular. "Your abdication has become necessary to save Germany from civil war and to fulfill your mission as a peacemaking Emperor to the end. The blood that is shed could be laid on your head. The great majority of the people believe you to be responsible for the present situation. The belief is false, but there it is. If civil war and worse can now be prevented through your abdication, your name will be blessed by future generations." He went on for twenty minutes but the Kaiser would not yield. He vowed to restore order in the country at the head of the army; the necessary instructions had already been issued.

Utterly dejected, Prince Max begged the Kaiser to dismiss him immediately and name a new chancellor. "You sent out the armistice offer," said His Majesty curtly. "You will also have to accept the conditions."

Deputy Hanssen was working his way with difficulty through the crowd in Potsdamer Platz as an infantry regiment wearing steel helmets marched across the square. "Machine guns were stationed on the street corners up towards Potsdamerstrasse, and on Lützowstrasse a few battalions were already prepared for battle." He went back toward the center of Berlin. "Everything was seething with unrest. Here and there large and small groups were gathered about speakers. It was evident that the storm would soon break."

Just before the Chancellor retired for the night, he was urged to take a step that might force the Kaiser to abdicate, while keeping the workers and troops in check. He would simply issue a notice to the press: "I am convinced of the necessity of abdication. I have demanded it and will force it through. The people must be patient until the armistice is concluded."

But he recoiled. "It was clear that what was being proposed to me was nothing less than a *coup d'état*. I answered that I would do nothing against the Kaiser."

2.

The following morning, Saturday the ninth, was cold and foggy. Prince Max wakened to more bad news. During the night the Independent Socialists had issued a call for a general strike in Berlin. The Prince's main hope was the Social Democrat leaders, Scheidemann and Ebert, who intimated that they would try to halt the demonstration if the Kaiser would abdicate. Unable to sleep, Scheidemann telephoned the Chancellery before seven. "Has the Kaiser abdicated?" he asked. Not yet, was the answer, but any moment. "I will only wait one more hour," said Scheidemann, "if he is not out by that time then I resign." Just before nine he called again and was told "perhaps at noon." "I don't need that much time to make up my mind," Schiedemann exclaimed. "Please inform the Chancellor that I am resigning. Within a quarter of an hour you will have my resignation in writing." Why such a rush? he was asked. "I shouldn't be in a hurry? I beg your pardon, one should never put off anything until it is too late."

About fifteen minutes later former Foreign Minister von Hintze called the Chancellery from Spa. The Supreme Command, he said, had decided to tell His Majesty immediately that the army could not and would not support him in any civil war.

"In these circumstances," replied Undersecretary of State Wahnschaffe, "there is no alternative left to the abdication." Getting no contradiction from Spa, Wahnschaffe promptly telephoned Ebert asking him to hold up the demonstrations. The Kaiser was going to abdicate!

"Too late!" said Ebert. "The ball has been set rolling. One factory has already come out on the streets." He promised to do what he could, but within an hour thousands of unarmed workers were marching toward the center of the city with placards reading, "Brothers, don't shoot!" A telephone call to the Chief of Police brought more disturbing news. The rebels had attacked one of the soldiers' barracks and blood had already flowed. Minutes later came a report that destroyed Prince Max's last hope: "The Naumberger Jäger battalions have gone over to the insurgents!"

At the Reichstag, Hanssen found spirits very low. "One could no longer doubt that the storm hung directly overhead." The last hour of the monarchy was at hand. A friend rushed up to him. "Machine guns have been put at all street corners," he said. "A bloody battle is about to take place, but the outcome cannot be in doubt. The Republic will soon be proclaimed." Hanssen went out into the lobby to find out how the meeting upstairs of the Majority Socialists on the floor above was going. At the stairs he met Ebert coming down. He was as calm and poised as ever, greeting Hanssen with his usual friendly little nod and winning smile. He went past sedately but his fellow Social Democrats were nervous and tense.

"Well," one named Schöplin told Hanssen, "it's all over now."

"Have you withdrawn from the Government?"

"Yes, there was nothing else to do. We were obliged to jump into the revolution, if we did not want to lose leadership of the masses."

The Minister of Finance joined them. "But that is terrible," he shouted excitedly, his knees shaking. "Was that necessary?"

"Yes, it was absolutely unavoidable," said Schöplin. "We cannot control the masses any longer. They have already ceased to work and have walked out of the factories. They have had enough of the swindle. *That fellow just will not go!*"

"We expect the voluntary withdrawal of the Kaiser any moment," pleaded the other. "If it does not come before noon, he will be deposed. For God's sake withhold your decision for a few hours!"

"No! Our decision remains fixed and cannot be shaken. The only problem is to prevent the spilling of blood."

The Finance Minister was desperate. "We will proclaim the dethronement of the Kaiser immediately. By all means do what you can to have the decision recalled!"

"No, the decision cannot be recalled!" said Schöplin. *"The die is cast.* What the Kaiser does or does not do is immaterial now."

At the Château de la Fraineuse in Spa, His Majesty had risen early that morning. He knew that today would determine his fate. The clang of telephone bells downstairs had gone on all night and still continued along with the almost constant hubbub of officers and orderlies, the clank of sabers, the clink of spurs. A thick mist lay around the château as he set out for his morning walk, "his face grave but with no trace of nervous agitation." He told the guard that he would be in the neighborhood in case the field marshal asked for him. Just then his adjutant, Major Niemann, joined him. Raindrops were falling gently from the trees together with the last leaves of autumn, and this atmosphere seemed to revive the Kaiser. He spoke of the outbreak of Bolshevism in Austria-Hungary and Germany. "In face of a peril which threatens the whole of Europe it would be absurd to continue the war," he said. "Such mania must be confronted by solid ramparts. It is to be hoped that the enemy will ultimately see the danger to the whole of European civilization if Germany is delivered over to Bolshevism."

At the Hôtel Britannique, Admiral von Hintze was bringing Hindenburg the latest dispatches from Berlin warning that unless His Majesty abdicated at once, revolution would sweep away the monarchy. The field marshal's face became a sickly gray as Hintze persuaded him to inform the Kaiser of the hopelessness of his position. Dejected, Hindenburg went to the Quartermaster General's office. Clenching his fists tightly, eyes red as from weeping, he hoarsely told Groener that he was now convinced that immediate abdication was necessary. It was up to the two of them to recommend this course to His Majesty.

The usually composed Groener was shocked. Why the sudden turnabout? He personally could not accept such a complete change of policy. Hindenburg apologized that he had "not been able to find time" to tell Groener earlier. On the drive to La Fraineuse, the two were silent. Hindenburg's lips trembled and he bit them in an attempt to regain his self-control. They were received at 10 A.M. in a closely curtained room overlooking the garden. It was chilly for the only heat came from a wood fire in the grate. The Kaiser was leaning against the mantelpiece, shivering from cold and anxiety.

He asked for a report on the situation but Hindenburg's voice choked. He could not speak. Tears ran down his cheeks and he begged leave to resign. It was up to Groener to say what Hindenburg could not: the situation of the army was desperate; the Fatherland was in the hands of revolutionaries. Some troops inside Germany had already gone over to the rebels. In Berlin civil war might break out at any moment. It would be impossible to lead the army against the revolution. In fact, the army was no longer in condition even to hold the front lines and an armistice must be concluded, on any terms, as soon as possible.

Both General von Plessen, the Kaiser's elderly Adjutant General, and General Count Friedrich von der Schulenburg, chief of staff of the Crown Prince's army group, protested that the majority of the troops were still loyal and there was hope a civil war could be avoided. But Hindenburg and Groener insisted that the army didn't even have provisions. The case was hopeless.

"His Majesty cannot simply and quietly capitulate to the revolution!" exclaimed General von Plessen, who had endeavored to shield Wilhelm from unpleasantness for forty years. Soldiers from the front must be immediately sent against the revolutionaries.

To Groener this was nonsense. If an order came to fight against the home front, he said, the soldiers would fight among themselves. The result would be utter chaos.

This impressed the Kaiser. Above all he wished to spare the nation a civil war. " I shall remain at Spa until an armistice has been signed," he said, "and then lead my troops back to Germany."

His Majesty could not realize that the entire revolution was directed against himself. "Sire," said Groener, determined to speak candidly, "you no longer have an army. The army will march home in peace and order under its leaders and commanding generals, but not under the command of Your Majesty, for it no longer stands behind Your Majesty."

Until then Wilhelm was composed. Now his eyes blazed with anger. "Excellency," he said, "I shall require a statement from you in black and white, signed by all my generals, that the army no longer stands behind its Commander-in-Chief. Have they not taken the military oath to me?"

"In circumstances like these, Sir, oaths are but words," was Groener's sad reply.

This infuriated Count von der Schulenburg. Forgetting he was in the presence of His Majesty, he shouted that neither officers nor men would desert their monarch in the face of the enemy.

"I have different information," said Groener.

Silent until now, Hindenburg felt obliged to come to his support. Like the Quartermaster General, he said, he was "also unable to take upon himself responsibility for the trustworthiness of the troops."

These words dissipated the Kaiser's anger. Uncertain and shaken, he asked that all the commanders-in-chief be queried as to the morale of the army. "If you report to me that the army is no longer loyal to me," he said, "I shall be prepared to go—but not until then." He adjourned the meeting and led the others into the garden. Here the discussion continued as he walked to and fro followed by his generals.

The Kaiser appeared entirely self-controlled and argued at length, but it was evident that Groener's statement had made a profound impression on him. "He was obviously undecided," recalled Baron von Grünau, who managed to spend a few minutes alone with him; "his general demeanor was that of melancholy resignation, and betrayed that he had realized the possibility of abdication, and would steel himself to this hard decision." He assured Grünau that he was ready to abdicate if such was the will of the German people. "I have reigned long enough to see how thankless is a monarch's task. I have no intention of clinging to power." It was now up to others to show if they could do better.

But Schulenburg and Plessen were still trying to convince His Majesty that he should stand firm. When the first learned that the Crown Prince had arrived, he hurried out to recount the morning's conference. He begged the Crown Prince to prevent his father from making a hasty and irretrievable decision.

The Crown Prince, frozen to the marrow, entered the garden to find his father surrounded. "Never shall I forget the picture of that half-score of men in their grey uniforms, thrown into relief by the withered and faded flower-beds of ending autumn, and framed by the surrounding mist-mantled hills with their glorious foliage of vanishing green and every shade of brown, of yellow and of red."

The Kaiser, passionately excited, was addressing those near him with violently expressive gestures. Catching sight of his son, he beckoned him to approach and himself came forward a few paces. As the Crown Prince stood opposite his father, he could clearly see "how distraught were his features—how his emaciated and sallowed face twitched and winced."

The Kaiser scarcely gave his son time to greet Hindenburg and the others before he began to spill out that he could not return to Berlin because a revolution had broken out, and that he would abdicate and turn over command of the army to Hindenburg. The Crown Prince tried to comfort him. All was not yet lost. If abdication as Kaiser were really inevitable, then he should at least remain as King of Prussia.

"Obviously," said the Kaiser.

Schulenburg grasped desperately at this idea. His Majesty should gather Prussian officers and men around him. They would support him to the end.

"Will they fight for their King against the people?" asked Hintze.

Deflated, Schulenburg had to confess they would not. "But in any case, the Kaiser must remain King of Prussia!"

The Crown Prince then urged his father to go to the front with him and march back at the head of his army group. Together they could win back Germany. This fantasy dissolved once Colonel Heye arrived with a report from thirty-nine important officers. They had been asked two questions: First, could the Kaiser lead his troops and reconquer the Fatherland by force of arms? Only one replied in the affirmative while twenty-three answered in the negative and the rest were ambiguous. To the second question, Would the troops fight the Bolshevists on the home front? eight said "yes," nineteen, "no," and twelve were "uncertain."

"The troops are still loyal to Your Majesty," said Heye, "but they are tired and indifferent, and wish only rest and peace. They will not march against the country at present, not even with Your Majesty at their head. Nor will they march against Bolshevism; they want simply and solely an armistice, and soon; therefore every hour is important."

Would the troops march home without me? asked the Kaiser. Schulenburg swore that they would not break their sacred oaths and desert their sovereign and chief warlord in his hour of need. At this Groener merely shrugged his shoulders. "Military oaths? Warlords?" he said bluntly. "Those are, after all, only words; those are, when all is said, mere ideas."

Schulenburg bridled. Such statements, he retorted, only proved that Groener "did not know the heart and mind of the men at the front." The army was still true to its oath and would surely not abandon its Kaiser.

This dispute was ended by Hintze, who said he had just talked on the telephone to Prince Max. The situation was so menacing in Berlin that only the immediate abdication of His Majesty could save the monarchy. Silent, the Kaiser looked appealingly to Hindenburg. The field marshal stood motionless and mute, with a look of despair.

The Kaiser finally spoke. His voice sounded hoarse, strange and unreal to his son as he instructed Hintze to telephone Prince Max that he was "prepared to renounce the Imperial Crown, if thereby alone general civil war in Germany were to be avoided, but that he remained King of Prussia and would not leave the army."

There was a long moment of silence, and as Hintze started for the telephone Schulenburg pointed out that it was essential to make a written record of such a highly significant decision. Thanking him, the Kaiser then instructed Hintze to draw up a declaration for him to sign. "After a good lunch and a good cigar, things will look better," remarked the Crown Prince, and went off to luncheon with the Kaiser and his entourage. It was a painful affair with scarcely a morsel eaten by anyone.

3.

All that morning Prince Max had waited patiently for news from Spa, and every time he rang La Fraineuse the château's telephone was busy. Just before noon he was confronted with the choice of either waiting and doing nothing, or taking action on his own responsibility. Knowing full well that he had no authority to do so, he sent a statement to the Wolff Telegraph Agency:

The Kaiser and King has resolved to *renounce the throne*. The Imperial Chancellor will remain at his post until decisions have been made on questions connected with the Kaiser's abdication, the Crown Prince's renunciation of the Imperial and Prussian thrones, and the creation of a regency . . .

No sooner had this news reached the streets of Berlin than

Prince Max was besieged by a delegation of Social Democrats with a demand that he turn over the Government to them for the preservation of peace and order. "In this matter," said their leader, Ebert, "we have both our party and also that of the Independent Socialists solidly behind us. Even the soldiers have been won over to our side."

Prince Max and his ministers withdrew to discuss their answer just as an army truck flying a red flag and armed with a machine gun rumbled down the Wilhelmstrasse to the raucous shouts from the crowd outside the Chancellery. The conference was short, for Prince Max recognized he had no alternative but resignation. His ministers did not try to dissuade him, for they too felt only a sense of relief. The Chancellor called in Ebert and asked if he was prepared to accept the office.

"It is a difficult post but I will take it over," he said.

"Are you ready to be head of a Government within the framework of the constitution?" asked Solf. He was. "Even with a monarchical constitution?"

"Yesterday I would have answered, yes, absolutely; today, I must first consult my friends."

"Now," said Prince Max, "we must solve the question of the regency."

"It is too late for that," said Ebert, and his followers chimed in like a Greek chorus, "Too late! Too late!"

While the new Chancellor remained in the building to interview prospective members of his cabinet, his associate Philipp Scheidemann hurried to the Reichstag to tell party comrades that Ebert was the new leader of Germany. Then he had a lunch of potato soup at the Reichstag restaurant. This was interrupted by a group of workers and soldiers who rushed in to demand that Scheidemann address the large crowd gathering outside. They said that Karl Liebknecht, leader of the leftist Spartacists, was already making a speech from the balcony of the royal palace and was planning to announce the establishment of a soviet republic.

To forestall the Spartacist plan, Scheidemann, dropping his spoon, rushed to the reading room. He went out to the balcony followed by Hanssen, who happened to be in the library. "It will have to be here," the deputy heard Scheidemann shout. "I must be on the balustrade!" As he climbed up to it, he noticed Hanssen and said, "Hold me by the feet while I talk."

There was a din from the great crowd outside, but as soon as Scheidemann began to speak there was quiet. "Fellow citizens! Workers! Fellow party men! The monarchical system has collapsed. Many of the garrisons have joined us. The Hohenzollerns have left." Then spontaneously he shouted, "Long live the Great German Republic!" There was a storm of applause. And Scheidemann, having proclaimed a republic on his own initiative, returned to his soup.

Hanssen made his way outside through the crowd to see what was going on. "Endless processions were marching along every street leading to the Reichstag building. Men and women were carrying red banners. All the street-cars were carrying red banners. Red flags were hoisted on nearly every house. The gods only knew from where all this red cloth could be procured in such a short time. Large trucks, carrying riflemen and machine gunners, whizzed through the streets and engaged in battle with the troops which still offered opposition. But most of the soldiers seemed to have gone over to the revolution and made common cause with them. Down at the palace cannon were heard, and here and there machine guns rattled. In a few places the streets were barricaded because fighting was still going on, but, on the whole, the revolutionists seemed to have won all along the line by early afternoon. The opposition of the old order was apparently completely broken by the first thrust."

He saw a group of "young brutes" stop a cab and pull out an elderly general. "I am no longer active," he protested. "I have taken an honorable part in three campaigns; give me leave to drive home." But his entreaties were in vain. His decorations were torn off and tossed onto the pavement. His helmet went the same way; his sword was broken; the chevrons ripped off his uniform.

At the Reichstag restaurant Scheidemann was still eating his soup when Ebert joined him. "You have no right to proclaim a republic!" the new Chancellor said angrily. The thoughtless proclamation had invalidated the existing constitution and the nation was technically without a government. "What Germany is to be—a republic or anything else—is for the Constituent Assembly to decide!" Ebert left in a fury but was forced to reconcile himself to his comrade's impulsive act. Thus it was that the German Republic came into existence, born in a decidedly informal and almost accidental manner.

After luncheon, the Kaiser and his entourage proceeded to the drawing room to discuss the draft of his announcement. Admiral von Hintze was in the next room telephoning the news to the Chancellery. But as he began to read the declaration, Undersecretary of the State Wahnschaffe interrupted. "That is of no use, complete abdication is to be pronounced, and Herr von Hintze must listen to what is now being telephoned to him." Hintze insisted on reading the Kaiser's declaration first. Then he was informed that Wilhelm's complete abdication as Kaiser *and* Prussian King had already been published by the Wolff Telegraph Agency.

Shocked, Hintze exclaimed that there had been no authorization from the Kaiser for such a step. At that point the ex-Chancellor, Prince Max, grasped the telephone and took responsibility for publishing the abdication as well as the renunciation of the Crown Prince.

Still holding the telephone, Hintze called the Kaiser and told him. He was stunned, and walked back to the drawing room in a daze, wondering if what he had just heard could possibly be true.

No one could speak for the next few moments. "The ground seemed to give way under our feet," recalled the Crown Prince.

"It is a *coup d'état*," said Schulenburg, "an act of violence to which Your Majesty should not yield. The crown of Prussia belongs to Your Majesty and it is absolutely necessary that Your Majesty, as Warlord, should remain with the army. I guarantee that the troops will remain loyal to Your Majesty."

"I am the King of Prussia," intoned the Kaiser, "and I will remain King. As such I will stay with my troops." He left with as much dignity and poise as possible but soon returned in a different mood. "Treason, gentlemen!" he cried. "Barefaced, outrageous treason!" Feverishly he began scribbling on telegraph forms "a manifesto of protest." Yet when his son begged him to resist and promised to subjugate the revolutionary elements at home with his troops, he refused to listen. He would have no war of Germans against Germans.

At 3:30 P.M. his counselors held a meeting at Hindenburg's villa. The generals asserted that they did have the military means of forcing Berlin to repudiate the published abdication, then Hindenburg insisted that the Kaiser seek safety in some neutral country. "I cannot assume the responsibility of having His Majesty taken by mutinous troops to Berlin and surrendered as a prisoner to the revolutionary government." Somebody suggested Switzerland, but Hindenburg insisted on Holland since it had a monarch and was only sixty miles away.

The group, with the exception of Count von Schulenburg, returned to La Fraineuse about 4 P.M. "My God [*Herrje*]," exclaimed the Kaiser. "You back already?" He told them that he had instructed his son to inform the troops that he would remain as King of Prussia but that he had abdicated as Emperor. Then he turned to Quartermaster General Groener rather sulkily: "You no longer have a Warlord."

It was now up to Hindenburg to admit that the army was not strong enough to put down the revolution. "I must advise Your Majesty to abdicate and to proceed to Holland." Plessen protested, "Above all, no flight!" he urged. The other generals argued that it was difficult to guarantee the Emperor's safety. The assassination of Nicholas II was in the back of everyone's mind. "Might not a similar fate threaten the Kaiser?"

Hintze interrupted the argument. In any case, he said, plans should be set on foot for the Kaiser's journey to Holland. Such negotiations took time. At this point, according to Hintze, His Majesty was suddenly convulsed with rage. "Do you by any chance think I am incapable of remaining with my troops?" he said. Hintze said nothing while the Kaiser paced the room. Finally he stopped and quietly told the former Foreign Minister to take the necessary steps with the Dutch Government.

Admiral Scheer and his staff were then admitted to make their farewell. "I no longer have a navy," Wilhelm told them, and left the room. Hindenburg sadly returned to the Hôtel Britannique, unaware that he would never again see his monarch.

In Berlin neither the announcement of the Kaiser's abdication nor the assumption of power by the moderate Socialists appeased the extreme leftists who called themselves Spartacists after the slave who had led a rebellion against the Romans. They took to the streets to make a real revolution. This was no *Gemütlich* Munich uprising. By midafternoon the center of Berlin was a truculent mass of humanity on the verge of violent action. Occasionally a shot was fired and in all a dozen people were killed, but nowhere did the mob get completely out of control.

Princess Blücher was watching the scene from her residence. "In between the dense masses of the marching throng, great military motor-lorries, packed with soldiers and sailors waving red flags were cheering and shouting vehemently, forced their way, the occupants apparently trying to stir up the strikers to violence. A characteristic feature of the mob was the motors packed with youths in field-grey uniforms or in civil clothes, carrying loaded rifles adorned with a tiny flag, constantly springing off their seats and forcing the soldiers and officers to tear off their insignia, or doing it for them if they refused. They were mostly boys from 16 to 18 years of age, who looked as if they were enjoying their sudden power immensely, and sat grinning on the steps of the grey motors like schoolboys out on an escapade. This, however, did not prevent their occasioning a good deal of harm in the course of the day, for of course some officers refused to obey them, which led to bloodshed and even death . . ."

The intrinsic feature of the rebellion lay in its elemental force, according to Richard Müller, leader of the shop stewards. "It was as though the millions of workers and soldiers had been guided from a single spot. But there was no direction of that kind."

To another eyewitness, Dr. Hjalmar Schacht, it was a bizarre sight. "People passed by the lorries looking depressed and indifferent—they did not even glance at them. The Red revolutionists shouted, brandished their rifles, and generally threw their weight about. In among them, before and behind, the usual midday Potsdamerplatz traffic carried on. A very curious significant scene, expressive of Germany's disrupted condition—revolution in lorries, apathy in the streets."

Near 4 P.M. Liebknecht, the Spartacist leader, was still addressing the crowd from the corner window where the Kaiser had several times addressed his people. "The day of liberty has dawned!" he was shouting to those below. "A Hohenzollern will never again stand at this place. . . . I proclaim the free Socialist Republic of Germany, which shall comprise all Germans. . . . We extend our hands to them and call on them to complete the world revolution. Those among you who want the world revolution, raise your hands to an oath." The answer was a choral roar of approval as a forest of hands shot to the air.

The events of that afternoon had brought about the actual, if not the technical, end of the Second German Empire. It had begun in France on January 18, 1871, with the proclamation of Wilhelm I, King of Prussia and grandfather of Wilhelm II, as the first Emperor of Germany in the Hall of Mirrors at the Palace of Versailles.

Probably the greatest shock to Germans was to find Friedrich Ebert sitting in the Chancellery. In a single day the Hohenzollern regime had evaporated and a man of the people, a former saddlemaker, had taken command. How could it possibly have happened? Ebert himself was uneasy in the seat of power. He realized that his presence would be an insult to those raised in imperialism. Moreover, he did not even represent the radical spirit of the streets. Whom did he represent? He was so panicky that when Prince Max appeared at dusk to say farewell Ebert begged him to remain in Berlin as "administrator" of the Empire. Prince Max had sense enough to know that his time was over. "Herr Ebert," he said, "I commit the German Empire to your keeping."

"I have lost two sons for this Empire," replied the new Chancellor sadly.

The news of the abdication came as blow to such ardent patriots as Corporal Adolf Hitler. He had suffered temporary blindness from gas and was recovering in a Pomeranian hospital when a dignified elderly pastor arrived to tell the patients that the Kaiser had abdicated and the Fatherland had become a republic. As the aged speaker eulogized the services rendered by the Hohenzollerns, so Hitler recalled, he "began to sob gently to himself—in the little hall the deepest dejection settled on all hearts, and I believe not an eye was able to restrain its tears." The pastor went on to say that the war must now be ended, that all was lost, and they had to throw themselves upon the mercy of the victorious Allies. To Hitler the revelation was intolerable. "It became impossible for me to sit still one minute more. Again everything went black before my eyes; I tottered and groped my way back to the dormitory, threw myself on my bunk, and dug my burning head into my blankets and pillow." Out of his black despair came a decision. "The great vacillation of my life, whether I should enter politics or remain an architect, came to an end. That night I resolved that, if I recovered my sight, I would enter politics."

Early that evening the Kaiser, after vacillating, decided to go to Holland and sent word to that effect to Hindenburg. A few minutes later Hintze arrived and, without preamble, informed His Majesty that all arrangements had been made for his trip. At about 7:30 P.M. the Kaiser was driven to the imperial train. On the way he told two officers accompanying him that he had agreed to leave "in the heat of the moment." Now he felt he should stay "even if only a few men remained loyal. I will fight with them to the end, and if we are all killed, well, I am not afraid of death. I should be deserting my wife and children. No, it is impossible. I am staying here."

The last-minute hesitations continued at the train. In the space of the next hour he changed his mind thrice, the last time striking a table in the dining car with his fist, then exclaiming, "I am staying here. I will not go away."

Dinner was a melancholy function and there was little conversation. As Wilhelm was leaving the dining car, Baron von Grünau informed him that the Foreign Minister had just telephoned that a definite decision had to be made. If their departure for Holland were delayed, the element of surprise in the plan would no longer come into play.

His Majesty reflected momentarily: "Very well, but not before tomorrow morning," he said, and, without a single look behind, strode off to his private compartment. This time he meant what he said and he explained why in a letter to the Crown Prince:

> My Boy,
> As the Marshal can no longer guarantee my safety, and can no longer vouch for the troops, I have decided, after a severe inward struggle, to leave the disorganized army. Berlin is totally lost; it is in the hands of the Socialists, and two Governments have been formed there—one with Ebert as Chancellor and one by the Independents. Till the troops start their march home, I recommend your holding out at your post and keeping the troops together! God willing, I trust we shall meet again. General von Marschall will give you further information.
>
> Your stricken father,
Wilhelm

He ordered the train to leave next morning at five o'clock.

The new Chancellor was still in his office, pacing the floor in his shirtsleeves, desperately attempting to conjure up some means of bolstering his fragile authority. Who would support him? What if the military turned against him? A telephone on Ebert's desk rang. It was the direct wire to the Supreme Command in Spa, and he knew his fate depended on what he heard. His hand trembled as he picked up the receiver.

"Groener speaking," said a martial voice. Was the new Government willing to protect the Fatherland from anarchy and to restore order? Yes, said Ebert unsteadily. "Then the Supreme Command will maintain discipline in the army and bring it peacefully home." He revealed that the Kaiser was fleeing to exile, leaving Hindenburg in full charge.

"What do you expect from us?" asked Ebert.

"The Supreme Command expects the Government to cooperate with the Officers Corps in the suppression of Bolshevism, and in the maintenance of discipline in the army. It also asks that the provisioning of the army be guaranteed and any disturbance of transport and communications prevented." Ebert almost wept with joy. What had seemed hopeless a few minutes ago was now reality. The army was behind him.

Perhaps the most fateful day in German history had come to its conclusion. It had marked not only the demise of a great empire but the end of an era. Forty-eight years earlier Bismarck had achieved his dream of unifying Germany and in so doing had created a new image of Germany and Germans, an image of solidarity and permanence that had abruptly vanished. Overnight the foundations on which rested the security of the Junker landowners in East Prussia and the great industrialists had crumbled; overnight the political philosophy on which the majority of Germans had based their conservative and patriotic way of life had apparently disintegrated with the lowering of the imperial flag.

4.

At two o'clock on Sunday morning the Kaiser's chauffeur, Warner, was wakened and ordered to lead a procession of some ten cars to a small railroad station not far from Spa. Warner was to remove the usual flag and any other signs that this was the imperial car. The cortege proceeded through the dark, foggy night at a moderate pace.

Two hours later the Kaiser's entourage collected in the railroad dining car. His Majesty came in, looking self-possessed and calm, and, as usual, gave each man a friendly handshake. Half an hour later, while they were having breakfast, the train started ahead of schedule without any signal, bearing with it a section of the imperial bodyguard. The train stopped at the designated station where the Kaiser and three officers transferred to Warner's car. It started off at once, preceded by one vehicle and followed by two others. A little after seven they reached the Dutch border near the village of Eysden. It being Sunday there was no frontier guard on duty, and it took repeated hooting of horns to rout a drowsy sergeant from the customhouse. Seeing German uniforms, he refused to lower the chains which barred the road. His demand for passports only brought out identity cards of illustrious personages. He was not impressed. The foreigners needed passports. While the Kaiser and his adjutants stood about in the chill smoking cigarettes, arrangements were finally made by telephone to receive His Majesty properly, and he was escorted to the railroad station. A few casual onlookers at the platform recognized him. *"Ah, Kamerad kaputt!"* shouted several; others called out, *"Vive la France!"* The embarrassment ended only when the imperial train rolled in and Wilhelm reboarded it.

While he waited impatiently on a siding at the little station, the Queen of the Netherlands was summoning her cabinet. In short order it was decided to give the German monarch asylum, and Count Bentinck, a fellow Knight of the Order of St. John, agreed, after persuasion, to give him sanctuary at his estate.

* * *

Berliners awoke that morning to find that the usual words of loyalty to the House of Hohenzollern no longer appeared on the mastheads of royalist newspapers. The Berlin *Lokal Anzeiger* was now *Die Rote Fahne* (The Red Flag), and *Die Norddeutsche Allgemeine Zeitung* was *Die Internationale*.

At noon Chancellor Ebert met with advisers, including men from the outgoing regime, to discuss the armistice terms and the request of the OHL that the Allied conditions be accepted "without delay and without change." There was no doubt what had to be done, and instructions were telegraphed to the Supreme Command in Spa to inform Erzberger to accept Foch's terms. At the same time a plea was sent to President Wilson asking him to use his influence with the Allies to mitigate the "fearful conditions" Germany had been forced to accept.

In the railway car at Compiègne, Erzberger only knew that the Kaiser had abdicated and a new popular Government had been formed under Ebert. Erzberger and the other delegates were bewildered. Was it a monarchy or republic? Would Ebert accept without delay the harsh conditions of the armistice? What about the Supreme Command? While waiting for official information from Germany, Erzberger and Oberndorff walked through the forest. It was a beautiful sunny day and they were allowed to wander in a spacious fenced-off area. The hours dragged slowly and it was not until about 7:30 P.M. that two messages finally arrived. One from Berlin, signed "The Imperial Chancellor, 3084," read: THE GERMAN GOVERMENT ACCEPTS THE ARMISTICE CONDITIONS OFFERED ON NOVEMBER 9. The other, from the OHL, authorized Erzberger to sign the armistice but instructed him to point out that the terms would cause famine in Germany and, if possible, to negotiate for better conditions so the people could get adequate food.

The two messages were transmitted to Paris. Clemenceau was annoyed at the second message from the Supreme Command. "What are they waiting for before they sign?" he said, and ordered Foch to demand immediate action. General Weygand showed the two messages to Erzberger. Were these the final acceptance? Yes, said Erzberger. The number 3084 attached to the Chancellor's signature made it authentic. But the rest of the German delegation refused to sign the final terms until they received a message from Hindenburg which was coming in code.

About 9 P.M. this message finally arrived. Hindenburg asked for modification of a number of terms, but if the Allies refused they were to sign. Now that he had authority to conclude the negotiations, Erzberger wired the OHL a recommendation to request Wilson "to institute without delay negotiations for the conclusion of a preliminary peace so as to avoid famine and anarchy." It was 2:05 A.M. by the time he at last informed Marshal Foch that the German delegation was ready for the final meeting.

Informed that the signing was about to take place, Colonel House cabled Wilson suggesting that he read the terms of the armistice to Congress and use the occasion to give another message to the world. "You have the right to assume that the two great features of the armistice are the defeat of the German military imperialism and the acceptance by the allied powers of the kind of peace the world has longed for. A steadying note seems to me necessary at this time. A word of warning and a word of hope should be said. The World is in a ferment and Civilization itself is wavering in the balance."

In London, Bonar Law was asking Lloyd George if he wanted to go down in history as the greatest of all Englishmen. "Well, I don't know that I do," he replied, "as I shan't be here at the time. But tell me your prescription! Do you mean to retire into private life now that the war has been won?"

"Yes."

Lloyd George took it in good spirit. You're right, he said. He himself might take to farming, and make just an occasional appearance on great occasions when he had something important to say.

5.

It was 2:15 on the morning of November 11 by the time the final armistice session began. "I tried with each separate article of the armistice to get even milder terms," recalled Erzberger, but the liveliest argument came over the article which provided for the continuation of the blockade. For more than an hour Erzberger and his colleagues pleaded. "In detail I pointed out that by means of this article an essential part of the World War was being continued, namely England's starvation policy, under which German women and children suffered the most."

During this argument, Count von Oberndorff explained that this was not fair. "Not fair?" exploded Admiral Wemyss. "Why you sank our ships without discrimination!" Even so, the British representatives promised to inform their government of the German wish to have the blockade lifted. It was also agreed by all the Allies that they would supply Germany with food during the armistice. At 5:05 everything was settled and, to assure hostilities ceasing as soon as possible, it was decided to type the last page of the text immediately for signatures. Foch and Wemyss signed first. Again tears were in the eyes of Winterfeldt and Vanselow as they forced themselves to sign. The last signature was affixed about 5:10, but it was agreed to set the time officially at 5 so that the armistice could come into effect six hours later, at 11 A.M., French time.

Erzberger then asked to be heard and read a declaration from the four German plenipotentiaries. It called attention to the short time allowed for evacuation and the surrender of essential means of transporrtation. This might make it impossible to execute the conditions "without its being the fault of either the German Government or the German people." The latter had held off a world of enemies for fifty months and would preserve their liberty and unity despite every kind of violence. "A nation of seventy millions of people suffers," it concluded, "but it does not die."

"*Très bien,*" said Foch, and declared the session ended at 5:30. As the two delegations parted there was not a single handshake. Foch at once sent a message to commanders-in-chief on all fronts by radio and telephone, ordering a cessation of hostilities at 11 A.M. Troops were not to go beyond the line reached at that time until further orders, and all communication with the enemy was forbidden until receipt of instruction.

It was 5:45 by the time General Mordacq in Paris got word of the signing. He was at Clemenceau's by six. He found the Premier already awake, for he had been sleeping fitfully. He hugged the general for a long time. They both were so moved that neither could speak for several minutes. Mordacq finally said, "The great work is finally accomplished. It was superhuman and I hope that France will appreciate all she owes you."

"Yes, to me and others," said Clemenceau emotionally.

While Mordacq left to inform President Poincaré and Colonel House, Clemenceau strolled in his little garden. It was just getting light. The sky was dull and the autumn fog enveloped the trees. He loved this kind of weather, for the heavy mist and fine rain reminded him of his beloved Vendée.

House already had the news from an American major. "Autocracy is dead," he cabled Wilson in their private code. "Long live democracy and its immortal leader. In this great hour my heart goes out to you in pride, admiration and love." The colonel was still in pajamas at eight when he received Mordacq, resplendent in formal uniform and medals. "I have come to tell you, at the express orders of the President of the Council of Ministers," he said portentously, "that the armistice terms have been accepted and signed. M. Clemenceau wished that you, who have contributed so notably to the happy result of the negotiations, should be first advised and by word direct from him." House's two aides, Bonsal and Frazier, were delighted by the acting performance of their chief. Pretending the news had come like a bolt from the blue, House thanked the general warmly and patted his hands affectionately. "He would have been mortified," House explained after Mordacq's departure, "if after 'deranging' himself at this early hour he had seen that the news he brought was a twice-told tale."

At nine Clemenceau, now at the Ministry of War, penned a warm note to House:

My very dear Friend:
In this solemn moment of great events in which your noble country and its worthy chief have played so fine a rôle, I cannot restrain the desire to open my arms to you and press you against my heart.

Half an hour later Foch and Wemyss arrived to give Clemenceau the details of the signing. The Tiger made no attempt to conceal his joy, wrote the Admiral, "and taking my right hand in his left and the Marshal's left hand in his right, Foch and I joining hands equally, we all warmly congratulated one another." According to Foch, Clemenceau irritably asked, "What have you yielded to the Germans?" Foch handed over a copy of the agreement. At eleven, he said, guns should be fired in Paris to announce the end of hostilities. "It is unthinkable that the Parisians remain in ignorance of it."

"Well," said Clemenceau, "let the guns be fired at eleven o'clock."

"My work is finished," said Foch crisply, preparing to leave. "Your work begins."

Lord Derby arrived, at Clemenceau's invitation, just before the marshal left, and warmly congratulated both men. "Foch very much moved," Derby wrote Balfour, "though I feel in his heart of hearts he regrets the armistice coming quite as soon as it did as he told both of us that within another fortnight the German Army would have been completely surrounded and would have been obliged to lay down their arms."

Foch next headed for the home of Poincaré, to inform him that the Tiger had abandoned his plan to keep the signing a secret until the meeting of the deputies that afternoon. Then he added, with the same disappointment that Derby had sensed, "that the Germans accepted the conditions that he gave them, but that they did not declare themselves vanquished and the worst is that they do not believe that they are vanquished."

Along most of the Western Front there was a miserable drizzle. Georg Bucher, who had fought since 1914, was awaiting another American attack. The Yanks were as full of fight as crazed animals and didn't seem to know that the war was about over. Bucher's unit sat huddled in their overcoats talking of the armistice, the homeland, their imminent collapse, and the possibility that they would be attacked again. A little after seven their company commander came rushing along the trench. Bucher thought he had gone mad. "Cease fire at eleven A.M.!" he was shouting. "Pass the word along—cease fire at eleven!"

So he wasn't mad after all. Bucher began to bellow the news and everybody took up the cry. A young recruit named Walter, wounded slightly but painfully a little earlier by a bomb from a low-flying plane, began to sob. "I shan't really die now that there's an armistice, shall I?" Bucher assured him he wouldn't die from such a tiny wound. "Is it really true? About the armistice, I mean?"

"Yes!" Bucher trembled violently as he answered in a choking voice. "Your damage is nothing and at eleven the war's over!" But all he and the others thought of as the minutes passed was: could they survive until then?

At the prisoner of war camp near Friedrichsfeld there was joy among the prisoners that morning. Overnight some bold spirit had nailed a Union Jack and French tricolor to the tops of two arc light poles. "The Jerries were furious about this," remembered Corporal Arthur Speight, a British infantryman captured in late May near the Chemin des Dames, "but I don't think they ever found out who did it. There was a distinct change of atmosphere now. Nobody would take any orders from the guards and some of the guards, especially those with the machine guns, packed up and went home. The German officers did not have much hold on them now and this led to a visit by the Officer commanding the lager who was an old dug-up general or something. He was furious at the slip-shod way everything was being done and when he was standing near our hut he was about purple with indignation. He drew his sword, waved it around his head, slammed it back in his scabbard and began to spit at anyone who was near. I know, because I was standing in the doorway of the hut. He was the nearest approach to a comic turn that I ever saw over there with his sword and scabbard dangling in front of him!"

Lieutenant Pat Campbell heard the news from Major Cecil, who rode up frantically waving a sheet. It announced that hostilities would stop at eleven. "Do you believe it's true?" asked Campbell. Cecil insisted there was no doubt. The official news had come through while he was at headquarters. Campbell looked at his watch. It was ten o'clock and there was no possibility now any of them would get killed. "I felt excited, and happy, but in an uncertain subdued way. I did not want to shout or to drink; there was nothing to drink anyway. I wanted to be with my friends, but none of those of my own age were left in the brigade." He felt alone and walked about in the lines but without going anywhere.

All along the line men were stunned and bewildered. There were few cheers. The one thought was: stay alive for the next hour and then go home. At 10:30 George Marshall, operations officer of the American 1st Division, thought he had been killed when he was suddenly blown out of his chair by a bomb landing in the garden outside. Luckily he had been saved because of the thick walls of the house. "A few minutes later a young aviator hurried in to see what had happened and he explained that he had been out in his 'plane with some small bombs, all of which he thought had been released, but it seems that one stuck to the rack and as he sailed down just over our roof to make his landing in the field beyond our garden wall, the remaining bomb jerked loose and fell just ten yards outside the window."

At American Headquarters everyone was sitting around, talking and glancing at watches. Pershing was alone in his office as Lloyd Griscom entered. He imagined the general must be experiencing some sense of exultation, but neither a gesture nor a word betrayed any hint. Pershing walked to the big map on the wall. "I suppose our campaigns are ended," he said, "but what an enormous difference a few days would have made!"

It was just fifteen minutes before eleven and the British troops who had taken Mons were east of the city. Moments after charging some German machine guns, a private galloped toward them. He was wild with excitement, had lost his cap, and couldn't stop his horse. "The war's over!" he shouted as he galloped by. The others thought the poor chap was suffering from shell shock.

Back in Mons the advance guard brigade was making the official entry into the city. Here the British had first engaged the enemy in August of '14 and it was appropriate that their advance on the last day of war should be in the historic little city. Correspondent Philip Gibbs watched columns of troops march into Mons behind their bands. Almost everyone had a flag on his rifle, the blue, white, and red of France or the red, yellow, and black of Belgium. "They wore flowers in their caps and in their tunics, red and white chrysanthemums given them by the crowds of people who cheered them on their way, people who in many of these villages had been only one day liberated from the German yoke. Our men marched singing, with a smiling light in their eyes."

Out front the battle still roared, for there were still several minutes before peace. The Allies kept on pouring lead into the enemy with no letup. "These orders," explained one American general, "were dictated by the necessity of taking every opportunity to render certain the complete acceptance by the enemy of the armistice."

Georg Bucher's area was undergoing a particularly severe bombardment that had been answered "with the utmost ferocity" by their own artillery, which was using up the last reserves of ammunition. A sentry in a gas mask staggered into Bucher's shelter, waved a warning, and dashed out again. Bucher jumped to his feet and helped the terrified young Walter put on his mask. "I knew that if I left him for a moment he would tear the mask from his face and shriek after me—I could see by the light of the flickering candle the thin mist of poison gas." Abruptly the barrage ceased. He removed the youngster's gas mask and silently held a wristwatch before his eyes. "Then I pressed my helmet firmly on my head, pulled my pistol from its holster, snatched up the bag of bombs and leaped out into the trench." Everyone who could hold a rifle or throw a bomb was standing ready. "Were the enemy going to attack us? We were taking no chances: but as we stood there waiting, hope and determination to live flashed in every eye." The final two minutes ticked by slowly. Then there was an abrupt silence. They stood motionless, gazing at the fumes which drifted sluggishly across No Man's Land. Bucher turned around and shouted, "Armistice!" Then he went back to Walter. "I couldn't bear to go on staring at No Man's Land and at the faces of the men. We had lived through an experience which no one would ever understand who had not shared it."

The sudden silence was uncanny. Some of the Allied troops came out of the trenches shouting joyously. But others, like the Scots Fusiliers, remained comparatively unmoved. "A few cheers were raised," recalled Deneys Reitz, "but otherwise they received the great event with calm. To me it was a supreme moment. I saw

the beginnings of a new era for the world and for my country."
But, after forming his battalion in a hollow square, and, astride his
horse, he began to speak he was overcome with stage fright, and
"the inspired thought of a moment before had vanished completely and I could only stumble through a few halting phrases.
The ceremony was a failure, but at any rate the guns were silent,
the war was at an end, and one could once again make plans for
the future."

When the firing stopped, A. Cunningham Reed was in the air.
As he groped his way through thick mist looking for his new
airdrome, he was relieved to see a Very light shoot into the air.
Below they must have seen him and were guiding him down. But
as he descended, there was no landing ground, only bursts of
colored lights on all sides. He thought he was in a nightmare until
he realized this was a celebration.

Most of the Germans stayed in their trenches, but the Allies,
and particularly the Americans, were romping around No Man's
Land. "The roar of voices," according to a correspondent with the
Second Army, "was like an outburst at some great college contest
in America." Then the enemy began to come out. "The rolling
plain was alive with cheering men, friends and enemy alike. Germans and Americans were coming along the narrow stretch of
ground so fiercely fought over, some shyly and awkwardly, like embarrassed schoolboys."

The Americans in Bucher's area were glaring angrily and con-
temptuously at the Germans. "They didn't seem pleased that we
still had hand-grenades hanging from our belts and rifles in our
hands; but if one of our men had made use of his weapons without most urgent necessity he would have got a rifle-butt hard
across the head—such had been the company commander's instructions." Bucher and a few others tried in vain to make friends.
"The Americans were too embittered by the events of the previous
day: which wasn't surprising, for they had attacked three times
and been beaten back with heavy losses."

In Mons correspondent Gibbs was writing: "The fires of hell
have been put out, and I have written my last message as war correspondent. Thank God!"

A submarine moored in the Seine opposite the Chamber of
Deputies began firing salutes at eleven. Bells rang and people
rushed into the streets of Paris shouting that the war was over.
"Then in a twinkling," remembered Prescott French, a doughboy
from Arlington, Massachusetts, "as if by magic, everybody seemed
to know everybody else, regardless of nationality, color, civilian or
military or for any other artificial barrier." Parades began forming
spontaneously. "Our group was caught up in the parade along Avenue des Champs Elysees and what a parade, row on row of civilians, male and female, soldiers of the different Allied Nations,
often alternating with a soldier then a girl, then another soldier all
the way across the broad Champs Elysees, arms locked together, a

singing, swinging, swaying, jolly jubilant mass of happy humanity." A middle-aged woman kissed one of the Americans to his astonishment, then apologetically said, "You are the very image of my own son killed in this awful war."

Marine Major Denig helped his one-armed roommate out on their balcony. The latter waved his stump and the people in the street below cheered him. Colonel House was also surveying the joyous scene in front of his house. It was "one of the pleasantest emotions of my life."

On the Rue Royale flags appeared at every window as the celebration developed with amazing speed. A troop of *chasseurs d'Afrique* mounted on spirited Arab horses came up the street "looking exceedingly picturesque in their pale blue tunics and red fezes," recalled Ernest Peixotto, "with their captain saluting at their head and bowing to the acclamations of the people. Grizzled veterans, in battered helmets and uniforms faded by years of campaigning, were singled out of the crowds, hoisted on youthful shoulders and, *drapeau en tête,* borne careering down the boulevard." Others were seizing small cannon from the Place de la Concorde and pushing them through the crowd. Factory girls and *midinettes* mixed with the soldiers and some were hoisted up to American trucks, swathed with bunting, and piled high with cheering soldiers.

The news reached General Wilson in London at 6:30 A.M. Three hours later the Cabinet met and it was decided to ring bells and have the bands play at eleven. At that hour Michael MacDonagh, the Irish journalist, was startled by the booming of maroons fired from police and fire-brigade stations. It was six months since these warnings of an air raid had been heard in London, and he rushed outside to see what was the matter. "The armistice!" shouted several people. "The war is over!"

It was gray and chill with a threat of rain, but this did not dampen the enthusiasm of the crowd that spilled into the street. "There prevailed everywhere throughout London an irresistible impulse to let business go hang, to get into the streets and yell and sing and dance and weep—above all, to make oneself supremely ridiculous." Car horns tooted, handbells rang, tea trays were banged, police whistles shrilled in an infernal orchestration. MacDonagh saw a colonel squatting on top of a car sounding a dinner gong; and a parson marching at the head of his parishioners, Union Jack stuck atop his silk hat, and singing lustily. It reminded MacDonagh of the wild rejoicing over the relief of the British garrison in Mafeking during the Boer War, "but today's orgy of rejoicing far transcended the other in complete surrender of self-control." And why not? The infernal war was over.

Disorder had broken out in Winston Churchill's headquarters at the Metropole Hotel. "Doors banged. Feet clattered down corridors. Everyone rose from the desk and cast aside pen and paper. All bounds were broken. The tumult grew. It grew like a gale, but from all sides simultaneously. The street was now a seething mass of humanity. Flags appeared as if by magic. Streams of men and women flowed from the Embankment. They mingled with torrents pouring down the Strand on the way to acclaim the King."

As the bells of Westminster Abbey and Westminster Cathedral rang out in a unison of joy, a huge crowd besieged Buckingham Palace. The Victoria Memorial was almost obliterated by swarming climbers. The staccato cry went up: "We—want—King—George!" At last he appeared on the balcony with the Queen. There was a roar. The King laughed without restraint and the Queen waved a Union Jack over her head. Then, with Princess Mary, they drove in an open car by the Strand to the City—unaccompanied by royal state.

"It was quite old English," commented Irishman MacDonagh. "It was Bank Holiday on Hampstead Heath on a vastly stupendous scale. The fantastic personal adornment of most of the revellers by means of face-masks and miniature flags—as well as the noise—recalled also the sights that were witnessed in London before the War on occasions of football matches and Cup Finals, when supporters of the rival teams invaded London from the North in the thousands."

Amid all the joy there were sober faces. To Lieutenant H. E. L. Mellersh the relief was mixed with regret. He should have liked to do a bit more since the ignominious March retreat; he should have liked to win the M.C. A munitions girl called out, "What's the matter? Cheer up!" He was surprised that he looked as gloomy as that.

And at the House of Commons, Lloyd George, who felt strangely depressed, was announcing in a voice broken by emotion, "Thus at eleven o'clock this morning came to an end the cruellest and most terrible war that has ever scourged mankind. I hope, we may say that thus, this fateful morning, came to an end all wars." The members cheered fervently. "This is no time for words," he said solemnly. "Our hearts are too full of gratitude to which no tongue can give adequate expression." He moved that they proceed in a body to St. Margaret's "to give humble and reverent thanks for the deliverence of the world from its great peril."

The celebration began in New York City before dawn with shrieking air-raid sirens. Lights illuminated the Statue of Liberty. Factory whistles and church bells took up the cry as people came to the streets to form into unruly parades. Crews tied down ship and tug whistles, put on lights, and ran up flags. Some sailors threw calcium flares into the war. The clangor spread all over the city and no one could sleep. Dawn found Fifth Avenue a mass of merrymakers cheering and waving flags in ecstasy. Men were weeping unashamed. As the great flag was being unfurled at the City Hall, a dozen musicians began playing patriotic songs with the crowd singing along. Mayor Hylan declared a municipal holiday, ordering a parade which grew with every block. There were, according to Mark Sullivan, "fashionable ladies jingling cowbells; street urchins yelling and dancing; stenographers in red, white and blue paper caps; sailors grinning under the floppy picture-hats of the girls and girls flaunting sailors' hats. There were autos bursting with vociferous passengers, one-horse carts, farm-wagons full of giggling girls, life-boats mounted on trucks, sight-seeing busses boiling with people." One truck carried a coffin from which an effigy of the Kaiser was hanged over and over again. Servicemen were waving signs: "No more beans! No more camouflaged coffee! No more monkey stew!"

Having gone to bed before news of the armistice arrived, President Wilson didn't learn of it until breakfast. He gave immediate orders that all government workers be given a holiday, and wrote out in pencil an announcement to the people:

> The armistice was signed this morning. Everything for which America fought has been accomplished. It will now be our fortunate duty to assist by example, by sober, friendly counsel and by material aid in the establishment of just democracy throughout the world.

After breakfast he retired to his study to write an address to Congress, then left for the Capitol at 12:30. The galleries of the House Chamber were filled to capacity by the time he entered and there was prolonged cheering while he shook hands with Speaker Champ Clark and the Vice-President. Wilson seemed the personification of vigor and did not look his sixty-one years, nor did his face show any effect of the last harrowing days. As he took out the small sheets containing his address, the audience hushed. "In these anxious times of rapid and stupendous changes," he began, "it will in some degree lighten my sense of responsibility to perform in person the duty of communicating to you some of the larger circumstances of the situation with which it is necessary to deal." When he told of the signing of the armistice there was only faint clapping, but upon revealing that Germany would immediately evacuate the invaded countries there was unrestrained delight. Applause also came for each of the countries to be evacuated—Belgium, France, Luxembourg. But when he announced that Alsace-Lorraine would also be evacuated, the spectators rose to their feet.

Then he said that everything would be done to supply the defeated enemies with food and relief. This brought only faint clapping, nor was there any demonstration after his concluding sentence: "I am confident that the nations that have learned the discipline of freedom and that have settled with self-possession to its ordered practice are now about to make conquest of the world by the sheer power of example and of friendly helpfulness."

By midafternoon the celebration in Paris was at its zenith. Marshal Foch's auto was mobbed on his way to a meeting of the

Council of Ministers. "It seemed likely they would drag me out of my car." He managed to slip away and get to his destination about the time Clemenceau was being kissed by his old opponent, Poincaré. "Since this morning," remarked the Tiger, "I have been kissed by more than five hundred girls." Victory, he said, was the work of everyone, and each person, from the highest to the lowest rank, had done his duty. They all headed for the Chamber of Deputies, where Clemenceau was scheduled to read the terms of the armistice.

Lord Derby was having great difficulty getting out of the courtyard of the British Embassy, as a dense crowd besieged his car. The Blue Band was playing the national anthem led by Decima Moore atop a taxi. She was dressed in the Union Jack and every so often would shout, "Rule, Britannia!" Then everyone sang *La Marseillaise* and also started for the Chamber of Deputies. Here there was bedlam with everyone trying to jam into a building already crammed full. At 4 P.M. Clemenceau was given an ovation by the six hundred emotional deputies. General Mordacq observed that there were tears in almost all eyes as Clemenceau read out the terms. After each clause came a roar of approval. "It was truly an unforgettable spectacle."

"For me," continued Clemenceau, "after the reading of the armistice agreement, it seems that . . . my work is done." He hailed the return of Alsace-Lorraine and concluded with a tribute to the poilu—"yesterday the soldier of God, today the soldier of humanity and always the soldier of the ideal." The deputies, who had made so much trouble for him and Foch in adversity, now voted their gratitude to both.

The Viscountess D'Abernon, a close friend of Lord Derby's, noted that he left the Chamber "looking less exuberantly cheerful than is his wont." He was perturbed because of Clemenceau's declaration that France had won the war. "No mention of Britain's share in it, nor, indeed of America, Belgium, or any of the other Allies." Later at the Café de Paris, Derby reported to Balfour, there had been a great demonstration "when an American got up and drank to the health of England 'who really won the war.' There is no doubt that the Americans are rather annoyed at the very little recognition that is given to our efforts."

Londoners were still cavorting unrestrainedly. A fire was started at the base of the Nelson Monument in Trafalgar Square. A huge New Zealander climbed high up on the structure and kept shouting to the crowd, "Come and feed the flames!" The long side signs on the London buses were ripped off and, along with wooden blocks coated in tar, were thrown on the fire. This and other lights kept the city brightly illuminated. From St. Paul's to Oxford Circus and down Whitehall to Victoria Station the streets were thronged from curb to curb with laughing, jostling, happy people.

Lloyd George, still subdued, was dining quietly with Winston Churchill and General Wilson at 10 Downing Street. They discussed many things but principally the coming general election. The Prime Minister did remark that he wanted to shoot the Kaiser. "Winston does not," Wilson wrote in his diary; "and my opinion is that there should be a public exposé of all his works and actions, and then leave him to posterity! Incidentally he has shown he is a coward by going to Holland."

6.

The Kaiser's flight to Holland set in motion the doom of his "dear brother" and ally, Karl of Austria. Fifty minutes before the signing of the armistice, Prime Minister Lammasch and Minister of Interior Payer had driven up to Schönbrunn Palace and presented to Karl a manifesto for his signature. In it he promised to take no part "in the affairs of state." This meant that the Habsburg dynasty was renouncing its power but not its crown. The agitated Payer begged Karl to sign at once before the workers massed before Schönbrunn "and then the few who refuse to abandon Your Majesty would fall in the fight and with them Your Majesty himself and the All-Highest family." Lammasch was equally eager. The manifesto, he pleaded, was scheduled to be distributed throughout Vienna at 3 P.M.

The ministers, recalled Empress Zita, pursued the Emperor in a panic from room to room demanding his signature, and he literally had to shake them off with the exclamation, "If you won't even let me *read* it, how do you expect me to *sign* it?" After studying the manifesto, he asked for Zita's opinion. "A sovereign can never abdicate," she said. "He can be deposed and his sovereign rights be declared forfeit. All right. That is force. But abdicate—never, never, never! I would rather fall here at your side. Then there would be Otto. And even if all of us here were killed, there would still be other Habsburgs!"

One of Karl's staff explained this was no formal abdication, and urged the Emperor to sign since the document left constitutional paths open for the dynasty in the future. As for the present, he added, "Madness reigns today and a madhouse is no place for a sovereign." After Karl signed the document in pencil, the two ministers hurried to their automobile and were rushed to the center of Vienna.

It was beginning to get dark by the time Karl finally left the palace after a short prayer in the chapel. He and the Empress Zita went up to the Hall of Ceremonies, where those who had remained were gathered. They bade farewell to the faithful few, thanking them one by one, then went down the stairway with their children. Cars were waiting to take them to a shooting lodge in the middle of the Lower Austrian countryside which was loyal by tradition. "Along the sides of the arcades, drawn up in two ranks," recalled Zita, "were our cadets from the military academies, sixteen- and seventeen-year-olds, with tears in their eyes, but still perfectly turned out and guarding us to the end. They had really lived up to the motto the Empress Maria Theresa had given them: *Allzeit getreu* (Loyal Forever).

"It was dark by now, and a misty autumn night. We got into the vehicles. The Emperor and I and all the children except Karl Ludwig squeezed into the back of one car with Count Hunyadi at the front . . . We did not risk driving out of the main gate in front of the palace. Instead we continued parallel with the main building along the broad gravel path that leads to the eastern side gate. We slipped out of this and left the capital by a special route. Late that night—without any trouble or incidents—we arrived at Eckartsau."

The streets of Vienna were still filled with jubilant crowds, celebrating the downfall of Karl. Officers ripped off the top button of each other's caps which bore the initial "K." These were replaced with buttons covered with the national colors representing the nationalities that had once composed the Austro-Hungarian Empire.

There was no holiday atmosphere in Berlin. As Franz Seldte's train pulled into the Potsdamer Bahnhof that evening, he could hear a wild yelling, then the spitting of machine guns. Bullets swept the full length of the train. The front-line cameraman darted out of the station to find the streets in wild tumult. From somewhere on a roof, bullets were spattering the pavement. Just a few yards in front, at the base of a lamppost, he saw a machine-gun crew firing fitfully at the station entrance. "Haven't you any trained machine-gunners here?" he asked. "That's not the way to handle it." No one answered, so Seldte jerked the belt and fired. Two shots. He tried again. The thing was hopelessly jammed. In a cold rage, he walked to the Wilhelmstrasse. He had been infuriated since learning that a republic had been proclaimed from the Reichstag with the silly lie: "The German people have won all along the line." He had been stunned to learn that the Kaiser had fled to Holland. It was all madness. Now he felt more than ever that he was in an insane asylum. Clusters of half-naked people hung on trucks, waving torches and red flags. "Just wait, you dogs," he muttered, "your time is coming."

From his hospital room in Baden-Baden, Lieutenant Binding was marveling at what a curious revolution it was that had come to Germany. In spite of the constant talk of violent convulsions, it was so superficial. "If the Workmen's and Soldiers' Councils imagine that they have given the people the freedom they want, they are much mistaken. This movement will soon show itself to be the most one-sided regime imaginable and reduce itself *ad absurdum,* after which it will probably give way to some stronger Government." As he was writing in his diary, he heard the people in the street. "The same fellows who marched through the town two nights ago singing the 'Wacht am Rhein' were singing today a new tune which had been produced for the occasion, 'We're going behind the Rhine-line, the Rhine-line, the Rhine-line.' " The one appreciable result of the Soldiers' Councils was that they had no sweet for dinner today. "I am quite overcome. Is that resurrection? Is that revolution?"

On the Allied side of the lines, almost all of those who thought the armistice was just another rumor finally realized the war was ended. A few like Lieutenant Patrick Campbell could not believe the horror was over. "Do you think it's real?" he asked Major Cecil, who told him to listen. Campbell could hear only the sound of horses on the other side of the farm. "There had never been a night like this. We could hear the silence, it was a little frightening, we had forgotten what silence was." He and Cecil prepared for bed. "It's been a bit flat," said the major. "I don't know what I was expecting, but certainly not this." Campbell found himself thinking of his dead comrades. "Now we should become aware of their loss, we had hardly done so until now, we had still been with them, in the same country, close to them, close to death ourselves. But soon we should have to go away and leave them, we should be going home, they would stay behind, their home was in the lonely desolation of the battlefield."

There were thousands of bonfires along the twisting front lines as the men tried to thaw out and get dry. Here and there would be a spontaneous flurry as troops fired off their last ammunition into the air, but most of the men were thinking soberly of what they had been through and what they faced in the peaceful life to come. "Got rid of my bandage," George Patton wrote in his diary. "Wrote a poem on peace."

Many were thinking of the momentous events of the past months. Had history ever seen such an eventful year? The end of tyrannic rulers in Russia, Germany, and Austria-Hungary. Even England and France would never be the same after the comradeship of the trenches. Rich and poor alike had bled and suffered miseries side by side. Life would never be the same anywhere in the world. But would the changes be for good or evil?

Winston Churchill was deeply disturbed by a recent memorandum of Bruce Lockhart urging the Allies either to make peace with the resurgent Soviets or destroy them by force of arms. Churchill decided that now was the time to wipe out Bolshevism in Russia before it gained more strength.

In Moscow, Lenin had left the Kremlin, for the first time since the assassination attempt, to address the crowds from a balcony. There was wild cheering from workers and Red Army soldiers. Radek noticed his "excited but profoundly anxious look" as he touched off a celebration that lasted until late in the night. They were not cheering for the end of the war but for the revolution which had erupted in Germany and Austria and would soon engulf the entire world. The isolation of the infant Soviet Union was at last over. But Lenin's secret doubts were only expressed to a foreigner, Philips Price. "I fear that the revolution in central Europe is developing too slowly to provide us with any assistance from

447

that quarter." Lenin was too wise not to realize that the West, now that it had conquered Germany, would try in earnest to crush Bolshevism. That very day the Americans and British had begun a bloody battle with the Red Army not far from Archangel.

In Vladivostok, General Graves, the commander of American forces in Russia, was becoming increasingly disenchanted with his country's intervention. He could see no good reason for it and was disgusted by the actions of White commanders such as Kolchak, Semyonov, and Kalmykov, with whom he was supposed to cooperate. "Semyonov and Kalmykov soldiers, under the protection of Japanese troops, were roaming the country like wild animals, killing and robbing the people, and these murders could have been stopped any day Japan wished. If questions were asked about these brutal murders, the reply was that the people murdered were Bolsheviks and this explanation, apparently, satisfied the world." Why, he wondered, was America joining with such rapacious forces in the name of democracy?

In Tokyo, Japanese leaders were celebrating the armistice and already calculating the gains they hoped to get for joining the crusade against the Kaiser: the German islands in the Pacific, the Carolines, the Marshalls, and the Marianas. These chains could be fortified into a formidable defense against any future danger from American warships based in Hawaii.

In Paris the Place de l'Opéra was ablaze with lights for the first time since August 1914. Every balcony and window looking upon it was filled with spectators, and crowd stretched far down the avenue. Then, despite the chill wind, the greatest singers in France came to the balcony of the Opéra so they could sing *The Star-Spangled Banner, God Save the King,* and *La Marseillaise.*

The crowd took up the choruses and finally, after clamorous appeals from soldiers, the Opéra stars sang *Madelon.* "It was a community song festival the like of which no city has ever seen," reported *Stars and Stripes,* "and the like of which may never come again. Though many lingered on the boulevards to cheer the flashing on an elevated screen of the pictures of the marshals, of 'Le Tigre,' of President Wilson, of Sir Douglas Haig, and of General Pershing, the singing brought the great and exultant day to a close." Then a French bugler, with a sense of humor, blew the *berloque,* the all-clear signal marking the end of an air raid. "And all Paris laughed the laugh of happy children after a day's glad play."

At the Rue de l'Université, House's elation was dampened by a cable from the President announcing that he not only planned to participate in the peace negotiations personally but assumed that he would be the presiding officer. The colonel was deeply disturbed. He had expected to head the United States delegation himself, and felt he would be much more qualified to press the peace program than its originator. House was becoming impatient of Wilson's shortcomings and feared that he would hopelessly alienate the other Allied leaders, who already had expressed their personal dislike and distrust. Until now the colonel had stayed in the background, subordinating himself to Wilson. Until now he had spared the President from hearing anything that might be disagreeable, but he decided that he must tell Wilson that the almost unanimous opinion of influential Americans in Paris was that it would be unwise for him to sit in the Peace Conference. A just peace must come out of the conference, and House felt sure that Wilson's overwhelming presence would antagonize the Allies into making it a harsh one. And that could create future trouble with Germany. While House's reasoning appeared sound, it was unrealistic to imagine that anyone but Wilson could lead the Peace Conference, since he was the symbol throughout the world of peace, international justice, and the League of Nations.

7.

Already millions of front-line German soldiers believed they had been betrayed by those back home—strikers and malingerers, Jews, profiteers and politicians. The front had not broken and they had been retreating in an orderly fashion when the civilians forced the generals to surrender. It was a stab in the back. From his hotel window that night Franz Seldte looked out on Unter den Linden. Bullets from sharpshooters began spattering to right and left of his lighted window. Seldte switched off the light. "The swine can't even shoot." They weren't even good soldiers. A private army of front-line veterans could quickly put this Red rabble to rout; and he would be just the one to lead them.

To the east in the hospital at Pasewalk, Corporal Adolf Hitler, who shared Seldte's convictions, still lay blind in his cot. The shame of the surrender in the forest of Compiègne had overwhelmed him. Life seemed unbearable until he was abruptly delivered from his misery by a "supernatural vision." Like St. Joan, he heard voices summoning him to save Germany. All at once "a miracle came to pass"—the darkness encompassing Hitler evaporated. He could see again! He solemnly vowed, as he had promised several days earlier, that he would "become a politician and devote his energies to carrying out the command he had received." He would keep his vow: enter politics and bring Germany from the depths of despair to the greatness she deserved.*

* The next month Oswald Spengler wrote a friend that the epoch of the World War had only now entered upon a new phase. "The master race, which from the time of Frederick Wilhelm I has been bred by old Fritz, by 1813, and by Bismarck and Hindenburg . . . is faced by a new task to which it is equal. I expect much from the leader natures which today are hidden nameless in the middle class element and in the *respectable* working class. . . . Actually our future lies, on the one hand, in Prussian Conservatism, when it is rid of every trace of feudal-agrarian narrowness, and on the other in the working class, after it has separated itself in disgust and pride from the anarchistical radical 'mob.' Much blood must still flow, for decisions of that importance will not be arrived at by national assemblies and party programmes, and they need time to ripen."

The President and his wife were driving down Pennsylvania Avenue where the peace celebration was at its peak. "I shall never forget how happy he looked," recalled his secretary, Tumulty. The fruits of victory were indeed sweet, but Wilson was already thinking of Europe and the final realization of his ideals, unaware that cold water would soon be doused on this dream by House's answer to his last cablegram.

The Wilsons continued their triumphant tour to watch the lighting of campfires which signaled the start of the War Work Campaign, another sign of a hopeful, fruitful future.

Great perils also lay ahead. For better or worse the world would be drastically, dramatically changed by the events of 1918. It was the end of an era in Europe for both victors and vanquished. Gone was the gracious way of life enjoyed by the privileged. What lay ahead seemed a better world for the common man. He could now enjoy the fruits of the astounding technical revolution that had been born of war's necessities. More important the war had accelerated the emancipation of woman, irretrievably altered the rigid class system, and given mankind the hope of lasting peace through a League of Nations.

But perhaps the only truth that would emerge from the cataclysm which had shaken the world was that war inevitably breeds war, that triumph eventually turns into defeat, and that only the brotherhood of suffering endures.

The night of November 11 was one of jubilation for the victors and despair for the conquered. But at any rate the most brutal war of history had finally ended. General Wilson, walking home to Eaton Place from his dinner with Lloyd George and Churchill, was breasting the enthusiastic crowd still swarming in front of Buckingham Palace. In the midst of unrestrained cheer, he came upon an elderly, well-dressed woman who was sobbing in loneliness. Distressed, Wilson said, "You are in trouble—is there anything that I can do for you?"

"Thank you. No. I am crying, but I am happy, for now I know that all my three sons who have been killed in the war have not died in vain."

Acknowledgments

I am grateful to the following archives, museums, and libraries in Germany, the United States, and Great Britain: the Bibliothek für Zeitgeschichte, Stuttgart (Werner Haupt, Gerhard Buch, and Dr. Jurgen Röhwer); the Institut für Zeitgeschichte, Munich; the Bundesarchiv, Koblenz; the Bundesarchiv, Freiburg; the Danbury, Connecticut, Public Library; the Library of Congress; the main branch of the New York Public Library; the Yale University Library (Judith A. Schiff); Columbia University, Oral History Research Office (Louis M. Starr); the U. S. Military History Research Collection, Carlisle Barracks, Pennsylvania (Colonel James B. Agnew, Lieutenant Colonel James C. Shepard, Michael Winey); the State Historical Society of Wisconsin (Paul H. Hass, Josephine L. Harper); the Hoover Institution (Dr. Agnes Peterson); the House of Lords Record Office, London; the Royal Marines Museum, Portsmouth (Miss B. Spiers); the Liddell Hart Centre for Military Archives, University of London, King's College; the British Library; and the National Library, Edinburgh.

This book could not have been written without the cooperation of U. S. Marine Corps Historical Center (Brigadier General E. H. Simmons, Benis Frank, C. A. Wood); the National Archives (Timothy Nenninger, William Leary, Paul White, James Trimble, Dr. James B. Rhoads, John Taylor, and James E. O'Neill); and the Imperial War Museum (Dr. A. N. Frankland, Roderick Suddaby, M. J. Willis, Terence Charman, and Rose Coombs). Besides providing me with hundreds of printed volumes and personal accounts, this museum made it possible for Miss Coombs to escort me on an extended tour of the major battlefields in France and Belgium.

Numerous agencies, organizations, and individuals made substantial contributions to this book:

United States: Fellow historians and authors: Richard Hanser, Dr. Harold J. Gordon, Dr. Bradley Smith, Dr. Edward M. Coffman, A. A. Hoehling, Dr. Betty M. Unterberger, Walter Lord, Frank Vandiver, P. J. Carisella, David Trask, and Professor Alfred Vagts; the American Legion (Ralph Burris); The Army and Navy Club, Washington, D.C. (George W. Hinman, Jr.); the Second Division Assocation (Dr. John P. Wakefield); Charles MacDonald, Office of the Chief of Military History, Department of the Army; Alexis Scherbatow; Frank Schaufler, Jr.; Captain Roger Pineau; Robert May; Frank Mason; Peter Kilduff; Lawrence J. Dugan; Colonel Eugene Prince; Wendy Jacobson and James

Moser of Doubleday & Company, Inc.; and my typist, Dorothy Vining.

Great Britain: Terence Prittie; Walter Henry Nelson; Roger Bell; the Royal British Legion; and the Black Watch Association (J. L. R. Samson). Also to the Earl Haig of Bemersyde for permission to use his father's papers, diary, and personal correspondence as well as his own unpublished autobiography; and to Major C. J. Wilson for use of Field Marshal Sir Henry Wilson's diaries.

Finally I would like to thank those who contributed outstandingly to the book: John Jamieson, Karola Gillich, and my two editors at Doubleday, Carolyn Blakemore and Ken McCormick, upon whose judgment and taste I relied.

1. 70/9/55
2. 165-BO-971
3. 111-SC-99973
4. 111-SC-98801
5. 165-GB-8153
6. 165-GB-7791
7. 165-GB-7981
8. 165-BO-1168
9. 165-BO-7908
10. 165-BO-839
11. 165-BO-1929
12. 165-GB-7996
13. Imperial War Museum Q 355
14. Imperial War Museum Q 11586
15. 165-BO-851
16. 165-GB-8318
17. 165-GB-8399
18. 165-GB
19. Imperial War Museum Q 35278
20. 165-GB-8776
21. 165-GB-8541
22. 165-GB-9506
23. 165-GB-8856
24. Toland
25. 165-GB-9506
26. 165-GB-8540
27. 165-GB-9814
28. 111-SC-94980
29.–30. 165-BO-766
31. Imperial War Museum Q 11538
32. 165-BO-1557
33. Maze
34. Imperial War Museum Q 6877
35. Imperial War Museum Q 9534
36. 111-SC-49024
37. 111-SC-18904
38. 111-SC-17592
39. 111-SC-10879
40. 111-SC-22472
41. 111-SC-94980
42. 111-SC-24644
43. 111-SC-26697
44. 111-SC-24649
45. 165-BO-1788
46. Imperial War Museum Q 03399
47. 165-BO-853
48. 111-SC-50094
49. 165-BO-1046
50. 165-GB-1000
51. 165-GB-10102
52. 165-GB-10136
53. 165-GB-9598
54. 76/76/29A
55. 165-WW-157D-11
56. Courtesy of Macmillan, London
57. 165-WW-157D-3
58. 111-SC-80488
59. Painting by John Singer Sargent
60. Imperial War Museum Q 54471
61. 165-BO-1891
62. 111-SC-14592
63. 111-SC-14592
64. No credit
65. Cooper
66. Maze
67.–68. Campbell
69. National Archives
70. Imperial War Museum Q 54381
71. D-721

453

72. 165-BO-855
73. 165-GB-11703
74. 76/76/18A
75. Imperial War Museum
    Q 54993
76. 165-GB-3100
77. 165-GB-9401
78. 165-GB-10654
79. 165-GB-9401
80. BO-1732
81. 165-GB-8471
82. 165-BO-1334
83. 165-BO-1326
84. Robert A. Niemann
85. 165-GB-7818

86. 165-BO-1635
87. No credit
88. P. J. Carisella
89. 111-SC-11887
90. Toland
91. Imperial War Museum
    Q 54399
92. 165-BO-958
93. 165-GB-9267
94. 76/76/31A
95. ABC-3372
96. No credit
97. 70/38/4
98. 70/38/12
99. 70/38/40

Sources

A. INTERVIEWS AND CORRESPONDENCE
(*partial list*)

Norman Armour (tape)
George W. Bailey (tape)
Douglas Campbell (tape)
Patrick Campbell
P. J. Carisella
H. Howard Cooper
The Earl Haig
F. Hodson (tape)
Brien Horan (tape)
Harry Hull (tape)
Edouard Izac (tape)
General Marshall-Cornwall
Paul Maze
Morden Murphy (tape)
Earl Packer (tape)
Don V. Paradise (tape)
Colonel Eugene Prince (tape)
Frank Rees
James W. Rose
Clinton Sherwood (tape)
Lieutenant General Merwin Silverthorn, USMC
Walter Stennes
John Terraine
General Gerald Thomas, USMC
George W. Tomek
Albert Vagts (tape)
George Vaughn (tape)

B. DOCUMENTS, DIARIES, RECORDS, AND REPORTS
Documents at the Bibliothek für Zeitgeschichte, Stuttgart; Institute für Zeitgeschichte, Munich; U. S. Army Military Research Collection, Carlisle Barracks, Pa.; Bundesarchiv, Koblenz; Bundesarchiv, Freiburg; Hoover Institution; State Historical Society of Wisconsin; Liddell Hart Centre for Military Archives, University of London, King's College; National Archives; Library of Congress; Yale University Library; House of Lords Record Office, London; National Library, Edinburgh; British Library; Imperial War Museum. Official histories:
British. *The Official History of the War: Military Operations in*

France and Belgium, 1918. Volumes I-V. Macmillan & Co., London, 1935–39.

United States. *The U. S. Army in the World War, 1917–1919*. All volumes.

Papers and original diaries:

British Library: Balfour, Cecil, and Derby papers.

House of Lords Record Office: Papers of Lloyd George, Lady Lloyd George, and Andrew Bonar Law.

Imperial War Museum: Henry Wilson diaries.

Library of Congress: Pershing diary.

National Library, Edinburgh: Haig diary and correspondence.

State Historical Society of Wisconsin: Raymond Robins diary and papers.

Yale University Library: Colonel House diary.

Personal accounts:

Imperial War Museum: E. C. Allfree, J. G. Birch, Patrick Campbell, R. S. Cockburn, H. Howard Cooper, R. von Dechend, R. D. Fisher, Gilbert Laithwaite, H. E. L. Mellersh, Arthur Speight, E. V. Tanner, W. A. Tucker, P. E. Williamson.

U.S. Marine Corps Historical Center: David Bellamy, Clifton Cates, Robert L. Denig, Don V. Paradise, Lemuel Shepherd, M. H. Silverthorn, G. C. Thomas.

U. S. State Department: *Foreign Relations of the United States, 1918, Russia*. Volumes I–III, Washington, D.C.

Foreign Relations of the United States, 1919, Russia. Washington, D.C.

C. MAGAZINES

Arpin, Edmund P., Jr. "A Wisconsinite in World War I," *Wisconsin Magazine of History*, Autumn 1967, Winter 1967, Spring 1968.

Dorpalen, Andreas. "Empress Auguste Victoria and the Fall of the German Monarchy," *American Historical Review*, October 1952.

Hammerton, Sir John, editor. *The Great War. I Was There.* Amalgamated Press, London, 1939. 51 issues.

History of the First World War. An international history published by Purnell and Sons, Paulton for British Printing Corporation Publishing, Ltd., London, in cooperation with the Imperial War Museum. 128 issues.

McCarthy, Joe. "The Lost Battalion," *American Heritage*, October 1977.

D. BIBLIOGRAPHY

Abbott, Willis J. *Blue Jackets of 1918*. New York: Dodd, Mead, 1921.

Adam, H. Pearl. *Paris Sees It Through*. London: Hodder & Stoughton, 1919.

Addison, Christopher. *Four and a Half Years*, Volume II. London: Hutchinson, 1934.

Aldrich, Mildred. *The Peak of the Load*. London: Constable, 1919.

Alexander, Robert. *Memories of the World War, 1917–1918*. New York: Macmillan, 1931.

Arnaud, René. *Tragedie Bouffe*. London: Sidgwick & Jackson, 1964.

Arndt, Richard. *Mit 15 Jahren an die Front*. Leipzig: Koehler & Amelang, 1930.

Asprey, Robert B. *At Belleau Wood*. New York: G. P. Putnam's Sons, 1965.

Asquith, Herbert. *Moments of Memory*. London: Hutchinson, 1937.

Aston, Sir George. *The Biography of the Late Marshal Foch*. London: Hutchinson, n.d.

Baerlein, Henry. *The March of the Seventy Thousand*. London: Leonard Parsons, 1926.

Baker, Ray Stannard. *Woodrow Wilson, Life and Letters*, Volume VIII. London: Heinemann, n.d.

Balfour, Michael. *The Kaiser*. Boston: Houghton Mifflin, 1964.

Barnett, Correlli. *The Swordbearers*. New York: Morrow, 1964.

Baumont, Maurice. *The Fall of the Kaiser*. New York: Knopf, 1931.

Baynes, Ernest H. *Animal Heroes of the Great War*. New York: Macmillan, 1927.

Bean, C. E. W. *Official History of Australia in the War of 1914–1918*, Volume VI, "The AIF in France, 1918." Sydney: Angus & Robertson, 1942.

Beaverbrook, Lord. *Men and Power*. London: Collins, 1956.

Behrend, Arthur. *As from Kemmel Hill*. London: Eyre and Spottiswoode, 1963.

Benstead, Charles R. *Retreat*. London: Methuen, 1930.

Binding, Rudolf. *A Fatalist at War*. London: George Allen and Unwin, 1929.

Bishop, William Arthur. *The Courage of the Early Morning*. New York: McKay, 1965.

Bittner, Oskar. *Kriegserlebnisse*. Brunn, self-published, 1936.

Blake, Robert, editor. *The Private Papers of Douglas Haig 1914–1919*. London: Eyre and Spottiswoode, 1952.

Blaxland, Gregory. *Amiens: 1918*. London: Muller, 1968.

Blücher, Princess Evelyn. *An English Wife in Berlin*. London: Constable, 1921.

Blumenson, Martin. *The Patton Papers 1885–1940*, Volume I. Boston: Houghton Mifflin, 1972.

Boatner, Mark M., III. *Military Customs and Traditions*. New York: McKay, 1956.

Bonham-Carter, Victor. *Soldier True*. London: Muller, 1963.

Bonsal, Stephen. *Suitors and Supplicants*. Port Washington, N.Y.: Kennikat Press, n.d.

Boraston, J. H. *Sir Douglas Haig's Despatches*. London: Dent, 1920.

Bouton, S. Miles. *And the Kaiser Abdicates*. New Haven: Yale University Press, 1920.

Boyd, Donald. *Salute of Guns*. London: Cape, 1930.

Bradley, John. *Allied Intervention in Russia*. London: Weïdenfeld & Nicolson, 1968.

Brook-Shepherd. *The Last Habsburg*. New York: Weybright & Talley, 1968.

Browne, D. G. *The Tank in Action*. Edinburgh and London: Blackwood and Sons, 1920.

Brownrigg, Sir Douglas. *Indiscretions of the Naval Censor*. New York: Doran, 1920.

Brunn, Geoffrey. *Clemenceau*. Cambridge, Mass.: Harvard University Press, 1943.

Bruntz, George G. *Allied Propaganda and the Collapse of the German Empire of 1918*. Palo Alto: Stanford University Press, 1938.

Buchan, John. *A History of the Great War*, Volume IV. Boston and New York: Houghton Mifflin, 1923.

————. *The Long Road to Victory*. London, Edinburgh, and New York: Nelson, 1920.

Bucher, Georg. *In the Line*. London: Cape, 1932.

Buckley, Harold. *Squadron 95*. New York: Arno, 1972.

Bugnet, Commandant. *Foch Talks*. London: Gollancz, 1929.

Bullard, Robert Lee. *Personalities and Reminiscences of the War*. Garden City: Doubleday, Page, 1925.

Bunyan, James, and H. H. Fisher. *The Bolshevik Revolution, 1917–1918*. Palo Alto: Stanford University Press, 1934.

Burdick, Charles B., and Ralph H. Lutz, editors. *The Political Institutions of the German Revolution, 1918–1919*. New York, Washington: Praeger, 1966.

Callwell, Major-General Sir C. E. *Field Marshal Sir Henry Wilson*, Volumes I and II. London, Toronto, Melbourne, and Sydney: Cassell, 1927.

Campbell, P. J. *The Ebb and Flow of Battle*. London: Hamish Hamilton, 1977.

————. *In the Cannon's Mouth*. London: Hamish Hamilton, 1979.

Carisella, P. J., and James W. Ryan. *The Black Swallow of Death*. Boston: Marlborough House, 1972.

————. *Who Killed the Red Baron?* Greenwich, Conn.: Fawcett, 1969.

Carpenter, Captain A. F. B. *The Blocking of Zeebrugge*. London: Jenkins, 1924.

Carr, Edward Hallett. *Soviet Russia and the World*. Part V, Volume III, "The Bolshevik Revolution, 1917–1923." New York: Macmillan, 1953.

Carver, Sir Michael. *The War Lords*. Boston: Little, Brown, 1976.

Catlin, A. W. *With the Help of God and a Few Marines*. Garden City: Doubleday, Page, 1920.

Chapman, Guy. *A Passionate Prodigality*. New York: Fawcett, 1967.

———, ed. *Vain Glory*. London, Toronto, Melbourne, and Sydney: Cassell, 1937.

Charteris, Brigadier-General John. *Field-Marshal Earl Haig*. London, Toronto, Melbourne, and Sydney: Cassell, 1929.

Churchill, Winston. *Amid These Storms*. New York: Scribner's, 1932.

———. *The World Crisis, 1916–1918*. Two volumes. London: Butterworth, 1927.

Clemenceau, Georges. *Grandeur and Misery of Victory*. London, Bombay, and Sydney: Harrap, 1930.

Coates, W. B. and Elda K. *Armed Intervention in Russia 1918–1922*. London: Gollancz, 1935.

Coffman, Edward M. *The War to End All Wars*. New York: Oxford University Press, 1968.

Collier, Basil. *Brasshat*. London: Secker and Warburg, 1961.

Cooper, John Milton, Jr., editor. *Causes and Consequences of World War I*. Chicago: Quadrangle, 1972.

Corday, Michel. *The Paris Front*. New York: Dutton, 1934.

Crozier, Emmet. *American Reporters on the Western Front, 1914–1918*. New York: Oxford, 1959.

Crutchley, C. E., compiler and editor. *Machine-Gunner 1914–1918*. Folkestone: Bailey Brothers and Swinfen, 1975.

Czernin, Count Ottokar. *In the World War*. London, New York, Toronto, and Melbourne: Cassell, 1919.

D'Abernon, Viscountess. *Red Cross and the Berlin Embassy*. London: Murray, 1946.

Davidson, Major-General Sir John. *Haig, Master of the Field*. London: Nevill, 1953.

Desagneaux, Henri. *A French Soldier's War Diary 1914–1918*. Morley, Yorkshire: Elmfield, 1975.

Dewar, George A. B. *Sir Douglas Haig's Command*, Volume II. London, Bombay, and Sydney: Constable, 1922.

DeWeerd, Harvey A. *President Wilson Fights His War*. New York: Macmillan, 1968.

Dickman, Joseph Theodore. *The Great Crusade*. New York: Appleton, 1927.

Dorpalen, Andreas. *Hindenburg and the Weimar Republic*. Princeton: Princeton University Press, 1964.

Dos Passos, John. *Mr. Wilson's War*. Garden City: Doubleday, 1962.

Falls, Cyril. *The Great War*. New York: Putnam's Sons, 1959.

Farrar-Hockley, Anthony. *Goughie*. London: Hart-Davis, MacHibbon, 1975.

Faulstich, Edith M. *The Siberian Sojourn*, Book I. Privately printed, 1970.

———. *The Siberian Sojourn*, Book II. Unpublished.

Fedyshyn, Oleh. *Germany's Drive to the East and the Ukrainian Revolution 1917–1918*. New Brunswick, N.J.: Rutgers, 1971.

Fischer, Fritz. *Germany's Aims in the First World War*. New York: Norton, 1961.

Fleming, Peter. *The Fate of Admiral Kolchak*. London: Hart-Davis, 1963.

Foch, F. *The Memoirs of Marshal Foch*. Garden City: Doubleday, Doran, 1931.

Foch, Joffre, and Ludendorff. *The Two Battles of the Marne*. London: Butterworth, 1927.

Fowler, W. B. *British-American Relations, 1917–1918*. Princeton: Princeton University Press, 1966.

Francis, David. *Russia from the American Embassy*. New York: Scribner's, 1921.

Freund, Gerald. *Unholy Alliance*. New York: Harcourt, Brace, 1957.

Frothingham, Thomas G. *The American Reinforcement in the World War*. Garden City: Doubleday, Page and Co., 1927.

Gatzke, Hans. *Germany's Drive to the West*. Baltimore: Johns Hopkins Press, 1950.

George, Alexander and Juliette. *Woodrow Wilson and Colonel House: A Personality Study*. New Haven: Yale University Press, 1931.

Gibbons, Floyd. *And They Thought We Wouldn't Fight*. New York: Doran, 1918.

Gibbs, Philip. *Now It Can Be Told*. New York, London: Harper, 1920.

———. *The War Despatches*. London: Gibbs and Phillips, 1964.

Gies, Joseph. *Crisis 1918*. New York: Norton, 1973.

Gish, Lillian. *The Movies, Mr. Griffith and Me*. Englewood Cliffs, N.J.: Prentice-Hall, 1969.

Goerlitz, Walter. *History of the German General Staff*. New York: Praeger, n.d.

Gollin, A. M. *Proconsul in Politics*. New York: Macmillan, 1964.

Goodspeed, D. J. *Ludendorff*. London: Hart-Davis, 1966.

Gough, General Sir Hubert. *The Fifth Army*. Portway Bath: Chivers, 1968.

———. *Soldiering On*. London: Barker, n.d.

Grange, Baroness de la. *Open House in Flanders*. London: Murray, 1929.

Gray, Frank. *The Confessions of a Private*. London: Blackwell, 1920.

Griffiths, Richard. *Marshal Pétain*. London: Constable, 1970.

Griscom, Lloyd C. *Diplomatically Speaking*. New York: Literary Guild, 1940.

"G.S.O." *G.H.Q.* London: Allan, 1920.

Hagedorn, Hermann. *The Magnate*. New York: Reynal and Hitchcock, 1935.

Haig, Countess. *The Man I Knew*. Edinburgh, London: Moray Press, n.d.

Haigh, R. H., and P. W. Turner. *The Long Carry*. Oxford, New York: Pergamon, 1970.

Halliday, E. M. *The Ignorant Armies*. New York: Award Books, 1964.

Hankey, Lord. *The Supreme Command*, two volumes. London: Allen and Unwin, 1961.

Hanser, Richard. *Putsch!* New York: Wyden, 1954.

Hanssen, Hans Peter. *Diary of a Dying Empire*. Bloomington, Indiana: Indiana University Press, 1955.

Harbord, James G. *The American Army in France, 1917–1919*. Boston: Little, Brown, 1936.

Hard, William. *Raymond Robins' Own Story*. New York: Harpers, 1920.

Hartney, Harold E. *Wings over France*. Folkestone: Bailey Brothers and Swinfen, 1971.

Headlam, Cuthbert. *History of the Guards Division in the Great War 1915–1918*. London: Murray, 1924.

Heald, Edward T. *Witness to Revolution*. Kent State University Press, 1972.

Heinz, A. Heinz. *Germany's Hitler*. London: Wingate, 1954.

Hendrick, Burton J. *The Life and Letters of Walter H. Page*, Volume II, 1915–18. Garden City: Garden City Publishing Company, 1927.

Hickey, Captain D. E. *Rolling into Action*. London: Hutchison, n.d.

Hilger, Gustav, and Alfred G. Meyer. *The Incompatible Allies*. New York: Macmillan, 1953.

Hindenburg, Field Marshal Paul von. *Out of My Life*. London, New York, Toronto, and Melbourne: Cassell, 1920.

Hoffmann, Rudolf, editor. *Der Deutsche Soldat: Briefe aus dem Weltkrieg*. Munich: Langer/Muller, 1927.

Hoover, Herbert. *The Ordeal of Woodrow Wilson*. New York: McGraw-Hill, 1958.

Horn, Daniel. *The German Naval Mutinies of World War I*. New Brunswick, N.J.: Rutgers University Press, 1969.

Horne, Charles F., editor. *Source Records of the Great War*. U.S.: National Alumni, 1923.

Hornsey, F. H. *Hell on Earth*. Leipzig, Berlin: Teubner, 1935.

Howe, Quincy. *A World History of Our Own Times*, Volume I. New York: Simon & Schuster, 1949.

Hutchinson, Lieutenant Colonel Graham Seaton. *Warrior*. London: Hutchinson, n.d.

Ironside, Field-Marshal Lord. *Archangel 1918–1919*. London: Constable, n.d.

Izac, Edouard Victor. *Prisoner of the U-90*. Unpublished.

Jackson, Robert. *At War with the Bolsheviks*. London: Stacey, 1972.

Johnson, Thomas M. *Without Censor:* Indianapolis: Bobbs-Merrill, 1928.

Johnson, Thomas M., and Fletcher Pratt. *The Lost Battalion*. Indianapolis, New York: Bobbs-Merrill, 1938.

Jones, A. H. *War in the Air*, Volume VI. Oxford: Oxford University Press, 1934.

Joynt, W. D. *Saving the Channel Ports 1918*. Wren, 1975.

Jünger, Ernst. *The Storm of Steel*. London: Chatto and Windus, 1929.

Kahn, David. *Hitler's Spies*. New York: Macmillan, 1978.

Kennan, George F. *The Decision to Intervene*. Princeton: Princeton University Press, 1958.

Keyes, Sir Roger. *The Naval Memoirs of Admiral of the Fleet, Sir Roger Keyes*, Volume II, 1916–18. London: Butterworth, 1935.

Kiernan, R. H. *Little Brother Goes Hunting*. London: Constable, 1930.

Knight-Patterson, W. M. *Germany from Defeat to Conquest*. London: Allen and Unwin, 1945.

Kurenberg, Joachim von. *The Kaiser*. New York: Simon & Schuster, 1955.

Lamm, Heinrich. *Das Frontkämpferbuch*. Leipzig: Hesse and Becker, 1930.

Langer, William L. *Gas and Flame in World War I*. New York: Knopf, 1965.

Lawrence, T. E. *Revolt in the Desert*. New York: Doran, 1927.

Liddell Hart, Basil Henry. *Through the Fog of War*. New York: Random House, 1938.

Liggett, Major General Hunter. *A.E.F.* New York: Dodd, Mead, 1928.

Lloyd George, David. *War Memoirs of David Lloyd George*, Volume II, 1917–18. London: Odhams Press, n.d.

Lloyd George, David, and Frances Stevenson. *My Darling Pussy*. London: Weidenfeld & Nicolson, 1975.

Lockhart, R. H. Bruce. *British Agent*. New York: Putnam's Sons, 1933.

Ludendorff, General Erich. *My War Memories 1914–1918*, two volumes. London: Hutchinson, n.d.

———. *The General Staff and Its Problems*, two volumes. London: Hutchinson, 1920.

Ludendorff, Mathilde. *My Married Life with Ludendorff*. London: Hutchinson, 1919.

Ludwig, Emil. *Wilhelm Hohenzollern*. London, New York: Putnam's Sons, 1927.

Lunt, James D. *Charge to Glory!* New York; Harcourt, Brace, 1942.

Lutz, Ralph Haswell. *The Causes of the German Collapse in 1918*. Archon, 1969.

———. *Fall of the German Empire,* two volumes. New York: Octagon, 1969 (Hoover War Library Publication No. 1).

MacArthur, Douglas. *Reminiscences*. New York: McGraw-Hill, 1964.

MacDonagh, Michael. *In London During the Great War*. London: Eyre and Spottiswoode, 1935.

Mangin, General. *Comment finit la guerre*. Paris: Plon-Nourrit, 1920.

———. *Lettres de guerre*. Paris: Fayard, 1951.

March, General Peyton C. *The Nation at War*. Garden City: Doubleday, Doran, 1932.

Marder, Arthur J. *From the Dreadnaught to Scapa Flow*, "Victory and Aftermath," Volume V, 1918–19. London: Oxford, 1970.

Marshall, George C. *Memoirs of My Services in the World War 1917–1918*. Boston: Houghton Mifflin, 1976.

Maude, Alan H., editor. *The 47th (London) Division 1914–1919*. London: Amalgamated, 1922.

Maurice, Major General Sir Frederick, editor. *The Life of General Lord Rawlinson of Trent*. London: Cassell, 1928.

Maurice, Nancy, editor. *The Maurice Case*. London: Cooper, 1972.

Max, Prince of Baden. *Memoirs*, two volumes. London: Constable, 1928.

Maze, Paul. *A Frenchman in Khaki*. London, Toronto: Heinemann, 1934.

McCudden, James T. B. *Flying Fury*. Garden City: Doubleday, 1968.

Miller, Henry W. *The Paris Gun*. London, Bombay, and Sydney: Harrap, 1930.

Mitchell, Allan. *Revolution in Bavaria 1918–1919*. Princeton, N.J.: Princeton University Press, 1965.

Mitchell, Brigadier General William. *Memoirs of World War I*. New York: Random House, 1960.

Monash, Lieutenant-General Sir John. *The Australian Victories in France in 1918*. London: Hutchinson, n.d.

Montgomery, Major General Sir Archibald. *The Story of the Fourth Army*. London: Hodder and Stoughton, 1919.

Moore, William. *See How They Ran*. London: Cooper, 1970.

Mordacq, General H. *L'Armistice du 11 Novembre 1918*. Paris: Plon, 1937.

Müller, Admiral Georg Alexander von. *The Kaiser and His Court*. London: Macdonald, 1961.

Nelson, Walter Henry. *The Soldier Kings*. New York: Putnam's Sons, 1970.

Noakes, F. E. *The Distant Drums*. Tunbridge Wells, Kent: Courier, 1953.

Norman, Aaron. *The Great Air War*. New York: Macmillan, 1968.

Noulens, Joseph. *Mon Ambassade en Russie Soviétique*. Paris: Plon, 1933.

Nowak, Karl Friedrich. *The Collapse of Central Europe*. London: Paul, Trench, Trubner, 1924.

Oliver, F. S. *The Anvil of War*. London: Macmillan, 1936.

Palmer, Frederick. *America in France*. New York: Dodd, Mead, 1918.

———. *Newton D. Baker*, two volumes. New York: Dodd, Mead, 1931.

Paxson, Frederic. *America at War 1917–1918*. Boston: Houghton Mifflin, 1939.

Peixotto, Ernest. *The American Front*. New York: Scribner's, 1919.

Pershing, John J. *My Experiences in the World War*, Volume II. New York: Stokes, 1931.

Pierrefeu, Jean de. *French Headquarters 1915–1918*. London: Bles, n.d.

Pitt, Barrie. *1918—The Last Act*. New York: Norton, 1962.

Playne, Caroline E. *Britain Holds On 1917, 1918*. London: Allen and Unwin, 1933.

Poincaré, Raymond. *Victoire et Armistice*. Paris: Plon, 1933.

Ponomarzvov, B., editor. *History of Soviet Foreign Policy, 1917–1945*. Moscow: Progress, 1969.

Possony, Stefan T. *Lenin: the Compulsive Revolutionary*. Chicago: Regnery, 1964.

Recouly, Raymond. *Marshal Foch: His Own Words on Many Subjects*. London: Butterworth, 1929.

Reed, A. Cunningham. *Planes and Personalities*. London: Allan, 1922.

Reitz, Deneys. *Trekking On*. London: Faber and Faber, 1933.

Repington, Lieutenant Colonel C. A'Court, *The First World War 1914–1918*, two volumes. London: Constable, 1920.

Reynolds, Quentin. *They Fought for the Sky*. New York: Holt, Rinehart, Winston, 1957.

Richthofen, Kunigunde Freifrau von. *Mein Kriegstagebuch*. Berlin: Ullstein, 1937.

Richthofen, Manfred Freiherr von. *The Red Baron*. Garden City: Doubleday, 1969.

Rickenbacker, Captain Eddie V. *Fighting the Flying Circus*. Garden City: Doubleday, 1965.

Riddell, Lord George. *Lord Riddell's War Diary 1914–1918*. London: Nicholson and Watson, n.d.

Ritter, Gerhard. *The Sword and the Sceptre*. London: Allen Lane, 1973.

Rogerson, Sidney. *The Last of the Ebb*. London: Barker, 1937.

Rose, James W. *My Experiences in World War I*. Unpublished.

Rosenwinkel, Fritz. *Kriegserlebnisse eines einfachen Frontsoldaten*. Stolzenau/Weser, Glenewinkel, 1932.

Roskill, Stephen. *Hankey, Man of Secrets*. London: Collins, 1970.

Rudin, Harry R. *Armistice 1918*. New Haven: Yale University Press, 1944. Archon, 1967.

Rupprecht von Bayern, Kronprinz. *Mein Kriegstagebuch*. Berlin: Mittler, 1929.

Ryan, Stephen, *Pétain the Soldier*. New York: Barnes, 1969.

Ryder, A. J. *The German Revolution of 1918*. Cambridge: University Press, 1967.

Savage, Raymond. *Allenby of Armageddon*. London: Hodder & Stoughton, n.d.

Saxe, Melvin. *Reminiscences*. Unpublished.

Schacht, Hjalmar. *Confessions of the "Old Wizard."* Cambridge, Mass.: Houghton Mifflin, 1956.

Schröder, Hans. *An Airman Remembers*. London: Hamilton, n.d.

Seldte, Franz. *Through a Lens Darkly*. London: Hutchinson, 1933.

Serge, Victor. *Year One of the Russian Revolution*. Chicago, New York: 1938.

Seymour, Charles. *The Intimate Papers of Colonel House*, Volumes III–IV, 1917–18. Boston, New York: Houghton Mifflin, 1938.

Silverlight, John. *The Victor's Dilemma*. New York: Waybright and Talley, 1970.

Sisson, Edgar. *One Hundred Red Days*. New Haven: Yale University Press, 1931.

Sixsmith, E. K. G. *Douglas Haig*. London: Weidenfeld & Nicolson, 1976.

Spengler, Oswald. *Spengler Letters*. London: Allen and Unwin, 1966.

Stallings, Laurence. *The Doughboys*. New York, Evanston, and London: Harper and Row, 1963.

Stallworthy, Jon. *Wilfred Owen*. London: Oxford, 1974.

Stark, Rudolf. *Wings of War*. London: Arms and Armour, 1973.

Steinberg, I. N. *In the Workshop of the Revolution*. New York: Rinehart, 1953.

Stevenson, Frances. *Lloyd George, A Diary*. London: Hutchinson, 1971.

Strakhovsky, Leonid. *The Origins of American Intervention in North Russia (1918)*. Princeton, N.J.: Princeton University Press, 1937.

Sullivan, Mark. *Our Times Over Here 1914–1918*. New York: Scribner's, 1933.

Sulzbach, Herbert. *With the German Guns*. London: Cooper, 1973.

Teilhard de Chardin, Pierre. *The Making of a Mind*. London: Collins, 1965.

Terraine, John. *Douglas Haig*. London: Hutchinson, 1963.

Thoumin, General Richard. *The First World War*. New York: Putnam's, 1964.

Toland, John. *Adolf Hitler*. Garden City: Doubleday, 1976.

Trask, David F. *The United States in the Supreme War Council*. Middletown, Conn.: Wesleyan University Press, 1961.

Tschuppik, Karl. *Ludendorff*. London: Allen and Unwin, 1932.

Udet, Ernst. *Ace of the Black Cross*. London: Newnes, n.d.

Ullman, Richard H. *Intervention and the War*, Volume I. Princeton, N.J.: Princeton University Press, 1961.

Unterberger, Betty. *American Intervention in the Russian Civil War*. Lexington, Mass.: Heath, 1969.

Valiani, Leo. *The End of Austria-Hungary*. New York: Knopf, 1973.

Vandiver, Frank E. *Black Jack*, two volumes. College Station, Texas: Texas A & M University Press, 1977.

Walworth, Arthur. *America's Moment: 1918*. New York: Norton, 1977.

Watt, Richard M. *The Kings Depart*. London: Weidenfeld and Nicolson, 1968.

Werkmann, Karl. *Deutschland als Verbündete*. Berlin.

Westman, Stephen. *Surgeon with the Kaiser's Army*. London: Kimber, 1968.

Wheeler-Bennett, John W. *The Forgotten Peace*. New York: Morrow, 1939.

———. *Hindenburg*. London, Melbourne, and Toronto: Macmillan, 1967.

———. *The Nemesis of Power*. New York: Viking, 1964.

Wilhelm II. *The Kaiser's Memoirs*. New York, London: Harper, 1922.

William, Crown Prince of Germany. *My War Experiences*. London: Hurst and Blackett, n.d.

Williams, Albert Rhys. *Journey into Revolution*. Chicago: Quadrangle, 1969.

———. *Through the Russian Revolution*. New York: Boni & Liveright, 1921.

Williams, John. *The Other Battleground*. Chicago: Regnery, 1972.

Wilson, Woodrow. *The Messages and Papers of Woodrow Wilson*, Volume I. New York: Review of Reviews Corporation, 1924.

Wright, Gordon. *Raymond Poincaré and the French Presidency*. New York: Octagon, 1967.

Wright, Captain Peter E. *At the Supreme War Council*. London: Eveleigh Nash, 1921.

Yardley, Herbert O. *The American Black Chamber*. Indianapolis: Bobbs-Merrill, 1931.

Zeman, Z. A. B. *Germany and the Revolution in Russia, 1915–1918*. London: Oxford, 1958.

Notes

Abbreviations

CHD	Colonel House diary
DP	Lord Derby papers
FRUS	*Foreign Relations of the United States, Russia,* Volumes I, II
HC	Field Marshal Haig private correspondence
HD	Field Marshal Haig diary
HFWW	*History of the First World War* magazine series
IWM-PA	Imperial War Museum, personal accounts
RD	Raymond Robins diary
TGW-IWT	*The Great War. I Was There* magazine series
USM-PA	United States Marine Corps Historical Center, personal accounts
WD	Field Marshal Sir Henry Wilson diaries

Prologue

page 1	"little prospect of military success for us." Gollin 553.
page 1	"If the war continues . . ." Riddell 303.
page 4	"No longer threatened in the rear . . ." Hindenburg 33.

Chapter One THUNDER IN THE WEST

page 6	Observance of German road traffic. Jones 269.
page 7	German code. Kahn 334–35; Yardley 223–24.
pages 7-8	"I expect a bombardment . . ." Gough, *Fifth Army* 251.
page 8	"strangely still and peaceful . . ." Blaxland 33–34.
page 8	"the only sign of bloodshed . . ." Asquith 315–16.
page 8	"The enemy is rather threatening . . ." HC, March 20.
page 9	"but all of us felt perfectly sure . . ." Gough, *Fifth Army* 259.
page 9	"No rest the whole night . . ." Stark 31.
page 9	"To-morrow there will be nothing . . ." Binding 204–5.
page 9	"They still believe . . ." Maurice 72.

page 10	"as soon as possible . . ." HD, March 2.
page 10	"Troop movements . . ." HD, March 3.
page 10	"I go by evidence . . ." Maurice 74.
page 10	"It looks now as if an attack . . ." Farrar-Hockley 262–63.
page 11	"On the whole I don't like . . ." HD, March 7.
page 11	Haig-Lloyd George conversation. HD, March 14.
page 11	"One can only be amazed . . ." Barnett 302.
page 12	"But had we really any grounds . . ." Hindenburg 345.
page 12	"Our superior training . . . hands of fate." Ludendorff, *My War Memories* II 597–98.
pages 12-13	"Do you know what it says . . ." Barnett 304.
page 13	Captive balloon escape. Blaxland 33; Farrar-Hockley 271–73.
page 13	Maze story. Maze 278–79.
page 13	"purred on the telephone . . ." Pitt 72.
pages 13-14	"quite inconceivable in detail . . ." Binding 204–5.

Chapter Two THE GREAT ATTACK·

pages 14-15	Campbell story. IWM-PA; Campbell, *The Ebb and Flow of Battle* 12–13 and *In the Cannon's Mouth.*
page 15	"as if the world . . ." Sulzbach 150.
pages 15-16	Bensen story. Bensen 146.
page 16	Behrend story. Behrend 53–56.
pages 16-17	Allfree story. IWM-PA.
page 17	Churchill story. Churchill, *The World Crisis* II 411.
page 17	Asquith story. Asquith 318.
pages 17-18	Gray story. Gray 157–58.
page 18	Gough story. Gough, *Fifth Army* 260.
page 18	"Machine-gun posts were blown sky-high . . ." Crutchley 131.
pages 18-19	Maze story. Maze 281.
pages 19-21	Jünger story. Jünger 254–58.
page 20	Lamm story. Lamm.
page 21	Campbell story. IWM-PA; Campbell, *Ebb* 15.
pages 21-22	Allfree story. IWM-PA.
page 22	Elstob story, Blaxland 44.
pages 22-23	Schülenberg story. Hoffmann.
page 23	Maze story. Maze 282.
page 24	"He hasn't got our manpower position . . ." Maurice 76.
page 24	"Only the valour of the British . . ." Repington II 254.
page 24	"It is one of the most decisive . . ." Hankey 785.

page 24	Air action. Morris 130.
pages 24-25	Gough story. Farrar-Hockley 277; Gough, *Fifth Army* 248, 266–67, 281–82.
pages 25-26	Elstob story. Gough, *Fifth Army* 269–70; Moore 58–59.
page 26	Jünger story. Jünger 259–60.
page 26	Muth letter. Hoffmann.
page 26	Campbell story. IWM-PA; Campbell, *Ebb* 14; correspondence.
page 26-27	Gough story. Gough, *Fifth Army* 271.
page 27	Gibbs dispatch. Gibbs, *The War Despatches* 328.
pages 27-28	Gray story. Gray 161.
page 28	Ross story. Moore 70.
pages 28-29	Campbell story. IWM-PA; Campbell, *Ebb* 17–18.
page 29	Birch story. IWMPA.
pages 29-30	Crown Prince story. William, *Crown Prince* 303–4.
page 30	Maze story. Maze 288–89.
page 31	Order to all corps, Fifth Army. Farrar-Hockley 285.
page 31	Haig letter. HC, March 22.
page 31	"no need to be anxious . . ." Griffiths 65.
page 32	Jünger story. Jünger 273.
pages 32-33	Campbell story. IWM-PA; Campbell, *Ebb* 19–22; correspondence.
pages 33-34	Asquith story. Asquith 326.
pages 34-36	Kerr story. TGW-IWT #39, 1559ff.
page 36	Boyd story. Boyd 285.
pages 36-37	Campbell story. IWM-PA; Campbell, *Ebb* 22–23, 29–32; correspondence.
page 38	Cockburn story. IWM-PA.
page 39	Gough telephone call to Pétain. Griffiths 65.
page 39	Lloyd George thoughts. Lloyd George 1687–88.
page 39	General Wilson postcard. Maurice 53.
page 39	Wilson description. Lady Lloyd George manuscript, House of Lords Record Office.
pages 39-40	Wilson-Clemenceau anecdote. Peter Wright 41.
page 40	Wilson on Haig. WD, February 25.
page 40	Behrend story. Behrend 81.
page 41	Cornwalls story. Moore 90.
pages 41-43	Paris Gun. Miller 13–25, 94–103.
page 43	Birch story. IWM-PA.
page 44	Maze story. Maze 291–292; correspondence.
page 45	Fisher story. IWM-PA.
page 45	VII Corps report. Moore 96.
page 45	Stark story. Stark 33.
pages 45-46	Gale story. Moore 87.
page 46	Mellersh story. IWM-PA.

page 46	Gough story. Gough, *Fifth Army* 252.
page 46	Haig story. HD, March 23.
pages 46-47	"The object now is to separate . . ." Farrar-Hockley 294.
page 47	"I invited the Staff to meet me . . ." Lloyd George 1727.
page 47	"War Cabinet in a panic . . ." Maurice 77.
pages 47-48	"The Cabinet much rattled . . ." Repington 255–56.
page 48	*"Le bon dieu est boche."* WD, March 23.
page 48	"The superiority of German leaders . . ." Horne 87–88.
page 48	Death of Ludendorff's son. Margarethe Ludendorff 130–31.
page 48	"The battle is won." Müller 344.
page 48	Pétain-Clemenceau story. Pierrefeu 229.
page 49	Lloyd George at dinner. Page 365–66.
page 49	"It was therefore decided . . ." Lloyd George 1731.
page 49	Derby description. Bonham 250; Roskill 497.
page 49	Haig letter. HC, March 23.
pages 49-50	Gaudy story. Thoumin 452–53.
page 50	Beddington-Seely conversation. Farrar-Hockley 295.
page 50	Amiens story. Williamson, IWM-PA.
page 51	Campbell story. IWM-PA; Campbell, *Ebb* 37; correspondence.
pages 51-52	Cockburn story. IWM-PA.
page 52	Mellersh story. IWM-PA.
page 53	"how much longer the officers and men . . ." Gough, *Fifth Army* 283.
page 53	Pétain-Herbillon story. Griffiths 66–67.
pages 53-55	Clemenceau-Poincaré story. Griffiths 76–78.
page 54	Foch-Loucheur story. Bugnet 219–20.
page 54	Footnote. WD, February 27.
page 54	Foch note. Foch 258.
page 54	Paris Gun. Miller 105.
page 54	Foch-Clemenceau conversation. Foch 258; Recouly 24–25.
page 55	Williamson story. IWM-PA.
pages 55-56	Laithwaite story. IWM-PA.
pages 56-57	Maze story. Maze 296–98; correspondence.
page 57	Cockburn story. IWM-PA.
page 57	"impressed by the horrors of the battlefield . . ." Müller 345.
pages 57-58	Wilson's day. WD, March 24.
page 58	Lloyd George-Riddell story. Riddell 320.
pages 58-59	Clemenceau-Pétain story. Griffiths 68; Ryan 160.

page 59	Pétain-Haig meeting. HD, March 24; Collier 309.
page 59	Footnote. HD, April 3, 1919.
pages 59-60	Haig cable and letter to wife. HD, March 24; HC, March 24.
page 60	"What are you doing there, gentlemen?" Pierrefeu 231.

Chapter Three "GOD GRANT THAT IT MAY NOT BE TOO LATE"

pages 60-62	Campbell story. IWM-PA; Campbell, *Ebb* 41–44; correspondence.
pages 62-63	Paris Gun. Miller 57–58, 106–7.
pages 63-64	Cockburn story. IWM-PA.
page 64	Wilson-Haig meeting. HD, March 25; WD, March 25.
page 65	"at all costs to maintain . . ." Gollin 502.
page 65	Meeting at Compiègne. Gollin 502–3.
pages 65-66	Haig-Wilson meeting. Foch 257.
page 66	Behrend story. Behrend 102–3.
pages 66-68	Seldte story. Seldte 188ff.
page 68	Maze story. Maze 299–302.
pages 68-69	Cockburn story. IWM-PA.
page 69	Foch-Wilson. Recouly 26; Foch 261; Collier 310.
page 69	Pershing-Pétain meeting. Pershing diary, March 25; Pershing I 356–57.
page 70	"Bomb and shoot up everything . . ." Lambert 44.
pages 70-71	Maze story. Maze 303–6.
page 71	Behrend story. Behrend 107.
pages 71-74	Meeting at Doullens. HD, March 26; Ryan 161; Clemenceau 387–88; Poincaré 86–89; Foch 262; Foch, Joffre, Ludendorff 166; Terraine 423–24; Barnett 327; Gollin 505.
page 75	Lunch at the Hôtel des Quatre Fils Aymon. Recouly 27; Poincaré 90; Foch 265.
page 76	Foch-Gough meeting. Bugnet 227; Gough, *Fifth Army* 305–8.
pages 76-77	Haig-Milner-Wilson meeting. WD, March 26; HD, March 26.
page 77	Gough telephone call to Lawrence. Gough, *Fifth Army* 309.
page 77	Corday recollection. Corday 328.
page 78	Foch story. Bugnet 225.
page 78	Addison recollection. Addison 499.
page 78	Milner-Wilson report to Lloyd George. Hankey 787; WD, March 26.
page 78	"If an English delegation . . ." Müller 345.

page 78	Ludendorff-Rupprecht telephone call. Foch, Joffre, Ludendorff 232–33.
page 79	"The enemy is now pushing westwards . . ." Monash 26.
page 79	"If there is a great disaster . . ." Gollin 508.
page 79	"The situation is very desperate . . ." Addison 500.
pages 79-80	Lloyd George message. Baker 57.
page 80	Wilson-Franklin Roosevelt conversation. Toland, *The Last 100 Days*, New York: Random House, 1966, 91.
page 80	"General Pershing expressed only . . ." Trask 81.
page 80	"Towns and villages razed . . ." Müller 345.
page 81	"I felt a great wave of bitterness . . ." Blücher 209.
page 81	"He then asked to see me . . ." Gough, *Fifth Army* 315.
page 81	Gough-Beddington story. Farrar-Hockley 310.
pages 82-83	Maze story. Maze 309–10.
pages 82-83	Pershing at Clermont-sur-Oise. Pershing I 364–65; Brunn 146.
page 84	Haig on King George and meeting with Foch. HD, March 29.
pages 84-85	Clemenceau at cathedral. Mordacq, *Le Ministère Clemenceau* I 250–52.
page 85	"There were breaks, plenty of breaches." Brunn 146–47.
page 85	Maze story. Maze 313–14.
pages 85-88	Seely story. TGW-IWT #40, 1584ff: interview with Frank Rees; Rees manuscript.
page 88	Churchill-Clemenceau-Rawlinson story. Churchill, *Amid These Storms* 165–77; HD, March 30.
page 89	"a curious atmospheric sensation . . ." Williams 250.
page 90	Footnote. Fowler 139–40.
page 90	Lloyd George at dinner. Riddell 322, Roskill 515.
page 90	Foch letter to Clemenceau. Foch 272–75.
pages 90-91	Lloyd George-Haig meeting. HD, April 3; Lloyd George 1744–45.
pages 91-93	Beauvais meeting. Pershing I 373–75; Dos Passos 327; HD, April 3; Foch 276–77; Lloyd George 1750; WD, April 3.
page 94	Haig-Gough meeting. Gough, *Fifth Army* 325; *Soldiering On* 169–70.
page 94	Cabinet meeting. WD, April 4.
pages 94-95	Binding story. Binding 216–17.
pages 95-96	Songs. Sullivan 340–41.

page 95	Footnote. Boatner 116.
page 96	*Hearts of the World*. Gish 199.
page 96	"What the English and French . . ." Ludendorff, *My War Memories* II 600.
page 97	"the acquisition of the iron district . . ." Gatske 264.

Chapter Four RED DAWN IN THE EAST

page 97	"They lay as they fell . . ." Schröder 263–64.
page 98	"by supplying reliable information . . ." Walworth 33.
pages 98-99	"God only knows who is right . . ." CHD, January 2.
page 99	"an answer to the demand . . ." Seymour III 322.
page 99	Wilson-House meeting. CHD, January 4.
page 100	"You will either be on the crest . . ." CHD, January 5.
page 102	"Senators and representatives jumped on chairs . . ." Dos Passos 306.
page 104	"The war with England and America . . ." Bunyan 504.
page 104	On Raymond Robins. Hard 3–9, 44.
page 104	Footnote. Maugham, *The Summing Up* 203–4.
page 105	Lockhart-Robins. Lockhart 195, 220–23; Fowler 167; Kennan 380; Hard 130–33.
page 107	"Now is the opportunity . . ." Ullman 73.
page 107	Lockhart-Trotsky meeting. Lockhart 227–29; Ullman 120.
page 107	"In our day wars are not won . . ." Wheeler-Bennett, *The Forgotten Peace* 261.
page 108	"What an hour!" RD, February 24.
page 108	Francis cable. FRUS I 387.
page 108	Lockhart meeting with Lenin. Lockart 233–35.
page 109	"There are still considerable possibilities . . ." Ullman 121.
pages 109-10	Robins-Trotsky meeting. Hard 134–44; Wheeler-Bennett, *The Forgotten Peace* 290–91.
page 110	Robins-Lenin meeting. Hard 148–49.
page 110	President Wilson message to Tokyo. Trask 110.
page 110	"Our proverbial friendship for Russia." Seymour III 399.
pages 110-11	Wilson message to Russia. FRUS I 395–96.
page 111	Sverdlov message to U.S. FRUS I 399–400.
page 111	"We slapped the President of the United States . . ." Francis 320.
page 112	Robins-Lenin meeting. Hard 151–53.

page 113   "The prospects which opened for us . . ." Hindenburg 351.

page 115   "Failing some readily outstanding . . ." WD, April 7.

page 115   Haig letter to his wife. HC, April 8.

page 115   Tucker story. IWM-PA.

page 116   "The assault battalion stormed on . . ." Westman 158.

page 116   Hornsey story. Hornsey 5.

page 117   Haig-Foch-Wilson meeting. Foch 284–85; HD, April 9; WD, April 9.

page 117   Hornsey story. Hornsey 5ff.

pages 117-18 Lloyd George's day. Hankey 522.

page 119   "I had written an article yesterday . . ." Repington II 271.

page 119   Lawrence letter to Maurice. Maurice File, King's College, Liddell Hart Centre for Military Archives.

pages 119-20 Tucker story. IWM-PA.

page 121   Wilson in Paris. WD, April 10.

page 121   "I was received and reassured . . ." Grange 315.

pages 121-22 Haig-Wilson meeting. WD, April 10; HD, April 10.

page 122   Haig Order of the Day. Terraine 433.

page 122   "where I frightened them . . ." WD, April 11.

page 122   "we cannot any longer make good . . ." WD, April 12.

page 123   Hutchison's story. Hutchison 243ff.

page 124   "We to whom it was addressed . . ." Fussell, Paul, *The Great War and Modern Memory*, Oxford University Press, 1975, page 17.

page 124   "If the section cannot remain here alive . . ." Terraine 433–34.

page 124   Tanner story. IWM-PA; Stoney Report, IWM-PA.

page 125   Hutchison story. Hutchison 249–50.

page 125   Hornsey story. Hornsey 32ff.

pages 125-26 Wilson story about Lloyd George. WD, April 13.

page 126   Tanner story. IWM-PA.

page 127   Abbeville conference. HD, April 14; Foch 291.

pages 128-29 Hornsey story. Hornsey 35–36.

page 129   Hutchison story. Hutchison 251.

pages 129-30 Prince Sixtus incident. Brook-Shepherd 145–51; Roskill 526–27.

page 131   "I plumped for Milner." WD, April 15.

page 131-32 Reaction in London to Haig's order. Playne 291ff.

page 132   Hornsey story. Hornsey 41ff.

Chapter Six "ST. GEORGE FOR ENGLAND!"

page 180	Lenin pass. Hard 191.
page 180	"The tide runs flood . . ." RD, May 14.
page 180	Lenin speech. Kennan 221–22.
page 181	Mirbach report to Berlin. Zeman 124–25.
page 181	Russian-German trade negotiations. Carr 80–82.
page 182	"It came up like an angry ball of fire . . ." Lockhart 278.
page 182	Lockhart story. Lockhart 280–81.
page 183	Wilson at Metropolitan Opera House. Kennan 351.
pages 183-84	Wilson note to Lansing. Kennan 356.

Chapter Eight "THE YANKS ARE COMING!"

page 185	Kiernan story. Kiernan 69–72.
pages 187-88	Cooper story. IWM-PA; correspondence and interviews.
page 189	Haig at 77th Division. HD, May 21.
page 189	Sulzbach story. Sulzbach 176–77.
page 190	Derby letter. DP, May 24.
page 190	"In our opinion there are no indications." Liddell Hart 324–25.
page 191	Rogerson story. Rogerson 24–26.
pages 191-92	Wiedemann. Wiedemann, *Der Mann, der Feldherr werden wollte*. Velbert, 1964.
page 192	Sulzbach story. Sulzbach 179.
page 193	Rogerson story. Rogerson 28–35.
pages 193-94	Kiernan story. Kiernan 75–78.
page 195	Sagewitz letter. Hoffmann.
page 196	Pierrefeu story. Pierrefeu 266–67.
page 196	Wilson-King George meeting. WD, May 27.
page 196	"a great victory . . ." Müller 358.
page 197	Sulzbach story. Sulzbach 181.
pages 197-98	"which was back on the Aisne . . ." Foch 313.
page 198	"I hope so. This would be good." WD, May 28.
page 198	Kaiser at Californie Plateau. Rogerson 137.
pages 198-99	Kiernan story. Kiernan 84–85.
page 199	Derby letter. DP, May 28.
page 199	"an absolutely incredible fury . . ." De Weerd 292.
page 201	Sulzbach story. Sulzbach 182.
page 201	Crown Prince story. William, Crown Prince 319–20.
pages 201-2	Matthaei story. Gies (bound galleys) 164.
page 202	"A tragic sight to see the General weeping . . ." Clemenceau 48–49.
page 202	Griscom story. Griscom 295–96.
page 203	Kiernan story. Kiernan 100.
pages 203-4	Clemenceau telegram. Foch 49–50.
page 204	Clemenceau-Poincaré meeting. Poincaré 198–99.

page 204	Clemenceau up front. Brunn 161–62.
page 204	Poincaré in his garden. Poincaré 200.
page 205	"It was nothing less than a rout." Palmer, *America in France* 217–18.
page 205	Matthaei story. Gies (bound galleys) 172–73.
pages 205-6	Clemenceau-Poincaré meeting. Poincaré 201–2; Gies (bound galleys) 171.
page 206	Haig-Foch lunch. HD, May 31.
page 207	Dinner at Versailles. Roskill 556–57; Hankey 809–11.
pages 207-8	"thoroughly tired of them!" HD, May 31.
page 208	"Tomorrow will be a critical day." WD, May 31.
page 208	"Writing now before breakfast . . ." WD, June 1.
page 208	Milner depression. Gollin 564.
page 208	"If the French had so readily . . ." Lloyd George 1842–43.
pages 208-9	Haig at Villa Romaine. HD, June 1.
page 209	Clemenceau-Poincaré. Poincaré 205–8.
page 209	"And so these people went on wrangling . . ." HD, June 1.
page 209	Supreme War Council meeting. HD, June 1; Pershing 71–73.
page 210	Haig letter to his wife. HC, June 1.
page 210	"He is quite intoxicated . . ." Müller 359.
page 210	Hitler feat. Toland 69–70.
page 211	Clemenceau-Poincaré meeting. Poincaré 212–13.
page 212	"I will hit here." Lloyd George 1844.
page 212	Afternoon conference. Roskill 559; Hankey 812; WD, June 2.
pages 212-14	Clemenceau at Chamber of Deputies. Clemenceau 51–54; Gies (bound galleys) 181–83; Brunn 162–63.
page 214	"This is a very good thing . . ." HC, June 5.
page 214	Meeting at 10 Downing St. Hankey 813.
page 214	Wilson to Lloyd George. WD, June 5.
page 215	Cates letter to mother. USM-PA.
page 216	Pierrefeu comment. *U.S. Naval Institute Proceedings*, November 1928, 940.
page 216	Hamilton story. Asprey 148–54.
pages 217-18	Gibbons story. Gibbons 306–8.
pages 218-19	Silverthorn story. Interview; USM-PA.
page 219	Catlin story. Catlin 114.
page 220	Paradise story. Correspondence; USM-PA.
page 220	Silverthorn story. Interview; USM-PA.
pages 220-21	Gibbons story. Gibbons 322.
page 221	Cates story. Asprey 184–85.
page 221	Cates story. Asprey 198.
pages 221-22	Shepherd story. USM-PA.
pages 223-24	Versailles meeting. HD, June 7; WD, June 7.

page 224	Griscom story. Griscom 398ff.
page 225	Pershing to Clemenceau. Pershing II 92–95.
pages 225-26	Milner letter to Lloyd George. Gollin 565–66.
page 227	Desagneaux story. Desagneaux 79ff.
page 227	"Those in the know maintain . . ." Müller 361.
page 227	Haig letter to wife. HC, June 14.

Chapter Nine INTERVENTION II

page 229	Lockhart story. Lockhart 283–84.
pages 229-30	Robins-Williams meeting. Williams, *Journey into Revolution* 306–7; RD, June 21.
page 230	Robins thoughts. RD, June 21–22.
page 230	"Specific evidence accumulates daily . . ." FRUS I 554–55.
page 231	Lockhart-Balfour wires. Ullman 190–92.
page 231	"If I had my own way about Russia . . ." Baker 219.
page 232	Francis letter to son. Francis 304–5.
page 232	Williams story. Williams, *Through the Russian Revolution* 247–50.
pages 232-33	Supreme War Council. Ullman 212.
page 233	"In short, President Wilson hoped . . ." Trask 123.
pages 233-34	Wilson meeting with Cabinet. March 124–26.
page 234	Wilson-Mme. Botchkarova incident. George 195.
page 234	Wilson's fear his failures at Princeton might be repeated as President. George 321.
page 235	"Wilson and his Secretary of State . . ." Kenman 406.
page 236	"I know exactly what the President has in mind." CHD, July 9.
page 236	Reading cable. Ullman 216.
page 236	Lloyd George's reaction to U.S. proposal. Roskill 573; Ullman 217–18.
page 237	Wilson's *aide-mémoire*. Ullman 226.

Chapter Ten THE TURNING POINT

page 238	"Immediately following this operation . . ." Ludendorff, *My War Memories* II 639.
page 238	"They were advising him to continue . . ." Barnett 336.
pages 238-39	"but was still high enough to allow . . ." Ludendorff, *My War Memories* II 638.
page 239	Pétain-Foch-Hellé conference. George Viereck, editor, *As They Saw Us*, Garden City, N.Y.: Doubleday, Doran, 1929, 135–38.
page 241	Aldrich story. Aldrich 217–18.
page 241	Clemenceau-Derby meeting. DP, July 14.

page 241   Quentin Roosevelt's death. Rickenbacker 152–53.

page 242   Lloyd George-Milner conference. Hankey 826–27; Roskill 575.

page 243   Crown Prince story. William, Crown Prince 332–33.

page 243   Adams story. Adams 240–41.

page 244   Hesse's story. Alden Brooks, *As I Saw It*, New York: Knopf, 1930, 194ff.

page 244   "Scores of these boats were shattered . . ." Dos Passos 353.

pages 244-45   Mitchell story. Mitchell 219ff.

page 245   Pétain-Fayolle telephone call. Gies (bound galleys) 231; Griffiths 82.

page 246   Crown Prince story. William, Crown Prince 334ff.

pages 246-47   Ludendorff-Lersner-Klewitz conference. Barnett 338; Ludendorff, *My War Memories* II 578.

page 247   Bucher story. Bucher 268ff.

page 247   Hesse story. Alden Brooks, *As I Saw It* 194ff.

pages 247-48   Binding story. Binding 235–36.

page 248   "His mood was slightly less ebullient . . ." Müller 371.

page 248   "Difficult question what to do next." Barnett 339.

page 249   Thomas description. USM-PA; interview.

page 250   McCord diary. USM-PA.

pages 250-51   Ganoe story. Catlin 203–9.

page 251   "which the men devoured after making . . ." Dos Passos 360–61.

page 252   Rose story. Rose; correspondence.

page 252   Teilhard story. Teilhard 218–19.

page 254   Hartney story. Hartney 170–71.

page 254   Gibbons story. Gibbons 371–73.

page 255   "Ludendorff was confident and eager . . ." Barnett 339.

page 255   "I think your proposals are pertinent . . ." Ritter 233–34.

page 255   "While the commanders were doing . . ." Ludendorff, *My War Memories* II 665.

page 256   Ludendorff-Hindenburg meeting. Barnett 340.

page 256   Rose story. Rose; correspondence.

pages 257-58   Kaiser-Hindenburg-Ludendorff meeting. Horne 376ff.

pages 258-59   Mangin-Pétain-Fayolle meeting. Mangin, *Lettres de guerre* 279–80.

pages 259-60   Sulzbach story. Sulzbach 204.

page 260   "It must have been someone . . ." Müller 372.

page 260   "It was certainly the most critical . . ." William, Crown Prince 339.

page 260	Hindenburg-Ludendorff meeting. Barnett 340; Goodspeed 205.
pages 260-61	Rose story. Rose; correspondence.
pages 261-64	Cates-Paradise-Denig-Brannen-Bellamy action. USM-PA; Cates 37; correspondence; New York *Times*, October 17, 1918.
page 263	Sulzbach story. Sulzbach 205.
page 263	Binding story. Binding 237.
page 263	Ludendorff story. Barnett 342.
page 265	Rose story. Rose.
page 265	Canright letter. *Wisconsin Magazine of History* 196.
page 265	Princess Blücher story. Blücher 238–39.
page 265	"even the most optimistic . . ." Frothingham 285–86.
page 265	Kaiser depression. *American Historical Review,* October 1952, 31.
page 266	Ludendorff-Mertz von Quirnheim meeting. Barnett 344–45.
page 266	Kaiser at Avesnes. Müller 373–74.
page 266	Mertz von Quirnheim's diary. Barnett 346.
page 267	Zöberlein story. Gies (bound galleys) 266–67.
page 267	Arndt story. Arndt.
page 267	Bucher story. Bucher 277–79.
page 268	Sulzbach story. Sulzbach 211–12.
page 268	Crown Prince on colonies. Gatzke 274–75.
page 269	Wilhelm on Belgium. Knight-Patterson 181.

Chapter Eleven BLACK DAY

page 269	Ludendorff directive. Barnett 346–47.
page 269	Wilhelm at Spa. Müller 376.
pages 269-70	"I have got a bad opinion . . ." Binding 240–41.
page 271	Lloyd George to Hankey. Hankey 830.
page 271	Meeting of prime ministers. WD, August 1.
page 272	Ludendorff secret order. Barnett 347.
page 272	Haig-King George meeting. HD, August 7.
page 273	"The British cavalry columns were paired . . ." Bean 524.
page 274	Bacon story. TGW-IWT #44, 1751ff.
page 274	Hickey story. Hickey 223.
page 274	Maze story. Maze 325–27; interview.
page 275	"Last night was our most critical . . ." HD, August 7; HC, August 7.
page 275	Montague story. Chapman, *Vain Glory* 648–49.
pages 275-76	Australians await battle. Bean 525ff.
page 276	Maze story. Maze 328.
pages 276-77	Bacon story. TGW-IWT #44, 1751ff.
page 277	"I had a feeling of being behind . . ." Bean 630–31.

page 279	Maze story. Maze 328–30; interview; correspondence.
pages 279-80	Montague story. Chapman, *Vain Glory* 650–51.
page 280	Württemberg artillerymen. Bean 572-73.
pages 280-81	Bacon story. TGW-IWT #44, 1751ff.
page 281	In Bayonvillers. Thoumin 497–98.
page 281	"It was said that masses . . ." Hindenburg 391–92.
pages 281-82	Maze story. Maze 329–34; interview; correspondence; Blaxland 171–72.
page 282	"already gained a complete impression . . ." Ludendorff, *My War Memories* II 680.
page 283	"Well, sir, au revoir until tomorrow." IWM-PA (letters of Major-General S. S. Cutter).
page 283	Haig's morning. HD, August 8.
page 284	"Today, for the second time, our troops . . ." Rupprecht.
page 284	"It's very strange that our men . . ." Müller 377.
page 284	Maze story. Maze 335.
page 284	Bacon story. TGW-IWT #44, 1751ff.
page 284	Haig letter to his wife. HC, August 8.
page 284	"Gentlemen, there was an attack this morning . . ." IWM-PA (letters of General Cutter).
page 285	"Ludendorff is constantly insisting . . ." Barnett 353–54; Rupprecht.
page 285	"I was told of glorious valor but also . . ." Ludendorff, *My War Memories* II 683.
pages 285-86	"All that I had feared, all that I had . . ." Rudin 20.
page 286	Ludendorff-Wilhelm meeting. Rudin 21–22.
page 286	"Don't ever forget that the history . . ." Griscom 431.
page 287	"Had Haig flung his army . . ." Lloyd George 1869.
page 287	Lloyd George love letter. Lloyd George and Frances Stevenson 22.
pages 287-88	Binding story. Binding 242–43.
page 288	"You don't know Ludendorff . . ." Goodspeed 208.
pages 288-90	Ludendorff, Hindenburg, Kaiser, etc., at Spa. Rudin 22–25; Ludendorff, *My War Memories* II 686; Ludendorff, *General Staff* 580ff; Lutz, *Fall of the German Empire* 459.
page 290	Footnote. Goodspeed 209.
page 290	Emperor Karl at Spa. Rudin 27; Brook-Shepherd 168–69.
page 290	"But has he the necessary force?" HD, August 17.
page 291	"fully and very frankly, but as . . ." DP, July 27.
page 291	Solf speech. Max I 325ff.

pages 291-92   Dechend story. IWM-PA.

page 292   Hitler incident. Toland 70.

page 292   Crown Prince story. William, Crown Prince 347.

page 293   Haig letter to his wife. HC, August 27.

page 293   Dechend story. IWM-PA.

page 293   "I must recognize for the first time . . ." Goodspeed 210.

Chapter Twelve THE RED TERROR

page 295   "What would you have?" Howe 648–49.

page 295   Lenin-Sverdlov incident. Serge 279; Possony 285.

page 295   Footnote. Interview with Norman Armour; Horan unpublished manuscript.

page 296   Chicherin telegrams. FRUS I 637, 640.

page 297   Footnote. Interview with Armour.

page 298   "You see what happens . . ." Kennan 455-56.

page 299   Lloyd George cable. Balfour papers, July 18.

page 300   Hellferich report and Hintze's rebuttal. Ullman 286; Freund 25–27.

page 300   Panic in Moscow. Lockhart 306–8; Ullman 286.

page 301   "a ruthless mass terror . . ." Howe 647.

pages 301-2   Attempted assassination of Lenin. Possony 290–91.

pages 303-4   Lockhart story. Lockhart 313–18.

page 304   Cheka retaliation. Steinberg 150.

page 304   Poole report to Washington. FRUS I 682.

page 305   German Consul General's protest. FRUS I 676.

page 305   Cromie funeral. FRUS I 683.

page 305   "It is impossible for me to believe . . ." FRUS I 678.

pages 305-7   Lockhart story. Lockhart 322–26.

page 306   "because although the United States . . ." Carr 88.

page 306   Landing at Archangel. Ullman 243–44; Halliday 50–53.

page 308   "I could not give a Russian . . ." Fleming 93–94.

page 308   "I have often thought . . ." Faulstitch I 124.

page 308   "In default of instructions . . ." Halliday 68.

page 308   "Department approves your action . . ." FRUS II 536.

Chapter Thirteen "AND WE WON'T BE BACK TILL IT'S OVER OVER THERE"

pages 309-10   Haig-Foch meeting. HD, August 29.

page 310   "The object of this telegram . . ." HD, September 1.

pages 310-13	Cooper story. IWM-PA; interviews; correspondence.
page 313	"If this is true, then the end . . ." HD, September 2.
pages 313-14	Hindenburg manifesto. Lutz, *Fall of the German Empire* I 163–65.
page 314	"Now we have lost the war!" Nelson 426.
page 314	"The Seventeenth Army has suffered . . ." Müller 383; Nelson 426.
page 314	"I have had a slight nervous breakdown . . ." Müller 386.
page 315	Wilhelm speech. Nelson 426; Ludwig 479.
page 315	Haig letter to his wife. HC, September 5.
page 316	Haig-Milner meeting. HD, September 10.
pages 316-18	Pershing-Foch meeting. Pershing II 244–55.
page 319	Tomek story. Tomek 39–40.
page 319	"When the shelling first started . . ." Blumenson 584.
page 319	Langer story. Langer 31ff.
page 320	"The exultation in our minds . . ." Pershing II 267.
page 320	Patton-MacArthur meeting. Blumenson 584.
pages 320-21	Denig, Bellamy stories. USM-PA.
page 321	"No enemy aircraft were encountered . . ." Buckley 124.
page 321	"everything was going well . . ." Vandiver II 949.
pages 321-23	Patton story. Blumenson 585–99.
pages 323-24	"I have experienced a good many . . ." Horne 312.
page 324	"completely broken man." Müller 388.
page 325	"I haven't had a wink of sleep . . ." Müller 392.
pages 325-26	Hertling address. Hanssen 294–97.
page 326	"We know our goal . . . but not in the way we wanted it." Müller 394.
page 326	"Can Department advise me . . ." FRUS II 544.
pages 326-27	"except the guarding of the ports . . ." FRUS II 547.
page 328	Mott story. Stallings 228.
page 329	"Sir, I have no doubt that your men . . ." Alexander 175–76.
page 329	"Just a word to you before . . ." Blumenson 609.
page 329	Rickenbacker story. Rickenbacker 212–16.
pages 330-32	Patton story. Blumenson 613.
page 333	Rickenbacker story. Rickenbacker 217–18.
pages 333-34	Kochli story. *American Legion Weekly*, January 30, 1925.
page 334	"Those Americans will lose our chance . . ." Liddell Hart, *History of the First World War.* London: Book Club Associates, 1970, 582.

pages 335-36	Noakes story. Noakes 170ff.
pages 335-36	Reitz story. Reitz 193ff.
page 337	Hintze document. Ludendorff, *The General Staff and Its Problems* 611–13.
page 337	Ludendorff rage. Goodspeed 211.
pages 337-38	Ludendorff-Hindenburg meeting. Hindenburg 429; Ludendorff, *My War Memories* II 722; Lloyd George 1945.
page 338	Monash-Haig incident. Bean 956.
pages 338-40	Campbell story. IWM-PA; Campbell 73; correspondence.
page 340	Maze story. Maze 348–50.
page 342	Campbell story. IWM-PA; Campbell 116–17.
page 342	"with suppressed emotion, with kingly . . ." Nelson 428.
pages 342-43	Hertling-Hintze-Kaiser incidents. Lloyd George 1951.
page 343	Hanssen story. Hanssen 306.
page 344	Maze story. Maze 350–53; interview.
page 345	"to have completely lost their nerve here." Rudin 60.
pages 345-46	Max story. Max II 4–5.
page 346	"Shall we ever see it again?" Müller 400.
page 346	Hintze-Ludendorff incident. Rudin 66.
pages 346-48	Max on October 2–3. Max II 9–17.
page 348	"Tomorrow will be a great day . . ." Hanssen 309ff.
pages 348-49	Max on October 4. Max II 18–23.
pages 349-50	Hanssen story. Hanssen 216ff.
page 350	"Whether there will be a cessation . . ." Lutz, *Fall of the German Empire* 166–67.
page 350	Max speech. Max II 42–43; Rudin 83–85.
pages 350-51	"How strange it is that there is no . . ." Hanssen 328.
page 351	Princess Blücher story. Blücher 250–51.

Chapter Fourteen

"I AM DEALING IN HUMAN LIVES—NOT IN POLITICS."

page 352	"General Weygand, I believe, left . . ." Pershing diary, October 1.
pages 353-54	Whittlesey story. Joe McCarthy, *American Heritage*, October 1977; Johnson and Pratt 21–108; Monograph, Captain Nelson Holderman, "Operations of the Force Known as 'The Lost Battalion,'" Infantry School, Ft. Benning.
page 355	Rose story. Rose; correspondence.
pages 356-59	Whittlesey story. Joe McCarthy, *American Her-*

itage, October 1977; Johnson and Pratt 109–285; Holderman monograph.

page 358	Rickenbacker story. Rickenbacker 243–44.
page 360	Footnote. New York *Times*, November 30 and December 1, 1921.
page 360	"It is stirring news that comes to-day." CHD, October 6.
page 361	"mild in tone and did not . . ." CHD, October 7.
page 361	"Pretty piece of impertinence." WD, October 7.
page 361	"I agree with LG . . ." WD, October 6.
page 361	"The state of chaos the fool has got . . ." WD, October 7.
page 361	"At present, the absence of any authoritative . . ." DP, October 7.
page 362	Wilson on October 8. HD, October 8.
page 362	"I can hardly describe . . ." Max II 63.
page 362	"the note spoke in a different tone . . ." Max II 65.
pages 362-63	Ludendorff at meeting. Rudin 68–69.
page 363	Riddell story. Riddell 366–67.
page 364	"The time is approaching . . ." Serge 316.
page 365	London celebration. Playne 368.
page 365	Lloyd George on October 13. WD, October 13; Riddell 370–73.
pages 365-66	Wilson and House in New York City. Baker 473–74; CHD, October 13.
pages 365-66	"It seems to me that it is impossible . . ." George 187.
page 366	"If we agree to an armistice . . ." Baker 475.
page 366	"I don't believe that things can ever be kept secret . . ." Clemenceau 65–66.
pages 366-68	Pershing-Weygand and Pershing-Foch meetings. Stallings 324–28; Vandiver II 972–76.
page 368	"I never saw him more disturbed." CHD, October 14.
pages 368-69	"Neither did he desire to have the Allied armies . . ." CHD, October 14; Dos Passos 428.
page 369	"I hope the President . . ." Rudin 124.
page 369	Wilson gives House note. CHD, October 15.
page 370	"All were very sarcastic about the note . . ." Roskill 614.
page 370	"It really is a disgraceful usurpation . . ." WD, October 15.
page 370	Max account. Max II 85–89.
page 371	"A black day." Müller 408.
page 371	"for generations to come every German . . ." Rudin 135.
pages 371-72	Princess Blücher story. Blücher 252–53.
pages 372-74	German Cabinet meeting. Lutz, *Fall of the Ger-*

Chapter Sixteen THE END OF THE BEGINNING

pages 432-33	Ebert-Groener conversation. Wheeler-Bennett, *The Nemesis of Power* 21–22.
page 434	House cable. Trask 172.
page 434	Lloyd George story. Riddell 379.
pages 435-36	Final armistice session. Rudin 381.
page 436	House cable. Seymour IV 143.
page 436	Mordacq-House meeting. Bonsal 11.
page 436	Clemenceau note to House. Seymour IV 192.
page 437	"and taking my right hand in his left . . ." Rudin 384.
page 437	"What have you yielded to the Germans?" *The National Review* XCII 369.
page 437	"Foch very much moved . . ." DP, November 11.
page 437	"that the Germans accepted the conditions . . ." Rudin 384.
page 437	Bucher story. Bucher 315ff.
page 438	Speight story. IWM-PA.
page 438	Campbell story. IWM-PA; Campbell 161; correspondence.
page 438	Marshall story. Marshall 199.
page 438	Pershing-Griscom story. Griscom 446.
page 439	"The war's over!" Chapman, *Vain Glory* 705.
page 439	Gibbs dispatch. Gibbs, *The War Despatches* 407.
page 439	Bucher story. Bucher 317–18.
pages 439-40	Reitz story. Reitz 238.
page 440	Reed story. Reed 1–2.
page 440	"The roar of voices was like an outburst . . ." Crozier 269.
page 440	Bucher story. Bucher 318–19.
page 440	Gibbs dispatch. Gibbs, *The War Despatches* 408.
pages 440-41	French story. *The Torch*, November 1974 (international publication for World War I veterans); correspondence.
page 441	Denig story. USM-PA.
page 441	"one of the pleasantest emotions . . ." CHD, November 11.
page 441	Peixotto story. Peixotto 182.
page 441	MacDonagh story. MacDonagh 327–32.
pages 441-42	Churchill story. Churchill, *The World Crisis* II 541–43.
page 442	Mellersh story. IWM-PA.
page 442	Lloyd George speech. Lloyd George 1986.
pages 442-43	Celebration in New York City. Sullivan 517ff.
page 443	Wilson announcement. Baker 580.
page 443	Wilson speech. Baker 580–81; Rudin 387.
page 444	Clemenceau-Poincaré incident. Poincaré 413.
page 444	Celebration at British Embassy. D'Abernon 48; DP, November 11.
page 444	Clemenceau speech. Mordacq 89.

page 444	"looking less exuberantly cheerful . . ." D'Abernon 49.
page 444	"No mention of Britain's share in it . . ." DP, November 12.
page 444	"Come and feed the flames!" Joynt 214.
page 445	"Winston does not and my opinion is . . ." WD, November 11.
pages 445-46	Karl of Austria. Karl Werkmann; Brook-Shepherd 212–16.
page 446	Seldte story. Seldte 273ff.
pages 446-47	Binding story. Binding 244–45.
page 447	Campbell story. IWM-PA; Campbell 162–64; correspondence.
page 448	"Semyonov and Kalmykov soldiers . . ." Stewart 250.
pages 448-49	Celebration in Paris. *Stars and Stripes*, November 15.
page 449	Seldte story. Seldte 278.
page 449	Hitler story. Toland xix-xx.
page 449	Footnote. Spengler 71.
page 450	"I shall never forget how happy . . ." Baker 582.
page 450	Wilson incident. Callwell II 149.

Index

Chapel Hill, 29, 32, 37
Chaplin, Capt. Georgi Ermolae-
  vich, 298
Chardin, Pierre Teilhard de, 252-
  53
Charlevaux Valley, 353
Charleville, 200, 246
Charteris, Gen. John, 166
Château de la Fraineuse, 423
Château-Thierry, 205, 212, 214-15,
  223, 238, 244, 248, 255, 258;
  German drive on, 204-05; 3rd
  U.S. Division attacks toward,
  206-07; German capture, 240-
  42; loss of, 268
Chaumont, 368
Cheka (Russian secret police) (see
  also Peters, Jakob), 294, 300,
  303, 305; murders Capt.
  Cromie, 302-03
Chelyabinsk, 181, 228, 294
Chemin des Dames, 189, 190-91,
  199, 201, 208, 212, 214, 224,
  247, 267, 438; described, 184-
  85; Germans attack, 193;
  French retreat from, 195
Cher Ami (carrier pigeon), 356-
  57, 357n
Chicherin, Georgi, 172, 229, 295n,
  296-99, 303, 305, 307; con-
  demns Japanese threat to
  Vladivostok, 172; advises diplomats to leave Vologda, 296;
  on intervention, 300
Chinese Labour Corp, 71
Churchill, Winston, 1, 7, 96, 441,
  444-45, 450; on Paul Maze, 13;
  at opening of Ludendorff's
  first offensive, 17; supports
  Lloyd George, 58; returns from
  France, 78; visits Rawlinson,
  88-89; on Zeebrugge raid, 154;
  House speech on mounting
  crisis, 157; tours front, 286;
  releases munitions workers for
  military service, 315; on Lockhart memorandum, 447
Clark, Champ, 100, 443
Clemenceau, Georges, 39-40, 41,
  53-54, 54n, 58-59, 64, 73-74, 77,
  88-89, 119, 129-30, 159, 190,
  199, 203-04; 209-10, 211, 225,
  434, 436-37, 444; becomes
  Premier of France, 2; predicts
  German offensive, 9; reaction
  to German successes, 48; suggested as over-all commander,
  69; on unity of command, 72-
  74; questions Amiens future,
  74; on Foch, 74-76; personality
  of, 84-85; on peace with Germany, 120; calls for consulta-
  tions with Lloyd George, 125;
  relations with Lord Derby,

158-59; berates British, 161-
  62; on British manpower figures, 166; on soldiers and
  politicians, 169; visits Foch,
  255, 258; Germans predict
  downfall of, 197; at the front,
  202; on fall of Château-
  Thierry, 211; attacked in
  Chamber of Deputies, 212-13;
  supports Mangin, 226; on Allied unity, 241; on Lloyd
  George, 291; criticizes Pershing, 334; works on Armistice
  conditions, 351; on plan to
  break up U.S. forces, 352; on
  Wilson's note, 363; insists on
  Pershing's dismissal, 366; plots
  against Pershing, 367; demands Pershing's relief, 378;
  on Lloyd George and the
  English, 388; on Pershing, 389;
  objects to inviting Germans
  to an armistice, 394; on Wilson's Fourteen Points, 396-97;
  on German suit for armistice,
  398
Clermont-sur-Oise, 82-83
Cockburn, Capt. R. S., 38, 51-52,
  57, 63-64, 68-69
Cologne, 400, 420
Compiègne (Pétain's headquarters),
  60, 74, 77, 208, 450; Foch
  confers with Pétain at, 65;
  Pershing visits, 69; Germans
  threaten, 225; counterattack
  near, 226; offensive stalled, 227;
  Erzberger party arrives at, 418;
  Armistice conference at, 434
Congreve, Lt. Gen. Walter N., 18,
  23, 25, 30-31, 79; abandons
  Péronne, 45
Conner, Col. Fox, 202-03
Cook, Maj. C. Fred, 416
Cooke, Lt. E. D., 221
Cooper, Pvt. H. Howard, 134-41,
  185-88, 310-12
Courcelles, 227
Cowan, Rear Adm. Walter H., 154
Cromie, Capt. F. N. A., murdered
  by Cheka, 302; funeral of,
  305; British reaction to mur-
  der, 307
Crozat Canal, 25, 26-28, 29-30, 39
Currie, Gen. Sir Arthur, 273
Cuxhaven, riots in, 411
Czech Legion (and Czechs), 232,
  294, 295n, 300
Czernin, Count Ottokar, 129-31;
  and secret negotiations, 129;
  resignation of, 131

D'Abernon, Viscountess, 444
Daffodil (ferry), 146, 149, 152
Daly, Gunnery Sgt. Dan, 217

497

505

509

continued . . .

THE NINTH DAUGHTER

"An exciting new mystery series set in revolutionary Boston. Abigail Adams could become my favorite historical sleuth."

—Sharon Kay Penman, *New York Times* bestselling author of *Lionheart*

"Barbara Hamilton plunges us into colonial Boston, where we walk beside the legendary Abigail Adams as she tries to find justice for a murdered young woman while also helping with the birthing pangs of a new nation."

—Victoria Thompson, national bestselling author of *Murder in Chelsea*

"[An] exceptional debut . . . While bringing to life such historical figures as Sam Adams and Paul Revere, Hamilton transports the reader to another time and place with close attention to matters like dress, menus, and the monumental task of doing laundry. Historical fans will eagerly look forward to the next in this promising series."

—*Publishers Weekly*

"Hamilton . . . has just the right touch to guide the intelligent Abigail through the dangerous shoals of being a patriot while seeing the good side of the colonies' English rulers. There are no missteps here in what should prove to be a captivating series for all historical fans."

—*Library Journal*

"The wry repartee between Abigail and John, together with the fact that this clandestine investigation of the murder of loose women would never have made the official record, make Hamilton's debut believable and gripping."

—*Kirkus Reviews*

"The story line provides a deep look at Boston as rebellion is in the air. Fans will want to join the tea party hosted by Ms. Hamilton with guests being a who's who of colonial Massachusetts."

—*The Mystery Gazette*

SUP WITH THE DEVIL

Barbara Hamilton

BERKLEY PRIME CRIME, NEW YORK

THE BERKLEY PUBLISHING GROUP
Published by the Penguin Group
Penguin Group (USA)
375 Hudson Street, New York, New York 10014, USA

USA I Canada I UK I Ireland I Australia I New Zealand I India I South Africa I China

Penguin Books Ltd., Registered Offices: 80 Strand, London WC2R 0RL, England
For more information about the Penguin Group, visit penguin.com.

SUP WITH THE DEVIL

A Berkley Prime Crime Book / published by arrangement with the author

Berkley Prime Crime Books are published by The Berkley Publishing Group.
BERKLEY® PRIME CRIME and the PRIME CRIME logo are trademarks
of Penguin Group (USA).

For information, address: The Berkley Publishing Group,
a division of Penguin Group (USA),
375 Hudson Street, New York, New York 10014.

ISBN: 978-0-425-25726-5

PUBLISHING HISTORY
Berkley Prime Crime trade paperback edition / October 2011
Berkley Prime Crime mass-market edition / September 2013

PRINTED IN THE UNITED STATES OF AMERICA

10 9 8 7 6 5 4 3 2 1

Cover art by Griesbach & Martucci / Bernstein & Andriulli.
Cover design by Judith Lagerman.
Interior text design by Laura K. Corless.

ALWAYS LEARNING   **PEARSON**

For Brandy & Joey

One

Horace Thaxter
Cambridge, Massachusetts

23 April 1774

Abigail Adams
Queen Street, Boston

Dear Aunt Abigail,

John (my cousin, not your esteemed husband) has told me upon many occasions of your extraordinary acuity in seeing through the riddles of criminal conduct, a veritable Alexander (if one may so term a member of your sex) cutting the nodum Gordium *of both puzzling circumstance and the* obstructio deliberi *of evildoers.*

Therefore, I write to you in a state of mental perturbation regarding events that befell me this week, which I am at a loss to interpret.

The events were made the more troubling because I was introduced to them by a letter from Mr. Adams (your esteemed husband, not his notorious cousin), which induced me to believe myself safe in entering a situation at best equivocal, and at worst giving rise to fears that I might have been—and may still be—in danger of my life.

Might I beg the pleasure of calling upon you on the 30th, when Mr. Adams will be returned from the circuit courts and propriety will permit you to receive a male caller? This is a matter that troubles and—though others have said it is the merest exiguum—*frightens me. I look forward to the favor of your reply.*

Your ob't h'bl svt,
Horace Thaxter

Propriety indeed. Abigail Adams, perched on the back of Uzziah Begbie's delivery wagon as it jolted its way along the extremely narrow streets of Boston's North End, reread her nephew's letter with mixed amusement and exasperation. *You'd think the boy was forty instead of barely seventeen.*

You'd think I was a sixteen-year-old village maid instead of a woman of twenty-nine with a husband—off at the Maine Assizes or not—and four children.

And you'd think we were in London instead of Massachusetts, where women have been going about their business in perfect freedom and safety since the Indians left. Does he think the neighbors are going to suspect him of an assault on my virtue?

Or suspect me of an assault on his?

On second thought, reflected Abigail, tucking the letter back into her smallest marketing basket, *considering some of my neighbors . . .*

In addition to Horace's letter, which had arrived late yesterday afternoon, the basket was stocked with apples, carrots, corn-bread (wheaten flour of any kind gave Horace migraines), a small crock of honey, and ten hard-boiled eggs, and rested beside her on the narrow bench that served as a wagon-seat. On her other side, the carter Uzziah Begbie clucked to his horse as the wagon made its careful way among the carts and barrows that cluttered the cobblestones of Prince's Street. To their right loomed the piled-up rooflines of Copp's Hill, a maze of steep alleyways and small yards; to their left, through a break in the roof-lines, Abigail could glimpse the placid green water of the Mill Pond. Wind from the river flicked her face, caught a strand of her black hair that had escaped her neat white cap. She smoothed it primly into its place again. Were she on the farm in Braintree, she reflected—the land that her "esteemed husband" (as Horace Thaxter described him) and his family had farmed for three generations—she would have pulled her cap off altogether, run to the top of Prospect Hill to let the wind of the bay have its way with her hair . . . would have revelled in the sweetness of May after so harsh and unsettling a winter.

But this was Boston, and people did talk.

Indeed, as they rounded the last of the brick and timber houses and came to Gee's Shipyard on the rocky nose of North Boston, people were doing nothing but talking. The boundaries of the street itself dissolved into a roughly defined apron of gravel and mud around the end of the hill, beyond which lay the hard blackish sapphire waters of the bay. Sailors, roustabouts, stevedores, and the lady who sold hot pies stood in knots among the piled timber and coiled cables, gesturing out toward the British warship that patrolled the bay and half shouting over the clattering symphony of shipyard hammers.

I hear the King's going to close the port . . .

He can't do that, can he?

They say in Salem there's a royal commission on its way to inquire . . .

Royal commission my backside, my cousin says they'll send troops from Halifax and hang the rebels that did it . . .

Sam Adams'll never let that happen.

Don't be a fool, Adams is the first man they'll hang. The King won't put up with rebellion . . .

No, agreed Abigail silently. *The King won't put up with rebellion.*

And she wondered for the dozenth time since leaving the house if she had any business going out of Boston even for an afternoon.

Her common sense told her that even if the King sent a Royal Commissioner to investigate the circumstances of last December that had resulted in over three hundred crates of East India Company tea being dumped into Boston Harbor, trouble wasn't going to erupt on the first day. For one thing, the Sons of Liberty—the semi-secret organization devoted to defiance of the King's arbitrary commands—would have to take the measure of the commission's mandate and decide what to do. And these days, Sam Adams—her husband's wily cousin—kept a tight rein on the Sons, cooling violence in one place, puffing it up in another, simplifying the issues at stake, and playing upon the angers and fears of men like a virtuoso playing upon a pianoforte.

A journey out to Cambridge for the afternoon would likely do no harm.

She hoped.

Begbie drew rein to let a half-dozen men pass, bearing on their shoulders the massive beam of what would be a ship's keel. Some of them called out greetings to him, asked after wife, children, that keg of nails they were waiting for . . .

Abigail returned her thoughts to the note she had received.

To what "troubling" events did John introduce Horace by letter? As far as Abigail knew, her esteemed husband—stout, peppery, brilliant, and maddening—hadn't had anything to do with any of the Thaxters other than John Thaxter, his young law clerk and Horace's cousin (*second cousin? Uncle? That was the trouble with being related to half the colony . . .*) for over a year, one whole branch of that well-off merchant clan having decided that she—Abigail—had stepped down in the world by marrying a farmer's son even if he *was* related to the extremely respectable (*back then, anyway*) Deacon Adams of Old South Church . . .

And into what earthly situation could John have pitchforked the boy that would have put him—so he believed—in danger of his life?

A man in the leather apron of a ship's carpenter emerged from a chandler's shop, crossed the gravel, and spoke to the deliveryman, quiet beneath the din of hammering. Abigail didn't hear his exact words, but she knew what they were.

Any news . . . ?

Begbie shook his head.

Only a few clouds spotted the bright April sky, but Abigail felt a chill and pulled her shawl close about her.

No news yet.

Six weeks for the news of the so-called Tea Party to reach England. Then whatever Parliament was going to decide to do about the rebellion growing in the colony. Then six weeks back.

Which meant that whatever was going to happen, was going to happen soon.

"Half a mo', Mrs. Adams." Begbie sprang down from his seat, darted down the split-log steps to the shipyard. From where she sat Abigail could see the broad, flat shape of the ferry scow and no sign of its captain or crew. A carter, a country minister in a black coat, and two stout farm-women in wide-brimmed straw hats clustered by the ferry landing, talking eagerly with a couple of men in sailors' slops.

Even the gulls that wheeled above the dumped remains of some fisherman's unsold catch seemed to be yammering rumors to one another.

Men came and unloaded an immense coil of ship's cable from the goods-wagon; Begbie took the horse's bridle, led the animal down to the ferry just as Obed Pusey and his crew reappeared and began collecting sixpences for the voyage. Abigail climbed down before they crossed the wet black wood of the wharf, and sought out the bench farthest aft and as close to the mast as she could get without interfering with the crew's work. Crossing through the confluence of the Charles River and the bay itself, the ferry would roll like a home-going drunkard and—a disgrace to her merchant heritage—Abigail knew she invariably became seasick in even the half-mile voyage from Boston to Charles Town across the harbor.

The sharp spring wind filled the sails as the men poled the scow off the wharf: Abigail resolutely fixed her eyes on the tidy cluster of brown houses, of orchards and farmlands, on the feet of the mainland hills. Like Boston, Charles Town stood on a peninsula, connected to the mainland by a neck of land, but from Charles Town you didn't have to wind around rivers and over bridges to get to the town of Cambridge, where young Horace Thaxter was presently in college.

A letter from Mr. Adams . . . which induced me to believe myself safe in entering a situation at best equivocal . . .

Of course, Horace always believed himself in danger of his life. Abigail recalled more than one conversation with the weedy boy devoted entirely to his recital of his latest symptoms, which ranged from *tremor cordis* to sanguineous congestion of the lungs. At the time of their last meeting he had been, she estimated, fifteen and "grinding" with a tutor to prepare himself for Harvard College. Horace was tall, thin, and filled to the hairline with Aristotle and medical quackery. That had been on a visit to Salem where his parents (as well as Abigail's sister) lived, shortly after Abigail's son Charley's first birthday.

Now Charley was three.

This is a matter which frightens me.

After long and complex circumlocutions in Latin, it came down to that. *This is a matter which frightens me . . .* Simple words in English.

And it was true—Abigail admitted it to herself—that she took a deal of pleasure in chopping through the Gordian knot of puzzling circumstance and the deliberate obstructions of evildoers.

It was also true that it was May, after a winter remarkable for the bitterness of its cold, and that once Mr. Begbie's goods-wagon was off the rocking waters of the bay and onto the road that ran along the feet of Breeds and Bunker Hills, the sweet-smelling quiet of the countryside made a blessed change from Boston's fishy reek and the stinks of sewage and backyard cows, the twitter of birds a delight after the rattle of carts and the shouting of boys playing in Queen Street and the clatter of hammers in Mr. Butler's cooperage next door . . .

The peaceful air a relief from that dread that seemed to have settled over the town like a pillow pressed to an uneasy sleeper's face.

What will we do if . . . ?

It should be any day we'll hear . . .

Massachusetts in the spring.

The countryside that lay between Charles Town and Cambridge was prosperously settled, orchard trees parting now and then to show Abigail tidy farmhouses, and fields of corn already shoulder-high. Cows chewed mildly in their pastures;

gray stone walls lined the road. In patches of woodland, finches and robins sang. Abigail dearly enjoyed the noise and excitement and conveniences of Boston—the ability to simply go down to the wharves for Spanish lemons or to a mercer's on the next street if she happened to decide her daughter Nabby needed a new dress. The ability to go to a bookstore and purchase the newest works of Goldsmith or Smollett, or the fact that John could bring in newspapers printed that day. The fact that in winter, snow did not mean utter isolation. Yet she had been raised in the parsonage of a very small village, and in her heart, she sorely missed the scents of deep grass and woodland in May.

As Mr. Begbie had a number of deliveries in Cambridge and was likely to pursue his second vocation—that of collecting and disseminating news and rumor—when they reached the outskirts of the village, Abigail bid him good-by with thanks. "I shall finish up at the Golden Stair, on the Common," said the carter—a neighbor of hers on Queen Street—shaking her hand in farewell. "You'll find me there in three or four hours—time enough to locate your nephew—and we'll still be back at the ferry long before the sun's down. Good luck, m'am!"

Good luck indeed, reflected Abigail good-humoredly, as she set off with her marketing basket in the direction of the College, whose cluster of brick halls she glimpsed through orchard trees, for she hadn't the faintest idea in which of its several buildings Horace was lodged. The open-sided quadrangle of Harvard College faced the town common, across a lane and a four-foot wall. A young man in a freshman's short gown emerged from the gate as Abigail drew near. He bore a wig box and walked swiftly, as if pursued or in fear of pursuit, and hesitated for an instant when she waved him over. "Are you acquainted with Mr. Horace Thaxter? Would you know—?"

"I say, I say—!" Another scholar in the longer gown of a more senior student strolled over from a group of his friends. "You there, Yeovil—"

The freshman gave Abigail a harassed look and turned.

"What are you up to, Yeovil?"

"I was speaking with this lady, sir," said the boy. He looked about fifteen—Horace had been sixteen and a half when he'd entered the college the previous September, but they took boys younger even than this one—with linen spotlessly white against the blue of his academic gown and a beautifully curled pigeon-wing wig, powdered like marble.

"Now, Yeovil," chided the newcomer, who looked rather like a ferret in a scarlet gown, "a *freshman*? Address a *lady*?"

"And so beautiful a lady," added another of the group, coming over and making Abigail a handsome leg as he bowed. *"Che il crin s'è un Tago e son due Soli i lume/Prodigio tal non rimirò Natura . . ."* Between a crumpled neckcloth and an elaborately curled wig, his face was plump and unshaven, and his eyes, set in little cushions of fat discolored by sleeplessness, had the twinkling and rather dangerous intelligence of a pig. The effect was of a dissipated baby who had been spending far too many nights in a tavern. "How may your humble servant be of use to you, fair stranger? You, Yeovil, run along . . . Where *were* you off to?"

In a taut voice that showed an unfortunate tendency to crack, the boy said, "I was taking this wig to be curled, sir." He held up the box.

The fat student viewed it through a quizzing-glass; his companion in the red gown, suppressing a grin, exclaimed, "Why, so you were! And whose wig is that, Yeovil?"

"Mr. Lechmere's, sir."

"Lechmere, Lechmere . . ." The older men—and the other

two of their group who had joined them—all made a great
show of trying to remember who Lechmere was.

"Egad, isn't he a sophomore?"

"Disgraceful . . . !"

"For shame!"

"Tell you what," said Red Gown, and produced from his
voluminous sleeve two pewter pitchers, "why don't you be a
good chap and, while you're in town, just hop on over to the
Crowned Pig and fill these up with our good host's best?"

John had told Abigail about the customs of the college:
Yeovil, a lowly fresher, was obliged to do the bidding of his
seniors. She also guessed that Red Gown was probably a
junior and thus able to preempt the boy's services (*How was
he going to carry both pitchers full of ale and also Mr. Lechmere
the Sophomore's wig box . . . ? Which of course was the point, the
wretched boys . . .*).

Thus she wasn't at all surprised when Yeovil had been
dispatched on his errand and the fat student—whose lush
yellow gown gave him the general appearance of a gargantuan squash—made another bow, to find her request for Horace's direction interrupted yet again . . .

"Excuse me, my very dear madame, I beg of you—Yeovil!"
the fat man yelled. "Yo, Yeovil, come back here, blister it!"

He was the senior, then, reflected Abigail with a sigh. Or
a bachelor-fellow, by the look of him. And privileged to preempt the junior's request for ale, which had preempted the
sophomore's demand for his wig to be taken to be curled . . .

The fat student's companions were stamping and slapping
each other and smothering with laughter to such an extent
that none of them saw another man—crimson-gowned and a
few years older than they—until he had crossed the yard
from the gate and reached Abigail's side. "Pugh, aren't you

getting a little old for this kind of trick?" he asked in a quiet voice.

Pugh turned, piggy eyes sparkling in their pouches of fat. "*Dulce est disipere in loco*, my dear Ryland . . . Have you a quarrel with educating the wealthy in the arts of humility?"

"When it involves rudeness to a stranger," replied his dear Ryland, "yes, I have. How may I serve you, m'am? My name is Joseph Ryland— Are you here in search of someone?" With a gesture he led her away from the group and farther into the quadrangle.

"I'm looking for Mr. Horace Thaxter, yes, thank you. I am Mrs. Adams, his aunt."

"I've heard him speak of you, m'am. Did Mr. Fairfield write to you, then, about Thaxter's illness?" Mended red gown billowing, Mr. Ryland led Abigail cattycorner across the yard to the old brick building that enclosed its southern end. "I'm sure it isn't as serious as Fairfield thinks it—"

"What happened?" asked Abigail, startled.

Ryland made a gesture of frustration. Unlike the refulgent Mr. Pugh and his friends, the young man—she guessed his age at nearly thirty, her own age . . . *A tutor, then, or a bachelorfellow waiting for an appointment somewhere*—wore his own hair, long and only lightly powdered; he spoke with the accents of Pennsylvania. "To be honest, Mrs. Adams, I think it was the food in the Hall. Do what they will, the Governors cannot keep the kitchen staff from buying the cheapest slops they can come by and pocketing the difference, and I know Horace's constitution is a delicate one. I was going to let the matter go another day—I am the Fellow in charge of Massachusetts Hall—and then write his parents . . ."

They entered the building by the most westerly of its several doors, and Mr. Ryland led her down a wide hall and then up one of the residential staircases. "He'll be in Captain Fairfield's room—he fags for Fairfield, a noxious custom . . ."

As they reached the first landing, a young man stepped from the room on the right, his dusky face and black Indian braids startling against the white of his neckcloth and shirt, and the sober darkness of waistcoat, breeches, and stockings. Ryland said, "Weyountah, how is Thaxter? Mrs. Adams, this is Weyountah—Mr. Enoch Wylie—one of our best men in the sciences. Weyountah, Mrs. Adams of Boston, Thaxter's aunt."

"Good Lord, get that woman out of here!" called a voice from the left-hand room, and the door opened to reveal a fair-haired, cheerful young man with a weather-burned complexion and a gray coat rather heavily laced with gold on the sleeves. "I knew it—Ryland's trying to get the lot of us sent down for bringing a female in here . . . Diomede!" he called back into the room behind him. "Get on out here and bring a rope—tie up Mr. Ryland and throw him into the river—"

"Don't be a fool, Fairfield, this is Thaxter's aunt come to see him."

"Doesn't matter," said Mr. Fairfield, in the slurry drawl of a Virginian. "The Governors will never believe a gang of towsers and tosspots like us . . ."

Spots of color appeared on Mr. Ryland's cheekbones, and he stepped back—with rigid reserve—as Fairfield led the way briskly into the left-hand chamber. The Indian Weyountah bowed to Abigail and gestured her to precede him, then followed her in, leaving Mr. Ryland upon the landing and the door open behind them.

Horace got quickly to his feet from the desk where he sat by the window. The chamber was the usual one for the College: small, very tidy, furnished with a desk by the window, a couple of chairs that young Mr. Fairfield had obviously brought with him from Virginia, a small fireplace, and a little table. On a neat sideboard were ranged a coffee-roaster, pot, and a lacquered Chinese canister, presumably for coffee beans; there was a smaller caddy for tea, spouted blue-and-white pots for tea and water, and tidily arranged cups and saucers, not all of them matching.

Horace Thaxter hadn't changed much in two years, Abigail reflected; she didn't think his weight had increased by so much as an ounce, though he'd grown a good five inches, and he had not been short when last she'd seen him at fifteen. All elbows, knees, and spectacles, he wore an extremely shabby suit of faded black coat and breeches, clearly handed down from someone both shorter and more robust. He said, "Aunt Abigail—!" and held out a bony, ink-stained hand.

From the doorway, Ryland said, "I'm glad to see you on your feet, Thaxter," a small crease of worry between his brows. "Captain Fairfield, if I may remind you—"

"I know, I know, dash it! That hell-begotten Greek class, may they all descend unto Avernus together—"

"Hades, actually," put in Horace, stepping aside as an elderly black man—who'd been arranging wood and kindling in the hearth—gathered his hearth-brush and ashes and slipped from the rather overcrowded room . . . Presumably Diomede, Abigail guessed. And presumably the one responsible for the room's spotless order. There was a chest in the corner that, by what John had told her of the Virginia and Carolina men when he had studied here, would contain the slave's blanket, upon which he would sleep on the floor . . .

"Avernus being the Latin . . . Aunt Abigail, you truly shouldn't have—"

"Horry, I shall smite you with the poker if you tell me

once more the difference between Latin and Greek . . . Yes, yes, Ryland, take your duty to the Muses as given, and I'll be along as soon as I've done my duty to decent manners."

"I shouldn't want you to be—"

"It's my business if I'm sent down or not," Fairfield snapped. "You're not my dry nurse. Dash it," he added, as Ryland disappeared into the shadows of the rather gloomy staircase, "now I've offended him again. If it's not one thing, it's another. Diomede"—he thrust open the door to the inner chamber— "go fetch some water for Mrs. Adams for tea—or would you be of the Rebel persuasion, m'am, like all the rest of the Adamses I've heard of, not to speak of every other scholar in this curst school? Or is the issue of *tea* now considered settled once and for all?" And he raised his brows in a quirky jest.

"Coffee," said Weyountah, "is I believe the proper alternative. Or cocoa." And he guided Abigail to one of the chairs beside the cold hearth.

"You sounded as if a visit would do you good." Abigail took Horace's hand with a smile and set her basket on the corner of the table. "You know your mother would never forgive me, were you left to languish without someone at least making sure you were still alive."

"Cocoa, then," said Fairfield, snapping his fingers as Diomede appeared in the doorway. "And sink me if that dashed Beaverbrook hasn't stolen my cocoa . . . Go upstairs and get it, would you? And thrash the little maggot if he's there. Shall we take ourselves off, Horace, while you visit with your aunt? I daresay Ryland only showed her up to make sure I came along to his Greek class and didn't get sent down, which old Hogden promised he would, if I'm late again. When class is done, m'am," he added with a bow, "I trust you'll join us for dinner at the Golden Stair? Diomede"—he leaned through the staircase door to call after the ascending slave—"after you've provided cocoa for Mrs. Adams, run along to the Golden Stair and bespeak a dinner for five. Oh, and fetch me my—"

Patiently, the servant reappeared, took from the seat of the other chair the red gown and four-square cap of scholarship—Abigail could see Horace's hanging on a peg on the wall—and held them out to his master.

"You're a wonder, Diomede . . ." Fairfield called back over his shoulder as he dove through the door. "And if you don't save me some of whatever's in that basket, Thaxter"—his voice trailed back up the stairs—"I shall tell Mr. Pugh you've been tupping his mistress—"

Weyountah said, "I'll be in the laboratory should you need me, Thaxter," and with a bow to Abigail, departed.

The room seemed suddenly, echoingly quiet.

Horace's breath blew out in a sigh. "Aunt Abigail, I beg a thousand pardons for having written. No consideration in the world would have induced me to do so, had I thought you would put yourself to the inconvenience—"

"Don't be silly." Abigail fetched her basket from the table and held it out to him; his pale face flushed slightly with pleasure when he saw what it contained. He moved the table closer to the hearth, which was cold, the afternoon being far too fine to need a fire. "And tell me, please," she went on, "what troubling events befell you and why you think John had anything to do with them?"

"That's just it, Aunt Abigail." Horace made a move toward the door as if he would have closed it, then hesitated—no doubt recalling the extreme strictures the College set upon its students having women in their rooms—and settled himself awkwardly in the chair opposite her. "I think Uncle John had something to do with it because Mrs. Lake had a letter of introduction from him—and from Uncle Mercer in

Connecticut—recommending her in the highest terms. But I suspect that she poisoned me—and I very much fear that she will try to do so again."

"Good Heavens, why?"

The boy shook his head helplessly. "I haven't the slightest idea."

Two

John Adams
Boston

16 April 1774

My dear Horace,

Let this serve as an introduction to Mrs. Lake, a woman of the highest probity, and as urging that you oblige her in her researches. She is a member in good standing in the Brattle Street Congregation, and in that capacity, I have known her for many years, and can vouch for both her character and her intentions.

Yrs obt'ly,
John Adams

"This is nothing like Mr. Adams's hand." Abigail set the letter down among the cocoa cups. "And I can assure you at once that there is no Mrs. Lake in the Brattle Street Congregation."

Silently, Horace held out the other letter.

It purported to be from Justice Mercer Euston—Abigail identified him as a connection on the other side of the Thaxter family and well-known across the border in Connecticut—but even to her inexperienced eye, the smudgy, spidery handwriting looked suspiciously similar. The paper, so far as she could tell, was identical.

"And who," asked Abigail, "is Mrs. Lake?"

"That's just it." Horace propped his thick-lensed spectacles more firmly onto the bridge of his nose. "I have no idea. We seem to be moving *per nocte ad tenebris*, unless she is some relation to Henry Morgan . . ."

"Henry Morgan the pirate?" Abigail experienced the momentary sensation that she and her nephew were not engaged in the same conversation.

An inexplicable pink flush crept up Horace's cheekbones. "He was Governor—and later Lieutenant Governor—of Jamaica . . ."

"Yes," said Abigail, "I know. Why would this Mrs. Lake's relationship to him cause her to poison you—if poison you she did . . . ?"

"I think she did," said Horace earnestly. "Though my symptoms bore a certain resemblance to my previous attacks of gastritis and the symptoms that sometimes accompany my headaches, in other respects they were such as to frighten me. Please believe me, Aunt Abigail. I have spoken of this to no one—not to Weyountah, who has been a brother to me here; not to George Fairfield, who has been so good as to take me under his wing . . . No one." He pressed his hands together, palm to palm as if praying, and rested his lips against them, an attitude Abigail remembered from his boyhood. For a moment she was prey to the curious sensation of seeing in the young man the reflection of an infant she had held—herself a fragile and studious girl of eleven—in her arms.

"I will believe you," she assured him. "But tell me everything, from the beginning, and leave no detail out. One cannot reconstruct the sense of a disputed text," she added, with a glance at the contents of the desk beside the window—a mountain of books in Greek, in Hebrew, and in tongues stranger still whose very writing was alien to her—"if one is given only fragments to work with."

"That's true," agreed Horace. "And it started with those texts."

Horace Thaxter—for all his youth—was virtually the only scholar at Harvard who made a study of Oriental Languages, by which was meant (Abigail gathered) Arabic, Persian, Russian, and Biblical Aramaic, there being no one in the colony (and probably not in Britain, either) who could understand Chinese. Horace had begun his fascination with these tongues as a child, getting his merchant father (baffled but indulgent and impressed in spite of himself) to arrange for him to be tutored in the first three by sailors who had come through the port of Boston at various times, and had continued a stubborn quest for further knowledge ever since. By the age of twelve he had begun correspondence with members of the Royal Societies in both London and Paris, and had amassed a small quantity of books in each of those languages, as well as lexicons treasured as if they were chests of gold. Abigail well remembered Horace's childhood reputation in the family: the boy had always been regarded as strange, but she now saw him, in his own element, as the man he would be, a pathfinding scholar on a road that no one she knew or knew of had traveled before.

He must somehow get to Oxford, she thought, listening to his brief preamble. *Here, we can do nothing for him, and 'twere shame to waste so mighty—if odd—a gift.*

"I have something of a reputation here in Cambridge," he continued shyly. "I can only attribute it to that, that Mrs. Lake sent me up a message last Tuesday—the nineteenth— asking me to meet her at the Crowned Pig on the Waterford Road and enclosing these letters from Mr. Adams and Uncle Mercer."

"Why the clandestine meeting?" asked Abigail. "Didn't that seem amiss to you?"

"Not really." The boy blushed redder. "Perhaps it should have, but one can be fined, you know, quite severely, for having anything to do with a woman—not yourself, of course, m'am, being family . . . But it's not unusual for care to be taken even in quite innocent meetings. I didn't think anything of it."

Remind me to keep you locked in your room if ever the Navy press gang comes to town.

The Crowned Pig was a tavern about a half mile beyond the last of the handsome mansions of the town, mansions built by the wealthy merchant families who—by staying in the good graces of the Governors and obtaining the best political appointments—ruled Massachusetts. Mrs. Lake proved to be a beautiful woman a few years older than Abigail herself—Horace estimated—who asked him, was it true he could read Arabic? Horace said that he could, whereupon the lady offered him twenty pounds to come with her in her carriage and do a job of translation from that language.

"What did she look like?" asked Abigail, adding—when her nephew merely looked confused by the question—"Other than *beautiful*. What color was her hair?"

"Dark. Brown, I think, not black like a Spaniard's."

"Eyes?" *Of course he didn't look her in the eyes* . . . "Nose large or small? How was she dressed?"

"Like a lady," said the boy promptly, but that was the best he could do—not unusual, reflected Abigail. Most men she knew—with the exception of John and her friend the silver-smith Paul Revere—could attest to whether a woman was naked or clothed, but were left blank by distinctions between a round gown or a jacket and skirt. Much less could they say whether the said garments were blue or green, wool or calico, English-cut or sacque like the French. At least "like a lady" could be interpreted to mean not, for instance, in the bodice-and-skirt of a tavern-wench or a farm-girl's faded linsey-woolsey hand-me-downs.

Something a woman couldn't get into without the assis-tance of her maid.

And Mrs. Lake had a carriage, a closed post chaise driven by a groom, in which she and Horace rode for some two hours before descending to what—by Horace's rather sketchy description—sounded like a well-to-do farmstead, a brown wooden house of two storeys set some half mile back from the road.

"The groom took the team around to the stable in the rear of the house when we descended," said Horace. "I noticed him particularly, because his face was scarred—" With two fingers he touched his hairline and drew them down across his left eyelid, until they converged at a point an inch or so above the right-hand corner of his mouth. "And his eyes were so light, a very pale blue under extremely dark brows. He looked like a rough man—a veritable beast—and I found myself hoping Mrs. Lake would accompany me back as far as Cambridge. Perhaps I should have been more cautious," he added unhap-pily, "but twenty pounds is a great deal of money—enough to pay for my board and room here for next year."

"*Clausum possidet arca Iovem*," sympathized Abigail. "And did she indeed have a document in Arabic, of all things, which needed translation?"

For some reason Horace's blush flared again, and he answered—his voice a little stifled—"Yes. And it was curious," he added, puzzlement returning him to some of his composure, "because it had clearly been copied by someone who didn't know Arabic—by someone who didn't even know that Arabic is written right-to-left, not left-to-right. I could tell by the way the letters were drawn. Even at first glance I asked where she had copied this from—because I'm always looking out for Arabic texts, you understand, and she said, 'Never you mind.' She sat me down with the text—it was about two pages long—and pen and ink, at the table in the study of this house, where the light was good, and the whole time I worked, she sat in a corner, watching me and playing patience—"

"Playing *patience*?" The solitary card game was an interesting choice, Abigail thought, for a lady—though of course there were plenty of ladies of the highest degree who hadn't the wits to read nor the domestic virtue to sew . . . a task that Abigail herself hated.

"Yes, m'am."

"And you translated this document?"

"Yes, m'am." His cheekbones had now gone a fiery pink. "Her message asked me to bring my Arabic lexicon, which I had."

"And what on earth was it, to put you so to the blush?"

Horace avoided meeting her eyes. "It was an account—quite—er—Petronian—of an . . . an encounter between Governor Morgan and a female pirate named Jezebel Pitts, which was supposed to have taken place in May of 1688 in Port Royal. It was written not in Arabic, but in English using

Arabic characters, as a sort of code-writing, and contained passages that would have been better suited to have been translated into Latin . . ."

"Good grief!"

"The tenor of the account would lead one to believe that the writer had been present, for it included a mix of veritable pornography and quite treasonous and conspiratorial assertions on the part of Governor Morgan—a plot to raid the colony's treasury with the assistance of—er—Mistress Pitts and her men, though there was no mention of where the bullion so acquired was to have been bestowed, nor of course any indication of whether the plan proceeded to—er—consummation."

"Consummation indeed," murmured Abigail, her eyebrows raised nearly to her hairline. "When was Port Royal destroyed?"

"Sixteen ninety-two, m'am."

"And lies full-fathom five, with nobody to miss the pilfered gold. How long did it take you to translate this remarkable document?"

"About three hours, Aunt Abigail. Mrs. Lake read it through without so much as a blush, and by her expression seemed most vexed that it had nothing to say about the whereabouts of the treasure . . . She asked me, two or three times, if I had translated it all, and I swore to her that I had. In the end she brought me a cup of coffee and some bread and meat, and went to summon her coachman, it being quite dark by then. I will say I was extremely hungry and rather vexed that all I might eat was a little bit of the meat, which is poisonous to my digestion but which would not bring on a migraine like the bread would. And coffee, I believe, is a pernicious drink, not suited to human consumption, so I poured it out after a few sips. To this abstention—for being of dyspeptic habit I depend upon regular meals—and to the exhaustion of concentration, I attributed the sleepiness that overwhelmed me.

Mrs. Lake and her coachman had to assist me into the chaise, and I so misliked the man's appearance that I struggled to remain awake and to observe if I could the countryside we traversed."

Abigail did a moment's mental calculation. "With no moon that night you're fortunate he didn't have you in the ditch."

"Yes, m'am. Yet I found the countryside wholly unfamiliar, as one does by starlight, and despite the fact that I was shivering violently, I kept nodding off. At last I woke to find the chaise standing still in what appeared to be a stand of woods. I called out to the coachman and had no reply. I tried to open the door of the chaise and for some reason could not—it was very dark within, since we were in the woods, and in my befuddled state I couldn't find the door handle. At last, convinced that something terrible was about to happen, I used my Arabic lexicon to break the window-glass and put my hand through to open the door from the outside—"

"Reasoning that Mrs. Lake could scarcely have you up for vandalism if her coachman had abandoned you in the wilderness?"

The young man's black eyebrows pulled together behind those thick lenses. "Aunt Abigail, at that point I know not what I was thinking. I staggered when I came down from the chaise, and it seemed to me that I could hear someone or something approaching me through the woods. It came to me, I know not why, that the whole of the events of the evening might have been orchestrated by one of the senior classmen—'tis precisely the sort of thing Black Dog Pugh likes to do—for my discomfiture . . . An' 'twere not that, I had not liked the coachman's face nor his mien. It may seem cowardly of me," he added in a stifled voice, "and foolish, too, but I fled into the woods."

His long, slender fingers toyed with the corn-bread on the

plate; he was caught between the shame of being teased the whole of his short life and the memory of very genuine terror.

"Have you any idea where you were?"

Horace shook his head. "Weyountah says that a farmer from Concord brought me here in his wagon, having deduced—in quite your style, m'am," he added with a faint grin, "that I was from the College by the circumstance of me clutching my Arabic lexicon to my breast when I was found in a ditch at the side of the Concord Road, raving of pirates and gold. I did not come to my right senses 'til nearly evening and then was vilely sick all the next day. I begged Weyountah and George not to breathe a word of my absence—George is the dearest of good fellows but a complete, er, rattlepate—for fear that I might be sent down for having to do with a woman and for getting drunk, though George has told me that had I been drunk my symptoms would have been quite different."

"Do Weyountah and Mr. Fairfield know—" She paused as a discreet tap sounded at the door, and Diomede put his head in to ask after the state of the cocoa pot. "Do Weyountah and Mr.—or is it Captain?—Fairfield—"

"Mr. Ryland calls him Captain because that's his rank in the militia troop he formed."

"Did he, indeed? Do they know about Mrs. Lake?"

"No, m'am. Weyountah says he thinks that I was poisoned—he has made a study of plants and says there's something called mad apple or Jamestown-weed that produces such effects—and I said I had gone to visit friends and had eaten of sallet at an inn. Such accidents do happen, he says, and naturally an innkeeper would have sent me on my way when I began to rave. In the light of Mr. Adams's letter, and Uncle Mercer's, I had almost convinced myself that something of the sort had indeed taken place—that it was an accident on the part of Mrs. Lake, and there was an innocent explanation. Then, four days ago it must have been, St-John Pugh—a most arrogant bullyboy . . ."

"Black hair, green eyes, and a nose like a suffused potato? Wears a yellow gown?"

"Even so, m'am—the Black Dog, he's called. I condole you to have made his acquaintance," added the boy, with his donnish smile. "He has been a senior here at least three years, they say, and has made my stay at this college a calvary. 'Tis only because George took me in as his fag that I've had some protection, though George doesn't truly need a fag the way other seniors have them: I mean, he has Diomede to keep his rooms for him and run his errands. But he lets me study here in his rooms—Pugh used to come looking for me in my own, to send me on made-up errands to the farthest end of town . . ."

"Does he not have a fag of his own?" John had always been philosophical about the fagging system in effect at Harvard— the freshmen attaching themselves to seniors as partial protection against hazing; it was something one simply had to endure in order to get an education. Abigail, aware that it was almost certain that her sons would one day be freshmen here, regarded it in a less sanguine light.

"He does, m'am. And slaves as well, two of them. But he likes to bully and is a positive *diabolos* for spiteful vengeances. As I was saying, Pugh caught me on Friday and sent me on an errand into the far end of the town, to the Pig; and when I came out of the inn, I saw Mrs. Lake's coachman across the road."

"Did you so?"

"I knew him, m'am. The scar on his face is like the mark of Cain. There were two men with him, one tall and powerful with a shaven head that poked forward like a turtle's, the other a man of medium size with an ear missing and his nose most horribly scarred. All three were swarthy, and the mutilated man wore his hair in a long queue, smeared with tar as sailors do.

They were looking about them, and as I knew no one at the Pig, I asked no questions but simply made haste to leave by the kitchen door. It was then—Friday evening—that I sent to you."

"As well you did," murmured Abigail. "We seem to have stumbled into a broadside ballad here—all we need is an endangered maiden who is true heiress to the treasure, though I reckon Mistress Pitts was very well able to take care of herself. How much do your friends know, or guess?"

Horace shook his head. "What they know is only that I went to visit friends and was found unconscious in a ditch the following morn. What they guess . . ."

His brow furrowed, and for a moment the boyish face with its pasty adolescent spots and its too-large nose seemed, suddenly, that of the man he would be. "Weyountah has taxed me, two or three times, with questions. He guesses I wasn't telling the truth, and he's seen that I'm afraid. George . . ." He grinned affectionately. "I'm sure George took him aside and told him that if I'd had the red blood in me to go off—er—drabbing, and ended up drunk in a ditch, I'd be the better not to have some praying Indian chasing after me for the details. They put it about that I was sick—"

"'Tis what Mr. Ryland seems to have thought."

"Well, he's the Fellow in charge of this hall, so if word of any of this reached his ears, he'd have to report it, you see. And he'd really rather not know."

Abigail raised her brows. "He seems to me a most honest man—"

"Oh, he is! *Amicus humani generis.* He does most of the work in George's troop—the King's Own Volunteers—if the truth be known. But by the same token, he knows that if George gets sent down, that's the end of the Volunteers. *Quod verum est* and all that, of course . . . but what Dr. Langdon doesn't know won't harm him."

Three

When George Fairfield returned after his Greek lecture ("Lord, how am I supposed to know the difference between Ajax son of Telamon and Ajax son of that other fellow?"), Abigail could easily understand the glow of hero worship in her nephew's eyes when he spoke his friend's name. Long-limbed and handsome, the young Virginian had the instinctive air of command that came—Abigail guessed—from ordering black slaves around for most of his life, and the exquisite manners acquired in a society where impressing landowners more wealthy than oneself (or their relatives) was the only way to advance one's family's fortunes.

Yet he had great kindness and an instinctive sense of justice. Over dinner at the Golden Stair Tavern on the Common ("Madame, God would send me to Hell if I obliged you to eat the food they serve in the Hall!") during a lively argument about how far democracy ought to be permitted in the government of each colony, he argued not from Locke or Rousseau ("Good Lord, m'am, I couldn't tell the one from t'other if they were both to offer me a hundred pounds!") but from the men he'd met in the backcountry beyond his father's plantation. "You can't put men like that in charge of making the laws of the colony, m'am! First thing they'd rule is that it's perfectly fine for them to close off the lands the Indians hunt on and chop them up into farms to sell to new immigrants, and then to shoot any Indian who tries to stop them."

Since Abigail had met hundreds of such men in Boston—particularly since the beginning of John's involvement with the Sons of Liberty—she was hard put to find an argument against this. "Just because a man owns no property doesn't mean he's a self-seeking savage . . ."

"No, m'am. But in my experience, it means he's *likelier* to be than a man who's had an education—"

Yet when Uzziah Begbie—as democratic a soul as one was likely to meet in all of Massachusetts Colony—came in seeking her, Fairfield beckoned him to the table and bade the innkeeper's wife bring beer and another plate, and asked him all about his carrier business and were the roads as terrible when one went west as they were in Virginia?

"He acted as protector to me when first I came to Harvard," said Weyountah to Abigail, under cover of this dialogue, "though he was only a year before me. No one wanted an Indian to fag for him, as you might expect, so I was very much on my own. He made sure I knew all the rules, like not wearing a hat in the Yard and not swapping gowns with anyone, so I wouldn't be boxed—"

"And telling us which seniors to watch out for," added Horace, with a glance across the tavern at Black Dog Pugh and his minions, who had gathered near the windows to drink and flirt with the innkeeper's spritely niece. "Pugh or his boys—the thin one is Jasmine Blossom, I think his real name is Jessamy, and the one in the blue coat is Lowth—will send freshmen into town for punch, knowing it's against the rules, and when they're caught by the provosts, will deny having done so. Then the fresher gets fined four shillings, which is a great deal, especially in winter with candles to buy."

"The rumor runs," contributed Weyountah, "that the neighbors of Pugh's father back on Barbados all take up a collection, once a year, to keep the Black Dog in Harvard and in the interest of maintaining good order on the island."

"And the—er—virtue of their daughters. Heaven only knows how he's remained here long enough to become a junior bachelor—"

"Well, he's not stupid," said the Indian, "and I understand he's made better use of his time here visiting merchants in town and learning of their business than he ever has studying his Latin. Perhaps he only courts their daughters."

"*Vincant divitiae*," concluded Horace with a grin, and then coughed violently in a drifting cloud of pipe-smoke from the direction of Pugh and his friends.

When Begbie had gone—with Fairfield's assurances that he would send Mrs. Adams home in his own chaise—Abigail and Horace told the other two young men of the true course of Horace's adventure last week: of the assignation with Mrs. Lake, the letters of introduction, the scandalous document, and the carriage-ride that was almost certainly intended to end in Horace's death. "Can you write out what you recall of the document?" suggested Weyountah at once.

"I think so," said Horace. "My memory is very good, and because I translated it, I paid particular attention to every word. It wasn't a treasure-map or anything."

"Not an obvious one," said the Indian. "But it might have contained clues—every third word, every fourth word . . ."

"Yes, but unless he can recall every single word that's of no use," protested Fairfield.

"No," agreed Abigail. "Yet 'tis a good idea, and once Horace writes as much of the document as he can recall, some pattern may emerge that strikes one of us that was not evident to him at the time. Take a look at these." She held out to the others the two mendacious letters, and Weyountah held them where the westering window-light could fall on them most brightly. "They're complete fabrications, of course, but does anything about them suggest anything to either of you?"

"Good quality ink," said the Indian at once. "And expensive paper."

"Moreover, a writer who knew how to cut quills and keep the flow of words going," pointed out Abigail. "The hand is a confident one, without hesitations or blots. Further, the writer is accustomed to forming complex words: *intentions*, *probity*, *researches*. He knows how to *sound* like a lawyer or a judge."

"He certainly convinced our Horace," said Fairfield with a grin and a gentle nudge at his friend's shoulder. "What do they say about the pure not seeing anything but purity?"

"With your permission," interpolated Abigail, "I shall take these two letters back to town with me. John's away, *naturally*," she added, unable to keep exasperation from her voice—*When WASN'T John away when you needed him?*—"but my friend Mr. Revere—the silversmith, you know—has a most acute eye for the details of handwriting and other telltale signs. He may very well see things in these that are hidden from us."

She half expected the young Virginian to object at the mention of Paul Revere's name, but he'd clearly never heard of the man in his life. Like most people outside of Boston, George Fairfield's knowledge of the Sons of Liberty was limited to Sam Adams and James Otis (who hadn't been able to be active among them for years, poor man) and some of their more spectacular exploits, like sacking the Governor's house, destroying shops, and dumping $92,000 worth of tea into the harbor.

Instead he declared, "And *I* am going to do the obvious and have a look around the ladies of the surrounding countryside to see who might be Mrs. Lake."

To which Weyountah laughed, "Why does it not surprise me that George is going to look around among the ladies?"

"Dash it, man, the woman wasn't just made up out of mud for the occasion. She has to have come from someplace, chaise, coachman, and all."

"For that matter," said Weyountah thoughtfully, "where would this Mrs. Lake—or whoever she really is—have gotten a text in Arabic, or Arabic lettering, to copy from? The only scholar in Harvard who had any Arabic texts at all was old Reverend Seckar, and Horace got all of his when he died."

"And lucky thing he did," said Fairfield. "Poisonous old screw was going to leave them all to the College and stick his poor wife and sister without a bean. You got a few too out of that lot, didn't you, Weyountah?"

"Are you also a scholar of Oriental languages?" inquired Abigail—though why a young man who'd been born in a two-room wigwam in the woods of Rhode Island shouldn't have as much of an interest in the wisdom from another portion of the world as one who'd been born thirty miles away in a two-room farmhouse in the woods of Massachusetts, she didn't know, once she thought of it.

The Narraganset shook his head. "No, natural science," he said. "Astronomy, chiefly, but really anything I can get my hands on. The books Mrs. Seckar was selling off were ruinously old and of little use, given the advances that have been made in the studies of things like atmospheric vapors and air and water pressure. I've begun correspondence with Mr. Franklin," he added, naming a little shyly the foremost scientist and philosopher in the colonies. "He's been good enough to recommend me to the Royal Society in England, which has been of enormous assistance. There's so *little* over here."

"So little of anything," sighed Horace wistfully.

"Which brings us back," declared Fairfield firmly, "to where we started. Where would that Arabic text have been copied from? Who would have written a document like that in *Arabic*, for the Lord's sake—"

"Obviously," said Abigail, "someone who knew Arabic writing and was using it as a code to keep a record of a disgraceful encounter—I assume for purposes of blackmail."

"Would Henry Morgan *care* if everybody on the Spanish Main knew he was having a—um—Latin lesson"—Fairfield hastily interpolated a euphemism, having clearly, for the moment, forgotten that Abigail was a respectable matron and his friend's aunt to boot—"with someone by the name of Jezebel Pitts? I don't imagine Mistress Pitts would mind. Besides," he added, "they've both been dead for years."

"The principal activity *Governor* Morgan was practicing with Mistress Pitts," Abigail reminded him starchily, "is called, without going into Latin, *conspiracy to commit embezzlement* . . . and given the fact that it involved assistance from pirates, it probably would be considered treason as well by an Admiralty Court. Reason enough to justify hush-money to someone, I'm sure, even if they did not manage to lift any actual gold. But as Mr. Fairfield so justly points out, both parties have been in their dishonored graves for decades. Sam might know . . ."

"Sam—Adams?"

Abigail remembered too late—just as Fairfield had forgotten that she was an aunt and a respectable goodwife from Boston—that her listener was a Loyalist to whom the name of her husband's notorious cousin was anathema.

"No, Sam Brooke," she extemporized hastily. "A neighbor of mine on Queen Street. An elderly gentleman who once—I suspect—had a great deal to do with the smuggling trade and may very well have known Mistress Pitts in her old age." She felt like kicking herself, because of course Sam Adams was precisely whom she meant. Three-quarters of the Sons of Liberty were mixed up in smuggling to one degree or another. Why put yourself in danger of an Admiralty noose, if it weren't to avoid paying the King's taxes on this, that, and the other, every time the King decided one of his friends needed a job as a special revenue collector?

Abigail had frequently deplored the fact that wily Cousin Sam seemed to be on a first-name basis with half the wharf-rats in Boston Harbor. *But on this occasion*, she thought, *he might as well do some good . . .*

If he wasn't packing to get himself out of Boston, she reflected grimly, before the King's vengeance—whatever it was going to be—for the tea came ashore.

Whatever it was going to be, it was almost certainly going to involve a warrant for Sam Adams's arrest.

What broke her sleep every night for weeks—and had caused her to warn her fourteen-year-old servant-girl, Pattie, and John's clerk, Thaxter (not Horace but his—and Abigail's—esteemed cousin), to stand ready to take the children to Uncle Isaac's house at the first sign of trouble—was not knowing how far beyond Sam the arrests would spread.

And what the Sons of Liberty would choose to do about the situation.

She picked up the two letters again and realized that the window light had faded to the point where they were difficult to read. "Good Heavens, it must be getting close to sundown," she said in alarm. "If I'm to be back to Boston—"

"Aunt Abigail, *mea culpa*—"

"Dash it, where's that lazy buck Diomede?" Fairfield sprang to his feet, strode toward the kitchen. "He'll have the chaise harnessed for you before a fly can wash his little hands, m'am—"

In fifteen minutes Abigail was being assisted into an extremely elegant English chaise outside the Golden Stair, with bows and thanks and assurances that Horace would be permitted neither food, drink, nor sleep that night until he'd finished a verbatim copy of Mrs. Lake's disgraceful document. In twenty, she was clinging to the brass rail of the vehicle as it bowled sharply along through the slanted evening sunlight on the road to Charles Town. Like most Virginians, young Mr. Fairfield favored spirited horseflesh, but Diomede—a big-shouldered man in his fifties—was a skilled and careful driver: Abigail was disconcerted and exhilarated by the speed, but never frightened.

When Diomede apologized for the pace—"But for a fact, m'am, we'll be fortunate to make the ferry before it closes down"—she felt encouraged to ask him, was he himself familiar with the countryside hereabouts?

"Not like a native, m'am," he said, in a deep velvet bass. "I came up with Mr. Fairfield in '70, and he's a personable young gentleman, as I'm sure you've observed. The year before last, when there was such a to-do about that revenue ship that went aground in Rhode Island and was burned by smugglers claiming to be against taxation, Mr. Fairfield formed up a company of gentlemen loyal to the King—the King's Own Volunteers, they call themselves—and so he's widely known from here to Medford and always being invited to stay at this house or that. Mr. Charles Fairfield—Mr. George's father—gave me instructions to make sure that he kept to his book."

The valet smiled as he reined in to let an oncoming wagon

pass in the narrow road where it swung around the base of Prospect Hill. "But it's true also that so far as I can see, the reason a young gentleman goes to college is to meet men of property and consideration, and to make friendships that will be of use to him later in life. So I guess one could say, I've seen as much of the countryside as a man can, traipsing behind a very popular young gentleman with his baggage."

Abigail laughed. "You have my sympathies," she said. "Do you happen to know the name of the farmer who brought Mr. Horace back to Cambridge on Wednesday? I think Weyountah said he was from Concord."

"From that direction," agreed Diomede. "Mr. Rutherford has a farm just this side of Lexington, on the Concord Road. He said he found poor Mr. Thaxter by the road near Pierce's Hill."

Abigail mentally placed the location, a wooded country of old farmsteads and stone field-walls. A two-hour drive from Cambridge would indeed put Mrs. Lake's "brown house of two storeys" somewhere between Menotomy and Lexington, particularly if the woman had taken the precaution of not driving straight there. *John would know.* And if John weren't yet home from the Maine Assizes, Revere—when she showed him the bogus letters—would very likely be able to tell her: the Sons of Liberty made it their business to know everyone in the countryside around Boston, if for no other reason than to know were they adherents to the Crown's policies and power, or in favor of colonial rights?

Yet for all its superficial resemblance to the little towns of the Massachusetts countryside—her family's village of Weymouth, or Braintree where John's mother and brothers lived— Harvard was different. In Weymouth or Braintree, everyone had known one another since childhood, and a strange face was instantly noted and commented upon. Hers certainly had been when nine years ago John had brought her to that little brown farmhouse as a bride, although everyone knew Parson Smith's three daughters and his gadabout son . . .

People came and went from Harvard all the time. Praying Indians like Weyountah from converted villages in Rhode Island. Gaudy exotics like St-John Pugh. She reflected uneasily on the openness of the buildings of Harvard College, the ease with which anyone could ascend any of those staircases . . .

"Whoa!" Diomede drew rein. "M'am, your pardon, I beg you, but it looks like Sassy's picked up a stone."

And indeed, even as the little mare slowed her pace, Abigail could see she was favoring her off fore.

It crossed her mind very briefly that the delay would cost her her return, but she said at once, "No, of course—"

She took the reins as the servant sprang down and hastened to the mare's head. She was carrying it low, Abigail observed worriedly, and holding her hoof from the ground— *She must really be hurt* . . .

Diomede worked gingerly, testing and probing in the woodland twilight. When he came back to the chaise, even in the gloom, she read consternation on his face.

"Is she all right?"

"She'll *be* all right, m'am," said the servant. "But she's cut the frog of her hoof—there must have been a nail or something in the road—"

Abigail sprang down from the chaise at once. "Poor little lady," she said. "And such a nuisance—but you know, I think I rather pushed my luck talking to those boys as late as I did, and having to walk back to Cambridge is no more than I deserve. Will she be all right to be led? I suppose we could leave the chaise here for a short time . . ."

The man relaxed—as a slave, reflected Abigail, he had

probably witnessed the human limits of bad manners and pet-ulance among those who considered a) that their convenience ranked higher than an injured animal's pain and b) that if they missed the ferry, it must be the fault of the driver. "I don't think there's call for that, m'am." He looked around him at the darkening woods. "It goes without saying that Mr. Fairfield will pay for a bed for you at the Golden Stair. I hope it's no inconvenience—"

"The only inconvenience," replied Abigail grandly, falling into step with Diomede as he turned the mare's head back toward Cambridge, "will be to my aunt and uncle, who will be obliged to look after my children tonight." In the shadowy trees, wrens and thrushes, mockingbirds and starlings all twittered and whistled as if to make sure of their territories before they settled down for the night. A breeze riffled the leaves, filled the world with the soft green scent of hay. "Of course I shall sleeplessly weep the whole night through at spending the hours apart from them," she added with a blithe-ness that made the servant grin, "yet I trust that somehow I shall survive the experience of not separating Johnny and Charley from killing one another when Charley hides John-ny's toys, and not being woken up twice and three times by Tommy wanting a story or a drink of water—"

"Oh, m'am," said Diomede, and clasped his hands to his heart, "please don't go on—I'm afraid I shall weep."

"I do beg your pardon," said Abigail.

They led the limping Sassy the two miles back to Cam-bridge in perfect amity.

Diomede left Abigail in one of the college parlors while he took Sassy back to the stables; in a few moments George Fair-field came running in, green robe billowing and Horace at his heels. "M'am, I am covered with shame—!"

"Nonsense! I was telling Diomede, I look upon the whole business as an excellent opportunity to get a complete night's rest, something one doesn't, you know, if one has three sons under the age of seven."

"Well, you'll have rest at the Golden Stair on my account—or rather my Pa's, since he's the one who settles them all," added the young man with a grin. "Poor old Sassy! Thank the Lord, Diomede saw her falter as quick as he did. She's taken no hurt—the man's a wonder with horses. With just about everything, come to that . . . I could have taken a whip to that brute Pugh for telling me only yesterday that I'd best sell him off cheap because he pilfers my liquor now and then. Lord, I'd trust Diomede with a bottle a lot sooner than I'd trust Pugh or either of those so-called grooms of his—wild savages straight off the boat from Africa! Diomede was born in Williamsburg and raised a gentleman, *and* his father before him!" He tucked Abigail's cloak around her shoulders and sprang to open the parlor door for her, seeming blithely unaware of any incongruity in the fact that he could describe a man old enough to be his father as a *gentleman* and yet possess the legal right to sell him off like a mule. "His manners are a sight better than Pugh's, anyway—though I suppose the same could be said about Sassy."

Mrs. Squills at the Golden Stair didn't appear a bit surprised at Abigail's reappearance with the two scholars: "The way those boys were talking to you, I knew you'd never get to the ferry in time," she said, her smile as she curtseyed making her look much older—she was missing several of her teeth. "Mr. Horace's aunt, I think Diomede said? Now, go along with you," she added briskly, flapping her apron at Abigail's escort. "Before you're fined for being out of your rooms after dark, *and* in a tavern—"

"They wouldn't fine me for being with my *aunt*," protested Horace, and the tiny innwife's face flexed into an exaggerated expression of astonishment.

"There's another college here in Cambridge that you've been going to all this time without telling me?" she demanded. "Because the Dean of *Harvard* would fine you for being out with your own *mother*, let alone an aunt . . . *And* I know full-well about the little minx *you've* got waiting for you out behind the stables," she added, with a glare at Fairfield.

"I—?" Fairfield pressed his hand to his heart and raised his eyebrows in innocent bafflement.

"Run along with you!" She shook her head as Fairfield made a dancing-master's leg to Abigail and saluted her hand before he strode off, laughing, across the dark of the Common, Horace trotting loyally at his heels. "They're good boys," she added, leading Abigail toward the stair. "For all they drive an honest woman mad with their, 'I'll pay you next quarter for a batter-cake today.' I don't know which is worse, George with his lady friends or Horace with his nose forever in a book!" She collected a couple of abandoned beer mugs from the table, as she passed it, to add to her tray. "Well, 'tis the peskiest kitten that grows to the best mouser, you know. I wouldn't give tuppence for a lad that didn't run about the town seeing what he can get himself into, would you?"

Abigail smiled, thinking of her own too-serious Johnny's hair-raising experiments with building mousetraps and measuring the current of the tides in the Mill Pond. "Nobody's ever shown me a lad that didn't," she responded, "so I wouldn't know."

Her mind returned to Johnny as she made ready for bed ("Now I've a clean hairbrush that I keep for those who're taken by circumstance unexpectedly . . . And let me lend you a shift for tomorrow, Mrs. Adams—I've one just laun-

dered, and I know you'll want a clean one in the morning . . .
No, no, just send it back when you're home . . ."). Unfair, of
course, to abandon her children to Pattie and Aunt Eliza—to
whom Pattie would unfailingly take them, once it was clear
that their mother had missed the ferry. Six-year-old Johnny
had an instinctive dislike of change, and little Tommy—at
eighteen months—was of an age to want things to remain
the same . . . and Nabby would worry. Abigail wished, as she
brushed out the raven cloak of hair that fell to her hips and
braided it for the night, that there was a way that she could
have sent them a note, at least, reassuring them, though it
would be obvious what had happened . . .

In time, she hoped, Johnny would be coming to Harvard,
as his father had. Abigail hopped quickly between the spotless sheets, blew out the candle . . .

But in ten years, she could not keep herself from asking,
would the college still be in existence? A year ago, or two, the
question would have been unthinkable. Harvard College was
the best and oldest school in the colonies. Yet in throwing the
King's tea into the harbor, the Sons of Liberty had effectively
declared their rebellion against the King's authority. Only a
fool or a child would talk himself into believing that the
retribution for this behavior wouldn't be severe . . .

And her acquaintance with the Sons of Liberty convinced
her that whatever the King did, their reaction would be
equally violent.

As she drifted toward sleep, she heard again, on the edges
of her dreams, the angry shouting of mobs that had at various
times attacked the shops and businesses of men who'd
denounced the Sons. Remembered the sparkle in Sam's eyes
when he'd related to her how he'd egged on a mob to even
sack the house of the Governor: the building had been gutted,
and the collected records of the first years of the colony,

painstakingly collected by that scholarly gentleman in order to write the first comprehensive history of Massachusetts, had been torn and trampled in the gutters . . .

Remembered, too, the crack of guns in King Street, the black pools of blood in the blue evening snow. It was too easy to picture in her mind the college buildings in flame or occupied by troops . . .

Though she had knelt by the bed to say her prayers before undressing, Abigail propped herself on the pillows a little and again folded her hands. *Whatever paths they tread*, she prayed, *ten years from this night or with the coming of this night's dawn, You have already laid out for them, for their good and Your best purposes. But as their mother, I beg of You, keep them safe, hold their hands in Yours . . .*

She must have fallen asleep in midprayer—as she almost invariably did when she prayed in bed with the featherbed up to her chin—because the next thing she knew, it was morning, and Mrs. Squills was knocking on the door of her room with the news that George Fairfield had been murdered in the night.

Four

"They're saying Diomede did it." Horace's face was white as paper, save his eyes, which were swollen and red—he had been weeping for his friend when Abigail had come into the Golden Stair's private parlor.

"Who's saying?" She took the chair on the other side of the small fire. Beyond the window, mist still lay on the Common, and the birds she'd heard twittering themselves to sleep last night when George was alive were waking in every tree and shrub.

"The Dean, and Dr. Langdon—the President of the College—and the sheriff, Mr. Congreve. He was drunk—Diomede was—but just because a man's had a dram or two . . ." Horace broke off in some confusion, with an expression of helpless guilt, remembering no doubt the numerous family discussions in which the consumption of alcohol was roundly denounced as the root of considerably more evil than grew from the greed for money.

"Of course not!" It said much, in Abigail's opinion, that

Horace's tolerance for the foibles of others had widened to that extent. Two years ago the boy had been an unconscionable prig on the subject. *One gift of a Harvard education . . .*

"Diomede would never have raised his hand against George." These last words came out as a whisper, and Horace sank into the chair in which he'd been sitting when Abigail— hastily dressed and tying a fresh, clean, and borrowed cap of Mrs. Squills's over her hair—had hastened into the room.

With astonishing good sense, the landlady—who must have been nearly as upset over the murder as Horace was— brought in a tray of coffee things. Abigail poured a cup for herself and hot water for her nephew, to which she added a little honey. "Drink that." When Mrs. Squills went out, through the open door of the ordinary blew the voices of men discussing the crime: *murdering nigger—drunk as David's sow—knife still in his hand . . .*

"What happened? You'll feel better. Who's there now?"

"Weyountah," whispered the boy. "He waked to the sound of George shouting at someone—not shouting, really, just raised voices . . . His room is across the landing. Mine is above Weyountah's—Mr. Beaverbrook from New York is above George, and you couldn't wake Beaver if you set his rooms on fire. But George often shouts at Diomede, you know . . ." He put his hand quickly to his mouth as if to catch back the present tense.

"What time was that?"

Horace shook his head. "When the bell rang for chapel this morning, Weyountah went across and knocked at the door— We all have to work to make sure George gets to chapel. It's Diomede's job, but the last two times Dio had a few drinks, George was fined, and Dr. Langdon warned him . . . So either Weyountah or I will check. When Diomede didn't answer, Weyountah went in and found him asleep—"

"In the study?" She remembered the small leather chest in the corner of George's little study, which contained the slave's pallet and, no doubt, every other item the man owned. In Virginia, she had been told, the house-slaves often slept on the floor of their masters' rooms, like dogs.

Horace nodded, struggling to speak in something resembling normal tones. "There was blood on his hand, and on the sheet—" His voice cracked, and he raised the cup to his lips, needing two hands to hold it steady. "Weyountah ran into the bedroom. George was lying in his bed, in his nightshirt. He'd been stabbed—there was blood all over the bed—"

Abigail put both of her hands over the boy's cold one. "Was there a knife?" She knew better than to believe what the men in the next room were yelling to one another.

Horace nodded. After a moment he recovered himself enough to reply, "On the floor next to Diomede's pallet, covered with blood." Then, when she came around to kneel beside his chair, he threw his arms around her shoulders and held her desperately, his body trembling with the impact of the first great grief, the first blow of loss and violence in his life.

Abigail held him, stroked his back as she did Tommy's when the little boy had a nightmare, saying nothing. But her mind raced. Her grief at the young man's death seemed to run in tandem with her shock at the manner of it, and totally separated from the thousand questions that formed themselves up, sharp and clear as if she saw them written down on a paper before her. *What kind of knife? Was it one of George's, or strange to the establishment? Diomede would know that—probably Weyountah also, he seems an observant young man . . . Was there anything missing from the room? When did George come in last night? Was Diomede dressed?*

Was there anything in the bedroom that seemed out of place?

But Horace was barely seventeen years old and had just

taken a wound as agonizing as the one that had killed his friend, and for a time she did nothing but hold him, letting him know that there was someone to hold.

He took a deep breath, let it go. Let go of George, as if he had been clinging to his friend's hand. He began to say, "I'm sorry—"

"Shush. Can you take me back there now? Are you able for it?"

Horace nodded, pushed his steamed and tear-blotted spectacles back into place, then removed them, and fumbled to clean them on the end of his neckcloth. "Diomede would never have done it," he said.

"Was he drunk? George said he drank . . ."

"Never to the point that he didn't know what he was doing!"

"But to the point that he wouldn't wake up if someone else put a bloodied knife into his hand? What is it Lady Macbeth says? *I'll gild the faces of the grooms withal* . . ."

"But no one *would!*" protested Horace. "George hadn't an enemy in the world!" He got awkwardly to his feet and gallantly helped Abigail to rise.

Not even the man George kept at his beck and call for four years, away from family and friends, only for his convenience in a foreign town? An American born and bred, gentlemanly and intelligent and kind, who had to sleep on the floor and live out of a chest the size of a breadbox, so that he was there to 'make him mind his book,' keep him away from unsuitable ladies, and wake him up in time for chapel?

It was the first thing the Middlesex County sheriff was going to say.

"It doesn't take a plot, or a lifelong foe, to do murder," she said quietly. "Only a moment's rage. Let us go and see what we can learn."

* * *

The entire student body of Harvard—some two hundred young men and boys between the ages of fifteen and twenty-five—were either milling around the westernmost hallway of Massachusetts Hall or pushing their way up and down Horace's staircase. Horace bleated, "Here, let me through— I have rooms up here— Please let me through . . ." to absolutely no effect.

Abigail caught the first brightly colored sleeve that came her way, yanked it purposefully, and said in a voice honed by six years of dealing with young Johnny at home, "Excuse me, sir, I am Mr. Fairfield's aunt— I beg your pardon, sir, but I am a member of the family— Please let us pass—" in so firm a tone that the young men so addressed either backed down out of the staircase or, farther up, squashed themselves flat against the wall. Abigail's normal conversational tones were brisk but soft, yet at need she could call up a particular timbre of voice that could cut flint. "I beg your pardon, we must get through— Please excuse us, sir, but we're members of the family—"

In Fairfield's study, men were packed tight, all of them shouting at the slumped form of Diomede, who huddled in a chair in the corner with a harassed-looking man in a blue coat before him, whom Abigail recognized—from years of association with John's legal practice—as Seth Congreve, sheriff of Middlesex County. Diomede was shaking his head, saying, "I don't remember, sir! I don't know—" He raised his hands, sticky now with drying blood that blotched and boltered the white sleeves of his shirt. "I swear I didn't—drunk or sober, I'd never have touched a hair of his head!"

His clothing stank of blood and rum, and tears of shock ran down his face.

"So you're saying you're so drunk you didn't even hear—Can you gentlemen please be silent!— So you didn't hear your master arguing with some other man—someone whom you weren't even aware was in the room?"

"He could have been," barked St-John Pugh. "I warned George about that nigger's drinking . . ."

And the weasel-like sophomore Jasmine Blossom demanded sarcastically, "You were so drunk you didn't even wake for a man walking in bold as paint and stabbing your master after a quarrel loud enough to wake the Injun? Oh, let me have another story, Papa, it's not nearly bedtime yet!"

"Mr. Pugh," said Abigail briskly, "would you and your friends be so good as to assist Mr. Congreve in clearing the room a little? One can scarcely do justice if one isn't able to hear oneself think. Mr. Ryland, just the man I wished to see—Might you detail some of the King's Own Volunteers to eject anyone not immediately connected with the investigation? Thank you—Mr. Pugh is also assisting me . . . Deputize whom you will—"

"Yes!" Congreve swung around with a gesture of a man with a sack of corn beset by pigeons. "All of you, out of here—Mrs. Adams!" he added in surprise. "What on earth—?"

"I was working with Mr. Fairfield," she said, "on a strange little puzzle that involved him and his friends; I am horrified to hear of this. And of course Mr. Adams will undertake to defend poor Diomede, who quite obviously had no more to do with the killing than Mr. Ryland or Mr. Pugh—You there, Mr. Yeovil, are you associated with the sheriff? No? Then please take yourself out—"

"What puzzle?" asked the sheriff, as Ryland pushed past him into the bedroom—even more crowded—beyond. "And why 'obviously'?"

"A man who's drunk so much that he doesn't know what

he's doing is unlikely to win a hand-to-hand fight with a sober one," she retorted briskly, though she was not, in fact, at all certain that this was true. "Certainly not as swiftly as this battle proceeded, in any case. Mr. Ryland, could you ask Mr. Beaverbrook to remain, and of course Mr. Wylie—" It took her a moment to remember Weyountah's baptismal name. "Is there a physician here?"

"Mr. Perry." Congreve nodded toward the bedroom door, then turned toward the task of ejecting the last of the stragglers. "Mr. Perry teaches medicine here at the college."

"Mr. Pugh," called Abigail, "might I prevail upon you to keep guard at the bottom of the staircase with your men? Thank you," she added, not giving the bachelor-fellow a chance to say yes or no. "You have been of inestimable assistance—" She caught him by the sleeve and thrust him through the door and into the faces of Lowth and Jasmine, just reascending after pushing the last of their fellow classmates out at the bottom of the stair. She closed the door on him, reopened it long enough for Ryland and another young man whom she vaguely recognized as one of the younger members of the Oliver family—relatives of the Governor—to push out the last few observers, then closed it behind them all.

Harvard men—and raised in the best traditions of good manners—they clearly had been taught that one doesn't push back against a lady, and weren't quite sure how to deal with one who summarily ordered them out the door.

"There," she said, and walked back to the corner where Sheriff Congreve still stood—looking rather amused—beside Diomede. "It wants but a little firmness—and getting the right people to think they're going to receive more than their due. Might I speak with the prisoner, Mr. Congreve? I truly cannot imagine the man would turn against his master— and Mr. Adams will want to know every detail I can glean."

"And Mr. Adams sent you out here?" He sounded doubtful about that, as well he might. Being a lawyer's clerk
required an education, something Abigail was sharply conscious that neither she nor any other woman was allowed to
obtain. Nor would she or any other woman have been permitted to exercise the skills of a lawyer if she somehow acquired
them. And a lawyer who sent out a woman—much less his
wife!—to do a man's work would have been, quite simply,
committing professional suicide.

Abigail lowered her voice, though the little study was now
empty except for themselves, Diomede, Horace, and a pale
and rather wizened-looking young man who was probably
Mr. Beaverbrook, who lived immediately above this room.
"The matter upon which Mr. Fairfield asked to see me," she
explained—*And it isn't QUITE a lie*, she reasoned, *as the poor
young man really did consult me for my opinion once he knew what
was taking place*—"was, we had thought, a family matter concerning my nephew Mr. Thaxter, and for this reason I hesitate to speak of it without consulting Mr. Adams. Whether it
has any bearing upon this shocking turn of events or not, I
have no idea, but Mr. Adams will certainly undertake to defend
Diomede, whom we both know would never have done such
a thing."

On the other side of the table, the servant raised his head,
the first flash of life returning to his eyes that Abigail had
seen since she had come into the room. The first flash of hope.

She went on as if it were the most natural thing in the
world, "The family side of the business not being completed,
Mr. Fairfield paid to have me stay in Cambridge last night, at
the Golden Stair. I will of course write at once to Mr. Adams,
who is at the Maine Assizes this week, and to his clerk in
Boston, Mr. John Thaxter, who graduated from here last year.
But I know Mr. Adams will want to know the precise details

of the scene, as they were before the rooms were disturbed, and will also want to know everything that can be recollected by both the witnesses and the accused—which as you know yourself can become very quickly distorted with the passage of time."

Congreve nodded and scratched at the edge of his wig—horsehair, Abigail guessed, and probably vastly uncomfortable: she could see the little rim of reddened flesh all around its edge where it irritated the skin. He said, "I see. And that's perfectly all right, Mrs. Adams—a very respectable gentleman, your husband is, and a fine lawyer. Mr. Langdon—"

He turned to the waspish, red-faced gentleman—resplendent in a red doctor's gown barred with black velvet and a startling full-bottomed wig—who appeared in the door of the bedchamber.

"Might Mr. Perry be spared for a few moments to describe to Mrs. Adams—here acting as her husband's amanuensis—the condition of the body and the room when you were summoned?"

"Actually," said Abigail, "what Mr. Adams would ask me to do—and on those occasions when I have acted in his name before this, he has been most emphatic in his instructions—would be to enter the chamber myself and compare my own observations with those of"—she could see President Langdon bristling up like a porcupine and the stooped, graying gentleman in black behind him who had to be Dr. Perry radiating disapproval at this display of womanish inquisitiveness—"of observers trained to analyze the smallest details. Mr. Adams has a horror"—here she could at least put the genuine ring of truth into her voice—"of information coming at third-hand, as you gentlemen"—she divided her deprecating smile among the three men—"must also abhor for its potential for mistakes. He has quite trained me to describe matters exactly as I see them, without the addition or subtraction of thoughts of my own."

John had done nothing of the sort, of course. But she knew he had always admired that quality in her, which she had possessed long before that sturdy, brilliant, opinionated, and passionate—not to say maddening—little gentleman had come into her life when she was fifteen.

Langdon and Perry looked mollified.

Horace—with singular and, to Abigail, surprising presence of mind—produced a memorandum-book from his pocket and said with the air of one deputized to stand ready on the fringes of events, "Your notes, m'am."

Abigail said, "Thank you, Mr. Thaxter," with her most serene air, and preceded the doctor and the college president into the chamber where George Fairfield's body lay.

Five

Dr. Perry stepped quickly across to the bed and drew the sheet over George Fairfield's face. Perry would have pulled the counterpane up to cover the splotches where the blood—turning dark now as it dried—had stained through the linen, but Abigail held up her hand and asked, "How was Mr. Fairfield lying when you came in, doctor? It's one of the things my husband will wish to know." Her words stayed him long enough for her to note that there seemed to be three or four sources of blood—wounds that had bled. *Plenty,* she thought, *for the killer to "gild the faces of the grooms" and, like the wily and wicked Lady Macbeth, transfer the blame with the blood.*

"He lay on his back," said Perry. "His limbs were composed and the sheet drawn up to his waist, for as you recall, 'twas a mild night. There was no evidence of struggle." With a sharp twitch of his wrist he flung the counterpane into place. Despite herself, Abigail felt relieved.

"Where was he stabbed?" she asked.

The man's upper lip seemed to lengthen at the idea of a woman wishing to know such things, even to pass the word on to her husband. "Thrice in the breast, two of the blows penetrating the heart. Once in the side, up under the ribs—"

Left side, Abigail noted. That's where the blood had flowed out, anyway.

Abigail had seen dead men before. There were families, she knew, who didn't believe in having their girl-children assist in the laying-out of the dead—grannies, uncles, younger children who didn't make it through sickly winters or the endless barrage of ailments that hammered the very young before their tenth year—but hers had not been one of these. And after one has prepared for burial the body of one's own child—poor tiny Susanna, who had barely passed her first year—no other death hits quite so hard.

She recalled going with her mother and her sister Mary to help one of her aunts lay out a cousin when she, Abigail, was barely seven: Mary was ten, and the dead child was Abigail's own age. It was Abigail who had helped her mother braid the little girl's hair. She remembered asking, Would Annie be angry that it was Abigail who was alive today and Annie who was dead? and getting an hour and a half on the subject of how much luckier and happier Annie was to be dead and with Jesus . . .

Probably true, she reflected, looking down at the worn linen where it lay over George Fairfield's face: the little mount of nose and chin, the silky tousle of blonde hair just visible at the top. Certainly true, in fact, and what she had told Nabby—only with greater brevity and, she hoped, greater tenderness—a few months ago when little Jemmy Butler next door had died. But she had thought at the time, *Will Annie miss her doll Penelope? Or her baby sisters? Or the way the sunlight makes crazy patterns of elongated diamonds on the plaster of the bedroom wall first thing in the morning? Or the first sweet strength of that first sweet spoonful of molasses on hot corn-pudding first thing on a cold morning?*

Would George miss driving Sassy full tilt along the roads to visit his friends, when he was *invited to stay at this house or that . . . widely known from here to Medford* as he was? Would he miss riding with his Volunteers in preparation for a rebellion they all guessed was coming but that he would not see?

She raised her eyes to meet those of Weyountah, who sat in such stillness as to be almost invisible on the room's single chair at the foot of the bed.

Would he miss his friends?

From the door, President Langdon commented, "Given the attitude of the body, and Mr. Wylie's testimony"—he nodded toward Weyountah—"as to raised voices and harsh words spoken to a man already laboring under the intolerable resentment of his servile condition, and given the presence of Mr. Fairfield's rum-bottle in the study and its contents all over the slave's clothing, it seems clear that Diomede drank himself into a state of rage while his master slept, and entering the room, stabbed him as he lay in his bed. Deplorable, of course, but no more than can be expected when a man practices the injustices of slavery upon his fellow creature—"

"But that gives no explanation for the blood on the floor of this room," said Abigail.

"I beg your pardon?" Dr. Langdon was clearly not used to having his diatribes against slavery interrupted by anyone, let alone a woman, for mere practicalities.

"There is blood on the floor," said Abigail, pointing. "It's been tracked and trampled about, but you see where the main stain of it lay, here, beside the desk by the window. Was the window open?"

President and doctor looked at each other.

"It was not." Weyountah got to his feet. A step—the

bedchamber was a tiny one—took him to the place; Abigail fetched the branch of candles from the little work-desk beneath the window, searched her pocket for flint and steel—which of course she'd left back at the inn . . . She caught up flint and striker from the bedside table. The room looked north onto the quadrangle of grass that lay between the college buildings and at this hour of the morning was gloomy. No wonder the poor boy had trouble waking up.

She knelt, holding the lights close to the floor. The main portion of the stain was clear to see. Not quite the diameter of a cider-mug, it was clearly outlined on the scuffed oak, as if it had lain there half the night. By comparison, the blots and tracks where the crowding students—and Dr. Perry himself, belike—had stepped in it were superficial. Her handkerchief, wet with a little discreetly applied spit, cleaned one of them up at once, but the original stain—which had lain hours longer—it could not touch.

There were two others, between that stain and the bed, in direct line. Round drips, and set, as if they, too, had lain there for many hours.

"He was stabbed here, by the desk," said Weyountah softly, "and dragged or carried to the bed. The wound under the ribs—"

"Which I cannot see how it could have been made," said Abigail, "by a man standing over him on the room side of the bed. You can see how the bed lies against the wall, with the head pointing south, the feet north toward the window. The left side, where the stab-wound is, would be away from a man standing in the room. But if he were stabbed here, standing up, of course the attacker would stab him in the left side—"

"And carry him to the bed and stab him thrice more, to make sure of him."

Abigail turned, frowning, back toward Perry and Langdon in the doorway. "And then proceed back to his pallet in the study and go to sleep? Without even washing the blood from his hands? When all the college was sleeping, and he could easily have fled—"

"The man was drunk," pointed out Langdon, in a tone of disgust. "I—and others—remonstrated with the boy about retaining a drunkard in his service, but he would not listen. Preferring, I suppose, the prestige—if one can call it that—of owning a Negro to the drudgery of making up his own bed."

"If your honor will pardon me for speaking," said Weyountah, "in my experience of the man, Diomede was not a habitual drunkard. He would go on an occasional spree for an evening if he thought Mr. Fairfield was not going to return to his rooms until late, as was the case, I believe, last night. But this is not the same thing as a man who punishes the bottle night after night."

"'Tis but a step, and a short one," replied the president coldly, "from the 'occasional spree,' as you call it, to greater and greater frequency as the demon takes hold. Surely *you* of all people do not deny the pattern?"

"No, sir." Weyountah's voice held level, despite the reference—which Abigail considered tactless in the extreme—to the notorious effect that white man's liquor had on many of the Indians who used it. "I speak only of my observation as to where Diomede stood in regard to that pattern."

"With what was he stabbed?" Abigail wondered if Perry would let her get a look at the wounds themselves and decided that a request to do so would only exacerbate a futile situation.

"The paper knife from Mr. Fairfield's desk was in Diomede's hand, m'am," said Weyountah.

"Would a paper knife be sharp enough to kill a man?" *And do I need to worry about Johnny getting his hands on John's from the study desk and murdering Charley while I'm away?*

The Indian edged between doctor and president—neither

of whom looked as if they would have made way for him, had either been able to find a good reason for standing on his dignity to that extent—and returned from the outer study a moment later with the bloodied weapon in his hand. "The edge is no sharper than it has to be to cut paper," he said. "But the point would surely be a deadly weapon in a strong man's hand."

A bit gingerly, Abigail took the hilt and touched the point with her fingertip. Aside from the smallness of the guard and the narrow blade, it would have almost served as an actual weapon: English-made, steel, with ivory plates on the hilt and a blade about seven inches long. Long enough and strong enough to reach the heart.

"And is there anything missing from the room? Where did Mr. Fairfield keep his money, for instance?"

"In his pockets, if he had any," replied Weyountah with a sigh. "Or in a desk-drawer or lying on the corner of the desk. Every excursion involved George searching for money—" A slight break flawed his voice as he remembered a hundred or a thousand tiny, trivial scenes. "And he never had a penny."

"I thought his father was rich!"

"He is, m'am. And George had credit all over town. But actual money in his pockets—"

"The boy was a gamester." Langdon's voice reeked with disgust. "And worse," he added darkly, meaning, Abigail guessed from Mrs. Squills's remarks at the Stair, given to wenching. Weyountah laid the paper knife on the corner of the desk and looked over the untidy papers there.

More than untidy, thought Abigail. Shuffled up together into loose bundles, the way Sam's were when he had been looking for something in his overcrowded study.

It could just mean that George Fairfield had mislaid his money and had searched his own desk. Still . . .

Two Spanish doubloons and a couple of Pennsylvania pound notes lay on the floor, as if they'd fallen when the desk was opened. A dozen or so books—the *Iliad* and the *Aeneid*, lexicons of Greek and Latin, Hoole's *Catonis Disticha de Moribus* and Ezekiel Cheever's *A Short Introduction, to the Latin Tongue, for the use of the lower forms in the Latin School, Being the Accidence abridged and compiled in that most easy and accurate method wherein the famous Mr. Ezekiel Cheever taught*, were piled on a chair higgledy-piggledy.

She remembered the tidiness of the front chamber. Looking around her, every portion of the bedroom save the vicinity of the desk attested to Diomede's housekeeping skills.

The stain on the floor was exactly between the desk—which stood beneath the window—and the bed.

She asked, "Does it look to you as if George had done any work at this desk? As if he'd been *able* to do work at it as it is?"

The Indian frowned and reconsidered the papers—the fact that no single paper lay in the center, that the inkstand and standish had been moved to the windowsill . . . the fact that, in effect, the desk looked as if someone had taken everything off it, then piled it back on . . .

"He did keep up with his work," said Abigail, standing at Weyountah's side. "He spoke of it last night . . . See, there's been wax dripped on the surface of the desk, fresh, it looks like, and *under* these papers . . . When did George come in last night, do you know?"

"The curfew is nine o'clock," pointed out Dr. Perry, rather severely, from the door.

Weyountah said nothing, but the glance he gave Abigail spoke clearly enough.

"Mrs. Squills spoke yesterevening of George meeting *a friend* out by the stables," she went on, turning toward Horace, who now stood a little behind the physician and the college president in the doorway. "Horace, you walked with George from the inn after he so very kindly saw to my lodging . . ."

In a stifled voice, Horace said, "We—George and I—parted between Massachusetts Hall and the brewhouse. I-I did warn him 'twas nearly nine, and he said he'd not be late."

And quietly, Weyountah added, with a warning glance toward Perry and President Langdon, "George had many *friends*. If he . . ."

Voices raised in the staircase outside, followed immediately by a thumping on the outer door. "Dr. Perry, sir—!"

At the same moment, Abigail became aware of voices in the quadrangle below.

Going to the window, she saw Pugh's tall, skinny follower Lowth slumped unconscious beside the door of the staircase, with two of his companions bending over him. Another young man lay on the ground, surrounded by his friends, a short distance away. She turned back as the excited young Mr. Yeovil burst into the study, crying, "Dr. Perry, Dr. Perry, they've been poisoned!"

Mr. Ryland, hard on his heels, added, "Dr. Perry, there's something very strange going on . . ."

Sheriff Congreve led Diomede away to the town jail while everyone piled and crowded after the stricken scholars as they were carried into the parlor of Massachusetts Hall. Since one of them was Mr. Lowth, Pugh and Jasmine Blossom had apparently lost any interest in guarding the staircase; even as she turned from the window, Abigail heard some of them coming up the stairs. *They'll trample over the room like cattle . . .*

She dropped behind as Langdon and Perry followed everyone out, then quickly turned down counterpane and sheet—she'd heard both John and her friend Joseph Warren speak of doing this with the victims of murder, and it made good sense to her— and caught up the paper knife, intending to compare the width of its blade with the size of the wounds. But as she turned back, she stopped, stood for a moment, and looked down into George's face: that young man she'd met but yesterday, that *personable young gentleman*, as Diomede had called him, who had talked of men as he'd found them, who'd never been able to tell Ajax son of Telamon from Ajax son of the other fellow, who'd come running from an assignation with a willing wench to make sure she, Abigail, was housed in the best inn of the town . . .

Someone killed him, she thought, and her throat tightened suddenly, her eyes flooded with tears. The slight changes of mortality had already taken hold, so that his face was not so disturbing as a man's new-dead. Her uneasy horror was gone, leaving only memory and pity.

Someone stabbed him, ended his life at the age of—what? Twenty-one? Twenty-two? With all the world before him . . .

Feet in the stairway; voices in the chamber.

What was it the Romans said? *Ultio prima, secundae lacrimae.* Vengeance first, then tears . . .

No, she corrected herself, as she laid the blade against that strangely ivory-colored flesh. *'Tis not vengeance I seek but salvation for the man who didn't do this crime . . .*

All four of the wounds looked a good half-inch wider than the width of the blade.

Swiftly, Abigail pulled down the young man's nightshirt, drew up the coverlet, even as she heard the doctor's voice cry angrily in the staircase, "Here, this won't do!" She dunked her handkerchief in the water-pitcher and was wiping the last traces of blood from her fingers when Joseph Ryland came in.

"Are you finished here, Mrs. Adams? Dr. Perry has sent for a litter to carry poor George's body to the infirmary—"

"What happened out there?"

The bachelor-fellow shook his head. "Lowth was suddenly taken queer, he said, and slumped down as if he'd been shot. In the next second Mosson went down, too—Waller and Blossom said they were feeling queer . . ."

Abigail stared at him for a moment, then said, "Oh, those wretches!" and dashed past him and out into the study.

The cut-glass rum-bottle that had stood next to Diomede's bloodstained pallet had been tucked unobtrusively behind a chair. It was empty.

"And it serves them right!" she exclaimed. "Only now of course there's no way of proving it—"

"Poison?" Ryland followed her, brow drawn down half in consternation, half in disbelief. "How could—?"

"*I have drugged their possets*, Lady Macbeth says." Abigail sniffed at the carafe, but could smell only the overwhelming reek of rum. "More likely laudanum than poison—"

"Meant for George?"

"Those idiots," said Weyountah, going to the window— meaning, Abigail guessed, Lowth and Jasmine and Waller and Mosson who'd thought it was so clever to sneak an extra drink while everyone was milling about . . . "'Twould serve them well if it *were* poison."

Ryland and Abigail—carafe in hand—were already hurrying down the stairs.

In the parlor where Abigail had waited last night for young Fairfield, dark little Mr. Blossom was being plied with hot coffee while half-a-dozen masters and students were trying to revive Lowth and Mosson. The smell of burnt feathers and panic filled the air. "They've been poisoned!" cried Mr. Yeovil again, and Pugh shouted to a little freshman named Pinkstone—presumably, thought Abigail, his own luckless "fag"—to run fetch coffee from his own room, which was on the staircase of the new hall directly across the quadrangle from that of Fairfield, Weyountah, and Horace.

"They have not," retorted Abigail, entering hard upon this line. "Mr. Blossom, did you drink the rum in the carafe in George's room? I thought so. Mr. Waller?" A tall young man with a long, horsey face—sitting with his head between his knees in a circle of frightened acquaintances—jerked upright shakily and gazed at her with pupils narrowed to pinpricks, even in the gloom of the parlor.

"I did, too—" gasped another young man in a green robe. "I-I feel so queer . . ."

"I'm sure you do," returned Abigail briskly. "There was laudanum in the rum, which would amply account for poor Diomede not waking up—"

"And for poor George—" cried someone else.

"The blackguard!" exclaimed another young gentleman. "To poison his master, then drink himself stupid in celebration—"

"Nonsense!" snapped Abigail, taken aback by this interpretation of her evidence. "Fairfield was stabbed, for one thing, and for another, a killer would have to be stupid to take a drug like that before even getting out of the room—"

"It's exactly what that nigger of mine would do," remarked Pugh, straightening up from beside the pile of coats where Lowth lay. "Only he'd probably drink off half the rum before drugging it, to give himself a little Dutch courage—" He put his hands on his hips, regarded Abigail's openmouthed indignation with some amusement. "They don't think the way white people do, m'am," he said. "You ask any man who's grown up among 'em as I have. They don't look ahead—not two minutes, not two feet. Like dealing with a lot of four-year-olds."

"That's ridiculous!"

Pugh raised one eyebrow. "Got a lot of 'em in Boston, have you, m'am, to know 'em so well?"

And a man with the accent of the Carolinas affirmed, "Ours sure don't think before they act."

As she looked from face to face, Abigail was shocked to observe how many of these young men were nodding—some of them unwillingly, but accepting the judgment as it stood. Someone said, "Poor old George!" and someone else, "My Aunt Caro was killed by a nigger maid—"

"And what do you expect," demanded Dr. Langdon, rising from beside Dr. Perry where both men had knelt beside the vaguely stirring Mr. Mosson, "when you have grown up in an atmosphere envenomed by the vice of slavery? When a poor Negro is driven to desperation by the ill-treatment of a vicious master—"

"Aunt Abigail—"

She was opening her mouth, breathless with anger at these assumptions about Diomede and anyone else of African descent, when Horace quietly touched her elbow.

"Aunt Abigail, I'm sorry, but . . . there is something missing from George's room. Two books," he said.

Six

"I'm afraid they were not terribly edifying volumes." Horace shyly pushed up his spectacles more firmly onto the bridge of his nose. "I only took note of them because—"

"You needn't explain," said Abigail kindly. The poor boy was only barely seventeen, and she recalled what her brother William had been like at . . . well, considerably younger than that. "And if they were as unedifying as all that, they might very well have gone the way of the rum." She glanced back over her shoulder as they emerged from the parlor into the open quadrangle and reentered the hallway to mount Horace's staircase. Even in here, Dr. Langdon's thundering peroration on why Diomede must have done murder because of his degradation under slavery could be heard with damning clarity. "What were they?"

"Aretino's *I Modi*, with the—er—illustrations by Raimondi," stammered Horace. "And Brantôme's *Les Vies des Dames Galantes*. Also illustrated." His blush went from his hairline down under his neckcloth. Abigail thought his ears were going to catch fire. He must have looked over Fairfield's shoulder at the illustrations, if no more. "And I don't think they could have been sneaked out of the room by anyone in the crowd this morning. Weyountah was in the bedchamber with George the whole time."

"Did he keep them in there?"

Horace nodded. "The desk has a false bottom in it," he said simply.

And Weyountah explained, "There are no locks on the doors of the chambers, so people are always pilfering things. Nothing big—there's not a man among us who would steal his neighbor's money—but if a man has tea, or coffee beans, or has just had a package from home with something sweet in it, he's likely to come back to his room and find less of it than there was when he went out. Of course no one is permitted spirits, so no one can report it if he comes back and finds his rum has been watered—"

"It's one reason, I think, that seniors let us fags study in their rooms," put in Horace. "So someone will be there, should they have something they'd rather didn't disappear— though in truth, Aunt Abigail, it isn't the nest of thieves we must sound like. For one thing, most of us are in the same lectures at the same times—"

"And for another," added Weyountah, as they approached the staircase, "everybody gets to know everything, pretty much, and if someone goes about pocketing coffee beans, it doesn't remain a secret for long."

They stopped at the foot of the staircase door to let a small procession descend. Mr. Ryland, his faded crimson gown giving him the archaic look of a priest, walked ahead; behind him, four college servants in rough tweeds carried a stretcher covered with the blankets that Abigail recognized from George Fairfield's bed. She moved to put her arm around Horace's waist in comfort, then restrained herself, recalling that Ryland was the Fellow in charge of the Hall. No sense having the poor boy fined four shillings on top of everything else.

"Will Dr. Langdon write to George's father?" she asked softly.

Horace nodded, unable to speak, and Weyountah said, "I imagine so, yes."

"Do either of you know the man? Or does Mr. Ryland?"

They looked at one another, shook their heads. "Only from hearing George speak of him," said the Indian. "He'll be coming, I'm sure, to—to take George home . . ."

"And to deal with Diomede?"

She could tell by their faces that this aspect of the situation had only begun to surface through shock and grief.

Horace said, "Oh, dear—"

And Weyountah, "Oh, Christ."

"*Dear Mr. Fairfield,*" said Abigail drily. "*I regret to inform you that your son's valet has murdered your son in a fit of drunken rage over his enslaved condition, which is no more than is to be expected. Shame on you for transforming him into a man so degraded as to do the deed, and it serves you right that he did. Please come and have him picked up for trial before the Virginia courts.* What is the penalty for a slave who kills his master, in Virginia? Hanging? And how likely is it that he'll receive even a hearing, let alone a trial?"

"Negligible," said Weyountah softly. "And no, it's not hanging. It's burning at the stake. When will Mr. Adams return from Maine?"

"Friday," said Abigail. "Possibly Saturday, though there's talk of him going down to Providence next week. I expect they'll hold Diomede here for Mr. Fairfield's arrival, rather than try him under Massachusetts law, which means that no matter how many affidavits we can collect attesting his innocence, he shall still face judgment entirely at the hands of a father mourning the loss of his only son and men who have spent the whole of their lives watching for the slightest signs of defiance and murder in their slaves."

"Can Mr. Adams have the trial moved here?" With a swift and rather guilty glance about them, to make sure that Mr. Ryland and his party were out of the hall, Weyountah led the way up the staircase again. "How would one go about that? Petition the Governor?"

"'Tis what I'll try," said Abigail grimly. "John hates the man, but the one time I've met him, His Excellency seemed kindly and well-disposed. I've heard nothing personal against him, save that he's a self-serving blockhead who gives all colonial offices and perquisites to his family and friends, and any man might do that. Even one who has written to the King advising that the harshest measures be taken against the colony for our disobedient persistence in wanting to have the rights accorded to the meanest ditchdigger in a British parish.

"The problem is," she added, as they slipped through the oak door and stood in the tiny study again, the stink of blood and rum very strong now in the close room. "The problem is, 'twill be difficult to convince His Excellency or anyone that murder—sufficiently premeditated to entail the drugging of a servant—was done for a couple of pornographic books. It seems a small matter to be the worth of a man's life."

"Think you so, m'am?" Weyountah, kneeling beside the rumpled and blood-smudged pallet that still lay along one wall of the study, looked up, his dark eyes somber. "My grandparents were killed, and three of my aunts, because a band of Massachusetts militiamen took the wrong path in the woods one day on their way to avenge the killing of four cows and a herdsman by the men of a Pocasset village that they couldn't manage to locate. Such was their desire for vengeance, however, that they followed the path, *knowing themselves to be lost*, and burned the village that they found at the end of it, though they *knew* that they'd come upon Narragansetts rather than Pocassets. About twenty people were killed—men, women, and children who had no more to do with the original cow-killing than had the islanders of Oatahite. My mother only escaped because she was down at the creek catching fish that afternoon. She was ten."

Abigail was silent, looking down at that young man, in his faded blue scholar's gown and his trim, dark, threadbare suit. The blood on the sheets nearby seemed to mutter and whisper of the violence done in the room beyond: that someone had considered something worth not only the life of George Fairfield but of his slave also . . .

But ten years of talking over John's cases with him had told her—if a childhood listening to the sins and enormities of an isolated New England village had not—that men walked the earth to whom the avoidance of inconvenience or embarrassment was sufficient justification for taking another man's life.

"Would a student caught breaking into another man's room stand in danger of being sent down?" she asked. "Particularly at night—"

"Absolutely."

"*Sine dubium.* The thing is," went on Horace diffidently, as he followed Abigail and Weyountah—rather white-faced but resolute—into the bedchamber beyond. "The thing is, George had only just gotten those books . . . what was it, Weyountah? Two weeks ago?"

"Exactly two weeks." Weyountah removed the stacked papers from the desk, handed them to Horace, his movements swift as if the two of them worked underwater, with only limited time available in the room that stank of their friend's lifeblood soaked into the mattress of the bed. "The twelfth of April. He kept them in here."

He opened the desk, revealing the shallow compartment inside empty of everything save a few sheets of paper and some broken quills.

"Was there usually more in here?" Abigail inquired. It looked nothing like John's neat desk at home, but then, Fairfield had not impressed her as a scholar.

"I think so," said Horace, his arms filled with papers, books, and Greek and Latin lexicons. "But I usually worked in the front room, not in here. The college provosts will sometimes search the rooms—I know Pugh pays the ones over in Harvard Hall and the Fellow in charge of the hall as well not to touch his—and last term Jasmine tried to blackmail George over some love-letters a girl had written to him . . . that's when he started keeping everything hidden in this desk."

Weyountah hooked his finger into an almost-invisible hole at one side of the desk's interior and lifted out the false bottom to reveal a second compartment beneath. This contained a vast rummage of disordered papers: bills—from tailors, bootmakers, the college stables for feed—mixed with letters and notes. Abigail picked one up, *Deerst Geo Ill bee back of the brewhous tonight dreemin of you ellie* . . . There was also a small sack of coffee beans and a flask of rum. "He kept the books in there," said Horace. "I know, because I came in yesterday morning earlier than he'd counted on, and he had the desk open and was looking at them—" Color crept up into his face again and faded almost at once, as he remembered not the pictures in the book, but the nearness of his friend who would never ogle questionable pictures again. After a moment he swallowed hard and went on, "And the same woman who sold them to him, sold me four books in Arabic."

* * *

Her name, said Horace—over a breakfast of Mrs. Squills's sausage and corn-cakes at the Golden Stair some half hour later—was Mrs. Seckar. "Her husband held the Vassall Professorship of Religion for about a hundred years," explained the boy. "He was very much a disciple of John Calvin and would hear of no innovation in the teaching of his master—"

"He was a pride-sick old bigot." Weyountah poured out coffee for himself and Abigail from a yellow pottery pitcher, while Horace sipped the mild tisane of honey, mint, and water that was all his fragile digestion would tolerate. "Cruel, too. He led his poor wife a frightful life, then left the house and bulk of his estate to fund a position here at Harvard. She was selling the books—which were hers—in order to have a little money to take with her when she went to live with her cousins in Medfield."

"The one Mr. Fairfield spoke of," said Abigail thoughtfully. "And she had books in Arabic? Not to mention volumes like the *Vies des Dames Galantes*?"

"Mrs. Seckar said they had probably been her great-grandfather's," explained the Indian. "I bought two texts in chemistry, though they're fearfully out of date—the most recent was Willis's *Pharmaceutice Rationalis*, 1674—and what I think was someone's journal, which contained tables of astronomical observations and several pages of various methods of calculating sidereal time. One passage was translated from al-Farghani—an Arabic scholar nearly a thousand years ago—and I think in the chemical sections there were translations from al-Jildaki, who was one of the early Mohammedan scholars of the discipline."

"The four I bought weren't anywhere near that erudite,"

admitted Horace. "I had an edition of the Alexander Legend, Ibn-Battuta's travel narratives, a commentary on the Koran, and a book about horse-doctoring."

"So obviously, Mrs. Seckar's ancestor was the last Arabic scholar in this colony . . . How long ago? Fifty years? Sixty years?"

"Longer," said Weyountah. "Mrs. Seckar must be in her seventies. The Reverend Seckar was eighty-five, but up to the day he died he'd walk from their house on the Watertown Road to the chapel"—he nodded in the direction of the Common and the college—"to supervise prayers."

"To make sure nobody strayed from the Master's doctrines by so much as an inch, you mean," put in Horace, devouring his fifth corn-cake. "Please don't get me wrong, Aunt Abigail," he added earnestly. "I understand the need for correct understanding of the Will of God, and I know that disregard of intellectual distinctions can result in some quite frightful misunderstandings of our own unworthiness to have received salvation that lies beyond our desserts . . . but I also think that no sin lies in sweetening the lesson."

"You're saying he was a trifle dry?" She hid her smile.

"Horace is saying the Reverend Seckar was long-winded, doctrinaire, and intrusive into matters that seemed to me no part of the Church's business."

"That was his point," said Horace apologetically. "That everything in life is God's business, in that it glorifies or affronts God. He abused poor Ryland like a pickpocket at the merest hint of Arminianism—"

"Is Mr. Ryland an Arminian?" Somehow she could believe it of that grave young man, that he could not endure the belief that a man's good deeds would not suffice to bend the will of an angry God.

"He claims not to be. Of course, the Reverend Seckar would say—"

"I think his quarrel with Ryland," put in the Indian, "was as much about Ryland taking a stipend from the Governor to support him here as it was about Free Will. Seckar never forgave Governor Hutchinson for being descended from a heretic. And the fact that Mrs. Seckar had four books in Arabic in her great-grandfather's collection doesn't mean that the other books she sold at the same time contained something that could have gotten the Governor of Jamaica hanged for treason, Arabic or not . . ."

"No," admitted Abigail. "But the coincidence of a murder, an attempted murder, and the disappearance of antique books from the murdered man's rooms all within a week makes me extremely curious to have a few words with Mrs. Seckar about what other books Great-Grandpa's collection might have contained."

From Mrs. Squills, Abigail borrowed pen and paper, and wrote a note to Mrs. Seckar in Medfield ("She's gone to live with cousins, poor lady, the Barlows, at Rock Farm out nearer Stonton than Medfield . . ." Mrs. Squills provided), asking the favor of an interview at her earliest convenience. After a moment's thought, she composed another, to Governor Hutchinson, and a third note, more brief than the others, she sent by way of Mrs. Squills's niece to a Mr. Metcalfe, who lived in Cambridge and whose most recent fines for infractions of the Navigation Acts John had been instrumental in having dismissed. Had she not done so, she feared that Weyountah and Horace would beggar themselves of candle-and-food money to rent her a chaise to return to Boston in.

While waiting for Mr. Metcalfe's reply—he had assured John on the occasion of their last meeting that *any help I can be, to you or any of yours*—Abigail walked from the Golden

Stair to the town jail, only to be told by Sheriff Congreve that Diomede, still half-stupefied, had slipped back into a heavy sleep. She gave the sheriff most of her slender pocket money to provide food for the prisoner and, returning to the inn, made arrangements with Mrs. Squills to send bread, cheese, and cider to him over the course of the following days.

"Last night you spoke of poor Mr. Fairfield meeting a young friend out near the college barns," she said, when these negotiations were satisfactorily concluded. "You wouldn't happen to know her name, would you?"

And Mrs. Squills laughed. "Lord love you, Mrs. Adams, that's like putting a name on one of those butterflies out there." She gestured toward the kitchen door, beyond which lay her vegetable garden and a rather weedy border of penstemon, buttercups, and wild roses just coming into bloom. "Poor Mr. George had a dozen of them, for all he was practically engaged to Miss Sally Woodleigh. I think my Ginny broke her heart for him," she added, in a quieter voice, "not that I'd ever let her go meeting him or any man living out behind the college hay-barn . . . But it goes to show."

The tiny landlady shook her head sadly. "He hadn't an ounce of vice in him, you know, Mrs. Adams. Please don't think so. And he'd never have harmed a soul. But he was like a walking sprig of catnip, and that's the truth."

"Had he enemies?" In addition to the marketing basket she'd arrived with, Abigail now carried a small satchel belonging to Horace, into which they had crammed the papers, bills, and letters that had cluttered the hidden compartment of George Fairfield's desk. "Barring the sweethearts of his lady friends, that is." Dozens of the letters in the satchel were love-notes in a score of different hands, and in the pocket of George's gold-laced gray coat—which had lain, tossed down with his ruffled shirt and his breeches, on the floor where he'd dropped them—she had found a small packet of them, along with a note in a delicate hand saying, *As you love me, be behind the barn at midnight* . . .

"Well—" Mrs. Squills frowned, as if speaking against her will. "He was a Tory, when all's said—though I like to think it was just a boy's fancy, because he was raised that way, you know. He'd have gotten over it." She sighed, and Abigail guessed that the local beauties weren't the only ones who'd fallen for George Fairfield's easy charm. "But most of the men at the college, they're all for our liberties and will be slaves to no man, nor no King either. And yes, sometimes there was bad feeling over that, and once or twice I understand it came to blows, though never here. I stand for nothing like that in my place." (There was a Mr. Squills, stout and ox-eyed, fussing about in the kitchen, but Abigail was under no illusions about whose *place* the Golden Stair was.)

"But that sort of thing, 'tisn't the sort of thing one kills over."

Isn't it? Mr. Metcalfe's chaise drew up before the door, and Horace and Weyountah—appearing in their college gowns with a bulky parcel for her—helped Mr. Metcalfe's young groom fasten satchel and parcel onto the back. Promises were exchanged to lose no time in searching the countryside round for the house to which Horace had been taken, for a dark-haired woman of respectable appearance, for anyone who might have been called George's enemy . . . Promises to visit Diomede and make sure he had food and a blanket, to write to Mr. Fairfield protesting his innocence . . .

'Tisn't the sort of thing one kills over, reflected Abigail, as the chaise pulled away.

Only wasn't the formation of the King's Own Volunteers— a fighting-force of the young men of the district loyal to the King—preparation to do exactly that?

Kill all men who would take up arms against the King in defense of their own liberties?

Was there not every chance that the King's ship, when it made landfall in Boston, would be carrying troops with precisely that mandate? To arrest—and kill if necessary—those whose politics differed from those of the King? *Including Cousin Sam*, she thought, her heartbeat quickening unpleasantly. *And maybe John . . .*

No. She thrust the thought aside. John had never involved himself with the Sons of Liberty—not much, anyway. She leaned back in the seat, and thought about the paper-wrapped parcel the boys had given her, and Horace's worn satchel with its muddle of love-notes and who-knows-what that George hadn't wanted prying eyes to see. *A personable young gentleman . . . widely known from here to Medford . . . always invited to this house or that . . .*

Politics, passion, and mysterious ciphers written in Arabic . . .

And none of them, reflected Abigail—gazing out between the horse's ears at the bright dapple of sunshine on the shaded road, the peaceful countryside of stone walls, prosperous farmhouses, hay, and corn—none of them sufficient reason to save a man's life from those who had decided beforehand that he must be guilty.

Abigail's uncle Isaac Smith dwelled on Milk Street in a house that wouldn't have looked out of place in London. He was one of the wealthiest shipowners in the colony, and his dwelling had its own stables, half-a-dozen apple trees, and gardens stretching back to join the open fields of the Summer Street Ward. Charley and Tommy—held severely to their good manners by Aunt Eliza and Pattie—were ushered into the parlor in a scrubbed and polite condition that made Abigail's heart glow with pride. "I am covered in abnegation," she said, stretching out her hand to her aunt. "And to you, Pattie, I owe you a thousand apologies. What must you think of me—?"

"I think you're a good lady who got talking too much to her nephew in Cambridge," retorted Aunt Eliza good-naturedly, "and ended up standing on the wharf watching the ferry pull away, like nobody ever has in the history of the world—"

"I promise you, Aunt, the horse picked up a stone—"

"Oh, aye, and there was an earthquake and an Indian attack . . ."

All three women laughed. "They were honestly no trouble," said Pattie, with a slightly nervous glance at Aunt Eliza, who was, after all, a well-off lady and might take exception to a servant entering into a conversation uninvited.

"Lord, no," chuckled Elizabeth Smith. "Johnny and Nabby went off to school this morning, good as gold. I'll send them on to you when they come back, unless you'd care to stay for dinner . . . You're sure? Let me at least have Cuffee carry that package of yours, then—"

Cuffee was one of the Smith household slaves. Virginians—and the sons of West Indian merchants like Mr. Pugh—weren't the only ones in the Americas to hold black men in servitude.

"'Tis only a few books, not a bale of hay!"

It was, in fact, seven books: rather large, heavy, and old, their thick leather covers smelling of mildew and smoke. As Weyountah had remarked, there was no reason for Abigail to think that George Fairfield's murder had had the slightest thing to do with the books he'd bought from Narcissa Seckar—there were plenty of other reasons someone might have wanted to make away with a young Tory captain of militia who had apparently tupped every woman in Middle-sex County. Considering the content of the missing volumes and the presence of young men like St-John Pugh in the vicinity, their disappearance last night from George Fair-field's room might have had nothing to do with their new owner's murder.

And the fact that part of the original collection had been in Arabic only coincidence.

But she had felt better, knowing that the books would not be in Horace's room that night.

Seven

Midmorning Thursday brought a note from Governor Hutchinson.

My dear Mrs. Adams,

I well remember our brief meeting and the kindly concern that you showed for an unfortunate stranger whom Fate had brought beneath my roof. Please do attend me this afternoon following dinner, and I will do what I can for you. If as you say the matter is 'not one of politics,' it will be a most welcome relief at the present moment.

Sincerely,
Thos. Hutchinson

Abigail suspected that had she not included, in her request for a few minutes of Hutchinson's time, the reassurance that her visit was not a political one, the reply would have been merely, *Send a petition to my secretary* . . .

And so it might prove, she reflected, glancing through the kitchen windows at the angle of sunlight in the little yard. Pattie was emptying the mop-water into the gutter of the little alley that connected the yard with Queen Street—it was shocking how quickly street-dust and the general griminess of town living accumulated in a house, even with only two days of not being mopped. Abigail ticked off tasks in her mind as she tucked the note behind the household tablet on the big oak sideboard: butter to be churned—thank Heavens Their Majesties Cleopatra and Semiramis were producing milk again after the winter's drought!—lamps to be cleaned and set ready for evening, dinner to be started, mending . . . And all before she could justify to herself even touching that satchel full of young Mr. Fairfield's papers.

The "worthies" of Boston ate their dinners later than workingmen and the wives of peripatetic lawyers, so probably she could walk to Marlborough Street at six and find His Excellency back in his office . . .

Oh, drat it, the bread needs to be got up . . .

My dear Mrs. Adams sounded promising, however. From a drawer in the sideboard, Abigail pulled out a piece of paper, then—considering its rough yellow surface—replaced it. When Pattie—fourteen years old, brisk, and pretty, the dark-haired daughter of one of their neighbors on the farm back in Braintree had lived almost as a daughter in the Adams household for over a year— came back in and hung the mop-bucket in its place by the back door, Abigail said, "Would you scald the dasher and the churn for me, dear? But do *not* get the butter started—I won't have you doing my work for me; you've enough to do on your own . . . Yes, my darling," she added as Charley—just a few weeks short of four years old and filled with resentment that he no longer had Uncle Isaac's garden to play in—"I'm sorry you can't go back to Aunt Eliza's, but you can't." She lifted Tommy as the younger boy held out his arms. Twenty months old, he had recently figured out how to untie his leading-strings from whatever piece of furniture he'd been fixed to and was running everywhere now with happy abandon and was going to get himself killed, Abigail reflected, before he reached his second birthday . . .

"I will be out in exactly two minutes— Yes, Charley, you can come with me . . ."

With the boys tugging at her skirts and at each other's, she went down the hall to John's study, sat the boys firmly on the chairs there (*For all the good that's like to do . . .*) and, on the fine smooth English legal paper from John's desk, wrote a quick précis of the events of Tuesday evening and yesterday: that George Fairfield, a scholar at Harvard, had been murdered in his room by person or persons unknown; that all evidence showed that his slave Diomede had been drugged; that items were missing from Fairfield's rooms that a robber could have taken; but that the Reverend Dr. Langdon (whom Abigail knew was no friend to Hutchinson) was stubbornly insisting that Diomede must be the culprit because as a slave he must have hated his master enough to do murder, despite all evidence to the contrary.

Without your assistance in the matter, the unfortunate Diomede will be returned to his master's father in Virginia and will surely suffer the extreme penalty for a crime of which he is almost certainly innocent. In the name of justice, sir, please consider either taking the necessary steps to have the case tried in the courts of Massachusetts, or at the very least, stay this unhappy man's deportation until some enquiry can be made into the actual circumstances of the event, for he surely can expect no justice once he leaves these shores. Yours sincerely, A. Adams.

And a blot, because Tommy, overwhelmed with the endless weight of enforced stillness, was moved to pull Charley's hair, setting off a train of circumstance that precipitated both boys against their mother's chair.

One day I am going to run off to the Maine Assizes myself and let John stay here and make butter . . .

Petition in hand and, for the sake of propriety (a convention she privately considered silly), escorted by her daughter Nabby, Abigail walked the quarter mile along Cornhill to Marlborough Street at six and presented the Governor's note to the Governor's butler at the handsome three-story brick mansion allotted by the colony to the representative of the Crown. *Just as well*, she thought, *that John IS away at the Assizes . . .* To her assertion a few months ago that she had never found His Excellency to be other than polite and considerate, John had simply roared, *And I suppose you'd think well of a WHOREMASTER who was polite to you?*

If he were not passionate, about politics as well as all other things, she supposed, he would not be John . . .

But it was best that she, and not he, was in charge of this particular portion of the effort to save an innocent man from death.

A dozen men—most of them well-off merchants, to judge by the quality of their clothing and wigs—occupied the chairs of the handsome tapestried parlor to which the butler showed her; the Governor's son-in-law Mr. Oliver got quickly to his feet and offered Abigail his chair, and a man whom she recognized as one of Uncle Isaac's extremely wealthy merchant rivals brought his own seat over for Nabby, who curtseyed her thanks in some confusion. At not quite nine, the plump, quiet girl was curious and a little proud to be taken out into company, but invariably shy once among strangers, and sat with hands folded in silence, wide blue eyes taking in the old-fashioned, elegant hangings and carved wainscot of the room. Abigail sent in her petition and took note of the men whom the Governor called in before her with abstract curiosity. She rated, evidently, below the merchants—who were probably relations of the Governor—but above the two she guessed were ship-captains.

Given that no one in Boston had the slightest idea what the King was going to rule appropriate punishment for the colony and the town, it was not surprising that His Excellency was being inundated with requests for audience, favors, and assurance of protection.

From her satchel she took the small packet of love-letters that had been in George Fairfield's pocket and glanced over them while she waited, as she would on another occasion have brought a book. Delicate and rather rounded handwriting, thin expensive French paper, passionate sentiments, a faint scent of attar of roses, and no signature. But obviously some wealthy man's daughter who had been taught, at least, to handle a pen.

"Mrs. Adams?" said the secretary from the inner door.

Governor Hutchinson—whom John habitually described as a *pusillanimous traitor*—was on his feet when Abigail came into his study, and himself held the chair for her when she sat.

"This sounds like a most serious matter, Mrs. Adams," he said in his soft voice, seating himself and touching the petition that lay before him on his desk. "And one in which there is certain to be some question from Governor Dunmore of Virginia, regarding the legality of distraining a man's property here in Massachusetts, should Mr. Fairfield, Senior, demand the slave Diomede's immediate return. Are you sure of what you contend, that the man was drugged and not merely drunk?"

"Two students who entered the room and—as young men will—drank off the rest of the rum in the carafe were rendered unconscious within minutes. Two others—I presume juniors who were only able to get a lesser share—were groggy and stumbling. No rum remained in the carafe, but I found the inference compelling."

"And the items removed from the room—?"

"Two old volumes, only recently acquired by Mr. Fairfield from a Mrs. Seckar."

The Governor's narrow face lightened: "Not old Professor Seckar's widow? Dear Heavens, if ever there was a man who would cut you to pieces over whether God's predetermination of the saved and the reprobate was active or passive—I remember that thundering lecture of his on infralapsarianism and the precise timing of the Fall of the Angels that went two hours over into the dinner hour, and all of us ready to tear apart the youngest freshman in the room and eat him, we were so hungry. Which I suppose," he added with a smile, "was proof in his eyes that we were none of us saved and all doomed to the eternal fires. But I thought he left the whole of his library to the college when he died?"

"I believe these volumes had come down to Mrs. Seckar from her grandfather."

"I wonder that—" He visibly bit back some epithet applicable to the Reverend Dr. Langdon, and continued, "I wonder that Dr. Langdon didn't insist on their inclusion in the bequest. That wouldn't be Barthelmy Whitehead, would it? By all accounts the man was practically illiterate, but with a heart like a counting-frame—one of the last men in the colony to attempt to sell Indians as slaves to the West Indies and one of the first to enter the Negro trade."

Abigail guessed that having written a history of the colony—his own troublesome ancestress having played no small part in it—the Governor was intimately acquainted with the affairs of every family from Cape Cod to Halifax.

"Perhaps Dr. Langdon did not consider them appropriate for inclusion in the College library," she replied. "I understand from my nephew—whom I was visiting in Cambridge on Tuesday night, when the crime took place—that they were of an *improper* nature."

"Ah." Hutchinson frowned. "Young men being what they are, that might account for their theft but surely not for murder being done over them."

"Among normal men, no, sir. But I'm sure Your Excellency is aware that where darkness corrodes a man's heart, even matters of insignificance become reasonable grounds for murder."

He shot her a sidelong glance—clearly thinking of Wily Cousin Sam—and murmured, "Just so."

"The circumstance of their theft so soon after their acquisition, and of poor Diomede—Mr. Fairfield's man—being drugged to prevent his waking during the theft, seem to me sufficient grounds to merit investigation, and intervention on your part to have the matter tried here in Massachusetts, where witnesses in the man's defense can be brought forward. Objectionable as the condition of slavery is, I do *not* see it as ipso facto proof of a slave's guilt in his master's murder when there are circumstances that so clearly point to another cause."

"I quite agree, Mrs. Adams. And yet, the law is established to defend a man's rights to his property, and I cannot subvert it—"

"The law is established, Your Excellency, to defend a man's *life*. And the slave Diomede's life will surely be forfeit if he is taken back to Virginia, for whatever witnesses can be found as to another motive for the murder will most likely not follow him there. In their absence, I very much fear that the courts—if a slave is even entitled to a hearing before Virginia courts—"

"He is," put in the Governor drily.

"I am thrilled to hear it," she returned. "But do you trust them? Do you trust them even to read the affidavits? Do you trust them not to take the simplest reading of the matter and avoid putting themselves to the inconvenience of delving for the truth? Would you wish to rely on such a court to defend your own life? Or the life of one of your sons?"

His thin lips pressed together—annoyed at her vehemence, she suspected, yet unable to refute her words. "I see what you mean, Mrs. Adams," he said at length. "Yet your position is based upon supposition, and your assumption of what a certain body of men *may* do or *might* do. Mine is based upon the law. It is beyond my power, as Governor of this colony, to abrogate the rights of property, particularly the rights of a citizen of another colony—and it is moreover quite properly beyond my power. Heaven forfend that a man should take a legal action based upon suspicion of what *might* be in another man's mind. Yet I shall certainly write to Mr. Congreve," he added, as Abigail opened her mouth to object, "that he is not to release this Negro man into the custody of Mr. Fairfield, Senior's, agents until he has communicated with me. I assume"—his voice thinned a little, like one forcing himself to be absolutely just—"that your husband will take it upon himself to defend this unfortunate valet?"

"He will."

"Then your best course of action—and his—will be to ascertain the facts of the case as quickly as possible, before communication from Virginia forces the issue one way or another. It will be at least two weeks, perhaps more, before Mr. Fairfield, Senior, arrives on these shores. With concrete evidence of a third person involved, I shall have more leverage against the law of property. Without it, I must yield. I hope you understand my position, madame?"

"I do." Abigail rose, and held out her hand. Her whole Christian soul revolted against what the Governor had said, and yet, as a lawyer's wife, she understood the principle from which he spoke. She forced back her temper, and said with an assumption of warmth that she barely felt, "And I thank you for what you can do, sir, and for what you are willing to do in this poor man's defense."

The Governor's slim fingers—cool and dry as a snake's back—closed around hers, and he led her to the door. "Mr. Oliver—?"

His secretary materialized, bowing, to conduct her out.

"Mrs. Adams!" Joseph Ryland got to his feet in surprise as she came back into the parlor, which was—despite the dimming of the daylight from the windows—more crowded than before. Nabby—to Abigail's approval—who had been about to leap to her feet and scamper to her mother's side, yielded at once to the dictum that the affairs of adults took precedence over the discomfort of eight-year-old girls abandoned in roomfuls of strangers, and settled back in her chair, grateful at least that her mother was in the range of her sight.

"Mr. Ryland." Abigail held out her hand, over which the young bachelor-fellow bowed. "Are you here also to speak to His Excellency on behalf of poor Diomede?"

He looked momentarily nonplussed. "Of course, I shall speak as to his innocence—"

"Not necessary," she assured him, a little drily. "Governor Hutchinson has agreed to intervene, insofar as the laws of *property* permit, to at least give us time to find the true culprit."

"I would have expected nothing less of the man." Ryland's shoulders relaxed, as if relieved of the weight of a water-yoke. "I know that your husband finds his politics objectionable." He spoke diffidently, but who in the colony wasn't aware—Abigail reflected—of the diatribes John had had printed, under his own name and pseudonyms like Novanglus and Mrs. Country Goodheart? "But in truth, m'am—as I'm sure you have learned, in even the briefest of encounters with him—that his nature is not only just, but generous and noble. Will your husband indeed take on poor Diomede's cause?"

"I shall see to it he does. But I did mean to ask you—"

He glanced around as another young man, trim and elegant in a suit of plum-colored velveteen, was shown into the parlor. "Mr. Ryland," the newcomer greeted him affably, casually handing off his hat to the secretary, and Ryland bowed.

"Mr. Heywood."

"Shocking business about poor old George, isn't it? So much for La Woodleigh's schemes to snabble his acres for her daughter—"

Abigail tardily identified La Woodleigh as the wife of Montgomery Woodleigh, who lived in Cambridge and owned five ships and considerable property in Boston.

"Anyone know if she's heard?"

"I myself informed Mrs. Woodleigh this morning." Spots of color appeared on Ryland's cheeks, and Mr. Heywood grinned.

"Not wasting a moment, are you, old boy? Going to get your bid in with the beautiful Sally?" But he laughed as he said it, as if he'd asked, did Mr. Ryland have plans to be crowned King of England in the near future? An absurdity, to think that a young Fellow of the College whose out-of-date coat was worn threadbare at the elbows and whose stockings showed neat mends above the re-dyed backs of his shoes would offer for the hand of a Woodleigh. Abigail felt a flush of anger rise along her neck, at his look of carefully controlled chagrin.

"More to the point," spoke up another young gentleman seated nearby—Abigail half recognized him as one of the younger Apthorps, whom she'd seen with his extremely wealthy parents at the Brattle Square Meeting-House—"d'you know when the Volunteers will be meeting, to select a new captain? I mean, we'll miss old George terribly and all that, but trouble could break out at any moment, you know. We can't be caught leaderless when it starts if we're to get any kind of preferment when the King sends in his regular troops."

"You sound very sure that he'll be sending troops, sir," said Abigail, and the young Apthorp rose to bow to her, Mr. Heywood acknowledging her with a deep salute as well.

"Mrs. Adams," introduced Ryland in a colorless voice. "Mr. Heywood, Mr. Apthorp."

She saw the glance that passed between them at her name.

"*Lieutenant* Apthorp, of the King's Own Volunteers . . ."

"If you'll excuse my saying so, m'am," replied Mr. Heywood politely, "the King can hardly do anything *but* send troops, you know. I mean, whatever is finally decided about colonists' rights and all that"—his gesture dismissed the question as if it were one of how many beads to pass along to the Indians—"Parliament isn't going to let itself be dictated to by a gang of hooligans dressed up as Mohawks. If you ask me, m'am, your husband and his friends did themselves a great disservice, resorting to violence that way. They're never going to get away with it."

"I'm not sure who you think my husband is," responded Abigail, "as there are a great many Adamses in Massachusetts—but if violence is not the answer, as you say, I don't entirely see how sending armed men into the situation is going to calm it. Surely—"

Young Mr. Oliver appeared in the doorway of the inner study. "Mr. Heywood?"

Mr. Apthorp went in with his friend; the secretary raised no objection. Nor, evidently, did the Governor, because the door remained closed.

Ryland turned back to his chair but waited until Abigail took the seat next to his before sitting down himself.

"And is Mr. Heywood a *lieutenant* also?"

A small sigh escaped his lips. "I had hoped—" he began, and then was silent.

Abigail said nothing, and in time, Ryland went on, with suppressed exasperation, "I shouldn't mind it, you know, if either of them had the slightest experience of arms or command—other than telling their grooms to saddle their horses, that is. George served in the Virginia militia; for my sins I volunteered, like the idiot boy I was, to join the King's forces when Pontiac and his Indians attacked in the west of Pennsylvania. I've *had* experience in war. And, His Excellency knows me. For six years I've worked in his library . . ."

He stopped himself again, and simply finished, "Well."

And you still ask why men in this colony find fault with Crown Governors who give positions of advantage only to those whose wealth will help them or to friends of the King? She didn't say it, but Ryland, looking at her face, must have seen the words there, for he sighed again, and said, "*Dura lex, sed lex . . .*"

"*The law is harsh, but it is the law,*" repeated Abigail softly.

"And things as they are, are harsh," said Ryland. "But the alternative—turning the country over to men who think the answer to a legal problem is the destruction of other men's property—is, I think, a solution worse than the problem."

He folded his hands and sat for a time looking at them. The Governor's butler came in with yet another petitioner and, as he passed Ryland's chair, nodded to the young man in a friendly way. She remembered someone saying yesterday— Weyountah?—that Mr. Ryland was one of the several young men whom Governor Hutchinson was sponsoring into Harvard, supporting not only the cost of their tuition and books, but in cases providing clothing and fuel in the cold New England winters as well. His faded green coat, with its old-fashioned, too-full skirts and threadbare cuffs, was of expensive wool and might well have belonged to the Governor himself ten or fifteen years ago. It was nothing a young man would buy for himself, even if he had the two or three pounds that such a garment would cost new.

At length he said, "I'm sorry, Mrs. Adams. There was something you wanted to ask of me, and I've let myself become distracted—"

"No, 'tis no matter." She put a hand briefly on his sleeve, and he raised his head a little, brown eyes meeting hers, then moving to the blue twilight beyond the windows. A servant came in with a taper and proceeded to light the candles in their holders all around the walls: beeswax and bayberry, not tallow, and all of them new. Abigail wondered what the Governor paid for lighting this great house, first and last, and if his half-burnt candles were passed along to his protégé?

"It is, though," he said. "And I see your very faithful and patient daughter is hoping that all of this will be over soon." He smiled at Nabby, which made Abigail smile in her turn.

"And so it will," said Abigail. "I wished only to ask you, Mr. Ryland . . . How difficult would it have been for someone to drug Diomede? To get into Mr. Fairfield's room, and to put laudanum into his rum? I think it must have been someone in the college, someone who knew the doors have no locks, who knew that Diomede was in the habit of sneaking his master's rum when Mr. Fairfield was out at night. Was Diomede generally in his master's rooms when his master was at lecture or in the library?"

Or meeting with "friends" behind the college barn—a practice which seems to have been common knowledge.

"Either there or close by," replied the young man. "Or Horace was there—doing George's work as well as his own, I fear." Disapproval deepened the lines at the corner of his mouth. "Two years ago—not long after the Volunteers were formed—Fairfield's rooms were vandalized: books torn up, clothing and bedding defiled. No one was ever punished for it."

Given Dr. Langdon's political views, this didn't surprise Abigail, but something inside her cringed. Though in principle she understood it when Sam said that the King and his minions would not pay attention to mere words, still she sensed that this kind of random violence did their cause no good, particularly with men such as Joseph Ryland.

"Surely students—" she began.

"It wouldn't have to be a student," said Ryland. "Laundresses, scullions, the cooks who work in the Hall . . . everyone knows everything in Cambridge. I daresay the Sons of Liberty know which staircase George lived on, and when he came and went." Bitterness tightened his voice like alum, and it occurred to Abigail to wonder what challenges and indignities this young man had encountered, both as a freshman and later, in a college population three-quarters or more given to the cause of the colonists. Every man in Harvard, practically, had been reading the broadsides John and Sam and Josiah Quincy had written denouncing his patron's venality and pigheadedness: who was it who had said that old Professor Seckar had abused him more for being Hutchinson's protégé than for his own—admittedly variant—views on a mere man's ability to alter by any human deed the abiding judgment of the Lord?

"Surely you don't think it was the Sons of Liberty who killed him?"

"Can you doubt it?"

"I've never heard that they sink to murder—"

"Have you ever seen a man who has been tarred and feathered, m'am?" The young man's voice dropped and his glance touched Nabby—engaged in a shy conversation about her schooling with a stout and fatherly merchant—then passed to his patron's shut office door. "Have you ever been there the next day, when his family and his doctor are trying to pull cold tar off his skin? Or the day after that, when the raw flesh suppurates? The mob covers their victim in feathers to make him look ridiculous, so that the onlookers don't fully realize what is being done in the name of this 'liberty' they're proclaiming . . . So those who hear about it think the object is to make a man look foolish, rather than to kill him in great agony and to terrorize the onlookers into acquiescence."

Abigail was silent, knowing what he said to be true. Then after a time she replied, "But the actions of the mob in no way alter the question of whether Englishmen here deserve the same rights that Englishmen deserve of Parliament and King."

"Perhaps they do not," replied Ryland. "Yet 'tis said, *He who sups with the Devil needs a long spoon.* However Mr. Sam Adams, and men like Josiah Quincy and Dr. Warren, may defend the question of their rights, they'll find themselves treated like savages if they employ savages to frighten those who oppose them. And, I think, rightly so, for there is no way of knowing when those savages may choose to take matters into their own hands."

Behind him, the study door opened and Messrs Heywood

and Apthorp emerged, joking and waving behind them to
Governor Hutchinson. Mr. Oliver said, "Mr. Brattle—" and
the stout merchant who had been talking with Nabby bade
her a courteous farewell and went in. Abigail rose, tucked
the collection of love-letters back into her satchel, and found
a silver bit in her pocket to tip the footman who had taken
charge of her lantern—congratulating herself on her fore-
thought as to how long she might have to wait for an
interview—and Ryland stood also, to shake her hand.

"Mrs. Adams, please forgive me if I've spoken too
vehemently—"

"You have said nothing untrue," she responded. Certainly
the men who'd gutted and looted the Governor's house nine
years ago—destroying much of his precious collection of
manuscripts—had acted far beyond Sam's intention. "And no
fault lies in vehemence of sentiment. 'Tis our actions by
which we are judged." She added, "Good luck, in the matter
of the Volunteers."

He managed a wooden grin. "Thank you for your good
wishes, m'am. I expect I shall continue as company sergeant—
the position I held under Captain Fairfield—and I can do a
great deal there in making sure that the Volunteers are fit to
fight. Because you were quite right in your observation to Mr.
Heywood: the infusion of armed men into a situation that
has already turned violent will beget still more violence. And
it is our duty, as subjects of the King, to keep matters from
degenerating to such a pass that the French or the Spanish
think themselves safe to come in and take over these colonies
for themselves in the chaos that will follow."

The butler entered again and in the hallway handed Abigail her lantern, the candle lighted already and shedding a
wan glow barely stronger than that of a couple of fireflies.
Abigail was glad that the way home led through familiar

streets and wasn't a long one. As the servant showed mother and daughter from the room, Abigail looked back over her shoulder to see Mr. Ryland patiently waiting, while Mr. Brattle emerged from the Governor's study and another wealthy merchant in a bottle green coat was shown in, in his stead.

Eight

"What did you make of the books, Sam?" inquired Abigail, when Surry—the slave-woman who was the sole remnant, along with the ramshackle old house itself, of the modest fortune old Deacon Adams had passed along to his son Sam—showed her into Sam's book-room the following morning.

Sam Adams looked as if he might have protested that he would never have been so impertinent as to pry into volumes left in his charge by his cousin's wife, then grinned, held Abigail's chair for her, and went to the secret panel to get the books. Upon her arrival in Boston from Cambridge late on Wednesday afternoon, Abigail had taken the seven volumes straight to Sam's old yellow house on Purchase Street. Though John's clerk—Horace's and Abigail's cousin—Thaxter had been for some months now living under the Adams roof, Abigail still felt sufficiently uneasy about George Fairfield's murder to want to get the volumes out of her own hands as quickly as possible.

Ryland might say what he chose about the Sons of Liberty—and might indeed, she reflected uneasily, be right—but the coincidence of there being *two* sources of Arabic documents in the colony within the past two weeks was a trifle difficult to swallow.

Besides, Sam was the only person she knew positively had secret panels in his house. Cellar to attic, there was probably enough treasonable material cached here and there—books, pamphlets, correspondence with the Crown's opponents in other colonies, and the true names of a hundred authors of sedition—to blow the roof off the Houses of Parliament. She guessed the hidden compartment beside the mantel in his book-room was one of a dozen.

"Not a solitary thing." Sam set the books carefully on the desk between them: a folio edition, four quarto-sized volumes, and two octavos, their leather bindings cracked, age-dark, and bearing signs of having been gnawed by mice. "Three of the Arabic volumes bear the imprint of the Medici Press in Rome. I had no idea typefaces existed in Arabic—I assume for the benefit of Christians in the Turkish Empire. We would have to have Dr. Warren"—he named a mutual friend and fellow member of the Sons of Liberty—"pass judgment on the chemistry and astronomy texts, but they must be shockingly outdated."

He passed his big, square hand gently over the cover of the folio, and Abigail remembered that in his youth, Sam Adams had also been a student at Harvard and had acquired there—along with a taste for fiery politics and the Rights of Man—the fascination with books shared by so many questing minds.

"Where did you come by them?"

"My nephew Horace purchased the Arabic texts from a woman named Narcissa Seckar," began Abigail.

"Good lord, not old Malachi Seckar's wife? I can't imagine

the old boy letting his wife sell so much as the kitchen drippings without his permission—"

"He didn't." Abigail gingerly opened one of the quartos, studied the curious loops and squiggles that surrounded a woodcut of a horse's backside, elaborately detailed. Presumably not the legend of Alexander. "She sold these upon his death—I understand, in order to get money to live on, her husband having bequeathed everything else he owned to the College."

"That sounds like the old—er—gentleman. Everything?" Sam's square, friendly face clouded. "She should have sued. John would have pried a living out of the College for her—"

"Indeed he would have. Just as well he knew nothing of it, for we'd probably have had to send Johnny to Princeton rather than Harvard as a result. In any case, these were hers—or rather, her grandfather's—"

"Wasn't he a pirate or something?"

It was Abigail's turn to startle. "Not to my knowledge. According to Governor Hutchinson—whom I called upon last night for a perfectly legitimate reason," she added, as Sam's frown returned in earnest at the name, "Barthelmy Whitehead was a slave-trader and a merchant, but a pirate I hadn't heard. Why," she inquired thoughtfully, "did you say pirate?"

"Oh, 'twas a great joke when I was at Harvard. That for all Seckar's thunderings in chapel about how nine-tenths of us were going straight to Hell, not for anything we'd done or resisted, but because God in his infinite wisdom had positively determined that we should do so, before the beginning of time for His Own Ineffable Purposes—and there was some frightful argument about whether this decision was active or passive and whether it had taken place before or after the Fall of the Angels—for all his condemnation of *us*, the Reverend Log-In-Thine-Own-Eye Seckar's wife was descended from a pirate. We used to think it a huge jest to chalk a skull and crossbones on the door of his study, just to hear him curse at the servants."

"And he probably went home and took his rage out on his wife. 'Tis odd," Abigail continued, "that you should speak of a pirate in connection with the books. Because there's a very strange story attached to them."

She hesitated, studying Sam's face—already lined, the gray eyes watchful but bearing no trace of sleeplessness, for all the waiting dread that had settled on the city. *If he was anything like John*, she reflected wearily, *he could probably sleep through the Lisbon earthquake* . . .

"Are you familiar," she asked slowly, "with a young gentleman named George Fairfield?"

"That young Tory jackanapes who's got up a troop of mounted militia?"

"The same."

Sam's eyes narrowed. "He was killed Tuesday night, wasn't he?"

"He was."

She saw his expression change as he realized the direction of her question. "Oh, for God's sake, Nab—!"

"'Tis what they're saying."

"'Tis what *who's* saying? We're not the Assassins, Nab. I promise you, masked patriots don't lie in wait for every young imbecile who takes it into his head to get himself a King's Commission by raising a troop of horse that'll likely schism itself into insignificance the next time the father of one of them cheats the father of another over a land-deal. The countryside is full of them."

He made a movement to pick up the folio, then set it down, regarding her with troubled eyes. "What evidence do they have?"

"None that I know of. Yet the man they've arrested for the deed—the dead boy's servant—is to my mind as innocent as my son Johnny. And there is something most curious going on." And, a trifle hesitantly—one never knew what Sam was going to do with any piece of information one gave him—she related what Horace had told her about Mrs. Lake's disgraceful document, about the events of Tuesday night, and the sudden indisposition of four Harvard students on Wednesday morning. "Does it not seem to you that *not* having found what she sought—or all of what she sought—in the account of Captain Morgan's and Mistress Pitts's embezzlement of Crown funds, this Mrs. Lake or her scar-faced henchmen are now in quest of other volumes from the same source? I have written Narcissa Seckar—she lives in Medfield—asking for the favor of an interview, to ascertain that Mrs. Lake's Arabic document was indeed connected with the only other source of texts in that language that we know of in the colony: I hope to receive a reply tomorrow."

"And you think that this Mrs. Lake—or one of her henchmen—knew only that young Fairfield had gotten books from the same source, not knowing what they might be." Abigail could almost see the flash and flicker of thought passing through his eyes. "Who's Mrs. Lake?"

"I'd hoped you might know someone of that name."

He shook his head and opened the folio. "Geof. Whitehead," he read the large, rather crooked signature that sprawled, in faded ink, across the title page of *The Sceptical Chymist*. "Sixteen eighty-two. The name isn't familiar—Mrs. Lake's, I mean—and probably isn't her own—"

"I'd thought of that, yes."

"But I'll make enquiries. Embezzlement of the Crown treasury of Jamaica—"

"Horace is recopying what he can remember of the document," said Abigail. Having paged completely through the quarto on horse-doctoring, she opened its front cover and ran her hand over the rather mildewed marbled paper of its inner binding, but she found no evidence that anything had been hidden beneath it. Nor had anything been written on it or on any of the blank pages that made up the ends of the last signature. "His memory is excellent—"

"There are notes in the back of the Paracelsus," provided Sam, who had evidently gone over the volumes with some care. "In English, Latin, Spanish, and what I think is Algonquian, which the writer—I presume Geof. Whitehead, whoever he was—seems to use interchangeably. And that thin quarto with the red cover is all notes—mostly about chemical experiments, the position of stars as they progress through the ecliptic, where he goes to harvest witch hazel, and how long it takes cranberries to progress from first leaf to jam on his breakfast table. Nothing about pirate treasure . . ."

But there was a soft thoughtfulness in the way he said those last words, and when Abigail looked up sharply at him, she saw a distant glimmer in his eyes.

"Did you have a look about young Fairfield's rooms?"

"I did. And found naught but a great quantity of tailors' and bootmakers' bills—which I shall pass along to Mr. Fairfield, Senior, when he arrives next month—and love-notes from about a dozen young ladies." The drawer had also contained several drafts on Boston moneylenders, a huge quantity of gaming-vowels, three promissory notes that young Fairfield had signed—hair-raisingly, for other men's debts, including one for Joseph Ryland—and two letters from his father, decrying his spendthrift ways in terms that gave Abigail little hope for liberality or pity where Diomede was concerned. But these were not Sam's business.

Nor were the love-letters that had been in Fairfield's pocket when he'd died—nor the note in the same dainty hand begging for an assignation behind the barn.

"You didn't tell Hutchinson any of what you've told me, did you?" Sam asked at length. "The man's a serpent; he couldn't crawl straight if he wanted to . . . *and* he knows everything there is to know about who did what in this colony ninety years ago. He'll know who Geof Whitehead was, and if he was burying pirate treasure . . ."

"I didn't tell him that there were other books, no. I had to tell him of those in Mr. Fairfield's room. As the slave Diomede stands in peril of his life, I didn't think it proper to withhold evidence. I left him with the impression that they had not been included in the Harvard bequest because of their nature, which I understand to have been eyeball-scorchingly obscene."

"The man's a trustee of Harvard. Belike he's already got his hands on the rest."

"He said nothing of it . . ."

"Good Lord, woman, d'you think he'd mention it to you if he sees you poking about on the trail of the stolen books? The man's a snake, I tell you. There's every chance 'twas he who hired Mrs. Lake in the first place, *and* the man who put laudanum in young Mr. Fairfield's rum."

"Now, that's ridiculous!" said Abigail. "I know you and John hate the man like poison, but even his enemies allow him to be a man of justice—"

"God save us," retorted Sam, "from a good man with a bad idea—though I reserve my judgment about our dear Governor Hutchinson's goodness. He's a merchant and a pedant who convinced the King to appoint him, first to the chief justiceship of the colony, despite the fact that he has exactly as much legal training as the kitchen cat, then to the governorship—on the grounds of his loyalty to the idea that the colony exists solely for what money can be wrung out of it and handed to the King's friends. And he's kept there by his adherence to the principle that any means are legitimate to keep its people in bondage to the merchants of London who support the King. If he so much as suspects that money embezzled from the Jamaica treasury a hundred years ago is floating about in 'undeserving' hands—"

"I think you're confusing the man with Cesare Borgia," replied Abigail resolutely.

"And I think you're confusing him with Solon the Good, Lawgiver of Athens . . . who had a few weaknesses of his own that they've kept out of the history books. Will you show me this 'reconstructed' treasure-key, when your nephew finishes with it?"

"So far as I know it isn't the 'key' to any 'treasure' . . ."

"Someone seems to think it is."

"I know," retorted Abigail. "I'm looking at him."

"Don't mock me, Nab." Sam's voice fell suddenly quiet. "And don't play hide-and-seek. The matter is serious."

"Of course 'tis serious! A man's life—"

Sam brushed aside the issue of Diomede's guilt or innocence with a wave of one square, blunt-fingered hand. "We need that treasure. If it's there, we need to be the ones who find it. Not this Mrs. Lake or whoever is behind her. In a week, maybe in a day, there'll be British troops landing in Boston—"

"How can you know—?"

"For God's sake, Nab, what else can the King do? He's not going to content himself with some watered-down Royal Commission as everyone seems to expect. We destroyed his tea, he'll send troops, and the whole colony will rise in rebellion. Everyone who's been sitting on the fence dithering about which side they'll hop down onto, will see that there *is* no middle course anymore: the choice is between rebellion and slavery. No, I'm not going to make a speech at you, Nab, don't look that way," he added. "You've heard it all before."

He spread his hands out over the covers of the books and leaned toward her. He was bulky and powerful in his gray coat, and compelling, for all Abigail's distrust of his alliance with every man who liked his politics simple and violent; for all the whiff of boiling tar, burnt feathers, and charred flesh that seemed to her, for a moment, to cling about him, like sulfur on the sleeves of a man who's had supper with the Devil.

"We need money," he repeated. "Every farmer in New England possesses a gun, but when those farmers come into Boston to work on the wharves or in the grist-mills, they leave their guns at home. And every gun needs powder and ball, flints and cartridge-paper—things we're forbidden to manufacture here and must purchase . . . and the King tells us, we can only purchase them from England. We need guns for those who have not the money to buy them, but only the willingness to shed their blood for their rights to choose where and how they'll spend their money *and* their blood. Will you help us, Nab? Will you tell us what you find? This could be a Godsend, if and when it comes to shooting . . . which it will very soon. When do you go out to Medfield to find this Mrs. Seckar?"

"Monday, I hope," she replied unwillingly. "If I hear from her tomorrow. John should be back—"

"If he isn't, I'll send a man with you," promised Sam. "Did you speak to this slave Diomede about his master's books?"

"I tried," said Abigail. "On Wednesday he was still too stupefied yet from the laudanum—and were he not, I should think he would have been too shocked and grieved at the death of a master he loved . . . for all what that imbecile Langdon said!"

"If I sent a man with you tomorrow—someone respect-able," he added, as Abigail opened her mouth to make a comment on the waterfront ruffians who were usually most at liberty to run Sam's errands for him. "Would you go?"

"Thank you. And if I could prevail on you to carry a message for me there this afternoon, with some food for that unfortunate slave, I would most appreciate it." As long as Sam was eager to make himself her partner in the enterprise, reflected Abigail, she might as well take advantage of the facilities he offered, even if those consisted of assistance from every scoundrel, idler, and illegal importer of French contraband from here to Halifax. "And whatever else you may learn of Seckar and pirates and Geof Whitehead . . . I must be circumspect," she added, gathering her shawl about her shoulders again. "Else John will divorce me, I shall be forced to enter a convent, and there will be no treasure for anyone."

Sam bowed. "I should be much entertained," he said, "to see what havoc you would make of a convent, m'am. There'll be a man by at noon to take your message, and a wagon to get you to Cambridge first thing in the morning. But you watch out for Hutchinson," he added. "I understand you wanting his help in getting that poor slave out of danger . . . but the Governor is a powerful enemy. The more so because he seems so *nice.*"

> *Cambridge*
> *Thursday evening*
>
> *28 April 1774*

Mrs. Adams,

Mr. Thaxter and I have spent this afternoon (following lecture and study) in making enquiries in and about Cambridge concerning either Mrs. Lake or the house in which Mr. Thaxter performed his translations. Though we have found no one of that name hereabouts, I believe that we have located the house. As it lies at several miles' distance from the town, we propose to investigate it on our half-holiday Saturday and will write you of our findings.

Moreover, young Mr. Pinkstone, who "fags" under the protection of Mr. Pugh, tells me that Messrs Pugh, Blossom, and Lowth were playing at cards Tuesday evening in Mr. Pugh's rooms, which face across from the staircase occupied by Mr. Thaxter, Mr. Fairfield, and myself, and that Mr. Pugh—clean against his custom—broke up the party at midnight and went out; this despite threats from Pugh that should Mr. Pinkstone reveal this fact he would have him killed and eaten by Pedro and Eusebius, Pugh's two African grooms.

Diomede is in good health, and Mr. Thaxter, Mr. Ryland, and I have endeavored to take food and clean linen to him at the gaol, and to see to his comfort and cheer.

Yrs respctfly,
Enoch Wylie

"Midnight," muttered Abigail to herself, turning Weyountah's note over in her fingers even as she shed her shawl and donned an apron. "A curious time to break up an evening of cards: I wonder if the Black Dog cheats? I see an interview with Mr. Pinkstone is in order—"

She glanced at the late-morning sunlight through the kitchen window, estimating the time before John would be home against the chores undone: Pattie's wooden clogs thudded on the floor overhead (doing the sweeping, by the sound of it) . . . Beds to be made, lamps to be cleaned and filled, and then the ironing of those wash-damaged linens mended yesterday . . .

At her feet, beside the heavy sideboard, Tommy played

contentedly with four walnut shells and two of Charley's toy soldiers and *where was Charley*???

His blocks were by the hearth, but her middle son was distinctly missing. Nor could his scurrying steps be heard upstairs, following Pattie from bedroom to bedroom impeding her work. Abigail's first thought—*The stable*—was succeeded by a more frightening one, *The street* . . .

Two steps took her to the back door, caught between her usual anxious spurt of panic about her increasingly adventuresome son making his way down the little alley to the street, and preparation for a stern talking-to if he was found digging around in the clean—but probably none too sanitary—straw in Their Majesties' stalls . . . And as she opened it, Charley swung into sight from behind it, clearly in disguise in the raggedy old coat that John wore to clean out the cowshed, and a knitted cap acquired from Heaven only knew where, into whose hem straw had been thrust to approximate a bandit's long, untidy hair.

"Stand and deliver, m'am!" the boy croaked throatily, brandishing a crooked stick. "For I'm a robber on the King's Highway."

"Gracious me!" Abigail flung up her hands in mock terror. "Have mercy . . ."

She broke off and took a closer look at the boy. "And just who are you supposed to be?"

"I'm Mr. Scar-Eye," replied Charley cheerfully. "I saw him, and I bet he's a robber and a villain."

He had made for himself, as a part of his disguise, out of wax and mud and Heaven only knew what, a V-shaped scar down his left eye and cheek . . .

Precisely as Horace had described.

Nine

And of course, the first thing John wanted to know of
when he returned that night—just as Abigail was
sweeping the coals from the lid of the Dutch oven, and
Johnny and Nabby were setting the table for dinner—was
about what everyone in town was saying about the King and
whether the ship from London had been sighted?

This was understandable, Abigail knew, considering the
possibility—remote but not unthinkable—that John himself
might be included on a list of suspected persons as Sam's
cousin . . . and as someone who had written any number of
inflammatory letters and pamphlets concerning Governor
Hutchinson. "The countryside is in arms already," he said,
when Abigail had outlined what she knew on this subject,
which was—as with everyone else in Boston—merely a collection of speculation and rumor. "From here to the Kennebec, every village and town has formed militia, elected
officers . . . They've spoken of reestablishing the minutemen,
as a first defense against an alarm, and are stockpiling powder

and muskets in Concord and a dozen other places. What good that will do against trained troops—"

He shook his head, his round face grave. "What frightens me more, Portia—"

She smiled a little, at his use of the old nickname from their courting-days.

"—is that the Tories are arming as well. If war breaks out, 'twill be civil war, with every local squabble about land-boundaries and who-cheated-who-out-of-Grandpa's-inheritance dragged into it, to confuse and embitter the quarrel. Sam has threatened the King: *If you don't give us our rights, we'll open the gates of Hell in this country* . . . But I think Sam has deeply misjudged what will emerge from those gates."

He who would sup with the Devil . . .

Abigail was silent, sitting beside the spent dishes—dinner over, Nabby and Johnny quietly clearing off and (thank Heavens!) fending aside Charley and Tommy as they clamored for their parents' attention . . . "How much danger are you in?" she asked at last.

"Not much, I don't think. I'm Sam's cousin, not Sam." John finished his cider, handed the empty cup to his daughter, who—Abigail feared—was listening more than was probably good for the little girl's peace. "I've done what it's within the rights of every Englishman to do: spoken for our rights as Englishmen. I've broken no windows, boiled no tar, hamstrung no man's horse—"

"What if they don't care?" asked Abigail softly. "What if the Crown gives Hutchinson extraordinary powers to disregard the rights of habeus corpus, to suppress disorders here as and how he pleases, and sends him the troops to do it with? You've marked yourself his enemy—"

"If the Crown has given its Governor the power to punish a man's thoughts and words," returned John, "it will have made me its enemy indeed . . . and every man of the colony as well. Now leave over the clearing-up for a time, and tell me of your endeavors these two weeks, dearest friend." He gathered her onto his knee. "And tell me how it happens that you left our children with Uncle Isaac and Aunt Eliza for a night while you went gallivanting about the countryside—"

"Gallivanting, is it, sir?" Abigail raised her brows. "Take the log from thine own eye, Lysander, before you go looking for specks in mine . . ."

He pressed his knuckles to his breast and inclined his head in penitence, with an expression so humble that Abigail couldn't keep herself from pushing back his wig a little to kiss the smooth skin of his forehead.

Then she rose, and while she helped Pattie and the children clear up and do the dishes ("Sit down, John, you've a dispensation for today . . ."), she recounted the tale of Horace's adventure and its increasingly disquieting chain of sequels. She did not speak of Charley's encounter (*HAD it been an actual encounter?*) with Mr. Scar-Eye until she had returned to John's side, on the settle by the fire, and the children were occupied with their studies or their play, but when she did, she saw how his face flushed with anger.

"How would such a man have known of you? Of our house?"

She shook her head. "As Mr. Ryland said, in some ways Cambridge is very like a village. Word gets about very swiftly, from servants at the college overhearing the conversations of their masters belike: it doesn't seem very difficult for Weyountah to have learned from the unfortunate Mr. Pinkstone what he was sworn not to tell under threat of being eaten by cannibals."

"And anything you happened to speak of to Ryland," remarked John, leaning to the fire to tong up a coal for his long-stemmed Dutch pipe, "has now gone straight to His Excellency—if he didn't know it already."

Mrs. Lake's note he turned over in his fingers and held to the strengthening light of the kitchen hearth: "It's a man's hand, anyway, so we can assume Mrs. Lake is a cat's-paw—"

"Or had the wits to guess that her intended victim might wonder why a Boston lawyer's handwriting was so girlish?"

John made the gesture with his pipe, of a fencer acknowledging a hit. He'd taken off his wig, and without its neat frame of snuff brown waves his round face seemed more relaxed: the at-home John, the evening-John who seemed to her like lover and brother and best friend in one.

"Is the hand anything like Hutchinson's? Do you have a letter of his?"

"In his own hand and not a clerk's? I doubt it. As I recall it, Narcissa Seckar's father was Emmanuel Whitehead, who held the Vassall Chair of Theology before Seckar did. I never heard anything about a pirate in the family—"

"I should imagine 'twas the sort of thing they'd hush up. Particularly after Sam making a jest of it."

"Well, 'tis nothing you'd think of, looking at Old Whitehead. The man was dry and cold as the Original Snake in the Garden. You'd never have caught him giving his books to a college. He left everything he owned to Seckar, who was his student—house, property, the very dishes in the kitchen— rather than turn any of it over to a member of the sex that was responsible for human perdition, he said—"

"Wretch. I take it Mrs. Seckar was his only child."

"I think there was another daughter who ran off with a horse coper or something. 'Twas all a very long time ago. I believe his father was a merchant—"

"And a slave-dealer, His Excellency said. Myself, I had

rather have a good, honest pirate than the pack of hypocrites I've heard about——"

"That's only," said John quietly, "because you've never found yourself in the hands of one."

"And in any case," went on Abigail, "there must have been a genuine pirate somewhere in the family, because from what I gather of the two books that are missing, they're nothing that would have been purchased by a man who held the Vassall Chair of Theology . . . unless he was a thoroughgoing hypocrite indeed. I've found nothing out of the ordinary about the papers in Mr. Fairfield's desk and will return them there tomorrow for old Mr. Fairfield to deal with; the love-letters I shall burn. Weyountah writes me that they think they've found the farmhouse where Mrs. Lake lured Horace, so we shall see what the place can tell us——"

"Not much, I daresay. Ten to one you'll find 'tis the house of a Tory family that lives in town these days and rents out the land——and if Hutchinson's behind it, they'll not even have asked why he wanted to borrow the key to the place. And don't burn the love-letters just yet." He took from the settle beside them the packet of letters that had been in Fairfield's pocket, unfolded one of them in the flickering hearth-light. "French paper, expensive scent, a hand that shouts 'governess'——would there be any chance that these were sent by the Woodleigh girl?

"Montgomery Woodleigh's fortune is sufficient temptation, given the right circumstances, for a man to want to kill a rival, and given the nature of the missing books, they may in fact have nothing to do with the murder. Ask Diomede about whose hopes these letters"——he gestured with the scented packet——"might have crushed. And be careful, Nab."

He took her hand. Abigail was about to disavow any danger in dealing with possible minions of the scholarly gentleman to whom she'd spoken the evening before . . .

And then glanced across the hearth at Charley progressing through the alphabet at Pattie's side. She had, of course, scrubbed off the V-shaped "scar" that afternoon the moment the boy had come into the house, and Charley denied that Mr. Scar-Eye had spoken to him or even attempted to do so . . . and later, that he'd even existed.

And yet, for a moment, it seemed to her that she saw the mark on her son's face still.

When Abigail returned from her marketing on the following morning, she found Sam's promised minion waiting for her, a grim old codger in his sixties who was reassuring John—as Abigail came down the passway into the yard—that he would treat and treasure Mrs. Adams as if she were the Queen of England, and the more so because it stood to reason the bastard King wouldn't marry any but a whore . . .

And for the hour and a half that it took for old Mr. Creel's wagon and team to reach Cambridge, Abigail was obliged to listen to that gentleman's opinions as to what ought to be done to those who were conspiring with the King to enslave the men of Massachusetts—as well as to the New Hampshire sons of whores who were trying to cheat the colony of the best of its lands, the heretic bastards in Rhode Island who were siding with the Indians in a conspiracy to massacre women and children because they (the heretic bastards) were in the pay of the French, and all Pennsylvania merchants who were all born cowards and thieves. Abigail made several attempts at rebuttal to his more outrageous statements ("Them praying-Indians they talk about got no more prayer in 'em than cats: they worship the Devil 'cause they're Devils themselves . . ."), but the old man was almost stone-deaf and violently obstinate, and by the time they'd crossed the narrow neck of land that joined Boston to the mainland, she gave up and sat fuming. The man was, after all, giving her a ride in his wagon for seven rather weary miles, and she realized she had the choice of shouting her objections to him at the top of her lungs—objections to which he wouldn't listen even if he could hear them accurately—or walking.

Even attempts to turn the subject availed little: his neighbors were all Tory traitors also, apparently. And heretics. "Served 'em right that their horses was blinded and hamstrung by the Committee—that'll show 'em not to go speaking against Mr. Sam Adams and Mr. Hancock— We took an' strung up Cal Lechmere's dog, hung it right in front of his door with a sign on its neck, *This'll be You . . .*"

"And what did the dog ever do to harm you?" demanded Abigail. "Or the poor horses, either?"

Which was a mistake, resulting in a long catalog of the late dog's transgressions—which seemed to consist merely in doing its loyal duty to drive off intruders—and the observation that a) Tory beasts deserved what they got and b) women didn't understand these things and should keep their noses out of men's doings.

Abigail was frothing with wrath by the time she was set down outside the gates of Harvard College, and the first thing she did was to take from her pocket Sam's letter of introduction to one Lazarus Dowdall—of Perking Hill Farm—asking him to oblige Mrs. Adams by returning her to Boston that afternoon, and tear it up. The man was probably the local sheep-thief anyway.

A man in shirtsleeves pulling weeds around the single great tree in the court informed Abigail that Mr. Thaxter was carrying a note from Mr. Pugh to Mr. Beecham in town and would be back any time; Abigail watched through the window of the parlor of Massachusetts Hall where she was seated until she saw Horace come through the gate carrying a package. When she intercepted him, he greeted her with obvious relief—"I've been carrying notes back and forth between Pugh and Jasmine half the morning, just to be bloody-minded . . ." She walked with him up the end staircase of Harvard Hall, when he went to knock on Mr. Pugh's door.

The door was opened by a very young-looking fair-haired boy in a short freshman's gown, over whose shoulder Pugh's voice called out, "Oh, is that you, Thaxter? Did you get the coffee? Good lad! Now I've one more errand, if you would be so kind—"

"I beg you'll excuse my nephew," said Abigail, and the baby-faced freshman stepped quickly aside out of the doorway as Pugh set aside the enormous white Persian cat from his knee and rose from the chair beside the window: the study reeked of beer fumes and stale smoke, and Abigail had the impression, looking in, of rather old-fashioned furniture—opulent and tapestried—and not a book in sight. "I've come from town this morning to visit him."

"Madame, I abase myself in shame." Pugh made a surprisingly graceful leg for a man that corpulent, sweeping aside the skirts of the brocaded banyan he wore over his shirt-sleeves as if it had been a court-coat at the Palace of St. James. From the mantle of the fireplace a black cat blinked down, like Satan surveying the world beneath his feet; a long-furred gray tortoiseshell was washing itself in the windowsill. "Had I known our Horace was expecting company, I would never have taken him from his morning tasks. Don't just stand there, Pinky, put the coffee away—"

The freshman hastened to relieve Horace of his package.

"Will you have some tea, Mrs. Adams? No? My heart shall never recover. Yes, yes, Horace, it is well, run along—Pinky, dearest, I fancy you'd better take this note on to

Jasmine's room—" He scooped up the tortoiseshell cat as it moved to wind itself around Abigail's skirts.

"That's Mr. Pinkstone?" asked Abigail softly, as they descended to the courtyard again.

Horace nodded as he took Abigail's basket. "Is that gingerbread?" he asked, sniffing the air rather wistfully—since gingerbread was one of the many things that brought on his hives.

"I brought it for Weyountah," she explained, "and some honey for yourself—"

The gratitude and delight in his face were almost painful to see. Honey was one of the few treats that her nephew could consume with impunity.

"—and a little extra gingerbread, for purposes of corruption. I take it Mr. Blossom lives in Massachusetts Hall?" Though Horace would have turned right toward the main door of Harvard as they emerged from Pugh's staircase, Abigail set out briskly across the courtyard for the hall opposite.

"How did you know?"

"I assume Mr. Pugh would not have been sending you back and forth with notes to someone who didn't live in the building farthest from Harvard Hall . . . I think the walk will do us good, both to unload the honey, which is rather heavy, and to lie in wait for Mr. Pinkstone, who—threats of cannibalism aside—seems ripe to do his master a disservice. Upon which staircase does Mr. Blossom reside?"

After lying in wait for a very few minutes within the entry of the hall that led to the various staircases, Abigail and Horace were rewarded by the sight of young Mr. Pinkstone emerging from Harvard Hall and scurrying across the open court as if pursued. The clock on the chapel chimed noon as he came, and from the doors of the hall a great number of students began to pour forth, gowns bright against the Indian red of the brickwork and the green of the new grass.

Abigail rather feared that Mr. Pinkstone would turn back or engage himself in conversation with one of them, but in fact he quickened his steps—probably fearing to be intercepted by some student more senior to Mr. Pugh and sent on some yet more tiresome errand.

He checked his steps as he approached the door, but Horace called out, "I wanted a quick word with you, Pinky, where the Black Dog couldn't see—and I'm sorry you got caught up in all his bloody-minded note-carrying. Here," he said, and took Abigail's basket from her. "My aunt brought Weyountah some gingerbread, but I think he doesn't need all of it."

The young man took what Horace handed him and began immediately to devour it, like a small dog who expects his bone to be seized by a larger dog. "That's decent of you," he said, and after the first bite, "Lord, that's good, m'am! Did you make it?"

"Catch me palming off someone else's gingerbread on my nephew's friends," said Abigail. And then, to Horace, as if they'd arranged the matter beforehand, "Ask him about the marzipan tea I'd sent you that was in poor Mr. Fairfield's rooms."

"What? Oh, yes." Horace looked momentarily startled, then nodded. "I've been thinking what you said about the Black Dog breaking up the card game early Tuesday night— You don't think he came across to poor George's room then, by any chance, do you? It's just that my aunt had sent me some marzipan tea, and I had it in the room with me when I was studying there—"

"'Twas in a Japan-ware caddy," corroborated Abigail, "that belongs to my grandmother. I'm afraid it sounds like a terrible thing to be concerned with, but she'll be very upset if it's lost. And while I wouldn't wish to accuse anyone of thievery, the tea is the sort of thing that someone might help themselves to, and you can't carry it off in your pockets, you know. And I only wonder—"

"Well, m'am, I wouldn't put it past Pugh." The boy rubbed his eyes tiredly. "I haven't seen anything like a tea caddy in his room— What color was it?"

Abigail described her Grandma Quincy's Japan-ware tea caddy, which was in fact safely on a shelf in Aunt Eliza's kitchen. "It just occurred to me when Horace mentioned the matter, that midnight is a tremendously early hour for a man like Mr. Pugh to be breaking up a promising game."

"He was winning, too," said Pinkstone. "Not that that's anything new—the fellow cheats like Iscariot. He'd heard Shallop from over in Hollis Hall had just got money in from his family, and was physicking him of it when he said, of a sudden, that he had a headache, and we were all to get out. I knew that was all stuff—Pugh wouldn't have a headache if you gave him a hundred pounds to do it and wouldn't stop a game if there was an ax sticking out of his skull . . . Myself, I thought he'd got a signal."

"A signal?"

"Through the window," said the boy. "He'd sat himself where he could see it, instead of where he usually sits in the corner by the fireplace. I thought later—when I was talking to Horace—that he might have been meeting a girl. He wouldn't have come across to speak to George anyway, because George's window was dark."

"Hmm," said Abigail. "Well, another theory gone west. Would George have been asleep at midnight, Horace? It sounds a trifle early for him."

"I don't think so," said Horace, and she saw the shadow of grief darken his eyes. "He—Weyountah and I stayed up until nearly ten thirty, at work on a—a *translation*—which I have yet to finish," he added, seeing that she understood that he meant his reconstruction of Mrs. Lake's naughty document.

"George hadn't come back from when he left me after we spoke to you at the Stair . . ."

"There was a light in his room earlier," provided Mr. Pinkstone. "But that would have been old Dio waiting up for him like a mother hen." He grinned sadly. "I say, that was all stuff about Dio murdering him, wasn't it? Old Dio wouldn't hurt a fly, and the way he quizzed George when he'd been out, and waited up for him when he was off with some girl or other, and tried to find fellows to do his work for him—that's a damned shame, what they're saying. But when Pugh broke up the card game, George's window was dark, because he looked out—Pugh did—and I was standing behind him, and him with one of those nasty cats sitting on his shoulder like a parrot. Besides," added the boy, "the Black Dog wouldn't have come across to speak to George anyway—they couldn't stand one another."

"Really?" said Abigail. "Whyever not? Mr. Pugh wasn't in favor of colonial rights, was he?"

"Not that I ever heard." The boy glanced up the stair, then back across the courtyard toward the window of the man of whom they spoke, as if Mr. Pugh might be standing in it, watching for his return. "No, the thing is, m'am, old George had cut him out with Sally Woodleigh, and had drawn his cork over it but two days before. So there'd be precious little that he'd have wanted to say to George at midnight or any other time."

"Did he, indeed?" murmured Abigail, as she and Horace made their way up Horace's own stairway to deposit the honey—and Weyountah's rather depleted stock of gingerbread—behind the books in Horace's room. "Did you know that?"

Horace shook his head. "I knew George and the Black Dog were at odds, but I thought . . . George never could stand a bully," he said. "I think even before Pugh started plaguing me, it raised George's dander. He was like that." He was silent a moment as they returned down the stair. Then, carefully controlling his voice, he added, "But I can't see even Pugh poisoning Dio in order to lie in wait for George . . ."

"No, of course not. Yet if George surprised him in the act of stealing from his rooms—an act that might end Pugh's career at Harvard and would certainly end any chance of his winning back the fair Mistress Woodleigh—it might be enough to make a man lose his head in anger or in fear. 'Tis only a theory," she added.

"One that takes no account of Mrs. Lake," pointed out the boy diffidently.

"On the contrary: the Black Dog might have been watching George's window, waiting for the candle to wink out, demonstrating that Diomede was well and truly asleep. 'Tis far more likely that he went across on account of Mrs. Lake's business than that of Mistress Woodleigh; what matters would be that he was in the room when George returned. 'Twill be something to bear in mind when we drive out to see this house that you and Weyountah have discovered."

Ten

Diomede bore out Horace's account of relations between George Fairfield and St-John Pugh, and to it added an eyewitness account of the combat that had taken place between them the preceding Saturday afternoon. "It was nothing much, m'am." The servant leaned forward on the bench in the sheriff's little watch room, his elbows on his knees. Abigail was pleased to see that Mrs. Squills had kept her word about seeing to it that Diomede had at least clean linen and food to eat in the jail. And the small brick jail in Cambridge—though it could never have been called comfortable—was at least habitable, unlike the "Hell on Earth," as it was described, of Boston's.

Through the window that opened onto Church Street, the sound of drums drifted from the Common, where the militia of Cambridge were beginning their drill. Mr. Congreve, slouched in a wooden chair (he had given Abigail his good one) by the door, moved his head now and then as if following the sound with his ears, though whether this was because he thought he should be among them bearing a musket or because he was waiting for the sound of a fight beginning, Abigail couldn't tell.

Diomede looked haggard, and—Abigail was distressed to see—older than he had only four days ago when he'd joked with her as they'd walked back to Cambridge in the twilight, leading the limping Sassy by the bridle.

"They'd always rubbed each other the wrong way, from the time Mr. Pugh was a junior ordering around Mr. George as a freshman—not that Mr. George would take any nonsense from him or any man, no matter what these college customs say. First day he was a sophomore, Mr. George thrashed Mr. Pugh, and him five years younger than Pugh and nowhere near his weight. Miss Woodleigh, I can't say she favored Pugh much over any of the others that courted her—if you'll excuse me saying so, m'am, she's a bit of a butterfly—"

"She's a damned little flirt," put in Congreve from the doorway, "and her father'll be the happiest man in the colony when she finally settles . . . and her new husband the most miserable."

"Well," said the slave carefully, "it's not my place to say, of course."

Not about a white girl, at any rate, reflected Abigail. "What happened?"

"What you'd expect, m'am. Mr. George and a dozen of the Volunteers rode over to Mr. Woodleigh's house on the Lexington Road after they were done with their drill; I think Mr. Woodleigh had invited them all for a bowl of punch. He—and Mrs. Woodleigh especially—had great hopes for Miss Woodleigh and Mr. George, and of course from the moment Miss Woodleigh saw George in his uniform, she'd had eyes for no one else. Myself," he added with a wry half smile, "I think the uniform might have had a great deal to do with it, for he did look mighty splendid. Mr. Pugh's nose was out of joint over it, as you'd expect."

"Everyone's was," put in Horace, glancing up from surreptitiously counting his own pulse. "*Varium et mutabile semper femina* . . . at least, she was variable and mutable to those wealthy enough for her to notice in the first place. She's above *our* touch, but every senior and bachelor-fellow who isn't a candidate for the ministry is courting her, and half the professors are as well."

"And the prettiest little thing under a bonnet in Suffolk County." Diomede smiled.

"The best-educated little thing under a bonnet in Suffolk County," added Weyountah thoughtfully. "Or at least the most comprehensively tutored. Entirely free of charge, I might add. They fall over one another to instruct her—Latin, history, theology, not that she'd know a sacrament from a syllogism. I taught her astronomy for about three months when it was first fashionable, but I made her father pay me, since there wasn't a hope he'd have let me court her if I'd wanted to. She burned off Ryland's eyebrows during a chemistry lesson, but he's still tutoring her, I think: he'll be lucky if she doesn't blow him to bits. She's clever, though . . ."

"She's clever enough to pick the handsome ones as tutors," grunted Congreve. "Makes the rest jealous. And who was it who said, there's no such thing as an ugly heiress?"

"Well, be all that as it may," continued Diomede, "Mr. Pugh was there when the Volunteers rode up. Of course Miss Woodleigh went into ecstasy over Mr. George. She always spoke of him as her affianced, but there was nothing formal to it, and to my mind he never favored her above the common run."

"I just don't think it ever crossed her mind that the man she adored wouldn't adore her in return," Horace opined. He coughed and cleared his throat and wiped his lips with one of

the half-dozen clean white handkerchiefs he habitually carried in his pockets. "I know he didn't speak of her when they
were apart—well, not more than any of the others."

"Which I expect is what fascinated Miss Woodleigh the
most," remarked Abigail. "No wonder she pursued him."

"That I wouldn't know, m'am," said the servant. "But Saturday she leaped up from where she was sitting beside Pugh
and cried out that she counted the days 'til she and Mr. George
could be wed, and Mr. Pugh got pretty red in his face and
said as how Miss Woodleigh would favor Pedro—that's one
of his own grooms, m'am, a savage straight from Africa—if
he was to dress up in a red coat, or a monkey for that matter,
and added that to get Mr. George's notice she'd have to stand
in line behind half the tavern-maids in the countryside. Mr.
George flung himself straight off Sassy's back onto Mr. Pugh
and threw him down the porch steps, then leaped down after
him and beat him to the ground. Made him look no-how,
and sent him off with a blooded nose and a lesson about ban-
dying a woman's name in front of a troop of cavalry. He was
like that," he added quietly, his voice altering. "No, she wasn't
his affianced—and it rubbed him, I think, to hear her go on
about it—but he wouldn't hear her slandered, not if she was
a scullery-maid."

In the stillness that followed, a sharp-shouted command
could be heard from the Common, followed by the ragged
thunder of musket-fire. It was only the men drilling, Abigail
knew, yet the sound made her shiver.

*From here to the Kennebec, every village and town has formed
militia . . .*

*Stockpiling powder and muskets in Concord . . . What good that
will do against trained troops . . .*

Civil war. The words filled her with dread, echoing the
bloody chaos that had brought down the Republic of Rome.

She remembered Joseph Ryland's grave face as he watched men less competent than he step ahead of him to take George Fairfield's place in command.

It is our duty, as subjects of the King, to keep it from degenerating to such a pass that the French or the Spanish think themselves safe to come in and take over these colonies for themselves . . .

And young George Fairfield, riding here and there through Massachusetts, raising *a company of gentlemen loyal to the King . . .*

She forced her mind back to the man before her. *One thing at a time . . .*

"And nothing further came of it?"

"No, m'am. Mr. George was a little more careful after that about hiding—well, hiding things that might get him into trouble if it should come to Dr. Langdon's ears that he had them in his room—"

"Like his rum?" asked Abigail. And then, sinking her voice to a whisper—though Congreve's attention had been drawn to a confusion of angry shouting from the direction of the nearby tavern on Church Street—"Or his books?"

"You know about his books, m'am?" Diomede's voice lowered to match hers, and behind Abigail, Horace coughed again and fished for another clean handkerchief.

"I know he had them."

The servant sighed, and his face creased with vexation. "I told him— Well, they were mighty tempting books. But I did warn him, after he wouldn't sell them to Mr. Pugh, that Mr. Pugh would turn around and use them to get him into trouble—report him to Dr. Langdon and get him sent down. Dr. Langdon being a great Whig and always crying out for the colony's liberties. Everyone in the college knew he was just looking for a reason to get Mr. George turned out . . ."

"Mr. Pugh tried to buy those books?"

"Yes, m'am." Diomede looked apologetic. "Right after Mr. George bought them from poor Mrs. Seckar, almost three weeks ago now it was. Knowing Mr. Pugh and half thinking the offer might just be a way of learning if Mr. George had them, so he could report him to the provosts, Mr. George refused to admit he had them. But the day after this to-do at Mr. Woodleigh's, the Sunday evening, Pugh sent Eusebius, that other black African of his, to me with five pounds, m'am—five pounds!—for me to steal them and get them to him—"

"How did he know of them in the first place?"

The slave shook his head. "That I don't know, m'am."

Abigail was silent, thinking about the young man who'd come striding breezily out onto the landing, crying, *Good Lord, get that woman out of here!*

About the handsome young face lying so still on the pillow in the instant before Dr. Perry had twitched the sheet over it.

It seemed impossible that she'd known him for less than twelve hours.

"Does Mr. Pugh have any white hangers-on?" she asked quietly. "A dark-haired gentlewoman whose name may or may not be Mrs. Lake? Or a man with a scar like this"—she made a *V* of her fingers and pressed it to the left side of her face—"over his eye? Have you ever seen a man with a scar like this in Cambridge? Or in the countryside round about?"

Diomede turned the matter over in his mind. "No, m'am. I wish—" He looked aside, his features twisting with the effort to control them. "This is my fault, m'am, and I know it's my fault—"

"'Tis nothing of the kind," said Abigail firmly.

"If I hadn't been drunk—"

"Then whoever did this would have found some other way

of drugging you. The drug was meant for him as well as you, Diomede . . ."

"But they knew! They knew I have this weakness—"

"Pish-tush! There isn't a servant on Earth who doesn't drink his master's rum when his master isn't looking. 'Twas only chance that Mr. Fairfield woke when the intruder came in, and cried out—"

"No," whispered Diomede, and clasped his hands together, pressing the knuckles for a moment to his lips. "I swear to you, m'am, when I woke up—when I heard what had happened . . . It was my fault, the same as if I *had* got up and used that knife myself—"

"Stop it!" ordered Abigail. "What you're saying does no one any good and will only confuse the search for Mr. Fairfield's real killer." But her heart sank within her, for she guessed that was precisely what Charles Fairfield was going to say when he came north from Virginia to collect his son's body . . . and to avenge himself on those responsible for his son's death. "Can you write, Diomede?"

"Yes, m'am. Mr. Charles's father—*old* Mr. George—he didn't hold with servants being ignorant. I was made to do lessons alongside Mr. Charles and his sisters."

"Could you write out what you've told me? About the fight with Mr. Pugh and his attempts to bribe you, and about Mr. George's books that he bought from Mrs. Seckar? Write it in your own words, everything that you can remember. Mr. Congreve, do you have any objection to that? Weyountah, if you could see to it that Diomede has pen and paper—"

The Indian—who at Horace's nervous insistence had been listening to Horace's heartbeat—nodded, and Congreve said, "For all the good it's like to do you, m'am. I tell you, I've met these Virginia planters—"

"Which is exactly why every effort should be made to get the case heard here in Massachusetts— Yes, Horace, I'm sure you're *quite* all right; your coloring looks just as it should. With sworn statements in hand, I think my husband will have a better chance of at least getting a trial here—"

The slave closed his eyes for a moment, his face immobile; then he whispered, "Thank you, m'am," in the voice of one who knows perfectly well that miracles do not happen. "I'll do as you ask and have it for you if you should come here again. But if you would, m'am—could I trouble you, if I were also to write out a letter to my wife and to our daughters back in Virginia? Would you see that it's sent to them?"

"Of course." Then another thought occurred to her, and she dug in her pocket for the elegant love-letters. Lowering her voice to exclude the sheriff—who might not approve of a young lady's letters being viewed by a slave—she asked, "Does this handwriting look familiar to you, Diomede?"

He responded immediately, "Yes, m'am." And—taking the letters, with his own swift glance toward Congreve, who seemed to be preoccupied with the shouting from the Common—he whispered, "It's Miss Woodleigh's, m'am."

"Let me see those—" Horace held up his hand to stay her from tucking them away, as he, Abigail, and Weyountah stepped into the sunlight of Church Street.

"Is he right?" Abigail glanced up at Weyountah, who was looking around Horace's shoulder. "You tutored her—"

"That's her hand, yes."

"Yes, but this—" Horace held up the note. *As you love me, be behind the barn at midnight . . .* "This isn't her paper. It isn't the same as the letters, look—"

Which was quite true. The note was stiffer and thicker, and of a warmer hue than the thin, slightly crinkly sheets on which Sally Woodleigh had poured out effusions of love.

From the pocket of his hand-me-down coat, Horace took an identical sheet—folded in the same fashion as the note, in quarters, rather than the longer letters, which had been folded rather elaborately and sealed.

Startled, Abigail asked, "How did you come—?"

"This one's not from Miss Woodleigh." Horace unfolded it. "It's the one St-John Pugh gave me to deliver this morning to his bootmaker. You can see the paper—and the ink, too, look"—he held both notes to the sunlight—"are exactly the same."

"Pugh," said Weyountah. They came onto the Common again, headed for Brattle Street and the College. "Pugh sent him a note in Sally's hand . . ."

"To get him out of his room at midnight." Behind his thick spectacles, Horace's gray eyes seemed to glow with somber eagerness, his fancied ailment forgotten. "Pinkstone said he was watching for something . . ."

Before them, men formed up uneven lines, officers—that is, the men they'd elected as their own officers—dashing back and forth among the would-be soldiers like distracted sheepdogs, shouting commands to load and fire. Light powder, Abigail calculated, and no bullets: Sam had not been exaggerating when he'd said how short the militia was of such supplies. Most lead had to be imported—illegally— from France.

"But if he'd got George out of his rooms. . . ." said Weyountah doubtfully.

The Indian's face was still soot-smudged. Abigail and Horace had found him that morning in one of the laboratory rooms in Harvard Hall, trying to focus beams of sunlight with mirrors through a choking cloud of sulfurous smoke ("This is nothing, m'am—last fall Ryland nearly suffocated everyone in the Hall with some phosphorous compound he

was working on . . ."). Horace had been coughing and checking his pulse ever since.

"He must have returned sooner than expected."

"Yes, but he was on his way to meet someone just at dusk
when he parted from me. Would he have met—I mean . . ."
Horace blushed again at the thought that his hero would
have dallied with one girl from eight 'til midnight to pass
the time before a second tryst.

"Diomede said he'd no deep fondness for Miss Woodleigh," recalled Abigail thoughtfully. "Contrary to what Miss
Woodleigh was obviously telling Mr. Pugh. Obviously, the
Black Dog thought that a lover so gallant as George would
wait at least an hour for his lady fair before coming back to
his room. George must have returned and caught him."

"How do we prove this?" Weyountah's voice was grim.
"'Tis all very well to guess at what the man did, but I doubt
a Virginia jury will free a slave accused of killing his master
on the strength of two sheets of paper. Particularly not to
convict a white man in his place."

"Even searching his rooms might not help us," said Abigail, "without other proofs in hand. Though we shall certainly have to try it. They are—as everyone keeps pointing
out—volumes that any young man might easily wish to steal
without also murdering their rightful owner; though by Horace's own testimony, they were in his desk that morning.
Where is George, by the way?" she added in a quieter voice.
"I mean, where has his body been bestowed to await his
father's arrival?"

"In the holding crypt behind Christ Church." Weyountah's lips settled for a moment into a hard line of grief.
"Would you like to go there?"

"When we return," she said. "If there's time."

"Sally Woodleigh has been there three times to leave

flowers," Weyountah went on drily. "In full mourning—and always with some solicitous gentleman offering her his shoulder upon which to weep. That night I heard George cry out." He had said this to her before, but it was as if he were driven to repeat the words, to understand what they meant and what they could not mean. "I thought it was only him angry at Dio for getting drunk—"

"Do you know what time that was?"

The Indian shook his head. After a moment he went on, "I heard nothing further."

I went back to sleep . . . I let my friend die . . .

"And George would not have thanked you," Abigail pointed out gently, "had you gone charging across the staircase while he was dressing down Diomede for stealing his liquor."

"No, m'am." The Indian's voice was nearly inaudible.

They had reached the quadrangle between Harvard Hall, Massachusetts, and Stoughton College. Most of the students—and a certain proportion of the younger masters—being on the Common, comparing cartridge-boxes and arguing about the merits of French over English powder, the only scholarly gown visible was Mr. Pugh, strolling in the direction of Harvard Hall with one of his "cut-faced savages" at his heels. This man—small, wiry, and black as ink—appeared so barbaric, with his head shaved, his face crisscrossed with tribal scars, and plugs of sharpened bone thrust through the septum of his nose and the lobes of his ears, that Abigail suspected his master of playing up his African customs to impress and intimidate others.

"I'll hitch up Sassy," said Weyountah. "Dr. Langdon lets me take her out. If you're to be back in Boston by sunset, we'd best start now to show you Mrs. Lake's farmhouse—"

"Then we shall linger only long enough to return Mr. Fairfield's bills to his own room." Abigail patted her satchel.

"Provided my going up there won't get you boys thrown out of the College."

"What, for an *aunt*?" Horace looked grateful—Abigail suspected that if she'd gone into the parlor and left her nephew to carry the bundle of papers up alone, he ran the risk of being sent to the other side of town on some foolish errand by Mr. Pugh.

Pugh himself bowed as they passed him. "Not going out to march with the traitors, Mr. Wylie?"

The Indian returned the bow. "No, I thought I should stay in today with the cowards."

Smiling to herself, Abigail followed Horace into Massachusetts Hall and up the middle staircase. "You said Dr. Langdon was taking charge of George's things," she said as they climbed. "Is the room kept closed up, or can anyone come and go?"

"Anyone can," said Horace. "It's just that—" His voice tailed off as they reached the landing and saw that the door to Fairfield's room indeed stood open. Horace's lips pursed and behind the heavy spectacle-lenses, his gray eyes hardened. *Of course*, thought Abigail, *the one day the building is certain to be empty*—

The boy strode ahead of her into the empty study, Abigail at his heels, and through it to the bedchamber beyond. "Who's in here?" he called out, in a hard voice completely unlike his usual mild tones. "And what are you— Oh!"

He stopped in the doorway, blocking Abigail's view.

Beyond him, a young woman's voice demanded, "And who are *you*, frog-eyes? I have every right to be here, I guess—"

Abigail looked around her tall nephew's shoulder and saw, standing beside the desk, a girl of seventeen or so—"well-set-up," John would have described her lush figure—in a short petticoat and coarse skirt of striped linen, tucked up to show off slim brown ankles, and a brown linen jacket, much patched. Wisps of black hair, straight and heavy as an Indian's, floated free from her cap, and so sun-browned was her face that were it not for the morning glory blue of her eyes, she might have been mistaken for one of Weyountah's relatives.

She nodded toward the bed, stripped of bedding and mattress. "Has his Pa come for him, then?"

"Not yet," Horace stammered.

"Then where is he?"

"Christ's Church."

Her eyes narrowed beneath butterfly-wing brows: "Doing what? They're not making him marry that Woodleigh cow, are they? Because if she—"

Abigail said quietly, "You have not heard, mistress? George Fairfield was killed Tuesday night." The girl pressed her hand quickly to her lips, and though her expression didn't change, she went sheet white under her tan. It was as if she'd been struck but would not acknowledge the pain of the blow. Then she whispered, in a small despairing voice, "Oh, George."

"And you are—?"

The girl said softly, "I'm his wife."

Eleven

"George said he'd keep the license." Katy Pegg—as she had said her name was—sat on the edge of the naked bedframe, brown hands folded in her lap. "There's no place at home I could put it that it'd be safe from my step-pa. We married in December, before George left for Virginia."

Abigail glanced at the desk beside the window. It had not been opened. Among all the tailors' bills, all the gambling-markers, all the love-letters she'd taken out Wednesday morning, there had been no marriage license.

"We rode down to Providence together. I don't know what he told Diomede—the man his Pa wished on him, to keep him from meddling with girls, George said. Tuesday night—" Tears flooded her eyes, and she almost slapped them away with impatient fingers. "I was with him—"

"He was killed by an intruder," said Abigail gently, "late on Tuesday night after he came back here to his rooms. A thief."

The girl closed her eyes, her face like a defiant child's, who'll take a whipping rather than ask a parent to stop.

"What time did you part?"

"Midnight. He said he was meeting friends, and the—the men I'd rid out here with would be leaving soon. My step-pa would skin me if he knew—"

She took a deep breath, some of the terrible tension going out of her slim shoulders, her oval face. "My step-pa hated him. He said he was a damned Tory and would break my heart for me, *and* leave me caught with a baby . . . which is what *he* was after himself, the—"

She stopped herself, looked down at her square, boyish hands, folded tight in her lap. "George said he'd come for me on Wednesday night. That's the night Mr. Deems—my step-pa—goes out with the Watertown militia. I wrote Thursday . . ." She raised her hands quickly to press against her lips again, then lowered them almost at once. "So I got a lift this morning from one of the farmers that was coming in for the militia. I knew George's Pa wouldn't stand for it, for George and me, I mean. But he said—George said—that marrying me made it all right, and they couldn't stop us if we were wed."

Abigail rolled her eyes heavenward. Carmody—the worst of her brother's ne'er-do-well friends—had boasted to William once when he didn't realize Abigail was in earshot of having "wedded" a girl who couldn't be persuaded and was too cagy to let herself get into a situation where she could be raped with impunity ("Well, they always cry rape afterwards," Carmody had shrugged . . .)

And the young scoundrel with Sally Woodleigh's love-letters in his pocket—! She felt sick with disappointment, as if she herself had been betrayed.

"What happened?"

"Mrs. Adams—" Weyountah's light tread sounded in the study. "If we don't leave now . . ."

He halted in the doorway, startled to see Abigail not alone.

"Mr. Wylie," Abigail introduced, "Mistress Pegg. Or, as she claims is the truth, so far as she knows it, Mrs. Fairfield."

Weyountah's jaw dropped for less than a second. He shut his mouth and bowed. "I'm very sorry, m'am," he said. "Mrs. Adams must have——"

"She did." Katy stood, her shoulders straight. "And as for, *so far as I know it* . . . It is the truth. We brought proofs of my age and that my parents were dead, and the county clerk in Providence made us out a license and a certificate, and married us——"

"In the courthouse?" asked Weyountah.

Katy shook her head. "In the back room of a tavern about a mile outside of the town. George's father has many friends in Providence, merchants who do business with him. George made this arrangement, so that we wouldn't . . ." She broke off, looking from Abigail's face to those of the two students, and her own cheeks reddened. Her chin came up. "And no, it wasn't as it looks—as I can see you're thinking. The man was genuinely the county clerk, and George gave him ten shillings to put it in his book at the courthouse that we'd been married there, though there's nothing in the laws of Providence nor of Massachusetts, either, that says a marriage isn't valid if it's not performed in some certain magical place."

"But it is the reason, m'am," said the Indian gently, "that they want witnesses and the presence of the families, to make sure the girl isn't being lied to——"

"Oh, and wouldn't my step-pa just *love* to see his girl married to a Tory? George didn't lie to me. He said he'd keep the license——"

"It wasn't in his desk."

"Look in his books," said Katy, in a small, steady voice. "He was always putting things he wanted to keep in the backs of his books . . ."

"That's true," said Horace. Abigail's heart went out to him, at the expression of wretchedness on his face, that his hero would have played so despicable a trick on a girl.

"But I did see it when 'twas signed, m'am," said Katy. "And the clerk did sign it after he'd read the service over us. And he truly was the county clerk."

"Be that as it may," said Weyountah firmly. "The chaise is at the door, m'am, and further delay will prevent Mrs. Adams from getting back to Boston, either by the ferry or through the town gates. Moreover, Mrs. Adams is Horace's aunt, and you—Mrs. Fairfield—are nothing of the kind, and we could all of us be in serious trouble if some mean-spirited bachelor-fellow were to happen along and report the lot of us to Dr. Langdon."

"Like that wretch Ryland? He'd do it—Mrs. *Adams*?" The name finally seemed to register, and her blue eyes stretched wide. "Not . . . Not *Samuel* Adams?"

"I am Mrs. *John* Adams," said Abigail. "Are you staying in Cambridge, Mrs. Fairfield? Or can we leave you somewhere?"

"Looks like I've been left somewhere as it is." Katy turned and picked up the small bundle she had left, almost out of sight by the end of the bed. "John Adams—that wouldn't be he who writes as Novanglus, would it? And those other letters he's done . . . You'll be Weyountah, won't you?" she added, turning back toward the Indian. "You'd never get the four of us into that little chaise of George's."

"It's why I borrowed Millard's old post chaise and Benton's horse. If Horace has no objection to riding on the back—"

"And if Horace does?" protested Horace.

"Then *I'll* ride on the back," said Katy, with a sudden flicker of a grin. "I've always wanted to, seeing the gentlemen coming into the tavern yard—" She followed Abigail down the stair, halting obediently at Weyountah's signal so that the Indian could step out first and make sure that the corridor was clear. They hastened to the door, where the dwarfish Mr. Beaverbrook was holding the heads of Sassy and the tallest, boniest black gelding Abigail had ever seen. As Abigail handed Mr. Beaverbrook a quarter of a silver doubloon and touched her finger to her lips for silence, Horace climbed rather gingerly onto the footman's stand on the back of the little vehicle. "I suffer from vertigo," he warned. "And sometimes even scotodinia . . ."

"Where do you go?" Abigail asked Katy, as Weyountah helped them into the four-wheeled post chaise and then went to mount Sassy, the harness permitting a rider.

"Home, it looks like." Abigail heard in the girl's voice the effort to keep it steady. "Mr. Deems is the head hostler at the Yellow Cow, if you know where that is?" She leaned from the door of the chaise to address this last to Weyountah, who was preparing to put the whole equipage into motion. "Where the road forks to go to Watertown—"

"Never tell me you walked!" protested the scholar. "That's almost to Concord!"

"Lord, you think I couldn't get a ride?" retorted the girl, with a quick flash of a grin. But as she settled back into the worn leather of the seat and Weyountah touched his heels to Sassy's sides, Katy admitted wanly, "But to be honest, I'm just as glad to have the ride, if go back I must. I'd hoped . . ."

She broke off her words and sat for a time, looking out at the handsome houses as they passed along Brattle Street and out toward the countryside beyond the town. The drumming of the militia faded behind them, the ragged crackling of rifle-fire like very distant lightning. Katy began to say, "George—" She stopped herself. Whatever George was or could have been, it was over now.

"What about Diomede?" she asked after a time, returning

her attention to Abigail. "I only ever saw him at a distance, but George told me about him, and I feel like I know him— just as I feel like I know Weyountah and . . . It is Horace, isn't it? Was Dio drunk when this thief came in? I know he drank," she added. "But according to George—I'm sorry, I can't seem to stop bringing up his name, like a grandmother . . . George said Diomede seldom got so fogbound he couldn't pull himself together and wake up at need. Diomede's a terrible mother hen, George said. Well, he had to be; it was his job, like those old Roman he-nannies they used to have—"

"Pedagogues," said Abigail, smiling.

"Yes . . . and about time the men found out what it was like, having to chase around after a child all day long. Not that they aren't sweet," she added, with a secret smile of her own and a small movement, to lay her hand on her belly, that made Abigail moan inwardly—*And the young blackguard made her pregnant as well!* "I know all this is bad for me, but the poor man must be devastated! To look after someone all those years . . . Is Diomede all right?"

"I fear not," Abigail said. "Diomede is being accused of the murder."

The girl's eyes flared with horror, and when Abigail sketched the circumstances—saying nothing of what was stolen, only that the rum had been drugged—Katy cried again, "Oh, *NO*! How *awful*—"

"Is there anyone you know of," Abigail asked curiously, "who might hate George enough to harm him?"

"Bruck Travers," replied the girl at once. "He's captain of the Watertown militia. He's also on the Committee of Correspondence. Mr. Deems—my step-pa—says Bruck is the greatest patriot in the county, and so he is. Twice he had the boys out to ambush George and Diomede when they were coming back from drilling with the Volunteers."

The heartfelt approval in her voice made Abigail raise her brows. "I thought you were a Tory?"

"What on earth gave you that idea?" Katy looked genuinely surprised. "I listened very carefully to the clerk when he read the marriage service, and I didn't hear a single thing about a woman having to cleave to her husband's politics if her husband's idiot enough to believe the Governor's Tory lies. George can take care of himself and whip a dozen of Bruck Travers. That is—"

Her voice stammered a little, and she looked aside again, fixing her attention on the open cornfields that lay beyond the tree-shaded road, the grazing cattle and the black circling shapes of crows. After a moment she went on, "Just because George let a bunch of lying Tory merchants talk him into believing a King who wants to put us all in chains, doesn't mean I don't . . . I didn't . . ."

She took a few breaths, her body swaying a little with the motion of the chaise. "If your husband were a raving Tory, m'am, would you cease to love him?"

"No," said Abigail, smiling. "No, I suppose not."

About ten miles along the Concord Road, Weyountah reined the team up a side-trace that ran through a woodlot, across a very rickety bridge, and past what looked like, in previous years, had been corn fields, now given over to pasturage of a herd of black-and-white cows. Twisting in her seat to lean out the window and holding perilously to her sunbonnet, Katy said, "It's the Chamberville place, isn't it?"

"Is it?"

"Of course." She returned to a normal posture and looked at Abigail as if surprised she hadn't heard the whole tale. "Lemuel Chamberville was the magistrate at Waterford when the King tried to force the Stamp Act down our throats, and Boam Travers—Bruck's father—and his boys hamstrung Chamberville's cattle and horses, and burned his barn, and half killed his coachman, and eventually Chamberville went to live in Boston and rents out his land to the Harters, who're Tories, too, but have about five sons and hold the debts on nearly everyone in the township. The house has been empty for years."

And through the window, Abigail heard Horace cry excitedly, "That's the house! I know it!"

Score one for John.

Weyountah tied up the horses as Horace—pale with mal de mer—sprang down from his tall perch and ran across the drive (which could have stood a few wagonloads of gravel, in Abigail's opinion) to the shuttered windows. "These were open," he said at once. "When we drove up, there were lamps burning inside."

"They show no sign of having been forced," remarked Abigail, bracing her feet on the foundation bricks and raising herself up a little to examine the wood. "Either that, or whoever did it was very skilled—I myself have no practical experience in the forcing-open of window-shutters." She led the way to the front door, and knelt on the single shallow step to examine the wood around the doorknob. "No fresh scratches here—"

"And we're far enough back from the road that there's no reason they'd have chosen the back door over the front," added Weyountah. But they went round to the back in any case, checking every shutter en route, and found the kitchen door likewise innocent of fresh evidence of a break-in. The stable was also closed up, but horses had certainly stood in the yard, and the droppings left there looked no more than a week old—

"And look here," called out Katy, emerging from around

the corner of the stable with her short skirts tucked up even shorter under her belt. "Someone's eaten an apple and smoked a couple of pipes of tobacco here by the corner—"

"That would be *Oculus Cicatricosus*." Horace turned back to look at the house. "I don't think the parlor I was in over-looked the stable-yard . . ."

"No, but Mrs. Lake left you, as you recall, to fetch you poisoned bread and coffee," pointed out Abigail. "And this corner lies in clear sight of the kitchen door."

"Were you here?" Katy hunkered like a child to prod at the nasty little wads of tobacco with a twig, where they lay all but hidden in the unscythed grass. "Did someone try to break into the house?"

"We think Horace—Mr. Thaxter—was lured to this house," explained Abigail, "by people who almost certainly were not the Chambervilles . . . On the other hand," she added thoughtfully, "they might well have been."

"Chamberville is a Tory of the deepest dye." Katy straight-ened up and tucked back into her cap—under the shading brim of her straw sunbonnet—the long wisps of Indian-black hair that seemed to have a tendency to stray everywhere. "A close friend of the Governor's and ripe to turn his hand to any villainy in the King's name. What happened?" She looked sharply from Abigail to Horace, then back toward the house . . . which certainly could have been easily opened, Abigail reflected, by someone who had simply been able to get the key from its owner, as John had said.

"And is there anyone that you know of," she asked, "whose face is scarred in a *V* over his left eye—" She demonstrated again the mark that Charley had so carefully duplicated in mud on his own pink countenance.

"Blue eyes," said Horace eagerly. "Very light blue, under

black brows—the one brow whitened where the scar goes through."

Katy frowned thoughtfully and shook her head. She trailed Abigail and the two young men as they circled the stable, all four studying the ground without any clear idea of what they sought or might find. "He doesn't sound like the sort of person Mr. Chamberville would employ," she guessed, which, Abigail reflected, was probably true.

"I daresay not. And I daresay he and his spiritual brethren could be hired for a penny a day on the wharves, by whoever knows Chamberville well enough to beg his key off him for a night, with the throat-cutting thrown in gratis."

"Were they going to cut your throat?" The girl regarded Horace's tall, bespectacled form with renewed interest.

"I don't know," said Horace uncomfortably. "It seemed so to me last Friday night, stopped in the darkness of the woods with these people . . . Now, I'm not so sure."

"You must be sure," pointed out the girl. "'Tis when you have doubts and hesitate that you become their victim—whether highway robbers or the Governor's men spreading lies to keep the people from acting for their rights. Only in certainty lies the attack, and only in the attack lies salvation and freedom."

"*Some craven scruple*," quoted Weyountah, shaking his head, "*of thinking too precisely on the event.*"

Horace replied, from the same play, "*But I am pigeon-livered, and lack gall.*"

"Well, you can't be all *that* pigeon-livered," reasoned Katy, "if the Tories want to kill you—"

"We cannot be sure they were Tories," said Abigail. "For the simple reason that it appears—at least at the moment—that they were also the ones who killed Mr. Fairfield."

The girl stopped still, thinking about that. Abigail saw

the tears rise to Katy's eyes, only to be pushed aside with a shake of her head. "Who are they, then?" she whispered.

"That's what we're trying to learn. Did you leave your stepfather a note?" she added, as they approached the chaise again. "When you set out to find George this morning?"

The girl nodded, her eyes bleak. "I told him . . . well." She gestured helplessly, letting the thought go. "I've wanted to leave him," she went on. "And I'll not say it wasn't in my mind, when George proposed marriage to me, that even if he later cast me off—which, mind you, I wouldn't put it past that pa of his making him do, in the end . . . But George wasn't the man to behave scaly to a girl. I know he wasn't. And I know it shocks you to hear it, m'am, and I really did marry him before a clerk of the county . . . Anything was better than staying with Mr. Deems."

She looked aside, and color crept up again to her cheeks.

"Did you tell him you weren't coming back?"

A slight move of the head that might have been a nod.

"Will he come after you?"

"He might. Because of Bruck," she added. "He had it all fixed up with Bruck that Bruck was going to marry me and take Mr. Deems in to work for him at his livery, because Mr. Deems never did like Mrs. Cousins who owns the Yellow Cow—Mrs. Cousins is my aunt."

Abigail nodded. Life was such that many people of her acquaintance ended up raising other peoples' children simply because they were thrown onto the world suddenly parentless. She knew, too, that stepsons and stepdaughters were often looked upon as a kind of bounty from Heaven, a cheap source of labor that didn't have to be paid or—frequently—fed with any regularity.

"That is, her first husband and my mother were brother

and sister, but she's never had much use for me, nor for Mr. Deems, not that I can blame her for that."

"Can you cook?" asked Abigail as they reached the chaise, wondering if she'd regret this. "And clean? And mend?"

Katy was nodding, her eyes suddenly huge with hope. She seized Abigail's arm. "M'am, I swear—"

Abigail held up her hand. "Can you take orders?" she went on. "'Twould be from a girl younger than yourself . . ." She was aware that not only Katy, but Horace and Weyountah were looking at her like overboard mariners gazing at a drifting plank. *John is going to kill me—*

"It cannot be permanent," she added firmly. "Yet I daresay you can remain in my house until we find another place for you—"

"Oh, m'am—" began Katy, and then—wholly to Abigail's surprise—the girl burst into tears.

When Abigail, startled, said, "Here—" and moved to take her hand, the girl pulled away, shook her head, made a gesture of denial.

"I'll be all right, m'am. It's just—I really didn't want to go back . . . But I can't—"

"You can." Abigail possessed herself of Katy's hand. "And the rest we can talk about in private. Now get in the chaise," she added, "because that's three o'clock I hear striking—is that the Concord church?—and if I find myself stranded in Cambridge once again Mr. Adams really *will* kill me."

Their speedy departure notwithstanding, Weyountah thought it better to take the land route back to Boston, swinging south through Cambridge at a smart clip and down through the sunny fields and scattered woodlands to

Brookline, and so across the salt marsh, shallows, and mud-flats in the lengthening spring sunset, then over the Neck to the town gate. "If we tried for the ferry and missed," reasoned Abigail, when Katy pointed out that from Cambridge the way was slightly shorter to the ferry, "then we'd have twice the distance to reach the Neck overland and might find the gate shut against us. This way, though 'tis a trifle longer, we'll be certain of getting home."

Katy looked askance at the red-coated guards, as Wey-ountah drew rein before the three brick archways and Horace sprang down to open the chaise door, and at the sight of them Abigail felt herself shiver again: *Has anything happened while I was away—?*

And yet when they'd passed through Brookline, though militia had been drilling on the Common there, there had been no uproar. In Roxbury, at the land end of the Boston Neck, the local volunteers had been clustered companionably around the door of the Sun.

All is well. I'll return to find the house as it always has been, the boys well—

She pushed from her thoughts Charley's counterfeit scar and vague assurances that he'd only seen Mr. Scar-Eye yesterday or the day before, he didn't know where . . .

—John safe . . .

"Are you able for the walk of a mile and a half?" she asked Katy, as she kissed Horace, shook hands with Weyountah, made a hasty exchange of promises to keep one another abreast of whatever might be found while the guards glared at them, and pointedly pulled the leaves of the gate half to. "The house lies on Queen Street; 'tis some little distance."

"I'm well, m'am." The girl glanced sidelong at the soldiers again as they passed through, the last of the day's traffic. The gate-guards shut the three great archways behind them as the last light flashed on the shallow waters, a hundred yards off across the rough field that was all that the Neck contained, and shot the bars. A number of men—rough-coated and jesting with one another—were also coming in on foot from Roxbury: Abigail guessed they'd gone across to drill with the militia. Darkness outlined the hills and trees beyond the river where it flowed into the bay. As the fields along Orange Street gave place to the brick houses of the wealthy, set in their own orchards and gardens, lights were coming up in the windows, a guilt-inducing reminder of those good housewives who had *not* spent the day gallivanting about with undergraduates in the countryside around Cambridge looking for villains, Tory plots, and pirate treasure.

Those Marthas of the world, who had prudently cooked the meals for the Lord's Day tomorrow instead of hastily giving instructions to servant-girls who were really too young to have the whole of those duties thrust upon them—though Pattie was *perfectly* capable of putting together chickens to roast and beans to bake . . .

And so it proved. When Abigail and Katy reached the house, the kitchen was redolent with the scents of tomorrow's dinner and filled like a jewel box with the amber warmth of firelight and lamps. John was, of course, still out at the Green Dragon—Abigail knew that it wasn't the ale in the place that kept him, but the conferences going on all day in its long upstairs room with the Sons of Liberty—and Charley and Tommy flung themselves on her with the frantic abandon of children who sense themselves set aside, however necessarily, in favor of matters that they cannot understand.

Katy was introduced, and when Abigail came downstairs from showing her the small attic room in which she would sleep (with no little relief that she was at least enough of a housewife to have extra sheets clean, ironed, and on hand),

Pattie handed Abigail a letter. "This came this afternoon, m'am. Will Mistress Fairfield be having her bath here in the kitchen, when the rest of us do?"

"If she does," said Abigail, "she'll go after you—I brought her in to help you as much as because she needed a place to stay. But she may not, tonight," she added, remembering that the girl had heard only that morning that her lover was dead.

She broke the seals.

> *Rock Farm*
> *Medfield*
>
> *28 April 1774*
>
> *Mrs. Adams,*
>
> *Thank you for your kind favor, which I have received today. How extraordinary, that strange matters seem to follow my great-grandfather's books! It is as if one of the old man's own curses has clung to them, and though I am indeed sorry to learn that one of these curses has cost a young man his life, still I yearn to hear more of the matter.*
>
> *Indeed I would be delighted to receive you at your soonest convenience. Rock Farm lies four miles beyond Medfield, down the second lane that branches to the left from the road that continues on toward Stonton. It is a fearful drive from Boston, and I shall speak to my niece to prepare a bed for you here.*
>
> *So retired is my state here that your visit would be attended with eagerness, even were it not in connection with that wicked old pirate's evil doings!*
>
> *Sincerely,*
> *Narcissa Seckar*

Twelve

The reflection that the books were indeed connected with a wicked old pirate's evil doings—not to speak of a possible curse—made it no easier for Abigail to keep her thoughts focused the following day upon the Reverend Cooper's sermons. As usual, these ostensibly concerned the doings of ancient Hebrew kings but showed a marked tendency to drift toward Parliamentary injustices and the modern misbehavior of monarchs whose deeds rivalled those of Ahab and Herod; Katy seemed to enjoy both morning and after-dinner discourses hugely.

To Abigail, this was a great relief. From the sound of it, Mr. Deems at the Yellow Cow—not to speak of his associates in the patriot militia—left much to be desired as a moral preceptor, and at intervals during the family baths in the kitchen on the previous night, she had experienced qualms about her generosity in offering roof and bed to a girl whose existence she hadn't even been aware of that morning—and pregnant to boot! But while Pattie was bathing Charley and Tommy,

Abigail had gone up to the attic to offer the facilities of kitchen, towels, hot water, and a screen before the fire to her new guest, and had found Katy, by the light of her single candle, on her knees beside the little pallet bed, weeping—as she had not let herself weep while anyone could see—for George Fairfield. It had led to a long talk, and by the time Katy had descended to take her turn at the end of the bath-line, Abigail had no more doubt that she might not have done the right thing.

"Which is fortunate," said John, when—Saturday night, clean and damp and smelling of soap—he had yanked shut the bed-curtains and tumbled in beside her, "since Sam's been pestering me to ride down to Providence to meet with the Committee of Correspondence there Monday. As you are deserting me again, you wayward woman, I had thought to see if Uncle Isaac and Aunt Eliza might be prevailed upon to look after the children once more. Heaven knows I've heard nothing all evening but about how they'd like to go back. You can send both girls along with them without fearing for Eliza's silverware. Alone at last!"

He sighed, and in the darkness filled his hands with her hair—which, though hidden all day beneath a very proper cap, was in its unbound state like a black silk cloak. "I would bless you a thousand times, my dearest friend, only for not snoring—unlike every traveler I've shared a bed with these past two endless weeks . . ."

She kissed him, those lips so surprisingly soft against hers, and stroked the shorn velvet of his hair. "Bless me, then, dearest friend."

It was good to have John home.

Thus it came to pass that on Monday morning, after helping John and Johnny with the cowshed and dispatching the older children to school, young Mr. Thaxter—John's clerk—

harnessed a horse borrowed from the neighbors to the very old Adams chaise. The prospect of three days in Aunt Eliza's garden had reconciled the boys—and almost reconciled Nabby—to their mother's absence; sitting between the younger boys as they drove slowly back to Milk Street with Thaxter, Pattie, and Katy pacing along beside the vehicle like the aldermen of London escorting the King in procession, Abigail heard all about Charley's plans to implement Johnny's design for a bird-trap, and Tommy's intention to dig a hole clear to China.

"I trust you'll see that he doesn't," said Abigail to Pattie, and both girls nodded. "At least not among Aunt Eliza's roses. Katy, I must beg your forgiveness for saddling you with these two ruffians while Pattie helps Johnny and Nabby with their lessons—"

"Never fear it, m'am," said Katy stoutly. "I'll teach 'em their rifle-drill, and march 'em up and down the garden 'til they faint with fatigue—"

"I'll faint before you do!" Tommy challenged Charley. To judge by their expressions, neither boy found the slightest objection to this program. All four children had taken to Katy with the aplomb learned early by those in large New England families, where unmarried cousins, maiden aunts, and hired girls came and went in farm households like birds of passage. Her ability to whistle, play cat's cradle, and whittle toys won her the loyalty of the younger boys, and her curiosity and eagerness to be instructed in Latin by Johnny sparked his immediate approval. The boy loved to instruct anyone in anything and was well on his way, Abigail reflected with a sigh, to being as much of a prig at that age as Horace had been.

Katy's hard life—harder, Abigail guessed, than the girl

would admit—had left her willing and happy to fit herself into any environment, and Abigail sensed that beneath her sauciness lay great reserves of strength and loyalty. And John, of course, had fluffed up like a pouter-pigeon at the news that she had read his patriotic essays and thoroughly understood and approved.

After kisses, embraces, admonitions, and promises in Aunt Eliza's kitchen, Thaxter helped Abigail into the chaise again, and minutes later they were passing beneath the central archway of the Boston town gates and into open country.

"Don't you worry, m'am," said the clerk, as Abigail turned in the seat to look behind her at the tall jumble of roofs visible beyond the curve of the harbor, at the black masts and hulls clustered along the wharves, the violet green islands floating in the water beyond. "Uncle Isaac will keep them safe, even if . . . well, even if the King's message arrives and there should be trouble. And—well . . ." The young man coughed apologetically. "If you'll excuse my saying so, m'am, but if there's trouble, it's just as well Mr. Adams is out of it."

"Mr. Adams is *not* a member of the Sons of Liberty," retorted Abigail acerbically—a little tired of her neighbors' assumption that just because he shared a great-grandfather with Sam Adams he was naturally hand in glove with his cousin's more nefarious deeds. "He has no more to fear from the King's edict than the Reverend Cooper would . . ."

"No, m'am," agreed the clerk, a stolid young man whom Abigail had known since his school-days. Their mothers had been sisters, and they were both part of a wide-flung family network that stretched over most of the eastern part of the colony. "All the same," he added with a fleeting grin, "if the edict should happen to mention Mr. Adams, it's probably best that he's out of Boston just now—and the children out of the house."

* * *

Medfield lay at a day's drive along the wide bend of the Charles, and was a cluster of brown, peak-roofed houses set among stony fields and woods that stood untouched since the days when the Indians had had them to themselves. A harsh country, Abigail knew, and in places, appallingly primitive. Beyond the town's fields the woods stood thick, a dark roof of oak and hickory shading ancient deadfalls and centuries of fallen leaves. Most of the houses in Medfield boasted two rooms plus whatever loft-space could be used beneath the steep slant of the roofs; more than one, she could see, had the enormous old-fashioned chimneys that spanned the whole of one wall, like the one in Sam Adams's ancient house on Purchase Street, that you could sit inside in perfect comfort while Bess cooked dinner. In the winter, even the village would be isolated for weeks at a time by snow—as her childhood home of Weymouth still was, and John's village of Braintree also—and she shivered at the thought of those outlying farms they passed. Only a hundred years ago, half the town had been burned by Indians, and only a few days' distance to the west, she knew, some of the tribes still lived . . .

Lived, and watched with festering anger the advance of the white farmers, whose cattle destroyed their village fields of corn and pumpkins, and whose craving for land ate away at the hunting-grounds that for the Indians substituted for livestock as white men understood it.

Ten years ago the French had armed the Indians as part of their war with England, and the King, Abigail knew, was anxious to keep the tribes on his side because of the enormous profits the Crown reaped from the trade in furs. If it came to fighting—and if the King landed troops, she knew that it would—would the King arm the Indians? Would he turn them loose upon those he perceived as rebels against his authority?

The thought was deeply unsettling. The more so, Abigail realized, because she recalled not only a hundred details of massacre-stories and farm-burnings, but the equal outrages done by the whites against the Wampanoag and the Abenaki, the Pequot and the Nipmuc . . . the summons to peace-conferences that had ended in slaughter of the Indian delegates, the burning of villages and crops. The tribes would side with the King, both in revenge and because the King guaranteed them their rights against the settlers, who bitterly resented the fact that they could not farm wherever they wished.

They can't reach Boston, she told herself. *As John said, every militia in the state is drilling . . .*

And may be off fighting British troops in the east if an uprising comes.

The thought that she'd left her children in the town—though how she herself would defend them in the event of riot, invasion, or Indian uprising she couldn't imagine—pierced her heart like a knife, and she barely heard Thaxter's humorous observation on a very young child attempting to drive a herd of geese across the town's unpaved street.

Rock Farm lay four miles beyond Medfield at the end of nearly a further mile of lane, and it was nearly dark when Thaxter finally guided the tired horse into the yard. A lantern hung over the door of the farmhouse—small, old, and crude-looking beyond belief—and a couple of men were just crossing from the barn to the lean-to with pails of milk on their neck-yokes. The oldest of them, bearded and grim-looking except when he smiled, set down his pails and strode to the chaise, holding out his hand and beaming, a huge yellow dog trotting at his heels.

"You'll be Mrs. Adams, I expect? Seth Barlow—my son Eben, our cousin Jehu. Tilly, go tell your mother and auntie Mrs. Adams is here—" A girl in faded hand-me-downs darted from the woodpile into the house. "Mr. Thaxter? Pleased to meet you— Down, Rex! Sit, sir . . . Thad, help Mr. Thaxter with the horse— Methusaleh, take Mrs. Adams's things—" Mr. Barlow seemed to have an infinite number of children and young adults on-call, some of the boys no older than Horace but clearly men who did men's work. "I can't tell you how much Aunt Sissy looks forward to your visit, m'am." He held out a hand like a pickled cutting-board to assist Abigail down. "Tell me if you will—and just yes or no, I've no intention to tire you after that drive!—what's the news from Boston? Has the King's edict come?"

"It has not," said Abigail, marveling at the reach of the Boston newspapers. She hadn't seen a coffeehouse or anything resembling one in Medfield—presumably the newspapers were left at the local tavern, though she hadn't seen one of those either. Sam would be pleased. "The town waits daily, and—I am told—every militia from the Kennebec to Martha's Vineyard is readying for trouble."

"And out to Springfield as well." Mr. Barlow named one of the westernmost of the colony's settlements as they crossed the yard to the house, where in the open doorway two women stood framed. One was stout and rosy even in the fading daylight, in a much-mended apron and a dress worn colorless by age and sun—Mrs. Barlow, Abigail guessed even before her bearded husband kissed her. The other, fragile and white-haired, held out her hand with a welcoming smile.

"Mrs. Adams? I'm so pleased you could come. I am Narcissa Seckar—and I knew that old sinner would cause trouble, though he's been in his grave for close to eighty years now! My

husband said there was a curse on those books— Do you mind
a bed in the kitchen tonight? Hannah and I are quiet as mice
when we start the fires up in the morning, I promise you . . .
I would say I'm pleased he was right—my husband, I mean—
save that it's brought death and grief to innocent men. Girls,
this is Mrs. Adams, she'll be staying tonight."

Abigail was introduced to Tilly, Hagar, Zilpah, Dinah,
and Susanna, all engaged in putting up their after-dinner
tasks of mending, knitting, weaving—a loom took up most
of one end of the sand-floored "keeping room" that combined
the functions of kitchen, parlor, dining room, wash room,
and nursery. They hurried about in a rustle of hand-me-down
skirts, setting the long table for a modest supper of bread,
molasses, and milk. Hot water was fetched for Abigail, and
her portmanteau set near the box-bed beside the fireplace
where, Abigail guessed, old Mrs. Seckar herself usually slept:
Thaxter would bed down in the loft with the boys. The
younger Barlows—and those of the company who were cousins or hired help or both—stood behind the benches of the
adults to serve, and to eat their meal standing in the old way;
one of them (*Hagar? Susanna?*) brought close a lamp, so that
Mr. Barlow could read a chapter of the Bible before the meal.
(Second Peter, and a very proper warning to the righteous to
avoid conversation with the unrighteous lest they be corrupted as the Children of Israel were corrupted by long association with Egypt.)

He quizzed the younger children on what he'd read,
prayed an extensive prayer that included thanks for Abigail's
safe journey and a blessing—rather surprisingly—on Rex the
Dog, the horses, cows, pigs, and cats in the barn, and proceeded, finally, to supper. After a day of travel, Abigail had
never encountered bread, milk, and molasses that tasted so
good.

A conscientious guest, Abigail helped the women and girls of the family clean up, while Thaxter went out to give the boys a hand bedding down the stock. When the young clerk sat down with Mr. Barlow, Eben, Jehu, Methusaleh, Josiah, and Cry-Out-at-the-Coming-of-the-Lord to discuss the latest news from Boston, Abigail was taken aside to the corner beside the enormous hearth to share a little tisane with old Mrs. Seckar and to talk of pirates and curses.

"He was my great-grandfather." The tiniest trace of admiration flickered in Mrs. Seckar's voice. "And a fearful old sinner he must have been, by all accounts. In addition to commanding a fleet of four vessels—with a flagship whose name was so scandalous my father wouldn't even tell me what it was—old Geoffrey Whitehead was said to be a sorcerer, able to call the storms or flatten the waves at will, and to turn common rocks into gold, though if that were in fact the case I'm sure he would not have spent so long on the high seas plundering Spanish ships. Old Beelzebub, they called him, and the Nipmucs worshipped him as a god."

"What on earth was he doing in Massachusetts?" By the light of the fire—and a branch of work-candles—Abigail was helping her hostess mend sheets that were so worn she herself would have converted them to dish-cloths . . . having the luxury of one of the busiest lawyers in the colony for a husband. "Spanish ships being rare in these waters, even a hundred years ago."

"I gather he'd hide here when he made things too hot for himself in the Caribbean." Narcissa deftly turned the heel of the sock she was making, her knitting-needles long darts of reflected gold. "He'd repaint his ship and change her sails, and come ashore pretending to be a Dutch merchant—he spoke over a dozen languages with ease, and could pass himself off as anything from an Arab to an Indian. It also turns out he had at least three wives that anyone knows about, in different colonies. The Massachusetts one was my great-grandmother, the daughter of a Boston merchant who didn't see anything odd in her sea-captain husband being gone for a year at a time . . . nor apparently questioned why he would return from his voyages so *very* rich. In addition to her, he was said to have married a Nipmuc chief's daughter and built a castle in the backcountry somewhere, where he'd retreat when his Boston in-laws got on his nerves . . . as I imagine they must have," she added, giving her ball of yarn a twitch, which immediately brought it under attack from two of the kittens whose brothers and sisters were virtuously asleep in the basket beside the hearth. "If they were anything like grandfather Barthelmy, whom they raised."

"A heart like a counting-frame, was how I've heard him described," Abigail remarked.

"I suppose I should be charitable toward him," sighed Mrs. Seckar. "Given that he, his mother, and his sister were deserted when he was small, and he was raised among her family as a poor relation—no wonder the man was grasping. Oh, I don't mean all poor relations are treated ill," she added, with a smile and an affectionate glance across at the group on the other side of the hearth. "The whole family here is poor, by Boston standards, and I could not be better treated if I were their grandmother rather than just their mother's aunt. But Mr. Seckar's mother and sisters lived with us, and when Mr. Seckar died, there was talk of me going—with my surviving sister-in-law—to Mr. Seckar's brother near Concord. I would . . ." She seemed for a moment to grope for a polite way of describing him, and Abigail's mind returned to Katy Pegg and the way her glance had dodged aside when she'd spoken of her stepfather. Abigail remembered, too, some of the tales her parson father told of how children—and the incapacitated elderly—within his own flock were sometimes treated by those obliged to take them unwillingly in.

"Then it seemed Providential," Narcissa went on tactfully, "that I *did* have great-grandfather's books to sell, so that I could contribute a little toward my own keep here—in spite of what my husband's family insisted: that the books, by coming into my possession, were in fact *his* and should go on to Harvard with the rest. I was grateful, too, that I could find buyers for them all so quickly—though mind you, I was not at all surprised that the indecent ones went first!"

She sank her voice, though the girls were chatting happily among themselves as they sewed and the men were totally preoccupied in slandering the King. "I was almost tempted to keep those. I'd had no *idea* . . ."

Among the deep lines of laughter and age, a dimple touched her cheek, and Abigail saw how pretty she must have been as a girl. "Such an amazing thing, is the human imagination!" Mrs. Seckar went on. "But of course, Mr. Seckar—my husband—was the first to cry out that they should be burnt, for if anything bore Beelzebub's curse, 'twas those. And alas," she added, raising troubled eyes, "that it seems to be so. No ill has come of the others, has it? The Arab texts—which I believe you said your nephew purchased?—and those that the Governor bought . . ."

"The Governor?" said Abigail, startled.

"Governor Hutchinson." Mrs. Seckar regarded her in some surprise. "He purchased the bulk of them. Fifty-four books, not counting those I sold to your nephew and his friends."

"He never spoke of them—"

"Perhaps the subject did not arise," said Mrs. Seckar, in her comforting, grandmotherly tone. "He might have thought—"

"No, we were speaking of the books," objected Abigail impulsively. "He's the one who told me about your grandfather's grasping heart, and said he was surprised your grandfather had owned books at all. The whole question of the slave Diomede's guilt or innocence is hinged to the theft of the books. Yet he didn't mention them at all."

Thirteen

"That is most curious." Mrs. Seckar's hands stilled on her knitting; she regarded Abigail for a time in the dim flicker of the fire. Mrs. Barlow was nursing the baby for the last time that night; the younger children had already scrambled up the ladder to the loft and bed. "He paid me twenty-five pounds for the lot of them, hard currency, which was extremely generous. I am sorry to say, the transaction annoyed Mr. Seckar's sister Reuel beyond speaking." Her lips twitched, but she put the un-Christian smile quickly away.

"How did the books come into your hand?"

"Now that," said Mrs. Seckar, shaking her head, "was entirely my doing. For years, I had asked my husband if 'twere possible for us to enlarge the rear wing of the house, which was used as a laundry. He argued I had done quite well there for the whole of my life, and 'twas only vanity that sought more room for ironing and primping . . . though an ill-ironed shirt was enough to justify the cancellation of supper—"

"For a *shirt?*"

The old woman looked for a moment as if she might have made some comment about her husband, but again, she mastered herself and put the thought away, this time without a smile. "He was as he was," she said at last. "I daresay it taught me care in my work—"

"He would cancel his *wife's* supper? 'Tis not the maid we're talking of?"

"We had no maid," Narcissa replied calmly. "He said, 'twas against the will of the Lord to bind another to servitude—"

"He seems to have felt no compunction about binding *you* to servitude."

"A good wife is given unto man for his comfort." Again that small silence, as she looked back over the years spent with Malachi Seckar, infinite tiredness in those surprisingly bright blue eyes. Then she repeated, "He was as he was. My father, while he lived, thought it no great matter, and worth an occasional missed meal himself, to school me, as he said. And I had old Mrs. Seckar, who lived into her nineties, and my husband's sisters Reuel and Rachel to share in the work, though toward the end, in that last ten years, there was only Reuel and myself."

Narcissa Seckar looked to be in her seventies, white-haired and rather fragile in appearance, and Abigail felt herself flush with anger at that selfish old man who had decreed that his wife could do the tasks of hauling water and wood, cooking and cleaning, with her only help a woman who was probably as old as herself.

Before Abigail could snap ungracious words about the dead, however, Narcissa forestalled her. "In any event, I did at last prevail after quite literally decades of asking. And when the workmen broke down the wall of the laundry, lo and behold, they found a sort of little chamber hidden between it and the newer portion of the house. The whole end of the room had been bricked across and plastered, and in the space behind the bricks were two shelves of books."

"Good gracious!" Abigail—a bit reluctantly—put aside the subject of this woman's father, who hadn't even protected his daughter against a domestic tyrant, in contemplation of a treasure trove more valuable, to her mind, than gold. "I take it the house had been in your family? Was it your father's house? I know the Reverend Seckar willed it to the college when he died—"

"The house was built by old Beelzebub." Again there was that trace of pride in Narcissa's voice as she spoke her ancestor's name. "By *Captain Whitehead*, as my father insisted upon calling him. Father pretended to the end of his days that his grandfather had been no more than a sea-captain in the West Indies and had not even sold slaves, much less stolen them from the Spanish and sacked towns in passing. One cannot really blame him, considering the position he held, in the college and in the Church."

"And Beelzebub was—?"

"My father's grandfather, Geoffrey Whitehead. Of course he hushed the matter up, and I think 'twas one reason my father pushed me so hard to wed Mr. Seckar, who was his favorite student and his amanuensis after Father had his stroke. He edited Father's sermons, and acted as his secretary in all his business with the college and with the other churches in the colony. He was the son Father had always wished he'd had, the more so after Phoebe—my sister—wed a man who danced and played the fiddle and spent all his little money on fine horses . . . which he bred, to a fair profit, though Father would never hear of that. Father told me when I was seventeen that he was leaving the house to Mr. Seckar, who came of poor family and needed property. Better that a man of Godliness and worth should have it, he said, than a girl who would only marry it away to one of the Damned. I could marry Mr. Seckar, he said, and continue to live there, or leave it upon Father's death."

"Was your father—" Abigail had to bite back the words *right in the head*? stifling her anger—the man was after all great-grandfather to Tilly and Hagar and Zilpah and at least some of the others . . .

Narcissa only regarded her, with slightly raised white brows. "I was—a defiant girl," she said matter-of-factly. "Rebellious of Father's authority and scornful of the Fifth Commandment. I'm sure had I been the boy Father wanted, I would have kicked up all sorts of riot and rumpus, a fact which he ignored completely when he bemoaned the fact that God had inexplicably saddled him with the wrong sex of children. My sister was younger, and very sweet and meek, until she ran away at age fifteen with Mr. Wellman, who was Sarah's father." And she traded an affectionate glance with Mrs. Barlow. "Mr. Seckar was modest of bearing, right in thought and deed, saw clearly the will of the Lord—in Father's words—"

"Meaning saw clearly the will of your father."

"That, too, though perhaps he did clearly see the Will of God. I have no way of knowing. He was always ready to smite the unrighteous, Father said—meaning spiteful to those who didn't agree with him—and upright to those who looked to him for guidance, meaning cruelly harsh to his mother and sisters when he brought them in to live with us. And if he was as filled with pride as a toad is with poison, where Father could not see, and sometimes used the rod as well as the word to smite and guide . . . I'm sure Father would have allowed that some latitude is to be given for one so filled with the zeal of the Lord."

She returned to her knitting, and the gray kitten stood on its hinder legs and snatched at the moving needle-heads with its white-tipped paws. The farmhouse had no glass to its windows, and outside the tight-barred shutters, Abigail heard the hooting of an owl and the noise of some larger creature, moving about in the woods.

"I'm afraid I've wandered rather far afield," apologized the old lady after a moment. "But indeed, the house was the one I had grown up in, and the rear wing—the laundry and the kitchen—had once, I think, been the main part of the house. 'Tis made of stone, and very long and narrow, and the floors only dirt. I believe 'twas my grandfather, the despicable Barthelmy, who had the main house built in 1683, and old Beelzebub went on living in his old stone wing until his death nearly ten years after that."

"I wonder what the good citizens of Cambridge made of him?" Abigail couldn't keep the amusement from her voice, at the thought of a pirate and sorcerer—and sometime collector of naughty volumes—retiring for his declining years to that quiet town of divinity students and Tory worthies. "Or he of them, for that matter. And what of his castle in the backcountry where Indians worshipped him as a god?"

"From what Father said—though he was quite capable of making it up—toward the end of his life, Old Beelzebub repented of his sins, gave up alchemy—"

"He was an alchemist?"

"Oh, good Heavens, yes. In his quest for the ancient formula for Greek Fire he is reported to have burned down half an Indian village. In addition to which he summoned the Devil, invented a flying machine, and, of course, turned common rocks into gold. His repentance, Father never hesitated to point out, would not have done him the slightest good, as he was clearly destined for Hell, and he—Father—became thoroughly incensed when I asked, *Should we then not trouble to encourage thieves and slave-traders to abandon their evil ways?* and told me not to be impertinent, though I thought it a perfectly reasonable question . . ."

"My son asked me that, too," sighed Abigail. "I told him that only God knows whether a man is ultimately destined for damnation or salvation, and that we must encourage the unrighteous to abandon evil, because it might be—but we do not know—that we are God's chosen tools in another's path toward righteousness, like the ass that bore Saul of Tarsus toward Damascus."

"Well, that explanation would involve my Father not knowing something." Narcissa finished off the top of the sock, clipped the yarn, and slipped it neatly into her basket, as if all the long years she spoke of had happened to someone else. "So it could not be true. In any case, according to my aunt Serafina—Grandfather Barthelmy's sister, who lived with us for some years while I was a child—her father, Old Beelzebub, built the stone house in Cambridge just after King Philip's War, so it might have been he was simply driven out of the backcountry by the Indians and felt himself too old to make a new start there. The newer portion of the house lies at right-angles to the old, in such a way that it was not at all obvious that about eighteen inches of its northern end had been bricked and plastered over, to hide the two shelves of books. Only when the eastern wall was broken out—how long ago it seems! But 'twas not even a month!—to make the enlargement was this secret space found and, in it, my great-grandfather's books."

Thoughtfully, Abigail said, "Which the Governor then bought." She frowned. "But you said your husband ordered the work done—"

"He died," said Narcissa, "not a week after the workmen broke down the wall."

"Will you ladies stay up and make a night of it?" Seth Barlow grinned good-naturedly as he crossed the keeping room to their corner. Thaxter and the older boys came back in from having a final piss and disappeared up the loft-ladder;

the yellow dog turned around a time or two where the benches and chairs had been. The farmer put the tin lamp he carried on the table beside his aunt-in-law's chair and felt the side of the red teapot. Mrs. Barlow and the baby had disappeared into the bedroom some time previously. The house had grown deeply still.

Abigail said apologetically "I should—" and Narcissa waved her small, work-rough hands.

"Don't worry for me, Mrs. Adams, if you're wanting to sit up a little longer. If you're not too tired after your journey—"

"Heavens, no! I only worry that you—"

"Well," said Barlow, kneeling beside them to bank the hearth-fire under a careful mound of ashes, "while you two ladies are arguing out which of you is being polite, I'm for bed. Are you warm enough? 'Tis a mild evening—" He got to his feet, dusted his hands, and brought shawls from the great, clumsy sideboard, one of the few pieces of furniture in the room. "The pallet's made up for you in the bedroom, Sissy—" He bent to kiss the old lady's wrinkled cheek. "Mrs. Adams"— he grasped her hand—"my wife promises she'll be silent as a mouse in the morning. And don't mind old Rex. He snores."

"Anyone who promises mouselike silence," remarked Abigail ruefully, when the bedroom door shut behind him, "has never heard the ones we get in our attic. Five minutes," she promised, "and then I shall let you go to bed."

"Five minutes." Narcissa hobbled to the cupboard, took out a small pot, and from it dripped a spoon of honey into her tisane. "Will you have—No?—Where were we? Oh, yes, selling the books to the Governor."

'Twas true, Abigail reflected, there had been no real NEED for Hutchinson to tell her he'd bought Mrs. Seckar's books . . .

But they had been discussing the books, and Barthelmy

Whitehead, and old Emmanuel Seckar. They had been speaking of Diomede, whose life hung in the balance depending on the events of the evening when two of those books had disappeared.

Only a dullard would not have exclaimed, *But here, I have the rest of those books right here in my study . . .*

And whatever else John and Sam liked to claim, His Excellency Thomas Hutchinson was not a dullard.

"How did that come about? I take it your husband was not ill then——?"

"Heavens, no. That is, Mr. Seckar's health was fragile by then—he was in his eighties—but he never really ailed. He always walked to the college. And he would not hear of selling the books. In fact he spoke of burning them."

"Did he have offers?" Abigail wrapped her shawl around her shoulders, though in fact, as her host had said, the night was a pleasant one. Outside the tiny glow of the betty lamp, the big keeping room was like a friendly cave. The gleam picked up for a moment the round gold reflection of Rex's eyes before that faithful retainer dropped his nose back to his paws, sighed, and returned to his well-earned sleep. He did indeed snore.

"Three," said Mrs. Seckar. "The first was from a West Indian bachelor-fellow named Pugh—who naturally enough offered for the disgraceful books, of which there were about five, as I recall—I think he offered for three or four other volumes as well. Mr. Seckar refused and swore he'd burn them before he'd sell them to the likes of Mr. Pugh."

"I have met Mr. Pugh," said Abigail. "I should like to think myself spiritually fit enough that I would sell him a map were he lost in a desert without water, but I am not sure of it—"

"Well, he's the one who thought it a hilarious jest," said Mrs. Seckar, "to stand up and ask at Mr. Seckar's lectures, was it true that a member of his family had once kept a harem of Berber dancing-girls, and how was the state of their salvation affected by being tupped by a Christian man? Father had managed to completely scotch the rumor about his grandfather," she added. "But Mr. Pugh's great-grandfather had done business with Old Beelzebub in Jamaica. Threats to have him sent down served to keep him from spreading these tales—yet he made the mistake of offering to blackmail Mr. Seckar on the subject when Mr. Seckar would not sell. Of course this only rendered Mr. Seckar quarrelsome. Not," she added drily, "that it took much to render Mr. Seckar quarrelsome."

"And of course the one he quarrelled with was you."

"One did one's best." Narcissa sighed, and her arthritis-crippled fingers stilled on the looped yarn of a new-started sock. "And one did one's best not to be pulled down by his ways. At any rate I did. Poor Reuel was forever trying to please her brother—and her mother, while she lived, who was in many ways worse." She shook her head and went back to setting stitches onto the needles. "I think one of the other offers was from a relative of yours—you said your Mr. Thaxter was your cousin? This young man's name was Thaxter as well, a nice boy with spectacles. He said he had heard that Mr. Seckar might have some books in Arabic to sell, only by that time Mr. Seckar had made up his mind that he would burn the books. That was because of Mrs. Lake."

"Mrs. Lake?"

"If that was her name." Narcissa's tone made Abigail's eyebrows—elevated already—ascend further. "A well-dressed woman who came in her own carriage and offered twenty pounds for the lot. Only Mr. Seckar took one look at the cut of her dress and the cost of her lace—for a man who claimed that God had no use for furbelows he was a sharp judge of them—and the quantity of white lead and cochineal she had plastered from bosom to hairline, and declared her to be the blood-sister of the Whore that Sitteth upon the Waters . . . A remark he made to her face, unfortunately. This provoked a response from her, and the conversation rapidly lost whatever dignity it had begun with. He called her a Babylonian harlot, and I do not even know the meaning of the terms she applied to him, but the interview ended with Mr. Seckar screaming at her to get out of his house and Mrs. Lake threatening to call in her footmen—her *boys*, I believe she termed them—and have him thrashed."

"Footmen?" said Abigail thoughtfully.

"Two of them, as well as a coachman who would not have looked out of place on the gun deck of great-grandfather's flagship—"

"Had he a scar on his face?"

The old woman nodded at once and held up her two fingers in a *V* before her left eye. "A frightful one, just here . . . He and one of the footmen came up as far as the front door as she opened it to go out. I was in the hall at the time and could smell them—rum and dirty linen. After that of course, your poor nephew—who arrived only hours later with his offer—received short shrift, accompanied by an accusation that he was in That Harlot's pay. Mr. Seckar worked himself into a terrible passion." Her lovely brows tugged down into a frown. "Such things left him exhausted as mere walking did not, and he still felt a heaviness in his limbs, he said, on the following day. And on the following night he died."

She fell silent, gazing past the tiny gleam of the betty lamp into the silent gloom. The cat woke in her basket and padded out through the hinged flap in the door to hunt; the kittens tussled a little among themselves, then returned to sleep. Rex turned upon his side with a profound sigh. Though it was nearly too dark to see anything, Abigail could hear in the other woman's voice, despite the outrageous conduct of the man who had been her master for nearly three-quarters of her life, a break of regret, of grief.

It had, Abigail reminded herself, only been a few weeks—after how many years? One might hate the husband who crushed and oppressed and bound one's life, but he had been, when all was said, Narcissa's nearest company for almost fifty years.

"How did he die?"

Narcissa shook her head. "I think in his rage, he had strained his heart," she said. "Then we all three came down ill that evening—Mr. Seckar, Reuel, and I. One of his students had given him a frumenty, a dish of which he was very fond, and I suspect that under all the spices it might have been a little unwholesome. The doctor, when he was called, bled us and said 'twas likely an influenza, but neither I nor Reuel had a fever, though all the next day I had a headache, and felt stupid and not myself, though that," she added, "might have been the bleeding. In a way I am grateful, for I don't even recall feeling shock when I woke—halfway through the morning and the sun high in the sky—and found him lying dead at my side. I staggered to the door wrapped in a quilt, and managed to get it unlatched and to call out to some boys in the lane to fetch a doctor. Beyond that I recall little of the day. They tell me they found me curled up asleep in the quilt on the floor of the hall when the doctor arrived."

She fell silent again, a little like Weyountah, Abigail thought, repeating his memory of last Tuesday night as if to fix it in his mind. To make it something which had once happened to him, rather than a gnawing and present pain.

After long silence, Abigail asked, "And were any of the books gone the next day?"

The older woman looked up from her contemplation of

the dark pit of the hearth, startled. "Why, I have no idea," she said. And then, "Good Heavens, Mrs. Adams, you do not mean to suggest that my husband and I were *poisoned*? So that someone could get at the books?"

"I don't know what I mean to suggest," said Abigail. "You say your husband was frail?"

"He was active," she said. "And alert. But his heart was not good, and after preaching or lecturing, he would often come home and sleep for hours."

"Then a drug administered to put the household to sleep might easily have been too strong for him."

"Good Heavens," she murmured again, her hands still upon her knitting, her bright blue eyes gazing for a moment into the darkness, as if through it she could see the face of the horrid old man who had forbidden her supper if his shirt was not ironed as he liked it, and who would not have in a servant to help two old women whose strength was nearly gone.

Then her gaze returned to Abigail. "On the other hand," she said, "if someone knew of his infirmities, 'twould be just as easy to poison him—you must inquire as to the source of that frumenty, Mrs. Adams, the moment you return to Cambridge!—knowing that I would sell the books afterwards . . . would it not?"

"You, Mrs. Seckar," said Abigail, "are too clever by half. No wonder your husband wanted to keep you a slave."

Fourteen

Firebells ringing. In the kitchen Abigail heard them, and panic seized her: four-fifths of the houses in Boston were timber, and of those, most were crowded in these dense neighborhoods around Brattle Street and Brattle Square, where flames could leap from roof to roof. Though the cold March evening was still (*March?* she thought cloudily, 'tis *the second of May* . . .), if the fire was close, it wouldn't save their house . . .

(*We left that house, didn't we? We went back to Braintree because of John's chest-pains . . . Tommy was born in Braintree . . .*)

She ran down the corridor from the kitchen of the house on Brattle Street, tiny Nabby and tinier Johnny clinging to her skirts. Her movements clumsy (*Because of the baby? Or because I'm dreaming . . .*), pregnant with the child who became Charley, she flung open the front door, the cold smiting her, snow on the ground.

Voices shouting all around her in the twilight as her neighbors came rushing to their doors. Men raced to pump water from frozen pumps, to form up the lines that every neighbor-hood knew by instinct to form, buckets passed hand-to-hand . . .

Only there was no smoke in the air. Just shouting from the direction of King Street, men's voices with a savage note in them that raised the hair on her nape. In her dream she knew what was going to happen and turned, shouted over her shoulder at her children, "Stay inside—"

A single shot cracked out in the icy twilight—going over it, dozens of times, with John later, she never forgot that sequence: a single shot. Then a volley of gunfire, like ragged thunder.

John had been out that evening at his club in South Boston, and her heart was in her throat that he might have been in King Street—she knew exactly what had happened. For weeks the citizens of the town—the prentice-boys, the layabouts, the Sons of Liberty, the children—had been hectoring and cursing and threatening the British troops that Governor Hutchinson had asked the King to send, to help him keep order in the town that hated both Governor and King. For weeks she'd seen the redcoats walking about the icy streets armed with their muskets, primed with the Governor's accounts of riots and dis-orders, and confronted every day with handbills and broadsides decrying the troops as slave-masters who must be cast out.

Even in those dark days, pregnant and ill and sick with grief at the loss of the tiny daughter who had died the month before, Abigail knew that it would come to shooting.

She reached King Street while the powder-smoke still hung thick in the darkening air, the sharp smell of it overrid-ing the characteristic stink of fresh-spilled blood. Bodies lay in the snow: a young boy in a pool of blood at the mouth of Quaker Lane, a black man and a white sailor sprawled in the rucked and muddy slush close by the little knot of British soldiers whose coats seemed dark in the twilight, like the blood spilled all over the snow.

* * *

Her eyes opened with a snap: *Where am I?* Unfamiliar smells, the close air seeming to press on her . . .

She put out her hand and instantly touched a wall, like the side of a coffin . . .

Her other hand, flailing, met curtain.

Rock Farm.

The clink and scurry of tiny paws beyond the heavy cloth.

Those dratted kittens . . .

Abigail slept again.

Firebells ringing in the cold March twilight, only this time she saw the kitchen of her own house in Queen Street. The house was burning, and she heard gunfire in the street; Nabby, Johnny, Charley, Tommy fled out the back door, Abigail calling after them in a voice that had no sound to it . . . *Why are they alone? Why is no one else in the house?*

The cowhouse was in flame, and so was the house next door. Johnny led the way down the smoke-wreathed alleyway that led toward the street, clinging tight to Nabby's hand on his left, to Charley's on his right, smoke-blind, terrified, stumbling.

Charley was holding Tommy's hand, and when Tommy stumbled, tripping on his long leading-strings on the sides of his dress, Charley's hand slipped from his.

Tommy screaming, shrill voice tiny against the roar of the flame, trying to get to his feet in the snow as his sister and brothers fled down the aisle of smoke and burning. Fled away from him, unaware that they'd left him behind . . .

Gunfire somewhere close. Men shouting as the city burned.

Tommy screaming . . .

*   *   *

Abigail jerked awake, ill with panic, heart hammering. In the kitchen beyond the bed-curtain something fell with a small clatter. More dashing little feet.

I will catch those kittens and dunk them up and down in the water-bucket by their little tails.

Then half-grasped fragments of a dream, of distant gun-fire and distant burning, very far-off now and visible in the darkness through the window of Governor Hutchinson's tap-estried study. The Governor raised his head a little where he sat beside the cozy hearth, listened. Then touched the rim of his reading-glasses to settle them and went back to his perusal of the book in Arabic that lay upon his knee.

"Did Mrs. Lake come back to buy the books after your husband's death?" Abigail took the breakfast plates from Tilly, Hagar, Zilpah, et al., and arranged them on a towel-draped corner of the table where the basin was brought for washing. Mrs. Barlow had already gone out to feed the chickens—at the wooden counter, two of the girls helped each other, dumping boiling water into the churn to scald it for butter, while two others gathered up straw sun-hats to start on the garden work. In the country, there was always something that needed doing. Abigail helped Narcissa and the youngest girl with the dishes, the stillness of the spring morning broken only by the crack of axes in the woods, where Thaxter obligingly lent a hand with the endless sum-mer task of cutting winter fuel. When Seth Barlow had asked them last night, *Would they remain a day?* Abigail had assented, despite her uneasiness about leaving her children.

To return to Boston would entail a drive of all the daylight hours. She knew there were things that she had forgotten to ask last night.

"She did not." Narcissa paused, frowning, a rag daubed with soap in her hand. "Drat it, there goes my theory that the murder was done without robbery. I wish I could remember how many of those books there were, hidden behind the wall and what they were about."

"You said, fifty-four."

"'Twas only what I sold to the Governor." The older woman rubbed briskly at the pewter, went to the counter to cadge the last of the boiling water to add to the basin. "And the list of them that Mr. Seckar made went with them. Once I had said that they were mine to sell or to keep—this was after your nephew's first attempt to purchase and Mrs. Lake's visit—Mr. Seckar took them away and hid them in his study."

"Hid them literally? Not just shut the door and turned the key?"

"Hid them," said Narcissa firmly. "He said he would not put it past me to try to steal one or two, to sell them, and to blame his sister for the theft . . ."

"Why would you do that?"

"To make up household money that I had overspent. 'Twas ever his fear," she explained, "that I would spend too much at market and that I would sell something of his to make up the difference. His mother and sister were both fearful pinchpennies, and I could not throw out so much as a torn napkin without accounting of it to them."

No wonder this primitive farmstead where she was obliged to sleep in the kitchen seemed to fill the old woman with such happiness. It did not include any of the Seckar family.

"So a thief who came in when the family was drugged might not have got them all," said Abigail. "He—or she— would not have known where to find them. Was there any who

knew the house well, besides yourself and your sister-in-law?"
Abigail settled the dripping plates on the towel—only six of
them, which had probably come across from England with the
original settlers: the children ate off trenchers made of the
dried heels of bread-loaves and shared a cup among them.

"Nary a soul," the old lady replied promptly. "You must
understand, Mrs. Adams," she added with a rueful smile,
"there was not a man of the faculty—and I think every single
one of the Fellows—that my husband wasn't in a quarrel with,
over everything from the Nature of Time as it existed *before*
God created the Heavens and the Earth, to whether women
should be permitted to learn to read and write . . . which my
husband said were not necessary to a woman's salvation and
were in fact a detriment, for with our limited understanding
we would only come to hurt in using such things."

She stepped aside to let one of the little girls—Hagar or
Susanna—sweep the sanded floor around her feet. "And then,
there were a number of men in the college who felt that my
father had been completely wrong in leaving the house to Mr.
Seckar, and this, too, was a fruitful cause of backbiting. As a
farmer's son, Mr. Seckar was considered by some to be undeserving of the Vassall Chair—though he was a great scholar
and well deserved the honors accorded him. He felt everyone
was in league against him."

"Did anyone come to try to purchase the books the day
after your husband died?"

"That evening young Mr. Fairfield came with food from
the College Hall—Heaven only knows who he bribed to get
it!—and to make sure we had all we needed. We were both,
Reuel and I, still very weak from being bled—and poisoned
into the bargain! 'Twas then I asked him, was he interested in
purchasing any of the books? Perhaps I'm as wicked as Mr.
Seckar and his mother were always saying," she added, and

though she kept her tone light, Abigail heard in her voice that it was something she had indeed believed from time to time. "And it may come from being the great-granddaughter of a pirate, but 'twas already in my mind that Mr. Seckar's brother would be taking us in—Reuel and I. I thought that I had rather have a little money of my own . . . and the books *were* my own, as Old Beelzebub's heiress, even if the house had been left to the college. In any case, I suspected Mr. Fairfield would be interested in those volumes that Mr. Pugh had found so congenial, and I was right. I think he at once told your nephew that I would sell, for young Mr. Thaxter and his Indian friend appeared the next morning to buy what they could afford, and later in the day the Governor sent a man to purchase the rest from under the noses of the College Board of Governors. Mrs. Lake herself never came back."

"Curious," said Abigail softly. "Curious."

Through the long spring day, Abigail helped the girls and Narcissa in the garden, took her turn minding Baby Mary, listened to Tilly, Methuseleh, and Josiah recite their lessons, and in general gave herself over to the peaceful rhythms of the deep countryside. In such a place, it was impossible to know what was happening in Boston and thus necessary to trust entirely in the mercy of God. The family kept insisting that she was here as Aunt Sissy's guest, and they were glad of it for they feared Aunt would miss the town life, and it wasn't necessary for her or Thaxter to do a thing . . .

And yet, Abigail missed the vegetable-rows back in Braintree almost as much as her children delighted in the open spaces of Aunt Eliza's garden, and she revelled in the smell of the earth as she pulled weeds in a borrowed sun-hat. In the forenoon she helped Sarah Barlow prepare dinner for when the men came in from the woods and the field, and looked over the stitches of the younger girls, and now and then sat with

Narcissa and came back to the subject of alchemical books and pirate treasure . . .

"How did you know your great-grandfather was a pirate?" she asked at one point. "If your father worked to keep the matter hushed, and his father as well . . ."

"Aunt Serafina told us." Narcissa deftly untied the strings of Baby Mary's clout, took the washrag Abigail handed her. "She was, as I said, Grandpa Barthelmy's younger sister and lived with us when I was a very little girl. She remembered Old Beelzebub—her father—very well. She said he looked like the Devil would have, if the Devil were ever to sit in a corner of the kitchen and play the fiddle. This was after he had changed his way of life, of course, so she never saw him in his glory, with a cutlass in his teeth and burning cannon-fuses braided in his beard. But she said he was very tall, with long gray hair thick as a horse's mane, and had a long mustache whose ends he braided, and that he was missing two fingers of his right hand so that he held the fiddle-bow strangely. She swore us to secrecy, Phoebe and I, and at night when Father had put out the lights, Aunt whispered to us about the Indians worshipping him and how he burned down half their village and summoned the Devil and all the rest of it—"

"Did she ever speak of him hiding a treasure?" Abigail handed her a clean baby-clout and made finger-waggles at Baby Mary, laid on the keeping room table, who caught at Abigail's fingers and threshed her tiny legs.

Narcissa frowned as she tied the clout in place. "In a general sort of way," she said after a time. "Though that may have been only something Phoebe and I made up later, because pirates are supposed to have buried treasures. Certainly I recall nothing being said of one buried in Massachusetts. And even if there had been, I can't see that it would have gotten past Grandpa."

"Did your grandfather ever search for one?"

"If he had, 'twould have been an admission that his father was a pirate." Narcissa picked up the infant and carried her toward the door, Abigail following with a blanket. "Not that it would have stopped the old scoundrel. I'm a little surprised he hadn't had all the walls of Beelzebub's original stone house sounded the minute the old man died. Perhaps he thought that in repairing his way of life, his father had given the money to charity . . . something it never sounded like the old sinner would have done, either after his reformation or before it, according to Aunt Sera."

Abigail spread out the blanket in the sun, shaded her eyes to catch a glimpse of those three little straw-bonnets bent dutifully over the garden rows. "Why did he reform?" she asked. "Did your aunt tell you that?"

"No." Narcissa's forehead puckered as she considered the matter, putting together old tales half recalled, which might— Abigail reflected—have been hearsay anyway . . . "Yet it must have taken some great event, don't you think? For a man given heart and body to the ways of sin—not only sins of the flesh, as all pirates do, but the sort of intellectual dabbling in alchemy and demonology that can be twice as fascinating to an intelligent man. For such a man to reverse his steps and try to walk back uphill to the Light. Particularly," she added, "when everyone around him is telling him, as they must have if he was living in Massachusetts, that 'twould not have done him any good anyway."

"Exactly." Abigail adjusted a portion of worn sheet over a long billet of firewood to make a sort of lean-to above the baby's head. "So why would he have done that?"

"Does it make a difference?"

"I don't know. But 'tis odd—one of many odd things about this whole adventure. Is his castle still standing? The treasure would be there if anywhere."

"I've never heard of a castle anywhere in the backcountry." Narcissa fished last night's sock from her workbasket. "It might only have been a sort of *palisado*, such as soldiers build of logs in enemy country, in which case, 'twould have been occupied by the Indians when he left it and certainly destroyed during the fighting with France, if not before. And it may not even have existed at all. If he'd ever had any claim to land in the backcountry, it's been long sold. For again, Grandpa Barthelmy would have got hold of it, had it still been in the family, and I can't imagine he'd have sold a square foot of his father's land without searching it for buried treasure."

"'Twould serve Grandpa Barthelmy right, and your father, too," retorted Abigail, "had there been land with treasure buried on it, and they sold it . . . *Was* Old Beelzebub in Jamaica when Henry Morgan was Lieutenant Governor there?"

"Oh, I should think so." Narcissa grinned cheerily. "Nearly every pirate on the Spanish Main passed through Port Royal at one time or another, did they not? If he'd wanted to blackmail Morgan for his congress with Jezebel Pitts, he'd have had plenty of opportunity to do so."

Fifteen

Abigail's sense of well-being—of a job well accomplished, and of new friends made—lasted her about a hundred yards down the lane toward the Boston Road.

Thaxter hitched up the chaise shortly after first light Wednesday morning, and they were sent off with much handshaking and the gift of fresh-baked bread, new butter, and several slabs of soft cheese ("The landlady at the Anchor on the road back to Boston hasn't washed a dish in twenty years . . ."). Mr. Barlow bade her tell Mr. Adams that he and all the men hereabouts stood ready to defend the colony's liberties (he obviously thought she was married to the *other* Mr. Adams).

But no sooner had the house disappeared among the trees behind them than the enormity of having been gone from Boston—and her children—for three days settled upon Abigail like the fall of night, and her dreams of the Massacre, of fire and peril, of Tommy left behind crying in the snow returned and tormented her like a persistent gadfly for the remainder of the day.

The reflection that Cousin Sam would have sent out riders to Medfield and every other town posthaste in the event of any real trouble gave her only momentary comfort. "If the British have not yet arrived, the whole household has come down with the smallpox," she sighed ruefully, as the chaise turned onto the main road. "Or the house has burned to the ground."

"I'm sure all is well, m'am," replied Thaxter soothingly, which caused Abigail to smile despite her anxiety. In his months of association with herself and John, her young cousin had yet to pick up their sense of humor. John would have immediately set himself to cap her visions of disaster: *I think a lightning-strike, rather than the smallpox . . . If the harbor hasn't risen in flood . . . No, wait, we've entirely forgotten the earthquake . . .*

Instead, for the next several miles, the clerk set himself earnestly to assuaging her fears with assurances of how secure and happy the four children would be at the home of Eliza and Isaac Smith . . . something of which Abigail was herself already aware. Yet he meant well, and she knew that to summarily silence him would hurt his feelings. So she settled herself to listen and to sort in her mind what she'd learned, like a card-player arranging clubs and spades, hearts and diamonds.

A frumenty was exactly the sort of thing a solicitous student might bring to an elderly professor about whose health he was concerned—and the old man was probably vain enough to believe assurances of concern even from a man with whom he'd quarreled. But it pointed back yet again to the college: to someone he knew. And from Abigail's experience with the dish, the dried fruit and assorted spices that customarily flavored the meaty porridge could easily conceal the bitter flavor of opium.

Mrs. Lake presumably had access to a kitchen, but 'twas certain Seckar wouldn't have taken a cup of water from her hand if he were dying.

Did they make frumenty for the students in the Hall?

There are two of them in it, she thought. *Mrs. Lake—whose name almost certainly isn't Lake—and someone connected with the college. Someone who knows Old Beelzebub was a pirate. Someone who knew about—or learned very quickly about—the books.*

All of which would amply describe St-John Pugh . . .

Were it not for the curious fact that the Governor had not mentioned to her, Abigail, that he'd bought Mrs. Seckar's books, and the ease with which Mrs. Lake could have gotten the key to the Chamberville house from the Governor's hand.

Mr. Pugh had forged the note designed to keep George Fairfield from his rooms past midnight, when he could feel safe in searching for the books . . . Had he searched for them before, in the Seckar house, while its owner lay dying at the side of his sleeping wife? Would a young and dissolute man need to believe a copy of Aretino's *I Modi*—complete with illustrations—might conceal a pirate's treasure-map, to move Heaven and Earth to take possession of it?

And would St-John Pugh—the son of a West India merchant who was almost certainly a smuggler—enter into alliance with the Governor? And if George Fairfield had come back from his tryst to find Pugh in his room, would he not have been slain in his clothing rather than his nightshirt? Had he come in before midnight and gone to bed?

"Why would the Governor have to use subterfuge, drugs, and burglary to enter George Fairfield's rooms in the first place?" asked Thaxter, when Abigail spoke of the matter just east of Dedham. "I realize he can't simply detain the Vassall Professor of Theology for twenty-four hours while having the sheriff search his house, but an undergraduate? He could have simply had Horace and the servant arrested."

"With a King's Commissioner due to arrive within the week, I should be careful—were I the Governor—about going on public record as having jailed the son of a Virginia planter who is moreover the captain of a troop of Loyalist light cavalry. Particularly if I had no intention of turning over to the King any treasure that I might find."

Thaxter said, "You think Cousin Sam is right, then? That there is treasure?"

"I think that *they* think so," replied Abigail grimly. "Whoever *they* are, they consider what they're looking for worth three men's lives . . . so far. That's what concerns me."

They passed through Dedham and through the wooded farming country along the Charles. Eschewing the slandered Anchor, they had a picnic-lunch in the overgrown ruin of what had once been a farmstead. "It must have been quite a fire," remarked Thaxter, after tethering the horse near the crumble of anciently charred timbers that marked where the barn had been. "To have jumped that distance, from barn to house—"

"I should say rather that the two fires were started separately." Abigail rose from spreading a blanket on the bare stones of the foundation and peeked behind a tangle of gooseberry at the old smoke-blackening of the walls. "To judge by the growth of the trees in the dooryard, I'd say 'twas King Philip's Indians that destroyed this place, a hundred years ago."

"Philip—" Thaxter frowned, counting back in his mind. "Was he King of France . . . after Louis? The old King Louis, the present King's . . . grandfather? Great-grandfather?"

"Great-grandfather," said Abigail. "And no, Philip wasn't King of France. He was a chief of the Wampanoags who united the tribes against us . . . for all the good it did them," she added sadly. "They might have chased us out of their hunting-grounds hereabouts when first we set foot in this land, but they didn't. Like Virginia and the Carolinas and Connecticut—and Massachusetts—each tribe of Indians saw itself as a separate nation: Nipmuc and Wampanoag and

Pocassett. They would not unite with their enemy tribes, and so all fell to a greater foe."

This led to talk, over bread and Mrs. Barlow's excellent cider and cheese, of the excesses of Virginia's Governor—every bit as arbitrary as Hutchinson, but at least Hutchinson had never stirred up war with the Indians on the frontier as a means of distracting the men of the colony from complaints for their rights, as Dunmore was said to be doing.

"Were the King to send troops to occupy Boston in consequence of the dumping of the tea," said Abigail, "I doubt the Virginians or the New Yorkers would raise a peep over it. They seem to think we should apologize for protesting against the King's tyranny *and* pay for the tea that we wouldn't pay for when we were commanded to buy it and none other—even Mr. Franklin"—she named the Pennsylvania philosopher whom many considered the intellectual head of the movement toward the colonies' rights—"has advised we do so . . . presumably so he will not be put in the position of speaking in favor of hooligans."

As they gathered up their much-depleted supplies and corked the remains of the cider, the young man looked around him at the ruined farmstead again and commented—with a town boy's ignorance—"I wonder they never rebuilt this place."

"The land's dreadful." Abigail nodded toward the shaggy remains of what had been an orchard. "'Tis all rocks among the trees, and I see no well here. And it may be the land was taken over by some wealthier farmer in the district, the records having been burnt with the burning of the town. All the good land is west of here, in the valley of the Connecticut. The whites took that from the Pequots long before King Philip raised his forces—killed them all, my father told me, by selling them blankets taken from men who'd died of the smallpox."

"Is that true?"

"Having met some of the merchants in Boston," replied Abigail drily, "can you doubt it? I wonder myself if Old Beelzebub did not change his way of living—move to Cambridge and build his house there—because the Indians no longer worshipped him, but drove him out."

"And he left his treasure behind?" The clerk's eyes brightened as he slipped the bit into the horse's mouth again, hooked the harness to the traces once more. "Then it might still be there! All we'd need to do is check the county landrecords in the State House . . ."

"And discover that Old Beelzebub lived on in Cambridge a good fifteen years past King Philip's War and maybe more, and had plenty of time to return in perfect safety and dig his treasure up himself. Or, in the years since his death, if he indeed owned land, his clutchfisted son would have done so."

"But if he did not find it? If the treasure were cleverly hidden, in a cave or a pit, and the direction coded to look like a disgraceful account of an assignation by a pirate queen and a government official who should have known better—"

"Then it might indeed," said Abigail, as the chaise pulled out of the weed-thick dooryard and down the dim trace back to the road, "be worth three men's lives . . . to somebody."

A s had been the case a week ago, Abigail and her escort reached the Neck of Boston just as the sun was touching the distant hills. Coming through Roxbury, acquaintances had waved to them as they passed the Common, and no one had run out to them shouting, *Turn back, turn back, the streets of Boston run red with blood!* . . . Nevertheless, Abigail was conscious of deep relief not to see the smoke-plume of a burning town rising before them. Thaxter put the tired horse into a smart trot, and they jolted along the track between the shining and fishy-reeking shallows, with the red-coated soldiers standing waiting—again—for them in the half-closed portal.

The Common lay as it always had, a great ragged pasture sloping upward toward Beacon Hill, fading into the twilight. The tinny toot of the herd-boys' horns as they gathered up the cows mingled with the clatter of wheels on the cobbled street. The familiar mix of fish, woodsmoke, and latrines seemed to welcome her as they rattled up Orange Street, and Aunt Eliza and Uncle Isaac greeted her with embraces and laughter and offers of supper. Even her self-important cousin Young Isaac— a clergyman who seemed to regard Abigail's marriage into the Adamses as the worst mésalliance since Persephone's nuptials with Pluto—forebore to chide her about John's associates. Nabby clung silently—as if she suspected that her mother preferred jauntering over the countryside hunting pirate treasure to remaining hearth-bound and cleaning lamps—while Johnny brimmed over with an account of how profoundly he had impressed his Latin master that day. Charley wanted to know why they couldn't have a garden on Queen Street, and Tommy was missing altogether—they had to go out into the garden and hunt for the boy among the beanpoles.

"We've taken turns going over to the house to milk the girls," said Pattie, as she and Katy herded the children to the Smith kitchen to get cleaned up for the return home. "Mrs. Butler offered to do it, but 'tis no trouble. We take Charley and Tommy with us—"

"We're due there now," added Katy. "I can hear the boys bringing the herd in."

The Butlers, and the Hansons on the other side, had offered to look after Cleopatra and Semiramis in the absence of the Adamses and to have their prentices clean the stalls in return for a dozen small favors John had done them over the past few years.

"We've put the milk in the coldest corner of the pantry, so there'll be a fair deal of butter to be made . . ."

"I went out to Cambridge yesterday," added Katy, a little shyly, "to see Diomede in the jail, as you said I might—"

"I did indeed," said Abigail, "and I'm glad you thought to do so. Really, Eliza," she added with a smile, "there's no need—"

"Nonsense, nonsense," declared her aunt, as the maid brought to the kitchen table a tray laden with Dutch coffee, bread and butter, marmalade, and cold meats, "after a journey like that you must be famished—"

"*I'm* famished," said Charley hopefully, looking at the marmalade.

It was well and truly dark, and Tommy and Charley were sound asleep on the seat of the chaise when the little party returned along Queen Street by lantern-light. The lamps in the houses they passed, even, were being quenched on the lower floors, leaving only the very dim squares of illumination higher on the brick walls, where bedroom candles flickered over the pages of Bibles or novels, while men took off their wigs and scratched their heads, and women brushed out their long hair. Eliza had handed Abigail a letter from John, who had been delayed in Providence—*Another night bedding down with snoring strangers, poor lamb*, reflected Abigail ruefully. *Just as well, I can get the house in order again before he arrives.*

The children crowding around her while Thaxter unharnessed Tom Butler's horse, she handed her lantern to Katy, unlocked the kitchen door, and banged her ankle very smartly against something hard that lay almost on the threshold as she stepped in.

She began to say, "Good Heavens, Pattie, we didn't accidentally leave Messalina indoors—?" but the smell of spilled vinegar smote her, and the faint sickliness of spoiled milk.

She held the lantern up to further throw its light.

She'd nearly tripped over a crock of butter—not broken, but lying on its side where it had . . . *Fallen? How could it?* Even had the cat been somehow trapped indoors, she could never have—

Slowly, the light penetrated through the kitchen and pantry, showing Abigail an appalling shambles. Chairs had been pushed about, every drawer of the big sideboard stood open, cupboards agape. Beside her, Johnny said, "Ma—" and Nabby's hand, cold and frightened, gripped suddenly at hers.

And Charley, delighted as all three-year-olds are with chaos: "Was it bears did this?" He darted forward and Abigail grabbed him by the shoulder, pulled him back, and backed out of the pantry, out of the house.

"Katy," she said, "hold on to the children—Nabby, run next door and get Mr. Butler and his boys. Pattie, go with her," she added, seeing the little girl hesitate in fear.

"You don't think there's anyone—" began Pattie hesitantly, and then, as if exonerating herself, "I was inside yesterday, to make sure all was well, and it was. Pfew, that vinegar is strong! What happened?" She looked back toward the stable, from which Thaxter emerged, bearing the other lantern. "Who would do this?"

Happily, Charley opined, "I bet it was Mr. Scar-Eye!"

Sixteen

While Katy and Pattie took the children next door to the Butlers', Abigail, Thaxter, Tom Butler, and the cooper's two apprentices went through the house armed with kindling-axes, barrel-mallets, and every lantern that could be borrowed up and down the street. They found no human foe on the premises, but the house had been ransacked from cellar to attic. Even Katy's pallet bed had been shoved away from the wall and its mattress torn open, hay strewn everywhere in the room.

Abigail and the children went back to Uncle Isaac's to sleep, leaving Thaxter to guard the premises until morning. She dreamed of being locked in the house while it was being searched, hearing the scrape of Mr. Scar-Eye's boots as he groped toward her in the dark.

When she returned in the morning, it was to find Sam Adams in the kitchen, with his wife Bess, his daughter, Hannah, and their maid Surry all engaged in mopping up the spilled vinegar from the broken kitchen cask and scrubbing everything in sight. Abigail groaned inwardly—it was John's unvarying contention that the scene of any crime contained at least some piece of information about the criminal. Though she had a strong suspicion that Charley had been right about the culprit being Mr. Scar-Eye, she had hoped to find something that might tell her where to look for this sinister gentleman and who might be his employer.

Yet she was far too grateful at the prospect of not having to clean up the entire house herself to quibble, only assigning to Sam and Thaxter the task of straightening the tumbled library (*John will never be able to find anything on his shelves ever again!*) while she made a careful tour of the upstairs.

It told her nothing she hadn't known before. It had been too dark to see much by lantern-light last night, and their only object had been to make sure there was no one still lurking in the house, so the tracks of the reconnaissance party— herself, Tom Butler, et al—did not penetrate beyond the doorway of any room. Morning light showed Abigail that there had been three burglars, men in rough boots . . . something she could have guessed, she reflected wryly, from Horace's account of the sinister coachman and his henchmen. She also knew they were sized Small, Medium, and Large from Horace's account, information borne out by their tracks, which were just barely visible in the bedroom she shared with John. The merest modicum of guesswork would also have been sufficient for her to tell from Horace's story that they were men used to burgling places—there wasn't a nook in the house that they hadn't plundered, a fact that made her very glad she'd left the household money and her pearls at Aunt Eliza's with the children.

Beyond those obvious indicators, the visitors had been annoyingly fastidious. No one had dropped so much as a button, let alone a dagger that might match the wound in George

Fairfield's side or a letter from Mrs. Lake bearing instructions to murder Horace. No bloody handprints (*thank goodness!*); no mysterious documents in Arabic or any other language.

But, Abigail reflected as she came downstairs, she'd had to look. If they'd left any of these things in the kitchen, well, Bess, Hannah, and Surry had taken care of them and there was nothing that she, Abigail, could do about it now. The best she could accomplish at the moment was to assign various tasks to clean up, and herself go to the market—which, though it was now late in the morning and nothing would be available but picked-over leavings, was a matter of critical importance, particularly if John was due back tomorrow or Saturday . . .

"And we need to get up laundry tonight," she added to Thaxter, as she passed the study door. "I will *not* have anyone in this house spend a moment on sheets those villains have pawed—"

A familiar voice called from the kitchen, "Is she in? Aunt Abigail—!"

Then Weyountah's, deeper and steadier, "Is there something we can help with—?"

"Yes." Abigail entered the big room, dusting her hands. "Horace, get my marketing basket from behind the pantry door, please. Weyountah, would you be able to stay and assist Mr. Adams in straightening up the study? Oh, thank goodness, Arabella," she added, as her next-door neighbor knocked at the back door with a plate of smoking-hot griddle cakes and a jug of molasses, "you are a choir of angels and all the saints in Heaven rolled into one! Speedy help is double help . . ."

"*Amicus certus in re incerta cernitur,*" quoted Horace automatically, and then, thin face flushing with excitement, "Aunt Abigail, I've seen him! I know who he is! Mrs. Lake's coachman! Dubber Grimes!"

Abigail set her marketing basket on the corner of the

table, cast a glance at the angle of sunlight in the yard—*There will be NOTHING left in the market . . .* !—and said, "Bess, would you and Bella do the honors? I *beg* you will excuse me, but if I don't get to the market now—"

"We'll save you griddle cakes," promised Arabella Butler with a smile, and playfully shoved Abigail toward the door.

"And coffee," added Bess, "if we can keep Sam from drinking it all . . ."

Abigail seized Horace by the elbow and thrust the market basket into his hands as she was pushed out the door.

"Tell me," she commanded, as she and the young man hurried their steps down Queen Street toward the big market square.

"'Twas entirely by accident," said Horace, and shoved his spectacles more firmly onto the bridge of his nose. *"Res hominum fragiles alit et regit—"*

"Yes, yes, I know the fragile affairs of men are guided by chance," said Abigail impatiently. "Where did you see him?"

"At the Crowned Pig. The seniors were ragging poor Yeovil again and I followed him to give him a hand, and when I walked into the tap-room, there was Grimes—the scar-eyed coachman—dicing in the corner with Black Dog Pugh! I ducked back out at once and asked one of the—er—young ladies who work there, who was that man with Mr. Pugh? And she said his name was Dubber Grimes, and he is from Charles Town, and the men with him—there were two others at the table besides Pugh—were Newgate Hicks and the Cornishman, and they all worked as bullyboys at a . . . a house of ill-fame in Charles Town called Avalon. While the girl was getting the ale for Yeovil, I watched them; they weren't only dicing, but talking with Pugh. He gave them money!"

"Only to be expected if they were dicing. Still . . . Avalon," said Abigail thoughtfully. "Well, well—someone has a sense of humor. In the tales of King Arthur," she explained, seeing her nephew look blank, "Avalon is the location of the lake, which has in it the Lady who gives Arthur his sword, if I remember aright . . . Your aunt Elizabeth"—she named her mother—"never considered fanciful tales proper for us children, but Aunt Eliza has a book of them and would read to us when we'd visit. Though I never thought to find the reference useful—"

"Mrs. *Lake?*"

"When you think of it," said Abigail, as they turned from Cornhill into the square before the great market-hall, "what other sort of woman might a man know that he could hire as a cat's-paw, to look respectable enough that a young man like yourself would get into a carriage with her? Would you have gone with Dubber Grimes on his own? Or with gentlemen named Newgate or—er—the Cornishman? Or even Pugh himself, for that matter?"

Horace seemed to be digesting the information that he'd ridden in a carriage with a bona fide Scarlet Woman while Abigail made her way to the stalls of the farmers whose chickens, rabbits, and lambs she knew to be freshest and most plump, and who picked their vegetables in the dark of early morning and not the afternoon before. And since everyone else in Boston knew who those farmers were also, she found, as she had feared, no lettuces left, no peas (*DRAT "Dubber" and his henchmen!*), and the only asparagus remaining was thick and tough as tree-trunks.

With a basket full of beets and carrots, some elderly lamb, an assortment of very small fish wrapped in rushes, some strawberries, and a huge quantity of rather raggedy spinach, she turned her steps back toward home. John would just have to make the best of it. "When was this?" she asked.

"Yesterday afternoon. 'Twas too late to come to you then—

we'd never have made it to the ferry before sunset—and Wey-ountah was at a demonstration of vacuum-pumps, which he would not forgo . . . But what is a vacuum? Nothing! What can we do?"

"I think the time has come," said Abigail, "for a search of Mr. Pugh's rooms. Those grooms of his are generally there, aren't they?"

"Either the grooms or Pinky."

"Not surprising, if he's in the habit of keeping indecent books about—not to speak of treasure-maps. John won't be home until tomorrow evening or Saturday morning, and thank Heavens there's not a great deal of laundry to be done, bar the sheets and assuming the weather stays fine. Our Black Dog had mortally offended the Reverend, but 'twould have been easy enough to send him a frumenty by the hand of one of his minions. Do the cooks at the Hall make frumenties?"

"Sometimes," said Horace, a trifle startled at this conver-sational detour—frumenties were utter poison to him, and it clearly wasn't something he'd ever considered. "I know he gets custards and syllabubs from them—and pays them extremely well not to speak of making him things, since he could be sent down for it, and *they* could be sacked for selling the College provisions that way."

"I see." Abigail paused at the corner of Cornhill to let pass a group of men: laborers from the ropewalks that abounded in Boston, rough-looking men talking heatedly, and she heard among them the words *God-damned lobsterbacks* and *bloody bleedin' Parliament* . . . "So our best course would be to attack the problem from the other end—which will entail a visit to the farm of the Reverend Seckar's brother."

"He has a brother? It's like hearing there was a fourth Gor-gon." Horace shook his head. "I always thought the Reverend Seckar was spontaneously generated from a vat of sour lemons."

"My only hope is that his family does actually live in Concord and not out in somewhere like Haverhill or Springfield. If I have to chase off for another three days to speak to the sister about who drugged the family, Heaven only knows what I'd return here to find."

O ver a nuncheon of Arabella Butler's griddle cakes ("Now, we must save a few for Nabby and Johnny when they get home—"), Abigail thought to ask Sam, who as a longtime rabble-rouser knew everyone in the Boston area, about Genesis Seckar. As she'd suspected, Sam knew all about him.

"His farm lies about seven miles the other side of town." Sam poured out coffee for Abigail, Pattie, and Katy—who had brought the younger boys back from the Smiths'—as they settled around the much-battered table in a kitchen now spotlessly clean (Abigail could have kissed Sam's womenfolk for sparing her the appalling task). "Your husband," he added, "likes to chide that two-thirds of the men in the colonies either enjoy being the King's slaves or don't care whose slaves they are so long as they're able to cheat the poor out of their rightful money—"

"That is *not* what John says!"

Sam waved away the objection. "Well, Genesis Seckar belongs in the category of men who wouldn't care if they were slaves of the Grand Turk, since everyone around them is going straight to Hell anyway, so how they or anyone else lives on the Earth doesn't matter, because they've no proof that the world won't evaporate in flames tomorrow, so there! He lets the militia drill on his pasture—the place is well away from prying eyes—because it doesn't matter to him whether there's going to be fighting or not. Bruck Travers with the Watertown militia tells me Old Man Seckar comes out and preaches during drill at the top of his lungs."

"Oh, *him*." Katy made a face. "He's down to two cows these days and doesn't take care of either of 'em, poor beasts. You're not thinking of going out there, Mrs. Adams?" She turned on the bench to regard Abigail worriedly. "He's about a hundred and fifty years old, and proof, I always thought, that his way of life is holy—"

"How's that?" asked Sam, hugely amused.

"Oh, because if it wasn't, God would have let him die years ago, only He knows that if he did, the old wretch would be in Heaven, and God just can't stand the idea of putting up with him."

"You don't think he knows where your treasure-map is hid, do you?" Sam's gray glance cut sharply across at Abigail. "Or the sister? Is that why you're going?"

"It is not," she retorted. "I'm not entirely convinced that there *is* a treasure or a map to find it with. But I'm not trying to find a treasure; I'm trying to prevent an innocent man from being hanged for a murder he didn't commit. And since it's nearly impossible to prove a negative, we are reduced to finding who actually *did* kill poor Mr. Fairfield . . ."

"Does it matter?" His voice was suddenly hard.

Horace and Weyountah, on the other side of the table, looked at one another uneasily, and Bess said, "Now, Sam . . ."

"I'm sure it matters to Diomede," replied Abigail evenly.

Sam waved as if chasing away inconvenient flies. "Let me take care of Diomede, then. What we need of you, Nab—what Massachusetts and all free men in it need of you—is that you find that treasure-map of this Mrs. Lake, and that you find it before that British ship lands . . . or before who-ever the damned Governor is paying to do his dirty-work for him decodes the cipher and scoops the money that *we* desperately need."

"Which reminds me," began Horace, reaching for his coat-pocket, "I have——" And Abigail, guessing what he was about to produce, kicked him hard under the table.

"You don't really think the Governor is behind the man who killed George, do you, sir?" Weyountah sounded worried. "George was loyal to the King——"

"You think that would matter to any red-blooded Tory merchant?" retorted Sam. "Old Hutchinson'll be falling over himself trying to figure out what the cipher is so he can get the gold out of there before the British land as well, lest he be accountable for it. I'll send a man out to Concord to talk to Old Seckar——"

Abigail remembered old Mr. Creel and his spite-filled diatribes; thought about the unshaven rope-workers, with their hickory clubs and angry voices and dirty hands, she had passed on the way home. "That's quite all right, Sam."

"And I'll send someone out with you to Cambridge to find this map or cipher, and the books it's hid in——I can probably get you someone to burgle the Governor's house for you——"

"That's *quite* all right."

Sam was silent a minute——his expression reminded Abigail of Johnny's when the boy had verbally given away something he was planning and was trying to think how to cover his tracks. But at last he said, quietly, "I don't think you realize how important it is that we find that gold, Nab. And find it soon."

Around the table, Bess and Hannah, Katy and Pattie, Charley and Tommy, Weyountah and Horace had all fallen silent, as if they had ceased to exist . . .

And they HAD ceased to exist, reflected Abigail, *for Sam.*
As Diomede had ceased to exist.

Because Seth Barlow had been right, the other evening out in the isolated darkness beyond Dedham, when he read the evening portion of scripture . . . Violent men spread violence like a contagion, and greed in a good cause was still greed. When you supped with the Devil, even the longest spoon would not keep his whispering out of your ears, long after you had thanked him for his hospitality and scurried out the door.

Sam and his patriots, just like the rest.

"'Tis worth more than finding who killed some Tory or who gets accused of it," Sam said. "'Tis worth more than my life or yours—" His glance flicked across the table to the two young men. "The offices of friendship are one thing, boys, and I can see you're shocked at my saying so. But I tell you this. Once the British land—once fat old King George lands his troops here, the first thing he'll do is either close the courts or put his own men in charge of them, which amounts to the same thing. Then it isn't going to matter a split grass-blade who killed your friend or why, because the only thing that *will* matter anymore is who the King's friends are . . . or who gains the favor of the Governor. To fight that, we need money: money for guns, money for powder, money for food for the men who'll have the manhood to take up arms. And beside that, nothing is important."

He stood and went to the sideboard for his hat. "The wind's inshore," he said. "That ship can be only days away. We must do what we can, while we can, and let all else go by the wayside. Nab," he added, returning to the table to kiss her cheek, "thank you for your hospitality—"

"No," she said, rising, "thank you—and Bess, Hannah, Surry . . ."

The tension of the moment was lost amid handshakes, embraces, farewells.

But it wasn't until Sam and his family were out of the

house, that Abigail asked softly, "Do you have your reconstruction of the cipher, Horace?"

"I do. I meant to tell you, but with everyone here—and seeing Dubber put it from my mind—"

She gripped his arm, shook her head, "'Tis well."

"Is it true what he said?" asked Weyountah, deeply troubled. "That the King will close the courts?"

"The truth is that I don't know," said Abigail. "And neither does Sam. But the truth is also that when a man starts saying that the cause of defending our liberties is more important than justice or truth or saving the life of a man who has no rights before the courts of law, then I start to wonder what he *would* stop at. And a man who'll stop at nothing . . ."

"Becomes very difficult to distinguish from a robber," concluded the Indian. "Come into the study, and let's have a look at Horace's paper."

Seventeen

When Abigail had finished reading the two pages of Horace's sprawling, uneven scrawl, she said, inadequately, "Goodness." Although, quite patently, none of the recorded proceedings had anything to do with goodness.

The language was stilted and old-fashioned and used a great number of plain English words not generally encountered in polite conversation. At least her nephew hadn't translated these passages into Latin, as any number of Abigail's male acquaintances would have, under the impression that a mere woman wouldn't understand what *futuo* meant. Between the farmers around her childhood village discussing their stock, and her younger brother's raids on the higher shelf of their father's classical library, there was very little that Abigail had not at least heard about.

Horace, who had gone to gaze out the study window while she was reading, turned around and tried to pretend he wasn't breaking out in hives with embarrassment.

Weyountah said matter-of-factly—since his friend was quite clearly incapable of speech—"It's as close as Horace could make it to the original wording, but of course it isn't word-for-word. I don't see how we could decipher it, if it is a cipher, without knowing that."

"No, we couldn't." Abigail turned the sheets over in her hands, trying not to remember that these were what the two young men had been working on the night George had been killed. "And yet—Horace, you said that it was English written in Arabic characters, as if the Arabic was itself a cipher. Did the prose itself seem labored or . . . or *odd*? Given the subject matter," she added drily. "And the fact that 'twas written a hundred years ago.

"What I mean is," she went on, when her nephew merely looked uncomprehending, "did you ever write one of those every-other-letter or every-third-word codes to your friends when you were a child? Your uncle William was forever getting me to do so when he was trying to slip information to those good-for-nothing friends of his that he didn't want Papa to see. He was terrible at it," she explained. "They always sounded hideously labored, and words like *gambling-debts* and *liquor* are nearly impossible to conceal, if you're supposed to be writing about the new shirt your mother is making for you. And writing the operative words in Latin didn't do any good because Papa reads Latin as if it were English . . . considerably better than William or his friends."

"So if 'twere every third word or something like that," said Katy, perusing the disgraceful account with interest from her perch on the corner of John's desk, "you'd expect there would be words like *tree* and *dig* and *paces* somewhere in it, wouldn't you? And there aren't. Except where Mrs. Pitts refers to a 'mighty oak . . .'"

"And letter-ciphers were even more of a nuisance," agreed Abigail. "I always had to go fishing about for words that had a *q* or a *y* in just the right place, until I was astonished that Papa couldn't tell at a glance that William's notes to his friends were ciphers, they read so clumsily."

Horace still looked a little puzzled, but Weyountah nodded. "I see what you mean, m'am. I expect one needs imagination to . . . to feel that there's something amiss like that. Is your father an imaginative man?"

Abigail smiled at the recollection of that kind and steady old scholar back in Weymouth. "He's an excellent man," she said, "and a compassionate man—which requires a certain type of imagination, and one that is in short supply generally in the world. But he's not fanciful. He can write a very fine sermon, but when he reads a text, the only thing that he sees is its meaning, not . . . not what might be implied about the writer by its form. What I'm saying is that the paper Mrs. Lake gave to Horace to translate might not have been a cipher at all."

"Then what was it?" asked the Indian in surprise.

"And why have me translate it?"

"She didn't *know* it wasn't a cipher, goose," said Katy, leaning forward to pluck the paper from Horace's hand again.

"I don't think she knew quite what it was," said Abigail. "'Tis why she—and whoever hired her—needed it translated . . . and didn't trust her, by the way: you said that the original had been copied by someone who didn't know that Arabic is written right to left . . ."

"Which should let out the Governor," put in Horace, taking the paper back. "Whatever Mr. Adams says of him, he's an educated man and knows that much."

"Might *she* have copied it, though?" Katy leaned around

his arm to look at it. "Got at it at the Governor's, I mean, and made her own copy to beat him to the treasure?"

"What I think happened," went on Abigail, "is this: who-ever broke into the Reverend Seckar's house found *some* of the books, one of which had what *appeared* to him—or her—to be a cipher or secret writing in it. The sheets were probably either written on a flyleaf or tucked in loose, as you say Mr. Fairfield tucked papers into his books. He—or she—took it, and only after 'twas translated, realized that it was no cipher at all but merely notes for blackmail that were never used."

"And that's when he started looking for the other books!" said Horace excitedly. "He must have known about Old Beel-zebub's treasure from the Governor, if it's not His Excellency himself we're talking about—Poor George! If he hadn't waked when he did . . ."

"Then it might have been you the following night," said Katy softly. "Or Weyountah the night after. And one of you *would* have waked—I can't imagine how anyone would poison you, Horry, you don't eat anything but vegetables and clab-bered milk—and seen someone in his room that he knew . . ." She looked over at Abigail. "'Twas why he was killed, wasn't he? Because he recognized whoever it was he saw."

"I think so, yes."

"If 'twas someone working for or with the Governor," said Weyountah, "'twould stand to reason that George would have known him from the Volunteers, wouldn't it?"

Abigail nodded. "I don't say it couldn't have been someone like Bruck Travers—did Bruck and the others in the Water-town Committee of Public Safety know where George's room was, Katy?"

"Of course. There's dozens of the college men in the Sons or the militia, and that's not counting the college servants. But for one thing Bruck wouldn't know one book from another, and for another, I met Seph Nuttall from the militia in the market day before yesterday and asked him about where Bruck was that evening, and he was drilling with the militia in Watertown. Two hundred men saw him. Are you truly going to desert poor Diomede?"

"What, because Sam Adams told me to?" Abigail sniffed. "But to remain on his good side—because we may very well need his help before all's done—I think 'twere best we go to Charles Town tomorrow, and at least have a look at this Avalon, and see what its weaknesses are and if we can catch a glimpse of its proprietress. And in the meantime—"

"She didn't . . . She was quite modestly dressed," protested Horace. "She didn't have the air of a—er—*meretrix* . . ."

"Obviously she knew enough not to dress like a bird of paradise," said Abigail, "for fear of frightening her own bird away. You'd never have gotten into the carriage with her," she explained, to Horace's inarticulate protest that he wasn't *that* much of a shrinking violet, "if she'd been tricked-out and tire'd up and painted to her eyes like Jezebel at her window. I claim no knowledge of ladies of ill fame," she went on thoughtfully, "but it sounds to me—does it not to you?—that she's more than the answer to some sailor's prayer. She could steal a key, but a carriage and pair is another matter, even for the madame of a house of accommodation. Would you know her again?"

"Of course."

"If she were dressed differently, I mean, and painted up?"

He blushed. "I think so. Her hair was her own; I'm not sure I'd know her in a wig."

"Then let us make a pilgrimage tomorrow," said Abigail. "I can do that in the morning before John gets home—and see what we can see before Sam takes matters into his own hands.

For when a man will truly stop at nothing, there is no telling who may be hurt."

She asked the boys to stay for dinner, and prepared the lamb (only she would have gone bail that it was actually mutton) dressed with spinach, and put up a pan of potatoes beneath the hearth-coals to roast and some corn-and-milk for Horace. Johnny and Nabby came home from school, and Abigail let them thoroughly explore the cleaned and tidied house before starting them on their chores. Though the spring evenings were long, she guessed that once darkness fell, the children would be uneasy in a house that had been entered and ransacked by strangers, had they not had the chance to patrol it by daylight and see with their own eyes that all was safe. The boys departed immediately after dinner with a basket of provisions for themselves and another to be delivered to Diomede in the Cambridge jail—and Weyountah returned fifteen minutes later with Charley, whom Abigail had not even missed in the confusion of good-bys and who had managed to follow Horace and Weyountah nearly to Summer Street.

Since the handsome Indian didn't return a second time she assumed he did, in fact, make it through the town gate by sunset, though he and Horace—unless they found a friendly farmer with a wagon—would beyond all doubt be walking the last mile back to Cambridge in the dark.

Between dinner and supper, she and the girls put up laundry to soak—Abigail's housewifely instincts revolted at not having spare sheets clean and ready at all times—and as she at last led her little household in Bible reading and evening prayer, she reflected that few Israelites in Pharoah's brick-pits had put in a more strenuous day than her own.

* * *

Friday morning was, fortunately, a mild one. While Katy and Nabby milked the cows ('twas miraculous what one more pair of hands would do for the household), starting the moment it was light enough to see, Abigail and Pattie beat and rinsed, beat and rinsed the lye-smelling oceans of laundry, and had sheets, shifts, shirts, and clouts flying like flags from the maze of clotheslines in the yard by noon. By one (Charley had disappeared again, to be rescued by Katy from almost beneath the hooves of a dray on Cornhill), Abigail and Katy were crossing the Charles Town ferry.

"No sign of them yet." Katy folded up the brass spyglass she had drawn from her pocket to look out past the steep promontory of Copp's Hill toward the bay. No need to specify who *they* were.

From here Abigail could see the brick walls of the British camp on Castle Island and thought with deep regret of her friend Lieutenant Jeremy Coldstone, the assistant to the Provost Marshal and a young man, she sensed, who might greatly assist her in the unraveling of this tangle of codes and books and treasure that seemed to appear and disappear. But with tensions rising every day in Boston, it would be impossible these days for Coldstone to enter the town unmolested—particularly if Sam got word of his presence.

And in any case, reflected Abigail, the young lieutenant undoubtedly had enough to deal with these days. But she wondered what the men in the castle fort were doing to pass the time while *they* waited for word from the King to come.

"Do you think there will be fighting when they come ashore, m'am?"

Abigail sniffed. "I think there'll be fighting the first time the Royal Commissioner's bodyguard attempts to get a drink in a tavern. 'Tis all the prediction I feel can be made with certainty. As for Sam's contention that we'll face a flotilla and an invasion-force, I can scarcely see where the King is likely to find, at short notice, soldiers enough to hold a city the size of Boston. My guess is that he'll send a Royal Commissioner, not an invading general, with orders to the colony to pay for the tea. 'Tis an understandable request but not worth battle in the streets."

"To Mr. Deems, 'twould be. And Bruck Travers and his father. And George, I'm afraid," the girl added sadly. "Just the thought that patriot militia would have the temerity to form in defiance of the King's rule had him red in the face. Joseph Ryland had to talk him out of taking the Volunteers on Saturdays to attack the militias while they drilled."

"That's all we would need." Abigail folded her shawl around her shoulders at the chill of the sea-wind.

"'Twouldn't have been much of a battle," pointed out Katy practically. "They're barely a handful, and half of them not mounted, nor armed. They'd only come to the drills to cheer the others on and wear the uniforms and drink punch. At least our men have guns."

"And massacring them would solve something? Besides giving Parliament a far better reason than a little saltwater tea to send in a few regiments to keep order?"

Katy was silent for a moment, considering this, tucking the trailing streamers of her black hair back beneath her cap. In a somewhat smaller voice she said, "Well, howsoever, Ryland talked George out of it. He's got a great deal of sense and is a fine soldier, even if he does look at me as if I'd just crawled up out of a drain."

"Because you're a patriot?" Abigail had heard the slight break in her young companion's voice.

"I daresay it's what he tells people—and himself. But me, I think 'tis because he's been writing love-poems to Sally

Woodleigh and sending her flowers, and she won't so much as turn her head to say hello in the street but makes—made"—she corrected herself—"sheep's eyes at George." She was silent for a time; the brass tube of the spyglass forgotten in her hand, she looked out across the violet chop of the bay toward Charles Town, rising on the slopes of its hills.

"I saw her Tuesday when I went to Cambridge," the girl continued after a time. "I went to the King's Chapel, to—not to *see* George, because of course the door's locked, but to . . . I don't know. He's dead—'tis only his body in there . . . cold clay. But 'tis the body I held in my arms. The mouth I kissed; the fingers that would braid my hair. His hair was so soft, like silk . . . I know he's not in there, but . . ."

She shook her head, looked away across the bay again, her eyes clouded with grief. "And Sally was there. All in black, with a veil on her bonnet, as if she'd lost a husband, instead of a man she'd talked herself into thinking wanted her. I don't think she even saw me there. She had her maid with her, and Mr. Heywood from the Volunteers. She was taken faint and leaned on his arm."

The Charles Town wharf was drawing near. Young Mr. Peasley, the ferry's captain, shouted himself crimson while the two deck-boys swung the yard this way and that, trying to catch sea-wind against the inshore gusts that blew off the hills behind the town. Abigail clung resolutely to the edge of the bench where she sat and fixed her eyes on the tall green summit of Bunker Hill.

"He didn't lead her on to think it of him, did he?" she asked, and remembered the young man's careless smile. The Sally Woodleighs of the world, at least, were not to be caught with faked marriage ceremonies . . . but even if she had not truly sent the message, asking for a meeting behind the barn, George Fairfield at least had believed that she *would* have.

"No!" retorted Katy. "At least—I don't think he did."

"Did she favor one above another, of the others?" Abigail asked. "The Black Dog, for instance?"

"Oh, you heard about the fight that Saturday, did you?" Katy managed a pale and crooked grin. "'Tis funny, in spite of the things Mr. Ryland called me—he and George got into a *tremendous* quarrel about me—I could almost feel sorry for the poor man. Teaching her chemistry and writing love-poems—he really does write his own, you know . . . Mr. Apthorp pays Beaverbrook to write his—'tis like watching some poor mouse in a trap, running round and round against the wires, and you know he's never going to get out. Look, there's Weyountah!" She pointed, her face breaking into a brilliant smile. "And Horace, there on the wharf! What are you going to say to this Mrs. Lake when you find her?"

"It depends," replied Abigail, as the ferry at long last was drawn up alongside the wet, dark bollards, "upon how we find her and where."

Though it had been the original capital of the colony, Charles Town was barely more than a bustling little village these days, built on the footslopes of two tall hills at the mouth of the Mystic River and slightly less than three-quarters of a mile end to end along the shore. The house known as Avalon stood a few hundred yards from the ferry landing, east of the town proper, in a discreet grove of trees just where the gentle slope of Breed's Hill began to steepen. Abigail wouldn't have guessed it was a place of ill repute, save that Weyountah and Horace had inquired at two alehouses and had received the same directions from both. Avalon certainly bore no resemblance to the slatternly taverns along the Boston waterfront. It was built in the old style, partly of tim-

ber and partly of brick, with tall gables and an upper story
that overhung the lower.

The sign above its door depicted—not much to Abigail's
surprise—a woman's arm emerging from the waters of a lake,
caressing rather than brandishing the upright sword.

"'Tis known in town as an alehouse," said Weyountah, as
the little party walked along the road that curved toward the
brick kiln at the foot of Moulton's Hill some half mile ahead.
"Though the man in the taproom at the Peacock gave me a
wink when I asked after the place—by which I assume that
it is indeed what we're looking for."

"With a nice, sheltered approach on the other side of the
hill," murmured Abigail, as they reached the place where the
road curved northwest again toward Bunker Hill. "Invisible
if you're coming in from Cambridge or Medford in the dusk,
I daresay." She looked back toward the Avalon. "I don't see
anyone about, do you? Though I don't imagine there's much
activity here 'til nightfall. Still, one would expect servants at
least and some sign of smoke in the kitchen chimney . . . and
grooms about the stables. Best you stay out of sight, Horace.
Shall I knock on the front door and see if I can at least get a
look at this Mrs. Lake?"

Horace looked shocked, but Weyountah only said, "Lend
Horace your spyglass, Katy; the trees across the road here
ought to be close enough. Can you see the door clearly, Horace? No, turn it—that way. Good. Mrs. Adams?" He offered
her his arm, and Katy drew her cloak-hood up over her head
and did her best to look like a respectable servant-girl as she
trailed Abigail and the Indian back toward the front door.
With the trees thick with spring leaf, the whole dooryard of
the house called Avalon was rather gloomy, and close-up the
shabbiness of the place was more evident: the dooryard muddy,
the path needing gravel, the backhouses quite obviously in

need of cleaning. The diamond-paned windows had not been washed recently, and the house had an air of uneasy quiet. Abigail felt herself reminded of a woman who has been struck and waits to see what will happen next.

She knocked at the door and assumed the expression of a righteous matron drawing aside her skirts to wade through garbage in a holy cause.

The footsteps inside approached the door at a near run.

The young woman who opened the door—plump, freckled, and matter-of-fact in the rather faded print dress of a servant—looked both wary and scared. And, when she saw Abigail, taken aback—

Who is she expecting?

"Please pardon this intrusion." Abigail inclined her head. "My name is Mrs. Percy. I was told I might find a woman here who calls herself Mrs. Lake, though that might not be her right name. Dark-haired, about my height"—this was a guess, from the fact that Horace hadn't noted either tallness or shortness—"a lady, I suppose you would call her . . ."

Something altered in the young woman's stance: shoulders slumped, mouth tightened, eyes . . . not grieved, but the eagerness died from her face and was replaced by anxiety.

"Is she not here?" asked Abigail. "I was told—"

"She's gone," said the girl. "She's been gone two days. I hoped you had word of her, for God's honest truth, there's not one of us that knows what to do."

Eighteen

"Have you spoken to the constable?"

Abigail's tone of genuine concern seemed to have its effect, for the girl's guardedness faded, and wry resentment took its place. "Oh, aye, *that* did us a world of good! 'Run off with some other man,' was all *he'd* say—and so he wrote to Mr . . . to Mrs. Morgan's friend, who was good enough to buy her this house."

"I daresay," remarked Abigail, "if Mrs.—Morgan, is it? It would be. If Mrs. Morgan's friend had ever instructed some one of the Town Council to quash objections by Mr. Munn"— she named the Charles Town constable, a member in good standing of the Sons of Liberty—"concerning Mrs. Morgan's way of life, he might well turn spiteful—"

"*Him?*" The girl sniffed. "Spite's old Munn's middle name, right after Hypocrisy, carrying on the way he does with his wife's own sister. And what's it to him anyway if Mr. Chamberville wants a little comfort from time to time and a woman who'll let him know he's welcome in her bed? When I was a little girl," the servant added, shaking her curly head, "and I'd cry 'cause we weren't rich, my auntie would always say, 'If we were Quality, you'd have to marry some old merchant whether you wanted to or not, old enough to be your da.' I didn't understand then, but Lord, hearing about when people marry for ships and lands and warehouses, I understand now. There," she added. "I've spoke too free, m'am, but it just makes me mad as fire——"

"You probably ought not to have," said Abigail encouragingly, "since you've your position to think of. But, though I've always counted myself a Christian woman, I'm afraid I agree with you——" She let the end of the sentence hang with an unspoken question.

The servant said, "Dassie. Dassie Mitchell. Please do come in, m'am; it won't do you any good if you're seen standing outside this house, the way folk around here talk as if they hadn't anything better to do with their days. Belinda!" she called out, as she closed the door behind Abigail and her party. "Nancy! No word," she said, to the two young ladies who appeared in an inner doorway, a blonde and a brunette clothed, like Dassie, as maidservants, but in dresses far newer and more stylish.

Abigail guessed it was Dassie who did the actual work in the house.

"This is Mrs. Percy. She came— Who was it who told you to come, m'am?"

As they crossed through the beautifully furnished parlor and proceeded to the kitchen, Abigail spun her story—freely lifted from events that had befallen one of her father's parishioners some fourteen years ago—of the daughter of a fictitious elder brother who had been lured into a pretend marriage with a Frenchman, who had (she said) abandoned poor Pamela in Boston. A friend of the family had recom-

mended Abigail inquire of the proprietress of the Avalon in
Charles Town, Pamela being young and very pretty—"That
frightful mother of hers seems to feel that sin is sin and that
the Avalon is no better than some of those . . . those *kennels*
down along the Boston wharves—"

"Your sister-in-law must be related to half the women in
Charles Town, then," remarked the dark-haired Nancy drily,
as she poured out her mistress's tea. "And to my stepmother
and aunts as well. It's not like this is a sailors' knocking-shop,
begging your pardon m'am for speaking so free—"

It was in fact, Abigail gathered, what John (and several
English novelists) referred to as a House of Accommodation:
a venue where those who could afford it could bring their
mistresses for a few hours' congress. Mrs. Morgan provided
for the rental of clean, youthful temporary mistresses along
with the rooms more as a sideline than a principal business—

"Though mind you, m'am," said Dassie earnestly, "you'd
think those sniffy mamas in this town would be glad the
girls are here, when you think that if those boys over at the
college didn't have a place to come visit—as boys will—"

Blonde Belinda winked at Weyountah, who inclined his head
to her politely and passed her the plate of slightly stale cakes.

"Why, think what trouble they'd get into with the
respectable girls in the town! Like your poor niece!"

Abigail's mind—always ill-regulated concerning points of
doctrine and morality—momentarily scouted the question of
whether this was more or less sinful than an out-and-out
house of prostitution: it actively encouraged double adultery
rather than simple fornication. Then she glanced sidelong at
Katy, who was looking around the kitchen with great curiosity and obviously didn't connect any of this tale of falsified
marriage-vows and wheedling seducers with herself. Did she
really believe that the young heir to five thousand acres of

Virginia tobacco would genuinely marry the daughter of the head hostler at the Yellow Cow?

And if she did, what then? That he'd take her home to the master and mistress of a plantation and present her to them as their daughter-in-law?

And a dyed-in-the-wool patriot to boot?

Gradually—by dint of interest, sympathy, and letting the three confused and worried servant-girls simply talk—the story emerged. Wednesday afternoon—May fourth—Mrs. Morgan had gone for a walk, as she generally did before dinner . . . dinner being served at the fashionable hour of five, rather than at three or four as working-folk did. The girls didn't think much of it when she didn't return for dinner. It happened—not frequently—that Mrs. Morgan's particular friend would cross over from Boston where he lived, and they would meet to go driving. Only when night fell—the moon being on the wane—did they begin to worry, but there was a gentleman scheduled to come calling Wednesday night with a lady friend, and with one thing and another, none of the three of them—Nancy, Dassie, nor Belinda—quite knew what steps to take.

"And did not Mr. Grimes or Mr. Hicks have anything to suggest?" inquired Weyountah, which caused the girls to look at one another worriedly. "It is Mr. Grimes who has charge of Mrs. Morgan's stables, is it not?" he asked, as if the matter were common knowledge, and Nancy nodded.

"They said not to worry, that she'd most likely met Mr.— met her friend—and would be back late." With her long face and wide, rather mannish shoulders, Nancy was nowhere near as pretty as Katy or Pattie, Abigail judged, but she had a smooth briskness to her and a lovely velvet voice. *She probably has half the boys in the college in love with her. And is certainly more obtainable than Sally Woodleigh.*

"Might she have gone to Mr. Chamberville's house near

Concord with him?" asked Abigail smoothly. "I believe you said she had a key—"

Again the girls traded frowns, not remembering whether one or the other of them had mentioned Mr. Chamberville's name and, if they had, whether they'd also mentioned the Concord house or whether or not Mrs. Morgan had the key to it. It was Dassie who said, "I don't think she'd have gone there, m'am. Not with rebels all over those parts, as they are, and every sort of rumor flying about. Mr. Chamberville hasn't been next or nigh Concord in months."

"And did *you* write to Mr. Chamberville about this? Or is Mr. Munn the only one he's heard from?"

"M'am, to tell you the truth we haven't the least idea what it's best we do," replied Nancy. "'Twould be different if any of the three of us had family, or a friend who'd so much as acknowledge us in the street—not that a one of 'em would recognize our *faces*! Begging your pardon, m'am," she added. "The household money's gone—that's the first thing we checked, unless she moved where it's hid again—and 'tis only a matter of time before Mr. C takes his house back. And Mr. Grimes—"

"Here he comes!" Belinda, who'd been sitting near the window, sprang to her feet.

"Grimes—?"

"Cornishman."

"Hide us," commanded Abigail sharply, and Nancy flung open the door of the backstairs, then caught Weyountah's arm as Abigail and Katy darted up the narrow, boxed-in flight.

"You stay. He knows someone's here—"

The door shut. Much as she wanted to get a look at one of the men whom she strongly suspected of breaking into her house, Abigail knew how these narrow, concealed kitchen flights carried the sound of ascending footfalls. If she stayed for a look through the door-crack, she couldn't later flee upward if the Cornishman had enough imagination to disbelieve the girls and checked the backstairs. Pushing Katy ahead of her, she ascended in almost complete darkness, thrust open the door at the top, and emerged into a hall furnished—as the parlor was downstairs—with the newest style of straight-legged chairs, a small marble-topped table, and a painting by an inferior artist of Venus putting on her makeup.

Abigail signed Katy sharply to stay where she was, then moved with all the silent care of which she was capable—and having grown up with William for a younger brother, there was little she hadn't learned about sneaking in silence—from one door to the other of the four rooms that opened from the hall.

Two bore the appearance of guest-rooms—beds with French hangings of brocaded silk—one was a parlor with a large mirror on the ceiling, and one, Abigail guessed, belonged to Mrs. Morgan—the Lady of the Lake—herself. She signed to Katy again—*Wait*—and slipped inside, stepping carefully on the worn oak planks. The dressing table bore silver combs and brushes—putting paid, reflected Abigail wryly, to Mr. Munn's theory that Mrs. Morgan had run off with another man—and investigation of the highboy showed that she hadn't taken any chemises or petticoats, either . . . or at least that she hadn't taken so many that it showed.

Abigail checked all the drawers of the highboy and between the mattresses of the bed—no book, no notes, no mysterious manuscripts in Arabic, and no household money. She crossed, stepping carefully, to the dressing table, examined its drawers, and found only an astonishing quantity of white lead, carmine, pomade, rice-powder, and kohl. *Drat the woman* . . .

And in a corner of the dressing table, an ink-bottle.

Half empty.

And a used quill. Much used, in fact, its tip was whittled down nearly to the feather.

Abigail gathered her skirts about her, knelt carefully, and reexamined the marble surface of the dressing table itself.

Ink-stains. Granny Quincy had owned a marble-topped table, and Abigail knew exactly what happened if you didn't wait until the ink was absolutely dry before you turned the sheet over to write on the back—you ended up having to rub and polish with solutions of oxgall and wood-sorrel and chalk, listening to Granny Quincy's lectures on cleaning all the while.

So what had Mrs. Morgan been writing up here that she wouldn't write at her very pretty gilt secretaire in the parlor downstairs?

Gently, Abigail removed every drawer from the dressing table in turn and found the papers tacked to the back side of the lower left-hand one. Four pages torn out of what looked like a housekeeping book; two bearing a laborious, crooked-lettered copy of Arabic writing; and two written over with the now-familiar dialog (and descriptive prose) between Lt. Governor Morgan and Mistress Pitts in a woman's strong hand.

Footsteps in the backstairs—Abigail knew she'd been correct, they vibrated all over the house—and a voice calling softly, "Mrs. Percy—!"

Abigail shoved the papers into her pocket, wiggled the drawer back onto its runners, and darted to the window in time to see a huge, hulking man in a corduroy coat crossing back to the stables: the Cornishman. His head was cropped so closely it might almost have been shaved, and he carried it thrust forward, rather like an animal that has only recently learned the trick of walking on its hind legs . . .

"He's gone," said Nancy, as she and Katy entered the bedroom together.

Abigail heaved a convincing sigh—not entirely feigned—and put a hand to her chest: "What did he want? I vow, I was ready to go under the bed—"

"And you'd have done well to," replied the dark-haired girl. "He's a foul one to cross, and the more so when Dubber's not around, for he hasn't the brains on his own to know when it would pay him to hold on to his temper. Your redskin friend's got a ready tongue in his head," she added, with her sidelong, triangular grin. "I was afraid he'd get himself into trouble when the Cornishman demanded what he was doing there—he'd seen there was someone at the house—but Lord! The excuses and the whining, and letting the Cornishman bully two shillings out of him before he slunk out of the house with his tail between his legs—our boy never even thought there might have been someone else here. But," she added, "it's best you go. He's a nasty piece of work, and you were right to hide. He wouldn't think twice of telling your husband you were here, and getting money to keep quiet about it . . . and maybe worse, for your girl here."

She put a brief arm around Katy's shoulders.

"Is the coast clear?" asked Abigail. "Dassie said there were three of them . . ."

Nancy smiled—very briefly—at her use of the smuggler's slang, but only said, "Grimes and Hicks went off to town this morning. Hicks and the Cornishman are straight off the boat this year, but Grimes has friends in town. And to tell the truth," she added, as she led Abigail down the main stair to the front parlor downstairs, "that has me worried, for I wouldn't put it past Grimes to sell us—Belinda and me—to one of those waterfront kens your sister-in-law spoke of . . ."

"*Sell* you?" Abigail stopped in the doorway.

Nancy regarded her with a dark eye full of wry amusement. "You truly are an innocent, aren't you, m'am? Girls with no family, no one to speak for us and—God knows—no way of making a living, save what she and I have done since we were thirteen . . ."

She put an arm around Belinda's shoulders, as she had Katy a few moments before, and hugged her, all the beauty leaving her face for an instant, shadow in her wry and tired eyes. "I could probably sew a straight seam for twelve inches if the salvation of humankind depended on me doing so, but Belinda would need six months' teaching by St. Martha herself to learn to sweep a floor. Don't you worry, m'am," she added, seeing Abigail's face. "I've saved a little and so has Dassie, and if Mrs. Morgan isn't back by morning, we'll be out of here. What was your niece's name, m'am? The girl you're looking for? Pamela, yes—Pamela what? Not that she'll use her right name . . . If I see her, m'am, I shall tell her you're looking for her and will help her . . ."

"Thank you," said Abigail, with difficulty retrieving her appearance of concern over that fictitious damsel's plight in the face of this tall young woman's genuine fears.

"And confusion to your nasty old sister," added Nancy with her tight-lipped grin. "And to my nasty old aunt as well, and Belinda's ma, and all them others . . . Well. Now best you be gone. Last thing any of us would need is for Dubber and Newgate to come strolling up and see you here . . . Ah, there's your chief, I see him in the trees. Good luck to you, m'am."

And with a smiling wave at Weyountah, Nancy closed the door, leaving Abigail with a good deal to think about as she and Katy crossed the road.

Nineteen

"That isn't my hand," protested Horace at once, when Abigail showed him the paper she'd taken from Mrs. Morgan's dressing table. "'Tis a fair copy, though, of what I wrote . . ."

"At a guess, I'd say Mrs. Morgan copied it for herself the moment you were out the door." Abigail handed him the other sheets, which he turned over in puzzlement. "Not the same ones you translated from? But the same text, no?"

"Yes. Copied left to right by rote again—"

"Precisely. Mrs. Morgan is working for someone: the Governor, possibly—dare I breathe a sullying word upon a reputation so spotless?—Black Dog Pugh—"

"Catch me," remarked Katy, "ere I faint with shock." They lengthened their steps as they came near to the first houses of Charles Town, and the bright sharp breeze from the harbor flapped at the women's cloaks.

"Do you see a rash on my neck?" asked Horace of Katy, as they dropped behind a little. "I think one of those trees was a poisonous sumac . . . And I was bitten to pieces by gnats . . ."

"Goose, the only mark there is where you've scratched yourself . . ."

"I thought Miss Belinda looked like the sort of—er—young person who might attract Pugh's attention," said Weyountah. "If he isn't corrupting some presumed-virtuous young matron in Cambridge instead. What have you there?"

"Letters purporting to be from my husband," said Abigail, "and my great-uncle, Justice Mercer from Haverhill . . . Look at the paper. And the ink." She held them against Mrs. Morgan's copies of both text and translation. "Not that 'tis proof—we couldn't take it before a court and hope to impress anyone with the existence of conspiracy—but it confirms what I've thought."

"Yet the hand on the forged letters is a man's." Weyountah paused in his steps, held the two forgeries that had brought Horace into the business up to the light as he had done not quite two weeks ago at the Golden Stair.

"Is it anything like Pugh's? It's disguised, I know," Abigail added, as the Indian opened his mouth to point out that very fact. "But is there any similarity?"

"I can see none, but that means nothing. Horace would know his writing—we've both seen it on enough notes we've been sent with—and we know he's a fairly pretty forger from his imitation of Mistress Woodleigh's."

"I wonder if she wrote him love-letters as she did to George?" Abigail frowned, thinking of those wholly conventional outpourings of passion that George had been carrying in his pocket on the night he died . . . on the night Pugh had lured him out of his room . . . *Why carry Mistress Woodleigh's love-letters when the rest were all chucked into his desk?* "Are you returning to Cambridge?" she asked, as they turned along the street toward the ferry landing.

"We were, yes," Horace replied, still rubbing uneasily at the completely invisible spots and rashes on his neck. "Ryland is holding a sort of seminar in his rooms on translation of Plato, and with examinations coming up, nobody wants to miss it. One has to arrive early to obtain a seat."

"Would Mr. Pugh also attend?"

"He has in the past," said Weyountah. "He's clever—always passing his examinations by just enough not to be sent down."

"Then I think the time has come," said Abigail, "to make a search of Mr. Pugh's chambers and see if there is more there than expensive coffee and brandy smuggled from France."

There was a certain amount of discussion in the ordinary of the Peacock Inn—where Weyountah had left Sassy and George's chaise—about who should ride back to Cambridge and who should walk. "I'm not going to abandon Mrs. Fairfield by the side of the road for a four-mile walk back to the college," stated Weyountah, as the hostler went off to harness up the little vehicle, which would take three people at a very crowded pinch.

"Don't be silly," Katy retorted. "You need Horace to get Mrs. Adams into the Black Dog's room to do the searching, and you to stand guard. If old Ryland sees me anywhere in the vicinity of the college I'll be shown off the grounds and like as not everyone will start asking questions. I'll walk—and I'll meet you at the jail, where I'll go to cheer up poor Diomede and let him know he's not been abandoned and everyone is doing all they can."

Since Abigail had repeatedly contended that an American woman—even one as young and pretty as Katy—could go anywhere afoot in the colony without fear of the kind of insult that by all accounts lurked everywhere in crime-ridden Britain, there wasn't much that she could say against the plan. Horace provided several moving little homilies in Latin on the subject of self-sacrifice before Weyountah heaved him up into the chaise . . . The afternoon was, in fact, getting on. The Indian whipped up Sassy, and they bowled away down the tree-lined road for Cambridge.

"Did George speak much of his father?" asked Abigail, as they passed the old cemetery, and left the town behind. "Of what sort of a man he is and how he's likely to react to news that Diomede killed his son?"

"He called him 'stern,'" reported Weyountah, after a little time of thought. "And I understand their relationship was stormy, though George loved his father very much."

"More than once he spoke of how his father and his friends were forever uneasy about the idea of a slave uprising," said Horace, lowering Mrs. Morgan's copy of his translation, which he was comparing with his later reconstruction. "Like the Romans, the men of Virginia have become *servos servorum eorum*—an attitude that outraged George, I might add. But he was forever quoting his father on the subject of this trusted mammy of some friend, who had smothered the babies under her charge, or that trusted cook who'd put Jamestown weed into the family ragout. The most their cook ever did, George said, was, when she was angry with the master, spit in the coffee before bringing it to table . . . something he never told his father, because, he said, she was a very good cook and didn't get angry very often."

Abigail said, "Remind me never to breakfast with a Virginian in his home."

"But it doesn't bode well," concluded Weyountah, "for Diomede's chances of a fair hearing."

Nor did it bode well, reflected Abigail, as the little vehicle passed along the Charles Town Neck toward the mainland, for the chances that Mr. Charles Fairfield would welcome a

pregnant tavern-girl with open arms, prospective grandchild
or no . . .

And she was acutely conscious that at this point there was
little she or anyone could do, save marshal evidence for John
to use when Diomede's owner arrived . . . if Mr. Fairfield
would even consent to see John or to listen to some Massachusetts lawyer explaining that George had been killed in
the course of a hunt for buried pirate treasure . . . *No, we cannot prove by whom* . . .

Too easily she could hear the man simply shout, *He's my
property, and he's coming back with me* . . .

Her fists tightened where they lay in her lap. *The law is
established to defend a man's rights to his property* . . .

Horace handed her the paper, and as the chaise passed
along between stone walls, quiet fields, and shading elm
trees, she read over her nephew's translation, which, as he had
said, was so close to his later reconstruction as to give little
encouragement to any alternate reading. At no point did it
mention paces, yards, directions, digging, or trees (beyond
the single reference to a *towering oak* in a context that was
clearly metaphorical), or in fact any words that could be con-
strued as being part of a simple cipher. Nor, to Abigail's practiced eye, did it have the style of the labored cadence of words
that have been selected because their fifth letter was *q*.

The only cipher involved was that Old Beelzebub had
written his blackmailing account in Arabic letters to protect
it from prying eyes until he should have call to spring it on
Lieutenant Governor Morgan and demand hush-money. She
wondered if he'd ever done so. Or was it only one more
scheme he'd tucked away in the back of his alchemy books
and carried north with him when he'd left the Caribbean
for good?

He looked like the Devil would have, if the Devil were ever to sit in a corner of the kitchen and play the fiddle . . .

She frowned in thought, eyes narrowed against the sprinkling of the sunlight through the trees.

Yet someone at least was fairly certain that there *was* a treasure.

Well, hundreds of thousands of people in New Spain are fairly certain that all Protestants are inevitably bound for Hell, which certainly doesn't make them right.

Why did her mind hark back to the question of what had made old Beelzebub turn his back on his past? Walk away from the man he had been?

What man HAD he been?

As the chaise swung around toward the gates of the college, Abigail's glance strayed toward the King's Chapel by the Common, and a flash of black, like a crow against the green of the grass, caught her eye. A young woman in black—extremely fashionable black. Even at this distance, Abigail could tell the sable skirts gathered into the latest style of polonaise, the elbow-length sleeves festooned with sable lace and bedight with inky ribbons. Even the maidservant who followed her was in deep mourning, and the lapdog borne in the maid's arms wore a sable bow on his neck.

Weyountah said at the same moment, "Good Lord, it's Mistress Woodleigh! And there's the Black Dog coming to greet her! And comfort her, I dare—"

Abigail estimated the approach of that massive yellow-robed figure—trailed likewise by a black servant . . . "Which servant is that?" she asked as the chaise rounded the corner toward the college stables. "He has two—"

"Pedro." Horace twisted his body around in the chaise to look back. "He'll have left Eusebius in his room—"

"Let me out here," said Abigail, and dug in her pocket for pencil and her commonplace-book. Quickly she wrote:

Mr. Pugh,

'Twould be to your GREAT ADVANTAGE to meet me at four o'clock—a glance at the clock above the King's Chapel showed that it wanted but ten minutes of the hour—*at the Crowned Pig. Wait for me there, as I cannot linger long; this matter concerns certain BOOKS that I understand you seek.*

Althea Mainwaring

"Who's Althea—?" began Horace, and Weyountah chuckled.

"Very good, m'am! And if Mr. Pinkstone is there studying, I'm to send him on an errand to fetch a hair from the Great Cham's beard?"

"Something like that." She sprang down from the chaise and handed Weyountah the note. "Do you know anything about this Eusebius? Anything at all that I can use to keep him talking when he gets here?"

"He has a wife in the West Indies named Violetta and is courting one of the maidservants at Mr. Vassall's house," provided Weyountah. "He was brought from Africa as a youth and was trained there by the local witch doctor—"

"Was he, indeed?" asked Abigail sharply, and the Indian's eyebrows went up thoughtfully.

"So far as I know, the only thing he's used his training on in this country is making up embrocations for the Black Dog's horses and cats."

"Ah," said Abigail contentedly. "I had forgotten the cats. While Weyountah is searching Pugh's room, Horace, perhaps—

to make sure we've covered all possibilities—you have a look through Mr. Ryland's, just to see if the Governor is in the habit of sending him on errands. It occurs to me that as His Excellency's pensioner, Mr. Ryland may well have been the one who undertook the purchase of the books and can testify that indeed the Governor took possession. Now, go—"

"*I go, I go, look how I go . . .*"

"*Aquilis velociores; leonibus fortiores!*"

St-John Pugh was still deep in conversation with Mistress Sally Woodleigh as Abigail came around the corner of Massachusetts Hall and crossed the road toward the chapel. Like a good servant, the man Pedro stood impassive, his scarred face expressionless, looking around him with dark uninterested eyes. Abigail called out, "Mr. Pugh!" and was greeted with a deep bow and an off-swept cap, and introduced to Sally Woodleigh.

"I am terribly, terribly sorry to hear of your loss," said Abigail, taking the two fingers offered her in the British fashion, and Mistress Woodleigh immediately began to shed tears, silently, tragically, and without any accompanying sobs that might have rendered her lovely nose red.

"Thank you," the girl whispered—she must have been sixteen or seventeen, Katy's age, Abigail guessed—and wiped her eye with a handkerchief, trimmed in Brussels lace a handspan deep, that her handmaiden stepped forward to offer her. "Everyone has been so good . . ."

Pugh took her other hand in his and pressed it expressively; Abigail noticed the squeeze of gratitude that Mistress Woodleigh returned.

"I was never more shocked," said Abigail warmly, "as when I heard the news. I did not know Mr. Fairfield well, though my nephew thought the world of him."

"All loved him," replied the girl simply. "And I—I never understood what the poet meant, when he spoke of one's

heart being in the grave. But it is, m'am. My heart is back
there in that chapel—" She turned and gestured, a trifle too
much like Juliet in an amateur theatrical performance. "I
only go to visit it . . . and him."

"Say not so." Pugh patted the small gloved hand still in
his. "Leave those of us who loved him—and others yet on
this earth—still with the blossom of hope."

Sally Woodleigh, Abigail reflected, watching the dewy
smile she gave him, though she had the air of one who has
talked herself into believing in a grief that made her the center of attention, was clearly in actual pain; the glint in Mr.
Pugh's eye could not be described as anything but amused at
the scene. It was just as well that the slave Eusebius appeared
at that moment, calling out, "Michie Pugh, sir! Michie Pugh!
Got a message here; he say it important for you!"

Abigail watched St-John Pugh's face as he read the note
she had written five minutes previously and was gratified to
see how his eyes narrowed. "Thank you, Eusebius," he said.
"Who delivered this—?"

"Michie Thaxter, sir. He say a woman give it to him, out
by the stable; say she couldn't come into the stair."

Good for you, Horace!

The Black Dog looked as if he might have cursed, had he
not been still standing next to Mistress Woodleigh. Abigail
guessed he had a Rabelaisian turn of phrase. He glanced
toward the Chapel tower, then turned back to the girl, and
bowed deeply over her hand. "Please pardon my haste, *bellis-
sima*; a matter of great urgency."

*Certainly more urgent than Mr. Ryland's opinions on translating
Plato or your own upcoming examinations*, reflected Abigail, as
the clock struck four.

In a sweetly pouting voice, Mistress Woodleigh chided,

"And who is this lady you're running off to see the instant she beckons?"

"A withered old trout who's done business with my father," replied Pugh at once, though Abigail had made up the name Althea Mainwaring out of thin air. "'Tis tedious, beautiful nymph, but she carries tales, and I wouldn't have my father's ill-will for worlds." He bent to kiss her hand. "I know 'tis an effort for you to shake off your grief, but for the sake of those of us who—who are deeply concerned for your feelings, will you permit me to call on you tomorrow and take you walking with me on the Common? You must have a care for your health."

"You are too kind . . ."

Abigail was afraid Pugh would prolong the scene and send Eusebius back to his room again, but evidently both men knew that Mr. Pinkstone had been left in the chamber; in any case, Pugh, after another bow and a further reverent salute on the hand of his beloved, set off at a smart pace for the far end of Cambridge, trailed by Pedro, and Abigail turned just as Eusebius was walking away.

"Eusebius," she said, as if trying to remember something about the name—and, well-trained slave that he was, the African came back. One did not walk away from a white woman who spoke to you . . . "My nephew tells me you know something of the ailments of cats?"

To her surprise the ferocious face, with its tribal scars, relaxed into a gentle smile. "Oh, pretty ones," he said in a deep bass voice, and made a gesture as if cradling a cat in his arms.

"Could you spare just a moment?" asked Abigail. "I know it sounds fond and foolish of me, but my poor cat has begun scratching at herself, constantly, poor thing . . ."

She described at considerable length symptoms displayed by Granny Quincy's sour old Black Witch the previous

summer, and Eusebius listened gravely, asking questions now
and then—What was m'aum chatte's age, did she have rough
bumps on the skin beneath her fur, was she losing fur on her
backside? Since poor Black Witch had suffered with precisely
these symptoms through the past three summers, Abigail
took notes of what Eusebius prescribed—putting garlic in
her food, braiding herbs into a collar for her if she would take
it, washing her ("She no like, so you make her do anyway,
m'aum") in a solution of mild aromatics.

With luck, she reflected, handing the servant half a Spanish reale, Mr. Pinkstone would have time to return from
whatever errand Weyountah had sent him on before Eusebius
got back to the rooms, sparing them both anxiety about
what to tell Michie Pugh . . .

She had to remind herself, as she walked round to the lane
by the college stables where Weyountah and Horace waited
for her with Katy—flushed and cheerful and not a penny the
worse for her long walk—that Eusebius's obvious expertise
with the ailments of cats was a sword that cut both ways . . .
and he would have known exactly how much to dose a frumenty to guarantee that it would transform an entire household into Sleeping Beauty's castle.

"We both went in to look," said Weyountah, as Horace
helped Abigail and Katy up into the chaise and the vehicle
set off at a smart pace—as the sun was, yet again, sinking
toward the hills and threatening to catch Abigail on the
wrong side of the Boston town gates. Katy turned around to
wave back at Horace, then clung to the rail of the little wicker
seat, smiling into the breeze that whipped back her long
black hair. "So there would be no doubt about who found
what, where—"

"And did you find anything?" demanded Abigail, hearing
already in his voice that they had.

"We found both George's books—the *I Modi* and the *Vies des Dames Gallantes*—in Pugh's room . . . along with considerable other literature from other sources, but along the same lines."

"And they won't tell me what the others were," added Katy. "Well, I'm a married woman," she added, as Abigail frowned at her.

"And in Mr. Ryland's room," Weyountah's voice cut inexorably over Katy's protests, "we found . . . all the rest of Beelzebub's books, save only for the ones Horace and I gave to you."

Twenty

"Hidden at the bottom of his clothes-chest, in every drawer of his desk, and four-deep beneath his mattress, Weyountah says," Abigail reported to John, who had been listening to Nabby's history lesson when—tired and famished—Abigail and Katy came into the lamplight of the kitchen after the mile-and-a-quarter walk from the town gates in the deepening dusk. Weyountah had—yet again—barely reached the gates in time, and there had been no question but that he was obliged to leave her and Katy there, and turn back for Cambridge by the thin light of the wasting moon.

"And he was certain they were Old Beelzebub's?"

"Well, aside from the question of what other fifty-four books the Governor's protégé would be concealing under his mattress . . . Please, no, I'm quite all right—" she added, when John forced her into the settle beside the kitchen hearth and went to the pantry.

"You're not," he called back over his shoulder, handing bread, butter, and slices of cold sausage and cheese back to

Nabby, who had hastened after him with plates. "Did you have any dinner at all? Or you, either, Katy? I didn't think so—"

Johnny came hurrying back to the fire with mugs of cider, followed closely by his sister and father, bearing food. Abigail had to reach up over the heads of Charley and Tommy to get her plate, both the smaller boys having flung themselves ecstatically into her lap. "Mr. Adams, really you shouldn't—!" Katy protested, and then tucked into the sausage and cheese like a starving cannibal.

"In fact," Abigail went on as John brought her small sewing-table close to the fire, "Weyountah recognized a number of them from Mrs. Seckar's house. Others had Geoffrey White-head's name written in them and dates ranging from 1630 to 1693, which was the year he died." Pattie carried lamps from where she'd been sewing and hung them on the wall near Abigail's head. "There were also exactly fifty-four of them, which was how many the Governor's 'man'—obviously Ryland—took away with him—"

"Only to learn that nine had been sold elsewhere." John had shaved and washed his face, but he looked deeply weary from two days on the road. Yet the fact that he had shaved told Abigail that he was going out again to meet with the Sons of Liberty at the Green Dragon while yet it was possible to do so.

"I can't really see Mr. Ryland stabbing his captain over them, even if they *had* quarrelled."

"Can't you?" He settled with his own cider on the settle at her side. "Friends stab friends every night in this colony, Portia, and for the stupidest possible reasons or no reason at all: drunkenness, politics, anger at someone else. Then they panic and blame someone else. You'd like to think 'twas Black Dog Pugh because he's a slaveholder and personally obnoxious—"

"And you'd like to think 'twas the Governor because he was appointed Chief Justice of the colony in 1760 with no other qualification than that he was a good friend to the Board of Trade. And we don't either of us seem," she added, spreading the soft pale cheese on the crusty bread, "to be much closer to the answer. Pugh definitely—or as definitely as we can ascertain from the paper of the note—forged Sally Woodleigh's hand to a note to get George out of his room at midnight. But whether George then lingered behind the barn in hopes of meeting the girl . . ."

"I think he did," said John. And when Abigail frowned and Katy looked aside, he went on, "Why else would he have taken the girl's love-letters, if not to return them? If not to honorably inform her"—he glanced at Katy—"that he had married another woman—even if he *had* bribed the quite-genuine clerk of the Providence county court to perform the ceremony in a tavern instead of the courthouse. 'Twas still a legal marriage. Easy there, girl," he added, as Katy flung her arms around his neck and kissed him, "I'm just the messenger—"

But he beamed upon the girl as she embraced and kissed Abigail as well. John was as faithful a husband as could be found in the compass of the world, but Abigail knew he had the same soft spot in his heart for pretty girls as she had for good-looking young men.

"Therefore, he could have waited—who knows how long?—for the girl to put in an appearance, and returned, disappointed, to his chambers and gone to bed . . . to be wakened in the dead of night by an intruder whom he recognized, an intruder who had thought him drugged and had, therefore, taken no precaution to keep silent while he searched for books that were already gone."

"It still doesn't mean 'twas Mr. Ryland."

"No," said John. "But there's a simple way to find out."

Abigail sighed, and said, "Drat. 'Tis a day's drive to Concord, so we'll not leave 'til Monday—are you away tonight, dearest friend?" She put her hand on his.

"I must." He glanced across the room to where Pattie was seating the children in a small halo of lamplight, ready for evening prayers. "In truth, Portia, none of us has the slightest idea how many nights we have left to meet freely and make plans—nor what conditions will prevail once the King's Commissioner lands."

"You won't—" She kept her hold upon his hand as he rose, and went with him to the sideboard to fetch the Bible. "There is not the possibility that *you'll* be arrested?"

"Governor Hutchinson hates me as I hate him," said John grimly. "If friends stab friends under the impulse of momentary fears, how much more will a frightened man be tempted to stab his enemy if someone puts a knife into his hand?"

Yet he went to the table smiling and asked among his children whose turn it was to pick a portion from the Holy Writ (it was Charley, so they got Samson trouncing the Philistines—with John's observations that 'twas only God's love for Samson that strengthened the hero's arm to defend the weak). Sitting at his side with the fire's warmth shining on her back, Abigail listened to her husband's voice and reflected that this man had far greater matters to deal with than one lonely and frightened black man sitting in the Cambridge jail.

That he would take up his cudgel and fight like that ancient Israelite hero for a slave's life she didn't doubt—if she pressed him to do so. He would always take on one more task, one more responsibility, one more foe, for justice's sake or his country's—until, facing an army of assailants, he went down before them in defeat.

Diomede's freedom was her battle.

Enslaved, as Samson had been enslaved (and with far less foolishness, in her opinion), and helpless . . .

Across the table she saw Katy startle, and in her wide blue eyes Abigail read sudden enlightenment, something realized that she had not guessed before . . .

When the children had been kissed and herded upstairs, and John was adjusting his wig and putting on his greatcoat, Katy came up to them, and whispered, "Can you prove my marriage to George, Mr. Adams? Weyountah looked in the back of both of George's books and found no trace of the license."

"I took notes of the date and the circumstances and the name of the clerk," said John. "I'll write them out for you if you wish—"

"Belike that scoundrel Pugh took the license to blackmail George with," sniffed Abigail, as she brought paper and pencil from the sideboard drawer. "Or to blackmail Charles Fairfield when he arrives next week. If you like, Katy, we can speak to the man—"

"Yes, later," she said breathlessly. "But if Mr. Adams will be so good as to write out at least proof that I *am* George's legal wife—and lend me Thaxter and the chaise tomorrow— then I'll go out to Cambridge and tell the sheriff that Diomede is to be tried here in Massachusetts after all. Don't you see?" She looked from Abigail's face to John's, her eyes shining with triumph. "If Diomede was George's property, then he's *mine* now, and I can arrange his trial where I please!"

Neither John nor Abigail thought this would actually work, "But you might as well give it a try," said John. Abigail had intended to send Thaxter—*who surely has enough to do just keeping up with John's legal copying so the lot of us don't starve!*—to the State House in the morning and look up if, in fact, Old Beelzebub Whitehead had owned land in the colony, with or without a stone castle and a tribe of worshipful Indians, and if so, where this had lain. But she agreed that the journey to Cambridge took precedence.

It would be another week, she calculated—as she went about her marketing, did the long-delayed mending, and prepared the usual Saturday double meals in anticipation of the following day's enforced rest and meditation—before Charles Fairfield arrived in Boston: he did not sound like the kind of man to welcome even a legitimate grandson whose mother was a tavern-maid. Having her claiming to own a valuable slave would not endear her to him nor help her cause—nor that of the slave. As she and Pattie dumped snowy mountains of ironing from their baskets to the towel-draped table (a task that should have been done yesterday, she reflected guiltily)— she mentally marshalled various schemes to help either Katy or Diomede should Fairfield prove intransigent . . . in between forays into the yard and once into Queen Street when Charley's silence indicated that he'd gone exploring again.

"At least, thanks to the Committees of Correspondence, we now know the names of Virginia lawyers to whom Katy can go," she remarked, as she sprinkled water from the bowl at her side over the first of John's shirts.

"But what if the King closes all the courts?" asked Pattie worriedly. "In Virginia as well as here."

"What?" Abigail rested the heavy iron's butt on the table-edge. "What has Virginia got to do with Sa—with *Persons Unknown*," she corrected herself, "destroying tea in Boston?"

"They're both colonies," reasoned Pattie. "You know how everyone talks about 'the Indians,' when Weyountah speaks of the Narragansetts and the Wampanoags and the Nipmucs all being completely different peoples—some of them sided with the French during the war and some with the English, and some just tried to keep out of things as best they could. What if the King and Parliament—who are farther away from us than we are from the Narragansett villages—just think of everyone over here as 'the colonies,' the way my father thinks of 'the Indians,' and think to punish us all alike?"

"It isn't the same," protested Abigail. "Each colony is a separate entity with its own government and its own agents in London. You'd have to be a fool to mix up someone from Massachusetts, for instance, with a Carolinian . . . or a Carolinian from the coast with the sort of savages they have in the northern mountains. Even the—oh, drat the boy!" she added, looking quickly around the kitchen as Tommy—fastened as usual to the leg of the massive sideboard by his leading-strings—set up a protesting wail that indicated that his interest in his toys had flagged and his elder brother was nowhere to be found.

"You, sir," she informed her errant middle son, when she finally located him in the loft above the cowshed, "are far too old to wear leading-strings, which means you are old enough to obey your mother. Where is it that you are allowed to play by yourself?"

"The house and the yard," replied Charley obediently.

"And is the cowshed part of the yard?"

"It's *by* the yard."

Abigail led Charley firmly back across the narrow expanse of bricks as Pattie reemerged from the alleyway to the street that she'd just checked—

And behind her, Thaxter and Katy, leading Balthazar.

"What happened?" Abigail let go of her son's hand, and he immediately darted to hug Katy and put himself in danger of being trodden on by the horse. "We didn't expect you back 'til near dark—"

Thaxter shook his head, and Katy flung up her hands: "'Tis all solved," she said, and beamed happily as she lifted Charley into her arms. "Diomede was broken out of the Cambridge jail last night—and old Sheriff Congreve is mad as fire."

Of course it was Sam. Even John thought so when Abigail took the news to him in his study, where he had been immured all day, sorting out depositions and writing case notes—neither the colonial courts nor the natural litigiousness of New Englanders having come to a halt just because the King might be irate over some spilled tea.

"Drat the man." John looked up from the drifts of papers on his desk. "He might at least have waited 'til we'd *seen* Fairfield—"

"He might just as well have taken out advertisements in the *Gazette* in Diomede's name saying, *I AM GUILTY*! Not to speak of making it impossible for him to ever see his wife and family again—"

"Do you think that the slave stood the slightest chance of having his innocence even considered in his master's home country? Either way, his wife and daughters would lose him, and he them. At least as things are he lives—"

"And I'll wager Sam did this," went on Abigail wrathfully, "just to get my mind off saving an innocent man's life and onto finding a treasure for him to spend on gunpowder. Beyond doubt, he didn't even ask poor Diomede if he *wished* to be saved!"

"If he didn't wish it, he's a fool." John wiped his pen carefully, set it down beside the sheet he was fair-copying—a task that was generally left to Thaxter, if that young man hadn't been halfway to Cambridge with Katy in the neighbors' borrowed chaise. "You know as well as I how difficult it is to prove a negative—even had the true murderer not cast the blame on the nearest convincing suspect. Do you truly think the father will seek truth when vengeance is right before him? Nine men out of ten will settle for the ease of heart that vengeance gives rather than press on for the more astringent taste of facts."

"Robbing Diomede of his good name, his wife, his family, his home, and all his friends . . . so that Sam can hurry me into the quest for treasure—"

"Before he himself has to flee the city?" John raised his eyebrows. "I could wish Sam would have waited to see if there were need for Diomede to flee—or be dragged—into hiding, but once Diomede's owner is present, it might have been far less simple to free him out of hand, you know. And as I have said, tomorrow or the next day or the next might have been too late for anyone to do anything."

Abigail's shoulders relaxed, and her head lowered. "You are right," she said quietly. "'Tis just . . ."

He reached across the desk and took her hand. As always his fingers felt very warm on hers, and strong. "Sufficient unto the day is the trouble thereof," he said. "Monday we'll speak to Sam and have a word with Diomede if we can. Or—" He hesitated, glancing at the mountain of work before him, clearly trying to calculate when on Monday he would have ten minutes to spare . . .

"I'll speak to Sam," said Abigail. "You needn't come with me."

"Sam is my cousin," returned John. "Thus it is incumbent upon me to keep him from being murdered in his own house—so I think 'tis best I come with you."

Abigail laughed, and returned to the kitchen and the ironing and the task of tracking down the errant Charley, who had managed to make it all the way down the alley and out onto Queen Street . . .

* * *

On Monday she and John did indeed speak to Sam, but by Monday, Diomede and his fate had been removed, suddenly and terrifyingly, from their minds.

In general Abigail had little trouble keeping her mind focused on the Reverend Cooper's sermons, for the man was a good speaker, and his arguments—if sometimes more political than theological—were well thought-out and proceeded in good order. But on Sunday, as she sat next to John for the morning sermon, she found her thoughts straying to Diomede, to the wife he had left behind him in Virginia, to the daughters he had begged to be able to write to. By breaking out of the Cambridge jail, he had virtually guaranteed that he would never be able to go home—for who would believe him when he had fled from justice?

And yet, she thought, Sam had not been obliged to do anything at all for the man. Diomede was nothing to him, save an obstacle preoccupying Abigail's thoughts and preventing her from concentrating on what Sam wanted her to do. And it was true, she reflected—as she listened to the long elaboration upon the adventures of King David and his men hiding out in the wilderness from the King whom the Prophet Samuel had deprived of his crown—that there was every chance that Sam had saved Diomede's life . . .

And how could I tell?

How can any of us tell what lies down the road we do not take?

Dr. Cooper's second sermon—after eating a cold Sabbath dinner, and reading a little to the younger children, and hearing Johnny and Nabby give their summaries of the earlier sermon to make sure they understood the matter—concerned such martial prophets as Gideon and Deborah: *Hear, o ye kings, give ear o ye princes; I, even I, will sing unto the Lord . . .*

One of the oldest songs in all the Holy Writ, her father had said: how the small nation had risen against those that would oppress it, and how the stars in their courses joined battle on the side that was right. *So let all thine enemies perish, o Lord; but let them that love him be as the sun when he goeth forth in his might.*

Sisera was coming—the King's Commissioner or whoever the King was going to send.

With who knew how great an army in his train? With who could tell what weapon in his hand?

And by what would that Commissioner be met?

Abigail walked home quietly through the beautiful light of the early evening, listening to Pattie and Katy's soft chatter behind her: the girls had remained at home in the morning to look after the smaller boys—Thaxter invariably spent Sundays with his mother, so John and Abigail took turns missing the afternoon sermon to mind the children so that the girls could attend. *If I speak to Sam just after the marketing is done tomorrow, 'twill give me time to go with him out to Cambridge or to wherever they've hidden Diomede. And if he DARE bring up the subject of Old Beelzebub's treasure, I really will strike him with a broom-handle . . .*

She turned from Brattle into Queen Street and saw, rather to her surprise—for Boston streets were quiet as a rule on the Sabbath—John. John hastening along with no hat on his head, looking right and left about him . . .

She quickened her stride in the same moment that he saw her. What she saw in his face shocked and chilled her; she gathered up her skirts and ran.

Before she could even ask him what was wrong he said, "Charley's gone."

Twenty-one

They didn't get the note until morning.

Before darkness fell Sunday evening, the whole of the neighborhood had been called into service: Tom Butler the cooper and his two sturdy apprentices, Ehud Hanson the shoemaker, Uzziah Begbie and his wife, Gower the blacksmith down the street . . .

No one had seen a sturdy fair-haired little boy, not even quite four weeks from his fourth birthday . . .

Please, dear God, Abigail prayed soundlessly as she walked along Cornhill toward Milk Street, *please let him see his fourth birthday. Let us all see his fourth birthday . . .*

The streets were Sabbath-quiet—*Thank you, God!*—without the carriages and cart traffic of the weekdays, without the cattle being herded along and the barrows, drays, flocks of chickens and geese that rendered the cobbled, crisscrossing ways so confusing for a tiny child. *He'll have set off for Aunt Eliza's*, Abigail told herself as she walked, *and gotten distracted by something else*—the handsome lawn of the Governor's house or horses being harnessed to take some fashionable "worthy" to church. In this part of Boston, at least, if a stray child was found wandering—even one of the ragged little urchins from the North End waterfront—someone would take him or her in, would ask, "Where do you live, dearie?" and if no answer was forthcoming would keep an eye on the street for a distrait dark-haired woman in her blue go-to-church gown looking up every alleyway, around every tree . . .

Eliza and Isaac Smith were horrified. Eliza and Abigail searched the garden, and Young Isaac—for all his usual talk about not profaning the Sabbath—instantly put on his hat and went out to search in the streets round about, returning only when darkness was settling over the town to offer to walk Abigail home. "Of course we'll send and let you know . . . We'll have Cuffee outside in the street watching for him . . ."

"And poor Johnny thinks 'tis his fault," said Abigail, as she and Young Isaac—still so-called though he was twenty-five years old and had his own church and congregation—made their way along Cornhill arm in arm. "Nabby was watching the younger boys and Johnny got into some kind of quarrel with her—as children do, with their rivalries over books and toys and slate-pencils. John came out of the front of the house and adjudicated the conflict, and by the time anyone looked round, Charley was gone."

"He can't have got far," opined Isaac firmly, despite the fact that his mother's house on Milk Street was far from Queen Street by anyone's stretch of the imagination and no one seemed to think that Charley had any other destination. And then—giving himself the lie—"Would he have found his way to the Common?"

Abigail looked up. Dark had fallen, and above the black jumble of rooflines, stars shone clear and glittering, like diamonds. The moon was in its last dwindle toward darkness. "*Why?*" she asked. "Your mother's house is nearer—"

"Would he have known that?" reasoned the young parson. "He could simply have gotten lost. And if he grew frightened, it could easily be that he'd hesitate to speak to a stranger . . . and there are few about the streets of a Sunday between dinner and dark."

"True," said Abigail, as they passed the tall brick tower of the Old Meeting-House and turned up Queen Street. "But Charley isn't the least shy of strangers. When he gets hungry, he'll turn to the first friendly looking stranger he meets to ask him to lead him home. And he knows he lives in—"

She broke off, seeing the men moving about the alleyway that led to the back of the house. She quickened her steps, almost snatching up her skirts to run. When she got close, she saw that in addition to her neighbors, there were four or five of the North End roughnecks whose assistance Sam could habitually call on if he needed a Tory's shopwindow broken or—for instance—a mob to storm the Governor's house . . .

Paul Revere was in the kitchen, talking to John.

"—almost certain 'twas the same woman," he was saying. "I'll tell Sam to get his men onto the Common, though I cannot imagine Charley wouldn't walk up to the door of the first house he came to and knock on it, asking to be taken home— or given part of their dinner on the spot, more like—"

"You've heard nothing, then?" Abigail's glance went from her husband to her friend. "Did Sam send you?"

And saw the look that passed between the two men, that turned her blood to water in her veins. "I came on another matter," Revere said. "Sam heard today that the corpse of a woman whom he believes might be this Mrs. Lake you spoke of—the one who kidnapped your cousin Horace—"

"She didn't precisely——" Abigail hesitated on the denial, realizing that, effectively, that was exactly what had happened. And then, as the silversmith's words sank in, "Corpse?"

"A couple of boatmen"——by which Abigail knew he meant *smugglers*——"found her washed up on the rocks of Bird Island, where the river's current sets around with the tide. She was well-dressed, they said, and dark-haired. They said they'd heard from Munn in Charles Town that a woman thereabouts had disappeared."

"Mrs. Morgan," said Abigail softly. "The owner of——"

"Good Lord, not La Fata Morgana?" Revere almost laughed—he clearly knew what Mrs. Morgan was known to be—but sobered at once. "Well, I'll be . . . She's William Chamberville's mistress, isn't she? One of our dear Governor's in-laws——"

"Was she drowned?" Abigail recalled uneasily the glimmer of the river through the trees past the foot of Moulton's Hill. "The house isn't far from the river——"

John shot her a sharp glance; Revere barely raised an eyebrow. But he only said, "No, not drowned. Her throat was cut."

Whyever Revere had come to the house, he wasted no time in sending one of his men to fetch Sam, and by midnight—when Abigail finally went to bed—every smuggler, rope-beater, and out-of-work apprentice in the Sons of Liberty was moving about the streets of Boston, lantern in hand, searching for Charley. Katy went out with them. Pattie remained with Abigail to comfort Nabby's guilty tears and Johnny's even more excruciating stoic wretchedness: "'Twas only his way, my Hercules," whispered Abigail, gathering her eldest son against her side as they sat together on the settle and stroking his baby-fine fair hair. "You know how he is. If it hadn't been you and your sister, he'd have gone for the door next time one or the other of you buckled your shoe or went to the backhouse—" She said it to make them giggle, which they did. "'Tis just how Charley is right now, always wanting to be off exploring. You remember how you were, Johnny. How you had to follow Ben Clayford and his brother when they went fishing, and you climbed out the window of your room to do it—"

"I was a baby then," protested the six-year-old. "All the more, I should have been watching Charley, and not giving in to my ill-temper and sinfulness."

Nabby, on her other side, clung to Abigail's arm and began to cry softly again. "If something hasn't happened to him," she whispered, "they'd have found him by now."

This, Abigail knew, was perfectly true.

And it was also perfectly true that there were a thousand places within a quarter mile of Queen Street where a well-meaning, inquisitive boy of only-just-three-weeks-short-of-four could come to terrible and irrevocable grief.

The Long Wharf. Endlessly fascinating, and extending close to a half mile out to sea: ships, boxes, coils of rope. Wet boards slippery and slanting. Mysterious ladders extending down to the cold beryl black chop of the water.

Merchant Street, every shop and warehouse shut up and secretive-looking on the late Sabbath afternoon: cellar-doors, stacks of barrels, piles of crates that could easily fall unheard by any, pinning a little boy underneath.

In the other direction the Common, whose grassy open spaces might tempt the boy to explore further. Yet if he'd gone to the Common, what harm could he come to—?

In her mind she saw the men, nevertheless, traversing the dark rise of the ground toward Beacon Street, where the lamps of Mr. Hancock's elegant house shone against the slope of the hill.

The Mill Pond—

Abigail closed her eyes in prayer that she couldn't even phrase. Then she said, "Come. 'Twill do you no good, nor Charley either, to have you sitting up and making yourselves sick just because he's been goose enough to get himself lost. The moment he's brought back—and you know he'll be brought back and have his hide well tanned by his father for worrying us all!—I shall wake you and fetch you down."

"Might Johnny sleep in with me and Tommy," whispered Nabby, "'til Charley comes back?"

Pattie carried the sleeping Tommy up to the small room at the end of the hall, and Johnny and Nabby snuggled in together in the girl's narrow bed, like two doleful little ghosts in their white nightrails. Abigail held them and sang to them and reassured them, though neither felt much like hearing a story. When she left them, by the light of her single candle she still saw the glimmer of their open eyes.

If something hasn't happened to him, they'd have found him by now.

She leaned her head back against the hard wood of the fireside settle, staring into the silky whispers of light as they played over the embers.

He didn't start his running away until I left him at Eliza's, she thought. *Because 'twas only then that he was old enough and strong enough to get far? Because 'twas only then that he realized that a world of delight existed in her garden, which our pokey little yard could not approach in wonderment?*

Because 'twas only then that his mother would leave him with Pattie and Katy while she swanned off to Cambridge in quest of mysteries and justice?

Admit it, Portia, she told herself, knowing it for the truth of her heart and hating herself. *YOU have supped with the Devil in meddling with justice that is John's work—a man's work. You* revel in "*seeing through the riddles of criminal conduct,*" in being "*a veritable Alexander . . .*"

She closed her eyes.

And this is what has come of trying to take a man's part. Her whole soul cried out in anger at this view, repeated to her throughout her childhood by her mother and aunts. She knew herself capable of more than just bearing children and washing baby-clouts . . . *It CAN'T be God's intent . . .*

Where your treasure is, there shall your heart be also, the Scripture said.

Your treasure should be here, in this house, with your children.

She could almost hear her mother saying it. And in her heart of hearts, she knew that the house was not where her treasure lay.

I am what I am! God made me what I am!

A woman, her mother's voice replied. *God made you a woman, with a woman's lesser part to play.*

"*Who can find a virtuous woman?*" the Psalmist asked, "*for her price is far above rubies.*"

Who can find her indeed, if she's left for Cambridge for the day to look for pirate gold?

"*The heart of her husband doth safely trust in her . . .*"

. . . and should be able to have faith that she won't mislay his children.

"*She will do him good and not evil, all the days of her life.*"

Abigail could almost see her mother, a tall stern woman and extraordinarily beautiful, despite the tightly pinned day-cap on her raven hair and the trim dark simple dress of a minister's wife. Long hands like a queen's, roughened and reddened by laundry diligently done each Tuesday and not pushed off until some later date, by dishes washed, by floors swept. A beautiful alto voice reading the verses of Proverbs to her three too-intelligent daughters: *She worketh willingly with*

*her hands . . . She riseth while it is yet night, and giveth meat to her
household . . . She considereth a field, and buyeth it: with the fruit
of her hands she planteth a vinyard . . .*

Abigail's heart protested furiously, *A man's life is at
stake . . . A dozen mens', or a hundred, depending on that wretched
Commissioner or whoever the King is sending that keeps John up all
the night planning and organizing what can be done . . .*

But that is not your business, Abigail. She could almost hear
her mother saying it.

The Scripture might proclaim, *She stretcheth out her hand to
the poor; yea, she reacheth forth her hands to the needy—*

But her mother would say—and she was right, Abigail
reflected in agony—that the first duty of a woman was to her
children, and her second to her husband, whose children she
must guard while he went and had all the peril . . .

And the excitement and the intellectual sharpening that
went with it.

She felt the guilt like a physical pain, an ache in her side
where Charley would curl himself up against her when, worn
out with the mischiefs of a three-year-old, he would come
back to her, cling to her, knowing she would keep him safe.

And she hadn't.

She woke up cold, her neck aching where her head had
tipped sideways, the kitchen dark around her. The faintest glow
of the unbanked hearth rimmed the pans on their hooks, the
queens-ware dishes on their shelves making copper mirrors of
Messalina's wide, demented eyes. She had dreamed of arguing
with John—shouting at him through iron bars that separated
them, *You left them! You left them, and you left me!* knowing he
would be taken away to Halifax, tried by a military court, and
hanged for treason. Knowing that it was somehow her fault.

For a time she listened in the stillness, wondering what it
was that had waked her. Then she rose slowly, stiffly, to stir

up the fire again. Not long after that John and Thaxter came in, their voices muffled in the yard, calling out to others, thanking them . . . arranging a meeting by the Mill Pond as soon as it grew light.

"You didn't find him," she whispered, when the men came in, and John gathered her in his arms. She clung to him, trembling, trying to shove the last stains of her dream out of her mind. Feeling in the rhythm of his breath the degree of his own dread and pain.

"We will," he said. "We will, Nab. 'Tis dark as pitch; we could have walked within a yard of him on the Common and not seen him. If he'd knocked himself senseless—falling out of a tree or off the back of a dray trying to hook a ride . . ."

He turned his head sharply at the sound of someone knocking at the front door. Thaxter, already in the hall, reached it—Abigail guessed—in two strides, for she heard the bolt clack, the hinge creak almost before the sound of the first salvo died. She and John were in the doorway of the hall an instant after that and saw by the light of the lantern the clerk still held that it was Revere and Dr. Warren in the aperture, Revere in the act of handing a piece of paper to Thaxter.

"This was on the door," he said.

> *GIV US THE BUKS*
> *WE GOT YR BOY*

Twenty-two

Aday passed before the second note reached them, nerve-racking hours that brought Abigail close to unforgivable words with Sam, with Sam's wife Bess, with John himself. Last night she had silently cursed her mother's iron insistence upon the role of womanhood. Now, in her calmer moments—when, from long practice in forbearance and patience, she was able to take a deep breath and hold her always-unruly tongue at Sam's suggestion that they bring in Horace for an all-out attempt to find the treasure-code in the seven books before they had to be surrendered—she blessed her mother for not causing her to break irretrievably with every Adams on the planet . . . not to speak of murdering Sam.

She only said, "Bring the books here, Sam. They're going to be handed over the moment someone tells us where and when."

He looked like the words *Try to stall them* were upon his lips, but to his credit he didn't utter them. He said, "Of course. You'll have them tonight."

That had been during last night's conference in the small

hours when Sam was called back to see the note, and Abigail forbade them—any of them—to do a single thing, even call on the constables, until Charley had been returned safe. As the men were leaving, only an hour before dawn, she had caught Paul Revere by the sleeve: "Will you go out to Mrs. Morgan's house in Charles Town? You, yourself, without any others and without telling Sam, go out and see if her scar-faced coachman and the two grooms are still there? Don't go near the place—if they have Charley there . . ."

She bit back the words, not even daring to think them.

Revere's dark eyes narrowed, but he nodded. "I won't be seen."

Unable to utter a word, Abigail squeezed his hand.

Throughout Monday, it took all her self-command not to speak of the note to the other three children or to Pattie—whose self-control she did not trust as she instinctively trusted Katy's. With the bred-in discipline of one who has spent her life taking care of animals, Katy made sure that the milking was done before the town herd-boys drove the cattle down the street to the Common in the first pink twilight of morning; Pattie saw to it that Nabby and Johnny were clean and fed and off to school. But it was Abigail who sat down with her older children before their departure, and told them that 'twas best they go to school as ever and keep their minds from Charley, whom they could not help. "The men will search the Common again today," she said, "and the fields on the other side of Beacon Hill." She repeated John's argument of last night about how impossible it was to find anything as small as a three-year-old boy in the open fields on a moonless night.

While she was comforting them, a knock sounded at the front door, and Pattie came into the kitchen a moment later with the news that Mr. Ryland, the Governor's young man, was here . . .

"You had best go," she said, and kissed the two children,

aware that her efforts at control had robbed those kisses of anything but perfunctory motion. "Pattie, will you walk with them to the school?" Both children opened their mouths in protest—being escorted by an adult was the ultimate of babyishness—but Abigail was already out of the kitchen, with barely more than a glance at the small mirror in the hall to make sure that her cap was straight and her eyes those of a Roman matron and not a wild woman.

Yet when she opened the door and saw Joseph Ryland sitting beside the parlor's cold hearth, for that first instant it took everything she had in her not to walk straight up to him and seize him by the hair: *What has the Governor to do with this . . . ?*

Then he stood and faced her, white with shock and distress. "Mrs. Adams, I beg your forgiveness, for coming to you at a time like this—"

What are you doing with Beelzebub Whitehead's books in your chamber?

She took a deep breath. "No—" She hoped her gesture would convey this forgiveness to him. "'Tis well."

Did you hire Dubber Grimes to kidnap my son? The question shattered, dissolved against the haggard suspicion in his face, the sickened expression of someone who is trying very hard not to see something that's under his nose. Faced with Ryland's honest integrity, she could no more ask that than she could ask, *Did you tell Dubber Grimes to murder Horace and leave his body by the side of the Concord Road?*

It was absurd on the face of it.

"They have found nothing?" he asked.

She shook her head wordlessly.

"His Excellency asked me—I have been at his house yesterday and today . . . He said, he has had his quarrels with Mr. Adams, but 'tis all politics; this is another matter entirely.

Have— Pray forgive me asking this, m'am . . . Have arrangements been made to drag the Mill Pond?"

"I believe so, yes."

He made haste to add, "Of course 'tis absurd to think—"

"He is only three," said Abigail quietly. "Boys that age have neither the judgment to keep away from places of danger, nor the strength to swim or climb or scramble to safety."

Silence stood between them, and Abigail's jaw ached with the effort not to shout at him: *What do you know? What do you suspect? What has Hutchinson said? What has he done?* In the young man's brown eyes she saw the agony of surmises that he was trying his best to thrust away. And how not, when Hutchinson was not only the man who had gotten him into a college he could never have afforded to enter, but *who was keeping him there now* and upon whose continued goodwill he depended for everything?

To the marrow of her bones she knew that if she spoke of her suspicions, his honesty would drive him back to Hutchinson: *Mrs. Adams says this of her son's disappearance—is it true?* Too clearly in her mind she heard Paul Revere's voice saying, *Her throat was cut,* of the woman whose discreet house she had been in Friday . . .

Rage and tears and dread fought within her; the Lord only knew, she thought, what he was seeing of this in her face. And he would, thank goodness, attribute it simply to anxiety for her son . . .

At length the young man said, "His Excellency—Please do not hesitate, or let political enmities prevent either you or Mr. Adams, from calling upon His Excellency for any assistance whatsoever: men, authority, vessels, Writs of Assistance, whatever you require. As a father, an uncle, and a grandfather, he is utterly at your disposal, and that of your husband. As am I."

She managed to say, "Thank you," and made herself repeat

for the third time John's argument about the moonless night and the possibility that Charley had been lying stunned somewhere, and she saw relief flood into Ryland's sensitive face. "You're quite right," he exclaimed, with an eagerness to believe that told its own tale. "And a sturdy and well-grown boy—especially of that age—could well have missed his direction to your aunt's garden, if that's what he was seeking, and finding himself in open country . . ."

Some of the awful tension left his shoulders, and his face relaxed a little and grew sad. "My mother lived in Germantown but a little distance from Philadelphia," he said. "When I was apprenticed in the city, I ran away—three or four times—only wanting to be back where the streets weren't brick, and the houses weren't tall, and there was space to walk alone among the trees and smell the earth and the river. 'Twould have been easy, I think, for your son to let himself run too far."

She met his eyes then, and asked—with a softness that surprised herself—"And is that what you think happened to him?"

And his glance ducked away, but not before she saw the pain at the back of his eyes. "I don't—"

The rear door opened and Katy came in, a pail of milk in either hand. She stopped on the threshold and regarded Ryland warily; his brow clouded as he recognized her, and his glance went sharply to Abigail's face. Abigail said, "Mr. Ryland? I believe you know Mrs. Fairfield."

His lips tightened and a dusky flush crept up over his skin, that she would give the name of his captain to the daughter of a stableman. "Servant, m'am." His bow was a vocabulary of obligation, scorn, and restraint.

Katy set down one pail and offered him two fingers, as the Tory ladies did. They were stained, where Semiramis (as she so often did) had dunged her tail.

"M'am." His bow deepened by a degree and a half from the upright over her hand. Then he was gone.

Only an hour after that, Paul Revere arrived with the news that the house called Avalon was closed up tight: shuttered, locked, the barns closed and the horses and carriage gone.

When the cows came home that night, the head herd-boy beat with his fist on the back door and handed Abigail a paper. "'Twere tied 'round Cleo's horn, m'am," he explained, "when we gathered 'em up, like."

LEAV EM DED CENNER OF Y YARD WTH LANNRN
BURNINNG MIDNIT TOMORO WEN LANRN GOES
OUT YR BOYLL BEE THER TRY AN STOP US AN
HEL BEE THER DED

"Should Dr. Langdon or Sheriff Congreve be informed?" Joseph Warren handed the note back to Revere and looked inquiringly toward Sam, John, and Abigail in the lamplight.

"I don't know Congreve well enough to know whether he can be trusted to keep his hands out of the matter." Paul Revere turned the paper over in his hands, letting the gleam of the parlor fire fall upon it. Examining the writing, the ink, the quality of the paper itself, as it was, Abigail knew, his habit to study everything that came his way. "Langdon would try to interfere," he added.

"Langdon would try to interfere if he got news of a war between the Chinese and the Hottentots," remarked Sam bitterly. "He cannot be kept from interfering . . ."

"And can *you* be trusted?" With a queer, cold sense of

being someone other than herself, Abigail turned her glance to Sam. Darkness had fallen by the time the men had reassembled in the parlor; by the low gleam of the lamps on the table his face had a slightly sinister look. He made a gesture of surrender.

"John and I will go," Abigail said, without even a glance at her husband. "Mr. Revere, would you be so good as to accompany us? For the rest of you, Sam, Dr. Warren . . . I forbid you to be part of this. Any of you. My son's life is at stake, and I *will not* have interference in doing exactly as these men demand."

Revere began gently, "Mrs. Adams—"

"*No.* We will do as the note asks and nothing else. I defy any one of you to explain to me why the filthy gold collected by some pirate, no matter what noble purpose you intend to put it to, is more important to me than my child's life."

She waited for a few moments. The unruly portion of her soul—the portion that her mother had always deplored, that wondered things like how exactly HAD Jesus managed to multiply five loaves and seven fishes (*What kind of fishes?*) to feed five thousand people: had each fish regenerated its head or tail when pulled in half?—*that* portion of her soul wondered if Sam actually *would* try to argue for her putting in an effort to find the treasure in the time remaining. And wondered if she would be able to keep herself from clawing his face if he did.

But Sam clearly sensed that if Abigail didn't kill him for such an attempt, his cousin John would, and only said, "If you need any help, please—"

Abigail forced herself not to say, *You've helped enough, Sam,* and repeated what her mother had always told her: *When there is nothing to say that will help a situation, say, Thank you.* "Thank you," she said. "But we are well." In a slightly more natural tone she went on, "And I must thank you also, John says, for removing the man Diomede from harm's way—"

"Had we waited," said Sam, "we might have lost our chance completely. John—"

Sam rose from his chair, and John—who had stood unwontedly silent (for John) beside Abigail's hearthside seat—stepped forward to shake his hand.

"'Tisn't that we have no trust in you, Sam," he said, "as I hope I've no need to tell you. But not all the men you command have so complete a command of themselves as one would wish."

Sam looked on the point of saying something else—Abigail could read it in his eyes when they met John's—and she knew that what he wanted to say was, *We have no guarantee that the boy isn't already dead . . .*

And John's answer, as clear as speech, *Don't say it, Sam. It doesn't matter.*

There were times when Abigail felt that John was the best and wisest man on the face of the planet.

In the hallway Sam turned to her, and said quietly, "If I've harmed or offended you, Nab, in any of this, I am more sorry than I can say—particularly now. I had meant to tell you earlier . . . I've spent the afternoon at the State House. 'Tis why I haven't those wretched books about me, that I said I'd return to you. I've been looking through every record and transaction recorded by the colony, hoping to circumvent our friends' quest for the cipher by finding Old Beelzebub's stone castle and the remains of his Indian village . . . For where a man's heart is, there will his treasure be also."

He cocked a wry eyebrow.

"And?" said John, and Sam shook his head.

"Nothing," he said. "Barring the Cambridge town-lot and three lots in Boston, no Whitehead in this colony owned land before 1693—the year after Old Beelzebub died."

"You mean," said Abigail slowly, "that there *is* no treasure?"

"There may well have been." Sam picked up his lantern from the bench in the hall. "Geoffrey Whitehead could have buried or concealed some kind of treasure in Massachusetts, either Spanish gold—if he really was a pirate—or whatever coin he had, if he happened to be staying in an area that was overrun by King Philip's warriors in '75. But 'twould have been a cache hidden away in haste and gone back for, I think, the moment the Indians were driven off."

"Which our Governor," said John grimly, "seems to wish to conveniently forget. You're sure there's no record of his owning land in the west?"

"Nothing." Sam flipped open the lantern's door, held it steady while John lit the candle within it from his own. "Which has never stopped Hutchinson from going after something he thinks is there for the taking. Well, I wish the man joy of those books, cracking his so-called scholarly attainments against Arabic chemistry texts and alchemical discussions of how to make gold out of lead . . . Believe me, I've been over all seven of them with a magnifier and calipers, and haven't found anything in them that looks like a cipher to me. Fear not," he added, and bent over Abigail's hand. "All will be well."

He turned to where Revere and Warren waited for him on the doorstep. Abigail folded her arms beneath her shawl and watched from the doorway as those three bobbing blurs of yellow light disappeared down Queen Street. Far off, the crier's voice could be heard in the still night, *Nine o'clock of a clear night, and all is well* . . .

Twenty-three

True to his word, Sam sent the seven books, made up in a package thickly bound with string and crusted with blots of sealing wax, via Paul Revere. The silversmith arrived in Queen Street midmorning, driving his own light chaise with his quick-stepping little mare Ginny tethered and saddled behind. Johnny and Nabby had been sent off to school with instructions to go to Aunt Eliza's in Milk Street when they were done: Pattie had taken Tommy there as soon as the house was tidied and the marketing done for Thaxter, who would remain in the house. Neither Johnny nor Nabby had been much comforted by John's explanation that he and their mother were going across to the mainland to widen the search ("How would he have got over there, sir?" had been only the least acute of Johnny's questions), and it cut Abigail like a knife to see the confusion and suspicion in her son's eyes as he understood that he was being kept outside of the truth.

She tormented herself on the drive by conjuring visions of some independent scheme of Johnny's to discover the truth of his brother's whereabouts for himself. Nabby, silent, had simply nodded, her blue eyes a world of wretchedness—as if she, too, understood that something was appallingly wrong beyond what was being said—and Tommy had only cried.

They crossed the Neck to Roxbury, Katy riding pillion behind Revere, and reached Cambridge a little after noon. Weyountah and Horace were horrified at Abigail's news and offered a) to immediately try to decode whatever might be in their books and b) to stand watch with as many of their classmen as required, all around Harvard Yard, that night at midnight, to apprehend the villains when they came to the appointed meeting-place. Abigail firmly quashed both suggestions.

"What I will ask of you," she said, "is that in the meantime you show us old Reverend Seckar's house, that was Emmanuel Whitehead's."

Revere went off in search of Sheriff Congreve—he seemed to know everyone in the colony—and returned with the keys to the Seckar house, which had been closed up upon the quarrelsome old professor's death, pending disposal by the College.

"'Tis the closest we'll come, I presume," added John, as they crossed the Common from the Golden Stair and made their way along the road that eventually led toward Waterford, "to this stone castle Old Beelzebub was supposed to have built."

"He *must* have had property somewhere," said Abigail stubbornly. "Mrs. Seckar was quite clear that he did built a fortress of some kind . . ."

"Stories get conflated, Nab," returned John patiently. "Especially family stories. You remember Tilda Farren back in Braintree? The one who's convinced her parents fled England because her mother was the true heir of King James—the daughter for whom the baby Prince James was substituted for political reasons in 1688."

Abigail privately suspected that their neighbor back in Braintree was far too partial to the medicine she took for her so-called rheumatics and back pains, but was too distracted with dread to reply. Part of her prayed that there was something at the Seckar house that would solve the entire question—some hidden map or cipher that Grimes and his cohorts were actually looking for that could be handed over to them . . .

Another part of her was despairingly aware that if a map of the colony had been drawn on one of the bedroom walls complete with large red letters saying, HERE LIETH THE TREASURE, such was her mental state that she would be incapable of realizing what it was.

Dear God, keep him safe, she prayed . . . Did the sun never move? Would sunset never come, let alone midnight? And that detached and disrespectful part of herself, looking at her prayer as through a pane of glass, wondered how she had ever thought herself a woman of faith, when nothing— NOTHING—as precious to her as her son's life had ever hung in the balance like this before.

Mr. Scar-Eye . . . Dubber Grimes . . .

God, keep my boy safe.

The Seckar house turned out to be one she'd seen a hundred times in passing through Cambridge, its newer portion—facing the Waterford Road—built of brick and timber in the '80s of the previous century, tall and old-fashioned like Sam's house on Purchase Street, with most of the lower floor taken up by a great keeping room and a fireplace at one end that a family of four could have set up housekeeping in. The older portion of the house was hid from the road, lying perpendicular to the new, and had been built of a combination of stone and "nogging"—clay mixed with twigs and horsehair—a single story with a loft over part of it.

"This must have been the original keeping room," surmised John, as Congreve led them through its ancient door and into the chamber that had—for as long as anyone recalled—been the laundry. The big coopered tubs had been moved, and its northern wall knocked out and rudely patched over with boards. The eastern wall—what had been the gable end of the original house—joined to that of the newer structure but had never been pierced with a door: one entered the old wing from the yard, with no communication between the old part of the house and the new. *Old Beelzebub's idea to keep his son at a distance?* About twenty inches in from the original eastern wall a second wall had been built of bricks, plastered and whitewashed to match the rest of the room. Between the two walls a couple of shelves still remained, smelling of whitewash and dust.

Is Charley frightened? Have they hurt him?

He is in the hands of God . . .

Abigail stood back while John—who must, she knew, be in as great an agony as herself—methodically examined the space and the shelves. She herself looked around the old laundry-room, toward the great fireplace at its other end, where the copper and the racks of irons still stood . . .

He looked like the Devil would have—she heard Narcissa Seckar's thin old voice in her mind, passing along the words of Beelzebub's daughter—*if the Devil were ever to sit in a corner of the kitchen and play the fiddle . . .*

Here in this long, narrow chamber, the whole tangled knot of circumstance had begun: at the great old table, worn marble-smooth and so big it could not have fit through the doors, Old Beelzebub had undoubtedly copied out his original notes about the Governor of Jamaica into script unreadable by anyone in the colony and shoved it for safekeeping into one of his books.

This was the room where he—or perhaps his sanctimonious son—had walled his books away.

Where he had turned his back on his studies, thought Abigail. Why?

A man who'd sailed the seas, burned Spanish towns for their gold, studied the writings of the Mahometans, practiced sorcery, chatted with Satan, been worshipped as a god?

Deeper than ever did plummet sound I'll drown my book, swears Prospero in *The Tempest* when he forgives the men who wronged him and returns to the human world again. *I'll break my staff . . .*

Why?

He was missing two fingers of his right hand, so that he held the fiddle-bow strangely . . .

For a moment in her fancy she saw him, with his long gray hair like a horse's tail, and the ends of his silvered mustache braided and tied with green ribbons.

Playing the fiddle strangely with his mutilated hand. Looking straight into her eyes with a gaze black as coal and smiling mockingly. Had he, too, supped with the Devil and afterwards found that he had started chains of circumstance that he could not call back?

The Devil carried off children, she thought.

No. The Devil puts it into the hearts of MEN to carry them off.

She had been taught from tiniest childhood by her father never even to think, *May God curse this or that person*. But she thought it now.

May God curse Dubber Grimes and his henchmen, and may they die.

"Aunt?"

Shadows darkened the old door into the yard: Horace, Weyountah, Joseph Ryland.

"Have they found aught?" Horace stepped inside, gazing

around him with deep interest at the smoke-stained plaster and the high, steep rafters of the ceiling.

And Weyountah: "Dr. Langdon had men in two weeks ago to take away the books in the Reverend Seckar's regular library in the main part of the house. About half of those had been bought originally by Emmanuel Whitehead, though a few must have belonged to Barthelmy."

"Mrs. Adams." Ryland bowed deeply over her hand. "Mrs. Squills at the Golden Stair said that you could be found here. His Excellency has authorized me to offer a reward toward which he will contribute. He is most distressed and most anxious to show your husband—and indeed all the citizens of Boston—that he bears no ill-will. If there is anything that he can do—if there is anything that I can do—"

"Yes," said Abigail softly, "there is." And taking Ryland by the shoulder, she guided the young man into the corner near the great fireplace and lowered her voice still further. "You can tell me what you were doing with fifty-four of Beelzebub Whitehead's books in your chambers."

Ryland looked aside, flecks of color slowly rose to mottle his colorless cheeks. "Please, Mrs. Adams—" He glanced toward Revere and John, still poking about before the hidden cache on the east wall. "I beg of you, tell no one—"

"Not His Excellency?"

He put his hands briefly to his face. "I don't know how you can know this—"

Horace opened his mouth to make the obvious remark that they'd searched his room, but Abigail cut in ahead of him with, "Mrs. Seckar told me that you'd purchased them."

"His Excellency—" began Ryland, and stopped. Then he let his breath out in a sigh. "His Excellency has never been poor," he said, in a tone of weary defeat. "He heard that Old

Beelzebub's books had been found and mentioned that the old man had been a pirate. I-I thought, I hoped, that there would be some mention . . . pirates hid gold along these coasts as far north as Philadelphia, I know." His voice faltered as he spoke, as if he could not easily find words. "He asked me to enquire and I—'twas the act of an ingrate, but I can only plead that I was poor. I purchased the books of Mrs. Seckar with the Governor's money and told him that they had all been sold to others before I came with my offer. I thought—if there was a map or a cipher in one of them . . ."

"You didn't try to buy them through someone else?"

He looked at her blankly. "Someone else?"

"A Mrs. Lake?"

He frowned a little, fishing through his memory for the name, then shook his head. "I mean only to hold them until I've had a chance to go through them—"

"You have not done so yet?"

"No, m'am. I—since the books came to my hand, I've been in Boston more than I've been here, helping His Excellency. The only times I've come to Cambridge have been to help my students prepare for the examinations, to drill with the Volunteers . . . and to"—he stammered just slightly on the words—"to be of service to a . . . a private pupil who has suffered a great loss . . ."

Sally Woodleigh. Who is in elaborate mourning for George Fairfield and fainting in the arms of any wealthy man who'll stand still for it.

And if you were wealthy, she reflected, looking into those deep-set brown eyes, *she would be fainting in YOUR arms . . .*

"Please." Ryland swallowed hard. "Please tell no one of what I did. I will make the money good . . . There's treasure out there somewhere, I know there is. His Excellency's records of the colony speak of—of old Whitehead . . . I know he must have left some . . ."

"And do they speak," asked Abigail, "of this stone fortress of his? Or of where he might have held land?"

Ryland shook his head. "He held none, m'am. I've looked through all His Excellency's records. He had a sort of stronghold on the coast up above Lynn, but that was all, and 'twas burned by the Navy in King William's War. 'Twas thought the old man's books were all destroyed then—he was well known as a scholar. So I was surprised to hear that they'd survived here."

"As indeed you might be. Does anyone know you have these other books?"

"Not that I know of, m'am."

"Then keep it that way," she said softly. "And if any man approaches you about them, deny it, or invent a tale that you've passed them along to the Governor. Mrs. Seckar spoke of them as cursed," she finished. "And 'tis true; ill things have befallen those who've had them in keeping. And I only hope and trust," she murmured, as with a deep bow Mr. Ryland took his leave, "that you survive the possession of them once our friends discover nothing in those books of ours but chemical formulae and notes concerning the treatment of horses' piles."

They set forth quietly from the Golden Stair at half-past eleven that night: John and Abigail, Revere and Katy, crossing the Common on its northern side by the slitted glimmer of a single dark-lantern held low. The new moon had set early. By wan starlight the world was formless, trees like black thunderheads and the fine brick houses of the village's worthies no more than dim cutouts of dark against darkness. Abigail carried the wrapped package of books in her arms. *Accursed things*, she thought . . .

Was it only that *love of money is the root of all evil?* Mr. Joseph Ryland had, from the moment she had met him, impressed her with his integrity: even his devotion to the King's cause sprang not from place-seeking, but from dread of civil war. The fact that he would embezzle money from his benefactor, lie to him, then take advantage of his collection of the colony's old documents to hunt for the location of the treasure, only for money . . .

For money and love?

Sally Woodleigh's lovely face floated for a moment in Abigail's thoughts.

Going to get your bid in with the beautiful Sally, haha?

She burned off Ryland's eyebrows during a chemistry lesson, ut he's still tutoring her . . .

He is young. And beneath that steady exterior, she sensed in the young bachelor-fellow the capacity for passion——for Sally as for the cause of his King.

The dark bulk of the college buildings rose to their right as they moved on into the open field of the Harvard Yard, where the young men ran their footraces on bright spring days and played at ball, and where the hay was harvested in June. A single lamp glimmered, high in some uncurtained room, like a dim gold star in the blackness, and a stirring of night-breeze brought the smell of the college stables. Revere had brought a long, forked stick with its straight end sharpened; this he drove into the ground in the center of the yard, then hung one of the lanterns on it, above the level of the tops of the long grasses that in some places grew thigh-high. At the foot of this, Abigail laid the wrapped package of the books.

Please, God, let all be well . . .

She was trembling as John took her hand in his, and

together they retreated back toward the college, her cloak and skirts flapping around her ankles, the yellow smudge of the closed-down lantern-beam bobbing on the ground before them in the dark. Her thoughts seemed to have narrowed, running in a blind circle of fear and hope and agony.

Charley. Dear God, keep him safe.

Stillness and the watching sparkle of the distant stars. John shut the lantern-slide and they stood in the darkness among the trees along the wall of the college barn, where Fairfield had met with goodness only knew how many young ladies in his short career. Nothing below the level of the sky was visible, save that single light out in the midst of the Yard. John's breath was a steady whisper beside her, and his arm circled her waist, his strength surprising. Katy's hand stole into Abigail's free one, chilled in the night. A bird cried somewhere in the trees.

Then silence.

The distant light went out.

Abigail's breath caught. She started forward; John's arm tightened around her: "Give them a moment to get away from him."

But she knew if Charley had the freedom of his own limbs he'd immediately start looking for them, would get lost in the long grass . . .

Then a rifle-shot cracked, like thunder in the darkness. Then another and another. Abigail gasped as if cold water had doused her—somewhere a man cried out . . .

Sam. Dear God. Dear God—

She tore the lantern out of John's hand and the two of them were running, running toward where the light had been. John shouted, "Nab—!" and his hand caught hers in the darkness, and then, "*Charley!*"

Don't be an idiot, John, he'll try to run toward us and get lost—

"Charley!" she screamed. "Charley, we're here—!"

Shouting ahead of them, in the direction of the Sever orchards, and another gun fired, and then, thready in the blackness, a child's wail, "Ma!"

"Stay where you are!" shouted John. "Stay where you are and GET DOWN!"

I'm going to kill Sam. I'm going to kill him—

"Ma!"

How she found her way in the whole blackness of the Harvard Yard she didn't know, but the jolting lantern-beam showed her Revere's forked stick, the quenched lantern, and Charley huddled down next to the stick—not in fear, but trying to untie the short piece of rope that fastened him by one ankle to the upright wood. Somewhere in the darkness men were shouting, a confusion of sounds—*Get him! Hold him! Tory bastard!* The child stood up at the sight of their lantern, held out his arms, and Abigail and John both fell to their knees, catching him tight—

"Are you all right?" gasped Abigail. "Are you—"

The soft skin pressed her cheek, miraculously, blindingly.

"I wasn't scared," said the boy cheerfully. "I knew you'd get me."

In the blackness behind them, two more shots rang out.

I'm going to kill Sam.

At John's insistence—obeying his direct order was one of the most difficult tasks in their relationship so far—Abigail remained in their room at the Golden Stair, lying beside the sleeping Charley while John waited in the common room downstairs for Sam to put in an appearance. On the walk back to the inn, Paul Revere swore with such soft-voiced fury at his fellow Son of Liberty that Abigail was inclined to believe that he hadn't been in on the plot, but cold rage at them all nearly stifled her.

"How dared he?" she began, when she and John carried their son up to the chamber, "How *DARED* he—?"

John stroked Charley's head—the boy had fallen asleep in Abigail's arms before they'd even reached the Common—and breathed, "Later, Nab. Look to the boy."

Do what you should have been doing all this time . . .

Look to your child. Let men do men's work.

Sick rage filled her: at herself, at them, at the world. At the Sons of Liberty. At Sam.

Listening—for their room at the Golden Stair was close to the staircase that led down to the common room—she heard when the Sons of Liberty came in: the sarcastic voice of Mrs. Squills asking, would Mr. Congreve care for some assistance in arresting them all for breaking the curfew?, and then the low-voiced rumble of explanations, arguments, accounts. Twice Abigail almost fell asleep only to jolt awake again from dreams of panic, dreams in which she reached the lantern-staff in the middle of Harvard Yard and there was no child sitting beneath it, or dreams in which the child beneath it—

She shook her head, forcing the image away in panic. *He's well. He's truly all right. He wasn't even frightened, he says . . .* Oddly, she believed him. His body bore no signs of mistreatment, just a little bruising on his wrists where he'd been tied—no worse, so far as she could tell by the candle-glow, than he got from some of his rougher games with Johnny. (Despite the strictest orders all the children had not to play any game that involved tying each other up . . .)

If Dubber Grimes and his minions hadn't been shot out of hand by the Sons of Liberty, she supposed she owed them a plea of clemency for that.

The voices faded.

John's tread on the stair.

His dim shape in the light of the candle in his hand as he

opened the door. She could see he carried the package of books beneath one arm.

"Did they take them?"

He set the light down on the small table beside the bed, barely large enough for the candlestick and the package he bore. It was still wrapped all around in string, the big red globs of sealing wax uncracked. "Two of them," he said. "The scar-faced man—Grimes, I think his name was—and the man they called Newgate Hicks. Both are dead, shot in the scuffle—"

"And I suppose Sam didn't give a thought to the fact that we might want to ask these gentlemen who was paying them for their services? Whether it was the Governor or Mr. Pugh or—"

"Sam is furious. Of course he wanted to know who the true culprit is."

"You astound me." Abigail heard the shrewish shrillness that cracked her voice but couldn't help herself. "I didn't think Sam had a thought in his mind except finding this accursed treasure, if there is a treasure, no matter what it costs . . . just like whoever it is who is behind this attempt. And will be behind the next one."

She was aware that she was trembling, almost sick with reaction to shock, with anger. She reached out, ran her hand over the package of books—

Then looked up at John and said, knowing it for the truth, "Were the books even in this package?"

"No." He sat on the bed at her side, and when she threw his hands off her—furious with him as with the others—and ripped at the thick paper, the heavy seals, he persisted and took from her the half-revealed copies of some of Sam's old Greek textbooks. Drew her against him, held her close. "'Tis all right," he said softly. "'Tis all right, Portia. 'Tis done."

"It isn't," she whispered, and leaned her head on his shoulder.

"It is for tonight."

Twenty-four

Abigail was calmer when she and John descended to breakfast the following morning, but the anger she felt, though colder, was no less real. Years of milking cows and doing farm-chores had made of them both early risers; they were halfway through Mrs. Squills's porridge, eggs, and coffee before Revere joined them.

While she and John were still alone, Abigail inquired, "Does Sam have the true books here with him? Or was he so sure he could get away with his trick that he didn't even bring them?"

"He has them," said John. "He's staying at the Indian's Head—"

"For fear I may have glimpsed him yester'even and guessed what he was about?" She poured a dollop of cream from the pitcher into her coffee, a drink of which she was not truly fond, but Mrs. Squills would serve no tea.

"For fear you'd stab him in his sleep afterwards, I think." John spoke lightly, but Abigail could see him watching her sidelong. He knew she was still very angry indeed.

Stab him as George was stabbed . . .

Revere felt it, too, she could tell, when he descended the stair and greeted her, and—though happily married to his lovely Rachel—flirted a little with Mrs. Squills as she brought out hot bread and more coffee. "Is the boy well?" he asked, and John nodded.

"He slept soundly—sleeps still. Katy's up there now with him."

"I want to thank you," said Abigail, holding out her hand to her friend. "More than I can say."

The silversmith shook his head. "All's well that ends well. I could have murdered Sam—"

"Yes," said Abigail. "Sam. All's well that ends well, as you say . . . But if you would, Mr. Revere, when you're done with breakfast, would you be good enough to go to the Indian's Head and tell Sam I want the thinnest of the quarto volumes—the handwritten one with the red cover that contains the astronomy tables and the chemical experiments and the accounts of what flowers bloomed when. Katy and I will be going on to Concord—"

"Nab, I can't leave Boston now!" cried John. "The King's ship—"

"I didn't ask you to come with me. I know what you need to do in Boston—and you, too, Mr. Revere. All's well that ends well—but the matter isn't ended. Horace and Weyountah will come with us to have a few words with Reuel Seckar about who it was who handed her vile brother that poisoned frumenty. Is Diomede still in the vicinity, by the way? Or has he been smuggled clear out of Massachusetts?"

"He's at a place called Phips's Farm," said John, his brow furrowed with uneasiness at her words. "Travers—the man who actually carried out the jail deliverance—tried to talk him into flight to New York or Philadelphia, but Diomede says, he will not leave this area until one or another of us has spoken with his master, when he arrives, that Diomede may learn in how much peril he actually stands. He is loathe to utterly separate himself from all chance of seeing his wife and children again—"

"Oh, the foolish, foolish man," said Abigail sarcastically, and dabbed butter on her bread. "Loathe to brand himself utterly a murderer by breaking jail and fleeing? Now who ever would have supposed a man could be so silly?"

"A man would consider the course a good deal less silly when he has a noose about his neck," returned John. "There are men in Concord who have said they will take him in and claim him as a servant of theirs—"

"Can he be sent for here?" Abigail glanced at the slow-graying darkness of the window. "To be honest, I could do with another outrider—"

"You could do with half a dozen," said John bluntly. "Sam has half a score of men at call who can bear you escort—"

"The men Sam would give me as escort," retorted Abigail, "if the local Sons of Liberty bear any resemblance to those of Boston, would be as dangerous to Katy and myself as Messrs Grimes, Hicks, and the Cornishman. At least they would who haven't any business in their lives more pressing than hunting pirate treasure, rather than starting to cut their hay or make silver teapots or organize the defense of our liberties or pursue their livings like honest men. Do you think," she added, when John opened his mouth to protest, "that ruffians like Bruck Travers and smugglers like Ezra Logan whom Sam gets to fetch and carry for him would stick at carrying off treasure if they could? Do you think Sam would stick at it if I spoke of doing a thing with the gold—if there *is* gold— besides handing it over at once to the Sons of Liberty?

"I trust Horace, John," she went on more gently. "I trust Weyountah. And I must do this now, soon—ere the King's ship lands and the Governor acquires more strength, as you know he'll do, whatever else the King's Commission decides. And if it isn't the Governor, but only Black Dog Pugh, do you think *his* strength will be less if the Crown's is greater?"

"You sound as if, having found the true culprit in Fairfield's murder, you intend to go on from Concord to seek this mythical treasure."

"I do, John," said Abigail. "I must. Whoever is behind the attempt to kidnap Charley—whether 'tis the Governor or Pugh or someone else we've no notion of—do you think his failure will make him shrug his shoulders and give the matter up? If this treasure is not accounted for and *seen* to be accounted for, one way or the other, these men will try again, to force me or Horace or someone else close to us to aid in its discovery. We might not be so lucky next time. Next time you or Sam or any of our friends may be in jail or in hiding, and unable to lend a hand. It must be done now."

And she knew that—whatever her mother might say of it—this was true.

"Where do you mean to look? Sam has been through the court records, and this Mr. Ryland of yours"—she had told him of her conversation with the young Loyalist—"has seen everything the Governor has in his private collection, and both agree Whitehead had no property in the backcountry."

"If he was living in an Indian village, he wouldn't have," replied Abigail. "And if land were registered in his name, after King Philip's War I'm very certain some good Protestant congregation made sure that the records were changed, and serve him right for living with the Infidel. I shall see what Katy and Weyountah—and old Beelzebub himself—can tell us of the matter. Charley!" she added, springing to her feet as Katy came down the stair with the boy's hand in hers.

"You've had an adventure, son," said John, moving over on

the bench to make room for the child. "Will you have coffee with us?" Which meant a great deal of milk and the tiniest bit of the bitter black fluid to darken it. "So tell me, lad, did they starve you and keep you in chains?"

Thus encouraged by the lightness in his father's attitude, Charley poured forth his account of his captivity from the moment that Mr. Scar-Eye had scooped him up in the alley that led from the yard to Queen Street (only Abigail suspected that her son had actually gone out to the street). Other than being tied up and locked in an attic somewhere near the waterfront, it didn't sound as if Charley had been mistreated, and Abigail marveled a little at John's handling of what was, essentially, an interrogation: *Where were you taken? What did they do? Could you recognize the place again?* By treating it as an adventure—when Abigail knew, from the redness of John's ears, that his rage was no less than her own at the men who had kidnapped his son—he drew the fear from the event and disabled nightmares to come. "I knew you'd save me," Charley said again, hugging his father's arm and pressing his face to his coat-sleeve.

All's well that ends well. Yet aside from the fact that the deaths of the scar-faced Dubber Grimes and his associate prevented learning who had paid them, Abigail felt no pity for them and tried not to be glad that they were dead. She was burningly conscious that "all" had come very close to *not* "ending well."

"Do you think you—and Weyountah—will be able to figure out at least where Old Beelzebub's fortress might have lain from the notes in his commonplace-book?" she asked Katy quietly, when Revere returned to the inn with the volume.

"If someone can read it to me." The girl turned the pages as—at the other end of the table—Charley negotiated for a ride back to Boston on the crupper of Revere's mare instead of at his father's side in Mr. Revere's dull old chaise. "Lord if

I ever saw handwriting to beat this! It seems like the old man took careful note of where he found things and what the woods looked like and whether the dirt was clay or—is that word supposed to be *gravel?* That bog he speaks of where he'd gather his cranberries—that sounds like the one over beyond Medway—I don't know another where you'd get twelve gallons of berries in a day in mid-September. But over here he speaks of walking out to gather witch hazel, which grows on higher ground, and it doesn't sound as if it's far. And I do know there's high ground just north of there."

Horace and Weyountah arrived shortly after that, driving Sassy in George's chaise and accompanied by Diomede, who had been mounted—and armed—by the local militia. Two other saddle horses were tethered behind the chaise, from the same source, Abigail assumed, though Sam had had the good sense not to show his face anywhere near her. The prospect of riding back to Boston with Mr. Revere—and of boasting of his adventures to those of his siblings who had not been so fortunate as to be kidnapped by villainous ruffians—had reconciled Charley to his mother not coming back with them. He flung his arms around her neck and kissed her before his father tossed him up onto the back of Revere's saddle: Abigail smiled a rather crooked smile.

"Take care," whispered John, and glanced at Diomede as he handed rifles to Weyountah and Horace.

"We should be back tomorrow near sundown," said Abigail. "With at least some idea of where this treasure lies . . . if anywhere."

"And if the King's vengeance comes to Boston whilst you are gone?"

"Get the children to Isaac and Eliza's," she said. "And I shall meet you in Concord."

She kissed him then, and he helped her up into the chaise—

and gave a good-natured boost to get Horace onto the obese and mild-mannered nag that one of the local Sons had lent to the expedition. Weyountah, with a rifle on his back and another scabbarded beside his saddle, was very different from the scholarly chemist Abigail had met only a few weeks before: quiet and grim and watchful as he prepared to return to the world on which he'd turned his back. Horace, in his ill-fitting black coat and hand-me-down boots, looked considerably less heroic—he'd coated his face with an aromatic compound designed to keep mosquitoes and gnats at bay.

But when he nudged his borrowed horse over to the other side of the chaise, to exchange words with Katy, Abigail saw suddenly in her nephew's eyes the way he looked at the girl . . .

And there are heroes and heroes, she thought. *And one doesn't have to wear a crimson coat or join the Sons of Liberty to be one. Only have a willing heart.*

And for herself, like the heroines of ancient Rome she'd read about in Livy and Tacitus, it was up to her to defend her family as well as she might while her husband dealt with the greater threat to the State. She did not, however, feel tremendously Roman as she touched Sassy's flank with the end of the whip, and the innyard fell behind them as they set off into the morning's brightness.

They passed over the bridge at the village of Lexington midmorning and a little over an hour later crossed the narrow wooden span over the Concord at the town that shared the river's name. Like Cambridge, Concord had the peaceful air of well-being so often to be found in New England villages: sturdy houses of brick or clapboard surrounding a Common where cows grazed on the rather shaggy grass;

wide house-lots and tidy fences of stone and hedge surrounding the fields of the nearby farms. The farmer to whom Diomede had been sent for concealment—a colonel in the local patriot militia—directed Abigail on to Genesis Seckar's farm, deep in the woods at the end of a rutted track: "Though if you're hungry for a little nuncheon, m'am, I'll get my good wife to bring out some bread and milk for you, for you'll get nothing from him, not if you was starving."

"If a son shall ask for bread of you, shall you give him a stone?" Abigail quoted the Gospel, and Colonel Barrett made a mouth of mock dismay.

"Now, m'am, that's doing the man injustice! He'd never part with a stone that could be put to work in a fence!"

"If it's all the same with you, m'am, sir," said Diomede, with a little half bow and a glance at Barrett, "and not wishing to treat your house as an inn—but I should feel a bit better to go on with Mrs. Adams here, and Mrs. Fairfield, to their destination to make sure all goes well. I'll keep well out of sight if any tries to stay us, and won't come next or nigh your place, if I think any would be after me—"

"Oh, Lord, man, don't worry over that!" The colonel laughed. "Every man in the militia's heard you'll be staying here—on the run from the Tories, I think Mr. Adams said? Bad cess to 'em! And those who aren't in the militia can come speak to me if they've a problem with it." He grinned. "And there's enough of us here in the town that there won't be a problem. Come and go as you please, man." He slapped Diomede's arm. "And stay as long as you wish! And if you're any hand with a musket, you'll find you'll be welcome in my company."

"Er—thank you, sir." The valet looked slightly disconcerted at the idea of joining the patriot militia so soon after riding in his master's company with the Loyal Volunteers, but—wisely, Abigail thought—held his peace.

"Tell me truthfully," said Abigail, once they were on the road again toward the Seckar farm. "You're the only man, among all those who're saying what you ought to do, who actually knows old Mr. Charles Fairfield: what are the chances that he'll listen to testimony that says your master was murdered by someone else? When I've spoken with Mistress Seckar, I hope to be able to put a name on the true killer—but will Mr. Fairfield listen? Out of all of this, what would *you* have?"

"What I'd *have*, of course," replied the slave slowly, "is for Mr. Charles to be so struck by your proofs that he'll take me home to where I can be with my Maggie again, and our girls . . . But to tell you the truth, Mrs. Adams, even if he said he agreed, I'd be afraid to go. Because once we'd get home, sure as grass grows in the spring, there'd be some among his friends who'd start in saying how I'd actually done it—and them not knowing a thing about it, only that they've been afraid all their lives that they'd die at the hands of one of their own slaves. And then I *couldn't* flee. Yet I know if I just run off, when he gets back to Albemarle County, Mr. Charles will sell my Maggie and our girls, and I'd never find them, not if I searched a hundred years."

"He won't," said Katy firmly. "Because when he gets here, I'm going to start proceedings—that is," she added, "if Mr. Adams is agreeable—to be recognized as George's wife with interest in you and Maggie and your daughters . . . And he can't very well sell them if there's a lawsuit going on."

Diomede grinned, a little wanly. "That's kind of you, m'am," he said. "And a good thought, for no man wants to buy a slave that might get him brought to law. Yet I think, to stand a chance of winning that suit, you're going to need all the pirate treasure we can find and more."

* * *

The Seckar farm was very much as Katy had described it: ruinous with neglect, the miles of winding lane that connected it with the Concord Road a river of potholes, while its aged owner concentrated on the salvation of his soul. Abigail and Katy both climbed down from the chaise after the first few yards, and were taken up behind Weyountah and Horace, leaving Diomede with Sassy and the vehicle. "One would think the man had little taste for company," murmured Weyountah, glancing about him at the woods that closed in around the neglected track.

"Or company had little taste for him," retorted Katy with a grin.

Reuel Seckar proved to be a gaunt giant of a woman, her untidy hair dirty beneath a dirty cap, her dress spotted with tallow and food. She and her cowed and delicately built sister-in-law—brother Genesis's wife—emerged from the house when the visitors first came clear of the woods, and Mistress Reuel strode toward them like some gaunt Titaness from an earlier phase of the world, her white hair flying like some grimy sybil's and bare feet slopping in the clayey mud. By the look of the house, Genesis either shared his brother's feelings about household help making women lazy, or more likely, he couldn't get anyone to stay. When Abigail brought up Narcissa Seckar's name, Reuel sniffed with contempt.

"The whore of Babylon," she said. "Given over to Mammon and to chasing the things of this world, and greedy as a Jew: What profit it for a man—aye, or a woman!—to gain the whole world and to lose her soul? And defiant," she added bitterly. "Sweet-mouthed as a honeycake, and a heart rotted with Satan's pride and defiance against the Lord."

Abigail—whose slender experience with Jews had exposed none noticeably more greedy than some good Congregation-alist slave-traders she had encountered—bit back the urge to remind this sour-faced bissom that she'd spent thirty years of her life under a roof that belonged to that Babylonian whore, and replied merely, "What a relief for you, then, to be no longer obliged to share a home with her."

The glare that Mistress Reuel shot Abigail amply informed her that Brother Genesis—whatever his other sins—had not been pleased to take his sister in when he'd thought he'd gotten her safely palmed off on Brother Malachi. Heaven alone knew what their mutual mother had been like, God rest her soul.

"I've no time for idleness," said Mistress Seckar. But instead of turning back toward the kitchen, she snapped at the woman who waited by the kitchen door—white-haired and almost toothless, with the bludgeoned air of one who barely realizes anymore that she is human—"Get back to the stew, or Gen'll be in a passion when he gets home."

The other woman moved heavily off.

"What is it you want?" Reuel glared at Weyountah, with his long black braids and his hunting-shirt, then transferred her scornful stare to Katy, sitting à l'Amazone behind him, her slim brown ankles visible beneath her rucked-up skirt. "Brother Genesis don't hold with visitors, and he's his medi-tations to do 'fore he sits to his dinner."

Abigail wondered if this woman did meditations also, rather than clearing up the piles of husks, peelings, cores, and cobs heaped knee-high around the rear door of the house. "I took the liberty of coming to see you," she went on matter-of-factly, "because my husband is attempting to trace the books that Mrs. Seckar sold: the ones found behind the wall in the laundry-room."

"Greedy slut." Mistress Seckar's face darkened with suffusing blood. "The books were part of the house, as 'twas willed to my brother, God rest him, by Mr. Whitehead—and a good Christian man he was who had the strength to abide the Lord's law. Threatened me, she did—threatened to go to law, bare-faced as Jezebel at her window—"

Horace looked as if he were going to point out that Jezebel had not been bare-faced at her window but in fact had been comprehensively painted, but Katy—Weyountah's horse was close enough beside his for her to do so—kicked Horace in the ankle and he said, "Ow!" instead.

"For shame!" cried Abigail—of Narcissa Seckar, not of Katy—and added, "And with her husband dead beside her in her bed! I understand her poor husband had had offers for them?"

"Devil-books." The old woman's lip lifted to show bare brown gum adorned by a single canine. "Wrote by the Devil, and give to that Devil that hid 'em. There isn't but one book in the whole of the world that won't damn the soul of him that reads it, and that's the Scripture. Gen tried to tell Malachi that, and Mother . . . As stubborn and willful as she was, in his way." She shook her head, and added, with a distinctly medieval relish, "And he's burning in Hell now on the unquenchable pyre of his own books. He'd never turn loose of them, though he saw right enough that those Devil-books were evil, and burn *those* he should have, with their filthy pictures and their heathen writing. I always thought that sweet that Mr. Ryland brought us that night was to butter him up, to get him to sell them books—"

"Mr. Ryland?" Abigail tried not to raise her brows in surprise.

"Governor's lapdog." Mistress Seckar nearly spit the words.

"A lying weasel. Hutchinson is the son of witches, that's never touched nothing that didn't turn to vileness. I wouldn't put it beyond that smooth-faced hypocrite Ryland to have poisoned that frumenty to get at the books for that heretic Hutchinson. For he had 'em in the end, all but eight or ten."

"He did indeed," agreed Abigail thoughtfully. "All but eight or ten."

Twenty-five

"What an archwife!" said Weyountah, when they were on the rutted lane once more, working their way back to the road. "I wonder she isn't poisoned by her own spit."

"*Mulier ira Jovis*," added Horace sententiously, then glanced across at Katy and blushed in confusion, though Abigail guessed that if annoyed, Katy could outdo many women in the *ira Jovis* line.

Katy murmured, "Mr. Ryland—"

"I don't believe it," said Horace, baffled. "Ryland, kill George for—for money? Or just the rumor of money? Not to mention shuffling off the blame on poor old Dio! He didn't have a bean, of course, but he would *never*—"

"Not for money, I don't think," said Abigail slowly. "For silence after George woke and saw him standing in his room—to protect his position in the college, his position with Hutchinson—"

"His Excellency would never have ordered Ryland to—"

"No," said Abigail. "In fact I think he'd have been

horrified, had he learned his protégé had broken into another student's rooms—particularly if all that could be visibly *proved* was that Ryland was trying to lay his hands on a couple of singularly disgraceful books. If Hutchinson knew *nothing*—of the treasure, of the books, of Ryland's attempts to have translated the one handwritten document that he *was* able to find at Seckar's that looked like a cipher—if Ryland was not entirely certain even that the treasure existed but hoped to present his patron with a fait accompli . . ."

"He may very well have done what he did." Weyountah spoke without taking his eyes from the dappled depths of the woods around them. "Once he'd killed a fellow student, he had to cover his tracks, even if it meant accusing an innocent man."

"And if George thought Ryland was looking for something else there," said Katy softly, and tightened her grip around the Indian's waist as the horse hopped across a little stream that had washed out the path. "They'd quarrelled over me the day before, George told me—Ryland told George he had no business meddling with tavern-wenches when Sally Woodleigh was breaking her heart over him and everybody in the Volunteers was watching. The captain must be worthy of respect in all things, he said. George told him to go soak his head. When he saw Ryland in his room—"

"He shouted," finished Weyountah. "And sprang out of bed—especially if Ryland had the desk open—"

"And of course the books weren't there," said Abigail. "Because Mr. Pugh had already been in and stolen them before George even returned."

When they reached the road where Diomede waited, Diomede listened, appalled, to what they had learned and what they surmised, but he confirmed what Katy had said. "I didn't know it was you they spoke of, m'am," he said, as the chaise moved off toward Medfield. "But it's true Mr. Ryland is in love with Miss Woodleigh, and he was angry for her sake. Angry, too, that Mr. George was 'bringing down' the Volunteers in the eyes of folks like Miss Woodleigh's father and Mr. Lechemere and Mr. Vassall. It was far from the first time Mr. Ryland had spoken to Mr. George about how he behaved."

"It must have gone to his heart," murmured Abigail, "to see the militia troop he worked for and the woman he loved, both taken so easily by someone who was behaving so unworthily—"

"That's still no reason to have Mrs. Lake and her bullyboys attempt to murder *me*."

"I'm not sure Ryland knew anything about it." Abigail glanced up at her nephew, jogging beside the chaise on his fat and amiable mare with dust sticking to the mosquito-grease on his face. "He may not have—even as elegant gentlemen like Mr. Hancock and my uncle Isaac don't *really* want to know anything about what happens to a Tory when he's tarred and feathered. Ryland would know about Old Beelzebub from the moment word got around that the books had been found in his house. And from associating with the Governor's household, Ryland would certainly have known about Mrs. Morgan and the Avalon. Perhaps he knew also about Mr. Chamberville's house. He may have thought Mrs. Morgan would bring Horace to the Avalon to do his translation . . . and he may not even have known she *had* the kind of henchmen one would expect to find, working in the stables of a house of accommodation—"

"Well, he jolly well should have known." Katy raised her head from puzzling out the pages of the notebook.

"I don't expect he had ever been to the Avalon himself, or to anyplace like it. But once Dubber Grimes got wind of the treasure—and since Mrs. Morgan made herself copies of both the original Arabic document and Horace's translation, it looks like she planned to go treasure-hunting herself almost from the start—Ryland had no more control of how the hunt

was going to be conducted than Sam had when he stirred up
that mob to attack Governor Hutchinson's house back nine
years ago over the stamp tax. Sam doesn't want to admit it—
and Ryland didn't want to admit it—but these things do get
away from one."

"And all the henchmen knew," said Weyountah, "was that
it was connected with a code . . . and that the code was to be
found in one of the books."

"So *is* there a treasure?" Katy wanted to know. "At the end
of all that?"

Abigail was silent for a time, watching the sun dapple
through the trees on Sassy's dark flanks. "I think so," she said
at length. "Though perhaps not the sort of treasure that Mr.
Grimes and his companions thought they'd find."

It was growing dark when they reached Framingham, famished and exhausted. At the single tavern there, Abigail
asked, first, after word from Boston—had any message come
concerning the King's reply? When the answer came in the
negative, she asked after the countryside west of Medfield,
and did my good host or his good wife—or the half-dozen
members of the local militia who'd come in at the end of their
chores to make the same enquiry about affairs in Boston—
know the whereabouts of Deckle's Farm? Her sister—"That's
Mrs. Deckle," she explained earnestly—had writ her that it
lay about a day's journey on from the village and that 'twas
near a stone Indian ruin, or maybe 'twas the Spanish that had
built it . . .

"Spanish?" The innkeeper shook his head. "Not never
heard of Spanish in this district, m'am—"

"That wouldn't be the Devil's Castle, would it?" A very
young militiaman looked up from his ale.

"Is it a castle, then?" exclaimed Abigail in assumed surprise. "I'd heard, 'twas built by the Indians—"

"Narh, Indians never built in stone, m'am." (Abigail already knew this.) "Never heard about the Spanish, neither. But there's supposed to be a stone ruin over near Hassanamisco Pond where there was a Nipmuc village onc't upon a time. Never seen it myself—"

Enquiries for Hassanamisco Pond elicited several sets of mutually conflicting directions, most of which began, "You take the Grafton Road . . ." and ended anywhere in the countryside. Descriptions of the countryside between Framingham and Grafton were not encouraging.

"Is there a cranberry bog nearabouts there?" asked Katy, and that brought better results. Three of the militiamen testified to the location of Shelby's Bog, but two-three miles from the Grafton Road.

"And Shelby is the name of the man who owns the land?" inquired Abigail.

"Not now it's not. 'Twas the feller who took it over after King Philip's War, after the Nipmucs was wiped out there, so I've heard—"

"Friend of the Governor in them days," put in somebody's white-haired grandfather.

And another, derisively, "Ain't it always?"

"Had the records changed, I heard, to prove 'twas always his," confided the oldster. "Didn't get no good of it. 'Tis bad, hard land."

"Good cranberries, though . . ."

Bad, hard land, as Abigail feared it would, translated to, *few farms, much woods, impassable roads, and nobody within ten square miles to ask after the whereabouts of Shelby's Bog.* Most settlement in this part of the colony had gravitated toward the easier land of the Blackstone Valley to the south. In the course of the following morning, the two farms they encountered, at the ends of overgrown lanes from the not-very-well-kept Grafton Road, appeared to have been burned out by King Philip's Whampanoag warriors a hundred years previously and not rebuilt. The track branched and branched again, the chaise wheels sinking in the clayey muck. Abigail watched the angle of the sunlight slanting through the woods, and with an acid sense of urgency, she calculated when they must turn back in order to make Boston by nightfall. *We must find the place. Find the treasure, or prove that there is nothing there.*

Else we will know no peace . . .

Ahead of the chaise, Weyountah rode imperturbably, drawing rein from time to time to listen to the woodlands that were growing steadily thicker around them, though Abigail heard nothing but the twittering of birds, the rustle of the wind. He was listening, she thought, as a hunter listens— or a warrior entangled in the endless, ancient woodland fights between tribe and tribe.

He had turned his back on that world, she thought, looking up at the tall figure in his hunting-shirt and boots. And she wondered why. A world where his family clung to the old ways; a world in which visions counted for more than the theorizing of mathematicians and the spirits of the land clung tight to the hearts of its children, holding them in corn-patch and longhouse forever.

He had made his choice and refused to be part of that past. At what cost, Abigail could only guess.

But turn away as he might, thought Abigail, the old world of the forest was in his blood nevertheless. As they moved on again down the less travelled of those forking traces, she could see him sorting out the sounds of birds, the scent of the wind in the woods. As a child he'd hunted and learned what the land should sound like if all were safe.

"Oh, thank Heavens!" exclaimed Katy. "The cranberry bog at last!"

Sunlight brightened through the trees. Bees hummed over milkweed and marsh marigold, and the heavy, peaty smell of wet ground and standing muck breathed through the sweeter scents of the woods. Abigail drew rein, and Katy produced old Beelzebub's notebook again, marked in a dozen places last night as the five of them had sat around the lamp in a corner of the ordinary of the inn at Framingham until the innkeeper had good-naturedly told them he was banking the fire and putting up the shutters for the night.

"The village should be no more than a mile or two northwest of here . . ."

"And it being noon," replied Abigail mildly, unwrapping the lunch that Mr. Buckminster at the tavern had put up for them, "if you can determine which direction *is* northwest—"

"Back that way." Weyountah pointed. "At least," he added, as he stripped the harness from Sassy and tethered her to graze, "that's where I'd put a village: up the stream that feeds the bog, on the higher ground where the soil is better. Look, you can see where the trees were cleared and have grown back. Will you stay here or come with us?"

"Stay here?" Katy stared at him as if he'd suggested she drown herself in the bog. "And miss finding the treasure?"

"And miss a hard walk of a couple of miles uphill." Horace attempted to spread the carriage-rug for her over a couple of dry tussocks, only to have her turn impatiently away.

"I'm two months with child," she pointed out. "I didn't lose a leg."

"Don't be a goose, Horace," added Abigail. "Katy will be fine."

They shared bread and cheese and cider, and proceeded up the hill.

Weyountah said, "Damn it!" and stopped where the trail steepened, holding up his hand.

Abigail followed his eyes down to the trail and saw in the soft ground the tracks of a man's boot.

Even to her totally inexperienced eye, she could tell they were fresh.

And that there was only one man.

Horace gasped, "The Cornishman . . ."

"Don't be silly." Abigail dropped her voice, knowing how sounds carried in the quiet of the woods. She nudged Weyountah, who put his foot next to the track. "The Cornishman's as big as an ox. At a guess," she said, considering the difference in length and breadth, which was barely any and that little in the Narragansett's favor, "'tis Mr. Ryland."

Horace breathed, "He must have found the location of this place in the Governor's records after all—"

"And lied to us about it?" Abigail mimed shock. "The scoundrel!"

Beside her, she was aware of the girl's eyes suddenly growing hard.

Weyountah signed Diomede to separate from them and follow through the woods some half-dozen yards to the right. Then he handed Katy his spare rifle and motioned her to do the same to the left. In this configuration—picking their every step in the brown leaf-mast—they moved up the hill to where the land flattened out a little. A century had eradicated all trace of the cornfield-patches, where beans and squash had been trained up among the stalks, and the trees seemed to Abigail no thinner or smaller than the surrounding forest. Yet she guessed that a village had been here simply from the shape of the land. There was a spring and level ground big enough for houses to be built by men and women who'd lived and died in this place, worshipping strange gods and minding their own business until the white men came.

Horace's hand closed tight around Abigail's wrist. Between the trees she saw it: stones scattered among the deadfalls and tangles of witch hazel, and a little farther on, the shape of a curved stone foundation and what had been a wall. Trees had grown up close to it, roots forcing apart the stones in places. Elsewhere what looked like shallow steps had been cut in the rock bones of the hill on which the fort had been built, and the ruins of what could have been a tower.

The Devil's Castle.

Her nephew tried to run forward, and both Abigail and Weyountah pulled him back. They moved forward slowly, Diomede and Katy edging inward from the sides. It was Diomede who reached the stone remains first, surmounted a sort of breastwork, then straightened up in an attitude of shock. He called out, "Mr. Ryland!" and scrambling over the wall, sprang down. Horace broke from them, ran toward the place at the same moment that Abigail saw Diomede lift the head of a man who had been lying on the broken foundation-stones, half hidden by the walls.

Ryland struggled a little, flailed one hand, then seemed to come to his senses and cried out, "Get away! Go back!"

And around them in the woods, half-a-dozen rifles crashed.

Twenty-six

Weyountah grabbed Abigail by the arm and nearly dragged her up behind the low walls of the ruins, thrust her down beside him, and peered over the tumbled stones. Another rifle crashed and the ball cracked against the barrier near where they lay. Abigail gasped, "Don't tell me the Governor has men out after us after all!"

Diomede dropped beside her, bleeding from where a rifle-ball had grazed his arm as he dragged Ryland to shelter beside them.

Through gritted teeth—not taking his eyes from the surrounding trees—Weyountah replied, "I'd say the Cornishman went and got some friends after Tuesday night."

"Drat the man! They're as bad as the Sons of Liberty for coming out of the woodwork—I daresay some of them *are* Sons of Liberty in their spare time . . ." Keeping crouched behind the wall as best she could, Abigail pulled open Ryland's coat and shirt; blood was welling from a fresh wound.

"He was hit just now, m'am," said Diomede. "When he sat up a little and cried for us to get back—"

A short distance away she could see a huge pool of the man's blood where he'd been lying when Diomede had found him.

"Give me your handkerchief or anything you've got . . ."

Close beside her, Katy got off a shot, then cursed vividly and added, "Horry, have you ever loaded a gun? Curse it . . . Dio, let Horry take care of Ryland, we need you to cover the other angle—"

Obediently the servant shoved his handkerchief into Abigail's hand and, catching up rifle, powder, and patch-box, sprang to the remains of the tower. "I can load." Abigail had performed that service on numerous occasions when her father or William had gone duck-hunting. "Just give me a moment . . . Horace, don't you *dare* faint—"

She dug in the pasty and staring boy's pocket, pulled out five handkerchiefs, and wadded them tight against the bleeding hole in Ryland's chest. The bullet was lodged—at least there wasn't a corresponding wound in his back—but it seemed to her for a time that the blood would never cease pumping out beneath the reddened linen, no matter how hard she pressed. Behind her she heard Katy swear again, and say, "I'd better go to loading. I can't seem to hit the whoresons—"

And another crack of gunfire from the woods.

A swift glance back across the stone foundation—it seemed to have been a rectangle some thirty feet by fifty with a tower at either end—confirmed Abigail's first, fleeting impression that there was a square hole in the flooring of the more intact of the two towers, where Diomede crouched on the high-point of the remaining wall. A broken paving-stone and a couple of pieces of wood lay next to it, the remains, presumably, of a trapdoor . . .

"Good Lord, don't tell me there really is a treasure!"

She looked back down at Ryland's face. It was wax white beneath horrible bruises. Shocked, she said, "He's been beaten!" When he reached to touch her hand, she saw the mutilated fingers, sticky with blood.

Katy dumped powder from her hand down the rifle-barrel, shoved in a patch and ball, and whacked the whole thing with the ramrod. "I thought they worked for him!"

Ryland turned his head a little and without opening his eyes managed to whisper, "Saw me. Harvard Yard."

Enlightenment flooded Abigail and she said, "Were you the one who shot Dubber and Hicks after the kidnapping?"

"Had to," breathed Ryland. "They'd seen me—Mrs. Morgan's—" His eyelids fluttered open and for a moment he looked toward Horace. "Sorry. Never meant . . ."

"And I suppose you never meant that old Professor Seckar would die, either," retorted Abigail tartly.

"*Had* to," he insisted. Pleaded. The long fingers—their ends bloodied where the nail beds had been crushed—tightened feebly on hers. "Destroy them . . . within their camps. *Defend this city, for mine own sake . . . for my servant David's sake . . .*"

"Did they take the treasure, then?" asked the girl, as Abigail sat back on her heels, shocked—and suddenly cold—at his words. "Then why the Devil are they still shooting at us?"

"Or was it gone when you got here?" Weyountah fired again, followed instantly by another shot from Diomede on the tower. "Quick—!" The Indian stretched out his hand for Katy's gun, and she pressed it into his grip and instantly reloaded, twice as fast, Abigail noticed, as William had ever managed to . . .

"Not gone—"

Softly, while Katy was reloading, Abigail said, "It wasn't gold, was it?" She understood then what the treasure was, what it had to be. Pieces falling into place . . .

Ryland shook his head. *"Defend this city . . ."*

So THAT, she thought, *is what he would have brought in triumph to Hutchinson. As vindication of whatever it had cost.*

And she had to admit, it would have brought him all the preferment, all the advancement, all the recognition he wanted and had never received.

Maybe even the hand of the lovely Sally Woodleigh.

She felt breathless with rage and horror.

On the tower, Diomede called out, "They're coming around to your downhill side—"

Weyountah nodded sharply in that direction, where the cover consisted of trees rather than the stone walls, and Katy snatched up rifle and ammunition, and darted across the open space of the foundation. "How many?" he called out to the servant.

His head on Abigail's lap, Ryland whispered, "Ten."

"And they didn't believe you," said Abigail, "did they, when you said the treasure consisted of . . . What? Other books?"

Ryland shook his head, closed his hand on hers again in a paroxysm of agony as more shots chipped the stone behind Abigail's head, fragments stinging her neck like bees. Weyountah called out, "Don't fire unless you have to! They're trying to draw our ammunition!"

"Didn't believe." Ryland's voice seemed to fumble at the words. "Followed me here . . . Excellency's papers . . . Shelby . . . records . . . Devil's Castle . . ." His eyes opened a slit under fluctuating lids, and he seemed for a moment to come back to himself. "Tried to buy them . . . The books. Excellency spoke of him . . ."

"Did you think 'twas gold you sought at first?" whispered Abigail. "Or did you know from the start it wasn't?"

". . . was a scholar, Excellency said . . . rumor of what he'd made . . ."

"Did Hutchinson know what you were doing?"

"Foolish." Ryland shook his head. "All tales. If it was real, he'd have used it. Knew it had to be here. Knew—somewhere in his books—had to be a way here. He'd write—Arabic—secrets . . ."

"And you tried to get Horace to translate," said Abigail. "Only to find you'd got hold of the wrong secrets."

Weyountah rammed home his load, swung the rifle to his shoulder, fired over the wall; a second shot immediately from Diomede told Abigail that someone had probably tried to rush them. How many shots had they left? How much powder?

And what would the Cornishmen and his friends be likely to do to two women in order to convince the wounded man—or the two other students—to tell them of the location of a treasure that didn't exist? Or didn't resemble any treasure they understood?

"And you knew George had some of Seckar's books in his rooms . . ."

"Wretched slut." The cold fingers picked anxiously at Abigail's hand. "Best—most beautiful—not worthy—untie her shoes . . ." Abigail realized he was trying to talk about Sally Woodleigh. "Loved him, and all he could see . . . some hostler's daughter . . ."

Well, reflected Abigail, *considering the nature of the missing books, 'tis no wonder he wouldn't admit having them to YOU . . .*

"Hush," she whispered. "Hush . . ."

"Had to find it." Ryland shook his head, pushing her admonition aside. "Came here—had to be here. Governor's papers . . . They followed. Cornishman . . . men with him . . . They think it's gold. Wouldn't listen . . ." He moved his head weakly, flexed his massacred hands. "Destroy the rebels. Destroy . . . utterly within their camps . . ."

Katy shouted, "Weyountah!" and a salvo of gunfire came

from the thicker trees on her side of the enclosure. Weyountah stood—Abigail had no idea where he got the courage to do it—for a better look through the trees, fired, dropped to his knees, and began loading with cool precise haste as a shot came from Diomede on the wall, and when Weyountah rose to his feet again, rifle at the ready, two more shots cracked out. He dropped behind cover again. Abigail could see blood on his coat.

"Followed me," whispered Ryland again. "Followed me here. Knew if I could get it . . . all those years of waiting and work. Knew if I could defeat them . . . kill the rebels in their camps . . . Sally . . . His Excellency . . . His Majesty . . . He'd made it. I know he'd made it. All the stories say . . . Beelzebub. He'd used it. Why he left, why he came to Cambridge . . . *I will defend this city, for mine own sake, and for my servant David's sake* . . ."

With a heart turned to ice, Abigail finished the passage from Second Kings: "*And it came to pass that night, that the angel of the Lord went out and smote in the camp of the Assyrians a hundred four-score and five thousand; and when they arose in the morning, behold, they were all dead corpses* . . ."

"*I will defend this city,*" murmured Ryland. "*I will defend this city* . . ."

And as Abigail had done, Horace whispered, "*What?!?*"

". . . *the angel of the Lord* . . ." Ryland's bleeding hand loosened in hers.

"It's what he thought was in the only handwritten Arabic document he found among Beelzebub's books," said Abigail softly, laying the back of her hand close to the unconscious man's nostrils to detect the thread of his breath. "And you have to admit, 'twould have made his fame not only among the Loyalists, but with the King as well." And as gently as she could, she began going through the pockets of his coat.

Horace turned and handed Weyountah the last of the rifle-balls, and by the way the Indian shook the lead powder-bottle, Abigail knew that was the end of the powder as well.

"Go to Katy, Horace," said Weyountah softly. "Get her rifle, cover that side of the enclosure—I should be surprised if she has shot or powder left either. Mrs. Adams, take Katy and flee up the hill into the deepest woods you can find. Go to ground as soon as you find someplace where you won't be seen; I doubt they're good enough trackers to follow. Stay there until dark—"

Abigail thrust the cracked and yellowed wad of papers she'd pulled from Ryland's pocket into her own. "We can't leave—"

"Do it. Crawl along the wall 'til you get to the woods—"

Crouching behind the ruined heaps of stone, Abigail darted and crept to where Horace and Katy knelt in the shelter of the trees, arguing in furious whispers—

"Don't be a goose, girl." Abigail caught Katy's arm.

"They need every gun—"

"And how many loads have you left? I thought so. Give it to him, and follow me—"

Abigail pulled her heavy skirts up and wrapped them tight around her hips and thighs; she dropped to the ground as close to the wall as she could. *John,* she promised, *I'll never follow my own course again in the face of your objection . . .*

And leave the possibility open, her non-Mother self whispered in her ear, *that one of those men would find those papers in Ryland's pocket and sell them to someone who DID know what to do with them . . . ?*

At the end of the wall the laurel grew thick. She and Katy slipped in among the glossy branches and crept uphill, trying to keep from thrashing the foliage too much. When they reached its end, Abigail heard behind them the thunderous crashing of rifles in the woods downslope, caught Katy's wrist in her hand, and ran. Her long skirts tangled with her legs, the uneven ground catching at her feet: deadfalls, rivulets, holes hidden beneath thick leaves. As a child she'd been swift as a sprite, but it had been a long while since she'd run full out any distance—not a thing a respectable matron was supposed to do.

A rifle crashed somewhere in the woods behind them, close enough that she could smell the powder. At the same instant a man sprang from behind a thicket: he was no taller than she but hard-looking as carved hickory, with a brown face burned by weather and the tarred pigtail of a sailor and the hardest, coldest eyes Abigail had ever seen.

He held a knife in one hand.

The two women swung around to find another man—a rough laborer of the kind that Sam routinely summoned to form his tame mobs—pointing a rifle at them at a distance of a few yards.

The man with the knife said, "An' the next shot goes right in your back, m'am."

The man Abigail recognized as the Cornishman—the hulking, heavy-browed ruffian that blonde Belinda had cried warning against at the house called Avalon—stood over the crumpled body of Weyountah in the old ring of the stone tower. One of his men held a pistol on Horace and Diomede. Others were slapping and shaking Ryland and pouring rum down his throat, with oaths fit to scandalize Satan in the Pit. Katy let out a cry of anguish and tried to run to Weyountah, and the hard little sailor laughed and grabbed her by the arm, yanked her back. A couple of the men grinned and called out, "That's the dandy, poppet!" and "Aw, 'fraid

we've broke his courting-tackle?" and "'Tain't all we'll break,
'fore we're done—"

Horace lunged at them in blind fury, and the man guarding him reversed the pistol in his hand and gave Horace a
crack in the head with it that dropped him to the broken
pavement. The Cornishman grunted, "'Ere, none o' that," in
a thick slow voice, like a semi-articulate pig's. He turned
beady eyes toward Ryland, who had given a sort of faint cry
that ended in coughing. Abigail could see blood trickling
from his mouth mixed with the rum.

The Cornishman took Katy by the hair, dragged her over
to Ryland, and pulled a knife the size of a small cutlass from
his belt. "You 'ear me, Ryland?" He kicked the young man's
ankle. Ryland managed to move his head. Abigail wrenched
herself from the grip of the man who held her—she counted
seven of them and wondered if Ryland had miscounted or if
three of them were lying wounded back in the woods—and
ran to Ryland's side. She dropped to her knees as one of them
reached to stop her, propped the young bachelor-fellow gently
against her, his head on her shoulder, instead of on the stones.

Three days ago she would have condemned the man who
had put in motion Charley's kidnappers—however little he
had had to do with the kidnapping itself—to the bottom-
most circle of Dante's Hell without a thought. But she knew
what she saw, looking at the color of his face and that drib-
bling line of blood. Probably the Cornishman did, too. And
wanted Ryland to last at least through questioning.

The Cornishman kicked Ryland again, and when his eyes
fluttered open, grunted, "Can you see, mate?" He slid the
knife under Katy's bodice and sliced the cheap cloth open to
the waist, jerked down the chemise beneath, and put the
knife-blade against the side of her breast. "I'm only gonna ask
this once," he said. "Then I starts cuttin'. Where's the gold?"

"Hutchinson has it," said Abigail.

Those piglike eyes narrowed. "Then why'd he say there wan't none?"

"Probably because Hutchinson told him there wasn't," she replied, with a dizzy sense of walking across a tightrope. "He sent him here to find what was in that pit—books and scientific implements . . . You know how His Excellency is about books."

The Cornishman blinked, thrust unexpectedly into the position—as Abigail felt she had been for weeks—of trying to prove a negative, and he was no better at it than anyone was . . .

He shoved Katy away from him, sending her sprawling to the stones. Before the other men could get to her, Horace reached her side, drew her up against him and away from the Cornishman as that hulking man stepped close to Abigail, knife extended inches from her face. "You lyin' to me, bitch? 'Cos if you are—"

Abigail never heard what he would do to her if she was, in fact, lying. In the same second, it seemed, that she heard a gunshot in the woods, the Cornishman's narrowed eyes popped wide, as if startled, and a rifle-ball exploded out of the front of his throat in a shower of gore. Abigail rolled aside, dragging Ryland with her, as the Cornishman dropped before them like a felled steer.

Two other shots cracked. The man standing nearest Horace and Katy fell, clutching his side and shrieking; with great presence of mind Katy grabbed the pistol away from him as he fell and shot the next-closest man through the body. Weyountah rolled and caught up that man's rifle, and the four remaining ruffians dropped their weapons and threw up their hands at once.

Diomede tossed one of their rifles to Katy and went around collecting the rest even as Black Dog Pugh—trailed by his two slaves, both armed to the teeth—emerged from the trees.

"Sink me, I thought I'd never find this place," Pugh exclaimed. "Wouldn't have, either, if they hadn't started shooting. And a damn good shot," he added, looking down at the Cornishman's sprawled body and the bullet-hole in the back of his neck, "if I do say so myself. Pity I can't scalp him as a trophy." He held down his hand for Abigail. "Don't you think, m'am?"

Twenty-seven

"Did you follow him?" asked Abigail, as the slave Eusebius rose from beside Joseph Ryland's body and shook his head. Abigail knelt also, to feel the young man's wrists and throat, though she trusted the African's judgment, and indeed, it was clear to her that Ryland was dead.

She looked up at Pugh.

"Lord, no. And just as well," the bachelor-fellow added, and rubbed his fat, unshaven chins. "If we'd been following him, instead of our upstanding friend here"—he nudged the dead Cornishman with his foot—"we'd probably have fouled on him like two dogs on the same lead. No, the fair Nancy—when she came to me rather the worse for wear, for having been locked up in some sailor's trap in Boston where Grimes had left her and the other girls—told me the Cornishman had come in and got himself a band of tavern toughs to find 'pirate gold,' as he put it—"

"You knew about Old Beelzebub's treasure, then?"

"Lord, who in the islands didn't? Is it here, then?" He

walked to the opening in the floor and squatted to peer in. "Grimes and his bravos were boasting about looking for it down at the Pig one afternoon, so I knew there was a rumor *someone* had found it. I had five shillings with Jasmine that the thing didn't exist. I should love to find out I'm wrong, though."

Abigail looked around her a little distractedly, and Eusebius—in the process now of tying the hands of their prisoners—wordlessly stripped off his coat and handed it to her to lay over Ryland's face. As she did so, Abigail drew out the knife that Ryland wore at his belt, noting the slender blade was only barely wider than a paper knife. Precisely the width, in fact, of the wounds in poor George Fairfield's side. Whether a judge would recognize this—or even look at it as evidence—she didn't know, but she pocketed the weapon just in case before she followed the Black Dog to the trapdoor.

"The treasure that Ryland was seeking," she said carefully, "I don't think was gold at all, but rather books and formulae of chemistry—or alchemy, as Beelzebub would have thought of it . . . Did Grimes tell you that?"

"Grimes? He swore it was gold, so much it wouldn't have fit into one shipload—sort of thing one talks oneself into after the second bottle of Hollands. I was buying the Hollands." He winked one long-lashed green eye. "A small investment, considering the money I took off him as the afternoon wore on. Doesn't look far down," he added. "And stap me if I see any gold. But when Nancy and the other girls came knocking at my door Tuesday night, asking shelter and swearing the Cornishman was off after the treasure, that was enough to get me to follow along and see. Hold this for me, would you, m'am?"

He put a candle in her hand. He had taken it from his pocket along with flint and steel.

"Are they all right? Nancy and Belinda and Dassie—"

"You've met 'em, have you, m'am? Good girls, and corky

as squirrels—" He cracked flint to steel briskly, then blew on the spark where it had taken on the loop of tinder through his fingers. "Grimes took 'em off to some crimp named Manchet down by the harbor who runs a nunnery out of his backroom. Kidnap, too, by the sound of it. Nan laid old Manchet out with a pintle Tuesday night after Grimes and his bravos had left, and the three of 'em came to me. Just bring that winker over here—"

He fastidiously removed his coat, then lowered himself down the trap, holding his hand up afterwards for the light. Abigail saw the small glow bob and shift beneath her in a hole that resembled a cold cellar, perhaps six feet by eight, beneath the stone foundation of the old fortress: "Coming down, m'am? That's the dandy!" He set the candle on a shelf and held up his hands for her as Abigail wrapped her skirts tightly around her legs and slid down into his grip. "What a mess, eh? And not a gold-piece in the lot."

He held up the candle, as Abigail looked around. The few books that the old pirate had left in this little strong room had mildewed into black blocks, but the glass vessels had survived the passage of years. Abigail recognized them from Weyountah's workroom in Harvard Hall, what she'd seen of it through his poisonous smoke: crook-necked distilling-bottles, thin measuring-flasks. Two carboys showed signs of having contained fluids of some sort, now dried away to glossy dark scum on the bottom and sides. In clay pots, a number of salts and something that smelled like sulfur remained.

"Weyountah would know what all this is," she said, trying to keep her voice casual.

"Wonder if it spoils with keeping?" Pugh held the light close to the largest vessel, where the liquid had dried and crusted with time. "Does Jasmine owe me five, or do I owe him? Would have been a jolly good sport if there had been something here . . ." He picked up a telescope from the shelf, pointed it at the sky and peered through it for a moment, set it down again. "Would have guaranteed me the fair Sally's hand, anyway. So this is what poor Ryland was after?"

"I think so, yes. He told me—in the course of the affray— that he'd hoped to gain some recognition from the Governor for it."

"I expect he would. The old boy's never given up the hope of putting together a history of the colony, and a find like this—proof that old Beelzebub did really do alchemy to get the Nipmucs to worship him—would turn him pink down to the ends of his prehensile toes."

Pugh chuckled, like the great black bulldog he was called. "Ryland was just wild that old Seckar wouldn't sell him the old man's books when they were found back in April. I'm afraid I muddied the waters there a bit . . ."

"And George got the two you wanted in the end," said Abigail drily, "didn't he?"

Pugh met her eyes in the dim glow.

She raised her eyebrows, and his heavy mouth quirked sidelong. "You know about that?"

"I have a good guess. Your note to George—sorry, *Sally's* note to George—was in his pocket when he came back to his rooms that night . . . on *your* notepaper. I take it George was still away from his room when you went in—"

"Oh, Lord, yes. Bed all made up and turned down waiting for him—Dio's a born chambermaid. Glad to see the old fellow here, by the way—did you arrange a jail deliverance? Good on you. I tiptoed in just after the clock struck twelve. I was pretty sure, with George gone, Dio'd be laid out stiff as a board on the rum, though 'fore God, m'am, if I'd known how stiff I'd have gone out to the barn and warned poor George something was afoot." He stood frowning, gazing at the dulled and dirty equipment crowded on the little bench. Then, more quietly, "Ryland really killed George for *this?*"

"When one chases the Devil's treasure," said Abigail, "one pursues the illusion that Satan conjures in the mind, not the handful of sticks and dirt that are often the reality. It's not only that the heart lies close to the treasure . . . sometimes one finds that the treasure exists only in the heart."

"Silly bastard." Pugh shook his head, placed the candle on the table's edge, and held out his hands to her. "George was worth a thousand of him. Well, I always said old George didn't care about Sally one way or t'other—not that I'd say so to the fair Sally herself. That young lady upstairs—" He jerked his head toward the hole above them, "would be the girl he married, would she? Katy Pegg? Thought I recognized her."

"Was the license in one of the books?"

"Wasn't sure what to do with it." Pugh shrugged. "No need to go waving it in front of Sally, of course. D'you think the girl would go halves with me for whatever we could screw out of old man Fairfield on the strength of it? You know he'll never let it stand up in a Virginia court."

"That," said Abigail sternly, "is something you would have to discuss with Mrs. Fairfield. I believe she would settle for ownership of Diomede, and Dio's wife and children—and some sort of maintenance for her child. If you're going up," she added, as Pugh whistled sharply beneath the trap-hole for Pedro, "would you be so good as to ask Weyountah to come down? I want to see if he can salvage any of this for himself."

Pedro held down his hands for his master, and when he'd been hauled (*Pedro must be stronger than he looks!*) up through, Abigail made a swift search around the cellar for any further papers or notes that might have been left. There were none. Joseph Ryland had had sufficient time, before his erstwhile henchmen had put in their appearance, to gather them all, into the thick block of folded pages that poked Abigail in the thigh beneath her petticoats every time she moved.

"*Do* these things spoil with keeping?" she asked Weyountah, when the Indian had dropped lithely down beside her.

"The phosphorous certainly has." He hastily re-stoppered a flask in which the waxy crusts of something white clung to the sides; Abigail stepped back, repelled by the smell of it. "I'm not sure what some of this is, even. But he was doing something with sulfur, and the sulfur is still good—"

"Let's take that, then," she said, "and pass it along to Sam or Mr. Revere . . . One makes gunpowder with sulfur, no?"

"Among other things, yes. It doesn't seem like that's what Old Beelzebub was doing down here . . ."

"No," said Abigail, a little quickly. "Can I ask you something, Weyountah? We can take the sulfur, but when we depart, would you stay behind and destroy the rest of this? Destroy it so that none of it can be used again? I shall explain later," she added, as the Indian looked quickly sidelong at her. "Beelzebub's treasure is . . . not something I want anyone else to happen upon by accident. It has brought too much grief and trouble to the world already. 'Tis a secret best forgotten."

The Indian looked puzzled for a moment, then turned his head to study the chemical apparatus—the retorts and alembics, the filtering coils and small furnace, the piston air-pump and oily crusts in the vessels—and she saw something change in his dark eyes, as he guessed, perhaps not what the treasure of Beelzebub had been, but the *sort* of thing it was. Softly, he said, "You can rely on me, m'am. I shall join you in Boston tomorrow."

I t was in fact late the following afternoon—Friday, the thirteenth of May—before Weyountah and Horace appeared on the Adams doorstep. Abigail—after a brief consultation with John—bade the two young men stay on for dinner with the family and to spend the night. Upon Abigail's return Thursday evening in company with St-John Pugh and his party—Katy, their various prisoners, and Joseph Ryland's body—John had listened to her account of the young Loyalist's death and her own theory about what Beelzebub's treasure had consisted of, and had agreed that it was a matter that must go no further.

From regard for their children—Charley seemed far more taken up with the equitable distribution of the wooden soldiers in the toybox than with the fact that he'd been kidnapped and held in the back-room of Mr. Manchet's tavern on Fish Street for forty-eight hours earlier in the week—the conference after dinner was held in John's study rather than the kitchen. But throughout the meal, Abigail kept glancing at Weyountah's face, reading her suspicions in the grimness of his eyes.

When John closed the door behind him and poked up the little hearth-fire—for the spring afternoon was chill—she asked, "What was it that Old Beelzebub had figured out how to make in the Devil's Castle back in 1675?"

Weyountah had spread out the notes on John's desk, a dozen folio-sized sheets, yellow with age and stained with time and mold. Notations of chemical formulae covered them, and writing both in Arabic and what Weyountah told her was Algonquian, the language spoken by many of the Massachusetts tribes. "All of this is written in Algonquian, but sometimes he'll use Roman letters for it and sometimes Arabic. No wonder people thought he was the Devil."

"But what is it?" Katy leaned from her chair at Abigail's side, tried to read past his shoulder. On the trip back to Boston, the girl had had a long, quiet conversation with Black Dog Pugh, presumably about whether half a loaf would be better than no bread once Charles Fairfield came to Cambridge. The West Indian had called again that morning, and conferred with both Katy and John. Diomede had wisely remained at Mr. Barrett's farm near Concord, under another name. "Why would anyone want a lot of chemical formulas so badly they'd kill for them?"

"Formulae," corrected Horace automatically.

"Killing is what they're about," said Abigail softly. "Isn't it?"

"I think so, yes," said the Indian. "I recognized a number of the experiments he's done. Beelzebub was working with combinations of poisonous vapors—mixtures of sulfurs and phosphorous a hundred times more deadly than the poisoned smokes the Romans used. Vapors that stuck to the skin and remained in the air for hours rather than dispersing."

"The Chinese used poison smokes, of course," said Horace. "The Persians, also—everything from balls of burning mustard to clouds of powdered antimony and chalk designed to asphyxiate the enemy . . . beastly. It sounds as if Old Beelzebub took a more scientific approach to produce clouds that would hang for hours in the air after they were shot by means of hollowed cannon-shells into enemy villages."

"Enemy?" said Thaxter, puzzled. "Who—?"

Weyountah held up the smallest of the sheets of paper, which contained not formulae, but simply writing in a firm, faded hand.

"*Evil Heart*," he read slowly, translating as he went. "*We the fathers of the Abooksiqun village have smoked over the offer you have made to us to deal with the white men who come against us, who have tried to take our land. We have talked and we have prayed to the spirits that guide us. You say that you can kill the white soldiers who will come to our villages before they can reach us; that you can rub them out before they can see a single warrior of the Nipmuc tribe; that you can stretch them dead upon the ground miles from us and destroy*

*their villages without a single warrior of the Nipmuck ever having to
enter there. This you will do, you say, out of thanks to us, for taking
you in when your own people had turned their faces from you."*

Weyountah turned the paper over, his strong-boned young
face grave and sad in the lamplight.

*"This we do not want and will not have. We the fathers of the
Abooksiqun village understand the greatness of this gift of death
that you offer to us, and thank you that we are in your heart and
your thought. Yet we find this gift that you offer us an abomination.
This is not what we wish to do or what we wish to become or how we
wish our sons to speak of us after we are gone. When we are gone, we
want our sons to say, Our Fathers were warriors, not, Our Fathers
were cowards who poisoned their enemies from afar."*

"He couldn't have done it," said Thaxter after a time.
"Could he?"

Horace regarded him in surprise. "Of course he could
have. 'Twas only a century ago that poisoned vapors were
outlawed, when the French would use them against the Germans during the wars of religion . . ."

"And he had the materials," said Weyountah. "And notes
for the making of phosphorous and other ingredients . . . He
had made the vapor in a small quantity already. 'Twas devilish
stuff, cleaving to the skin, both outside the body and inside
the nostrils and throat. It would blind and blister where it
did not kill, and apparently it rendered at least some of its
subjects permanently paralyzed. Moreover, it sounds as if he
were working on means to make it in quantity, and cheaply,
and to lay it down everywhere in the forests where the militia would come to attack the Indian villages."

"And that's what Ryland wanted?" asked Katy, both
shocked and sad. "Not gold, but a weapon to use on those
who stand against the King?"

"Worth a thousand times as much as gold," John said,

from his chair by the little hearth-fire, "if one side has it and the other doesn't. As Ryland would know. 'Twould be a guarantee of advancement, more so than mere money, in the eyes of the Governor and the King."

"And the elders of the village decided they'd rather die," said Katy, a little wonderingly, "before they'd use it. Before they'd let themselves turn into people who would use it."

"People like Beelzebub," said Horace. "No wonder he left the village when they told him that."

"Because he couldn't bear to see them killed, as he must have known they would be?"

"Or because," said Weyountah, "he couldn't bear to see himself through their eyes. We found no evidence, by the way," he added, looking across at John and Abigail, "that His Excellency had sent anyone to follow Ryland. I'm inclined to think Hutchinson really didn't know." He shuffled the deadly papers together, passed them back to Abigail. "He was out in Cambridge this morning—Hutchinson was—and they say he seemed deeply distressed to see Ryland's body, but he didn't ask about the books or make any attempt to see his rooms—"

"Which is just as well," added Horace, "since we'd already moved the books to *my* room."

"You can have a look through them," offered the Indian. "They're just perfectly ordinary old books, you know. We had a look through them this morning when we got back—here's the list of them—" He withdrew a handwritten sheet from his jacket pocket and held it out to John. "The cover-papers had all been slit with a paper knife, and to judge by the smudges everywhere, Ryland had searched through them pretty well."

"That may have been before he got word back from Mrs. Morgan that what he'd hoped was the formula for a poisonous gas was just some old notes for blackmail," surmised Abigail. "Since afterwards, he certainly didn't waste any time trying to get his hands on the other books. Which is just as well," she said slowly, "because even if he had not intended the deaths of Seckar and George, having encompassed them, he would have to cover his guilt . . . in any fashion that he could until he had the formulae and equipment in hand. I don't imagine—"

Sharp knocking sounded on the front door, making them all look around. John rose and opened the study door as Pattie's swift footfalls passed in the hall. An instant later a familiar voice called, "John, it's Sam—"

Sam Adams strode into the study, greatcoat flapping open and a small portmanteau in his hand. "I've just come from the harbor," he said. "The *Duke William*'s been sighted coming past Calf Island—from London. She'll be docking at Castle Island before dark."

"Anyone go out to it?" asked John, with an eye on the portmanteau.

"The harbor pilot. And some traders with water and rum." Sam's voice was grim. "General Thomas Gage is aboard—the commander in chief of the British armies here up 'til last year . . ."

"They've sent him back?" asked Thaxter, a little apprehensively.

"They've sent him back," replied Sam. "Not *only* as commander in chief . . . He's now Governor of Massachusetts as well."

"Governor—" began Abigail, shocked.

John's voice was hard and strange. "They've put a *military commander* as our *Governor*?"

"Has he troops?" asked Weyountah.

Sam's mouth twisted, and he picked up his portmanteau. "Some. And you can bet your Sunday hat there are more on the way. From Halifax, from Ireland . . . And that's only the beginning. The King has signed something called the Boston Port Bill; it goes into effect in June. They're closing down the port of Boston: no shipping, no trade, no vessels of any kind to land at all until we knuckle under and give them money for their damned tea. Justices in the Colony Courts are henceforth to be appointed by the Crown. Juries selected by the Crown. All town governments in the colony—not just Boston—are to be disbanded . . . There are other provisions, but I'm not waiting here to learn of them. John—" He clasped his cousin's hand. "Can I rely on you for messages? John Hancock and I are bound for Concord. The militia's already starting a weapons depot there, where a British warship can't shell us—"

"Won't they be watching the gates?" asked Horace, and Sam grinned.

"We'll make a patriot of you yet, my boy. Hancock's got a couple of lads who're taking us across before the warships turn up in the harbor in earnest. Nab—" He turned to Abigail, bowed over her hand. "Barrett in Concord tells me you had sent on from Framingham about thirty pounds of sulfur you'd found in old Whitehead's fortress. You didn't happen to find anything of that mythical treasure there as well?"

He spoke lightly, but as the dying fire set up a little spurt of light, it seemed to find reflection in his eyes: anxiety, fighting-spirit, a mind that was already sorting a thousand things at once and racing ahead. Mentally rallying his troops and readying his response . . .

Troops coming into Boston.

The British military commander made Governor of the colony . . . and of how many other colonies, she wondered, besides? Town governments disbanded—to be replaced by what? The Crown controlling the courts. She was aware of John watching her, of the rough, worn texture of the papers beneath her fingertips on the table. British troops converging on Boston, and how long before they were marching out into the countryside? To Lexington where the militia was drilling. To Concord where the weapons would be hidden . . .

She took a deep breath, gathered the papers together, and said in her lightest voice, "I fear that a myth is all that it was, Sam. Myth and rumor that reached the degree of obsession, to the point that men would kill for what might only be a myth in their dreams." She crossed to the hearth, with the air of a woman tidying up the last household details before starting her mending, and dropped the papers into the flames.

"If there was treasure there," she said, "'tis gone now. We will do what we can, within the bounds of honor, to defend ourselves against the British."

"And more than that," added John, and in the new, sharp flare of light from the burning paper, he caught her eye and nodded his agreement, "more than that, we cannot do."

FROM

BARBARA HAMILTON

A MARKED MAN

AN ABIGAIL ADAMS MYSTERY

**Passion can be as dangerous as politics in
the Massachusetts colony . . .**

1774: Ten weeks after the Boston Tea Party. Abigail Adams, wife of attorney John Adams, who is deeply involved with the Sons of Liberty—a secret organization opposing the Crown—remains as committed to the cause as her husband. And the arrest of one of the Sons comes as a shock to both of them. Because it isn't for treason, it's for murder . . .

The accused is young Henry Knox; the victim, a royal representative to the colonial court. Rumors begin swirling—did the murder indeed arise from the competition between the two for the affections of the daughter of a prominent Loyalist—or was it politically motivated? Abigail and John believe Knox to be innocent, as he claims, though the evidence against him is strong.

While John works to clear his client's name, Abigail begins her own investigation, and soon learns several unpleasant facts about the dead man, things that greatly increase the number of possible suspects. But as she pursues the truth, the killer pursues her—threatening not only Abigail, but her vulnerable family . . .

"A captivating series for all historical fans."
—*Library Journal*

penguin.com

"Exciting . . . Abigail Adams could become
my favorite historical sleuth."
—Sharon Kay Penman

FROM

BARBARA HAMILTON

THE NINTH DAUGHTER

AN ABIGAIL ADAMS MYSTERY

Abigail is shocked when she visits her friend and fellow
patriot Rebecca Malvern, only to find a dead woman in
the kitchen and Rebecca missing. The gruesome crime
was seemingly perpetrated to obtain a secret Sons of Liberty document—and there are many who would benefit
by seeing John accused of the murder. Using her keen
prowess to prove him innocent and find their missing
compatriot, Abby uncovers a conspiracy that could cost
them all their freedom—and their lives.

"Barbara Hamilton plunges us into colonial Boston,
where we walk beside the legendary Abigail Adams as she
tries to find justice for a murdered young woman while
also helping with the birthing pangs of a new nation."
—Victoria Thompson

facebook.com/TheCrimeSceneBooks
penguin.com

M1107T0512